The Private Marjorie

Florida A&M University, Tallahassee
Florida Atlantic University, Boca Raton
Florida Gulf Coast University, Ft. Myers
Florida International University, Miami
Florida State University, Tallahassee
University of Central Florida, Orlando
University of Florida, Gainesville
University of North Florida, Jacksonville
University of South Florida, Tampa
University of West Florida, Pensacola

University Press of Florida

Gainesville · Tallahassee · Tampa · Boca Raton · Pensacola · Orlando · Miami · Jacksonville · Ft. Myers

Edited by Rodger L. Tarr

THE PRIVATE

Marjorie

The Love Letters of

Marjorie Kinnan Rawlings

to Norton S. Baskin

09   08   07   06   05   04   6   5   4   3   2   1

Library of Congress Cataloging-in-Publication Data
Rawlings, Marjorie Kinnan, 1896–1953.
The private Marjorie: the love letters of Marjorie Kinnan Rawlings to
Norton S. Baskin / edited by Rodger L. Tarr
p. cm.
Includes bibliographical references and index.
ISBN 0-8130-2783-7
1. Rawlings, Marjorie Kinnan, 1896–1953—Correspondence.
2. Authors, American—20th century—Correspondence. 3. Baskin,
Norton S.—Correspondence. 4. Love-letters. I. Baskin, Norton S.
II. Tarr, Rodger L. III. Title
PS3535.A845Z483 2005
813'.52—dc22
[B]   2004058080

The University Press of Florida is the scholarly publishing agency for
the State University System of Florida, comprising Florida A&M
University, Florida Atlantic University, Florida Gulf Coast University,
Florida International University, Florida State University, University
of Central Florida, University of Florida, University of North Florida,
University of South Florida, and University of West Florida.

University Press of Florida
15 Northwest 15th Street
Gainesville, FL 32611-2079
http://www.upf.com

For Carol Anita and Clayton Carlyle

Contents

. . . .

Acknowledgments

I am especially indebted to Meredith Morris-Babb, the assistant editor-in-chief of the University Press of Florida, who asked me to edit the *Love Letters* and who arranged for the necessary permissions. Too often we fail to acknowledge our senior editors, but in this case this volume would not exist if it were not for the efforts and support of Meredith. Susan Fernandez offered advice before she left the press. Susan Albury, my project editor, was excellent in every way, as was Susan Brady, my copy editor. Deidre Bryan, who edited my three previous books on Rawlings, was there once again with her encouragement.

I am particularly grateful to Frank Orser, the curator of the Rawlings Collection at the University of Florida, who supplied me with the texts and illustrations, offered suggestions, and contributed substantive information on many of the complex references. It is difficult to imagine this volume without Frank's invaluable participation. Carla M. Summers, head of Special Collections at the University of Central Florida, helped with the texts.

David Nolan, a pioneer in the Rawlings Society and close friend of the late Norton Baskin, as always proved to be a fountain of knowledge. David's wise counsel and enviable historical sense are ever-present in this work. I am also indebted to James M. Stephens, whose invaluable *"Cross Creek" Reader's Guide* (2003) helped me to see fully many of the important allusions. Philip May Jr. supplied me with texts from his incomparable collection. Special thanks must go to Richard Young, the son of Owen D. Young, who painstakingly sorted out the Van Hornesville references.

I particularly wish to acknowledge Maggie Kinser and Brent Kinser: the former entered many of the letters into the computer, and the latter not only aided in the input but also proofread, did research, and contributed substantive material. Maggie and Brent in no small way are responsible for this volume.

There are, of course, myriad others. Jamie Lane, my honors research assistant, worked wonders on the text. Sally B. Hooker helped with the Baskin family names; Bob Williams with those of the Brice family; J. T. "Jake" Glisson with the Cross Creek references, relying in part on his invaluable book *The Creek*; Frank Upchurch with the St. Augustine names; and William McGuire with the Gainesville and the St. Augustine names.

Kevin McCarthy, executive director of the Rawlings Society, has as always been unfailing in his personal and substantive support. His wise editorial discretion is found throughout. Sandra J. Birnhak, CEO of Worldview Entertainment, has provided much-appreciated support; and Veronica Makowsky has offered excellent suggestions on both text and context. I must also thank the anonymous University of Florida reader for the splendid commentary, and John Lowe for the blurb, assuming the two individuals are not one and the same.

Idella Parker, Rawlings's "Perfect Maid," who lived much of what these letters chronicle, remains with us, providing stories and inspiration as only she can.

I owe a personal debt to my beloved friends Phil and Gloria May, Ron and Betty Kinser, Bob and Edwina Davis, and Bob and Barb Middendorf, who offered both wit and wisdom.

To Anita, devoted partner, excellent scholar, and wise counselor, written acknowledgment seems hardly sufficient.

Editorial Note

The holographs of the *Love Letters* are in the Rawlings Collection at the University of Florida. Some of these letters came to the library through the Rawlings Bequest, and others came from private sources. In spite of the vastness of this collection, there are, no doubt, letters missing. On rare occasion, parts of a letter are gone. A lengthy period of time—weeks or months—without letters obviously could indicate that Rawlings and Norton were together, hence no need for letters. Still, it is likely that there were more letters written, especially in 1942. These letters may have been destroyed or may still be in private hands. And we know that on at least one occasion, Norton, Rawlings's second husband, destroyed a whole cache of manuscripts. Any missing letters could have been among them. Also, there are a few letters printed in the *Selected Letters* whose holographs I have not seen; the location of these holographs has not been determined. It is remarkable that so many letters have survived, especially since the letters sent to Norton in India/Burma during World War II had to be brought back by Norton, who was an ambulance driver on the front lines and who was seriously ill at the time of his return.

If the extant letters were published in full, this volume would be about one-third longer. Although it would have been ideal to print every word of each letter and to annotate each letter fully, practical considerations ruled this out. I have therefore chosen what I consider the most important material in the letters, and I have used ellipses to alert the reader that words, sentences, and/or paragraphs have been dropped. Such choice is difficult, often fraught with danger, for choice always depends upon the knowledge, ingenuity, and prejudice of the editor. In making my selections, I have adopted the guise of a biographer, hoping to choose the details and events that will disclose for the reader, as fully as possible, Rawlings's complicated character. I am grateful to the University Press of Florida for being so generous in the allotment of space.

By using ellipses I was able not only to present the substantive parts of each letter but also to include nearly every extant letter. On rare occasions, I have dropped a letter entirely. Letters were eliminated only when they contained no substantive material or addressed purely incidental matters—for example, notes such as: "I will see you in Ocala tomorrow," or "Do not forget the whiskey," or

"Be sure to pick up my prescriptions." These notes were easy to excise. What became more difficult was truncating or eliminating description that could be considered substantive. I was ruthless when it came to certain subjects. For example, I eliminated most of Rawlings's lengthy descriptions of bridge hands, menus, flowers, gardens, acquaintances of little or no import—especially those in St. Augustine and Van Hornesville—and, sadly, most of her lengthy commentary on her pets. Rawlings especially loved her cats and dogs, and she wrote endlessly on their antics, illnesses, and deaths. However, I did retain the more poignant moments with her animals to provide insight into her often-ignored sentimental nature. On another issue regarding excision, I struggled. Rawlings on occasion was brutally frank about others' sexual proclivities. Several of the individuals she wrote about are still alive, and to protect their privacy, I decided to excise potentially embarrassing comments on their sexual exploits. I trust I have made the honorable decision. I have not retained Rawlings's own excisions unless they inform the text. Such informative excisions are indicated within angle brackets < >.

I was equally ruthless in deciding which of Rawlings's subjects to retain. Because her life at Cross Creek was what was most important to Rawlings—and is thus key to understanding her—I have tried to include everything involving the Creek. These letters provide an in-depth history of Cross Creek. Much of what we learn here about the Cracker and black cultures is new, and what is not new is certainly told with more frankness and detail. I have also retained a great deal about her activities in St. Augustine and environs. Norton's Castle Warden Hotel and her Crescent Beach cottage were immensely important in her life, and much of the detail presented here is new. I have also tried to preserve her descriptions of her life in Van Hornesville, New York, but especially those stunning accounts of Owen D. Young, the renowned business and political leader, and Robert Frost, who was already thought of as America's poet. And, of course, I have retained anything that has to do with her literary life. All commentary on other writers and their books has been kept to document Rawlings's critical acumen. Maxwell Perkins especially admired Rawlings's critical verve. Her vibrant commentary on the literary events of the day certainly supports Perkins's opinion, and her comments on Perkins himself add a new chapter to the Max and Marjorie saga. Finally, I also have retained all of her remarks on the political, social, and cultural events of the day.

As for the editorial use of ellipses themselves, I have indicated where material has been dropped in the middle of sentences and at the end of paragraphs. Ellipses at the beginning of a paragraph indicate that one or more previous paragraphs have been dropped, or that material from the beginning of that paragraph has been dropped. I have tried to avoid, however, the awkward occurrence of having one paragraph end with ellipses and the next begin with them. Thus, on occasion ellipses at the end of a paragraph might also indicate that subsequent paragraphs have been dropped. When some editors use ellipses, they also count and list in a footnote the number of words and paragraphs dropped. I will not quarrel here with this procedure, except to say that I find it both intrusive and space consuming. To add, literally, hundreds of such nonsubstantive footnotes robs the reader of what the reader desires most, as much primary text as possible. Therefore, I have not provided a paragraph and word count. As for the descriptive footnotes, I have tried to keep them to a minimum, for precisely the same reason—space. The more I write, the fewer words by Rawlings we can read. However, I have provided editor's notes when necessary to explain an allusion, to identify a person, or to enhance understanding of an event.

The letters themselves are presented in chronological order. "TLS" stands for "Typed Letter Signed"; "ALS" for "Autographed Letter Signed"; and "Wire" identifies a telegram. There are also a few postcards. The number of pages of the letter is given, although length can be deceiving since the length depends upon whether the letter is typed or handwritten and on the size of the paper. Rawlings wrote in a large, bold hand. Thus, six pages of holograph can be a relatively short letter. For the sake of uniformity, the sequence of address is place followed by date. Greetings and closings are given when present. Rawlings's signature is dropped unless it is special, such as when she signs "Dora," her alter ego. Rawlings's printed stationery misspells her post office as "Hawthorn," which is properly spelled "Hawthorne." Such idiosyncrasies are not corrected. When she does not use printed stationery, and when she does not supply place, the location of Hawthorne is inferred as [Cross Creek, Fla.]. Undated letters are inferred using the postmark or using the partial date given in conjunction with the perpetual calendar. Using this method, nearly all undated and/or partially dated letters have been dated. Any question about a date's accuracy is indicated by a question mark, such as [7? January 1953].

Rawlings's language has not been altered. Her spelling, especially the coining of words, can be creative. These quaint spellings (including names and dialects), are retained, although obvious typos ("teh" for "the," for example) have been silently corrected. On occasions when a word is unusually bizarre, [*sic*] is used. Her miscues were often the result, as she freely admits, of alcohol, or anger, or both. If the wrong word is used, it is followed by the correct word in brackets. Most of the letters are typed and thus present few transcription problems. Rawlings had the habit of using an uppercase *I* for a 1, as in I947, which infuriated the meticulous Julia Scribner. In this volume, the *I* has been silently corrected to 1.

Rawlings's handwritten letters present one problem. She employed, depending on her mood, various lengths of the dash. In an effort to represent her style, I have used an em-dash (—), a medium dash (——), and a long dash (———). This system is entirely arbitrary. Emendations to the text appear in square brackets. Punctuation is supplied only where it is necessary to convey meaning, and brackets are used to indicate editorial intrusion. Underlining is indicated by italics;

double or triple underlining is noted in brackets. Wires are printed in small caps. Editorial notes explain peculiarities in text.

A chronology is provided to indicate the major events and publications in Rawlings's life and career. A section titled "A Guide to the Major Figures and Places" is intended to facilitate identification of those names mentioned most often. A brief biographical sketch appears at the beginning of each year of the letters to account for Rawlings's activities that are not necessarily covered in the letters.

The Scribner lineage always causes confusion. The following is an accurate enumeration: Charles Scribner I (1821–1871), Charles Scribner II (1854–1930), Charles Scribner III (1890–1952), Charles Scribner IV, aka Jr. (1921–1995), Charles Scribner V, aka III (1951–). Arthur H. Scribner (1859–1932) was the son of Charles Scribner I.

Introduction

· ·

Marjorie Kinnan Rawlings should need no introduction. From 1933 until her death twenty years later, she was one of the best-selling novelists at Charles Scribner's and Sons. She was the protégée of the famed editor Maxwell E. Perkins, who considered her one of his outstanding pupils, an elite group that included F. Scott Fitzgerald, Thomas Wolfe, and Ernest Hemingway. Perkins once bragged that she was the only novelist he knew who had three novels—*South Moon Under* (1933), *The Yearling* (1938), and *Cross Creek* (1942)—adopted by the Book-of-the-Month Club, to him no mean achievement. When *The Yearling* was awarded the Pulitzer Prize in 1939, Rawlings became a star at Scribners, and only after the death of Perkins in 1947 did her star begin its eclipse. Even so, *The Yearling* has never been out of print, and *Cross Creek* only on occasion, and each has been made into a successful Hollywood film. The fact that today Rawlings is not widely read in academic settings says more about the fickleness of academe than it does about her accomplishments. However, with eleven books published on Rawlings and her works since 1988, her former reputation is being restored.

Yet there is a great deal that we still do not know about Rawlings, especially about the intersection of her personal and professional life. The more we know about Rawlings the person, the more we will know about Rawlings the writer because she was, more than most other writers, a part of her fiction. Further, the more that is revealed about Rawlings, the more we come to realize the stellar position she once held among her peers. She is at present considered a regionalist, an appellation she always detested and vigorously challenged. Her peers knew better. Margaret Mitchell once wrote to her: "Your versatility is a marvelous thing. . . . Yours is truly an American gift. You are just a born perfect storyteller" (copy, 12 June 1940, Tarr collection). Perkins was equally effusive, assuring her that she wrote in the descriptive tradition of Mark Twain, once saying of *South Moon Under,* "It is wonderfully good material, as good as *Huckleberry Finn*" (Rawlings, *Max and Marjorie,* 56). Words of high praise, and words Perkins meant.

What is not generally known about Rawlings is perhaps what makes her most intriguing, her life outside of literature. Except for what is revealed about her personal life in the *Selected Letters* and *Max and Marjorie,* the only attempt at a full biographical study is Elizabeth Silverthorne's *Marjorie Kinnan Rawlings:*

Sojourner at Cross Creek (1988). This popular biography—there are no notes or citations—lays a few foundations but fails to explore in depth the character of Rawlings, whose intriguing life spans the spectrum from honors graduate from the University of Wisconsin to frontier personality at Cross Creek.

Indeed, when Rawlings moved to Florida in 1928, her life quickly became a matter of survival. An urban woman intruding upon a rural backwoods culture, she faced constant danger, living precariously among the poisonous snakes, alligators, and black bears of remote North Central Florida. Mosquitoes were her constant companions. She had to get along with her Cracker neighbors and manage her help, nearly all black, or risk failure if not death. The Mary Steenburgen characterization of Rawlings in the film *Cross Creek* (1983) as a lithe, transcendental idealist, while appealing, could not be further from reality. The unvarnished truth is that Rawlings was a frank-spoken, hard-drinking, tough-minded, often overweight individualist who, until her work gained recognition, had to live off the land. Most remarkable of all, she managed to survive in the rudimentary white male–dominated culture that surrounded her. When provoked, she would face her male antagonists with a resolve they finally came to admire. She settled disputes over cattle gaps, put neighbors' hogs back into their pens or shot them, and oversaw a seventy-two-acre orange grove through killer freezes and unexpected droughts. Those who disliked her most when she first arrived at Cross Creek soon became her friends. For all her faults—and, as these confessional letters reveal, her faults were legion—the Crackers and the blacks came to realize that she was honest, fair, and, most important, charitable. She always kept her word.

When Rawlings was divorced from her college sweetheart turned cruel husband, Charles Rawlings, in 1933, her life took on new meaning. Faced with the challenge of forging a life among her Cracker neighbors and her black workers, Rawlings entered a period of increasing self-awareness that is dramatically anticipated in her novella "Gal Young 'Un" (1932). Once she committed herself to the Crackers whose stark lives enriched her literary soul, and once she was *en rapport*, as she called it, with her black help, Rawlings found her literary voice. Her first novel, *South Moon Under*, gained her critical attention and much-needed cash, and it was followed by *Golden Apples* (1935), not a commercial success, but a novel of technical merit. *The Yearling* (1938) made her one of the most famous writers in the world.

However, in spite of the myriad rewards resulting from the international success of *The Yearling*—she not only had to learn to live with wealth but also with being in constant demand—Rawlings was both lonely and alone. Fame fed her ego, but fame could not be her companion. A conversationalist since childhood—a born storyteller, as Margaret Mitchell said—Rawlings needed more than her sympathetic editor Perkins could give her. She needed companionship, a voice to listen to her voice, a spirit to share her spirit. Sometime in late 1937 or early 1938, Norton S. Baskin became both her soul mate and her lover. After nearly three years of trial and error, they were married, with little fanfare, in October 1941. The letters gathered here are a record of this extraordinary courtship and marriage.

If Marjorie had ever met her match and her opposite, it was Norton. Largely self-educated, he was a debonair raconteur from Union Springs, Alabama, who possessed the qualities Rawlings needed most—a patient strength, a quiet demeanor, and a wry humor. He could make her laugh, even in those bleak days when her creative spirit abandoned her. Norton was also a good listener and wise counselor. He was, as Wordsworth said of his hero Michael, an "unusual man." He indulged her tirades, suffered her foibles, and deflected her criticisms. Rawlings, as these letters repeatedly illustrate, was not an easy person to live with. In a real way, Norton, who had considerable responsibilities of his own as a hotelier—he managed the Marion Hotel in Ocala, then owned and managed the famed Castle Warden Hotel in St. Augustine, and finally managed the restaurants at Marineland, south of Crescent Beach—devoted his life to her. It is sad that we cannot print here the letters—now at the University of Florida—of this wonderful man many of us had the privilege to know. Norton was always kind, ever generous, and forever cordial. His letters to Rawlings are a testament to his devotion to her and in themselves represent a valuable history of the times. Norton now rests beside Rawlings in the rural cemetery at Antioch. The words he chose to put on her gravestone speak to his ever-present humility:

MARJORIE KINNAN RAWLINGS

1896–1953

wife of

NORTON BASKIN

THROUGH HER WRITINGS SHE ENDEARED

HERSELF TO THE PEOPLE OF THE WORLD

What, then, does *Love Letters* add to what we now know about the tapestry of Rawlings's life and by extension Norton's? Most important, the letters allow us for the first time to see the naked truth of Rawlings's extraordinarily rich but immensely difficult life. In them she confesses her fears, confronts her inadequacies, and conjures her demons. The letters are not sensual love letters, although Rawlings is never above using barnyard humor to express her love for Norton, once writing playfully that she missed her "bull" (16 April 1944) at Cross Creek. But as a whole, most are not really love letters at all, at least not in the romantic sense, even though Rawlings often uses them to express her devotion. They are instead an epistolary diary of Rawlings's life from 1938 until her death in 1953, given impetus by the fact that she seemed determined to write Norton each day she was apart from him.

At times the letters are not pleasant to read. Their detail can make the letters exposés—often painful exposés—as Rawlings confesses all manner of prejudices and problems. They take us inside the recesses of Rawlings's psyche, making us privy to what she describes as her "unspeakable torments" (9 September 1949). Divulged here for the first time are the trials and the tribulations that even those most intimate with her, save Norton, did not know. And some of what is revealed is heartbreaking. Her need for a son, hauntingly addressed in "A Mother in Mannville" (1936), and later rekindled in her thoughts of adopting her brother's child, is a recurring subject. Her lamentation at one point about the "false alarm" when she once thought she had "killed the rabbits" (7 April 1944) was not lost on Norton.

Through it all, her courtier Norton was always there, skillfully balancing her needs against his obligations. Even though I had had the rare privilege of discussing Rawlings candidly with Norton, I was still surprised by much of what I found in these letters. They are frank, often brutally frank. Rawlings seldom spares the rod; it simply was not in her. Invective, barely hidden by irony and sarcasm, is her tool. Only Maxwell Perkins, Robert Frost, and Owen D. Young were spared. Even her beloved Norton felt the sting of her wrath.

Love Letters is a chronicle of a writer, too often sick both physically and spiritually, searching for but never finding a full measure of happiness. In frustration, she turned to food, to booze, to nicotine, and in consequence to rebuke, each and all contributing to bouts of ill-health, to increasing periods of despondency, and finally to thoughts of suicide. It would be easy to dismiss her suffering and to say that Rawlings suffered only what all sensitive artists suffer. Perhaps true. But hidden in these letters is something more, something universal, another literary woman looking desperately for and never quite finding a room of her own.

The letters are also disturbingly contradictory. Rawlings's racism is particularly frustrating, because, although it was not unusual in her time, we expect more from her. As the letters carefully chart, Rawlings acted as a champion of the blacks at Cross Creek and by extension as a spokesperson for the cause of equality nationwide. She lectured the editor of a Jacksonville newspaper on his racial bias; she stayed in the president's house at Fisk University to call attention to her position; and she repeatedly debated with Norton (and others) the best way to advance the cause of equality. In seeing the rights of blacks through the lens of female suffrage (22 May 1944)—the latter providing the example for the former— Rawlings was ahead of her time. And yet, while Rawlings chastised her closest friends for their racism, in the next breath she would call her "Perfect Maid," Idella Parker, a "nigger," or refer to her ancient servants, Will and Martha Mickens, as "Nigger Will" and "Nigger Martha," or, more incredibly, dispatch her good friend Zora Neale Hurston to the "nigger" quarters to sleep when she visited Rawlings at Cross Creek. Such actions make no sense, particularly within the context of her Herculean efforts to stem the tide of racism. On the subject of race,

Norton Baskin, 1940. By permission of the University of Florida Libraries.

Rawlings is an enigma. She tried so hard publicly to change the face of America, yet in private she routinely employed racially charged stereotype and slur.

However, if we are able to look beyond Rawlings's racist language and its context, there opens up a whole new world of white-black relationships in the otherwise staunchly segregated Cross Creek. There is a definite love, however paternalistic, between Rawlings and her black workers. The folk wisdom of individuals like Martha Mickens became a part of Rawlings's own education. She learned to appreciate black culture, and by appreciating the culture, she came to understand it. Indeed, to a large extent Rawlings became a part of that black culture. Idella Parker, who experienced firsthand Rawlings's racism, is the first to acknowledge Rawlings's sympathy with the plight of blacks. Ironically, Parker, more than anyone else, was the subject of Rawlings's taunts and epithets, usually the result of too much alcohol. Yet Parker stood beside her, helping Rawlings to survive the war years, the writing of *Cross Creek*, and the subsequent "invasion of privacy" lawsuit. Parker was also instrumental in the preparation of *Cross Creek*

Cookery (1942), contributing many of the recipes and checking all of them. And it was Parker who came to Rawlings's aid during much of the Van Hornesville period, when she was plagued with finishing the transcendental *The Sojourner* (1953). In Rawlings's own words, "Idella is a black angel" (19 August 1949), although we cannot overlook that Parker is a "black angel," not just an "angel." Context here is everything. Nevertheless, when it comes to the volatile issue of racism and the often offensive nature of Rawlings's language, I would ask the reader to consider that there is much that is commendable in this collection of letters, which provides a chronicle of race relations in the 1930s and 1940s that is perhaps unprecedented in letters. Zora Neale Hurston recognized Rawlings's sincere efforts at reform when she wrote about *Cross Creek*: "You have written the best thing on Negroes of any white writer who has ever lived. Maybe you have bettered me . . ." (Hurston 486).

Rawlings's curious blend of vituperation and sympathy was not restricted to blacks. Her treatment in the *Love Letters* of her Cracker friends—many of whom she brought to life in her fiction, especially in *Cross Creek*—was equally conflicted, reflecting both contempt and compassion. Yet here again, context is everything. Her frustration with the Crackers more often than not is followed by an acknowledgment of her debt to them. She not only owed them the subject matter of her fiction, but she also owed them the knowledge that saved her life. Their names are legend, and include Barney Dillard, Fred Tompkins, Leonard Fiddia, Cal Long, Tom Glisson, and Chet Crosby, each of whom—by taking her on bear hunts, alligator hunts, deer hunts, bird hunts, and fishing trips—taught her to survive in the hammock and the scrub. Her close friend Ross Allen, the herpetologist at the Silver Springs tourist attraction, made sure she was properly introduced to poisonous snakes. With the help of these men, Rawlings soon became an expert naturalist.

The Cracker women were no less important to her. The most famous of them was Dessie Smith Vinson, herself a venerated pioneer and expert naturalist, who took Rawlings on hunting and fishing trips, the most famous of which was down the St. Johns River, a trip that became the subject of Rawlings's celebrated chronicle "Hyacinth Drift" (1933). Another woman who dominates these letters is Zelma Cason, the census taker, who took Rawlings throughout the scrub, and who later sued her for "invasion of privacy" for what Rawlings wrote about her in *Cross Creek*. There seems no doubt that this celebrated trial and its lengthy litigation exacerbated Rawlings's severe bouts with diverticulosis. Certainly the trial and its aftermath interrupted her creative flow. Rawlings came to appreciate what it was like to be a Cracker woman in the Cracker male–dominated culture, and she almost always turned to the women to help—and to be helped. To celebrate their bravery and fortitude, she made fictional heroes of them, most notably Quincey Dover, whose feminist antics and strength in adversity served as an emblem for the women at Cross Creek. Rawlings on Cracker women provides a

Martha Mickens and Idella Parker, ca. 1939–40. By permission of the University of Florida Libraries.

unique history of Cracker culture, splendid descriptive accounts of the minimal, day-to-day existence of these singular individuals. The characterization of the youthful, destitute Cracker girl Florry, in "Jacob's Ladder" (1931), celebrates the inherent nobility Rawlings discerned in these women. It was the tragic story of Florry that drew Maxwell Perkins to Rawlings. *Love Letters* provides a dramatic, often sad account of Rawlings's devotion to these proud individuals who lived on the margins of poverty.

There is a host of other Cracker men and women who become a part of the *Love Letters*. Rawlings drank with them, ate with them, and took care of them. As J. T. "Jake" Glisson—the crippled boy Rawlings befriended and used as a prototype for Fodderwing in *The Yearling*—recently said to me, she had a "quiet way" with the Crackers; she "made them feel comfortable." Rawlings became the Crackers' benefactor. She took food to them, lent money to them, and when necessary buried them. The story of her rescue of the Bowen family from "starvation" is especially telling (21 February 1950) and is but one example of her repeated eleemosynary efforts.

The *Love Letters* provides, of course, much more than the accounts of life with the blacks and the Crackers at Cross Creek. The letters also offer fresh insight into Rawlings's life with the social elite of St. Augustine, Florida's oldest city. When Norton opened the exclusive Castle Warden Hotel, just north of the ruins of St. Augustine's Spanish Fort Matanzas, in January 1942, a whole new social world was opened to the already famous Rawlings. The list of the Baskins' friends reads like a page from *Who's Who*, with names like Flagler, Young, and Du Pont commonplace. Among the most prominent were State Senator Verle Pope and his novelist wife, Edith Taylor Pope. The latter became a close friend of Rawlings and the subject of considerable chit-chat in the *Love Letters*.

Friends led to new friends. Ernest Hemingway was there, visiting the bar at the Castle Warden on a number of occasions and later—with his wife, Martha Gellhorn—staying late into the night at Rawlings's cottage on the ocean, south of St. Augustine. Wendell Willkie, candidate for president of the United States, visited the Baskins both at Cross Creek and at St. Augustine, as did N. C. Wyeth and his younger and not yet famous brother, Andrew. Owen D. Young, among other things head of the Radio Corporation of America, director of the Federal Reserve, and trusted advisor of several presidents, and Louise Young, his wife, were also close friends. The Youngs and the Baskins often played bridge into the middle of the night, and it was the Youngs who convinced Rawlings to buy the farmhouse in Van Hornesville, New York, a small village near Cooperstown, a decision that would change her literary and personal life forever. Also at Cross Creek and St. Augustine was Robert Frost, who like Owen Young became an even closer friend during the Van Hornesville years. Rawlings's descriptions of Frost's visits to Van Hornesville add new insight into both of their robust but fragile characters. Her lengthy letters on Frost are nothing short of a treasure. The *Love Letters* also provides a new perspective on the relationship of Frost and Young, who, as Rawlings came to discover, were inextricably linked, not wholly to Frost's liking. Of all the male friends Rawlings had in her life—excluding of course Norton and Maxwell Perkins—it was Young she respected most, always referring to him as "Mr. Young," and it was Frost she revered most, nearly always referring to him with affection as "Robert."

Yet another prominent personality who bridges Rawlings's life in Florida and New York is Julia Scribner, the daughter of Charles Scribner III and Vera Scribner. Julia was the child Rawlings never had; Rawlings often referred to Julia as her "goddaughter." As the *Love Letters* documents, Julia spent countless hours at Cross Creek, Crescent Beach, and Van Hornesville, and Rawlings spent equally countless hours trying to deal with Julia's unfathomable eccentricities. The love they shared was always being tested. Julia was rich beyond imagination, spoiled to a fault, but loving in full measure. She was given to more psychological maladies than even Rawlings could handle. She tortured Rawlings, and Rawlings loved it. Their conflicting yet complementary personalities led to frequent arguments, legendary drunks, and lyrical moments. Julia, an accomplished photographer, loved hunting and fishing, and somewhat surprisingly managed to endear herself to Rawlings's Cracker friends and black workers. Rawlings, never shy when it came to offering her opinion, tried unsuccessfully to pick a husband for the eccentric Julia. She suggested suitors, once lobbying heavily for the Reverend Bertram Cooper, but in the end Julia married a High Church Episcopal priest, Thomas Bigham, whom Rawlings at first did not particularly like but for the sake of diplomacy tolerated.

What all this demonstrates is exactly how connected Rawlings was to the Scribner family. Scribners was not just her publisher; the Scribners were, largely through Julia, her extended family, even though Rawlings found little to admire in Vera, on more than one occasion referring to her as a "bitch." This language says a great deal about Rawlings's possessive jealousy when it came to Julia. One can only imagine how difficult it was for Maxwell Perkins to negotiate this situation. Julia Scribner's importance in Rawlings's life cannot be overstated. It is not surprising that she named Julia her literary executor. Julia saw Rawlings's posthumously published children's book, *The Secret River* (1955), through publication, and until her death she protected the valuable documents Rawlings had entrusted to her.

The *Love Letters* also offers wry political observation. Wendell Willkie, until he lost the Republican presidential nomination to Thomas Dewey, was a sort of hero to Rawlings, an image partly encouraged by Russell Davenport, the husband of the novelist Marcia Davenport, who had been Willkie's campaign manager. There is even a tradition—difficult to put to rest at Cross Creek—that Rawlings was a ghostwriter for Willkie. Not true, of course, but the tradition of the story tells us a lot about the myth surrounding Rawlings at the Creek. Whether it was a presidential election, or a race for governor, or a run-off for county sheriff, Rawlings kept herself in the thick of political things, and her political commentary while Norton was in India during the war rivals that of *Punch* or the *National Lampoon*. She despised Dewey, once calling him a "little shrimp" (19 September 1943), although she was not ready to spare the Democrat Harry S. Truman from the charge of "mediocrity" (13 April 1945). Clare Boothe Luce, a congressperson of considerable renown, was a "female ass" (25 February 1944).

The candidates for governor of Florida seldom escaped her acid pen. The prominent St. Augustine attorney Frank D. Upchurch, who was a frontrunner for governor, was dismissed as a "famous ass," followed by Rawlings's reluctant conclusion that she would support the venerable Claude Pepper, in spite of his "patent demagoguery" (16 April 1944). Rawlings's politics were nearly always moderately conservative until she came in contact with right-wing conservatives. Her letter to J. Edgar Hoover reporting the "insidious air" (13 October 1943) of an anti-Semitic chain letter attests to her liberal leaning. Her support of unpopular ecological issues is another example of her willingness to embrace liberal causes. On the lighter side, she found Emily Post's social strictures, purporting to represent a national identity, absurd.

Yet what fascinated Rawlings most was local politics. In one of her more satiric short stories, "Fish Fry and Fireworks" (written in 1940), the politicos, with names like Turnbuck and Crapson, are linked to a rattlesnake brought to a political rally. At one juncture Rawlings reports to Norton that she went to see "backwoods democracy in full swing," a "famous half-wit . . . running for County Commissioner" (22 April 1944). Norton himself was very much interested in the political scene, and when Rawlings was in Van Hornesville, she would fill him in on the nuances of state and national politics as conveyed to her by Owen D. Young, who had the ear of the president. In fact, the otherwise gregarious Rawlings considered it a privilege to sit quietly and to listen to Young, among the most powerful men in America and to her mind one of the most astute. The Young family included her in their many dinners to honor political figures from throughout the world. Indeed, with the Youngs as well as the Scribners, Rawlings was considered family.

If there is any one disappointment in the *Love Letters*, it is the lack of commentary on such prominent literary personalities as F. Scott Fitzgerald and Thomas Wolfe, a silence that can perhaps be attributed to these writers having died before most of the letters were written. The *Love Letters*, however, provides more than adequate compensation, as Rawlings writes extensively of other writers of the period, many of whom have now faded from the limelight. Marjory Stoneman Douglas, the famous Everglades naturalist, is treated with reverence. The tragic death of her good friend Margaret Mitchell left Rawlings numb. Langston Moffett, a Florida writer, is much admired, and Sigrid Undset, the Norwegian Nobel laureate, was a valued correspondent. A. J. Cronin, the Scots novelist with a penchant for telling dirty stories, seemed always at hand. Robert Frost, as these letters confirm, became a close friend and valued advisor. And Ernest Hemingway is written about extensively. Rawlings once lamented that her writing was of no value when compared to Hemingway's, although she did not especially like his "high thin voice" or the "inhabited" hair on his chest (3 May 1944). As Norton said to me, Hemingway was their friend, but not a "close" friend. Nevertheless, Rawlings spent time fishing with him at Bimini and drinking with him at Crescent Beach. Her analysis of the autobiographical *Across the River and into the Trees* is especially noteworthy (23 August 1950).

The famous Virginia writer James Branch Cabell, who was a close friend, introduced Rawlings to the celebrated novelist Ellen Glasgow. In 1949, Rawlings undertook to write a biography of Glasgow, and Cabell secured her the necessary entrée to the Glasgow inner circle. The revelatory letters Rawlings writes on the secrets divulged to her by the Glasgow intimates add a new chapter to the Glasgow story. As one reads these letters, one can only lament that Rawlings died just as she was about to turn her extensive notes into what surely would have been a sensational biography. Everyone of consequence in Glasgow's life confessed his or her secrets to Rawlings. What might have been is, of course, speculation, but certainly we could have had a modern-day Elizabeth Gaskell writing on modern-day Charlotte Brontë, an author of renown on an author of renown.

Of the myriad personalities discussed in detail in the *Love Letters,* several stand out. For the sheer brilliance of description, Rawlings's commentary on Pearl Primus captivates. Rawlings deeply admired the celebrated dancer, choreographer, and anthropologist credited with combining African rhythms with American and Caribbean sound. Primus came to Van Hornesville in 1950 to stay with Rawlings, in part to discuss her interest in becoming a creative writer. These invaluable letters on Primus document their developing friendship and offer yet another example of Rawlings reaching out to embrace black culture.

Norman Berg, an editor with Macmillan in Atlanta, emerges as another notable personality. Rawlings and Berg struck up a genuine friendship, although Rawlings was always somewhat suspicious that Berg's motivation was to get her to bolt from Scribners. Constantly inviting her to come to Macmillan, Berg implied that he would make a better editor for her than Maxwell Perkins, who was considerably irritated by Berg's poaching. Although Rawlings managed to stay one step ahead of Berg, the letters demonstrate that he was persistent to a fault. After Perkins's death in 1947, Berg increased the pressure, offering to help Rawlings with the manuscript of *The Sojourner* and telling her that he is a "good critic, and of course he is, but . . . I need Max, and I don't have him, and that's that" (27 July 1949). No one seemed able to help Rawlings. Charles Scribner III and Whitney Darrow, old friends, were loath to look at the evolving manuscript. Julia Scribner read bits and pieces, but Rawlings rightly kept the whole manuscript from her, understanding that the pressure on Julia would be too great. Rawlings never found another "Max," nor for that matter did anyone else. But for Rawlings the loss of Perkins was devastating. The death of Charles Scribner III in 1952 was the beginning of the end for Rawlings: "It is unspeakable. To lose Max and Charlie together in so few years. I don't see how I can bear it" (12 February 1952).

Rawlings was not always kind when it came to her fellow writers. In truth, she could be downright nasty. To be Rawlings's friend required both tolerance and forgiveness. The young poet Gene Baro, whom she met while he was at the University of Florida, provides a good example. Baro was living openly with his partner, the artist Albert Stadler. Although Rawlings publicly welcomed them, even permitting them to live at Cross Creek while she was at Van Hornesville, she was conflicted about their homosexual relationship, complaining at one point about their "Bohemian ramblings" (22 August 1949). Yet in another moment she writes of them fondly as the "gourmand-gourmets" (23 August 1949). Baro and Stadler were frequent visitors at Cross Creek and at Van Hornesville, and Rawlings found them both intriguing and stimulating. She never hesitated to ask them to "come out and eat shrimp" at the Creek (21 February 1950). Yet when Baro, who seemed always to be struggling financially, suggested to Rawlings that he be her housekeeper at Van Hornesville, she declined because he was a "congenital homo" (3 November 1950). Both Baro and Stadler (the latter painted the famous surreal portrait of Rawlings) must have been aware of Rawlings's feelings, but they never abandoned her or she them. On more than one occasion they had to depend upon Rawlings's goodwill and charity. Nevertheless, Rawlings was a creature of her time and was quite willing to use the stigma of homosexuality as a weapon to marginalize them and others. Once she suggested to her brother, Arthur, that "he was likely to make Jeff [his son] not only totally unadapted to normal living, but even homosexual" (26 August 1952).

Should we postmoderns be critical of Rawlings for displaying such prejudice? Perhaps. But at the same time we must remember that prejudice of this sort, just like her prejudice toward blacks, was part of her culture. Similarly, should we be disappointed in her for calling the Japanese "Japs" while her husband was dodging real bullets in Burma? Perhaps. But we must also remember that prejudice often emerges from cultural imperatives. Moral hindsight is easy; social context is complex. Certainly Rawlings's complex responses are no worse than those of most of her contemporaries, and they are almost always more forthright.

What is perhaps most intriguing about the confessional nature of the *Love Letters* is that Rawlings was constantly confronting her prejudices. She worried incessantly about her mistreatment of Idella Parker; she fretted over her growing dislike for Louise Young; she realized that many of her negative feelings toward Julia Scribner resulted from her own cultural biases; she examined her own motives of jealousy when it came to the success of Edith Pope; and, most important, she understood that her problems with Norton could more often than not be traced to her own insecurities. Understanding her shortcomings and then attempting to address them kept Rawlings in constant turmoil. Rawlings's confessions to Norton are particularly instructive. There are intense moments of anger, usually brought on by alcohol. She could be cruel, and often Norton became the object of her self-torturing ridicule. Part of this came from her need to excel as an artist, part from her upbringing by a distant father and (to her) an unloving mother, part from her native penchant for sarcasm laced with irony, and part from the fact that she and Norton had to live apart for much of their marriage.

What strikes one immediately in reading the *Love Letters* is how much of the time they were apart. Early in their relationship her life was at Cross Creek. She stayed there while Norton managed the Marion Hotel in Ocala. Just after their marriage in October 1941, he purchased the Castle Warden Hotel in St. Augustine, partly with funds borrowed from her. At this juncture their relationship became increasingly complicated, for they now lived apart even more. Norton had a suite built for her at the hotel, and she did spend time there, but it was not Cross Creek; it afforded her no privacy, and, more important, it took her away from the source of her inspiration. She did have the cottage at Crescent Beach, south of St. Augustine, which she had purchased in 1939, and overnights and weeks there brought her closer to Norton. Yet she seemed unable to do her writing there and would inevitably drift back to Cross Creek and again away from Norton.

When Norton enlisted as an ambulance driver in the American Field Service in July 1943, was attached to the British Army, and then sent to India, they were separated again until October 1944. It was during this fifteen-month separation that she wrote to him nearly every day, creating the letters that are the heart and soul of this volume. In a curious way, this separation brought them closer together. Rawlings devoted herself to the letter writing, and we now are the fortunate benefactors of this devotion. After returning from the war, Norton sold the Castle Warden and in 1946 became the manager of Marineland, a well-known resort south of Crescent Beach. The thought was that they would be closer. He could live at the beach, and she would come for frequent visits. The best-laid plans did not work; she stayed at Cross Creek much of the time. Meanwhile, through Owen D. Young, Rawlings was introduced to the remote village of Van Hornesville, New York, and in July 1947, she purchased a home there. Her hope was to complete *The Sojourner*. Whatever her expectations, the fact was that her lengthy stays in Van Hornesville took her farther away from Norton, who was struggling to keep Marineland profitable. Their marriage became, in the words of the poet William Butler Yeats, a "continual farewell."

All was not doom and gloom, however. Rawlings loved Cross Creek, and she developed a fondness for certain of her black workers. Most prominent of them was Martha Mickens, the matriarch whose folk tales and "voodoo wisdom" left Rawlings mired between admiration and dismay. The *Love Letters* provides significant new insight into the relationship of Martha and Rawlings. Martha was the glue that held the Rawlings menagerie together. Various maids came and went, including the venerable Idella Parker, but Martha was always there, loyal to Rawlings when loyalty was difficult to find. Martha was especially clever, on occasion deceitful, and more often than not she got the best of Rawlings, who was amazed by Martha's ability to pretend ignorance in the face of understanding. Rawlings also makes Martha the subject of humor, some of it unfortunately racial, but the letters attest to the fact that Rawlings admired the way Martha and her ancient husband, Will, learned to survive in a cruel, often uncompromising white world. According to Rawlings, Martha never cooked properly, never cleaned properly, and never behaved properly. She could not even ward off unwanted visitors properly. Yet, in spite of these and other perceived deficiencies, Rawlings was devoted to Martha. One of the more telling examples of Rawlings's affection for her is in the report of Martha's "rather fabulous" response when asked about the surreal portrait of Rawlings done by Albert Stadler:

> Ain't got my mind composed, but it means a whole lot to me. The way it's looking direct, just like you fixing to pray. Wish he could of had your hands in it. Your hands has meaning.
> Just to stand up and look at it, makes you think way back, way back.
> He couldn't of done a better thing.
> It brings a half-sorrow to me. (14 March 1950)

Martha became an institution at Cross Creek, and, together with "Old Will" and the other members of the Mickens family, she took care of Rawlings to her death, asking for very little and providing a great deal.

Another inscrutable personality who dominates the *Love Letters* is "Aunt Ida." Ida Tarrant was actually Charles Rawlings's great-aunt, but Rawlings soon adopted her, feeling that Aunt Ida was more her mother than her real mother. Aunt Ida was a constant source of humor. Her malapropisms became legendary, and in the *Love Letters* Rawlings uses these celebrated malapropisms as comic relief. Aunt Ida's "grand little cute letters . . . saved my life" (28 November 1939), she writes Norton from the St. Moritz Hotel in New York. Aunt Ida never ceased to interfere, oblivious of the problems she was creating. Rawlings complains that "there's just no use trying to type and listen at the same time. What she practices is a sort of mental rape. You are deep in typing or reading, and she invades you, violates you" (27 November 1943). Still, the endless malapropisms and faulty syllogisms kept everyone laughing. Aunt Ida would call Chattahoochee, the home of a state mental institution, "Catchahoochie" (20 March 1944), or she would report that, "The old gentleman died, after lying in a semi-comma for over a week" (22 April 1944), or she would reject Christ with the logic, "'When we have God, why do we have to have a son?'" (9 July 1944). Rawlings's patience with her on occasion wore thin: Aunt Ida is "driving me nuts. . . . She is reading 'Grapes of Wrath' . . . and said, 'This is a wonderful book for anyone to read that's moving'" (11 July 1944). All of this left Rawlings to lament, "I really should have made notes down the years of her malapropisms, for a side-splitting story could be made of them, though no one would believe a word of it" (12 July 1944). Rawlings's litany persists: "Aunt Ida has literally driven me to drink the last two days. . . . [I]f she knew how much I was drinking in my ready-to-scream despair, it would only bring on a moral treatise" (17 July 1944). But as the letters amply demonstrate, Rawlings's love for her adopted aunt never abated. Ida Tarrant died suddenly on

18 June 1952, at the age of ninety-two. As promised, Rawlings took her ashes back to Cincinnati, and yet another important chapter in Rawlings's life was closed.

The *Love Letters* also provides lively commentary on the literature, art, and film of the day. Rawlings was an inveterate reader, as was Norton, and her observations—especially when combined with those in *Max and Marjorie*—offer a fascinating critique of the literary scene of the 1930s and 1940s. To be sure, her remarks are often only one-liners, but those one-liners are sometimes reflective and are invariably trenchant, such as her acknowledgment of *The Catcher in the Rye* as a "lovely sensitive job" (8 September 1951). Maxwell Perkins and Charles Scribner and later Norman Berg of Macmillan sent her most of the books she read. Rawlings had her likes and dislikes, of course. Faulkner's style was obtrusively dense; Hemingway's was lyrically simple. Rawlings found Hemingway exceptional. After reading the first three chapters of *Across the River and into the Trees*, she put it aside with the comment, "It makes my stuff seem worse than ever" (23 August 1950). James Joyce's earlier work inspired a similar response. Rawlings admired *A Portrait of the Artist as a Young Man*, and *Ulysses* she called "a *magnificent* thing, and completely lucid and intelligible," an observation she followed with, "It seems asinine to turn out my trivial tripe when the Big Boys have already said about all that needs saying" (17 October 1943). But Rawlings's positive impression of *Ulysses* was short-lived; later she lamented that Joyce had ventured into "obscure shadows" in *Ulysses* (5 September 1943), reporting that parts of *Ulysses* shared "the stream-of-consciousness unintelligibility of 'Finnegans Wake,' and I was so disappointed" (18 October 1943). Rawlings's critical voice is like that—visceral yet cogent.

Of the numerous writers Rawlings mentions and analyzes, Edith Pope, her close friend, is written about most. Although Edith Taylor Pope's name is barely recognized today, her novel *Colcorton* (1944) was one of Scribners' best sellers. Pope became a celebrity. At first Rawlings was thrilled by Pope's success, but there came a point at which Rawlings became jealous. Rawlings saw Pope as her protégée, in a sense her pupil. Pope's sudden fame was difficult for the then-struggling Rawlings, and even more disturbing to her was that Pope now had the attention of Maxwell Perkins. To Rawlings's credit, she overcame such pettiness, and Pope remained a favorite. Pope was also a source of humor, principally because of her extreme myopia. She once unwittingly got close to a deadly coral snake, exclaiming, "Gosh it's pre-e-e-tty" (21 April 1944). Pope survived this and other scrapes with nature at the Creek, but Rawlings was never certain that she was good to have around, fearing that if she took her blackberry picking, "Edith would attract all the rattlesnakes in the county" (27 May 1944).

Just as the *Love Letters* provides a history of literature of the period, it also provides an informal history of film. Rawlings loved the cinema, as did Norton. Thus the letters are replete with commentary on the films of the day. When Norton was gone to war, Rawlings would often drive into Gainesville to see a matinee and then stay for an early evening feature. Her analyses of the films and the stars provide a cultural overview of what was popular at the time, although in many instances Rawlings's preferences went against the grain of those of the general public. For example, although she was a great admirer of Ingrid Bergman, she thought Bergman's role and that of Gary Cooper in *For Whom the Bell Tolls* the "weakest parts" (29 July 1943), and she was appalled when she learned that Bergman was being considered for the role of Ma Baxter in *The Yearling*: "What ARE those asses up to?" (6 May 1945). Rawlings's taste in movies was not exclusive. The war influenced what was available for her to see. Thus the movies she critiques in these letters range from features such as *Sunny* (1941), which she found "utterly *lousy*" (November 1941), to hits such as *Lifeboat* (1944), starring Tallulah Bankhead and William Bendix.

Rawlings's satiric wit naturally surfaced when it came to film. She laments that Deanna Durbin in *Hers to Hold* (1943) has a "wonderful personality and still has a lovely figure, but her little face has gotten as round as my behind" (27 September 1943). Rawlings was expecting to "weep buckets" over *Lassie Come Home* (1943), starring the ingénue Elizabeth Taylor. She found Carmen Miranda "a *riot*" (30 April 1944) in *The Gang's All Here* (1943). *Jane Eyre* (1944), starring Orson Welles and Joan Fontaine, was "perfectly wonderful," although Welles "overacted" (8 May 1944). On the other hand, she found *Tender Comrade* (1943), starring Ginger Rogers, "tripe" (15 May 1944). *Madame Curie* (1943), starring Greer Garson, was a "sad Hollywood mess" (21 June 1944).

Rawlings was, of course, no innocent when it came to Hollywood. She watched helplessly as the 1941 filming of *The Yearling*, starring Spencer Tracy, floundered and finally was scrubbed, the result of expensive delays and actor disenchantment. Cross Creek lore still has it that Tracy, drunk, hired a taxi to drive him to Chicago to escape. Later Rawlings wrote the screenplay for *The Sun Comes Up* (1949), starring Jeanette MacDonald, which MGM intended as a "Lassie" movie, but which ended up as a musical to highlight the talents of MacDonald. Rawlings's contributions are barely noticeable, although her compensation was in the six figures. She failed in her attempt to complete another screenplay, *A Bad Name Dog* (1948). The *Love Letters* offers new insight into these notable failures. Curiously, however, there is no mention of *The Yearling* (1946), starring Gregory Peck and Jane Wyman, a film that remains a Hollywood classic. And, even more curious, there is no mention of her and Norton being the special guests of Margaret Mitchell for the premiere of *Gone with the Wind* (1939).

These letters are particularly valuable for Rawlings's critiques of the traumas she experienced while writing, although there is less commentary on her works as a whole than one might expect, and certainly not as much as in her correspondence with Maxwell Perkins. Still, her constant complaints to Norton serve as a road map of the demands she placed upon herself as a writer. Her complaints about *The Sojourner*, the writing of which plagued her for more than a decade, are deafening, and finally a source of conflict with Norton. When it came to her work, she seldom invited response from Norton. However, her failure to ask him is not so much because she lacked confidence in his judgment; rather it was because she had Maxwell Perkins until his death in 1947. And after that it was too late; she had lost both energy and inspiration. She had suffered through the war years writing daily letters to Norton, and to the military personnel who, with their Armed Services Editions of *South Moon Under*, *The Yearling*, and *Cross Creek* before them, deluged her with letters—often very personal letters—about the war and their fear of battle. If history should credit Rawlings with anything beyond her literary contributions, it should credit her with enriching the lives of hundreds of servicepeople by writing detailed responses to their letters of appeal. She often received more than one hundred letters per week, and to answer them—work that she found debilitating—she had to employ secretaries to help her. And she became attached to a number of the servicepeople, the most notable of whom was Caleb Milne, who wrote her lengthy, poignant letters of appeal, only then to be killed in battle. Responding to the sorrow of the Milne family, and to her own, Rawlings agreed to write a preface to *I Dream of the Day: Letters from Caleb Milne, Africa, 1942–1943* (1944). The strain of writing these war letters, coupled with those to Norton for over a year, took its toll on Rawlings, who was also embroiled in the *Cross Creek* "invasion of privacy" lawsuit. To compensate, she turned to drink, to nicotine, to pills, and to food. To be sure, she had her good moments, even days and weeks, but on the whole her increasingly profligate lifestyle took its toll. These letters are a history of her addictions and a record of her guilt. She suffered, indeed suffered more because she was fully aware of what she was doing to herself. Through it all Norton stood by her, unwavering in his devotion.

If there is one measure of good that came from Rawlings's conflicted life in the 1940s and early 1950s, it was Norton Baskin, the anchor in her shifting sea. I am reminded of the distress of Lord Byron's unrequited Julia, who laments: "'Man's love is of man's life a thing apart, / 'Tis a woman's whole existence'" (*Don Juan*, canto 1, stanza 194). I can think of no greater compliment to Marjorie Kinnan Rawlings and Norton S. Baskin than to say that for once, at least, Byron was wrong. Norton's love for Marjorie was never qualified, never a thing apart. And, in spite of seemingly insurmountable obstacles, Marjorie enjoyed and returned a love Byron's Julia never knew. If anything, these letters are a testament to their enduring love and to those many individuals, great and small, fortunate enough to have shared in it.

Chronology

. . . .

MKR's major publications are included below. For a complete catalogue of her writings, see Rodger L. Tarr, *Marjorie Kinnan Rawlings: A Descriptive Bibliography* (1996).

1896	Born 8 August, Washington, D.C., to Arthur Frank Kinnan and Ida May Traphagen Kinnan. Father was an examiner for the U.S. Patent Office; mother taught school before MKR's birth. The Kinnans also owned a dairy farm in Maryland.
1900	Arthur Houston Kinnan, MKR's brother, was born.
1910–1912	Publishes a number of letters and award-winning stories in the *Washington Post*; "The Reincarnation of Miss Hetty" in *McCall's Magazine* (1912); and several stories in her high school magazine, *Western*.
1913	Father dies.
1914	Graduates from Western High School. The family moves to Madison, where MKR enters the University of Wisconsin and majors in English, with serious interests in journalism and theater.
1915	Begins to publish articles of current university interest in the *Wisconsin Literary Magazine*. Acts in various plays.
1916	Achieves sophomore honors and is elected to Mortar Board. Is on the staff of the school yearbook, *The Badger*. Initiated into the sorority Kappa Alpha Theta.
1917	Elected Phi Beta Kappa and vice president of Red Domino, the women's drama club, and has the leading part in the junior play *Lima Beans*.
1918	Announces engagement to Charles Rawlings. Writes a senior English thesis, and graduates from the University of Wisconsin with honors.
1919	Works at various editing jobs and for the Y.W.C.A. in New York City, while trying unsuccessfully to sell her stories. Marries Charles Rawlings, and they remove to his hometown of Rochester, New York.
1920	Rawlingses move to Louisville, Kentucky. MKR becomes a feature reporter for the *Louisville Courier-Journal*. Writes a feature column called "Live Women in Live Louisville."

1921	Rawlingses return to Rochester, where MKR writes feature articles, mostly on social issues, for the *Rochester Evening Journal*.
1922	Continues to write for the *Rochester Evening Journal*, but has no success in selling her own work.
1923	Mother dies.
1924	Lands a job as the society editor for the popular magazine *Five O'Clock*, writing under the nom de plume "Lady Alicia Thwaite."
1926	Begins, in May, for the *Rochester Times-Union*, a series of poems called "Songs of a Housewife," a syndicated feature that appears almost daily until February 1928. There are 495 of these domestic poems, which run the gamut from advice, to recipes, to gardens, to anecdotes on the "Romance of the Housewife." See Rawlings, *Songs of a Housewife* (1997).
1928	Completes her autobiographical novel, *Blood of My Blood*, which is published posthumously in 2002, largely about her conflicted relationship with her mother. Calls it "poor Jane Austen." Buys a seventy-two-acre orange grove near Cross Creek in remote North Central Florida and moves there with Charles in November.
1930	Sells "Cracker Chidlings" to *Scribner's Magazine*, followed by the novella "Jacob's Ladder," which brings her to the attention of the famed editor Maxwell Perkins.
1931	Publishes "Cracker Chidlings," about her impressions of her new neighbors; "Jacob's Ladder," about a young Cracker bride who must learn to survive in a male's world; and "A Plumb Clare Conscience," about a moonshiner whose Cracker ingenuity prevails over civil authority. Writes "Lord Bill of the Suwannee River," about a railroad foreman whose exploits rival those of Paul Bunyan, published posthumously in 1963. Lives with the Fiddia family in the Big Scrub to gather material for a novel.
1932	Publishes "Dutch Oven Cookery," which features her talents as a cook; "A Crop of Beans," about how a man, suffering from avarice and pride, is saved by his wife; and the expressly feminist "Gal Young 'Un," about a woman who empowers herself after suffering humiliation at the hands of her abusive husband. The last was awarded the O. Henry Memorial Prize for the best short story of 1932. Works on the manuscript of her novel about the Big Scrub.
1933	Publishes *South Moon Under* and enjoys immediate critical acclaim. Perkins compares the novel favorably to *Huckleberry Finn*. Lives with Cal Long family and learns more Cracker lore, part of which later finds its way into *The Yearling*. Goes to England to gather material for a novel Perkins does not want her to write. He encourages her to write a "boy's book" instead. Publishes "Hyacinth Drift," an account of the boat trip she and Dessie Smith took up the St. Johns River; "Alliga-

tors," a chronicle of her alligator hunts with Fred Tompkins; and "Benny and the Bird Dogs," a satire about a man who sells his dogs knowing that they are trained to come home. In the last story she introduces Quincey Dover, a recurring female foil based loosely on MKR herself. Divorces Charles Rawlings in November.

1934   Publishes "The Pardon," about a misfit who is unexpectedly pardoned from prison for a crime he did not commit, and who returns home to find his wife living with another man. Completes draft of *Golden Apples*.

1935   Publishes *Golden Apples*, a psychological novel about an Englishman who finds himself unsuited to life in Florida. While not a critical success, Perkins thought it had great technical merit. Abbreviated version appears in *Cosmopolitan*.

1936   Publishes "Varmints," about two slippery friends who own a mule, but who avoid responsibility for its burial when it dies; and "A Mother in Mannville," about an orphan boy who invents a mother to hide his shame, one of MKR's most celebrated stories. It was later adapted for the so-called Lassie story, "Mountain Prelude." Fishes with Ernest Hemingway in Bimini; hunts with Barney Dillard in the Big Scrub; and meets F. Scott Fitzgerald in Asheville, North Carolina.

1937   Works on the manuscript of *The Yearling*, the "boy's book" Perkins had wanted her to write. Meets Thomas Wolfe in New York City at the urging of Perkins, who hopes she can convince Wolfe to shorten his manuscripts.

1938   Publishes *The Yearling*, which becomes an international best seller, and sells the film right to MGM for $30,000. The novel is serialized in the *New York Post*. Becomes a celebrity and goes on the lecture circuit, which impacts her health.

1939   Publishes "Cocks Must Crow," where Quincey Dover learns the lesson that "Man-nature is man-nature, and a woman's a fool to interfere." Elected to the National Institute of Arts and Letters. Receives the Pulitzer Prize for fiction. Buys the cottage at Crescent Beach.

1940   Publishes "The Pelican's Shadow," in part a retrospective of MKR's marriage to Charles Rawlings, about a woman who purchases a life of ease at the expense of her dignity; "The Enemy," about frontier justice set in the cattle county of Central Florida; and "In the Heart," about racism with the twist that she treats black prejudice toward other blacks. Also publishes a nonfictional essay, "Regional Literature of the South," in which she disavows the term *regional*. Publishes *When the Whippoorwill—*, a collection of previously published stories. Completes "Fish Fry and Fireworks," about Quincey Dover introducing a rattlesnake to a political rally with near tragic consequences, which was published posthumously in 1967. Begins work on the manuscript of *Cross Creek*.

1941   Publishes "Jessamine Springs," about an itinerant preacher whose meaningless commitments lead him to loneliness and despair; and "The Provider," about a railroad fireman who gives coal to a destitute family, only to be fired for his charitable spirit. MGM begins production of *The Yearling*, starring Spencer Tracy, only to scrub it later because of weather, costs, and actor disenchantment. Marries Norton Sanford Baskin.

1942   Publishes *Cross Creek*, a collection of semi-autobiographical vignettes about her life at Cross Creek, which becomes a best seller; *Cross Creek Cookery*, a collection of recipes with anecdotal interlinear commentary; and the nonfictional "Trees for Tomorrow," about the need to preserve the forests. Awarded Doctor of Humane Letters by the University of Florida.

1943   Begins work on the manuscript of *The Sojourner*, the writing of which plagues her for nearly a decade. Zelma Cason files a lawsuit accusing MKR of libel—later changed to "invasion of privacy"—for the characterization of her in *Cross Creek*. Norton enlists in the American Field Service and is assigned to the India/Burma campaign.

1944   Publishes the nonfictional "Florida: A Land of Contrasts," another ecological appeal; and "The Shell," about a retarded young woman who, when rudely turned away by the Red Cross, walks into the ocean to join her soldier husband who is at war. MKR is coming under increasing pressures caused by the lawsuit, by Norton's absence, and by her determination to answer literally hundreds of letters from servicepeople.

1945   Publishes the nonfictional "Florida: An Affectionate Tribute," yet another ecological appeal, which is entered into the *Congressional Record*; "Black Secret," about a white boy who learns accidentally that his favorite uncle fathered a child by a black woman; and "Miriam's Houses," about a girl who is envious of her friend who seemed to have everything, only to learn later that the friend's mother was a prostitute.

1946   Publishes "Miss Moffatt Steps Out," about a teacher who mistakenly abandons the ideal of books for life in the raw. In the *Cross Creek* trial, MKR is found innocent of "invasion of privacy." Cason appeals the decision to the Florida Supreme Court. The film *The Yearling*, starring Gregory Peck and Jane Wyman, is released.

1947   "Mountain Prelude," the so-called Lassie story, is serialized in the *Saturday Evening Post*. Publishes "The Use of the Sitz-Bath," one of many contributions to the *Dumpling Magazine*, an annual publication by the family of Owen D. Young. The Florida Supreme Court reverses the *Cross Creek* trial decision and orders MKR to pay a one-dollar fine and court costs. MKR rents and then buys the farmhouse in Van Hornesville, New York. Maxwell Perkins suddenly dies, "an unspeakable grief" to MKR from which she never recovers.

1948   Continues work on the manuscript of *The Sojourner*, which is made more difficult because of the death of Perkins.

1949   Publishes "The Friendship," about a boy who learns the value of friendship after lying to his policeman friend. Continues to be frustrated by her inability to finish *The Sojourner*.

1950   Publishes "Portrait of a Magnificent Editor," about the importance of Maxwell Perkins as an editor and friend.

1951   Begins revision of the first draft of *The Sojourner*.

1952   Suffers a coronary spasm. Convalesces at Crescent Beach. Robert Frost visits her. Completes the revision of *The Sojourner*. Begins preliminary work on her biography of Ellen Glasgow. Takes a trip to England and Ireland with NSB.

1953   Publishes *The Sojourner*, a novel that explores in transcendent terms the subjects of betrayal, redemption, and brotherhood. It receives mixed reviews. Removes to Richmond, Virginia, to continue research on the Glasgow biography. Five-part autobiographical sketch appears in the *Los Angeles Times*. Suffers a ruptured aneurysm on 13 December, and dies the next day at Flagler Hospital, St. Augustine, at the age of fifty-seven. Is buried at Antioch Cemetery, near Island Grove.

Guide to Major Figures
and Places

· ·

The following is a guide to the individuals who play a major role in these letters. It is intended as a quick reference tool. Since MKR uses first names almost exclusively, the guide begins with first names, except where appropriate to use last names. The guide is not intended to replace the index, where the names of and page citations to the literally hundreds of individuals mentioned in the letters can be found.

ADRENNA MICKENS SAMSON—a maid to MKR and daughter of Will and Martha Mickens. She is described in *Cross Creek* as an "angular creature" whose "butt stuck out sharply. She was a *femme fatale*" who was "careless in dress and cleanliness. . . . She could seduce any man she wanted. . . . She did my work for several years and there was a true love and exasperation between us" (22–23). Adrenna was married to B. J. Samson.

ALBERTA MICKENS—the "fat lazy" wife of "Little Will" Mickens (*Max and Marjorie*, 480). Alberta worked for MKR on occasion, tending the garden and the chickens, and on occasion helping with the laundry (Parker, *Perfect Maid*, 29). MKR hoped to train her as a maid, but once married, the "homeless orphan . . . announced that her working days were over" (*Cross Creek*, 202).

ARTHUR H. KINNAN—brother of MKR, whose unsettled domestic and business life was a constant torment to MKR. Married three times, under what MKR considered dubious circumstances, Kinnan aspired to sail the seas. MKR helped him purchase a charter boat, with the plan that he would take tourists into the Alaskan waters from Seattle. The venture failed. Kinnan seemed always in debt and at various times borrowed money from MKR, whose love for her brother never wavered in spite of the frustration he caused her. It was Kinnan's son, Jeff, whom MKR once hoped to adopt.

ATCHLEY, DR. DANA—New York City physician who treated MKR at Harkness Pavilion, Columbia-Presbyterian Hospital, and who later became a friend and confidant. He was also Norton Baskin's primary physician upon Norton's return from India.

Aunt Ida Tarrant—great-aunt of Charles Rawlings, beloved by MKR, and especially known for her malapropisms. She first lived in Ocala, then in St. Augustine. MKR's recounting of Aunt Ida's banter at Cross Creek gives rise to much of the humor in the letters.

Barney Dillard—the old hunter from whom MKR learned Cracker lore. His bear-hunting exploits were later used in *The Yearling* (*Cross Creek*, 289–90). MKR describes him as the "marvelous old pioneer," a "famous 'bad man,' but honorable and respected" (*Max and Marjorie*, 250).

Bernie: Charles Bernie Bass—a commercial fisherman whose family seemed always to live on the brink of poverty. They were proud yet on occasion had to ask for MKR's help. Once Teresa Bass asked for a dime to feed her child, only to pay it back a year later, which led MKR to reflect in admiration: "When one has a basic integrity, one's standards are high" (*Cross Creek*, 139).

Bert: Bertram C. Cooper—Navy chaplain and good friend whom MKR pushed as a suitor for Julia Scribner. MKR's intrigues did not work. In June 1945, Julia married the Reverend Thomas Bigham, whom MKR first tolerated, then came to like.

B. J. Samson—helped to manage MKR's grove.

Bob: Robert C. Camp—an artist and close friend who did the drawings for *Cross Creek Cookery* (1942).

Bonny—nickname for NSB.

Buddy: Ernest Wayne Bass—the boy whom MKR befriended, brought into her home, and for a time treated as her own.

Carl Brandt—New York agent of MKR.

Carol Brandt—New York agent of MKR.

Castle Warden Hotel—St. Augustine resort hotel owned and managed by Norton Baskin.

Cecil Clarke—Clarke, Norton Baskin, and Robert Camp were the "three musketeers who are like brothers to me" (*Max and Marjorie*, 359). Manager of the Marion Refrigeration Co. in Ocala.

Charlie: Charles Scribner III—president of Charles Scribner's Sons, MKR's publisher, husband of Vera Scribner, and father of Julia Scribner.

Chef: Clarence Huston—chef at the Castle Warden Hotel.

Chet: James Chester Crosby—MKR's grove manager, a favorite hunting and fishing companion who also trained MKR's hunting dogs. Crosby was especially enamored of Julia Scribner.

Chuck: Charles A. Rawlings Jr.—first husband of MKR. Marjorie and Charles were college sweethearts at the University of Wisconsin, and after graduation they courted in New York City, where she worked for the Y.W.C.A. while seeking publishers for her own work. They were married in 1919, and after nearly a decade of unfulfilled goals moved to Cross Creek in remote North Central Florida in 1928, with the idea of living off the land while they pursued their writing careers. The marriage was doomed, for Charles was unable to accept Marjorie's success. They were divorced in 1933. MKR's short story "The Pelican's Shadow" (1940) offers, in some ways, a retrospective view of the volatile, often violent, nature of their marriage.

CLIFF: CLIFFORD LYONS—chair of the English Department at the University of Florida, later dean at the University of North Carolina, Chapel Hill, once a close friend of MKR with whom she had a falling out later in life. MKR was fond of Lyons's wife, Gladys.

CRESCENT BEACH—the oceanfront cottage, now in private hands, that MKR bought from Ralph Poole of Scribners. She loved the ocean atmosphere, particularly because it brought her closer to NSB, who owned and managed the Castle Warden Hotel in St. Augustine to the north, and who later managed the two restaurants at the Marineland resort to the south. However, in spite of the inviting nature of the cottage, she could never sustain her writing there and always longed to return Cross Creek.

DESSIE SMITH VINSON [later, Prescott]—a Florida pioneer and barnstormer who offered friendship when MKR was struggling early in her career, and who taught her a great deal of Cracker lore. Dessie was one of MKR's favorite hunting and fishing partners. MKR celebrated their now-famous trip down the St. Johns River in "Hyacinth Drift" (1933).

DICK: RICHARD YOUNG—son of Owen D. Young, who became a favorite of MKR, publishing her work in the family journal, the *Dumpling Magazine* (Tarr, *MKR: A Descriptive Bibliography*, 234–35).

DORA, DORA ROLLEY, OR DORA REGINA—MKR's self-created alter ego, not to be confused with MKR's prize milk cow named Dora.

DOUG: DOUGLAS THOMPSON—manager at the Castle Warden Hotel when NSB was in the American Field Service.

EDIE: EDITH TAYLOR POPE—close friend and American novelist whom MKR introduced to Scribners. Verle Pope was her husband.

ELLA MAY TOWNSEND SLATER—wife of "Snow" Slater.

ESTELLE MICKENS SWEET—a maid and oldest and "best" daughter of Martha Mickens (*Cross Creek*, 22). Wife of Sam Sweet.

FREDDIE: FRED FRANCIS—a wealthy St. Augustine socialite and a favorite bridge partner of MKR. He was once married to Jean Francis. Fred owned the lavish estate called Hunta Hunta Hara.

FREDERICKS: ELLIS J. AND LILIAN FREDERICKS—farm neighbors at Van Hornesville. Lilian would help MKR on occasion.

FRED TOMPKINS—a special favorite of MKR who took her on hunts and who inspired the article "Alligators" (1933). MKR went often to Tompkins for advice on how to portray Florida wildlife. He was characterized as Uncle Benny Mathers in "Benny and the Bird Dogs" (1933) and perhaps as Will Dover in "Cocks Must Crow" (1939). MKR called him an "amazing person" in *Cross Creek* (314).

GENE BARO [Baroff]—poet whom MKR befriended while he was at the University of Florida. Baro and his companion, Albert Stadler, visited regularly at Cross Creek and at Van Hornesville. MKR came to admire them both, even though she professed to be offended by their homosexuality.

GEORGE FAIRBANKS—described as the "last of a once proud and prosperous line" (*Cross Creek*, 126), whose "modest income" was administered for him by "Old Boss" Brice. He lived west of the Creek in a shanty, and once tried to court MKR, in whom he confided weekly.

GRACE FLORA BRICE WILLIAMS—daughter of "Old Boss" Brice, and wife of Hugh Williams.

GRACE KINNAN—a favorite aunt of MKR.

HENRY FOUNTAIN—a grove man who worked for the Glissons and the Brices, and on rare occasion for MKR. He was married to Sissie Mickens. On New Year's Day, 1939, Fountain shot B. J. Samson, the husband of Adrenna Mickens. MKR filed charges against Fountain, which were subsequently dismissed, causing MKR to conclude, "It came to me that I had never been in a court of justice less touched by truth and honesty" (*Cross Creek*, 200).

HETTIE LOU FOUNTAIN—daughter of Zamilla "Sissie" Mickens Fountain.

HUGH: G. HUGH WILLIAMS—a neighbor at Cross Creek.

IDELLA PARKER—one of the central figures in the letters and arguably the most important figure in MKR's life after Norton Baskin and Maxwell Perkins. Although a maid, Parker was MKR's confidante and for years her close friend. Together they entertained the rich and the famous, and it was Parker who was responsible for many of the recipes in *Cross Creek Cookery* (1942). Parker was formally educated and could welcome individuals as diverse as Robert Frost, Zora Neale Hurston, Julia Scribner, and Owen D. Young. The major conflicts between MKR and Parker came when the former would get drunk or when the latter would leave, on occasion without notice. This perhaps accounts for one of the enigmas of the letters: how cruel MKR could be, in language, toward Parker at one point and how loving at another. Certainly, what is said in these letters, both good and bad, should be read in the context of Parker's own reminiscences of MKR: *Idella: Marjorie Rawlings' "Perfect Maid"* (1992) and *Idella Parker: From Reddick to Cross Creek* (1999).

J. T., or JAKE, GLISSON—son of Tom and Pearlee Glisson. The importance of his presence at Cross Creek cannot be overstated. As a child, he visited with MKR repeatedly, the Glisson home being just north of hers. She treated him, as she did other boys like Buddy Bass, as the son she always wanted. In *Cross Creek*, MKR describes him as a "tragic little cripple . . . hobbling down the road on his crooked legs, with the luminous expression on his face that seems peculiar to those we call 'afflicted'" (14). J. T. was the prototype for Fodderwing in *The Yearling*. Glisson fully recovered from his boyhood affliction, and is now an artist, author, and "born storyteller" of considerable renown. His book *The Creek* (1993) is an invaluable historical resource.

JAMES BRANCH CABELL—the Virginia author who introduced MKR to Ellen Glasgow and who subsequently aided MKR in preparing Glasgow's biography, never completed, by connecting her with Glasgow's family and intimates. Cabell and his wife, Priscilla, were favorites of the Baskins. When Priscilla died, MKR introduced Cabell to Margaret Freeman, whose subsequent marriage to Cabell became a social event, arranged by MKR, in St. Augustine.

JEFF: JEFFREY KINNAN—son of Arthur H. and Grace Kinnan, whom MKR once thought of adopting because of the strained relationship of his parents and because of MKR's need for a son.

JOSEPHINE YOUNG CASE—poet and daughter of Owen D. Young, and wife of Everett Case, president of Colgate University.

JULIA SCRIBNER—daughter of Charles Scribner III and Vera Scribner, and later Mrs. Thomas Bigham. MKR considered her a "goddaughter," and Julia soon became her closest female friend, visiting her repeatedly at both Cross Creek and Van Hornesville. MKR's antipathy for Vera is no doubt the result, in part at least, of her motherly feelings for Julia, whom MKR later named the executor of her estate. Julia saw MKR's posthumously published children's book, *The Secret River* (1955), through publication and until her death oversaw many of MKR's unpublished manuscripts, including the autobiographical novel *Blood of My Blood* (2002).

LEONARD FIDDIA—general handyman. MKR lived with Leonard, his wife, Margaret, and his mother, Piety, in the Big Scrub to learn more about the Cracker culture and language and to gather material for *South Moon Under*. During this time, MKR hunted and ran moonshine with Leonard, and cooked and made quilts with Piety (*Selected Letters*, 339–42). It was Leonard who coined the expression "them Christian-hearted sons of bitches," which MKR took delight in using in her letters. Leonard was the prototype for the hero Lant in *South Moon Under*.

"LITTLE BOSS"—nickname given NSB by the employees of the Castle Warden Hotel.

"LITTLE MARTHA"—daughter of Zamilla "Sissie" Mickens Fountain and Henry Fountain.

MARCH MICKENS—son of Will and Martha Mickens, husband of Katie.

MARINELAND—resort south of Crescent Beach. NSB once managed the two restaurants there.

MARION HOTEL—Ocala hotel once managed by NSB.

MARTHA MICKENS—the black matriarch at Cross Creek and one of the most important figures in the MKR household. In *Cross Creek*, MKR speaks of her importance: "As I look back on those first difficult times at the Creek, when it seemed as though the actual labor was more than I could bear, and the making of a living on the grove impossible, it was old black Martha who drew aside a curtain and led me in to the company of all those who had loved the Creek and had been tormented by it" (19). Martha and "Old Will," her husband, helped MKR when she was in desperate need of help, and they asked for little in return. When MKR was poor, Martha worked for ten cents an hour, more when MKR could afford it. She was, says MKR, a "natural aristocrat," perhaps "descended from old African kings and queens" (25). As these letters show, clearly for the first time, it was Martha to whom MKR turned for loyalty and respect, which was returned in full measure. It was Martha who welcomed MKR to Cross Creek, and it was Martha who was there when MKR left for the last time.

MARTIN, MR.: O. E. MARTIN—lived west of the bridge at Cross Creek and was notorious for letting his hogs roam. On several occasions, they rooted MKR's favorite petunia bed. In anger one night she shot the barrow hog dead, had it dressed, and threw a barbecue for the locals. Martin was outraged and confronted MKR. She offered to replace the hog. Martin refused but later took cash in recompense (*Max and Marjorie*, 507). The whole affair is described in the chapter "A Pig Is Paid For" in *Cross Creek*.

MAX: MAXWELL E. PERKINS—MKR's beloved editor at Scribners. It was Perkins who discovered MKR, nurtured her, and brought her to success. When he died suddenly in 1947, the lamp of MKR's literary life was in effect extinguished. Her relationship with and tribute to him are portrayed in "Portrait of a Magnificent Editor as Seen in His Letters" (1950) and in *Max and Marjorie: The Correspondence between Maxwell E. Perkins and Marjorie Kinnan Rawlings* (1999).

MISS BINNEY: FLORIDA BINNEY SANFORD BASKIN—mother of NSB. MKR had great respect for her and the Baskin family in general, and she visited them often in Alabama.

MOE—MKR's second pointer dog.

NETTIE MARTIN—Ocala friend and accomplished fox hunter (*Cross Creek*, 286). Martin's companionship with John Clardy frustrated MKR.

NORMAN BERG—a trade manager for Macmillan in Atlanta who tried to recruit MKR from Scribners. Berg and his second wife, Julie, who liked to stay at Crescent Beach, were considered close friends but a nuisance: "Norman is an odd sort of egotist," MKR wrote to Maxwell Perkins (*Max and Marjorie*, 595).

"OLD BOSS" BRICE—William Riley Brice, who lived just north of MKR and who owned the country store in the village. Brice was a recalcitrant old man who served as a counselor to the blacks of the area (Stephens, *Reader's Guide*, 5). One of the most talked-about events at Cross Creek was that of MKR hitting and killing the Brice mule, which had wandered onto the road. The scene was witnessed by J. T. Glisson, who relates the cause and the aftermath in *The Creek* (167–70).

"OLD HEN"—nickname for Annie Tompkins, wife of Fred Tompkins. MKR used her henpecking character in several of her short stories.

"OLD WILL" MICKENS—husband of Martha Mickens. By the time MKR came to Cross Creek, Will was in his sixties and not capable of sustained work. He did, however, occasionally work around the house and in the grove. MKR felt that he suffered from "arrogance" and that he was "belligerent." "He looks," she says in *Cross Creek*, "for all the world like Uncle Tom, with grizzled hair and whiskers, and walks with a cane. The cane is a badge of his independence, indicating that he is frail and cannot or will not stoop to labor." Yet she concludes, "When I am his age, . . . I think I too shall walk with a cane and accept a livelihood as my right, after years of toiling" (26).

PAT—MKR's first pointer dog.

PEACHES—nickname for MKR.

PEGGY OR MARGIE: AUDREY HUSTON—hostess at the Castle Warden Hotel, wife of Clarence Huston, the chef.

PHIL: PHILIP S. MAY SR.—MKR's attorney, who represented her at the *Cross Creek* trial. May and his wife, Lillian, became MKR's close friends. MKR was also fond of Philip Jr. and Anne Hill, the stepchildren of Lillian. In 1988, Phil May Jr. founded the Rawlings Society.

PREACH—nickname for Henry Woodward, "Old Boss" Brice's field hand.

R. J.: R. J. SHORTRIDGE—husband of Thelma Shortridge.

ROBERT FROST—preeminent poet and close friend. Frost visited MKR at Cross Creek, at Crescent Beach, and at Van Hornesville.

ROSS ALLEN—famed herpetologist at the Silver Springs tourist attraction who took MKR on rattlesnake hunts, one of which is described in *Cross Creek*, where MKR concludes, "I discovered for me rattlesnakes represented the last outpost of physical fear" (168).

RUTHIE: RUTH PICKERING—close friend who perished in the fire at the Castle Warden Hotel.

SISSIE: ZAMILLA MICKENS FOUNTAIN—nickname of the wife of Henry Fountain. Sissie was once shot in a "jook joint" defending her husband, whom MKR liked except when he was drunk: "I know of no darky who more deserves shooting when drunk" (*Cross Creek*, 22). Sissie worked for MKR on occasion.

"Snow": Feldon Slater—MKR's grove man, son of the Widow Slater.

Stad: Albert Stadler—artist and companion of Gene Baro. Stadler did the famous surreal portrait of MKR.

Thelma Tompkins Shortridge—rural mail carrier in Island Grove, daughter of Fred Tompkins, and wife of R. J. Shortridge.

Tigerts: John J. and Edith Tigert—the former president of the University of Florida and his wife.

Tom Glisson—a central figure in MKR's life, although not mentioned as much as others in the letters. In *Cross Creek*, MKR says of him, "Tom raises hogs and some cattle, has built up a little grove, and he and his wife [Pearlee] do anything profitable they can turn their hands to." MKR had a number of "harsh encounters" with Glisson—once over her allegation that he had poisoned her dog, for which she later apologized; once over the need for a cattle gap, for which she finally paid; and once over the reasons for the shooting of B. J. Samson, for which she had to admit she had no proof: "I was in the wrong, and . . . now I know him for a friend and would turn to him in any trouble" (15). In 1950, Glisson accidentally drank poison, thinking it was water, and died "after hours of unspeakable agony" (*Selected Letters*, 352).

Widow Slater: Annie Slater—one of the earliest settlers at Cross Creek.

Wilmer Kinnan—a favorite aunt of MKR.

Young, Mr.: Owen D. Young—one of MKR's most influential friends. Lawyer, executive, bibliophile, and ambassador, he had an estate at Van Hornesville, near Cooperstown, N.Y. MKR was a frequent guest of Owen and Louise Young, his wife, and they frequent dinner guests of hers. MKR especially liked to listen to Young speak of the affairs of the world. She became a part of the Young family, which opened up rich sources of stimulation for her while she struggled with the writing of *The Sojourner* (1953). It was the Youngs who convinced MKR to buy her home at Van Hornesville. MKR always referred to him respectfully as "Mr. Young."

Zelma Cason—the census taker who in 1930 took MKR throughout rural Alachua County in order that she might come to a greater understanding of Cracker life in the scrub. MKR devotes a chapter to the experience in *Cross Creek*, describing Zelma as "an ageless spinster resembling an angry efficient canary" (48). Zelma took offense and filed a lawsuit against MKR. The trial was a sensation. The jury acquitted MKR, but on appeal the Florida Supreme Court reversed the lower court's decision, finding MKR guilty of "invasion of privacy" and ordering her to pay one dollar in damages plus court costs. The trial and its aftermath had a serious impact upon MKR's health and thus upon her literary production. For a complete accounting, see Acton, *Invasion of Privacy*.

The Letters

1938

1938 was a banner year. In the early winter, MKR revised proofs of *The Yearling* and then watched in triumph as it was published on 1 April. Illustrated by Edward Shenton, the novel became an instant best seller and stayed on the bestseller lists for ninety-three consecutive weeks, selling 60,000 copies in sixty days, 177,000 in six months, and 265,000 in the first year. It went through eighteen printings in 1938, and within a year it was translated into Burmese, Danish, Finnish, German, Italian, Japanese, Polish, and Swedish. Other translations were soon to follow. MKR became an international celebrity. The film rights were sold to MGM for $30,000 dollars. In June and again in July, MKR was hospitalized with what was to become chronic diverticulosis. By the end of the year, Scribners was planning a book of short stories and a special edition of *The Yearling*, the latter to be illustrated by N. C. Wyeth. In all this excitement and anxiety, MKR's relationship with NSB grew from companionship to love.

. . . .

(Wire)

JACKSONVILLE, FL

AUG 3 1938

DO HOPE YOU CAN COME TOMORROW HAVE SUDDENLY BEGUN TO FEEL WHIPPED DOWN DOCTOR CASON[1] SAYS ITS NORMAL REACTION I CONTROL MY OWN VISITING HOURS BUT SUGGEST NOT COMING BEFORE ELEVEN THIRTY BECAUSE OF MORNING TREATMENTS WART WILL BE SUFFICIENT IDENTIFICATION MUCH LOVE

1. MKR entered Riverside Hospital, Jacksonville, for "ten days of rest and rigid diet," as she wrote to Maxwell Perkins (*Max and Marjorie*, 364). Dr. T. Z. Cason is the brother of Zelma Cason, who later brought a lawsuit against MKR for libel, finally "invasion of privacy," for MKR's depiction of her in *Cross Creek*. This is the first known correspondence between MKR and NSB.

1939

1939 proved to be a year of literary triumph. In January, MKR was elected to the National Institute of Arts and Letters, and in February she was given an honorary degree by Rollins College. In May, *The Yearling* was awarded the Pulitzer Prize for fiction. MKR was now in great demand on the lecture circuit. Seemingly undaunted by her celebrity, she began historical research on Zephaniah Kingsley, an early-nineteenth-century Florida planter who married a black woman, an idea suggested to her earlier by Philip May, her attorney. The project was never completed, but it gave her ideas for a novel that later became *Golden Apples*. Beginning in June, *The Yearling* was serialized in the *New York Post*. MKR conceived and began a nonfictional book that was later published as *Cross Creek*. In July, she rented an oceanfront cottage at Crescent Beach, where she began work on several stories as well as the vignettes for *Cross Creek*. She continued to experience bouts of diverticulosis and was once again hospitalized in Jacksonville. Ignoring warnings that she must curb her profligate lifestyle, MKR continued to lecture, most notably before the National Council of Teachers of English in New York in November. As her love for NSB grew stronger, so did her need to justify herself to him. Each time that she left him, she regretted it. The absences caused frequent arguments, which were always followed by apologies and promises of reform.

. . . .

(*Selected Letters*, MS not seen)

[Cross Creek, Fla.]
[Spring 1939]

To Whom It May Concern:

This is to certify that Rear-Admiral Norton K. O. Baskin, B.B., being desirous because of advancing years to devote the remainder of his active life to a broader field of action, is of his own volition withdrawing from the service of her Majesty the Queen. His time of service has been long and arduous, and his efforts noble and unflagging. With no gain or profit to himself, spurred only by an unfailing sense of duty, making untold sacrifices, he has never let the Queen's sheets be furled by any hand but his own. Not even the crashing of bedsteads in the thick of battle has caused him to lower his colors or to drop his flag.

Her Majesty discharges him honorably and reluctantly, and by this document does set him free of the royal will. In commemoration, this day shall be known as Baskin Day, all shorts to be lowered at sunset to half-mast.

In testimonial thereof, we do hereby give our sign and seal.

Signed,

Dora Regina[1]

1. MKR is referring to her alter-ego.

. . . .

(*Selected Letters*, MS not seen)

[Cincinnati, Ohio]

[1? May 1939]

Hello, darling:-

We had a good trip, but I was furious to find we missed the mountains!

. . . Mean to rest and think up what I'll say tonight to a thousand "Christian-hearted sons of bitches," and will pull out for Columbus early in the afternoon.[1] After the affair tonight, will begin to enjoy myself.

Darling, I miss you painfully. I'm not going to ever leave you again. Well, hardly ever. Maybe just often enough to make you glad to see us come home. I despise being away from you. You see, I enjoy you anywhere.

I do love you.

Saw the Pulitzer announcement in my morning paper.[2] I'm glad for Scribner's sake. Publishers get an awful kick out of those things. I really thought I'd already had as much luck as I deserved on one book, and I sort of hate to think how blue the unsuccessful candidates are feeling this morning, when I wouldn't have minded particularly.

1. MKR, who always loathed talks because they made her so nervous, delivered a lecture at the Ohio State University. She got this expression from her Cracker friend Leonard Fiddia.
2. MKR was awarded the Pulitzer Prize for *The Yearling* (New York: Scribners, 1938).

. . . .

(TLS, 2 pp.)

Hawthorn, Florida

Thursday morning

[1939]

Mister Honey:

. . .Where are you? . . . I kept Monday, Tuesday and Wednesday open, to come in, but decided there was no telling what you were into, and life must go on, so accepted Mrs. Tigert's invitation to go in to Gainesville tonight to dinner and to hear Cornelia Skinner. . . .[1]

Poor Netty has her g— d— John[2] to herself this week, and hinted at their coming out, so will ask them for tomorrow night—will have to be very subtle, and say I want him to tell me fox-hunting stories, or he will be scared at public coupling and run for ambush. Will sound out Netty on asking you, though it may not suit you at all. If you do come, suggest you come in your own car, so the poor soul can have him to herself. Us women want such funny things, and a ride some place alone with her b-st-rd is Netty's idea of Heaven.

Am all upset, what with hard-worrying days and lonesome evenings. Am worrying over the fourth story,[3] which Cosmopolitan refused but the Post accepted, but the Post wants the end changed and I can't get it right. Collier's took the third story,[4] so feel I earned my salt this summer after all. Now Carl[5] is bullying me for more.

My love,
Dora

1. Edith Tigert, wife of the president of the University of Florida. Cornelia Otis Skinner, known for her dramatic readings and solo performances.
2. John Clardy and Nettie Martin, who MKR believes are having an affair. Martin kept cattle near Cross Creek.
3. "The Enemy," *Saturday Evening Post* 212 (20 January 1940): 12–13, 32, 36, 39.
4. "In the Heart," *Collier's Magazine* 105 (3 February 1940): 19, 39.
5. Carl Brandt, MKR's New York agent.

. . . .

(TLS, 4 pp.)

[Crescent Beach, Fla.]
Thursday
[10? August 1939]

Dear Norton:

I not only despair of making you understand me, but I have a great embarrassment in attempting it, for it comes to me that you really do understand, and have only pretended to be puzzled, since you didn't see things the way I did, and it is something that is very hard to bring out into the open. When a woman has wanted more of a man than he has wanted of her, it puts him on the spot to talk about it, and is very humiliating for the woman. But I want to try to give you a clear statement, so that at least, if your not understanding has been genuine, you will know the conflict in my mind.

All the time of our close relations, I have not wanted less of you, but more of you. It was dreadful in the early days, when you seemed actually afraid of me, and showed no desire to be with me very often, and came moseying out once a week at eight or nine o'clock at night after you had fooled around with miscellaneous people. I came so close to putting an end to everything, just out of self-respect, but something told me you really did care for me and things would work out. Things did work out, to a large extent. We reached a greater understanding and closeness. You came to trust me and to trust my affection for you, which you certainly did not in the beginning. And as time went on, my mere hunch about you, ever since I had known you at all, was verified: that you had a wonderful quality to give a woman, and there could hardly be a more lovable companion.

So: what did I want? Frankly, marriage. You did not. You said once that you did. You said once also that you had nothing to offer me. Let me try to give you my idea of marriage. I am not concerned with the legal or social or ethical aspect of it. It is just that I am convinced that the greatest good can be had of life when a man and a woman who love each other and are happy in each other's company, live it together.

I loathe living alone. I need more solitude, more privacy, than most women, but even I can get all I want in the course of a day. My work does not satisfy me as the end and aim of my life. It is something I have to do, but it does not fill and complete my life. Neither am I satisfied with what might be called weekend love, romantic and charming as it really is. I want the quiet satisfaction of living with a man I enjoy.

I certainly am not appealed to by a very usual type of marriage, where it seems as though the poor man and woman were handcuffed together, and neither could move an inch without the other. Loneliness—and weekend-love—are much better than that. But I want the solid base of a joint life.

All right. Where does that put us? First of all—and the thing I resent so deeply, and makes me flare out at you in my ill or drunk unguarded moments—you not only do not want that kind of life, but you have very obviously avoided it. You have a deep and actual horror of it. You have changed a great deal in your feeling about me, and are much closer to feeling about such things as I do, than you used to be. But I think it is very deeply rooted in your nature. All right again. Supposing that in time you came to want the same sort of life I want. Your profession seems to me to make it impossible. I not only could not live the hotel life, but I think there are very few instances where a wife fits in it. When I was younger, I could have adapted myself to a man's life, whatever it was. Now certain aspects of life are as necessary to me as love.

I am torn most of the time between my real love for you, and my desire for a type of man and woman life that I think is impossible for us. If I could accept my loneliness and just go ahead and enjoy you when we are together, as you enjoy such an arrangement, all would be well. If I could make up my mind to break with you entirely and set out on a deliberate and somehow shameful man hunt, I would not be so tormented. But I love you too much and appreciate too much the large measure of happiness that we do have, to be able to do it. Yet our life together is not what I want and it does not complete or satisfy me.

It is poor sportsmanship for me to subject you to my feelings, when there seems to be nothing, according to the circumstances of your profession—which is as right for you as writing is for me—that you can do about it. I made up my mind some time ago that at least while our relationship was close, I could keep my torment to myself. But when my guards go down for one reason or another, I'm not strong enough to do it. I am terribly sorry not to make you easy in mind and entirely happy with me while I'm at it.

Now I have done my very best to be frank, although it embarrasses me, and to try to make you understand what is back of my apparently meaningless fits. I know that you love me very much in your own way. But it makes me feel cold and ugly sometimes when I stop to think that you don't want of me what I wanted of you.

I can't begin to tell you what a cruel thing that was for you not to come to see me Saturday when you could. You had told me that you would not be able to come over for a long time . . . and it never occurred to me to question it, when you called me. If you had been here to stop my damn work for a while, and give me the comfort and release of your companionship, I don't think I'd have gone down for the count the way I did Monday. I told Edith I was desperate, so she and Verle got a friend and came down Sunday evening to play bridge.

Now I do hope I have made you understand.

Love,

. . . .

(*Selected Letters*, MS not seen)

[Crescent Beach, Fla.]
Wednesday morning
bright and early
[6? September 1939]

Dear Honey:

Was lying on the floor listening to the early war news before going out for a pre-breakfast walk, when I heard a tap on the door. It was nigger Will and of course I had visions of Cross Creek in flames, or Adrenna returned with ten men, or what-have-you. He had a little package for me that Martha had forgotten to put in the car. It was half a dozen small cheap napkins—. I could have bought their duplicates in St. Augustine for fifty cents. Counting Will's time, it costs about three dollars for the truck to make that trip. But the sense of virtue with which Martha must have dispatched him to bring me the damn things—. And we are in the midst of the grove fertilizing and need both truck and Will there—. Have put him at cutting the grass while I write you, so he can mail it on his way home.

Drove over in a terrific rainstorm. Could hardly see most of the time. The rain was actually attacking the cottage—had driven in under the front door. It was so beautiful over the river, had to open the door to watch, then in for the mop to keep from getting flooded. It would have been very cozy and wonderful with you here. It was cozy, actually, but not wonderful—. Your bathing suit, the radio, the two reading lights, and so on, made me very homesick for you. I don't know why, but this seems more your place than Cross Creek.

The weather cleared about seven at night and Pat and I walked to the mile and nine-tenths house and back. The sky and sea were gorgeous—salmon and deep violet. The pools of water on the receding tide were violet. As we got back to the cottage, met the Popes. They visited a while, then we went riding on the beach and Verle cast the cast-net for pompano. He got only mullet but plenty of that and it looks fun. Billions of donax, but I thought, "Well, as Norton says, I don't *have* to gather them."

My clean typewriter fools me—I don't get the usual timing.

Have got my mental kinks straightened out again. Am wondering if salt air is all I need for my aberrations. And thanks for your patience. After spending all your life with sane people (or don't we count the Baskins?) you must wonder how come you now to be [are] hanging on trapezes etc. I insist that I'm good for you. And I know you're good for me.

. . . Well, will send Will on now. God, when I look at that little package of un-needed napkins—. You know, if the niggers get turned loose, it will be awful, but won' it be funny? Just a little sense is worse than none at all.

Lots of love, my sweet.

. . . .

(*Selected Letters*, MS not seen)

[Crescent Beach, Fla.]
Thursday
[7? September 1939]

My dear:

It certainly was good to find a parcel of mail in my box just now. Curtis sand-papered out the "Poole" and I painted "Rawlings" in very droopy-drawers black letters and the postman came across.[1]

Sorry you've been hot—it's been divine here. The cross ventilation here is marvelous. There's always at least one place that's breezy and cool.

Put in an infuriating day yesterday. Was all set for hard work, total abstinence except for one small drink just before dinner at night, a slimming diet, lots of exercise. Had just gotten turned around after Will and the truck left, when he popped up at the door again. The truck had broken a spring about two miles across the river. Had to hustle around and get the garage at Dupont Center[2] to tow the truck in, go to town for a new spring, etc. The truck wasn't done until nearly six o'clock. It discouraged me so that I just collapsed with the bottle, ate like a pig, read two books and wondered if I would ever write another word.

This morning all is well again, have had a walk and a marvelous swim—the water is rough now, but then was flat and smooth on the low tide-and think I can hold my appetite down and my typewriter up.

Am going in to Edith's for supper and female bridge, and I enjoy a day's work when I have something to look forward to at night.

In my mail was an express notice of what is almost certainly Julia's rye, though would imagine two bottles weighed more than 5 lbs. Am enclosing the notice, and will write the agent that you will call for the package. Assume you won't mind so pleasant an errand. You may even peek.

Phil May wrote me warning me that I am to be introduced in Jax. by Marcus Fagg,[3] from one of whose addresses to a Baptist Sunday School, Mencken[4] quoted as an incredibly priceless bit of Bible Belt Americana. Afraid I had better not tell Leonard's Christian-hearted sons-of-bitches story—. Though I may never have a better target—.

Lots of Love,

1. MKR purchased the Crescent Beach cottage from Ralph Poole of Scribners. Now in private hands, it is near the intersection of A1A and State Road 206.
2. DuPont Center, where U.S. 1 crosses State Road 206, west of Crescent Beach. The DuPonts were early settlers of the area.
3. Marcus "Daddy" Fagg, state superintendent of the Children's Home Society of Florida.
4. H. L. Mencken, American journalist, critic, and essayist.

. . . .

(ALS, 2 pp.)

[Louisville, Ky.]
Thursday afternoon
[5? October 1939]

Hello honey!

Dr. Rankin[1] was swell. Said my innards were anything but useful, but absolutely would not advise operation. Said it was too dangerous, and too much of the colon is involved for it to do any good to take out the worst part. Said I'd just have to expect the attacks, but it wouldn't matter. Said of course I ran the risk of a perforation, but might never have one. If I ever did, there would be time for me to take a 'plane and go to him, or to some good place.

He gave me much more lee-way on diet than before. Said not to ever let anyone tell me a highball was bad for me! Said a couple of highballs were the best thing in the world for this condition! What a doctor! And would not let me pay *any fee*!!!

The lecture went off fine. Will tell you about things when I see you. . . .

Love and thanks,

1. Charles M. Rankin, M.D., Lexington, Ky. MKR was in Louisville to give a reading at the University of Louisville and while there visited with her good friends Edward and Lois Hardy.

(ALS, 3 pp.)

[Louisville, Ky.]
Saturday morning
[7? October 1939]

Dear Norton:

. . . Have had almost enough of the social whirl. I love the people I see here, but I get bewildered with all the confusion. The damn telephone rings every four minutes. God, how I love Cross Creek!

Have gone it just a bit too hard, of course, but feel real well. Eddie[1] goes to the World's Series in Cincinnati today and tomorrow. I should love to have gone, but tickets are unobtainable—they sent back $400,000 to fans—and it never occurred to him, I know, that I would like it. I didn't say anything, for fear he'd do something chivalrous and drastic, like taking a ticket away from one of the two big customers he is taking with him.

Am a broken-hearted woman this morning. . . .

Lots of Love,

1. Edward J. Hardy.

. . . .

(*Selected Letters*, fragment, MS not seen)

[Cross Creek, Fla.]
Friday morning
[October 1939]

My sweet:

. . . Can't say I've had much rest. Didn't really need but one night, anyway, and feel pretty good. Found a pile of work waiting for me, including proofs on both the New Yorker and the long Post stories.[1] The dirt that I thought was bothering the New Yorker, they left intact and the dirt I thought very funny and wouldn't disturb them, was out with a vengeance. They had rearranged a sequence to eliminate it, and I had to admit it carried just as well as the original. Had some fun with the Post. I had Quincey Dover say she blazed up higher than the fire in a Presbyterian hell, and they queried the "Presbyterian," so I just put: Author's note: Fix the fires of hell to suit the Post's religion.

So far, Jeff[2] and I split 70¢ as the return to date on our squash field. But there has been frost to the north, so we think from now on we will do better. The hard-working creature has cleared a quarter-acre of land ready for the Cornell lettish [lettuce]. If the original Jeff Davis had worked as hard, the South might be free. . . .

Until tomorrow, my love

1. "The Pelican's Shadow," *New Yorker* 15 (6 January 1940): 17–19; and "Cocks Must Crow," *Saturday Evening Post* 212 (25 November 1939): 5–7, 58, 60, 62–64.
2. Jefferson Davis, who was named for the president of the Confederacy, and MKR planted on a share basis; she provided the land and materials and he the labor.

(ALS, 4 pp.)

The St. Moritz
New York [N.Y.]
Friday evening
[24 November 1939]

Honey:-

Arriving in New York alone is just as horrid as I knew it would be. However, I'm going to have a good time if I have to stay drunk to do it.

Had a marvelously comfortable trip up. The Seaboard has it all over the Atlantic Coast Line.

My room at the St. Moritz is on the 18th floor, and I look straight up the whole length of Central Park. As I arrived, all the ducks were swimming up the pond to go to bed, and now all the lights are lit, and the moon is up, and if you were here it would be swell, but as it is, the ducks and moon are much prettier at Cross Creek.

The Scribner people had all left for the week-end when I got in, and although I had expected just to climb into bed, find I can't quite take it, so will go to one of the musical comedies. Couldn't make a reservation by 'phone, but they said at the Winter Garden that you could always pick up a good single seat.

My room, itself, isn't enough more attractive than your house to pay five dollars a day, but the view is worth four of the five.

Lots of love,
Dora

People who eat peanut soup
Soon grow as round as Betty Boop,
But people who eat hotel oysters
Grow slim as virgin nuns in cloisters.

. . . .

(ALS, 2 pp.)

St. Moritz Hotel
New York. [N.Y.]
Tuesday 6 P.M.
[28 November 1939]

Honey:-

Have been getting along fine yesterday and today, but when I came back to the hotel an hour ago to rest up for the theatre tonight (your show, "Too Many Girls")[1] I ran smack into the lonesomeness that is so bad. The toddy hour, and New York at its loveliest and saddest, with the evening haze over everything. I lay on my bed and watched the lights come on over Central Park and wished for you. There was one of Aunt Ida's grand little cute letters waiting for me, and that saved my life.

Saw "Yokel Boy"[2] last night, and it was delightful. Our Florida Buddy Ebsen and Judy Corona are tops. There are so many hit songs in it—"Comes Love,"

"Let's Make Memories Tonight," and "A Boy Named Lem and a Girl named Sue," etc. A *beautiful* chorus of girls.

. . . Am all upset trying to make up my mind as to whether to accept a limited lecture contract, for 3 weeks in the fall and 3 weeks in the spring. Offhand, it looks so immensely profitable, but Bernice Baumgartner (who handles foreign rights at Brandt's)[3] said I'd be ducking what I should be doing, to do it. She said, "You feel if you make all that money that way, you don't have to write—and you ought to write instead." She said it takes writers months to get over those things and I guess she's right.

Love,

1. *Too Many Girls*, a musical by Richard Rodgers and Moss Hart.
2. *Yokel Boy*, a musical by Sam Stept.
3. Carl and Carol Brandt, MKR's literary agents in New York.

. . . .

(ALS, 4 pp.)

St. Moritz Hotel
New York, [N.Y.]
Thursday
[30 November 1939]

Honey:-

Was surely glad to have your letter this morning. Had an awful hang-over and was all ready to feel worse if there wasn't a letter from you!

Went to the Christmas punch tasting meeting yesterday afternoon of the famous Wine and Food Tasting Society at the Sherry-Netherlands, and oh God.

Thought I was being discreet and just sipping, but when my hostess and I ran into some jolly company, including that famous Pierre, of Pierre's, and we agreed the champagne punch was the best, we settled down to a little right steady tasting.

Then I went to Malvina Hoffman's[1] studio for dinner and had 3 cocktails, and wine with dinner, and a long drink later in the evening, and the man who brought me home thought some ale on the way would be a good idea——and the feeling this morning was familiar, but a little plus. So your letter and the good coffee picked me right up after all my howling about too much time in N.Y., am being pushed to get in everything. Had a hard time working in all the shows I want especially to see. . . .

Am staying through Wednesday (my lecture at Columbia is Tues. night) because my aunt[2] got swell tickets for Wed. Night for The Man Who Came To Dinner,[3] and it is sold out for 12 weeks.

So glad the Atlanta date seems likely. Have wished for you at everything here.

Love,

1. Malvina Hoffman, American sculptor.
2. Wilmer Kinnan.
3. *The Man Who Came to Dinner* (1939), a play by Moss Hart and George S. Kaufman.

(*Selected Letters*, MS not seen)

St. Moritz
New York, [N.Y.]
Monday Morning
[11? December 1939]

Honey,—

Well, the worst is over, and I think from now on I can come closer to enjoying myself. The National Council affair[1] went off with very little suffering as far as I was concerned. I made my proposition to let them publish the essay and just talk, and they burst into grateful Applause, so the officers had nothing to say. They were a grand audience, 2 or 3,000 and I had a good time.

Went alone to Hellzapoppin'[2] Friday night and it was so insufferably lousy that . . . I walked out on it at the intermission. . . .

It was the tackiest kind of burlesque, not even enjoyably dirty, and as un-funny as possible. New Yorkers are the biggest *hicks* in the world. They stand in crowds watching a silly electric sign.

I put in a God-awful week-end with Auntie.[3] After Saturday luncheon, she said, "Now there are two things that will rest you," and I said, "They are both a drink." I had made up my mind I would do anything she wanted except suffer for a drink. . . . I ploughed ahead to a bar and she drank ginger ale in great martyr-dom while I had a couple, and it certainly ruins the pleasure to drink with any-one like that.

Then she took me to "The Little Foxes"[4] and it was so swell I'll wait to tell you about it when I see you. Tallulah is *marvelous*, and the whole cast was grand.

Yesterday was *awful*. Wilmer took me to *church* in the morning (a big new thought church), then to a Health Food restaurant for dinner. . . . I thought work-ing on my soul and on my stomach would do for one day, but she had only begun. She took me at night to one of a series of lectures she is attending, and this one was "The Rejuvenation of the Face." It was the damndest *medicine show* I've ever seen perpetrated. . . .

I did insist on drinks after that, and fell back on Wilmer's preacher, who had said that while human beings were individualizations of God, that material things were God's thoughts. So I told Wilmer liquor was one of God's thoughts, and in my opinion, one of the best ideas He ever had. . . .

Lots of love,

1. On 2 December, MKR gave a lecture at the National Council of Teachers of English meeting. Her subject was literary regionalism and how such appellations stigmatize the creative writer. The lecture was subsequently published as "Regional Literature of the South," *English Journal* 29 (February 1940): 89–97, and was also published in *College English* 1 (February 1940): 381–89.
2. *Hellzapoppin'* (1938), assembled by Ole Olsen and Chic Johnson, was at the time one of Broadway's longest-running musicals.
3. Wilmer Kinnan.
4. Lillian Hellman (1906–1984), *The Little Foxes* (1939), starring Tallulah Bankhead.

1940

1940 provided an especially productive year. In the winter, MKR finished reading proof for the collection of short stories entitled *When the Whippoorwill—*, which was published on 2 April. She then left for a two-week lecture tour after deciding to abandon the work on the Zephaniah Kingsley project and instead to concentrate her efforts on *Cross Creek*. In the spring, she enjoyed the company of prominent authors, among them James Branch Cabell and Ernest Hemingway. Julia Scribner visited in March and again in August. In October, MKR returned to the University of Wisconsin for an Alumni Scholarship Fund lecture, at which time she met Sinclair Lewis and Frank Lloyd Wright. Idella Parker came to work for her. The work on the manuscript of *Cross Creek* progressed, not without difficulty, into the winter. The sudden death of F. Scott Fitzgerald on 21 December seemed to cast a pall over the holidays. NSB was learning the painful but obvious truth; he was going to have to learn to share MKR with the world.

. . . .

(Wire)

GAINESVILLE, FLO

1940 JAN 24

SO GLAD YOU CAN COME OUT. IF NOT TOO MUCH TROUBLE PLEASE BRING QUART FRENCH VERMOUTH TWO QUARTS CHOICE RYE BLANK COMMERCIAL CHECKS AND FIFTY IN CASE. PLEASE SAVE TOMORROW EVENING IF HUMANLY POSSIBLE TO HELP ME ENTERTAIN SCRIBNERS. HAVE ALL THREE TIGERTS AND THE LYONS FOR SUPPER[1] LOVE

1. Charles Scribner III and Vera Scribner, John J. Tigert and Edith Tigert, and daughter Mary Jane, and Clifford and Gladys Lyons. Charles Scribner was president of Charles Scribner's and Sons, John Tigert was president of the University of Florida, and Clifford Lyons was chair of the English Department at the University of Florida.

(ALS, 4 pp.)

The Battle House Hotel
Mobile, Alabama
Tuesday night
[2 April 1940]

My dear:-

Made Mobile by dark—didn't leave home until 10 this morning—

The drive was so beautiful it hurt—but I felt like Cousin Polly—honeymooning all by myself—

Had to take a double ($6.) to get me a bed—

The Battle House is historic and all that, I know, but a swell example of how not to furnish in case you take over the Ocala House. The two buildings are certainly sisters under their mangy-looking skins.

Had very good food for dinner, and very reasonable. Ate in the vast dining-room with its mammoth pillars like the Temple of Karnos[1] (except for the acanthus), with only two other tables occupied—one by a wizened young aristocrat (obviously), the embarrassing end no doubt of a long proud line, who chatted with the head waitress though his mother had been sending him down here to eat his dinner to get rid of him, for years and years. The other table had a fluent Japanese and a man who looked like an American Jew but talked straight Alabaman, and his wife or lady-friend, who talked to the Jap as though he were just another Alabama boy—

"Mah Mothuh is jus' as Ami'cun as the day she was bohn. She had six children."

Whereupon the Jap went into polite convulsions, like a little brown cat sneezing. I wondered if he was here buying oil to put out the lamps of China, or what.

1. MKR is probably referring to Karnak in Luxor, Egypt.

. . . .

(ALS, 10 pp.)

Eola Hotel
Natchez, Miss.
Wed. night
[April 1940]

. . . Reached New Orleans for lunch, and with the Atlantic article fresh in mind, went to Galatoire's—

. . . I prowled on in through the old silver shops, and bought some English Sheffield serving dishes much too nice for the way I live, at the Creek or the Cottage. . . .

Forgot to tell you that the waiters at Galatoire's were the only distinguished group of men I've seen in many a day. One was a dead-ringer for Cliff Camp, but younger and more intelligent-looking. Another, with white hair and pink cheeks and a look of impeccable wisdom and conservatism, would make the perfect candidate for the Republican party—

Made Natchez before 8 tonight, and had to buy a $6 double again in order to get put up. They quite frankly don't reserve singles "this time of year!" It seems that this time of year in Natchez means the garden pilgrimage to the homes of the impoverished elite, who, I am sure, scrub the portal, and quite rightly, after the tourists have come and gaped and gone—

It occurred to me that my good friend Herschel Brickell,[1] who is on a Guggenheim Fellowship to do a book on Natchez, might be here, so I called the local newspaper, who referred me to a friend of his. He is here, and the friend is trying to locate him. I shall either see him or collapse, being very tired. From Baton Rouge to Natchez after dark was a bitch of a drive. . . .

In case I mail this without further word, will you pay my help this week? Snow at $2. per day. Will at $1.35 per day. Adrina $4.50 for the week.[2]

I have wished for you so hard it isn't funny. And loved you——

1. Herschel Brickell, book critic for the *New York Post*.
2. Feldon "Snow" Slater, MKR's grove man and son of the Widow Slater. Will Mickens, husband of Martha Mickens. "Adrina" is Adrenna Mickens.

. . . .

(TLS, 6 pp.)

[Crescent Beach, Fla.]
Wednesday
[12? June 1940]

My dear:

I hope you aren't as heavy-hearted as I am this morning. The Barclay's quarrel was of course all my fault. I cannot understand how I could have developed a chip on my shoulder, for I was so happy to have you and Cecil[1] with me. Of course, the chip meant nothing at all. My ugliness never does mean anything, which makes it all the uglier.

Any ugliness from you is so rare that it is a different matter, and no matter how I have provoked you, I feel that you mean it. The terrible things you said, that all I wanted was a man—did you say "a little man"—to dance attendance— must have come from a profound mistrust and resentment of me. It explains the wall I often feel you put up against me—the withdrawal—the lack of any desire or need to be with me as much as I like to be with you—which haven't fitted in with the affection I know you have had for me. I have wanted something so much closer than you have wanted and have had an awful struggle to accept the fact that what meant closeness to me, meant something irksome and "regimented" to you. I have a great respect for and understanding of, a self-respecting man's need of freedom, and have tried my very best not to let my loneliness make unreasonable demands on you. I am sorrier than I can tell you, that you have interpreted my pleasure in being with you, as only the vanity of a predatory and arrogant woman. That you are both wrong and unjust doesn't help the situation at all, for there is nothing more I can do about it. If I thought that the only thing that stands in the way of our having the closeness I have wanted is your mistrust of my nature, I should just go on loving you patiently, as I decided to do last summer when I ran away to the cottage to make what adjustment I could to the shock of your feeling of regimentation. But I am awfully afraid that the thing goes deeper than that. I am afraid that we simply ask different things of a very lovely relation. What I ask would give you everything I have. What you ask, leaves me still lonely. You feel that I ask too much of you. I feel that you do not ask enough of me. Many times I have thought that the wisest and best thing for both of us was to call it all off, and I haven't done it for two reasons. One is that I have cared too much for you and enjoyed you too much to give you up if it wasn't necessary, and if I could make the adjustment to your point of view. The other is that I have been afraid that once it was over, you would realize the potentialities we have for something close and beautiful and permanent, something that would end my loneliness—and that then it would be too late. Your psychology and your way of life—with people all the time—sharing your bedroom with someone you are fond of—so that I represent, not your whole life, but someone you go to as just a pleasant adventure—make me unnecessary to the inmost core of you.

I know that my own psychology as well as the typical female psychology have a great deal to do with the difference in our requirements. But there are men who feel and know that the only complete unity in the world is that between a man and a woman—between the right man and the right woman. My misfortune, like the misfortune of most such men, has been in not getting the proper combination together. Your misfortune in not feeling this way is also your good fortune. You simply do not feel this need. It takes much less to satisfy you than it does men who want the same thing I want. You will probably always be able to find what you need to satisfy you. The only danger you face is as you grow old or older, and I can foresee for you the same loneliness that I have felt for many years. But the way you look at this is probably safe and wise for you and I can't run the risk of upsetting what is right for you. I have evidently cramped your style, without meaning to. You'll just have to take my word for it that it has been only because I preferred being with you to being with anyone else—not because I wanted you "dancing attendance."

I am terribly afraid that we've done something that can't be fixed. The revelation you gave me of what you think I am is too painful. I don't think anything has ever hurt or shocked me more. I'd suggest that we not see each other for a while. Then if we find that our mutual trust and affection are strong enough we'll try again. It didn't seem to me that I was making any demands on you, but you evidently can't be with me three or four days in a row without feeling coerced. It's possible that I'm asking of a man that he act as buffer for me against the strange despair that hits me and that I can't seem to lick. Only I've hoped that a man I could care for would be glad to help me. But I suppose there are some battles that we always have to fight alone.

Well, cheerio. I'll probably go alone to the cottage today and stay there until I come home next Thursday to entertain Aunt Ida's friends. Think it would be better if you don't come over even if you want to, for seeing things as you do, you'd feel I was just putting it over.

Please understand that I have no criticism of you in any way. You are the sweetest, kindest, most generous person I've almost ever known.

1. MKR once wrote to Maxwell Perkins that Norton S. Baskin, Cecil H. Clarke, and Robert Camp were the "three musketeers who are like brothers to me" (*Max and Marjorie*, 359).

. . . .

(TLS, 3 pp.)

[Crescent Beach, Fla.]
Wednesday Morning
[7? August 1940]

Dear Norton:

Won't be able to get this in the mail until tomorrow—sorry to leave you so long without word of me. Am slightly marooned on top of the dune, due to having walked my four miles on the sand *bare-footed* the first evening I got here. Soles and heels actually bruised, and a big blister on one foot. Set out just to swim yesterday evening again, and it was such a beautiful sunset, limped along a bit, felt better, and ended up taking quite a walk. Came in practically crippled with the blister broken, and think I just missed a bad infection. Had boric acid and soaked the foot twice and this morning the blood-poisoning type of pain is gone, but after making it down to the beach to swim and back, it's all I can do to get to the johnny. . . . Certainly wish I had Martha. It's just one of those troublesome trifles, and if the cottage was on fire or I saw Norman and Julie[1] showing up, I could run like a deer—.

. . . Well, was quite disappointed to find the cottage in very good shape. Had hoped for a mess so I could get real mad. The only thing that wasn't really all right was the bathroom, tub and toilet dirty, but the kitchen was in perfect order. Also a solemn lofty note from Norman, which I expected. I knew the bastard would put me further on the spot by being terribly grateful. "The cottage was his Shangri-la, etc. etc. etc." Hell, it was mine, too. "His heart was full not only of Julie but of you and Norton and your measure of friendship" etc. etc. I've looked back and tried to figure just when he clamped himself on me to such an extent. All he did was keep showing up and I was polite to him, and now here we are. And there is truly a strange obligation to people who are attached to you, even if you yourself could live very happily without ever seeing them again. . . .

Edith and Verle[2] saw my light Monday night and came in. I knew I should have written her warning her about the occupants of the cottage. She said she knew I was due back here after the week-end we went to the Gulf, and when she heard nothing from me she knew I was here and was beginning to feel quite affronted. Then they saw the light and came in and she said that even to her near-sighted eyes it was plain that neither of the two people was Marjorie, and after a minute's blinking she recognized Norman. Norman told a beautiful story of my having graciously "offered" the cottage. She felt that as long as I was doing all I could for these, my bosom buddies, it was up to her to cooperate, so she had the pair in for dinner Friday, and Verle invited Norman to go turkey-hunting this winter. I assured him not to worry. Norman would come. When I told the true story, including the wife and two children and the fur coats, the unvirginal bride, the snatching of the cottage from my unwilling breasts, they almost had hysterics. It was a shame to destroy their picture of this fresh and lovely idyll on which they had stumbled, but it was too funny not to pass on.

Edith asked Julie if she had done any cooking "before she was married." Julie said no, but that Norman hadn't minded doing the cooking over here. (Of course he had nothing to cook but bacon and coffee). Norman said that if Julie would hunt and fish with him, he'd just as soon live on toast. And I'm the damn fool who made myself sick cooking up a breeze for them!

It is simply grand here, and I hate to think of you slaving away twelve hours. The water is milk-warm in the evening, and in the morning is just crisply cool enough to make you feel good. Down below the dune it is blistering, but up here inside the cottage you are conscious only of utter comfort....

Love,

1. Norman and Julie Berg, the latter Berg's second wife.
2. Edith and Verle Pope.

. . . .

(TLS, 1 p.)

[Crescent Beach, Fla.]
Thursday Evening
[8? August 1940]

My dear:

Had to give in on the foot yesterday and sent a wire to have Will bring Martha over. It seemed silly to limp around in the middle of a mess when I am paying the old gal to clean up after me. She came with a devoted and martyred air, making it plain that she had worked herself into exhaustion at the Creek since I've been gone, and has risen from her bed of pain only because she is of a noble nature. I shall probably send her back with you when you come, but meantime, it is good to have things straight and clean again. The foot incidentally is infinitely better tonight and I can make it in to Edith's for dinner, having been afraid I couldn't.

May not have a chance to get in touch with you again. Hope you can make it Saturday. Do really need you.

Love,

. . . .

(TLS, 2 pp.)

[Crescent Beach, Fla.]
Wednesday
[21? August 1940]

Dear Norton:

. . . Well, I had begun to hope that Norman had felt just a touch of indifference in my invitation to a meal and had passed by, but just a touch of anything bounces off that hard hide of his like a butterfly brushing by. The pair of them arrived at 3 yesterday afternoon, and we had a swim and many drinks—I drank a good half pint of rye alone in my desperation and Norman and Julie put a quart of rum well down toward the bottom. Dinner, and then thank heaven they left early for their night at Marineland. It was a very painful gathering, at least as far as Julia[1] and I were concerned. She is simply violent on the subject of Julie, and you'll have plenty of fun getting her going. She is even furious at her beloved Pat because he lay at Julie's feet. She said that the girl is obviously not in love with Norman and says she will get sick of the bargain first, and I agree. They argued so violently, Norman and Julie, over some war matter that it was embarrassing. Julie was very ugly about it and Norman just gave in. When he was alone with me a minute, he said, "I'm very happy," then giggled and said, "I don't know whether it's going to last." Then leaned toward me with that leer and whispered, "I've been giving her hell." Delicate guy, eh?

After they had gone and Julia cut loose, she said all through the visit she had kept lamenting, "Oh, for darling Norton and Bob and Cecil and our nice times! . . ."

It would also be much easier for me if we did stay in town Saturday night, either with Bob or with you if your house is not full. Dorothy[2] has already spoiled me for coping with Martha's droopiness and incompetency. Certainly wish I could take the little nigger home with me for the winter, but have no illusions about its working. Dreamt last night that Adrenna was back at the grove.

Am on pins and needles about Jacksonville and imagine to you it's swords and bayonets. Am keeping my fingers crossed against a Dupont[3] double cross.

Lots of love,

1. Julia Scribner and MKR soon became inseparable. MKR looked upon her as a daughter and once described herself as Julia's "godmother."
2. Dorothy, the maid at Crescent Beach.
3. Will DuPont owned the land in the area.

(TLS, 1 p.)

[Cross Creek, Fla.]
Wednesday morning
[4? September 1940]

Good morning, my sweet-

Just wanted to take a minute off from my work and bless you again for the fan. The rear of the house is like an oven, but the porch, usually very bad in the morning sun, is almost as comfortable as the cottage (where I hope the usurpers[1] are quarreling violently). I have the fan about three feet from the table, and a cool breeze eddies around the largest and warmest part of my anatomy.

The morning mail brought old Will a special delivery from Adrenna. Will is in Gainesville, seeing about his—some perfectly unintelligible big word—if it was Henry,[2] I'd say it was his testimonials. Martha and I are all agog to know the news. But being honorable about the letter.

Since I let you get away half the time without showing you choice bits that I often save for you, I'm enclosing today's crop. The Winchell comment is from Danton Walker's Broadway column, and he makes a neat point about the length of the Profile.[3]

Your noble example has inspired me and I am putting in the day on liquids. I don't mean rye. Martha is churning fresh buttermilk so it won't be too hard. Wish you could have some of it with me.

See you tomorrow, with delight as usual.

Aunt Ida would enjoy the *Pegler*.[4]

1. Norman and Julie Berg.
2. Henry Fountain.
3. Walter Winchell, especially known for his Sunday night radio broadcast. Danton Walker, a columnist for the *Broadway Spotlight*.
4. Westbrook Pegler (1894–1969), American journalist and writer. Perhaps a reference to *The Dissenting Opinions of Mister Westbrook Pegler* (New York: Scribners, 1938).

. . . .

(Wire)

ISLAND GROVE, FLO
1940 NOV 23
DR ROLLEY[1] HAS BEEN RECOMMENDING A VACATION FOR YOU BUT I THINK A LITTLE HUNTING MIGHT DO YOU AS MUCH GOOD MEET FRED TOMPKINS AND ME AT CITRA AT TWO OCLOCK IF YOU WANT TO SHOOT QUAIL OTHERWISE WE WILL COME BACK TO CITRA TO MEET YOU AT FIVE OCLOCK FOR DOVES LOVE

1. Dora Rolley, MKR's self-created alter-ego.

Marjorie Kinnan Rawlings at Crescent Beach. By permission of the University of Florida Libraries.

. . . .

(TL, 2 pp.)

> [Crescent Beach, Fla.]
> Tuesday afternoon
> [November? 1940]

Dear Norton:

Well, turned out 3,000 words today and they seem all right, so feel a little more entitled to living. Lots of people don't feel that peculiar obligation to earn their salt, but I can't get away from it. That's one reason I have my earthly hell—picture the world's laziest woman with a gnawing conscience to work—

The menace of the National Park turned out to be a real one, but think us Crescent Beach-combers can nip it in the bud. It seems that a small group of men who own developments at the north end of the Island have slipped the project over, as any stop to further development here would profit them. The man who owns Davis Shores etc. Verle Pope is ostensibly against the project, but he is one of the committee that has put it through so far, and I have always had a strange feeling of not trusting him in a business way. We had a meeting last night, and I was amazed at the ability of common men to get up and express themselves well. We are all in accord that we will not allow our places to be condemned away from us, or bought at government prices, and have already sent in our protest to the Dept. of the Interior, the two senators etc. The group of men who tried to put it over had worked in secrecy, and we just got wind of it. It is lots of fun and I am sure the plan will be stopped. One old Cracker asked if the Park plan was to grub-hoe the palmettos. It seemed it was. He said, "We got nothin' to worry about. If they start at the north end they'll never reach here."

Had to fire my other sweetheart, with much heart-break all around. The little devil came yesterday evening to water the zinnias. I noticed that I didn't hear the pump cut on and off, and looked out to see him playing with a weed on a string, like a kite. He started to walk away. I called out to him that he hadn't watered the flowers. He said that he had, two buckets to each bed. An hour later I went down to go into town, and the beds didn't have a drop of water on them, dry as a bone. The watering can was on its side where it has been for several days, and it too was dry as a bone. I examined the rose beds and the petunia boxes to make sure he hadn't just misunderstood the places I meant, and everything was bone dry. He had tackled me for money yesterday, saying he needed it to order pants for school and didn't have the money. Think now that was a lie, too. So this morning I just told Curtis to tell him I didn't need him any more and he could have the money as a present. Later Frank came up in tears and said his mother said if I didn't want him to work he didn't deserve the money, and he threw it down and went away. I was terribly upset and when Curtis brought me a message later I told him the whole thing, and he said his brother, and also his older brother, "said they had done things when they hadn't." Further questioning brought it out that Frank is a congenital liar, due to being spoiled by his grandmother. You know how I love little boys, but I have always had a funny feeling about the kid and just couldn't like him. I told Curtis to try to teach him that he couldn't get along in life lying. Funny how in the same family you get such different characteristics. I have always thought environment had everything to do with it, and of course a spoiled younger child does suffer from that, but there must be something inherent in the natures, so that one is honest and with integrity, like Curtis, and the others do not have those qualities.

I spent most of the morning cleaning up and hating it. I can work up a breeze when I have to, but it just takes too much out of me to do it and try to do the goddamn writing too. . . .

Often wish I was a dumb cluck (or am I?) with a husband to look out for me, and nothing to do but put the meals on the table. Oh well. I have fun.

1941

1941 was one of the most eventful years in MKR's life. She married NSB on 27 October, a marriage of genuine love that brought stability to her otherwise chaotic life. Earlier in the year, in April, she was the honored guest of Eleanor Roosevelt at the White House. Before returning to Florida, MKR visited with Ellen Glasgow in Richmond. In May, MGM arrived in Florida to begin the filming of *The Yearling*, to star Spencer Tracy, which was finally shelved because of actor disenchantment, location difficulties, and director problems. MKR was sanguine. The work on *Cross Creek* continued, with the subject of libel being raised by Rawlings and dismissed by Perkins. The marriage in October came amid the usual tumult, given impetus by the fact that NSB was in the throes of preparing to open the Castle Warden Hotel on 7 December, as it turned out, the "day of infamy" when the Japanese attacked Pearl Harbor. Yet MKR was able to write in reflection to Glasgow that being with NSB was "like coming into harbor after long storms." This observation, although tested, never altered.

. . . .

(ALS, 10 pp.)

> The White House
> Washington [D.C.]
> April 1, 1941

Dear Norton!—

I should probably be doing something more serious, here at Lincoln's desk, than writing impudent letters, but I can't think of anything more pleasant than writing you, so may the shade of Lincoln forgive me.

The usher showed me into a room somewhat larger than your dining room, and asked me if I thought the room would be large enough! It is the Lincoln room—and Lincoln's bed—and I simply don't feel good enough to sleep in it. Do you suppose he might possibly have liked "The Yearling"?

The vast room is comfortably shabby, and the draperies are almost a duplicate of my English material that is on my davenport—and there is dust on the marble-topped center table—so I feel almost at home——And the help has as easy a welcome as Martha——

I haven't met Mrs. Roosevelt[1] yet, but was told to appear for tea at five in the West Hall. All the newspaper women here simply worship her. And it is not that they are being diplomatic, for they say the most indiscreet and disreputable things about the great and the near-great.

The luncheon today was nice—Margaret Mitchel[l][2] was there. . . .

I went to a British cocktail party yesterday afternoon, and had dinner with my friend Sigrid Arne—Jim Rawlings's old girl.[3] She had with us such a jolly Australian girl, who used to be a champion swimmer, Pat Jarrett, and is now living at the Australian Embassy, covering the U.S. for the big Melbourne paper. And she's Dessie's double! Voice, mannerisms, and all.

The dinner tonight promises to be a delightful brawl. All kinds of women, from Clare Boothe Luce and Mary Martin, to Eve Curié.[4] And by the way, a funny thing happened about the luncheon at Pierre's today. Mrs. Herrick, the hostess, told the head waiter that Margaret Mitchell and Marjorie K. R. were coming, and he bustled about nobly. Then later he said to her, "You said it was Mary Martin coming, didn't you?" and when she said no, he lost all interest.

It is pouring rain—Washington at its typical spring worst—but still warm.

Wednesday morning
[2 April 1941]

Ashamed to report that I am suffering from a hang-over in the White House ——. It's a long story, but I did your trick of being the last one at the party—Mr. and Mrs. Eugene Meyer[5] and I had a grand time together and ate and drank at two in the morning after everybody else had gone.

I have been quite an orphan at the White House. It was, of course, just a gesture from Mrs. Roosevelt, in thanks for my cottage gesture. I must say I'm happier where I know I'm really wanted! I'll have to see you to tell you everything.

Love,

Hay-Adams House
Washington, D.C.

Back at the hotel to pack my other bags to be moved over to the White House. Just after I finished my letter there to you, I called Miss Thompson, Mrs. R's very jolly secretary, and asked to see her. I told her I'd never been as lonesome in my life as at the White House! Mrs. Roosevelt took an early 'plane for New York this morning, and I had heard her very gay voice and laughter, going off. Miss Thompson and Mrs. Helm,[6] the social secretary, came into my room and we had a grand visit, and I stopped feeling like an orphan immediately. I even felt that I was wanted as they told me Mrs. Roosevelt had looked over the Press Club guest list and picked out the ones she wanted to stay in the White House. Eve Curie and Genevieve Tabouis[7] were the others, so I didn't feel so much that I was just the victim of Courtesy——

Mrs. Helm insisted on my staying on at the White House, so I am checking out here at the hotel. I could have a good time here for days, but will go home either tomorrow or Friday, arriving in Ocala 10:49 A.M. either Friday or Saturday. I had a note from Miss Glasgow[8] and will stop over to see her in the afternoon.

You *could* have had a note for me here.

I'll let you know my definite plans, later.

Love,

Editor's note: The first nine pages are written on White House stationery.

1. Eleanor Roosevelt, writer and humanitarian, wife of Franklin Delano Roosevelt.
2. Margaret Mitchell and MKR were good friends. Both MKR and NSB were Mitchell's guest for the film premiere of *Gone with the Wind* in December 1939, which MKR characterized to Maxwell Perkins as a "riotous occasion" (*Max and Marjorie*, 435).
3. Sigrid Arne, journalist with the Associated Press; Jim Rawlings, brother of Charles Rawlings, MKR's first husband.
4. Clare Boothe Luce, playwright, later ambassador to Italy; Mary Martin, American singer and actor; Eve Curie, daughter of the renowned scientist Marie Curie.
5. Eugene Meyer, a friend of MKR at the University of Wisconsin.
6. Malvina Thompson and Edith Helm.
7. Genevieve Tabouis, French journalist.
8. Ellen Glasgow, American novelist, later the subject of MKR's unfinished biography.

. . . .

(*Selected Letters*, MS not seen)

[Crescent Beach, Fla.]
Thursday
[26? June 1941]

Dear Norton:

Well, I am on my feet instead of my back today, to my amazement. I had my initiation into floundering last night, and Verle darn near killed me. My only satisfaction is that he must have ruined himself, too. He invited the Harrolds[1] to go with us, for they are flounder fiends, too. Fortunately Edith decided to stay home. She could never have stood it. We set out at nine o'clock at night, at low tide, and parked the car down one of those roads that lead toward the ocean, on the island here, up where you're so crazy about the cedar trees. (If that is a clear direction.) Verle carried a big gasoline lantern and we all had gigs. We walked along in the shallow water for about a mile before we got the first flounder. The place is one of those sort of bays, with a strip of marshy land between it and the ocean. The floundering itself is fascinating. You can barely see them, for they take on the color of the sand, and are sometimes almost buried, so that you just see the shape. They don't move when the light is on them, and you joog them with your gig, then reach under them and somebody puts them on the string. I don't know how far we walked, all in the water. All of a sudden even the men admitted they were tired, and we had all that way to go back again. Verle overdoes things like that terribly. We must have gone about three miles then. Meantime, the tide had come in and was close to high, and everything looked different. We walked and walked, and all of a sudden we were lost. The lighthouse was on the wrong side and so was the moon. We thought we'd passed the car and worked back, then decided we hadn't come far enough. We walked and walked, and there were deep creeks and sloughs where there had been dry land. Sometimes things would just drop from under us and we were in over our waists. That was plenty spooky. Verle left us to reconnoiter and then couldn't find us again! We could see his light, but he couldn't see us. We called and whistled and the sounds were deceptive and we could see the light go off the other way. At last we got together again and walked and walked, pushing through the deep water. We could hardly put one foot ahead of the other. Mr. Harrold had played 18 holes of golf and hadn't had any dinner, and I had been fool enough to take Pat for a three-mile walk! We found the car at 2 o'clock in the morning, having walked steadily for five hours. We had to deliver the Harrolds back in town, divide the flounders—we got twenty—and get my car, and I reached home at three-thirty, hardly able to crawl up the steps.

When we set out and didn't get any flounder for so long, I said snootily, "So this is floundering." Then we caught a lot fast and I said with enthusiasm, "So *this* is floundering!" As we struggled in at the end, I said bitterly, "So this is *floundering*."

I was so wet and sticky and muddy and shelly and achy, I soaked in deep hot water, and am all right today.

The work has me chewing all of my nails, but it goes steadily.

Verle told me last night about the deal, and said he wouldn't be willing to have you pay more than $22,000.[2] Said you were running into danger past that, counting what you'd have to put in for fixing and fixings, and much as he wanted you over here, he didn't want to see you get into trouble. I thought that was pretty white of him and it made me feel better about him.

The war looks worse again, doesn't it? . . .

Much love,

1. Frank and DeVene Harrold.
2. NSB was negotiating to purchase the Castle Warden Hotel.

. . . .

(TLS, I p.)

[Crescent Beach, Fla.]
[September 1941]

Dear Norton:

I have no intention of making any mystery of what I am feeling. The street was simply no place to have it out. And I don't think it can be had out in any case.

You gave me a first class shock when you turned on me after my sputtering and said that you hated people who had fits. Your face was appalling. You really hated me. You changed instantly from my sweet Norton to someone with whom I could not possibly be close. And since you are capable of feeling that way toward me, if only for a moment, you don't want to be close to me either.

I make no excuses for my "fits." I am ashamed of them. But I exercise as much control as is possible for me, and when I make a trivial fuss, as in that case, or really boil over, I simply cannot help it. My temperament is what it is, volatile and high-strung—and you may use any other adjectives you want to. My virtues—if any—come from exactly the same temperament as my faults, and each is a part of the other. I couldn't write books, I couldn't have a warmly emotional nature, if I were a placid pond. A man who was right for me would never be upset by my fits, and certainly would not hate me for them.

When we have stepped on each other's toes before, my heart has been like a lump of lead. Now it is just a chunk of ice and I don't even care. You aren't Norton any more. Your sweetness has been the happy aspect of a passive nature, and without the sweetness I don't want you. I certainly am not going to make myself liable to spells of being hated. Probably you don't care to be annoyed into hating.

Your charm is devastating, as nobody knows better than you, and I don't know whether I am permanently immune. In any case, I want to say that regardless of our future personal relations, the hotel deal is still a business deal.

. . . .

(*Selected Letters*, MS not seen)

> Harkness Pavilion
> [New York, N.Y.]
> Wednesday afternoon
> [1 October 1941]

Dear honey:-

And what an afternoon! Gorgeous! Wish to Heaven I'd come directly here. Have the most divine HOTEL room on the 12th floor looking out over Hudson and the Palisades. The food as good as Longchamps. Darling nurses. A bathroom big enough for Badminton. Feel rested enough already to whip Hitler single-handed.

Well—JOKE on you and Edith. The first doctor to come in is an eminent psychiatrist! Hate to think they signed me up at once as nuts.

Actually, he is the coordinating diagnostician. They get all the physical data together, and he tries to see the whole picture. He said, "Emotional disturbances may be causing most of the trouble." Of course, I knew that nervous tension had a direct effect on both stomach and colon. Anyway, he said he wanted to go into the mental and emotional angles. He said, "I may or may not give you any advice at all, but I have to get a picture of the patient as a person." You should be here to tell him!!

Have had just the routine things checked today. The resting is divine.

Forgot to say that the psychiatric diagnostician is an intimate friend of John Marquand and Stephen Benet.[1] He knows you don't get books out of contented cows.

Had to have my vulgar fun, of course, with somebody. The intern doing the blood pressure etc. took himself pretty seriously. The nurse tuned down my bed jacket so that my bosom was exposed for something or other, and the intern had a 6-inch ruler in one hand. I said, "You don't need to measure. I'm a rather droopy 36."

Only the nurse thought I was funny.

Evening

Julia came up to see me this afternoon, and that was grand.

Maxwell Perkins sent me books later yesterday evening by messenger. There has been no mail from you. Perhaps a letter is there now and Max will send it up late as he did the books.[2]

Can't see how you can let me be away without wanting to keep contact. If there's nothing by tomorrow afternoon, when Dr. Atchley[3] begins our probing, I'll just have to tell him my man doesn't love me—and what can a psychiatrist do about that?

I will be through here Saturday afternoon. If Julia is ready to head forth then, think I'd rather do it than fool around in town.

Saw "The Corn is Green" Monday night, alone. A mess! Like something out of the Ladies' Home Journal forty years ago. Nothing much in town very good. We'll see "Arsenic and Old Lace" sometime.[4]

Will drop a line as we go along. Weather suddenly cooled.

I love you, but I think it's awful for you not to write to me.

1. John P. Marquand, American novelist; Stephen Vincent Benét, American poet.
2. On 12 October, MKR wrote to Maxwell Perkins: "The Medical Center verdict is that nothing can be changed or helped physically, but that I am to ease up on nervous tension. The diagnostician said I had an engine too big for the chassis" (*Max and Marjorie*, 502).
3. Dana Atchley.
4. Emlyn Williams (1905–1987), *The Corn Is Green* (New York: Random House, 1941); Joseph Kesselring (1902–1967) *Arsenic and Old Lace* (New York: Random House, 1941).

. . . .

(Wire)

NEW YORK, NEW YORK

1941 OCT 7

THERE ARE OTHER BUMS THAN THE DODGERS. SEE NO REASON FOR RE-TURNING AT ALL. NO MESSAGE FROM ANYBODY. DORA

(*Selected Letters*, MS not seen)

Harkness Pavilion
[New York City]
Saturday morning
[11? October 1941]

Dear Honey:-

Your sweet letter of Wednesday just came, forwarded by Max.

I am hoping that the time is past, or soon will be, when I snap at you so. Had a long session with Dr. Atchley yesterday, and he identified the cause and source of my unreasonable rages—which I told him about—so simply that I can't see why I couldn't have figured it out for myself. But he said that an outside, disinterested, objective point of view is absolutely necessary—no one can get the perspective on his own picture for himself. The rages, as I suspected, have nothing to do with you.

It's a long story, and I'll have to see you to tell you all about it. But there is one thing I want to tell you now so that you'll have a chance to be thinking about it by yourself before I come home.

I presented my immediate problems to Dr. Atchley—principally our considering the matter of marriage, and the way I am torn at the thought of giving up the Creek way of life—wanting to be fair to you, and not wanting to worry if it would mean I went on rebelling. I just had to tell him the cute thing you said about the Will o' the Wisp.

Well, honey, he is perfectly certain that you are Willie. He said, laughingly, "What the Hell are you waiting for?" He said I needed exactly what you are, as I described you. I didn't go into any great detail, of course, but I had to tell him about you, as I feel at a crossroads in my life.

I gave him an outline of my life, and the things that I could identify as having disturbed me. He clarified so many things for me. Will have to tell you when I see you, as it's a long story.

Anyway, we'll have to talk things over, and so I'm giving you the chance either to run like everything or to propose to me! My heart ached a little about the telephone and cottage business—I thought what a wonderful time for you to suggest the other alternative—of your really taking me under your kind wing, permanently.

So you think things out from your point of view, decide what you *really* want, and we'll figure from there.

. . . Dr. Atchley won't know until he has gone over all the tests, by this afternoon, how long I am to stay here. Neither Julia nor I is in any hurry.

(ALS, 6 pp.)

Hotel New Weston
New York, N. Y.
Monday Morning
[13? October 1941]

Dear Honey:—

. . . Julia and I leave at two this afternoon. It seems you can make the Berkshires easily in 3 hours from New York, and we plan to make them today. We'll take everything very leisurely—both by inclination and doctor's advice.

Won't go into details on doctor's findings, but briefly the medical picture is exactly the same—physical condition neither better nor worse. Nothing can be done about the intestinal condition. However, nervous tension and emotional disturbance have such an effect, that by learning to ease up that way, I should be able to avoid attacks. People with diverticulosis as extensive as mine, but who do not tie themselves up in knots, are perfectly comfortable as long as they stay on their diet.

Angel, I did not mean to indicate that I would not take a strange doctor's "Stop" or "Go" on anything as important as *us* [underlined twice]—but he did identify the source of my peculiar, spasmodic belligerence to you—and I had to wonder, as I know you must have, whether it meant that I was trying to reject you. Anyway, we will have a good talk about everything when we are together.

. . . I will telephone Perkins about Wednesday or Thursday, so if you need to communicate with me for any reason, you can leave a wire in his care, or if necessary, word for me to telephone you at a certain time and place. Otherwise I'll just pick up my mail at his office about Saturday.

I do wish we were together to shop for the Castle. . . .[1]

Lots of love,

Feel almost rested—think leisurely driving in lovely new country will finish the job—better than staying in bed. Have wondered if you've run into trouble getting building and plumbing materials. They are howling about it up here. Hope things are going smoothly.

1. NSB had just purchased the Castle Warden Hotel and was furnishing it for the official opening, 7 December 1941.

(ALS, 3 pp.)

Hotel New Weston
New York, N.Y.
Tuesday morning
[14? October 1941]

My dear:—

. . . I didn't mean to give the impression of cold second thoughts—but I did think it might seem to you as though I were letting an outsider influence me, which is not the case.

Anyway—last morning—no, I won't even be facetious about it—when you ask me, the answer is the right one. . . .[1]

You can reach me at the Creek through Friday.

I love you very very much, and my labyrinth is coming out on a good straight lovely road—

1. MKR is alluding to NSB's forthcoming proposal of marriage.

. . . .

(Wire)

GREAT BARRINGTON MASS
(14 OCTOBER 1941)
HAPPY BIRTHDAY TO MY BULL FROM YOUR EVER LOVING PSYCHOANALYZED
DORA.

. . . .

(Wire)

ISLAND GROVE, FLO
23 OCT 1941
JUST MISSED YOU BY TELEPHONE LONG PLANNED WEEK END IMPOSSIBLE
UNLESS YOU THINK WE NEED FORTY EIGHT HOURS OF TALKING[1] BELIEVE
IT WOULD BE PLEASANT TO ASK LYONS[2] UNDER THE CIRCUMSTANCES WE
CAN TALK SATURDAY AFTERNOON LETTER MAILED YESTERDAY EXPLAINS
THIS UNWILLING SUGGESTION LET ME HAVE A WIRE MUCH LOVE

1. MKR is reflecting on their impending marriage.
2. Clifford and Gladys Lyons.

(Postcard)

[Cross Creek, Fla.]
Monday [Sunday] 4:30
[26 October 1941]

Hey, honey:—

Sat down this morning in the middle of the cigarette butts, empty bottles and general mess (the way I work best) and finished my story about noon. In walk Leonard and his whole damn family. No hope, then, of editing the story or starting a new one, so I cleaned house & turned the cottage over to the Fiddias[1] and cleared out. See you at the wedding tomorrow.

Love,

1. Leonard and Piety Fiddia.

. . . .

MARJORIE AND NORTON WERE MARRIED
IN ST. AUGUSTINE ON 27 OCTOBER 1941

. . . .

Marjorie and Norton on their wedding day, with (*left to right*) Edith Pope, Ida Tarrant, Verle Pope. From the collection of Philip May, Jr.

(ALS, 4 pp.)

[Crescent Beach, Fla.]
Tuesday
[November? 1941]

Dear Norton:-

. . . I used the week-end or rather Sunday to do my duty by Phil May. Anne Hill is looking very attractive and the boy has lost most of his fat and is getting tall and will be quite a fellow.[1] Poor little Phil had such a good time. Having Edith here was a big help in entertaining. . . .

. . . Saw a movie item in the Jax paper that The Yearling had been permanently abandoned, after throwing $400,000 away! The sissies![2]

. . . Saw "Sunny"[3] on your recommendation, and think it utterly *lousy*. Despised Neagle much as ever. She has a lovely figure, but I just can't stand her Goddamned face.

Any chance of you coming over this week-end? Do hope so.

Lots of love

1. Anne Hill May and Philip May Jr., daughter and son of Philip May, MKR's attorney.
2. Metro-Goldwyn-Mayer began filming *The Yearling*, starring Spencer Tracy, in 1941. The filming was scrubbed as a result of expensive delays and actor disenchantment. In 1946, it was produced, starring Gregory Peck and Jane Wyman.
3. *Sunny* (1941), starring Anna Neagle and Ray Bolger.

. . . .

(TLS, 2 pp.)

[Crescent Beach, Fla.?]
Monday
[November? 1941]

My dear:

Didn't we have a good time! It was a shame you had to leave us, because we kept right on. Bob and Edith Pope found they had been to school in Switzerland within a few Alps of each other, knew all the same French resorts, and had even, both, been bitten by a dog in the garden of the same Swiss hotel! It was two different dogs, however, so they could not quite claim blood relationship. Verle was not particularly thrilled over the rapprochement, especially as I quoted Bob on the very high price of the lot I want, as an alibi for hedging on buying just yet. I think Verle must have an occasional qualm over having taken Edith out of her sophisticated world. He should not, for she is very happy with him, and he is probably a much better mate, and balance, for her than some white-plumaged literary neurotic. Anyway, it was his turn to be jealous, for he had made one of those tactless remarks that honest men sometimes make. He had taken me by the arm, and all but shouted, "God! You have the softest skin I've ever touched." And Edith didn't like *that*. Like the time I was so entranced with the texture of your shirt, any woman wants to think that her skin *feels* the softest to a man of any he's ever touched.

...I had another bad night and morning, but this afternoon it is better, and if it continues to lessen, I sh'n't bother with a doctor. It has been such a funny pain. It flutters about in the middle, then ripples over to where my appendix used to be, and shoots into a meteoric sort of pain, like a rocket going off. Then it ripples back again and explodes on the other side like a smaller rocket. Then it settles down to a steady chewing in the middle, like a crab feeding itself with those harsh sharp mandibles. I think either that I caught cold by swimming indiscreetly, or that I did something silly like swallowing a lemon seed, that may be raising hell in one of my pet diverticulae. If I could only make pearls out of such things, as an oyster does with an irritating grain of sand, what a valuable person I should be! ...

Lots of love,
Dora

1942

1942 was yet another year of literary success, tempered, however, by the events of 7 December 1941. After much revision, *Cross Creek* was published on 16 March, and like *The Yearling* it became an immediate best seller. By June 455,000 copies were in print. The effect of such acclaim was dampened, however, by NSB's desire to enlist in the war effort. Meanwhile he had built for them an apartment atop the Castle Warden, but MKR still often escaped back to Cross Creek, where she felt at home. Her frequent sojourns caused tension. The Armed Services Editions of *South Moon Under*, *The Yearling*, and *Cross Creek* were distributed to the servicepeople, and the response was immediate. MKR was deluged with letters, each of which she was determined to answer, which in turn compromised her literary production. Still, she forged ahead, and on 16 November she published *Cross Creek Cookery*, illustrated by her good friend Bob Camp. The year ended on an ominous note. While Perkins was encouraging her toward another book, MKR got word that Zelma Cason was preparing to file a libel suit against her for her depiction of Cason in *Cross Creek.*

. . . .

(Wire)

ISLAND GROVE, FLO

1942 JUN 26

ARRIVING SIX THIRTY PROBABLY FIVE POUNDS HEAVIER FROM TESTING RECIPES[1] DORA AND DORA

1. MKR is referring to her testing of the recipes for *Cross Creek Cookery* (New York: Scribners, 1942). She reached paranoia about getting the recipes correct. In the words of Idella Parker, who assisted in the preparation of the cookbook: "I can't tell you how many times we cooked some dishes. . . . When something didn't come out right, we'd cook it again and again until it did" (Parker, *Perfect Maid*, 69). NSB would have enjoyed the humor of Dora, MKR's alter-ego, being "Dora and Dora," or double in size.

(ALS, 4 pp.)

Atlanta Biltmore
Atlanta, Georgia
Wed. A.M.
[30 September 1942]

Dear Honey:—

It was so good to talk to you last night. Finding your nice letters here made me so lonesome for you, and I thought it wouldn't be so bad to wake you up that late if you were in the apartment—but couldn't resist calling anyway.——

We just had to make Atlanta last night, or we'd have run still another day late. My material has been getting more interesting, as I talk with different kinds of people. The story is beginning to shape up in my mind.[1]

Julia is feeling fine again. She said when we got in last night that she was tougher than she thought, and asked wistfully if I thought she could go ahead and do something if she just kept going. Evidently her fear of the same sort of collapse that I get, has held her back from getting into some work.

It is really cold here, but due to warm up today. Will try to buy some red flannel underwear or its equivalent before getting into the mountains.

If possible, without missing something I should catch, I'll try to skip the S. Carolina part of the trip and get on back on schedule, after we "finish" the mountains.

Will be mighty glad to get back.

Lots of love,

1. MKR and Julia Scribner traveled throughout the Southeast with members of the U.S. Forest Service. MKR was gathering material for an article on American forests, in part inspired by her defense of the forests in *Cross Creek* (New York: Scribners, 1942). The nonfictional appeal for conservation was published as "Trees for Tomorrow," *Collier's Magazine* 117 (8 May 1943): 14–15, 24–25.

· ·

(Postcard)

Murphy, N.C.
October 2, 1942

Up in beautiful mountain country. The only good part of the trip ruined by having an Atlanta stuffed shirt attach himself to the party for the duration of the trip! It may drive me out—will try to stick it out to finish getting my material.

Love,

1943

1943 was not a kind year for MKR. In January, Zelma Cason filed the lawsuit for libel, a complaint later changed to "invasion of privacy." MKR spent much of the spring rounding up character witnesses to refute Cason's charges. The legal maneuverings escalated as MKR's counsel, Phil S. May Sr. of Jacksonville and Sigsbee Scruggs of Gainesville, addressed charge and countercharge. The affair began to exact an emotional toll on MKR, who at the time continued to answer the myriad letters from servicepeople. All of this brought on more attacks of diverticulosis, exacerbated this time by the need for a hysterectomy. In June, NSB delivered the shattering news; he had enlisted in the American Field Service, and in July, he shipped out for the India/Burma theater. MKR went to Michigan to visit her mother's side of the family, the Traphagens, where she got the idea for *The Sojourner*, the writing of which was to plague her for nearly a decade. It was during this tumultuous period that MKR began her immense, almost daily correspondence with NSB, who as an ambulance driver was in constant danger.

. . . .

(ALS, 4 pp.)

> The Gotham [Hotel]
> New York City
> Wednesday noon
> In bed
> [17 February 1943]

Dear Honey:—

Mighty glad you threw me out and made me come—I really need attention. Am knocked out, but haven't much pain, so I don't mind. Thought Damon[1] would want to wait to make his examination, but he thinks it should be done right away anyhow. Told me to stay in bed today (talked on 'phone) and come to his office at 9:45 tomorrow, Thursday morning. If he decides to operate, then we'll make plans at once. I'll suggest next Tuesday unless you are coming—in that case, I'll make it Wednesday or Thursday—all provided, of course, Damon doesn't want to do something immediately.

... Julia and Charlie Scribner met my plane, to my surprise and pleasure, and brought me in. Julia stayed and had dinner with me in the grill here.

Recognized George Carger[2] in a corner—and in a moment in came Sinclair Lewis[3] and another man and sat almost opposite. I sent notes to both of them, and am sure the waiter thought I was shamelessly drumming up trade. George came over and chatted a few minutes and sent his regards to you. Sinclair Lewis and his friend, a doctor, joined us after our dinners—and we talked about an hour. He still looks like something abandoned to the vultures in the Libyan desert, but is so nice.

Julia is coming in some time today.

The plane trip was wonderful and I loved it. Am thoroughly sold.

The Gotham is nothing extra, but is all right. . . .

Loads of love,

1. Virgil Damon, M.D.
2. George Carger, American artist.
3. Sinclair Lewis (1885–1951), American novelist.

. . . .

(ALS, 2 pp.)

[Harkness Pavilion]

[New York, N.Y.]

Thursday noon.

[25 February 1943]

Sweetheart——

I don't think flowers have *ever* thrilled me more than these. You sweet angel to cheer me up so.

Aside from being *so* happy to have you think of me, they came at a moment when I could do with a bit of cheer. I was on the john in a state of collapse, not at all sure which end of me should be there, for they had just finished pulling a stomach tube out of my mouth and an anuscope out of my tail. I thought of Arthur's description of sea-sickness, and when my stomach gave a quiver, I thought to myself, "Don't let go—that would be the anuscope."

The nurse pushed open the bathroom door to show me the flowers, for they are so unusual, and I knew I'd live.

I was all upset to get at the card, and I thought "If they're from anybody but Norton I'll cry." There was no reason for you to send them—except your sweetness—but they were from you and I'm very happy. . . .

All my love,

(ALS, 6 PP.)

Harkness Pavilion
New York, [N.Y.]
[26? February 1943]

Dear Honey:—

... Had thought they would be through with me tomorrow afternoon, but Edith's Dr. Damon[1] said today it would probably go over into the beginning of the week. They took some more blood today for some other tests. Had my abdominal X-ray yesterday, and was relieved, in a way, to have the doctor say, as he watched the barium percolate, "You really have a dandy diverticulosis. There's certainly enough here to cause all your symptoms." Think I told you, I had begun to think they thought I was just another neurotic.

Well, after my first session with the psychiatrist (he said he isn't one, in the limited sense)——he *laughed* at me!! *Such humiliation.* The last thing I ever expected. My tail is between my legs. It's awful to find out you're just plain *funny.* Not even *queer!*

He is having another session today, but I have an idea we'll just tell dirty stories——

Julia and I had already decided not to set out until Monday morning, as getting out of N.Y. on a Saturday afternoon or Sunday is too awful. May have to put it off a bit, but I'm so comfortable here, don't mind.

I had a letter from Aunt Ida. She doesn't sound quite adjusted yet. I shain't waste any more sympathy on her. If she can't be happy there, even without me, she can just mope, for all of me. But think it will work out....

Lots of love,

1. Dr. Virgil Damon removed MKR's uterus (*Selected Letters*, 256).

. . . .

(ALS, 6 pp.)

Harkness Pavilion
New York, [N.Y.]
Friday
[26 February 1943]

Dear Honey:—

... Everything is going well.

Dr. Damon is very proud of me. Incidentally, the nurse told me that part of my recovery is from having a top-notch job done by an expert. Dr. Damon says that nothing could have prevented the operation eventually, so I am glad it's over. He also says that of women who come to him from all over the country with the same recommendation from local doctors, he sends back 4 out of 5 with no need of being touched. ...

Got rid of the night nurse, the old one, after 3 nights. She drove me crazy. I told Dr. Atchley you could sum her up by saying she was the kind of nurse who can't find the hole in your rectum.

...Marcia Davenport[1] sent me a spray 24 inches long of small brown orchids.

Vera Scribner[2] sent today 4-foot long white stock Easter lilies, wishing they were for my bier, probably.

Julia came over this afternoon for the first time, looking rather peaked. It was not a strep infection after all....

Harriette[3] sent me a lovely case you hang at the side of your bed, for tissues, etc.

John Marquand is in the room next to me and both Brandts[4] came to see him with a huge jar of Martinis and what a racket. They, the Brandts, spoke to me and I refused a drink naturally. Carl was so drunk his tongue was thick. He said he had had a "relapse" from his pneumonia—said it seriously. That is awful....

Must stop so Miss Reynolds[5] can mail this on her way out tonight.

She is a dandy.

Much love,

Give my best to everybody

1. Marcia Davenport (1903–1996), American novelist.
2. Vera Scribner, wife of Charles Scribner III, mother of Julia Scribner Bigham.
3. Harriette "Biscuit" Bigelow, a favorite source of St. Augustine gossip for MKR.
4. Carl and Carol Brandt, MKR's literary agents.
5. Miss Reynolds, MKR's nurse.

. . . .

(ALS, 3 pp.)

Harkness Pavilion
New York, [N.Y.]
March 1 [1943]

Dear Honey:—

Would like to be cross as a bear today but can't find anybody to be cross at. Am feeling well enough to be very restless in bed, but without strength to do anything about it. The blister on my fanny has given me a lot of trouble—the skin got rubbed off and made an awful place.... The nurse says it will leave a scar, but we agreed it would not be conspicuous!

Julia was here from 11 to 3:30.

I got permission to smoke today, as I was so fidgety—and I never tasted anything so nasty. Took 3 puffs and had to put it out.

Now honey, I told you Carlos Sowrance[1] had never meant anything to me, and that he was certainly nobody to give a second thought to. He and his whole family were nice to me when I was in N. Carolina, and then a year or so after I left, he suddenly decided I was the girl of his dreams. He is an awful ass. His family is sweet, though.

The fan mail is appalling. . . . Several more good letters for Phil[2] to use.

One forwarded letter was from Fred Tompkins' sister.[3] He is at the Veterans' Hospital in Lake City, not expected to live. I am terribly distressed. The whole family is at the hospital and I wired Thelma. Fred has meant a great deal to me, and I can't imagine my neck of the woods without him.

Wish I was home, and *drunk.*

Love,

1. Carlos Sowance, an admirer who made NSB jealous.
2. Philip May Sr., MKR's attorney, who was preparing for the *Cross Creek* trial.
3. Maggie Tompkins Turner.

. . . .

(ALS, 6 pp.)

[Harkness Pavilion]
[New York, N.Y.]
Monday noon
[1? March 1943]

Dear Honey:—

Just could not believe it when there was no letter from you in the morning mail. Have had nothing since last Friday morning. We don't get a Sunday delivery. It was bad enough to go all Saturday without word, Sunday couldn't be helped—but I certainly expected something this morning. Will say, like Bing,[1] "You have no imagination." Otherwise you would picture how forlorn it is to be ill and alone and not get a message *every day* from the person you love most in the world. Maybe you feel that a wife who isn't willing to live all the time in your house and darn your socks, doesn't deserve to be treated kindly every day. But it isn't like you to feel that way.

A letter from Thelma[2] gives me the heart-breaking news about Fred. I feel the most terrible sense of loss. He was one of the staunchest friends I have ever had.

Marcia Davenport came to see me yesterday afternoon—a life-saver, as Julia was in the country. I haven't felt like seeing any casual friends. She is very dynamic and I liked her a lot. She is also just as Jewish as can be.

. . . Had such a sweet letter from Idella. She is all ready to come back and take care of me. Between her and my Elizabeth Arden kit and what I hope will be a continued loss of weight, you will have a much more attractive wife. . . .

Loads of love,

1. Bing Crosby, American singer, to whom MKR was indebted for his praise of *The Yearling* on the Kraft Music Hall radio program in July 1938 (*Max and Marjorie*, 364).
2. Thelma Shortridge, daughter of Fred Tompkins, who had just died.

(ALS, 6 pp.)

Harkness Pavilion
New York, [N.Y.]
Wednesday
[3 March 1943]

Dear Honey:—

. . . I "dangled" today. Dangling is a new hospital ritual, and means that the day or so before being allowed out of bed the first time, you sit on the edge of the high bed and dangle your legs in space. I felt fine. Got Dr. Damon to let me slip onto the scales for a minute—and have lost 11 pounds so far. Am so thrilled. It has almost killed my nurse to bring up my deliberately puny trays, in the midst of the luxurious plenty here, but it was my choice, plus the absence of liquor. Will sit up tomorrow for half an hour in a chair. My behind is healed.

. . . Julia and I shrieked with laughter at your thinking Dr. Atchley shouldn't have left me. It all depends on who does the leaving, doesn't it?

He also walked out on Mme. Chiang kai-shek,[1] to the fury of his colleague who didn't want the responsibility alone for her while she was in New York. She has been very ill and exhausted between speeches. I felt much less abused by Dr. Atchley when I found he was leaving her, too. And of course, Dr. Damon sees me every day.

I knew you weren't complaining about Moe, but a runaway dog is a frightful nuisance, and I was afraid you'd be inclined not to baby him or bother with him, unless I pled for him.

It is snowing heavily today, 8 inches predicted. I can't see the river or the Jersey shore. . . .

. . . Carl Brandt said when I felt like it, lots of people wanted to come and see me, but even though I feel perfectly wonderful, Julia once a day is enough company and I've laid low. I really feel grand. Julia gave me Saroyan's "The Human Comedy."[2] Think you'll like it. . . .

Love,

1. Chiang Mei-ling, author especially known for bringing Western culture to China. Wife of Chiang Kai-shek, Chinese statesman and general.
2. William Saroyan (1908–1981), *The Human Comedy* (New York: Harcourt, Brace, 1943).

(ALS 3 pp.)

Harkness Pavilion
New York, [N.Y.]
Thursday
[4? March 1943]

Dear Norton:

Well, maybe you have written and it is the fault of the mails. Maybe you caught Julia's cold and are sick.

Anyway, I have had one letter from you in the 5 days you have been gone, and you promised you would write me every day. It is very depressing.

Have seen no one. Julia is better though and is coming to see me tomorrow.

Today when the last mail was in and nothing from you again, Dr. Atchley came in and told me he is going to Florida for a week with his son, leaving Saturday. It was the last straw and I made a fool of myself by bursting into tears. . . .

Please don't let anything happen to Moe. Moe would write every day if he could write.

. . . .

(ALS, 8 pp.)

[Harkness Pavilion]
[New York, N.Y.]
Friday
[5? March 1943]

Dear Honey:—

. . . The mule arrangement is all right. Henry[1] is planting beans on shares and am afraid it will be a nuisance for me. Yet I do feel I should put all available land into production, especially of vegetables. If I can get glass jars and rubber rings, plan to put in a good-sized vegetable garden and do quite a bit of canning. Hope the freeze didn't get the orange bloom. I had seen a few signs of bloom before I left. Haven't added up any checks from Talmadge,[2] but am making enough on the grove this year to have lived on—for the first time in 15 years!

Was amused at your having Doug Whidden[3] be polite to you and your guests. You remember that I told you that Fred Tompkins almost knocked him down for saying ugly things about me. He asked Fred if he and Thelma "were still speaking" to me, after being written about in C. C. A letter from Bob said he had heard Doug was one of Zelma's backers and had told her he considered her maligned by the book. Doug has had it in for me ever since I broke with Maxcy[4] and wouldn't let him bully me when he threatened to take me into court. And I had no contract with Maxcy and wasn't obligated in any way! I expect he lost face by losing an account. Anyway, I have recognized him lately as a *real* enemy.

Was allowed out of bed yesterday for the first time, to sit half an hour in a chair. Was *so* disgusted, after having felt so fine, just *collapsed* when I got back into bed. Miss Reynolds called to another nurse to bring arom. spirits of ammo-nia, and called for a doctor. I couldn't speak, but near-unconscious as I was, I wanted to say, "The hell with a doctor. Send me a St. Bernard dog." It took her 45 minutes to get a doctor. She had me pretty well out of it by the time he got here. He prescribed brandy, bless his heart, and that did the trick. Was pretty well knocked out all day.

Things went much better today and I sat up twice, half an hour each, with no ill effects. But I begin to see where the long convalescence comes in.

Dr. Atchley's wife has been in twice to see me. She is a dear.

Vera Scribner, the bitch, came up ostentatiously one afternoon. Charlie prob-ably had to make awful threats to get her to do it. Probably reminded her that "Cross Creek" was paying for her East 67th St. winter apartment. When she left she said, "Well, remember me to Norton when you get home," indicating that she had done her duty and was washing her hands of me.

Mrs. Atchley, on the other hand, invited me to spend a few days at her place when I left the hospital. Wouldn't dream of accepting, of course.

I told Idella that after making her clean house just before she left, I would have it done before she came back. Told Martha to have Sissie help her do it the first week in March.

... Honey, I just don't know how we are going to work out the living arrange-ments, but I know you will cooperate in helping me to try to do it. I know only that I love you—and that I cannot live at the hotel. But long visits ought to be lots of fun. And then when I go to the cottage for the summer, it will be grand. They are taking off the ban on using 2 or 3 gallons of gas any way people want to, so between us we can go back and forth as much as we want. . . .

Loads of love,

1. Henry Fountain.
2. Talmadge DuPree, MKR's groveman and the manager of Citra Packing Co.
3. Douglas Whidden did grove work for MKR.
4. Maxy [Maxcey] ran a citrus packing house and once supplied MKR with trees and fertilizer (*Selected Letters*, 87).

. . . .

(ALS, 5 pp.)

[Harkness Pavilion]
[New York, N.Y.]
Saturday
[6? March 1943)

Angel——

If you don't write to me pretty soon, I'm going to make love to the nicest of the three nice interns—

And when you come up, I shall hide the cute blonde nurse I've been saving for you——

... Come up when convenient, and write me—OR ELSE!!

All my love,

(ALS, 4 pp.)

[Harkness Pavilion]
[New York, N.Y.]
Saturday
[6? March 1943]

Dear Honey:—

Do hope I get a letter from you before the day is over. Had a nice one yesterday, after a two-day gap.

... Have been *so* lonesome for you. Listened to sentimental music on the radio last night and longed for you.

Julia goes to the country for the week-end so won't see her until Monday. However, Marcia Davenport is coming tomorrow afternoon and I look forward to that.

Had a most interesting visitor this afternoon, a friend of Julia's and a Scribner author—the Dean of the Episcopal Cathedral in Buffalo.

Young, attractive, and no more like a clergyman than I am. He would be *wonderful* for Julia—but he has a wife and two children.

Well, the last mail is in and nothing from you.

A gorgeous box of 2 ½ dozen tulips in Spring colors came from "Mr. and Mrs. Huston and the Employees."[1] I could *weep*. They shouldn't have. But they are *beautiful*.

Love,

1. Clarence M. Huston was the chef at the Castle Warden Hotel. His wife, Audrey, ran the dining room, and their son, Robert, did odd jobs.

. . . .

(ALS, 6 pp.)

[Harkness Pavilion]
[New York, N.Y.]
Monday
[8? March 1943]

Dear Dr. Baskin:—

Your letter this morning was a good tonic——

... My dear, if the trip to see me seems too difficult, don't try it. My morale is swell and I'm so glad I came that even starvation seems a trifle. I'd adore to see you, but there isn't too much comfort in a short hospital visit, and if it seems too hard to come, I'll be disappointed, but I'll understand. . . .

I am more than content to lie quietly and just smell the flowers. The starvation—68 hours—and subsequent 1000 calories a day (not enough to keep old Jib going) and the pain and weakening from the treatments, have me with my head on my paws. But I can tell already how right it was to do it.

I needed some more nightgowns and sent Br'er Cecil to buy me a couple. Told him to get one of them real seductive. Told him it would be just my luck to encourage the wrong man with it. Sure enough, Sunday, thinking you might come up, I was all dolled up—and in pants Phil May, red and sweating with a handful of wild flowers he had gone out into the sun to gather for me. He all but put his fore-paws on the bed and licked my face, and I know damn well he wagged his tail. Poor Phil.

When you bring me wild flowers, I think it's the sweetest thing in the world for you to do for me (the second sweetest), and when Phil does it, I think there's probably poison ivy in the bouquet. Like the old saying of the two black crows, "Even if it was good, I wouldn't like it. . . ."

My love,

. . . .

(ALS, 6 pp.)

[Harkness Pavilion]
[New York, N.Y.]
Tuesday
[9? March 1943]

Dear Honey:—

. . . Dr. Atchley returned yesterday, sunburned and feeling fine. Says he doesn't think Mme. Chiang appreciates him as much as I do.

. . . Jean[1] spent the afternoon. Was so glad to see her but it made me terribly homesick. She is going to do my shopping for me, which is wonderful. She has charge accounts everywhere and will pick out a bunch of stuff and have it sent to the hotel for me to try on, so I don't have to go out at all. If I get thin and Elizabeth Arden and some good-looking clothes, will have to stay in St. Augustine to show off! . . .

. . . Am having fits to get home. Gosh, I love Florida, not even Zelma can spoil it for me. And I love you. I long so for the Creek, and I long so terribly for you. . . .

Loads of love,

1. Jean Francis of St. Augustine, the ex-wife of Fred Francis. After their divorce, the Francises remained close and were favorite bridge partners of MKR.

(ALS, 7 pp.)

> Harkness Pavilion
> New York, [N.Y.]
> Wednesday
> [10 March 1943]

Dear Honey:—

   ... Am going to try to go to Marcia Davenport's Sunday for supper with just the Willkies and Max Perkins.[1] Won't stay long if I go.

> Loads of love,

1. Wendell Willkie, Republican candidate for president in 1940. Russell Davenport, husband of Marcia, was his campaign manager. MKR refers to this dinner in a letter to Perkins on 13 April 1943 (*Max and Marjorie*, 555).

. . . .

(ALS, 5 pp.)

> [Harkness Pavilion]
> [New York, N.Y.]
> [10? March 1943]

   ... Actually thought the Big Guy was gunning for me last night and this morning. Was sure things had ruptured, and the doctors did at first, too. Then the blood-count tests showed an infection, but they are sure it's not serious, and that things have not ruptured, or the count would be higher. Temperature jumped up last night, but has not been bad today.

A lovely hypodermic stopped the almost unbearable pain, after 6 hours of it.

Now that the scare is over, they think this is just an inexplicable sudden inflammation in the bad area, and it may clear very quickly. It might even be possible to go home earlier than Sunday if it quiets as quickly as it came.

What a sweet, patient love you are—....

Knowing Dessie's Cracker slyness, think she had heard the gossip about you and me and was just trying to trap you.

Well, don't worry about me. The Master Bug Squasher will have to put His foot down pretty darn hard to get me. I'm a tough beetle!

And inside the toughness is a very real love for you.

(ALS, 4 pp.)

[Harkness Pavilion]
[New York, N.Y.]
Wednesday
[10 March 1943]

My Dear—

The birthday wire made me very happy—but it's just like you to do such a thoughtful thing. I actually forgot the day. I'm so glad you included the "and yesterday," for the birthday itself left much to be desired, while the preceding "yesterdays" could not have been much fuller or more satisfying in every way. . . .

They are turning me loose tomorrow afternoon, and I am so glad I put in these extra days, even though I have gotten homesick and restless. They have done me more good than all the rest—or perhaps I am just beginning to get a favorable reaction—and perhaps Dr. Baskin had something to do with it. . . .

I shall come straight home Thursday, reaching home before dark, of course. . . .

If you can come up Thursday evening, if only to say Hello, it would be lovely, but if you can't, I'll be good and not paw the earth.

So much love—

. . . .

(ALS, 3 pp.)

Harkness Pavilion
New York, [N.Y.]
Saturday
[13 March 1943]

Dear Honey:—

. . . I am going to be a puny thing for a while—and please lay the wires to keep people away—they wear me out worse than anything I do. Just have to expect and accept the weakness for a while.

Dr. Atchley is torn up about Stephen Benet's[1] sudden death—heart trouble. It is a great loss. He dropped work on an epic poem to do war writing—*wrong*. . . .

Lots of love,

1. Stephen Vincent Benét (1898–1943), American novelist and poet.

. . . .

(ALS, 4 pp.)

Hawthorn, Florida
Wednesday afternoon
[17 March 1943]

Dear Honey:—

Well, home on the range!

However, home is where you are, and I'm impatient at the stop-over. There was a wash-out 15 miles north of Gainesville, and they had to detour the train via Dunnellon, but sent cars, autos, to take Gainesville passengers from the wash-out to Gainesville. The agent gave Idella an inaccurate picture, and the poor thing dashed back here to see if there was a wire from me directing her elsewhere. Knew I could count on her intelligence, so just waited and sure enough she showed up in due time.

Things in modestly good shape at the Creek. Little Will is sending Alberta[1] away for good today. Think he wants to bring his previous family here.

... Have so much to talk about, can hardly wait. Will stop now, as Will can mail this in Citra as he takes Alberta through.

All my love, my very dear one.

1. Alberta was a companion of "Little Will" Mickens, brother of Martha Mickens. "Little Will" worked in MKR's grove when he was not "drunk" (*Cross Creek*, 23).

. . . .

(ALS, 11 pp.)

[Cross Creek, Fla.]
Monday morning
[22 March 1953]

Dear honey:—

Smoky is playing on the floor about two inches from Moe's nose. However, the rapprochement is anything but complete. Smoky gives a coy come-on, Moe takes on a kinder look, then at the last moment Smoky spits and Moe lunges. Each is increasingly intrigued, and Smoky even began to play with Moe's tail before it suddenly dawned on him it was dynamite.

... Drove in to see the young grove apparently ruined. It looks as though fire had swept through. The valuable Valencias are too damaged for shipping, but a portion of the crop can be salvaged for juice or pulp. The young trees may not be as badly hurt as they appear. There were altogether seven days, or rather nights, of severe cold, in ten days. The temperature went once to 17°. I lost my broccoli, but strangely, the flower garden survived. The stock has been stunted, but is blooming. ...

Martha in one of her practically-at-death's-door moods. Knew it meant guilt or a build-up to asking a favor. It was the favor—. Wanted Idella to drive her to Hawthorn today while she helped Estelle[1] dress two hogs! Favor refused, as I could not be left alone, and I don't think the Ration Board would approve of using gas for this purpose.

Lay on the day-bed on the porch yesterday, and Tom Glisson came in. "I don't want to worry you, but—"

There is a new war on at the Creek, he said. He was getting his innings first. A most complicated matter, as are all our wars here. Mr. Brice's[2] unpleasant son in law, Hugh Williams, has bought Brice's piece of grove between me and Tom. Is having his lines surveyed—quite wisely, I think, as Brice and Tom and I all end together in a tangle of swamp and marsh—and access to the Creek. Tom thinks they are planning, with the support of Mr. Martin,[3] his rival as fishing Czar, to block him from the Creek. Tom wants to get up a petition to have a public road declared through his property to the Creek. He suggested that "in a few days" I walk down to the swamp with him and look things over. Assured him it would be a month before I could do so. Meantime, told him when I was able, I would talk with Mr. Brice and see what was what. Thelma[4] has been coming to the Creek every two weeks to buy fish, ostensibly. Tom said he told her he didn't see how she had a case, as her full name hadn't been used. Knowing Tom, think this was a hint that as his full name *was* used, my participation in the road war on his side was indicated.

Before Idella could bring me my over-due lunch, Chet came. Frank Greene[5] hasn't been able to finish up his deed and mortgage and give him my check, as he had to have a quick-claim deed from Mrs. Cason[6] on a piece of the property that she owned and never properly transferred some thirty years ago. Chet left the quick-claim deed for her to sign three weeks ago. Now finds Thelma has refused to let her sign it, until she can "go over" the papers in the court house in Gainesville. Am sure she has no idea of my connection with the deal, as I told no one but you and Frank and Chet said he had not mentioned it. He thinks she will try to hold him up for some money. Said he would rather pay a lawyer to bring title-suit than be blackmailed. Nice gal, eh?

As Chet was leaving, Dr. Cason[7] drives by, stops. I ducked for bed. He talked with Chet a long time, then drove on without coming in.

Got my lunch at three o'clock.

This morning Henry[8] came to begin hauling the wood out of the young grove preparatory to unmounding the trees, so Chet can cultivate at the end of the week. Found Martha had gotten a ride to Hawthorne—taking with her the keys to the truck and gas tank.

However, it is all fun and I am enjoying myself hugely. We had a grand rain yesterday, and today is very cold. Will just live in the bedroom today with the hearth-fire and the animals.

Loads of love,

1. Estelle Mickens.
2. William Riley "Old Boss" Brice. Hugh Williams was married to Brice's daughter, Grace.
3. O. E. Martin.
4. Thelma Shortridge.
5. Frank R. Greene, MKR's lawyer from Ocala, who introduced MKR to NSB.
6. Charity Cason, Zelma Cason's mother.
7. T. Z. Cason, M.D.
8. Henry Fountain.

(TLS, 2 pp.)

[Crescent Beach, Fla.]
Friday
[26 March 1943]

Dear Norton:

Have gotten myself caught high and dry without cash. . . . Could get Verle Pope to go to the bank with me here, but have the uncomfortable feeling of not wanting to ask the slightest favor of him, as I begin to see every sign of his asking me to finance him on his tourist court. If some people were running the project, I should jump at it as an investment, but the St. Augustine beach section is simply crawling with such places, several new ones, and Verle somehow impresses me as a terrific gambler and definitely scatter-brained, and I can visualize a fiasco. Wish I saw it differently, for Edith's sake, and I may be very wrong. . . . Verle's unreliability, financially, much as I like him personally, is a definite conviction with me. . . .

The ocean continues marvelous for swimming. Went crabbing yesterday and got six in an hour. They were just beginning to come in when I left. I was a little early.

Love,

. . . .

(ALS, 6 pp.)

Hawthorn, Florida
Monday
[29 March 1943]

Dear Honey:—

. . . Weather still cold, but no harm done.

Am in the living room by the fire.

Poor Henry[1] is dragging himself around, but is really very ill.

. . . Idella gave me a grand massage today. I seem to be holding my own on the weight and not gaining.

Love,

1. Henry Fountain.

. . . .

(ALS, 6 pp.)

Hawthorn, Florida
Thursday
[1 April 1943]

Dear Honey:-

Certainly wish your car would drive in! It is a heavenly quiet afternoon, no sound but the birds flying in and out of the feed basket and the bees humming in the orange blossoms. The bloom is light and I smelled it last night for the first time. The tea olive smells deliciously.

Didn't feel as well as usual today and was glad to stay in bed, but got as nervous as a witch this afternoon. Took a Phenobarbital and while it didn't put me to sleep it quieted me down, and I came out on the porch with Moe and Smoky and am on the couch.

. . . I found that Henry had put in 26 rows of Fordhooks before he was sick and they are up several inches and thriving. Martha and George[1] fertilized them yesterday and one of the Townsends[2] was to come today and use Mr. Brice's[3] mule to cultivate them but never showed up. The help situation out here is desperate. . . .

Wish you were here.

Love,

1. George Fairbanks.
2. The Townsend family once lived at Cow Hammock, just south of Cross Creek on Orange Lake. They are the subject of "The Pound Party" in *Cross Creek* (chapter 4).
3. William Riley "Old Boss" Brice.

. . . .

(ALS, 6 pp.)

Hawthorn, Fla.
Thursday
[1? April 1943]

Dear Honey:—

Well, I can mind my own business and NOT write a book—and still get into trouble! The new war is a showdown between Tom Glisson and cohorts, and Mr. Brice and cohorts, and each side has put it up to me in such a way that I don't see how I can side-step. After figuring what seemed expedient for my own interests and not being satisfied, tried to figure the thing on the basis of abstract justice— and there is still something to be said on both sides. Will tell you the details when I see you.[1]

Henry is in dreadful shape and I've written to the Lake City hospital to see if they can take him. I told him I'd take care of Sissie and the children while he was gone, and he said he would have gone before, but just had to have the few dollars he could scrape up, to feed them. Now surely a system of social security can be managed to take care of things like that.

All is amiable between Moe and Smoky, except that Moe is so big and rough that his kiss or pat of the paw knocks Smoky flat, and then Smoky gets sore as hell. Moe used Smoky for a pillow this morning, until his weight finally made Smoky yowl bloody murder. . . .

. . . Heard the first whippoorwill last night—and no help available to put the corn in the ground. Henry didn't have the beans in, and perhaps just as well.

I am feeling grand, so good I have to watch myself for I automatically tackle everything.

Love,

1. The dispute between "Old Boss" Brice, Hugh Williams, and Tom Glisson was over a road and cattle gap. MKR wrote to Maxwell Perkins about the incident: "These Creek battles are the most complicated I have ever known" (*Max and Marjorie*, 545). MKR and Glisson had a complex relationship. She once believed that he had poisoned her pointer dog Mandy, and later that he had cut her fences. Their feud embarrassed everyone at the Creek, and their tearful reconciliation is recounted in *Cross Creek* (361–63).

. . . .

(ALS, 6 pp.)

Hawthorn, Florida
Friday
[2? April 1943]

Dear Honey:—

My Lord, life without W.D.!! even for a while. May I be the first to extend my heart-felt sympathy? And gone at the same time as Smoky and me!! Just pray to your spiritual though living ancestors that he and Leila don't fall for racial equality and high wages. I do know he was satisfied with his earnings, as Idella said they both told her she certainly left at the wrong time, as everybody had been making money. She said they had completely furnished their house, and very nicely. Also, did they leave the key to their house, in case we are in St. Augustine before they're back? Idella left all her clothes there except her uniforms and two dresses. But here's hoping they'll be back first. If anybody wants to stay North, it will of course be Leila. When Idella got back, Leila came into the laundry where Idella was washing sheets and said, "Well, Idella goes off to become a beautician and comes back a laundress." Idella said she said, "Well, it just happens I *like* it."

God, I hope she means to stay with me.

. . . Old Will is unmounding the young orange trees, for lack of any other help. Idella drove the truck into the grove while Old Will loaded fat wood on it to bring to use at the house. Idella said, "I guess this is what they mean by sharing in the war effort."

. . . Three bi-motored bombers just flew over, low. I wondered if the Germans had come to Cross Creek. . . .

Love,

(ALS, 4 pp.)

[Cross Creek, Fla.]
Sunday Morning
[4? April 1943]

Dear Norton:—

I think that your putting Jean[1] in our apartment was the height of indiscretion. I guarantee that you have started a scandal that will take a long time to lay. I know that you were only attempting to be accommodating to a good customer and incidentally a friend. I know that you would never do any cheap double-crossing. I know that you have too much contempt for Jean's vanity and selfishness to be interested in her. St. Augustine knows none of those things. They will know only that she is in our apartment during my absence. And where are you?

Cecil came by yesterday about 6. Said he had a hunch I was here. Also said he had 'phoned the hotel before he left the air field. He asked, with that sideways secretive look he can get, "Is Jean back?" It suddenly struck me that he knew damn well she was back, and had probably recognized her voice on our apartment telephone, or she may have identified herself to him. I told him the trouble she had given you about a reservation and said that when she finally arrived you probably had no room for her, so had given her the apartment.

He said, "If he didn't have a room for her, where the hell is *he* [underlined twice] sleeping?"

All St. Augustine will ask that question.

I said you had probably taken one of those small back rooms without a private bath. It occurred to me you might even be doing the night shift for lack of help, and sleeping on a couch in the lobby.

In either of those cases, where are you bathing? If you had literally no room for her, she should have done what any other dilatory customer has to do—go somewhere else. If you had one of the little rooms without a bath, it would have been wiser to give her that and let her bathe in Ruth's[2] bathroom while Ruth was out.

And since when have you added our presumably private apartment to the room roster of the hotel? You will probably think I am being dog-in-the-mangerish if I am unwilling to have a good friend use something I cannot use. She is not so good a friend but that you charge her room rent.

I do not think the inevitable scandal will hurt your business, but it will hurt you personally. People will be of two opinions:—that I walked out on you, perhaps *because* [underlined twice] of Jean; others will think you used an opportunity while my back was turned.

And you have outraged whatever sense of haven I had of the apartment's being an oasis, removed from the public commercialism of the hotel itself.

Please do not put this to Jean as I have put it to you. She is an innocent if selfish victim herself. And it would only make matters worse. But if she lingers on longer than you expected, as I venture to guess she will, I suggest that the moment you have a habitable room you inform her that you have a room ready for her, and that it is always possible I may have to return at any time. . . .

I am *furious*, but I love you.

1. Jean Francis.
2. Ruth Pickering.

. . . .

(ALS, 2 pp.)

[Cross Creek, Fla.]
Friday
[9? April 1943]

Dear Honey:—

. . . A letter from Phil May, that I hoped was notice of the suit being thrown out, was just a favorable statement from some lieutenant.

A recent letter from one of my rather steady soldier correspondents says they have him in the neuropsychiatric ward, telling him to forget "Economics" for a while. I'd better quit writing to all these guys—there'll be a whole insane asylum coming to see me after the war. And me none too sensible myself—.[1]

Smoky is hollering bloody murder for some fish—somebody brought us some. Think I'll take the rest of his sulfathyazol myself. I took the wrong puss to the doctor.

Hope W. D.[2] is back—but he is really on the spot, isn't he? Could he have a good physical exam to determine if possibly if he's likely to be taken in the Army? . . .

Lots of love,

1. MKR undertook an extensive correspondence with armed service personnel, who had been reading the Armed Services Editions of *South Moon Under*, *The Yearling*, and *Cross Creek*. Many of these letters are in the MKR Collection at the University of Florida Library.
2. W. D. Williams, a porter at the Castle Warden.

. . . .

(TLS 3 pp.)

[Cross Creek, Fla.]
Saturday afternoon
[10? April 1943]

Dear Honey:

. . . Well, my God, I just don't know nothin' about nobody. Of course, why I should ever expect even the most demure negro woman of 28 to be a virgin, I don't know. Anyway, I thought Idella was. A few days ago, she told me she had been married in West Palm Beach, and one reason she came up here was because she wanted to get entirely away from him. I asked what was the matter with him, and she said, "A little of everything."

. . . Do you ever feel OVERCOME with ignorance? At the moment, I don't know what anything is about. I should set up in business to write about human nature! Yeah, me and who else. Anyway, I can write just to spite other ignorant people. . . .

Love,

. . . .

(TLS, 5 pp.)

Hawthorn, Florida
Sunday afternoon
[11? April 1943]

Dear Honey:

Will probably be over Wednesday. Possibly Tuesday. Depends on when I get someone to put in the rest of the Fordhooks and whether my rose bushes arrive. They should have been in by now. After I got over my first shock about Idella, remembered her report described the type as "Late latent." So a day one way or the other won't matter, for her next treatment. . . .

Found Leonard[1] has been working all winter at Crosy-Wartman in Citra. Chet saw him, and he came out this morning and put the Kohler system on its feet again. I fair sat up and cheered when I saw him coming.

. . . Wilmer[2] knew I was in Harkness most of the time I was there! She wrote that she went to the phone a dozen times, or to the door, to call or just walk in, but kept waiting for a signal from me. She finally called—the day after I had left. She didn't sound sore—just said it was a typical Kinnan trick. Think I was well justified, as in telling me about Uncle Will's last illness and death, she criticized everything that the doctors did, and told me what she thought should have been done! She'd have had every one of my stitches out, and different ones in.

Love,

Monday morning
[12? April 1943]

It looks definitely as though I could leave here Wednesday afternoon. A man has promised to put in the rest of the beans tomorrow. It will take him all day and perhaps Wednesday morning, if I can get him to cultivate the ones that are already up. Henry[3] planted them too shallow, and about one bean out of ten is up, the rest just lying on top of the ground.

Had as unpleasant an evening last night as I've almost ever had. Had Idella drive me in to see Mrs. Tompkins,[4] and on the way home that bastard of a Doug Whidden and his wife and Dick Dewey[5] followed me home and of course I had to invite them in. I have never had any sort of persecution complex, but I certainly felt a ring of evil hemming me in. Doug just came to get some new grievance. Will tell you all about it when I see you. After sticking knives in me for two hours, he had the audacity to say, "You know, I'm your friend." I said, "Are you? I have been informed otherwise." I did not intend to have it out in front of his wife, who I am sure has nothing to do with it, and told him if he would stop by some time when on his way to Brice's, I'd like to tell him just what was what.

1. Leonard Fiddia.
2. Wilmer Kinnan, youngest sister of MKR's father, lived in New York City at the time.
3. Henry Fountain.
4. Annie Tompkins, wife of Fred Tompkins, known as the "Old Hen."
5. Doug Whidden and Dick Dewey, Cross Creek neighbors.

. . . .

(TLS, 4 pp.)

Hawthorn, Florida
Monday
[19? April 1943]

Dear Honey:

. . . Am feeling fine, somewhat to my surprise. Chet Crosby came by yesterday at five o'clock and took me bass fishing on the lake. It was the first time I had done any casting in three years, but the knack came back to me, and I stood up and cast until dark three and a half solid hours. Expected to be stiff and sore but wasn't at all. I only got one and Chet got five. We took Moe along and he loved it. But when a large bass flopped toward him with open mouth in the boat, he piled up on the little tiny seat in the bow and stayed there the rest of the time. When and if you come over, Chet will take us out.

Imagine I'll come over on Wednesday. Idella wants to go to West Palm Beach then to meet her husband[1] who will be there on furlough then, as they both want to get a legal separation or divorce. . . . There will be enough for canning next week from the first picking, then I will have a marketable crop, a good one, from the second planting. Henry (Preacher) Woodward[2] is keeping them cultivated. He also turned some land down toward the lake and old Will is setting out 300 sweet potato cuttings.

Heard from Dr. Atchley, to whom I wrote, but no help. He said they made no special investigation of the intestines, as it is important not to handle them any more than necessary. He said it was most unusual to have bleeding like that from diverticula. Said I should go to Jacksonville and have a good man do a proctoscopic examination to determine whether there were hemorrhoids—which is the very first thing Dr. Harris[3] did, and there was nothing like that. . . .

I am about to go nuts again over my correspondence. Feel the soldiers' letters just have to be answered, but am about to begin to ignore the ordinary ones. I can't get down to work at all. Also, dashing back and forth like this makes work impossible. Will do better when I get settled at the cottage. . . .

Love,

1. Bernard Young, Idella Parker's first husband.
2. Harry "Preach" Woodward, "Old Boss" Brice's field hand.
3. Robert D. Harris, one of MKR's favorite physicians.

. . . .

(ALS, 4 pp.)

> [Cross Creek, Fla.]
> Sunday
> [25? April 1943]

Dear Honey:—

Gosh, I'm lonesome.

. . . If you're not ill—just don't know what to think. All kinds of disturbing things. Do you love me? Would you rather I didn't write you so often? Are you stuck with Jean in the apartment, and waiting to write me until you have her moved, or she goes?

It would do a good deal to mitigate the gossip if she stayed a while in a regular room, instead of just taking off from the apartment.

. . . Mr. Brice's son in law, Mr. Williams,[1] is coming up this afternoon to see me, and I know it is to put pressure on me to pitch in on their side. If it weren't for the damn law suit, I would just tell him he is in the wrong, and to hell with him, but I can't afford to alienate Mr. Brice[2] if the suit does come to trial, as with Fred[3] gone, he would be my best witness.

. . . Edith Pope; has had the measles—quarantined, and Max Perkins harassing her to finish the corrections on her manuscript,[4] and she not allowed to work or mail out a letter full of germs! She is all right now. . . .

> Love,

1. Hugh Williams.
2. "Old Boss" Brice.
3. Fred Tompkins.
4. Edith Pope, *Colcorton* (New York: Scribners, 1944).

. . . .

(TLS, 2 pp.)

> Hawthorn, Fla.
> Monday night
> [26? April 1943]

Dear Honey:

It is ten o'clock, very late for the Creek, and I'm tired and in pain, but will write in case you don't come over. I felt very selfish at abandoning Edie, and even worse when I talked to you and found you'd been buying flowers for me. . . . I wanted so much a few days with no rush or hurry or commotion, and watching the oranges and the red birds. I was willing to be selfish, to have it. All of us get our strength from different sources, and mine comes from this. My need, that is more than a mere pleasure, in being here, is spoiled by feeling that I'm deserting you and that you are a little hurt. I wouldn't do it if I didn't have to. That's probably as far as I can ever explain.

. . . The hunt through rough country was exhausting and blistered my feet, but I felt I owed it to Moe. He retrieved almost all the birds all on his own, Chet says he has a wonderful nose, and after the second bird knew just what we were after and hunted like a veteran.

Tuesday morning

My God, it's dark at seven o'clock. Chet came for me at eight, and being cloudy it was still dark. Thought early this morning I was in for a worse attack, but feel much better now and think I'm over the hurdle. Everything was very dry and we only found one covey in the time Chet could be out. I held Moe while he shot, and Moe went a little bit wild when I released him, but made a wide circle and then came in when I called, and retrieved one of the two birds. He is very promising and Chet says once he has made and held his first point, he will be a trained bird dog. Not the least bit gun shy.

. . . I have given up trying to get a three-minute egg out of Martha and have switched to bacon—.

Lots of love,

. . . .

(*Selected Letters*, MS not seen)

[Cross Creek, Fla.]
Tuesday afternoon
[27? April 1943]

Dear honey:

It's a good thing I didn't try to go to Jax with you, as it took me two and a half hours to do my various errands and I didn't reach the Creek until 3 p.m. as it was. And no Idella! And she has not come yet. . . .

I had been in the house about five minutes when Mrs. Williams (Brice's daughter) and Doug Whidden, whom they had called on to help in the rumpus, came up. Mrs. W. had a contract that a lawyer had drawn up, whereby Tom Glisson leased his right of way and paid for a cattle gap, and Tom was making objections and wouldn't sign it. The contract seemed extremely fair to me in every way—and it was up to me to get Tom to fall in line. Tom had telephoned me to St. Augustine just before I left, asking when I was coming, as things were getting worse. To make an involved story short. Armour Brice and I went with Tom to the controversial land this morning and worked out an arrangement satisfactory to all. To swing it, I am paying for a second cattle gap and one line of fence myself, for I felt that Tom would balk at paying out any more, and it is well worth a hundred dollars, say, to me, to have everybody feel all right about it. Armour and I walked down the road together, and I said, "Do you remember what it says in the Bible? 'Blessed are the peacemakers, for they shall see God.'" He said, "That doesn't promise anything but seeing God. I'm afraid they'll let us have one look, and then throw us out again." Anyway, the contract is signed.

I also had it out with Doug Whidden and we both felt better about it.

Found a week-old letter here from Marcia Davenport, saying that she and her husband . . . were going to Hobe Sound, and would I like to have them spend a day or two at the Creek on their way back. Wired her I was delighted, and am now wondering what the hell if anything of any sort has happened to Idella. . . .

Mrs. Cason has absolutely no claim on the 64 feet of Chet's property. She sold the land 30 years ago to Ed Johnson, and Ed owned it 20 years and sold it to Chet's uncle who owned it 10 years. Now Zelma is going around saying she (Zelma) is going to throw Chet out, and is foreclosing right away. She or her mother has no more legal right to foreclose on Chet than on me. She has an appalling nature. . . .

It is a gorgeous day, but the Idella situation has me depressed. Feel sure there is a reasonable explanation, but am only afraid somebody, perhaps she, is seriously ill. . . .

Loads of love,

. . . .

(TLS, 2 pp.)

[Cross Creek, Fla.]
Wednesday
[28 April 1943]

Dear honey:

Idella safely home. Found her ill. She had been to Dr. Strange[1] for her shots and they had knocked her out, as she said they often do. Brought her back with me, but must take her to him next week. The poor thing would have been all over it if she had had the shots regularly.

As I drove in, found Tom Glisson and Armour Brice waiting for me. Old Boss had asked Tom, as a guaranty of good faith, to burn the petition Tom had to have the controversial road declared a public road. Tom wanted my opinion as to whether I thought the Brice's would keep their side of the agreement and I said I did. So I donated a match and there was a dramatic ceremony beside the cow lot of burning the petition. Everyone feels very noble. . . .

Love,

1. J. L. Strange of McIntosh.

(TLS, 2 pp.)

[Cross Creek, Fla.]
Friday
[30 April 1943]

Dear honey:

Have just listened for a steady half hour to old Will's droning account of what ails him. He is on his way clear to Palatka to a doctor who guarantees to cure him in three treatments. The doctor said that after all Will had been through, "ain't a thing ails you but lumbago and your right kidney"—which seems plenty. George Fairbanks, who is cutting the grass, leaned in fascination on the lawn mower through the account. I am exhaust[ed].

It was such a thrill to see you yesterday. Hope you got back without trouble. We certainly wrecked that quart in a hurry. Feel pretty dubious about Norman's new project. He'll have Julie hungry yet.[1] Agents have to have so many magazine contacts—but maybe he plans to go in just for books. At present would certainly not consider giving him my account. Carl is likely to kill himself with liquor or end up in an asylum, and in that case, believe I'd prefer Carol.[2] Have always had the uneasy feeling that Norman was cultivating my friendship with an ulterior motive. May be doing him a great injustice. His policy of watchful waiting is a little creepy.

Lots of love,

1. Norman S. and Julie Berg.
2. Carl and Carol Brandt.

. . . .

(TLS, 2 pp.)

[Cross Creek, Fla.]
Saturday 5:30
[22 May 1943]

Dear honey:

Gosh, I wish you'd walk in. I'm lonesome and bored as the devil and not even interested in beginning Proust[1] over again. Had the screaming fidgets last night and today, worked hard all morning and got tight before lunch to get relief, slept it off and don't care about starting over again without company. If 'twere unrationed days,[2] I'd light out for St. Augustine, Saturday or not. It's the first dose, I guess, of the type of nervousness I was warned about. Glad there hasn't been any more of it. . . .

Had another extremely fascinating and beautifully written letter from Caleb Milne IV. My last letter to him, written in November, reached him the end of March! Fool that I am, I had raved about my Julia (with not too subtle motives) and he said for heaven's sake to tell her to wait until after the war and not do anything rash meantime. I do pick out the damnedest bets for her. . . .

... Mr. Brice's Henry Woodward worked on the beans today and will finish Monday. Some of them look very promising.

God, I'm lonesome.

Love,

1. Marcel Proust (1871–1922), French novelist.
2. MKR is referring to the government rationing of scarce supplies during the war.

. . . .

(ALS, 8 pp.)

> Hawthorn, Florida
> Friday morning
> [28 May 1943]

Dear honey:-

Made the trip without undue fatigue. The potato fields were fascinating, strewn with sacks of potatoes and with the harvesters, many of them the deep black Bahamians. I stopped and bought a sack.

Moe went wild with joy when I drove in. Idella said that every day he had sat for hours in the middle of the road, watching toward Island Grove. Smoky of course didn't give a damn. He had killed and *eaten* one of my biddies yesterday. Idella overheard a conversation between Moe and Smoky. They were agreeing on the chickens. Moe said, "I'll chase the big ones and you chase the little ones." Smoky said, "What are we waiting for? Let's go."

My lawn grass is a foot high. George Fairbanks refuses to come. Martha and Idella tried to cut it, but could manage only a small patch.

... Caleb Milne 4th was killed in Tunisia in the final action. During the battle, four stretcher bearers were called for to go right into the thick of it and he volunteered and a bomb got him. I had a touching note from his mother, who said he had mentioned his pleasure in hearing from me. She enclosed also a copy of a letter he had left to be given to her in case of his death, and it's one of the most beautiful things I have ever read.

Women's pride in their men being brave is a strange thing—prehistoric, somehow—full of nobility—and as much to blame for the continuance of war as any other factor. I am terribly proud of you for what you have done, even while rebelling against it with every fibre, and while feeling that this war, while plainly as "necessary" as any war can be, is in the last analysis asinine, and no sacrifice toward it makes sense. Yet I have nothing to say to you about your decision, for it is so intimate a thing that it is yours alone. And I understand how you feel. One of my soldiers, with a bombing squadron, a boy who was in the class I talked to at the University, wrote that while the whole business was alien to his tastes and nature, that "a man feels he just can't let other men do his fighting for him." I suppose that is the true male answer.

Idella is making me stay in bed today, even though I feel pretty well. Moe keeps me company, and Smokey is stretched decoratively over the little red velvet sofa, ignoring me pointedly. He doesn't know that he's destined not to grow up as tough as he plans at present, he is a Siamese Studs Lonigan. . . .[1]

Lots of love,

1. Studs Lonigan, a fictional hero created by James T. Farrell (1904–1979). Lonigan's moral disintegration in the face of the Chicago underworld became legend.

. . . .

NORTON BASKIN ENTERED THE AMERICAN FIELD SERVICE ON 6 JULY 1943

. . . .

Norton Baskin, American Field Service, India. By Permission of the University of Florida Libraries.

(TLS, 4 pp.)

St. Augustine, Fla.
July 29, 1943

Dearest:

My Odyssey[1] seems very dull by the side of yours, but I'll trace it so that I can begin writing you the news from day to day. I have been most grateful, in a way, that we were both ill when you left. I know that I was so numb that nothing registered too painfully. I did have the same germ that you had, and decided it was just as cheap to move up to the hospital as to stay in the hotel. The germ was soon taken care of, and by that time I was into the diverticulitis, which proved fortunate, as Dr. Atchley had been hoping to catch me in an attack so that he could try bella donna and luminal—which work gorgeously. From now on, I should be able to get through an attack with no pain at all. The damn thing is embarrassingly neurotic in any case. I got restless and told Dr. Atchley for God's sake to let me out. He did, protesting, I spent the week-end with Sigrid Undset[2] and Marcia Davenport—and felt perfectly all right from that moment on.

Sigrid Undset was the stoic rock I had expected to wash against, but she rather failed me at leaving, by going into tears and embracing me with a certain desperation. She is living in quite depressing quarters, three narrow steep flights up in an old brownstone Brooklyn front, her living room small and cluttered, the air unbearably hot and close. "There isn't enough shade in Brooklyn," she said, "for a cat". . . . She is doing a secret job for the American government. She indicated its nature, but I still wish, in spite of the importance of her job, that she was doing creative writing instead. The Norwegian sense of humor is amazing. She told me a Norwegian story of how an English spy was caught by the Germans in Norway, and how a German spy was caught by the English in England. In Norway, there was apparently a Nazi officer—arrogant, insolent, brash. But the Germans realized he was *not* a German officer—he had no parcel of choice food secreted on his person. In England, on the other hand, there was apparently an English officer, reticent, hesitant of speech, modest. But the English realized he must be a German spy—he had lavish dinner at the Savoy, and tipped the waiter threepence. She was most optimistic about the war, in contrast to her gloom of a year and a half ago. She said that after the war it is likely that the Norwegian government will send her back to America. After seeing her friends and relatives, and Norway, again, she said that she thought she would be happy to return here to live. She is living from hand to mouth, and has to drop her war work often enough to do an article "to keep my pot boiling." I asked if she would come to Florida, but she said she cannot afford the trip. If I thought either she or I could go on with our work under the same small roof, I should risk offending her by sending a round-trip ticket. Am afraid she would send it back in small pieces. For one who gave the Nobel prize to charity, it would be hard to accept a hand-out, I suppose. Julia would have come back with me at the drop of a hat, but I shall burst if I don't settle down to work, so did not invite her. But we plan to have her come down to the Creek during the hunting season.

I sent a wire to Idella, asking her to come to see me at the hospital. Toward the end of my time there, she 'phoned. She said, "You know I don't want to see you, don't you?" "Why not?" "I'm too ashamed." I told her never to mind, to come on that afternoon. She said she would—and never showed up. She had 'phoned the hospital every day to inquire about me, and I do feel a little better in knowing that she does, or did, have a certain affection for me. But I shall have to mark her off, at least for the time being. I am wondering when my unusually long run of bad luck will give out. Not even Adrenna could have left me at a worse time.

Max came to the hospital one day, and I had lunch with him the day I left, and he gave me the green light on the book.[3] I am scared to death about it, for every word will have to be placer-mined, and it seems to me as though all my bones will have to go through a duck-press to squeeze out anything worth while. But the concept is still clear, so I shall go ahead.

I stayed from Saturday night until Monday with Marcia and we had a good quiet time, Russell was hard at work on a post-war economic plan at the order of the government, for which he said neither he nor LIFE will get any credit. He was thinking of expanding his report into a book. I didn't see Willkie. Sunday afternoon Marcia and I went to a Toscanini[4] broadcast and that was fun. Russell met us for dinner at the Plaza, and they fell ravenously on a $3.75 wisp of steak, not having had any beef in New York for a month. Marcia has a cook, maid-waitress, laundress and secretary—and I have never eaten such frugal meals, served so early, so on the dot, with such fear on the part of the hostess. She is paying terrific wages. I should rather do the work myself than be so terrified and so bullied. Sunday night she and I went to the Hemingway movie,[5] and I do hope you will have a chance to see it. It is superb—yet the love story, and Gary Cooper and Ingrid Bergman, are the weakest parts. Most of the reviews said the same, though TIME went all out for Ingrid Bergman—who so annoyed Marcia and me that we often covered our eyes while she was smirking. The minor characters were wonderful, and the whole show was stolen by Katina Paxinou, who played Pilar to take your breath away. Paxinou was the leading actress of the Greek theater, and Marcia had seen her in Athens in a Euripides play. I wept a dozen times at the perfection of her artistry.

All my love,

1. MKR went with NSB to New York, where he was to board a ship for deployment. Because of war secrecy, he never knew exactly when he was to depart and on what ship. Without any good-bye, he was secreted away to become an ambulance driver in the American Field Service, assigned to the British Army in India.
2. Sigrid Undset (1882–1949), Norwegian novelist, was awarded the Nobel Prize for literature in 1928.

3. *The Sojourner.* It took MKR ten years to complete the novel, which was published by Scribners in 1953.

4. Arturo Toscanini (1867–1957), Italian conductor.

5. *For Whom the Bell Tolls* (1943). Hemingway agreed with MKR, lamenting that Hollywood "flunked again" (Baker, 383).

. . . .

(TLS, 4 pp.)

St. Augustine, Florida
July 29, 1943

Darling:

I wrote in my first letter of my time in New York after you left. I wired my mother's sister in Michigan asking if I might visit her for a few days, and not to be a hypocrite, said that I wanted to talk about the old days on Grandfather's farm. A wire came back saying please to come—for the summer. This hospitality rather appalled me, not only from horror at a summer with Aunt Ethel,[1] but horror at the thought that some day she or her offspring might think it entirely natural to ask to spend a winter with me. . . . . There were no porters and I had to carry my heavy bags. I tackled an idle colored man in the Michigan Central station and said I was desperate for a porter and would he help me. He said insolently, "I ain't no porter."

The negro question in Michigan throws new light on the problem. I questioned everyone I met about it. There seem to be two angles to it in that section. Most of the people I talked to *hate* the negroes with a venom that is astonishing to those of us who love them. Then I ran into a woman who has charge of all the school cafeterias in Pontiac, (where there is still an Osmun Street, named for my Grandmother's pioneer ancestors). Pontiac is now a city of about 100,000. Negroes there have for years had "equal rights." They have gone to the same schools as the whites, had the same advantages and opportunities, are not segregated in any way. These have made desirable citizens, some of them prominent lawyers and doctors, though this woman said that on the whole the negroes had never done as well in school as the whites. She said there has never been any trouble with these negroes. She has *absolutely no* race prejudice and said that she would have no feeling about marrying a colored man if his character and intelligence were acceptable. She said the trouble is coming from the ignorant Southern negroes who are flocking to the high-paid defense jobs and who are totally unable to appreciate their wages and privileges. She said, as did the other Midwesterners who hate the negroes, that this group is arrogant, pushing, without manners. They delight in intruding on white resorts and driving out the whites. It is they who have caused the race riots in Michigan. A General Motors executive, the sweetheart, or fiancé or what-have-you, of one of my cousins, who is among the negro-haters, (and who is a Fascist of the first water, incidentally) said that the white mechanics and factory workers resent having these ignorant apes move in beside them at the machines and draw the high wages toward which they have spent their lives working—and then be arrogant to boot. This checks with the story of a woman who has no race prejudice and shows one thing certainly: that the mass of Southern negroes is not ready for equality. Yet her story would indicate that under equality, the negro becomes a desirable citizen. Mr. Gay, who runs "the" store in Hawthorn, told me that the negroes were being organized. He said that a group of twenty or thirty went by his house the other night, shouting things about their rights and what they meant to do. He said they were buying up all available guns and knives. Chet Crosby verified this. I wondered if foreign agents were behind this, in an effort to cause trouble, and Chet said that the FBI was investigating now in our section. If trouble comes, there is only one outcome, and it will be at the expense of the negroes. Even a die-hard Southerner like Chet is in favor of education and better wages for the negro. It would be a great pity if the negroes were misled by spies and fifth columnists. It could not harm the country, but it would set the negro back a hundred years.

I enjoyed my week's stay with my aunt to a certain extent. I had not seen her for twenty years, since my mother's death, and had always been fond of her. But she is a high-strung almost hysterical woman, and shocked me by suddenly *screaming* at her nice, if dumb, husband. My visit was ruined for me by the advent of her daughters whom I never cared for. . . . But my aunt proved a fount of knowledge of the old days, and also had the most fascinating family letters dating back as far as 1822. I read box after box, and it was exciting to re-create the personalities from the correspondence. My great-grandmother turns out to have been an inveterate writer of poetry, painfully religious and of dubious quality. Now and then she turned a neat phrase. In one poem, speaking of her weariness, she wrote, "The Savior's heart and hands were weary, too." And she wrote a grieving sister, saying, "Do not let your sorrow drink your blood." I had thought the curse of the urge-to-expression came all from the Kinnan side, but the Scotch-Irish great-grandmother seems also to blame. The earliest Traphagen came to New York from Holland in 1663. His grandson, William, built an inn at Rhinebeck, New York, which is still being run and is today advertised as "the oldest hotel in America." William and his son Arent operated it from 1700 to 1769 and "Washington slept there." Arent's son moved to Michigan, having married the daughter of a French Huguenot leader, Du Bois. Aunt Ethel had an old ledger with the names of both Du Bois and the first Abraham Traphagen, grandfather of my grandfather Abraham, dated 1822.

I spent a day with a great-aunt, sister of my grandmother, Fanny, in Pontiac. Aunt Effie's first husband committed suicide because of ill health and the old gal came to life after years of frustration. She made money in Florida real estate and married an old codger when she was nearly 70, who proved an awful flop. She hasn't lived with him for 8 years, She showed me his picture and I said, "I don't like his face." "Well," said Aunt Effie, (aged 84), "you wouldn't like his hind end, either."

Guess I come by my ribaldry honestly.

... Have a good time. Oh yes, there is a book out by a Capt. Geer of the Field Service, "Mercy in Hell,"[2] which you may want to write me for, as it tells of the AFS. I despise his personality and his book. I don't like his face and know I wouldn't like his hind end, either, but you might be interested. Eve Curie's "Journey Among Warriors"[3] is worth asking for if you want a topnotch war book. Dorothy Baker's (Young Man with a Horn)[4] new book is brilliant technically but the Lesbian subject-matter is repulsive. Can't recommend it.

Loads of love, darling.

1. Ethel Traphagen, MKR's aunt. The following are prominent members of the Traphagen family: Abraham and Fanny Traphagen, MKR's grandparents; William and Arent Traphagen, MKR's ancestors. Ida May Traphagen Kinnan was MKR's mother.
2. Andrew C. Geer, *Mercy in Hell* (New York: Whittlesey House, 1943).
3. Eve Curie, *Journey Among Warriors* (Garden City, N.Y.: Halcyon House, 1944).
4. Dorothy Baker (1907–1968), *Young Man with a Horn* (Boston: Houghton Mifflin, 1938).

. . . .

(ALS, 6 pp.)

[Cross Creek, Fla.]

July 29, 1943

Dearest:—

... When I got in last night, I invited Martha to have a drink with me. We got high as kites and swore undying loyalty. Whoever leaves me, "Old Martha will be here right on, Sugar."

She estimated Chrissy's breeding time badly and the calf has not arrived yet. From all signs, she is "expecting" hourly. Her bag is huge, and if Martha takes proper care of her, she should be a fine milker. I am swapping surplus butter to Mr. Martin for fish for Moe and Smoky.

... I asked Edith Pope to spend the week-end at the cottage with me, and will pick her up when I go back tomorrow. She will be in St. Augustine a week longer. Verle was to leave today, and expects to get overseas after from 6 weeks to 6 months at some other camp. Edith said he was turning into a psychiatric case from the frustration. He has taken John Cooley (Coolee?) into partner-ship to keep his business from being entirely wrecked.[1] No word from Lois—have wondered if Ed[2] was in on the Sicilian invasion.

Loads of love,

1. Verle Pope owned an insurance agency in St. Augustine.
2. Lois and Ed Hardy of Louisville. Lois was MKR's sorority sister at the University of Wisconsin.

(TLS, 6 pp.)

[Crescent Beach, Fla.]
At the cottage
August 1, 1943

Darling:

. . . I was infinitely relieved to know that you had gotten over your flu germ and were wallowing in comfort rather than the trough of the sea. Biscuit[1] thought it highly probable that you are on an especially interesting ship. I can't wait to hear the details when possible to write them. I stopped at Ocean Manor Friday night to pick up Edith Pope, who is spending an English week-end with me at the cottage. . . .

Wanting to be alone with my grief, I had rather dreaded three days of Edie's interminable anecdotes, droned like Bob's. . . . But I had a huge box of books that I ordered at Scribner's, and I have sat at one end of the davenport and Edie at the other, devouring books the way the rats devoured the pecans. We have come out of it only to eat and sleep. And I think I have done better with someone here, than being alone. Everything reminded me so of you, and when we went swimming, I kept turning Edie's bones into your marrow and hearing you say something through the waves.

Almost everything at the cottage is out of order. None of the lights on the north half of the cottage work; there was no drinking water; the path to the ocean is so thick with weeds that Moe went on tiptoe, seeing a rattlesnake, as I did, under every partridge pea; Smoky's pan is not to be found high or low, and I had to place a pie pan (pun permitted) for him, with a bit of cloth at the side to suit his peculiar aesthetics. It works, but using the bathroom must depress a house guest. . . .

The day I returned here from the Creek was one of the nightmares for which I have an unwilling penchant. I had wrestled in Gainesville with the rationing board, tire inspection, the Welfare Board on the subject of Martha's old age pension, etc. I had arranged to bring to Mr. Huston as many chickens as the Glenn Basses[2] could dress. The Basses have been thrown out of the hovel and have bought a very nice place at Lochloosa. I am doomed to lend them money for new furniture but am sure I will get it back. They got only twenty chickens dressed and I had to take the other hundred, alive, and crawling with chicken mites, to the grove, to dispose of at a future date. . . . Today's paper said that the sale of turkeys was forbidden until the quota was made up for the holiday turkeys for the Armed Forces, until fall, and I hope he will come on bended knee asking for Glenn Bass's chickens, which I shall delight in selling to someone else at any inconvenience. I melted toward him when he followed me to the car and put his hand on my shoulder and said they would do anything at all at any time to help me.

I had finished my trip, I think quite naturally, under the influence of Barclay's, and had two drinks at Ocean Manor, but Edie said she didn't realize I was high *until we started out.* Brave girl, for I had only one parking light down the ocean highway, I overshot my road and blithely *backed* from Junko's to my turn.

. . . Henry Fountain has had another operation and Sissy says they tell her there is no hope for him. We have made a tentative arrangement for Sissy to work for me at the Creek this winter if Henry does not return. I will have to teach her from scratch, as I have all the others, but she is clean and "willing."

I am horrified at the thought of returning to the airplane spotting at work, as now we have to know the *types* of planes, and there are about a hundred. . . . Julia passed her examination on this 100%, and the bitch Vera failed completely, causing tension in the Scribner household.

Edie is deep in Thomas Wolfe's letters[3] to his mother, and her eyes are as big as saucers.

. . . The bitch Jean is due to return this week, and the nice Ruth the first of September.[4] Your hostelry was full the Friday night I came in, and Mr. Huston said there are endless reservations ahead for the future. . . .

Well, it is 2:30 and I had better stop and feed Edie. She eats like a starved horse but is not fussy about quality. I do love her but she has little mannerisms that annoy me, such as using the public butter knife to spread her toast—.

My love,

1. Biscuit, nickname for Harriette Bigelow.
2. Glenn and Elma Marie Bass.
3. Thomas Wolfe, *Letters to His Mother* (New York: Scribners, 1943).
4. Jean Francis and Ruth Pickering.

. . . .

(TLS, 2 pp.)

[Crescent Beach, Fla.]

Aug. 2, 1943

Dearest:

. . . I'm really alone, for the first time, and being very sensible. I took Edith in today and when I came back drank milk instead of Sunnybrook and took a long walk up the beach with Moe instead of cussing.

. . . Let me know what kind of mail reaches you the quickest. Unless it makes much better time than regular air mail, I just don't like the V-mail. It doesn't look at all personal! By the time our letters make a round trip, it will be Palm Sunday. . . .

I miss you so that I can't talk about it—.

It's dark enough to draw the blackout shades, and as hot as it is, bed is the only answer.

A note from "Jimmy" Cabell asked for news of you and both sent you their love.

All of mine,

(TLS, 3 pp.)

[Crescent Beach, Fla.]
Aug. 3, 1943

Dearest:

Wrote letters today and did some very sketchy housework. Mr. Leyvraz came to check repairs on the cottage and while we were on the terrace the longest damn snake I have ever seen slithered in front of me. It was big around, too, and at first I thought it was a moccasin, but it was a coach whip—it must have been seven feet long. It investigated the dog-brush under the shower, thinking it was an edible animal. Mr. Leyvraz heaved a piece of wood at it with little enthusiasm, with no results. It went under the house and a few minutes later Smoky went under, too, for the first time. I was scared to death, for I know the thing was big enough to eat rabbits. I enticed Smoky out with chicken livers. There have been no rats around—and the coach whip undoubtedly is responsible. They are harmless, of course, except to swallowable animals, but they are one's least favorite people. If you had tripped over it, know you would never have come to the cottage again.

I didn't do as much work as I planned, having made the mistake of opening the short stories of Saki (H. H. Munro).[1] They are utterly adorable and you would love them. Riotously funny and charmingly written. . . . If you would like this book, ask for it, "The Short Stories of Saki." There is also a "The Complete Novels and Plays of Saki," which couldn't help but be good. But you have to request specific things.

Moe and I went to town in the late afternoon. The glamorous colored girl couldn't come, as her mother didn't care to have her alone at the beach. If Mama thinks she is protecting any café au lait virginity, she is a couple of years late. But a gray-haired colored woman who has worked off and on for the Young's says she will give it a try. If she doesn't run into the coach whip, I see no reason why the job wouldn't just suit her. . . .

All my love,

1. H. H. Munroe (1870–1916), *Novels and Plays of Saki* (London: Lane, 1933); *Short Stories of Saki* (New York: Viking, 1930).

. . . .

(TLS, 4 pp.)

[Crescent Beach, Fla.]
August 4, 1943

Dearest:

. . . [Edith Pope] got it out of Miss Grace[1] that it was Zelma who said that wicked thing about your going. That was my theory, that she had at least tried to start it—but why Miss Grace thought she had to pass it on to you, I still don't see. Miss Grace told Edith she was going to tell Zelma not to come to her shop anymore—she found Zelma reading her stack of telegrams—told her not to—Zelma went right on reading.

A letter from Dessie said that she was at the Blue Bird and Callie Horne was there. Callie began slapping an officer's face—where-upon he took her by the scruff of the neck and set her out of the door literally on her fanny.

... More gossip: Edith said a friend of hers, Mary Kay Brown, was riding with Zelma and Zelma shrieked at a small boy, "Don't forget that bicycle! Don't forget I'm going to give you a bicycle when I get my money!" Zelma later said to the Brown person, "Don't think Jimmy (her nephew, Dr. Cason's son) isn't making up to his Aunt Zelma these days. He knows in the end he'll get most of the money I'm going to get out of my suit. He knows which side his bread is buttered on." !!!!!!!!

Didn't write you half the funny Michigan things. The old great-aunt had gone to a book review of Cross Creek and was asked to tell of my childhood. She told how damn cute I was, and that at a certain very young age, when dressed up, I went around lifting my skirt and asking everyone if they wanted to see my fairy petticoat. That's what I mean about revolting little girls. The younger aunt asked if I remembered, which I did not, of periodically disappearing at Grandpa's farm, sitting under a willow tree by a distant brook, and showing up with a story or poem. The escapism evidently goes way back. . . .

All my love,

1. Grace Bugsbee, owner of a St. Augustine florist shop.

. . . .

(TLS, 2 pp.)

[Crescent Beach, Fla.]

Aug. 6, 1943

Dearest:

... Edie is either a genius or a precocious 12-year-old. Could I go to town on business alone today? No, both Edie and Moe had to go for the ride. I do love her, and she drives me nuts. She wipes her lipstick on my linen towels.

A Dickensesque little carpenter came today and fixed the screens, so at least I don't have to battle mosquitoes. He left notes all over the house, held down by his tools, telling me what was wrong with this that and the other, and what he would bring next time to fix them. It was like an Easter egg hunt, finding the billets doux. . . .

All my love,

(TLS, 3 pp.)

[Crescent Beach, Fla.]

Aug. 7 [1943]

Dearest:

I am glowing with virtue. I *was* glowing with sweat. I realized that what was irking me was *planning* to work, against insuperable obstacles. There is no chance of settling down to the book this month, so I just accepted it and am all right. . . .[1]

I celebrated my mental liberation today by cleaning the cottage as it hasn't been cleaned before. It looks elegant. I am seriously considering not bothering with trying to get a maid. I am determined to lose weight, and nothing uses every bit of you like ordinary housework. And it is certainly more peaceful than having a darky of dubious cleanliness and disposition. I talked with one colored woman whose mother in law is coming to visit and wrote that she wanted a job "to keep her mind together." No consideration for my mind, at all—.

Dora wanted me to stop and write you before I finished the house, but I know her tricks. She was looking for an excuse not to finish. When I had finished scouring every inch of the bathroom, I washed my hair and had a wonderful bath and dressed all clean. Whereupon Smoky went to the bathroom, and with all good intentions, missed the pan—.

. . . Was afraid I would never get Edie out so I could go to it. She had made an appointment for 9 this morning with the plumber at Ocean Manor, so of course I had to drive her in. I finally got her to breakfast, telling her she must hurry. At 9 exactly she disappeared into the bathroom. I hated to nag her there so just waited. At 9:30 she emerged dreamy-eyed, still studying "Florida Wild Flowers."[2]

I think a storm is making up. . . . The ocean tonight is metallic and somehow uneasy, in spite of the breathlessness.

Good night, dearest. I love you so.

1. MKR is reflecting here on the very beginnings of *The Sojourner*.
2. Mary Francis Baker (1876–1941), *Florida Wild Flowers* (New York: Macmillan, 1926).

. . . .

(TLS, 4 pp.)

[Crescent Beach, Fla.]

August 8, 1943

Dearest:

Edie wandered out to breakfast this morning in Julia's old gingham bathing suit (she had used up all her clothes), her clattering charm bracelet, and what is left of day-before-yesterday's elaborate hair-do.

"You know," she said, "I need time just to dream."

. . . Crescent Beach must be crawling with weird old men who live in the palmettos and creep out when Junko sends out word that someone needs the weeds cut. He introduced me to an awful old fellow who had done my cutting while I was away. He may be the Ancient Mariner,[1] for he fixed me with that kind of eye and tried to hold me to listen to his saga. . . .

Well, I must go and stick another fruitless fork into the dandy hen. If you were here, we could get nice and high and listen to the rain, and the hell with the hen.

All my love, and rather teary thanks for remembering the birthday.

1. MKR is referring to Samuel Taylor Coleridge (1772–1834), "The Rime of the Ancient Mariner" (1798).

. . . .

(TLS, 4 pp.)

[Crescent Beach, Fla.]
Aug. 11, 1943

Dearest:

How I wish I might hear from you. . . .

The Field Service sends out cables twice a month, and on the chance that one would reach you en route, I sent one, telling the at least temporary good news about the lawsuit. The Gainesville judge threw out the suit, after making a long personal study of the case, which he wrote both lawyers had intrigued him very much. Zelma will be allowed to make an amended declaration within 15 days, and Phil said she would almost certainly do so—and that the judge would almost as automatically disallow it again. Her only chance this time is to claim specific damages, and if she claimed there had been such, they would certainly have been mentioned in the original declaration. If the amended declaration is thrown out, they can ask for a hearing before the Florida Supreme Court, which Phil says they will also probably do. I have no qualms about it if it goes that high. It isn't over yet, but Phil feels it's in the bag. When it is once over, in Zelma's disfavor, God knows what she will attempt. I told Phil we should take out an injunction against her if she continues her petty persecution and he said we could sue HER for libel! I said we certainly should not!

. . . Jean Francis' good maid Ruby returned to town Monday and W.D., leaving the next day, had pounced on her for me. I saw her yesterday and she will come, and I think means it. I offered high wages, but it will be worthwhile. After my burst of cleaning, things got piled up again and I realized I could never work and keep up with the house, too. She is used to living at the beach and has a puppy she wanted to bring, so am sure it is all right. She is probably just as good as Idella.

I was walking along the beach, the ocean very calm, and the porpoises were playing and feeding in the *third* shallow wave, the closest I have ever seen them. I felt they were the Marineland porpoises, hanging around close to home for the duration, and looking forward to life in the Oceanarium afterward. I wonder if they have gone back to their normal sex life.

. . . I am toying with the idea of making a year-round home of the cottage, enlarging it to the north and south. A bathroom and swim-shower room could be added to the north. A glassed-in room where the outdoor fireplace is on the terrace, could be added as a combination dining-room and sun-parlor, and an enclosed corridor built from the kitchen to it. French doors from the present living-room could lead to it. There is no hope of ever *living* at the Creek. All I need is a *home*, sufficiently remote from people and town. The distance will be nothing after the war.

I do not *Love* the ocean. It is too much like a vast Smoky, colossally indifferent and with partly-sheathed claws. But the river-view is sympathetic, and I could plant trees on the west flat.

All my love,

. . . .

(ALS, 8 pp.)

Hawthorn, Fla.
Sunday morning
at the Creek
[15? August 1943]

Dearest:—

Mr. Frank Jones,[1] of Seals and Pennington, has come and gone. He arrived on the dot of the appointed hour, shook hands with great formality, worked out your neat books and my incoherent scraps with accurate dispatch, smoked one (no doubt carefully allotted) cigar in the process, shook hands formally again, and, revealingly, said, "I've enjoyed being here very much."

. . . Anyway, something about us and our income tax represents glamour to Mr. Jones. It may be our recent marriage. It may be the excitement of income based on books that people read. Anyway, Mr. Jones with his one cigar "enjoyed being here very much." I could die of shame that I am ever depressed, having so full a life, when working on our income and out-go represents adventure to Mr. Jones.

You are working a grand profit. Your *net* [underlined three times] profit to date, after a $4,000 depreciation is deducted, is $8,000.

At the moment, you are making a *minimum net* (probably more) of $12,000 a year. Your 1943 tax is $2,000.

Monday morning
[16 August 1943]

Must head back to the cottage, as I have to spot today.

I had invited Dessie to come over yesterday with "another" Wac, and she brought five! They were a tough bunch of pistol-packing' Mamas. They were definitely in undress—shorts or slacks, and their hair every which-a-way. Two of them had long straight hair and it just strung down their backs. They were high and very noisy. They seemed to be, though all quite different, of *a type*. Only one of them actually mannish, yet none of them really *feminine*. I suppose it is that self-sufficient sort who would go into the Wac's in the first place.

Almost had a catastrophe about feeding them. Had counted on using some of my own chickens, but Martha failed to receive my note telling her I would be here, with company, and to dress three chickens. Fortunately, I was able to get fish from Tom Glisson, so we can manage.

Well, darling, everybody is working post-war plans, so you and I should make some. We can have a heavenly life if you will work it out. I'm passing the buck!!!

I have made so many guesses as to where you are—N. Africa—the Middle East. I dreamed last night that you were in actual battle action. You didn't like it, but you did your part and came out all right!

All my love,

1. Frank Jones, the Baskins' accountant.

. . . .

(ALS, 4 pp.)

[Cross Creek, Fla.]

Aug. 15, 1943

at the Creek

Dearest:—

. . . Jean Francis' Ruby[1] came Friday and cleaned up and I am to pick her up on my way through St. Augustine tomorrow morning to stay for the summer. It is too good to be true.

Martha has a grandson—Adrenna's son—23,[2] who is going to work on the place here until October. He has contracted to work at Hastings, in potatoes, then. If he is any good, and is contented here, perhaps he will stay. Adrenna is coming next week to visit. . . .

Martha, as you might expect, made a classic remark when I told her you had already been more than a month on the ocean. She said, "Don't you know he's wore out with all that water."

I had a letter from Henry Heyl[3] from the Fitzsimmons Gen. Hospital, Denver, Colorado. He is in for two years of convalescence. He has bought a farm in Vermont and will go there in the spring. He has been writing some *charming* sketches, based on his experiences, and the *Atlantic Monthly* took two or three. He enclosed three for me to read and pass on. He said he had to do something to keep from going crazy.

. . . What about *Henry Heyl* for Julia? . . .

All my love,

1. Ruby Dillard, the maid of Jean Francis.
2. James Mickens.
3. Henry Heyl, a well-known neurosurgeon, was in the Army Medical Corps at this time and was later instructor in surgery at Dartmouth Medical School.

. . . .

(TL, 2 pp.)

[Crescent Beach, Fla.]
Aug. 16 [1943]
Back at the cottage

And glad to be here—it turned frightfully hot again. Did my 12–2 stint at the Post, and despair of learning the 'planes. But I am needed, even though I have to still turn them in "unknown." Maxwell Anderson,[1] who has been spotting in New York, thinks we should be doing something more useful. He says we aren't going to be bombed now. But it seems far too soon to stop the spotting.

Martha took advantage of a chance this morning that she's been watching for, for a long time. Told her I would like coffee at 7 A.M. She was in the kitchen dropping pans around and running the Kohler at 5:30!! It never takes her more than 15 minutes to make coffee and what she calls bread toast. There was no sleeping, of course, and at 7 sharp she called demurely to ask if I was ready. Even Moe went back to bed after breakfast and Smoky refused to stir at all. . . .

The Glenn Basses spent 3 ½ hours with me Sunday!!!! Glenn played my dulcimer[2] and sang hill-billy songs. He used to be with the Orange Grove String Band. But he wasn't good enough for 3 ½ hours. They drank a quart of rum and wished you were there.

[Remainder of letter missing]

1. Maxwell Anderson (1888–1959), American dramatist.
2. The dulcimer, now lost, was given to MKR by the Kentucky novelist and poet James Still (1906–2001).

. . . .

(TLS, 4 pp.)

[Crescent Beach, Fla.]
Aug. 18, 1943

Dearest:

Such wonderful news from A.F.S. headquarters. They passed on word of a cable saying that all was well with your unit en route.

Moe and I are just in from a long walk on the beach. I was paced by one of the young Dupont boys on a bicycle! I asked him, just to make conversation, if he'd seen any rattlesnakes. Just as casually he informed that a six-foot one crossed my road yesterday! They had nothing to kill it with, and by the time they got back with a weapon, it had disappeared. He said its length spanned the entire width of the road. Was sorry I'd mentioned it. Moe and Smoky are both wary and so probably safe, but one glimpse would certainly send Ruby back to town! Am keeping my fingers crossed about her, for she is a wonder.

. . . My tree article in Collier's[1] brought an unexpected repercussion. I had a four-page letter from a member of a committee in Congress that is investigating the timber and lumber situation, asking if I would do some more articles if they provided me with confidential information. I think I'll try to find someone else to do it. I just do not want to give the time to it. Yet I feel that if I could be of help in such a critical matter, perhaps I ought to. My literature is painfully likely not to be deathless, but I might go down in history as the gal who saved the nation's trees! Maple-tree Maggie.

All my love,

1. "Trees for Tomorrow," *Collier's Magazine* 117 (8 May 1943): 14–15, 24–25.

. . . .

(TLS, 3 pp.)

[Crescent Beach, Fla.]
Aug. 19, 1943

Dearest:

Would you be interested in a little study in the relation of psychology and perhaps psychoanalysis to one of the simpler and more primitive four-letter words?

For a long time I have been awakening at about three or four o'clock in the morning and going into a black abyss, in other words, having the heebie-jeebies. This goes back long before you embarked for parts unknown. It is usually preceded by a nightmare, customarily the one in which I am homeless, and wandering around in strange places looking for an abiding place. The nightmare last night was quite a hopeless one. I was celebrating Christmas all alone at the Castle Warden and feeling properly forlorn. The scene changed, and I was at the Creek, and feeling equally frustrated. My mother[1] was there, and I cried out to her, "Help me to get out of this awful place!" Now psychoanalysis would undoubtedly enter here, and trace some connection whereby some sort of betrayal on the part of my mother made me feel without ground to stand on, while at the same time leaning on her.

Last night I had no reason to be jittery. I had done without liquor, I had cut down on cigarettes, I had listened to the radio until a sleep-able hour—and just could not go to sleep. Finally, waking up after the homeless nightmare, I took one of his capsule knock-out drops. Well, to begin with, the rains came. This morning my bed, and Moe's chaise longue, were completely soaked, and I had noticed nothing. Also, Moe had evidently raised the roof trying to get me to let him out—and I had been sunk too deep to hear him. The most house-broken dog in the world, he had used the clean white rug in the living room—. So there is your connection between neuroticism—and ****! Fortunately, his condition was a little costive, so I could hide our joint shame before Ruby appeared to get breakfast. She overslept.

I think this is really a neat lesson in relativity—. The connection between a human being's tormented soul and a bird-dog's bowels is definitely intriguing.

I wish I could figure out what the hell it is I want, what the hell I am afraid of, and what the hell I am fighting. It seems to me that I want one of two things: roots in the earth, a home life that radiates from that earth; or an absolutely gypsy-like existence, without ties, without dogs or cats or material belongings. I think I could live either life. I cannot live a vague back-and-forth existence. And while you have time and detachment to think about it, try to figure out a life we can have together that will satisfy both of us. We should be able to work out something wonderful. Would you rather we were Darby and Joan,[2] or a gypsy king and queen? How about gypsying after the war for several years, then settling down?

Marjorie and Dora.

1. Ida Traphagen Kinnan.
2. Darby and Joan, a designation for a loving, old-fashioned, virtuous couple, from the broadside ballad *The Happy Old Couple* (1748).

. . . .

(TLS, 7 pp.)

Crescent Beach, Florida

Aug. 23, 1943

Dearest:

How I wish we could be reading John Marquand's new book[1] together. It calls for whooping aloud. It is the most wicked and delicious satire, as though a beautiful amber poison fell drop by drop. Yet the people he slays break your heart. I haven't finished it, and it is rather plainly headed for defeatism. Marquand is a better man than I, for he can love and pity people while he poisons them, while I have to feel extremely one way or the other. When I am loving them I make every excuse for them and have every hope, and when I hate them I can see no good at all.

Of course the crux of human beings is never what they do or say, but what they think and feel—their hidden motives. That is why so many "good deeds" are a mockery, and why "crimes" are sometimes not criminal.

I have wondered if my unknown friend Caleb Milne IV may not be a case in point. His mother has gathered together parts of his letters, intending them at first for private publication, but is being urged to submit them first to a regular publisher. She wants me to do a brief foreword.[2] She sent me a copy of the address given in Africa on Bastille Day by a Frenchman, who singled out Caleb as a symbol of American generosity, even to giving one's life, for France. It seems

Caleb was killed when he volunteered to bring back a wounded French soldier from under fire. The Frenchman seems to have known and admired him. His relation with his mother was very close. In her last letter she wrote that she had worked at anything she could get to do to keep her family of three boys together

I am in a mellow mood about human beings, for the Negro writer, Zora Neale Hurston,[3] has done one of the most beautiful things I have ever known. After several months, in which she must have thought I had taken offense at her letter about "Cross Creek," I wrote her a good letter. I am ashamed to say that I alibied about taking a river trip with her, telling her I should love to (which is true) but that I was deep in work on a book. I mentioned that I was in trouble as to getting the work done with all my energy free for it, as Idella had "gone Harlem."[4] I said that though I put no high value on my work, still I had thought Idella felt she shared in it in giving me an unirked background, and that surely there was nothing menial in her work, since the wives of countless creative workers of one sort and another did exactly the same things for their husbands and were glad to participate in that way. I said that I had felt, evidently mistakenly, that in treating and considering Idella as a friend, in sharing my books with her, talking with her, I gave her something she would not ordinarily get. Well—.

Zora Hurston is working on a book of her own. She said—I think I shall just quote from her letter:

"I know just what you need. You are certainly a genius and need a buffer while you are in labor. Idella is much less intelligent than I took her to be. What a privilege she had! Well, it is inevitable that people like you will waste a lot of jewelry by chunking it into hog pens. Even though I am busy, if it gets too awful, give a whoop and a holler and I will come and take everything off your hands until you are through with your book. I really mean that. I am already looking around for somebody who would really do for you permanently.

"Really now, Miss Rawlings, if you find yourself losing your stride, let me help you out. I know so tragically what it means to be trying to concentrate and being nagged by the necessity of living. Of course yours is not financial as mine was at one time but still with the scarcity of help in these war days, it might call for all sorts of annoyance just to get fed and bedded."

I shed tears over the woman's offer. She is an artist in her own right, and if ever the "nigger" was going to come out, it would presumably be in one who had gone as high professionally as she has. She and Dr. Carver[5] seem monumental to me. To transcend the humiliation of their position and being at the peak themselves, to have such graciousness—. Such bigness. I feel so small, thinking of my alibi to her. When she and I have finished our present books, I shall take the trip with her if it costs me the lawsuit and you your business, not, God knows, in any spirit of condescension but with a desire to learn and to know. Her offer settles in my mind all doubts I have had about throwing myself into the fight for an honest chance for the Negro. The mass of people, black or white, is always bound to be the hoi polloi. The rare, choice individual is the one who carries the torch, and nothing must stand in the way of such an individual. And of course, when the individual is big enough, as she is, and as Dr. Carver was, any Deep South obstructionism, any Jewish-radical "fight for rights," is a candle before a great wind.

1. J. P. Marquand, *So Little Time* (New York: Collier, 1943).
2. MKR wrote the introduction for *Letters from Caleb Milne* (New York: Woodstock, 1944).
3. Zora Neale Hurston (1903–1960), whose autobiography, *Dust Tracks on a Road* (New York: Lippincott, 1942), was already completed. Perhaps the reference is to her next work, *Seraph on the Suwanee*, which was not published until 1948. MKR was so impressed by Hurston's letter that she sent it to Maxwell Perkins (see *Max and Marjorie*, 551–53).
4. Idella Parker left MKR briefly to work for a family on Long Island (see Parker, *Idella Parker*, 80–83).
5. George Washington Carver (1864?–1943), former slave and renowned agricultural scientist at Tuskegee Institute.

. . . .

(TLS, 6 pp.)

Crescent Beach, Florida

Aug. 25, 1943

Dearest:

. . . I got your $3,000 in bonds, and was able to take them out in our joint names, so the hotel could cash them if necessary. Have not needed to validate your power of attorney, which relieves Willard Howitt no end.

. . . The pluperfect Ruby couldn't take the nights alone in the bottom-of-the-sand dune apartment and had every intention of not appearing again. She didn't show up Monday morning, and I left a note at her house suggesting that she take the bus back and forth every day and not stay at night, so she called me up and is apparently willing to try that. She reappeared today, into a fine mess.

Aunt Ida spent the week-end with me, and I was so damned lonesome I really enjoyed her. And of course, she is at her very best, now that she feels sorry for me. When Ruby didn't come on the bus Monday morning, Aunt Ida offered to come down and keep house for me. Dear God. You can imagine how much work I'd get done. And you can see me letting an 84-year-old sweep my rugs.

Cecil 'phoned this morning and is coming to the ration board this afternoon and will drive down here to see me. Am terribly afraid I will cry on his shoulder, for I know how he loves you and misses you. Forget when or where it was, but he said to me, "You and I are the only ones left."

Did I write you that Zelma's lawyer[1] is appealing direct to the Fla. Supreme Court on the case? At least that saves one step, the amended declaration.

Perhaps the most important news!—one of the Duponts killed the big rattlesnake I spoke of, right in my back yard! It was over six feet. I have the hide. Mr.

Canova (who seems a distant relative of Junko's and takes care of his store when Junko is drunk, and is a snake-catcher. I mean Mr. Canova is a snake-catcher. Junko probably never catches his!) told me cheerfully that the snake's mate must still be around my place. I begged him to come and hunt for it. He gave me some turtle eggs and I had a wonderful supper of the eggs and bread and butter and ale. . . .

Loads of love,

1. J. V. Walton.

. . . .

(ALS, 10 pp.)

[Cross Creek, Fla.]
Saturday Aug. 28, 1943
at the Creek

Dearest:—

The radio and press have carried the news that Mountbatten[1] has been placed in charge of over-all operations in S.E. Asia, with a view to making a push to open the Burma Road. This is not military secret, evidently, being broadcast. He is in Washington now and will go to India, where the monsoon season ends about October first, the radio said.

I gather that you will arrive wherever you are going about the time the monsoons end! And I know what that means. Well, you can never complain of a dull life.

. . . Poor Henry Fountain died yesterday in the Veteran's Hospital. The Western Union operation at Hawthorn did the most callous thing I've ever heard of. The wire was a long one, sent yesterday afternoon, and specified that it was to be delivered and delivery charges checked with the hospital. It informed Sissie of the death, asked permission for an autopsy and went into great detail as to the choices she had—free government burial in the national cemetery at St. Augustine or a certain allowance for burial other places etc. and said to have a return wire collect to them by this morning, otherwise they would have to do as seemed best to them. That white-trash bastard at Hawthorn made no effort to have the wire delivered—just stuck a 2¢ stamp on it and dropped it in the mail! It arrived at noon today and meantime Sissie, knowing only that Henry didn't have much longer, had hitchhiked to Gainesville to get a Lake City bus to go to see him. I went to Island Grove and telephoned the hospital. Poor Sissie hadn't arrived—must have missed the morning bus. They had had to proceed without the autopsy, which they had been most anxious to do. All because the telegram was to Zamilla Fountain,[2] *Colored*, Route 1. The hospital was as upset about it as I was and is going to take the matter up. Meantime it has messed up all of us. The funeral will probably be at St. Augustine Tuesday morning and I'll wait over an extra day and have the truck follow me, so the whole bunch can go. But I think the guy who didn't give a damn just because it was another dead nigger, will find he's been a little careless with government orders.

I asked Martha if she had a message for you, and she said to tell you she "thinks about you a whole heap of the time," and to tell you "she was cutting wood and a chunk came up and hit her over the eye and she feels so bad."

Her grandson has been working very well, but had his physical this week so will probably be in the Army shortly. He has things looking extremely neat.

. . . Had thought I would have to move back here, for lack of help at the cottage. Am terribly afraid my friend Jean tried to double-cross me about Ruby. Ruby just didn't show up a week ago. I left a note at her house telling her I could understand if she couldn't stand the nights alone, and that I could manage if she would come down every day on the 9 o'clock bus and go back on the 6 o'clock, and to call me. She did, and that arrangement was agreeable. . . .

. . . I reviewed Cabell's St. John's River[3] book for the N.Y. Herald-Tribune. He did a delightful job.

Had to have my car battery charged before driving over yesterday, and waited at the hotel for it. Doug[4] wanted to talk, so I listened. He said he was getting more temperament than he ever dreamed of, but as he described the way he had handled various matters, think he is using infinite tact and diplomacy. The Chef is over-working as usual and Doug has tried to work out some sort of vacation for him. . . . And he still refuses to pay high enough wages to the kitchen help, so they come and mostly go. He said to Doug, "I won't waste the Little Boss's[5] money that way." Doug tried to tell him he would waste it worse if he became ill and they had to close the dining room! Lots of women have that strange kitchen jealousy—they are willing to slave without help, to be sure they get all the credit! It is a form of egoism. . . .

Oh yes, Cabell et. al sent their love to you. He pretends to be hard-boiled, but isn't at all, and is very fond of you.

As who isn't?

All my love, darling,

1. Louis Francis Albert Victor Nicholas, Lord Mountbatten (1900–1979), head of the Southeast Asia Command, commanded the Allied operations against the Japanese in Burma.
2. Zamilla "Sissie" Mickens Fountain, wife of Henry Fountain.
3. James Branch Cabell and A. J. Hanna, *The St. Johns* (New York: Farrar and Rinehart, 1943). MKR's review appeared in the *New York Herald Tribune Book Review* (5 September 1943): sec. VIII, p. 3.
4. Douglas C. Thompson, who, after NSB sold the Castle Warden, became the St. Augustine city treasurer and tax collector. He and Chef Clarence Huston were often in conflict.
5. "Little Boss," a nickname for NSB.

(ALS, 4 pp.)

[Cross Creek, Fla.]
Aug. 29–Sunday
at the Creek [1943]

Dearest:—

The most magnificent rain came in just now to break the heat. Smoky got caught outside, and when I called him, he ran so fast for the door that he skidded right by it. It is thundering and lightning, and he is now under a bed. Moe is under my feet, pretending to be very brave.

. . . Dear God, I miss you so. And hit a rainin'—.

The daughters and grandsons and grand-daughters of the man from whom I bought the place[1] (the daughter married a son of Old Boss) were visiting at the Brice's today and I invited them to stop by. They were very nice about the changes I have made. The place I put the first bathroom they used to call Mosquito Heaven!

I also had as callers the Hoyt Hamons,[2] who own the land adjoining mine toward Island Grove, and on whose account I had to sell Ferdinand, because they didn't want him breeding his Jersey blood into their beef cattle—which he was doing with a right good will, fence or no fence. They own the shack where the Glenn Basses lived, and ran them off, and the Basses have bought a nice place at Lochloosa. Today Hoyt killed two huge rattlers, over six feet, he said, back of the former Bass house. They were fighting, and he took one shot when they had their necks crossed, in fighting. Old Will killed a big cottonmouth moccasin by their house.

This is rough country. While I was trying to 'phone the Veterans' Hospital from the Red Derby, a local yokel, who made his lunch on a bag of pretzels, a beer, a Pepsi-cola and an Orange Crush for dessert, somberly played the jukebox.

"Put that pistol down, Babe, put that pistol down. Pistol-packin' Mama, put that pistol down."[3]

. . . Old Will sure is glad Henry is being buried in St. Augustine. He said if he was buried in the Old Mickens lot over in the piney-woods, he knew he'd haunt him.

Love,

1. The Rawlingses bought the seventy-four acres of land from Mr. Armstrong in 1928 for $9000.
2. Hoyt Hamons [Haymans], owner of Cow Hammock, near Cross Creek.
3. The song was written and recorded by the country singer Al Dexter in the summer of 1943. Bing Crosby and the Andrews Sisters recorded versions in September 1943 and made it a hit.

(TLS, 1 p.)

[Crescent Beach, Fla.]
[30? August 1943]

Dear Honey;

Clifton Fadiman[1] wrote me about something or other, and in answering I spoke of the torment of the creative worker in war time—that I, for instance, was beginning a book when I felt I should be emptying bedpans in a hospital, yet I felt writers could only say what they had to say through an objective medium. I added post-script, for some unknown reason, pride in you, I guess, saying I felt a vicarious virtue in what you had done.

This is the result!

I wrote this woman[2] that you were a peculiarly modest person, a man of deep feelings who said little about them, and I could not do anything of the sort without your O.K. . . . .

1. Clifton Fadiman (1904–1999), writer, critic, book editor at the *New Yorker*, and moderator of the popular radio program *Information Please*.
2. In a letter dated 28 August, Rita Hill Kleeman of the Writers' War Board asked MKR write an article on NSB. MKR declined, and typed the above letter below the Kleeman letter.

. . . .

(ALS, 6 pp.)

[Cross Creek, Fla.]
The Creek
Tuesday Aug. 31 [1943]

Dearest:—

I began to be afraid we were never going to get Henry underground, and I kept remembering that Mr. Martin's daughter said, "You couldn't keep him, weather like this." War Department red tape held up the O.K., but the funeral is definitely to be tomorrow at the National Cemetery at St. Augustine, so the black rascal will go out in a blaze of glory.

My car will carry the chief mourners, and go ahead of the farm truck, which will have quilts in it and an assorted load of Fountain pickaninnies, Henry Woodward—and the Glisson's new maid,[1] who never laid eyes on Henry, but wouldn't miss the ride for anything. I didn't think the family would want her to horn in, but Martha said, "It's mighty nice to have comp'ny at the cemetery."

Will pick up Aunt Ida to add to the prestige. Only hope Moe and Smoky will stay in the car! They would love to help out.

Am running the risk of having Martha's grandson[2] drive the truck without a driver's license, but as he expects to be "abducted" into the Army, as Martha put it, could not see putting out $5 for the one trip.

This morning Martha and James were burying worm's nests in the pecans, Sissie was dressing a chicken for me, and Henry Woodward was putting out tobacco dust on my lawn to kill the bugs that are about to win out. All of a sudden the most violent Negro quarrel broke out—mostly Martha and Henry. It seemed Henry had mentioned he had cramps in his arms and Sissie said it was old age creeping up on him. Whereupon Henry, who has showed an amazing solicitude for Sissie's approaching widowhood, got furious and said he was young enough to marry a sixteen-year-old girl. Martha shouted that he was as old as she was, and they threw the ages of their respective children at each other like chunks of lighter'd. I joked them out of it, and Martha went off muttering, "That Henry! He's deep as a convict!"

Think I wrote you that Sissie will help me this winter.

And think I forgot to write that Smoky killed an enormous rat in the kitchen at the cottage. I heard a commotion and got out of bed, and here stood Smoky holding a rat so big, I thought at first the rat had Smoky. . . .

All my love,

When I told Martha we'd leave at 7 in the morning, she said, 'Then I can bring you your breakfast about 4 o'clock.' !!!!!

1. Estelle Mickens Sweet.
2. James Mickens, son of Adrenna Mickens.

. . . .

(TLS, 4 pp.)

[Crescent Beach, Fla.]
Sept. 2, 1943

Dearest:

Steinbeck[1] used his overseas feature the other day to say that men abroad just are not getting their mail, especially air mail, although the ordinary ship mail does a little better, as sinkings are at a minimum. I have written you almost every day, skipping an occasional day when I didn't have a thought in my head and even Moe and Smoky did nothing cute. . . .

I'll occasionally repeat a bit of news, in case some of my letters go astray. The lawsuit has been thrown out the second time, on appeal, by Judge Murphree,[2] but the enemy has three months in which to present it to the Florida Supreme Court. Phil thinks they will wait until the last few days, and present a practically complete brief of their case. He is getting his material ready in advance so he can present it in a hurry if necessary, in rebuttal.

W. D., after only three days at the Naval Station to which he was assigned, was sent to the hospital and is still there. He wrote Doug. I hate to have him that ill, but maybe he will be sent back after all. Well, poor old tramp-Henry's funeral in the national cemetery at St. Augustine yesterday was a most *impressive* thing. He was a veteran of the first War. Everything was arranged as nicely as could be, a canopy over the grave, seats etc. I found they do not provide a chaplain, so called a colored preacher, and he gave a *beautiful* short service, very quietly, in a rich voice, which consisted mostly of some of the finest Bible verses, recited. He did not try to say much about Henry, but did say that if he had served his God as he served his country, he knew he had an honorable discharge from the world of life. Of course, Henry paid God mighty little mind, and when the preacher said that, Martha snorted out a very audible "Humph!" Henry Woodward watched the coffin being lowered with the damndest expression, and I knew he was pleased as Punch, for one reason or another. The coffin was covered with a large American flag, and I thought of course they used it over again. When the service was over, the superintendent of the cemetery folded it just so and presented it to Sissie, from the U.S. Government. It was most moving, and even the sometimes insensitive Aunt Ida (who kept slapping the mosquitoes noisily with a palm leaf fan) said it gave her a terrific pride in the Government.

One thing did give me the creeps, and took away any last doubts about the desirability of cremation. The grave had been dug deep enough so Sissie can be buried there, too, if she wishes, and the coffin hit bottom with a *splash*. Water seems even messier than earth to lie in, unless it were clean clear ocean water.

Martha informed me that she had had a special delivery letter from Idella the day before and had meant to show it to me. She said she didn't know what to make of it. She promised to mail it to me, but said I must never let Idella know she did so. It seems to me that it could only mean Idella was ready to come back. Since I have engaged Sissie for the winter, Martha may have been torn in her loyalties. Sissie will get a pension, and help from the state for the children if necessary, so I should have no qualms about her if there is any chance of having Idella again.

I ran into a woman who had known Barney Dillard's mother-in-law, a woman weighing some three hundred pounds. My acquaintance said that she met old lady Kelly on the road, sobbing loudly. She inquired the reason, and Mme. Kelly said her feet hurt. My friend asked what was the matter with them, and Kelly said, "How the hell would I know? I haven't seen 'em for twenty years."

Loads of love,

1. John Steinbeck (1902–1968), American writer.
2. John A. H. Murphree, circuit judge.

. . . .

(TLS, 5 pp.)

[Crescent Beach, Fla.]
Sept. 4, 1943

Dearest:

. . . Phil May sent me his bill for the suit to date—$500, plus expenses of about $30. If his total bill isn't over a thousand dollars, I'll let it ride without complaint. I suppose that having a lawyer who knew his business made a great difference in

Judge Murphree's throwing the thing out of the local court. If by ill luck the Florida Supreme Court allowed the case to come to trial, and we win, I shouldn't mind paying Phil anything he asked, but if the thing dies a-borning I think $1,000 as big-time money. I feel sure I can take the $530 deduction from my income tax, for it is certainly a direct expense attributable to book profits!

Phil and his wife[1] are coming down for dinner next Friday, with Aunt Ida, as Phil wants to get notarized testimony from Aunt Ida on some remarks Zelma made to her last summer. Aunt Ida casually mentioned that when Zelma told her she was definitely going to sue, she, Zelma, said, "I'm going to get some of her easy money. And I'm going to sue Norton, too. She needn't think she can make over everything to him and get out of it." This alone establishes greed as Zelma's motive, rather than delicate, crushed feelings. Miss Binney[2] wrote me that her dressmaker . . . mentioned that she used to live near Zelma's mother's family in Georgia, "and they were the money-maddest folks you ever saw, and Zelma's mother, the one named Charity, was the worst of the lot."

I think that I mentioned that my ex-brother-in-law, Jim Rawlings, wrote that he would be glad to come to Florida and take the stand in my favor, as he thought he had heard Zelma call on the deity as often as anyone. Don't think I mentioned that he said that he remembered particularly the time her female dog got bred against her wishes (against Zelma's, not the female dog's) and Zelma administered what Jim called "Preventative medicine." I recalled the incident then—and what Zelma did was to use her own douche on the dog, right out in public!

I have been trying to answer some "Nut" letters. . . .

I have still not been able to get to work on my book. . . .

It seems silly to send these trivial items across thousands of miles! If you received them every few days, it would give you a feeling of home details, but I hate to think of 50 letters of this sort waiting for you. The only advantage in your not having a Katharine Mansfield[3] for a wife is that I am not dying of T.B. I am amazingly well, which surprises me, for I am nervous as a cat. . . .

The only alternative to my inane and casual letters, would be discussions of my torment in relation to the cosmic universe—and I think that would be even more inane! . . .

All my love,

1. Lillian May.
2. Florida Binney Sanford Baskin, NSB's mother.
3. Katherine Mansfield (1888–1923), especially noted for her short fiction. MKR later wrote a preface to her *Stories* (Cleveland, Ohio: World, 1946).

(TLS, 3 pp.)

[Crescent Beach, Fla.]

Sept. 5, 1943

Oh darling—

I have decided to celebrate my birthday *today*, because I feel re-born. Your cable came, three weeks earlier than I expected it, and I didn't know I could be so happy. . . .

. . . Your cable had across the top, "Sans origine"—so I'm betting my bottom dollar you are NOT in India. Be SURE and tell me whether you will get a chance to practice your French wherever you are. Your French is so good, and it will mean a great deal to me to know whether you will be able to use it. . . .

All my love, darling. I am so happy.

. . . .

(TLS, 4 pp.)

[Crescent Beach, Fla.]

Sept. 7, 1943

Dearest:

I had a strange let-down after I had your cable. I had a good hard cry for the first time since you left. I have put in two completely lazy days, but now I think I am ready to get to work. The trouble is, there are three stories[1] that clamor to be done for the New Yorker, and I know it's just Dora having fun, and trying to keep me from serious work!

. . . I stayed in bed late this morning, reading for the first time James Joyce's "Portrait of the Artist as a Young Man."[2] It was published in 1915, and it is amazing to recognize the fountain from which Hemingway and Farrell and Dos Passos and the rest of them took so deep a drink.[3] The book is completely intelligible, and the stream-of-consciousness technique is not overdone. It is a pity that Joyce went farther and farther into the obscure shadows, for he had a great deal to give. It seems actually spiteful of him to have done "Finnegans Wake," as though he held food just out of reach of hungry people. Perhaps, he thought, if you were avid enough, like Thornton Wilder,[4] you would make great leaps and get hold of the meat.

I have too a short collection of some of Katherine Mansfield's stories, which I'll send in one of your Christmas boxes. . . .

All my love,

1. "The Shell," *New Yorker* 20 (9 December 1944): 29–31; "Black Secret," *New Yorker* 21 (8 September 1945), 20–23; and "Miriam's Houses," *New Yorker* 21 (24 November 1945): 29–31.
2. James Joyce (1882–1941), *A Portrait of the Artist as a Young Man* (London: Egoist, 1916).
3. Ernest Hemingway (1898–1961), James T. Farrell (1904–1979), and John Dos Passos (1896–1970).
4. Thornton Wilder (1897–1975), American novelist and playwright.

(TLS, 5 pp.)

[Crescent Beach, Fla.]
Sept. 8, 1943

Dearest:

... I think I told you that Phil May and his wife are coming to dinner Friday, arriving in the afternoon to get some notarized testimony from Aunt Ida about some of the things Zelma said to her—both because of her age, and because we know she should be incoherent on a witness stand. Phil is sure Zelma will make her appeal to the Florida Supreme Court and will submit practically a complete brief, and will do so just a few days before the time limit expires Nov. 1st—so Phil wants our case all ready, too. We are hoping, and I really believe, the Supreme Court will throw it out also. But it is smart of him to be prepared.

I had a note from Norman Berg saying he would be in Jacksonville this week and would like to come down to see me, and where would I be, especially over the week-end. I shall have to go to the Creek Saturday. . . . Could easily take Norman to the Creek with me, but feel I should be very careful of appearances, as I am in a position to be criticized at the least little thing. I even felt a little uncomfortable when poor brother Cecil was here and went down to Junko's to buy beer and cigarettes to be charged to me! So will just ask Phil and Lillian to bring him along with them Friday, and then he can go back with them. Only hope he doesn't take one of his queer dislikes to Phil (or Lillian) so that he would sit all evening with that stony stare! I am probably crazy to pay any attention to gossip, as long as my own conscience is clear.

... Margaret Mitchell wrote to ask me if it was I by any chance who had sent her a gallon of sorghum from Wauchula! Of course I had not, and I wrote her the story of the postmaster and the "parcel" and the "parasol," and his comment, "people send funny things."

Rita Hayworth and Orson got married![1] With her beauty and his brains—they'll fight like Hell! Your friend Veronica Lake[2] was doing a picture, seven months pregnant, had a fall, the child, a boy, was born prematurely and died in a few days. And Bette Davis'[3] husband fell in the street and died shortly after, apparently from the effects of a bad fall he had had a couple of months before. Think that brings your favorites up to date.

Won't the censorship allow you to give an indication of the general part of the world in which you are stationed? I know you can't be as specific as giving even the country. If you are allowed to do nothing more, hope you can say "I am not in India," if you are not. I have an idea you may be seeing action already.

I suppose you have read, and know, that EVERYBODY is scared on going into action. Only a fool would not be. But they all say, fighter pilots and all, that once they are at work, doing the job, there is no further fear—until it's all over again and then they wonder what's wrong with their stomachs and their knees!

All my love,

1. Rita Hayworth, actor, and Orson Welles, actor and producer.
3. Veronica Lake, actor.
3. Bette Davis, actor.

. . . .

(TLS, 3 pp.)

[Crescent Beach, Fla.]

Sept. 11, 1943

Dearest:

I have just gotten together your first Christmas package, and it is depressing how little it holds and how small it is. . . .

Norman Berg decided to go back to Atlanta last night, so 'phoned that he'd like to come down in the morning. He missed the 9 A.M. Marineland bus and hitch-hiked, and finally I drove up the road after him. He passed four snakes within 150 yards, two of them rattlers. They are rampant this year. I have two six-foot hides already, one from the cottage back-yard and one from the Creek. Ross Allen is having them dressed for me. If you'd like one or both of them for exotic American gifts, ask for them. The censor will probably think, What the hell, when a man writes his wife, Please send me two rattlesnake skins. Norman and I had a good visit, and he went to the spotting post with me, then I drove him in when I went to meet Phil May to get Aunt Ida's testimony.

. . . I had been wondering why I hadn't heard from one of my most faithful Navy correspondents, Jimmie Maddox, (Not the one who escaped from the Lexington with "Cross Creek"). I was reading the third installment in the New Yorker of the story of an American-Italian seaman who was on a raft 82 days— and Jimmie Maddox died on the raft, after great physical and mental suffering. I feel as sad as though I had known him. It seems to me as though the very men who were reaching out toward unattainable ideas and ideals are the very ones who were doomed from the beginning. Another of my "queer" Army correspondents, Louis Dallarhide, who wrote long letters about once a week, was dismissed from the Army because of his neuroticism. He is now teaching in a Southern college, and while God help his pupils, I feel that I am relieved from any obligation in keeping up with the correspondence. James Still is somewhere in the South Pacific, and calmly wrote me asking me to send him a copy of a poem he sent to me a year and a half ago! I have it somewhere, but cannot find it.

Phil May's wife is really a very lovely person. Unfortunately, she tears herself to pieces trying to be witty, and comes out with such things as "The canine does not know how to accept the feline," thinking this will be devastating. What she was trying to say was that their little toy Boston didn't know what the hell to make of Smoky! Such things are more embarrassing than if she had taken off her clothes in public.

Martha sent me Idella's letter to her, and it certainly sounds as though Idella were ready to "come home." Idella wrote that she wished I would live all the time at the Creek, as she would like to live there, but she did not want to be in St. Augustine, having her reasons. Of course, this contradicts her statement to me that she got tired of the lonely life. Anyway, I wrote her, telling her that I was moving to the Creek October first, and if she was ready to come back, all would be forgiven and forgotten. I shall have to make sure that she doesn't just use me to get railroad fare to Florida to see her mother! It is depressing to have one's servants out-smart one!

. . . I 'phoned Dessie, who had asked to bring "a friend" in the WACS who wanted to meet me. She called back that she would love to come to spend Sunday, and was sure I wouldn't mind if she brought five or six with her! I can understand why Dr. Vinson[1] burned down her cabin. Meekly, I wrote Martha to kill four frying chickens.

All my love,

1. J. C. Vinson, MKR's doctor and friend, once married to Dessie Smith Vinson.

. . . .

(TLS, 3 pp.)

[Crescent Beach, Fla.]

Sept. 18, 1943

Dearest:

. . . A wire came today from Cliff and Gladys Lyons, from Hollywood, Fla., asking if we would be in St. Augustine Monday. I wired them where you were and where I am, and to stop by. They will be ill to miss you. And I won't enjoy them half as much without you. And the good bridge game we'll miss—.

. . . I had a typically delightful letter from Julia. The man she was so in love with for five years had married, and I'm hoping that may help free her from the obsession. She had run into three Belgian officers of the R.A.F. and has fallen very hard for one of them. She described "André" as tall, dark and spectacularly handsome, so that women turn to look after him. She said she seemed to pick out the ones that every other woman wanted, too. But they have the same tastes in art and music and literature, and he gave her his wings and a beautiful compact—the kind you use for powder, not for an engagement. . . . I hope something comes of it, if she wants him! . . .

All my love,

. . . .

(TLS, 4 pp.)

[Crescent Beach, Fla.]

Sept. 19, 1943

Dearest:

. . . There was a square of wooden grating from a ship on the beach—burned half through. It gives you such an awful feeling—you feel personally to blame, somehow, and that you must stop it all, again personally. All of us "just people" feel that way—I think even the run-of-the-mill German people must, except for that paranoidal indoctrination to which they have been subjected. Yet a nation is to blame, the man in the street is to blame, when he accepts what he knows is wrong. Every Cracker at the Creek is to blame, for allowing national greed to prepare the way for war. That is the key to Ortega's "The Revolt of the Masses"[1]— that the common man demands rights, without wanting to take the corresponding responsibility that goes with every right.

. . . Along the social-thinking line, Julia writes me the most appalling things about the way her people think. Of course, they are not her people, and that is the greatest thing that is tearing her to pieces and making her ill. Imagine living in an almost constant state of nausea about the ideas and standards around you! Yet she has no place to go—. Her father brings home "the Revolution is upon us" ideas from bank meetings and clubs. The latest is that his class is sure that rationing is a deep plot of the New Deal to make sure that the rich will get no more food and no better food than the poor. It is a preparation for a permanent rationing after the war. Money will buy no more than the poor man can buy— money will therefore become no good—behold the finish of "private enterprise." Those people are so much more dangerous than the ignorant or indifferent "masses," because they do have power. I mean dangerous as to making wars possible. You can see why Willkie is anathema to them. That little shrimp of a Dewey[2] is leading in Republican predictions.

I read Edith Wharton's "Age of Innocence"[3] last night and today, which I had never happened to read before, so ordered with the flock of Modern Library books I sent for. Wish I knew whether you had read it. You would enjoy it. It is on a par with "The Late George Apley"[4] for a pitiless revelation of our so-called aristocracy.

I also finally got around to reading, for the first time, Rousseau's famous "Confessions."[5] I had always had the idea they were the height of pornography and morbidity, and was never so surprised in my life. After "Studs Lonigan,"[6] they are Sunday School material. The *horror* comes in the perfectly unconscious revelation of an advanced case of *dementia praecox*. The man was so thoroughly selfish and egotistical as to become evil. For instance, he lived for many years until his death with a much put-upon woman, making the most noble excuses for not marrying her. He had seven children by her—and again, with the most lofty of reasons, put every one in a foundlings' home the moment it was born and never knew what happened to any of them! Under the guise of his nobility and frankness in exposing himself, he sticks a knife, or tries to, in every person who was ever kind to him—and sums up by saying that he knows he has presented a picture of the most magnificent soul ever to inhabit a human body, and that anyone who doesn't agree with him should be choked! He considered himself the victim of constant persecution and treachery—and between the lines, one can only wonder why someone didn't quietly smother him. Apparently, some of his works were the forerunner of, or had an influence on, the French Revolution. Otherwise, his great Opus would have no more consequence than the adolescent "nut" letters I get—although something about the style, and the smugness one feels in deciphering the hideous character underneath the self-righteousness, makes one read on with utter fascination. I don't know whether to send you the book or not. His psychology is astonishingly that of Hitler in "Mein Kampf."[7] The only difference is that Rousseau carried out his self-righteousness in an individual way, while Hitler transposed it on the psychology of a nation. But they are cut off the same piece of cloth. Hitler will go to his grave feeling noble. . . .

Some of the big bombers come frightfully low, and Moe barks fiercely when they just skim the roof or roar right past the window. . . .

All my love,

1. José Ortega y Gassett (1883–1955), *La rebelión de las masas* (1930).
2. Thomas E. Dewey, American politician who won the Republican nomination for president in 1944. He was defeated by the Democrat Franklin D. Roosevelt.
3. Edith Wharton (1862–1937), *The Age of Innocence* (New York: Appleton, 1920).
4. John P. Marquand, *The Late George Apley* (Boston: Little Brown, 1937).
5. Jean Jacques Rousseau (1712–1778), *Confessions* (1781–1788).
6. A trilogy by James T. Farrell: *Young Lonigan* (New York: Vanguard, 1932); *The Young Manhood of Studs Lonigan* (New York: Vanguard, 1934); *Judgment Day* (New York: Vanguard, 1935).
7. Adolf Hitler (1889–1945), *Mein Kampf* (1924).

. . . .

(TLS, 3 pp.)

[Crescent Beach, Fla.]
Sept. 21, 1943

Dearest:

. . . Cliff and Gladys Lyons drove in yesterday a few minutes after I returned from the spotting post, and I was certainly glad to see them. . . .

Since Jean was driving back, Ruby stayed, and we got together a good dinner out of scraps—meat pie with crust, baked potatoes, green beans, home-made bread, quince jelly, home-made peach ice-cream and cake—and a delicious salad of avocado and hearts of palm, canned, from Brazil, that I ordered from New York. The palm was delicious, and I have no qualms about eating off the flora of Brazil. Cliff ate more moderately than usual, rather to my disappointment! We slept late and had a good breakfast—cantaloupe, scrambled eggs and bacon, toast of home made bread and Dora's butter, marmalade and good coffee. Let me know whether you want me to repeat good menus, or keep my mouth shut! I think I never had a letter from Grandma Traphagen[1] or any of that family, that did not tell what they had had for dinner!

Cliff and Gladys have just left, and they did me a lot of good. They send their love and said to tell you how much we all missed you. . . .

And I have been unable to get down to actual work on the book. It is probably not time wasted, for when I woke up at 6 this morning I found myself thinking about it, and a title came to me that pleases me, so evidently it has been fermenting all the time.

I am calling off my request for three little boys from the Children's Home. I had a letter—and questionnaire to be filled out—. . . such an arrangement is so *regimented* that I cannot accept it. Among other requirements, you have to promise to take them to church or Sunday School every week—and Island Grove only has an itinerant preacher once or twice a month. Also, the Society's investigator comes around regularly—and I was asked what I planned to have the children do and what I planned for them, . . . it was obvious that he was suspicious that my preference for 3 boys from 8 to 12 meant that I was going to put them at hard manual labor on the grove! My one thought was to utilize my space and income and shreds of maternal feeling to make a real home for some kids that were temporarily without one, but the Society puts one in the position of accepting a great favor from them—so evidently things are not desperate. I am sending the Society a large check instead—not what I should have chosen, but it is probably just as well, as when the war is over and you are back, the kids could conceivably be still without a home, and it wouldn't be fair to you to present you with a ready-made family you had had no hand in choosing. I still think that some day you and I might enjoy taking in a whole batch of kids, but I cannot work under such rigid rules as the Society imposes. . . .

All my love,

1. Fanny Osmun Traphagen.

. . . .

(TLS, 4 pp.)

[Crescent Beach, Fla.]
Sept. 22, 1943

Dearest:

. . . Your birthday present, if and when it reaches you, is a new Rolls Razor blade. I could only send 8 ounces without a specific request from you.

. . . Do write as often as you can. General Mark Clark[1] writes his wife twice a week, and since he is in the middle of the battle of Italy, know he can't be less busy than you! Remember that mail means just as much to me as to you, maybe more, for it is always harder to stay at home.

I am not too happy over your location, as I felt the Middle East would be healthier, both from the standpoint of climate etc., and battle activity, for the German push will obviously be over long ahead of the Japanese one. Wish I had some way to get you news. Will send a clipping now and then. We took Sicily in no time at all, but even though Italy surrendered in a couple of weeks, the Germans are making something of a stand there and our casualties are heavy. Russia is pushing back the Germans steadily. Denmark practically revolted against German rule and is under strict military rule now, everything censored. Sweden is talking back to Germany for the first time and some think she may eventually declare war, or at least cooperate with the Allies. She has refused to allow Germany to transport troops across her any more, and the Germans have taken it. I mean, taken the refusal lying down. Yugoslav guerrilla troops have taken some Balkan ports. The British Eighth and American Fifth Armies recently made a junction from the west and east of southern Italy where The American Fifth under Clark was having a tough go with the Germans at Solerno. The Germans are sacking and burning Naples, just like the Huns of old. They have Rome, and under military rule. A Second Front on the west coast of Europe is prophesied by all commentators for the near future, but of course it may not come just there. But things are going very well, and the conquered small nations are presumed to be ready and waiting for the word to go. We are putting some new types of planes into action.

. . . Lois Hardy wrote me that the son, Mark Ethridge Jr., of my Louisville friends, Mark and Willie Ethridge,[2] is in the A.F.S. in your section. She asked you to look him up if possible, that he is young and would appreciate it.

I'll write you *every* day, darling, so if you don't hear that often, it will be the fault of the A.P.O. or German sub. . . .

I love you so.

1. Mark Wayne Clark (1896–1984), at this time commander of the Fifth Army in North Africa and Italy, later president of The Citadel.
2. Mark Ethridge Sr. was editor of the *Louisville Courier-Journal.* MKR worked for the newspaper in 1920–1921.

. . . .

(TLS, 3 pp.)

[Crescent Beach, Fla.]
Sept. 23, 1943

Dearest:

. . . I hope that once I feel *settled*, I can really get to work on my book. I got fed up with Florida this summer, partly from my restlessness at having you away, and not heard from, and would have gone to the Carolina or even New England mountains if it were not for the lack of gas to use a car, which was necessary to transport my animals, whom I could not leave behind. Something of my old desire to keep moving on has been on me. It seemed to me I could leave Florida behind forever. I still, or rather, again, have my nightmares of homelessness. Almost every night I am wandering in a strange place, lost and alone. I am usually trying to arrange my belongings in the new alien room or apartment. Sometimes I am missing trains that will take me to my home. It is all probably Freudian in that I have never had a true home since my father's death, yet I have understood and outgrown my childish attachment to him. Yet as Thomas Wolfe said, we are all lost, and you can't go home again.[1] And I can't accept it. Somehow, surely, even in maturity, one should be able to be at home.

Please write me all the details of your life—whether you are in barracks, or what. What and how you eat. And whether I need to worry about your being attacked by a tittsy fly-by-night. Which reminds me, that when Ruby would not stay here nights, I realized that it was the boogie-man against the boogie-woogie man.

Your tale of 30¢ a week for a servant, against high prices, is appalling. . . .

All my love, darling. And please call me "darling" as you did in your first letter. Your second, after you had had my mail, was only "Dear Honey," and since you call all your gals "Honey" or "Love," "Darling," or something like it, seems so much more personal. Surely my letters didn't sound cold! I was only trying so hard not to sound weepy! It is awful without you.

1. Thomas Wolfe (1900–1938), *You Can't Go Home Again* (New York: Harper, 1940).

. . . .

(TLS, 2 pp.)

[Crescent Beach, Fla.]
Sept. 24, 1943

Dearest:

. . . Had a bad night, caught in a typical Fred Francis upheaval, and drank too much in the excitement, and to keep going, and he wouldn't let me go home. Was overtaken by the lonesome blues, so drove Ruby in and went to see Jean. Fred was there, having returned the day before from California, where he bought the Palomino horse. They were already drinking warm champagne poured over ice and Jean had been crying. Fred put in some time being ugly, and jumping on me about all kinds of things. One was that he claimed I had once said to him that he couldn't buy my friendship, and I know I didn't. . . . Then when Jean began to fight my battle, for I would not quarrel with him, he turned on her and I became his bosom buddy, the only one who understood him. He went all to pieces and cried and kissed my hand and it was a nightmare. He said he was terribly sick—and he had been in the hospital in California with a strep infection—and of course he is so mentally ill that it probably has physical effects. He had evidently promised Jean to go to John Hopkins to see a psychiatrist—but I don't think the poor devil can be saved. . . . Had a frightful hangover—and had to spot. Fortunately my relief was 15 minutes early. . . . Fred also said, "I suppose you know I have left you Hunta-Hunta-Hara[1] in my will," which was probably something he thought up on the spur of the moment. . . .

Am struggling to write a foreword for the collection of Caleb Milne letters, which his mother was advised to submit to a publisher, and they are really excep-

tional, to my notion. It's a hard little job to do, without sounding gushy or plati-
tudinous. . . .

Will be following news of Mountbatten anxiously.

All my love,

1. Hunta Hunta Hara, the estate of Fred Francis.

. . . .

(TLS, 2 pp.)

[Crescent Beach, Fla.]
Sept. 25, 1943

Dearest:

. . . I am re-reading, after nearly twenty years, "The Education of Henry
Adams,"[1] which I think you would enjoy. You will be interested in the things he
says about Harvard and about all college education.

Martha's grandson[2] goes into the Army the first of October, so that is that.

Henry Woodward plans to leave Old Boss as soon as their partnership hogs
are fattened (in the field I rented Brice), and I mean to buy his share and put the
meat in storage for curing.

. . . Forgot to tell you that one of Freddy's grievances against me was that he
was never invited to the Creek, although two of Jean's beaux had been. The two
times he was asked apparently did not count, as he said we knew damn well both
times that he couldn't come! When I told Ruby how I happened to have such a
hangover, she said she had been through it with Herman more times than she
could count. She said he, Fred, kept them all up all night, again and again. . . .

. . . Ruby . . . has been completely faithful, and is just as good as Idella in every
way. All but one way, come to think of it—she is death on dishes, and among
other things broke one of my Spode plates, which I can replace—and the spout
off my cherished tea-pot that the old nurse gave my mother when I was born. If I
am back at the cottage next summer, it is likely that Jean will be away, and in that
case think Ruby would be glad to come to me again. Have had no word from
Idella since I wrote her, after her letter to Martha, which certainly seemed a hint
that she wanted to come back. But I can manage with Sissie very nicely. And I
should never feel the same about Idella again. I'll have so little company that it
won't matter. Marcia Davenport wants to come alone to the Creek some time
this winter. Am afraid the glamour will wear off for her if she sees too much of it!
Her daughter's engagement was announced in the Tribune—and the man's
name is most Jewish, which with Marcia's phobia, accounts for her objections.

Loads of love, darling.

1. Henry Adams (1838–1918), *The Education of Henry Adams* (Boston: Houghton Mifflin, 1918).
2. James Mickens.

(TLS, 5 pp.)

[Crescent Beach, Fla.]
Sept. 26, 1943

Dearest:

. . . We are having another north-easter, right on the heels of the big one. The wind came up at bed-time and fair shook the cottage. It is howling now like the spirits of the damned.

Which reminds me that Ruby had a headache all yesterday, the aftermath over hysterics that came from an incident on her bus coming down. A colored girl sat down next to her, trembling and with eyes as big as saucers. She said to Ruby, "I jes' seed two h'ants. I got to leave town. I'll tell the lady I work for, then I'm leavin.' I can't stay in a town where you can see two h'ants in the daytime."

Ruby asked her what they looked like. The girl described them—dressed all in flowing black, with black hoods and white faces. She had seen, for the first time in her life, two Catholic nuns!

Ruby said everyone on the bus, including the driver, had hysterics.

. . . A letter from Norman Berg said that he would probably take me up on my offer of the cottage, in November, as he thought he was likely to be drafted, and it would be his and Julie's last chance at vacation. Remembering the shape they left the cottage in after their honeymoon, I am not enthused, yet he is so good to me and sends me so many grand books, that it is little enough to do for the poor devil. . . .

All my love. When I went to bed with a book last night, how I wished you were here!

. . . .

(TLS, 3 pp.)

[Crescent Beach, Fla.]
Sept. 27, 1943

Dearest:

. . . Dinner at Castle Warden, where I took Mrs. White[1] and Aunt Ida, was superb. Fresh melon cup, wonderful squab, glazed sweet potatoes, banana muffins, etc. etc., and an enormous choice of desserts. I took them home as soon as was decent, and slipped off to a movie. Not very good, Deanna Durbin, with Joseph Cotten,[2] of all rather strange people to mix with her. She has a wonderful personality and still has a lovely figure, but her little face has gotten as round as my behind, and it was hard to glamorize her in the close-ups.

. . . I stopped by the Drysdales[3] on my way home to tell Drys that one of his peacocks was loose outside the place. Made a date with him and Evelyn to come to the Creek for some quail shooting. I haven't been able to get 20-gauge shells, but Drys has them, and will furnish the shells.

A Christmas box of books will arrive, if it arrives, in Aunt Ida's name. I sent you one box with several cheeses in it, and the next box will contain the beaten biscuits to go with them. Could not get things together at one time. Probably one box or the other will not arrive!

Must hurry, as I have to meet the mailman at the box.

All my love,

1. Mrs. Reginald White, Aunt Ida's St. Augustine landlady.
2. *Hers to Hold* (1943).
3. Cliff and Evelyn Drysdale, St. Augustine friends and bridge partners.

. . . .

(TLS, 5 pp.)

[Crescent Beach, Fla.]

Sept. 28, 1943

Dearest:

. . . Yesterday was my last day at the spotting post, and there was an alert on of some sort. A Coast Guardsman was stationed on the beach, and another stayed on the post with me. I asked no questions, of course. They didn't seem to be watching at sea particularly. You do wonder so. While I was on the post a couple of weeks ago, a young man in shorts came up and presented apparently proper credentials—said he was at the Naval Air Station. He asked all sorts of questions about how we made contact with the main observation headquarters, etc., his story being that he wanted to work out a way for quicker contact in case of a training plane crash, yet he knew absolutely nothing about the way the posts work. . . . I have often thought that if an enemy raid were planned, they could at least get inland without getting caught if they could knock out one post. It makes you feel a little creepy, and from the two Coast Guardsmen being at and near the post, and apparently not strung out the way they are for a sub alert, I thought that they may have had wind of some such thing. It makes you feel good that they are so very much on the job.

I simply don't know what is wrong, that I haven't gotten to work on my book. Perhaps it is because everything, from you to Ruby, has hung over me with such uncertainty. I shall go at it when I get to the Creek, whether or no. I did do several very short stories, but they are not good and I sha'n't send them out.

. . . I wrote you that Henry Heyl is at Fitzsimmons General Hospital, Denver, Colorado, and that he had been working on some sketches (literary), and sent me some for criticism, and had sold one to the Atlantic. He said he had bought a Vermont (or N.H., I forget which) farm and would go there next Spring. I wrote him among other things, about Julia, with the usual effect. I have always wished I had had a chance at the one man she cared for, for I seem able to sell her so that they fair fight at the auction. I told Henry Julia and I had always planned a spring, flower-hunting, in New England, and if my work went well enough—or badly enough—we might do it this spring, and suggested he invite us for a week-end at his farm. . . .

All my love,

. . . .

(ALS, 6 pp.)

[Crescent Beach, Fla.]
Sept. 29, 1943

Dearest:—

. . . I had such a nice letter—as usual—from Miss Binney—opening their doors wide to me. I don't think I shall try to go up for Christmas. . . .

. . . I am really not keen about isolating myself at the Creek with inadequate help. Martha's grandson has gone to the Army, Henry Woodward is leaving, and there is no one to do garden work, wood toting etc. Yet I do like running my own establishment, especially the kitchen. . . .

I believe it is Martha herself who keeps me so tied to the Creek. She takes it for granted that it is my home, mourns so when I am away, and is so joyful when I return. When she dies I may be free of the terrible and sometimes onerous pull. Yet she will probably live 20 years more and even outlast me.

I love you so much.

. . . .

(ALS, 4 pp.)

[Crescent Beach, Fla.]
Sept. 30, 1943

Dearest:—

I'll say Hello to you before I settle down to my packing and sorting. It is simply gorgeous today and it seems insane to leave. Yet Jean is expecting Ruby and Martha is expecting me, and I have to get my garden started so the wheels grind and I have to go the way they go.

. . . I have nearly finished re-reading "The Education of Henry Adams" and shall certainly send it on to you. Don't miss a word of it. It is *hard* reading. My mind is out of practice on hard abstract thinking, and it takes me a long time to absorb it. None of my usual hop scotch reading! . . .

All my love,

(TLS, 4 pp.)

Hawthorn, Florida
At the Creek
Oct. 1, 1943

Dearest:

For some reason, I simply hated leaving the cottage. I felt very sad driving over. It seemed as though I had been pushed back in time about five years, and was beginning the battle of the Creek over again, alone. Yet this morning it seems like home again, and I am already overlooking the floors that are caving in and the patches where the paint has flaked off! Martha wanted me to be sure and notice that real house cleaning had been done, so all the pictures were hanging as though monkeys had been swinging on them, and the draperies were turned up over the rods.

. . . Just before I left the cottage I had a letter from Martha, dictated to Sissie, almost unintelligible. I finally made out that the cow had been sick, but Henry Woodward was helping Mr. Brice and Jack[1] had to go, and the housecleaning would be finished Wednesday, so they would be looking for me, so the cow was all right now.

With my coffee this morning, Martha said, "Sissie wrote you about Chrissy being sick?" I said, yes, and that I had wondered which cow it was. "Yessum, she was right sick. A moccasin bit her." There is something disconcerting and screwball about putting the cart before the horse that way. If a cottonmouth bites a cow, the cow is automatically right sick, but a cow can be right sick without having been bitten by a moccasin!

Martha and Jack took a trip to Mackintosh for Martha to visit Jesus and Jack to visit a girl, and twice on the way home the truck just stopped perfectly dead. The second time, they were crossing the River Styx, and Martha walked all the way in to have Tom Glisson come and start them. Tom reported there was nothing the matter with the truck, Chet told Jack to take it to Boyt's[2] for a check and Boyt's reported there was nothing the matter. Martha solved it, of course. Henry Fountain stopped the truck. I expect Henry will make a lot of trouble, when convenient. Chet said that it was simply that Jack had driven the truck too fast through a flood and got the spark plugs wet.

. . . Well, your devoted cousin, Dora Rolley,[3] is very much disappointed over her failure to mail you the type of Christmas package she wanted you to have. She put some maple syrup, much better than Leonard's, in a brandy bottle, sealed the top with paraffin, enclosed some pancake flour so that you and the censor would both know it was maple syrup, added a small Bible and a sea-shell, and a message on a Christmas card to dear Cousin Norton, hoping the little package would be both useful and of spiritual guidance. She told me she was so afraid the censor would open the bottle, thinking it might be that curse, liquor, and once the bottle was unsealed, the maple syrup would leak out. She asked me to mail the package, and the first thing they asked was whether it contained glass. I said that I thought glass was allowed, if well packed, and the man said it was, but all such things had to be opened, in case it was lighter fluid, which being inflammable could set a whole ship on fire, and which I know Dora had never thought of, or poison, which again poor Dora would never have thought of. So I said I would just take the package back to her and check it. She is simply heart-broken, as she says you have never had a Christmas morning without maple syrup. When she and I pour ours over our Christmas pancakes, we will weep for you. I told Chet about it when he came out this morning, and he said he would have loved to send you maple syrup, too.

Yesterday, when I tried to get off for the Creek, was one of those days when the horoscope would tell you to go into the bathroom and sit there and not stir out all day. The Service Laundry said they would wash the big white rug from the living room. Ruby and I toiled and tussled and got it in the trunk of the car. A Negro twice as big as Joe Louis[4] came out to take it into the laundry, lifted it as though it were a feather, and I saw it was caught on the sharp edge of the steel supports. I yelled, "Look out," and he gave a heave and ripped the rug through three layers. Aside from cousin Dora's trouble with her box, one I had ready to mail, with just what I wanted in it, proved an inch too wide and 12 ounces too heavy. I thought I had 3 gas coupons left and when I stopped at the filling station, didn't have a one. Etc. etc.

Ruby all but wept when I left, and if Jean is away next summer, as is likely, Ruby will come back to the cottage to me. They love me—but goddam, they leave me! No word from Idella. It will be an awful job to train poor Sissie.

Phil May wrote that T.Z.[5] had sent for him, making a pretense of being disturbed to "discover" that Zelma had libel as one of her charges, and asked if Phil would advise his making one more attempt to get Zelma to call it off! The hypocritical bastard! Phil said he told him that unless he was reasonably sure of success, there was no point in his putting himself out, which I thought was damn cute of Phil. . . .

All my love,

1. James Mickens.
2. Boyt's, a service station in Citra run by Henry and Raymond Boyt.
3. MKR's self-created alter-ego.
4. Joe Louis, the celebrated heavyweight boxer.
5. Turner Z. Cason.

(TLS, 5 pp.)

[Cross Creek, Fla.]
The Creek
Oct. 2, 1943

Dearest:

Well, Mr. Brice's son-in-law Hugh Williams just came up, and wants me to act as go-between to start the damn land thing with Tom Glisson all over again. He is right in wanting it settled, but I do hate being the goat.

. . . I stole some roses yesterday, from a yard near Island Grove where no one is living. There is a huge old-fashioned bush there, covered with the most beautiful saffron-pink roses, that look like the ones in the old French flower prints. I have a bouquet in the antique glass sugar bowl and they look good enough to eat.

I got fish from Mr. Martin yesterday, and Smoky ate almost a two-pound trout all by himself, then ate a part of mine and some of my cornbread. His little belly bulged as though there were another cat inside him, just one size smaller.

I was able to get a large battery, what they call a farm battery, good for 1,000 hours, on which to run your radio that we had at the apartment, so am all set for the winter. I had the radio worked on, and the tone is fine now. It is impossible to get small batteries for my portable.

I just did not have room to bring over Bob's lovely-gloomy evening-crow painting, but will bring it the first time I go to the cottage. I decided to use it in the back bedroom, for which Cohen's is making new draperies, which will pick up the gray-blue in Bob's painting, yet have a good deal of life, too. The painting will go over the fireplace, and I'll put the pale green Audubon over the bed. If the room looks as well as I hope, I'll probably move back there. I like the big red bedroom, and in winter the heating is easier if I keep fires going there and in the first bathroom, but the Turk's-cap bushes have grown up so high outside that I have rather a shut-in feeling, and can't see much outside. . . .

Two of the most beautiful butterflies I ever saw are mating on the pomegranate bush. . . . It reminded me of the time Dessie and I watched a pair of chameleons happily mating, and Dess said, "Come on, kid. That's nothing for a widow-woman to be watching. . . ."

All my love,

. . . .

(TLS, 4 pp.)

[Crescent Beach, Fla.]
Oct. 5, 1943

Dearest:

. . . But short of an accident—and I mean to avoid horses—I expect to be all right. Have been amazed, really, that I have had practically no trouble with the insides. Have been wonderfully well since I left New York, only one very minor attack since, that cleared in two days. As I wrote you, Dr. Atchley experimented with luminol and bella donna, and it works. Really expected to have trouble, as I have been so anxious and terribly nervous, but aside from drinking and smoking too much, have been and am in perfect shape.

All my love, darling.

. . . .

(TLS, 4 pp.)

[Crescent Beach, Fla.]
[October 1943]

[page missing]

. . . I had an extremely nice letter yesterday from Idella. . . . She said she hated it in New York and thought about the Creek all the time—that her greatest pleasure had been in working for me. She said her husband, "Reggie,"[1] had just been moved, she did not know where (if her story is at all straight, he is in the Army) and that he had asked her not to leave until she heard from him and he knew something about his future whereabouts. Yet she said nothing about coming back. . . . I expect she will show up about the time I've taught Sissie to make Crab Newburg. For the moment, I feel hopeless, for Sissie doesn't even know how to butter bread for our kind of sandwich. If Idella ever does show up, am sure Martha will hail it with joy, for she is stuck with Sissie's kids during most of the day.

Idella said she was really praying for your safety, and to remember her to you.

Had something happen that amused me. Had a letter from a man I knew only slightly in college—older than I, and one of the big shots, as those things go, asking me to recommend his daughter for my sorority,[2] "if I had ever forgiven him for taking me out in such bitter cold weather to get scenic effects for the Junior Play." Well, I played a part in the play, "The Admirable Crichton,"[3] and it was the girl I have told you about who took most of my beaux away from me, the very beautiful one who sort of *waved* her behind when she walked, whom he almost froze to death! I remember well, for Mim[4] was living with us that year. How she would hate having his memory confuse us. I had the strangest combination of very great love and hopeless jealousy of her. She was terribly dear to me and we were very close, but I suffered half the time, for she had only to lift a finger—or wave her behind—to walk off with any man I liked. Jane Austen could have written about the pair of us.

Hope for mail every day—. Maybe today!

All my love.

1. Bernard Young, Idella Parker's first husband. MKR was angry that Idella Parker had "gone Harlem," but to her relief Idella returned in January 1944.

2. Kappa Alpha Theta.

3. J. M. Barrie (1860–1937), *The Admirable Crichton* (1902). MKR played the role of the maid Tweeny.

4. Mim, MKR's classmate at the University of Wisconsin.

. . . .

(TLS, 4 pp.)

[Crescent Beach, Fla.]

Oct. 6, 1943

Dearest:

Well, the big news is that the airplane spotting has been discontinued, except for a few hours once a week just to keep the machinery ready to use again if necessary. . . .

Conditions between Tom Glisson and the Brice-Williams are worse than ever. Although my sympathy is with Tom, he is being utterly unreasonable and unnecessarily suspicious. I sent for Mr. Williams yesterday and offered, as a possible solution, selling him my strip back of his grove which he has always wanted, and selling Tom the little corner at the other end which would give him his access, if Williams would sell Tom, in turn, the little patch of his that Tom crosses. Nothing doing—which would seem to verify Tom's theory that they do mean to block him eventually. I really think they expect him, sooner or later, to do something that will give them a moral excuse to cut him off. And the way he feels, he probably will!

In lieu of my $25 rent on the 16-acre field back of Brice's, which they have in chufas for fattening their hogs, I am taking a "gilt," bred to a thoroughbred boar, and will try to raise some hams and bacon of my own. Plan to buy some of Henry Woodward's hogs, if I don't have to go through a lot of red tape with the OPA and give up a whole book of points.

Martha's Jack is making seed beds for broccoli and lettuce and parsley and flowers. I am using a piece of land—don't know whether you were ever down there or not—at the back of the house grove near the lake, for extra vegetables, beans and beets, cabbages for Martha, etc. Old Will raised a magnificent sweet potato patch back there, on shares. As I wrote you, cornmeal and grits are almost unobtainable. Southern farmers use their own corn, and mid-Western farmers are saving theirs for fattening stock, or in hope of a higher price ceiling. I commissioned Martha to buy a bushel of water-ground meal from her farmer-son at Flemington, and he sent it to me as a *gift*. . . . I shall make it up to him, of course. Martha thinks pecans would be acceptable. If I can keep off the squirrels! Moe and Smoky spend half their time chasing them, and the squirrels sit up in the orange trees and cuss the daylights out of them—but they come in to the pecan trees much earlier in the morning than Moe and Smoky and I are up! I get my breakfast coffee at seven-thirty, after being awakened at seven by Mickens clattering in the kitchen, and on a cloudy morning particularly, it is so dark at that time that I feel as though I had only just gone to sleep. Shall have to ask for eight o'clock service instead, though doubt whether that will help, as Martha is going to be throwing milk pans around at seven, come hell or high water. But how fortunate I am, to have anyone to throw milk pans!

Dora Rolley and I used the maple syrup she had wanted so much to send you. We thought of you with every delicious and guilty drop. . . .[1]

All my love,

1. MKR had put maple syrup in a liquor bottle as part of a Christmas package to Norton, but when the post office refused to mail the glass bottle without first opening it to check for flammable material, MKR decided against sending it (see letter of 1 October 1943).

. . . .

(TLS, 3 pp.)

[Cross Creek, Fla.]
The Creek
Oct. 7, 1943

Dearest:

. . . If anything puts the Republicans in on the next election, it will be the nausea everyone feels at the thousand and one *petty* rules that have developed under this long bureaucracy. Am afraid I waited until too late to register and can't vote. But no one has a chance of beating Roosevelt but Willkie, and if Willkie runs, I just should not know what to do. If that ass of a Dewey runs, I shall stump the country against him. He seems to be leading Willkie pretty far at present.

The radio announced this morning that Mountbatten had arrived at Delhi and action is expected to follow soon. Oh God.

The enclosed story from today's paper about the Duke and Duchess of Windsor[1] takes the cake, to my notion. It is the first thing the gal has done that disgusted me. I believe from this that she would be insufferable if she found herself in a position of power. Of course, one can look at it that it was rather a pathetic attempt to insist on his prestige, but under the circumstances it would be better taste for her to let any gestures come from the other quarter.

. . . Wish you could have seen Smoky and one of the game hens trying to figure each other out. The hen was fascinated and moved closer and closer to Smoky. Smoky crouched low and switched his tail and gave that queer little hunting snarl that cats have, and I wondered what he would do, for the hen was as big as he. About the time he looked ready to pounce, the game rooster came around the corner, and Smoky dived under the plumbago bushes!

. . . If you have never read Arnold Bennett's "Old Wives' Tale,"[2] ask for it. I am re-reading it and love it. . . .

Have gotten by today without a drink, for the first time. Your letters were so much better than a quart of Barclay's! . . .

All my love, darling.

1. Edward VIII, Duke of Windsor, abdicated the throne in 1937 to marry the twice-divorced Mrs. Wallis Warfield Simpson.
2. Arnold Bennett (1867–1931), *The Old Wives' Tale* (London: Chapman and Hall, 1908).

(TLS, 3 pp.)

[Cross Creek, Fla.]
Oct. 8, 1943

Dearest Norton Baskin, Owner:

... The house and grove are beginning to look a little tidier since I have been home and putting everybody at it. Even Sissie's little pickaninnies are "employed," picking up the fallen pecan boughs that the worms have cut off. They are also to get 2¢ a pound for picking up pecans, which are beginning to mature and fall. The grove has been tractored and Jack has been cleaning along the edges.

Training Sissie is an appalling job, not for any lack of willingness on her part, but from her abysmal ignorance. I think she has lived an even leaner life than Martha, poor soul. I've explained three times where things go on a tray, and they still look as though Sissie had stood off at a distance and held the tray and Martha had pitched over the silver and dishes like a drunken quoit player—and for all I know, that may be exactly the way the trays *are* laid.

I had a vast mass of papers, letters etc. to be sorted and was at work on it. I came out to the porch to find Sissie leaning over a huge box. She said, "You through with all this, aren't you?" "All this" being letters marked "Immediate," manuscripts, notes on the book, etc. Then I said that *nothing* was to be thrown out that wasn't actually in the waste basket—since then a stray scrap of wrapping paper stays on the floor, by God, until I put it in the waste basket.

... You must not think of me as not well, for I am wonderfully well. It may be too soon to brag, but believe I really managed to get on the wagon. If I can go one day, as I did yesterday, the battle is usually won, for the nervous desire stops at once. And if anyone tries to get me off, ... I shall hurl the nearest full bottle. Don't know how I'll come out when and if I get to work, but perhaps I can bribe myself with, say, two drinks before my evening meal only. A day's work really deserves a couple of drinks. And I want to get some weight off before you come back, so that I'll be "encitin.'"

Am so glad you had a chance to go on a good bender! Would give anything if I could send you an occasional quart, but it's absolutely taboo, as you know. I wish I could swap with you, and be some place where I could not get it. Understand tobacco is to be short—will so gladly be rationed!

The radio yesterday said to watch Burma and India—as if I weren't. It said that up to the moment there had been secrecy about India, but now it was known that there were large American forces there, as well as British. ...

All my love,

(TLS, 4 pp.)

[Cross Creek, Fla.]
Oct. 10, 1943
Sunday

Dearest:

. . . Am just back from Citra, where I went to mail today's letter. With fall and hunting coming in, I missed old Fred so. I went by and had a visit with the Old Hen,[1] and longed to have you there, though I'm afraid you could never have kept a straight face. She talks, apparently, the English language, but it is such a stream of utter irrelevancies that you feel maybe it's another language. It dealt largely with births and deaths in the family, but every name reminded her of another, totally unconnected, or some incident with no bearing on the immediate story, and all staccato, like a muffled machine gun. At one point she threw in an aside to the effect that Fred's family had no call to look down on her or hers, "all my people were rich people, they all had homes, why I had an uncle was killed for his money." Fred's sister, "Aunt Maggie," whom I am so fond of, is visiting her, but was not there today. She isn't especially well, and the Old Hen wants her to stay with her and let her nurse her, "why, I told Maggie, look at the shape Presh was in when she come to me, dying, that's what she was, dying." She claims to have in infallible instinct for the approach of death. I saw why the Ocala Tompkins family wouldn't let her stay there when Fred's brother was ill, and died.

Chet came by late yesterday evening and asked if I'd like to go fishing this morning, so Moe and I went with him. It was a beautiful day, but we didn't even get a strike. We went to Lochloosa, then after three hours of no luck, turned back to Orange Lake, but left within an hour. They just weren't biting, but I enjoyed it anyway. There were so many birds flying over, and along the channels, egrets, ducks, coots, herons, that Moe almost went crazy and twice I had to pull him back from where he was perched precariously over the bow of the boat.

. . . Oh, the Old Hen sent her best to you, and so did Thelma. The Old Hen said, "If Thelma dies, R.J.'ll be one of the richest widowers in the county." This again was apropos of nothing in particular, except that the Old Hen sees anyone as likely to drop dead at any minute, and that she was incidentally making the point that her young un had been smart enough to make money, and it wasn't all Tompkins blood in her that made her smart. . . .

All my love,

1. MKR is recounting a visit with Annie Tompkins, the "Old Hen," the widow of Fred Tompkins. Those mentioned here are members of the family.

(TLS, 3 pp.)

[Cross Creek, Fla.]
Oct. 13, 1943

Dearest:

. . . I am reading a new book laid in India, and reading fast to finish before tomorrow, as I would like to include it in your last Christmas box if I decide it would interest you. The details about the life would perhaps have value for you in understanding the place. The book, "Indigo,"[1] almost made the Book of the Month.

Jack asked Martha, I don't know how seriously, whether I was raising white rats. It seems there is an albino rat in the barn, pure white. I am sure that I know him. He is The Rat Who Rode to Gainesville. You remember my telling you of the one who went all the way, back and forth, got out on the hood and peered through the windshield at me, holding on desperately, with the wind blowing his fur backwards, then scurried around and inside and sat up on the package of groceries washing his face with nervous relief. That is the rat. His hair turned white from the experience.

I have found that Martha and Sissie use me to keep Sissie's children in order. Mrs. Baskin will get them if they don't behave. And Mrs. Baskin also keeps a bear in the house. They are in consequence extremely quiet. Now and then one cries lustily, and stops abruptly, and I know that stopping crying is the alternative to being eaten alive, or cooked in her strange fashion, by Mrs. Baskin. I had hoped to raise a new generation of servants for my old age, but they will certainly run away from such danger as soon as they are old enough. I always bring them a little something from town, but I suppose it is like gifts from Bluebeard.

I received an anonymous typewritten letter a while ago, mailed from New York, that at first sight was only one from another nut. But on close reading it had an insidious air. It damned both Roosevelt and Willkie and included among other things designed to appeal to the ignorant, a demand to get the country out of the clutches of the Jews and to throw them out. It suggested that the receiver send it on to ten others to make a chain letter, with the usual statement that breaking the chain was the worst of luck. There were no names on my copy. I slipped the thing, envelope and all, in an envelope with a note to the effect that it was perhaps only the work of an individual crank, but that if it was an organized affair, it would seem to have a certain danger and mailed it to the FBI in Washington—and yesterday I had a personal letter from J. Edgar Hoover, so it is evidently a type of thing they are on the watch for. If enough ignorant people take such things seriously, you have just the sort of internal trouble that the enemy would like to see us get into. Hoover wrote that if I obtained any more information, to send it to Miami headquarters. . . .[2]

All my love,

1. Christine Weston (1904–), *Indigo* (New York: Scribners, 1943), which MKR thought "splendid" and sent it to NSB in one of his "Christmas boxes" (*Max and Marjorie*, 556).
2. The Hoover letter is reproduced in Rodger L. Tarr, "MKR and the FBI," *Rawlings Newsletter* 11 (June 1998): 2–5.

. . . .

(TLS, 3 pp.)

[Cross Creek, Fla.]

Oct. 14, 1943

Dearest:

If I'm not mistaken, today is your birthday. No Chef to bake you a cake—that you don't want!—no champagne, which you do! But I'm thinking of you and wishing you were here—or I there. . . .

It may dawn on the government some day that the "populace" is not a batch of children. Being limited to mailing only one box a week overseas from the period Sept. 15 to Oct. 15, a great howl was put up by the postal authorities last week that only about half of the Xmas mail expected, had come in. They should have said how much each person or each family could send, tell the advantages of mailing early, let it all be mailed whenever desired in that time, and the result would have been more satisfactory all around.

I finished the book on India, "Indigo" this morning, and believe it would interest you very much, so am sending it. Also "The Old Wives' Tale." Am about out of good books myself now, but more will be coming along, from Max and Norman[1] and an occasional decent one from other publishers who hope for blurbs.

. . . The book is evidently milling around in my sub-conscious while I'm dawdling about, for every now and then out of a clear sky an episode, or a certain angle, occurs to me, so I guess it is just a matter of time until the final coherence hits me and I go to work. I should so love to have finished it by the time you come back, for you know what a horrible inhuman wretch I am with unfinished work.

All my love, darling.

1. Maxwell Perkins and Norman Berg.

. . . .

(TLS, 2 pp.)

[Cross Creek, Fla.]

Oct. 15, 1943

Dearest:

I have such a lovely bunch of stolen roses on the big round table! From that deserted yard in Island Grove. Some day the old shack is going to be occupied and I'll get buckshot in my fanny.

. . . Moe and I were taking our evening walk last night about sunset, and I was amazed to find a letter addressed to me by the side of the road. Further on, there was another. I picked up five altogether. At last I came to a place where Jack had hauled off my rubbish and simply dumped it by the side of the highway! It consisted largely of discarded correspondence! There was nothing anyone couldn't have read but Cross Creek and Island Grove could have had a field day with that pile. Of course, Sissie was supposed to have been burning all such stuff daily in the specially-bought incinerator. I sent Jack back at daylight this morning to pick up every scrap and bring it back and burn it.

. . . Thelma and Aunt Maggie[1] came out yesterday. We talked a lot about old Fred. Before Thelma got back from Lake City, the Old Hen had sold Fred's car to a Citra nigger, and now Thelma has to go through the shock of hearing it drive up to Boyt's garage. Fred's car was as much a part of him as his hands and feet.

I don't know how much news you get. Italy has declared war on Germany and come in on our side as a co-belligerent, but has not been accorded the status of an ally. And I suppose your mother has written you that the Yankees took 4 games out of 5 from the Cardinals to win the World Series.

When I thought Martha's Jack was gone with the draft, I engaged George Fairbanks to come once a week, and now I am stuck with him. He comes faithfully. If I were desperate for him, suppose he would not appear. I have him replacing a broken window-pane and you never heard such a crashing and chipping.

. . . Marcia Davenport is doing an original screen play for Paramount, her subject dealing with "the public and private life of an ambitious American woman of these times." Look out, Clare Luce![2]

Notre Dame has a powerful football team this year. They are mopping up. You remember old Alonzo Stagg, who was Chicago's coach for so many years. He took a job as a coach—he is nearly 80, I think—at a *tiny* little college[3] in California, and his team is licking all the big boys, U. of California etc. It begins to feel like football weather and I'd love to see a good game. Maybe I can get together with the Lyons for one. . . .

Henry Heyl wrote that he should much prefer Burma to the Balkans as a battlefield, which encouraged me.

All my love,

1. Thelma Shortridge and Maggie Tompkins Turner of Island Grove.
2. Clare Boothe Luce, American playwright and diplomat.
3. College of the Pacific.

. . . .

(TLS, 1 p.)

[Cross Creek, Fla.]
Oct. 16, 1943

Dearest:

It is such a divine morning—bright sunshine, but crispy cool. Jack is cutting the grass and the sweet smell is even stronger than the tea olive. . . . I walked down to the back garden and the late-planted green beans are six inches high. Unless the rabbits get them, I will surely have a crop before frost. Beets and carrots are up, and the lettuce and broccoli will soon be ready to transplant. It is a good time, and I am as contented as possible under the circumstances.

I think the enclosed letter will amuse you as much as it did me. I just got around to answering it, and told the fellow I was intrigued to hear from one of Dessie's far-flung husbands—and realized too late that "far-flung" could scarcely be a more ill-chosen adjective!

I am gathering my courage and having Thelma and R.J. and Aunt Maggie and the Old Hen out to Sunday dinner tomorrow. The combination is not a happy one, with the Old Hen's mad garrulity and R.J.'s sullenness, but I have broken hell out of their bread so often that it must be done. It did give me a chance to tell Martha that I should need two more sweet potatoes. The other day she brought me four from the patch old Will planted on shares with me, and said casually that Jack dug those four just to see if they were "making." When I went down there this morning, I found they had dug a whole damn row! Perfectly all right, since they could be considered their row—but the best of them can't help that funny little slyness. . . .

I love you heaps.

. . . .

(TLS, 4 pp.)

[Cross, Creek, Fla.]
Oct. 17, 1943
Sunday morning

Dearest:

. . . Yesterday afternoon Martha and I looped the loop on an excursion. We set out for Citra to do our Saturday marketing, and because I wanted to ask Thelma and her family for dinner today. It was a gorgeous day, so I decided to go to Hawthorn, where the stocks are better, and to try to find the wood man. Mr. Gay[1] had some wonderful Swift steaks and he insisted on my having what I wanted, regardless of points. He said he had extra points and the steaks would be on him. How I wished you were coming out so we could get high and broil them together! I shall save them in case someone drops in, for Heaven knows when I'll have anything like that happen again.

Then it occurred to me to pick up Sissie's little boy, who is boarding with Sam and Estelle[2] in Hawthorn while he goes to school, and take him home for the weekend. Sam is still working at Camp Blanding and making huge money, I guess $10 or $12 a day—and they charge poor Sissie for the child's groceries—and no children of their own. The little darky looked so clean and cute and well-dressed. I don't see how they do it. Then we set out to find Davis[3] the wood man. We went to Windsor and got directions—seven miles beyond. We wound around through the most God-forsaken country you ever saw—a swampy sort of pine land where they had been cutting trees. They had dug up the pine stumps and they lay like Dali[4] nightmares all over the landscape. We found the place and no one was home. It was so broken-down that the only way we could tell it was inhabited was by a small washing on the line. A mammoth half-dead live oak loaded with moss stood over the house, which looked out over acres of swamp and twisted stumps. Martha said, "Sugar, let's us get out of this boogerish place." I left a note on the door and was as glad as she to leave it behind.

You can't spend an hour with Martha without having her say something that tickles you. We talked about Henry, and I said that I had been glad she had "viewed the remains" at the funeral in St. Augustine, which Sissie would not do, as otherwise there would always have been the question as to whether they had really sent us Henry. Martha said, "I thought of that. That's why I smoked him over."

We passed Mr. Martin's place—and passed Mr. Martin in his truck—at the end of our loop toward home, and Martha told me that his wife, whom he threw out with the bland announcement that he had divorced her, spends almost every week-end with him! She said he was on his way then to meet her and bring her back. She said, "Man and wife is a meculiar thing." Which seems, in an eery way, a satisfactory summing up.

She asked anxiously if Sissie was doing to suit me. Of course Sissie is not, but through no fault of her own. I just haven't had the hope and the enthusiasm to pitch in and go through each day with her, step by step. The hopelessness of cream sauce, of Hollandaise, of Mayonnaise, when soft-boiling an egg is something revolutionary! And I suppose I have had it in the back of my mind that Idella might show up. Martha has it planned that Sissie is to stay with me permanently. Martha takes care of the children while Sissie is here, and they are all living, crowded and happy, in the tenant house together. Martha "raised" Jack, and he lived alone in the woods with her and old Will over near the Guthrie[5] place for years, and Cross Creek apparently seems quite a lively place to him. And there is certainly something in having one large family under one roof. I am beginning to think that I might be smart to do my betting on Sissie, and pitch in and train her as I did Adrenna and Kate and Beatrice.[6] She is just as sweet and dear as can be, and terribly eager, and Martha says she's happier than she has been in years. She has enough to live on and take proper care of the very nice children for the first time, for Henry, between his temperament and his semi-invalidism, kept her up against it most of the time. And I can see the possibilities of training at least one boy and one girl out of the two of each that she has.

I just have a hunch that when the first winter weather hits New York and Christmas is in sight, Idella will want to see her mother, and will put up a song and dance about coming back, to work me for railroad fare for a nice little winter visit. And I don't see how I could ever trust her again. It might be worth while to let her go hang and put in a lot of time on Sissie, on the chance of her and her children being the permanent answer. How does it strike you? I've got to decide what to try for. Idella is so damn perfect when she's on the job. Yet someone I could count on is of more use than perfection for a few months, then an awful blank.

From the ridiculous to the sublime—I am reading Joyce's "Ulysses"[7] for the first time, and am bowled over by it. It is a *magnificent* thing, and completely lucid and intelligible. Once in a while I lose a link in his chain of thought, but not often. And there are classical allusions sometimes that are over my head, but if I had an Encyclopedia Britannica I could cope with that. There are some of the most beautiful lines and passages, pure poetry, that I have ever read. The occasional "dirt" doesn't seem at all dirty, the way "Studs Lonigan" is dirty. It is either so apt, so suitable at the moment, that you don't question it, so natural, or as funny as a crutch, the way the dirt you and Cecil and Bob and I toss about seems funny to us [MKR then quotes a long passage]. . . .

His sense of humor is grand. In one place he is making fun of the pretentiousness of the rich. . . .

Reading all these really great books that I ordered from the Modern Library isn't doing my work any good! It seems asinine to turn out my trivial tripe when the Big Boys have already said about all that needs saying. It makes me feel like a rag-picker, pawing through the cosmic dump.

How I wished for you last night. We would have had drinks by the first hearth-fire of the season and broiled the steaks and read aloud from "Ulysses". . . .

All my love, sweetheart.

1. Mr. Gay, grocer in Hawthorne.
2. Sam and Estelle Sweet.
3. Davis, not identified.
4. Salvador Dali, surrealist painter.
5. The Guthries lived near the River Styx.
6. Kate and Raymond were MKR's help after Beatrice left. They were fired for their incompetence (*Cross Creek*, 180–89). Beatrice, nicknamed "Geechee," was MKR's maid in the spring of 1934. MKR devotes a chapter to her in *Cross Creek*: "I shall never have a greater devotion than I had from this woman" (85).
7. James Joyce, *Ulysses* (Paris: Egoist, 1922).

. . . .

(TLS, 4 pp.)

[Cross Creek, Fla.]

Oct. 18, 1943

Dearest:

Still quite cold, and I love it. Last night I put cushions in front of the living room fire and lay there until bedtime with no other light, listening to the radio. I get more stations on your radio with the big farm battery than I've ever had here before, and I'm enjoying it very much. But how I hate Frank Sinatra's alleged voice. Most of the time I have to turn him off. Bing Crosby makes me feel so sad, but I listen. Out of a clear sky yesterday, with no thought of your nickname, I began to sing "My Bonny lies over the ocean," and when the connection hit me, damn fool I burst into tears. When I took my evening walk, I had to torment myself with singing it all the way through, and went along the highway yowling "Oh bring back my Bonny to me," with the tears running down and Moe chasing quail in the swamp.

My dinner for Thelma and Aunt Maggie went off nicely. Thelma has had no maid for some time and they eat at a little dump in Citra, so a real country dinner made even R.J. good-natured. I had chicken casserole with sherry, rice (very hard to get now) and gravy, baked sweet potatoes, squash, beets, head lettuce with Russian dressing, biscuits (Sissie made them and they were pretty sorry) hot gingerbread with whipped cream and coffee. Sissie did quite well at serving. The minute she appeared with a dish to pass—and from the first serving it was plain that she would pass it to everyone at the table—the Old Hen would call out in a loud voice, either, "I'll have a biscuit!," or, "I wouldn't care for any more of that!" I'd hate to have Sissie get the idea that she is to serve first whoever yells first. She was nonplussed, as this contingency was one I had not taken up!

Thelma thinks Sissie is my best bet. She says Idella is just a little too smart for her own good.

Well, I bragged too soon about understanding "Ulysses." When I picked it up again, in a few pages it went into the stream-of-consciousness unintelligibility of "Finnegans Wake,"[1] and I was so disappointed. The "stream" may clear a little later on, and the few rays that are coming through are so choice, so I'll stick with it. I had the feeling somehow that Joyce had laid the manuscript aside for a long time, at the point where I noticed the difference in clarity, and when he went back to it, used the "Finnegans" technique. I feel more encouraged than when the book was so wonderful, for I think, "Hell, I can talk plainer than that!"

Portugal has granted Britain (and so, us) the use of bases in the Azores, and plans to drive the Nazi espionage system out of Lisbon. Cordell Hull[2] has arrived in Iran to meet the British representative in Moscow for the first joint conference with Russia. Hull managed to kick Sumner Welles[3] out of the State Department—a pity. Hull is an old fogey, and most people blame him for the pussy-footing diplomacy we have practiced with Spain and with the French in Africa.

"B" gas coupons have been cut in value to only 2 gallons. Yet the queerest people seem to have plenty of gas. . . .

All my love,

1. James Joyce, *Finnegans Wake* (London: Faber and Faber, 1939).
2. Cordell Hull, secretary of state
3. Sumner Welles, undersecretary of state.

(TLS, I p.)

[Cross Creek, Fla.]
Oct. 19, 1943

Dearest:

I didn't think I could do any greater labor of love for you this morning than to copy, word for word, Edie's long letter. It has taken nearly an hour and a half to follow that hieroglyphic writing but I felt it was worthwhile. I should just have sent on the original, but I keep all her "good" letters. I am betting so heavily on the touch of genius in her that I feel they may someday make a collection almost as interesting as Katherine Mansfield's.

. . . Jack chose the cold spell to go visiting in Macintosh, and it has been a job keeping the fires going. I feel so guilty to have Sissie and Martha chopping fat wood for me, but I should certainly cut my foot off if I tried it. I carry in a good deal of the wood myself, for I am so extravagant with it. I peer down the road for the woodman, hoping he found my note in the boogerish place, like one of the old maids of the Civil War, watching for the unreturning lover.

I had one of the usual letters from a schoolgirl asking for material for a report on her "chosen" author, and as usual, wanting it by return mail as her time was almost up. She said, "I put off writing because I wanted to make sure that I wanted to know all about you." It would serve her right if I told her all about me.

I also had a letter from Arthur's daughter Marjorie Lou,[1] whose marriage is planned for December, when her fiancé will be on furlough. Something about it disgusted me and made my blood run cold. She gushed so about wanting me to know, and she was so thrilled, etc., and of course all she is doing is making sure of as sizable a check as possible. I couldn't possibly mean a damn thing to her—we spent one day together when she was about nine years old. I'm just the rich relative who by God ought to come across. It makes you understand why old aunts and uncles ignore nieces and nephews and leave millions to homes for cats and dogs!

All my love,

1. Marjorie Lou Kinnan, daughter of Arthur Kinnan, MKR's brother.

. . . .

(TLS, I p.)

[Cross, Creek, Fla.]
Oct. 20, 1943

Dearest:

. . . We are having one of our periodic periods of mechanical jinxes. The water wheel on the Meyers pump won't turn and we can't water the garden until I can find someone to fix it—the cord on the electric iron broke and Sissie had to finish with the old fashioned flat irons on the range—and Jack hasn't showed up and the woodman hasn't come and we are fair scrapping around for wood for the fireplaces. But I think the cold spell is breaking.

Chet says Moe must be trained this year or he will be ruined for life, and he is trying desperately to find shells for us. Some can be bought on the black market at $4 a box. Not so awfully black at that—they just belong to private individuals who got them last year. The to-be-expected story has sprung up, about the soldier on furlough who stopped a good-looking girl on the street and asked for a date. Sure, so much cash and 15 points. Well, he didn't have any points. The next girl named her price, with 10 points. Finally he stopped a neat colored girl, who named her price. No points? "No, suh. You'se dealin' in the black market." Silly. . . .

And I love you.

. . . .

(TLS, 2 pp.)

[Cross Creek, Fla.]
Oct. 20, 1943

Dearest:

. . . I had another choice letter in my "fan" mail. An inmate of an Alabama penitentiary, doing five years for grand larceny, wants me to be his friend. Said he didn't want any help of any sort, just wanted my friendship. Probably wants my signature so he can forge it when he gets out next year! Think I'd be foolish to answer at all. Even if he's sincere and has become honest, you can't go around being friends with lonesome jailbirds.

Zelma has appealed her suit, wretched woman.

. . . I sent Julia a copy of the Emily Post shandy-gaff take-off that I wrote for your amusement, and she was *disgusted*.[1] She said she is a vomitophobe, and often sits miserably through lunch or dinner in a restaurant, in fear that some nearby drunk will be ill. I don't think being ill is funny, either, but nausea seemed to me the only satisfactory answer to Emily Post!

Julia suspects me about Henry Heyl. But is keen about visiting there. I sent her the snapshot he sent me of the place, taken from a wooded hill over-looking some fields and then the house and barns, and she wrote that it looked like Heaven to her, and she just pored over it. She has a passion for New England. I really don't think she would ever fall for Henry, and it's nothing I should be *anxious* to have happen, but you never know, and I am so worried about her. She is in a perilous neurotic state. Dr. Atchley has failed to cure her migraine. He said he never had such a poor result from that gynogen. He wants her to go to a real psychiatrist, which verifies my own hunch. She wrote that she had no objection to going into physical matters with one, but did not want any invasion of her spiritual privacy. I am convinced that there's nothing wrong with her that a good man and I don't mean a doctor couldn't cure. A job would help, but I think that prospect is hopeless. She just lacks the energy to go out and make a life for herself. . . .

Got the water-pump fixed, but Jack has not returned. Martha is much more disturbed than I. Think I could count on George Fairbanks coming once a week anyway, to cut and carry wood, which is about all that we are desperate for. Martha said Mr. Brice, who had charge of George's annuity or whatever it was, only gives him a dollar a week now. She said that a few years ago George showed up with the bean pickers and Mr. Brice said, "What does he want to pick beans for? He's got enough to live on the rest of his life." She thinks there's something fishy about that lone dollar.

Lots of love,

1. Emily Post, American writer on manners, best known for *Etiquette* (1922). See Brent Kinser, "'The Least Touch of Butter': Marge and Emily on Manners," *Journal of Florida Literature* 10 (2001): 1–9.

. . . .

(TLS, 2 pp.)

[Cross Creek, Fla.]
Oct. 22 1943
Mailed same time as V-Mail

Dearest:

. . . The wandering Jack showed up today, and Martha had so plainly given him down-the-country, and he was so crushed, that I didn't have the heart to say a word. I just told him that it was perfectly all right for him to be away when nothing was pushing, but not to go off again and leave a bunch of women to cut and tote wood during a cold spell.

. . . I keep finding appalling mementos of my fall off the wagon yesterday. I asked Sissie if she had wax-papered and put in the ice box the bread I baked yesterday, and astonished, she said it was already wrapped and in the ice box. I found a bunch of the pink roses from the abandoned house in Island Grove, on the kitchen table, and said brightly, "Who stole the roses?" When I was answered with a blank stare, I realized that I must have picked them myself on my return from Citra to get Yank Carleton[1] to fix my water pump. The only thing I am sure of, is that I did nothing immoral! I fixed up a cock-and-bull story for Sissie about the shattered windowpane—my foot slipped when I was taking off my stockings. Shame on me. But I have felt swell today.

I worked out a system of answering the couple of hundred fan letters—I just scrawl a hand-written note, "Just to say Thank You—I am hard at work." I got off about a hundred and fifty. That alone would drive anyone to drink!

Oh darling, I do miss you so! It is awful.

All my love,

1. Yank Carleton of Citra.

(TLS, 2 pp.)

[Cross Creek, Fla.]
Oct. 24, 1943

Dearest:

I've just finished reading a book that even Julia wrote was a "must"—"Under Cover,"[1] a man's story of four years of pretended working with the Nazi underground system in this country, in order to get the facts. The angle that he went in for was not factory sabotage or the military spy system, but the carefully thought-out system of confusing and lethargizing the American mind. The book has caused a great stir, for he gives the names of everyone who has worked, either as a deliberate Fascist with the intention of over-throwing the democratic form of government, or as one motivated by unreasonable hate of Jews, of Roosevelt, of the New Deal, or what-have-you, with the paid Nazi agents. . . . He shows how the Park Avenue element gets involved, through their selfish hatred of the New Deal, and their fear of some sort of Communist movement that will deprive them of wealth and privilege—and we know this is true, from Julia's own horrified reports from the inside. The book is proving very valuable in making people aware of what must be combated—of the *deliberately planned* whispering campaign for instance—and is selling like hot cakes. And by the way Russell Davenport was the one who subsidized this chap Carlson while he did his investigating. I can understand now why J. Edgar Hoover acknowledged my letter personally and gave me an address to use in case I got any information, for that very type of thing that was sent me is part of an organized campaign.

You should have seen the stew we got into at Cross Creek yesterday. Thelma Shortridge came dashing out to ask if I knew that it was the last day for getting No. 4 ration books. I did not and was properly alarmed and she said she would take our No. 3's in with her to Citra, as they must be presented to get 4. Sissie dropped her work and ran to the tenant house and got all their books and I sent Old Will out to tell the neighbors. He went off like a black Paul Revere, and Henry Woodward came limping up with his book, and Mrs. Glisson dashed up—but insisting that we could get them Monday and Tuesday. And so we could—it turned out to be just Marion County that was winding up. I went in to Thelma's last night to get the books, for Old Will was having a fit about his No. 3 which he said he needed this morning. And after all the commotion, Thelma hadn't been able to get them for us—because we weren't related to her! I told her I didn't know what I would do then about getting the books for all the black folks—that there wasn't room in the car for all of them—and they were certainly no kin to me. I could say they were my black cousins, but I balked claiming Sissie's children for my own. But I realize Martha can go with me and take care of them. . . .

All my love,

1. John Roy Carlson (1909–), *Under Cover* (New York: Dutton, 1943).

(TLS, 2 pp.)

[Cross Creek, Fla.]
Oct. 25, 1943

Dearest:

I have never thought there would be a musical menace at the Creek. "J.T.," the youngest Glisson,[1] has acquired a cornet or something dreadful of the sort, and if anything was needed to make impossible reconciliation between the Brice's across the road, where the radio usually is not heard, occasional blasted notes tear your ear-drums. You can come just close enough to recognizing "The Old Gray Mare," "Yankee Doodle Dandy," and even, God help us, "The Star Spangled Banner," to go nuts trying to correct for yourself the missed notes. After all we have been through at the Creek, we did not deserve this.

Poor Sissie got herself into the usual nigger jam yesterday. A daughter of Henry's first marriage, about Sissie's age, became suddenly affectionate—never having seen Sissie, and not having seen her father since she was 8 years old—and announced a visit for the week-end, from Jacksonville. Sissie got the time of the bus wrong—reached Gainesville to find no Henry's daughter, and of course just sat and waited patiently for other buses and got a ride home about midnight. Meantime, Martha and I went marketing to Hawthorn, and returned to find the visitor waiting in a car. She had taken a bus to Hawthorn when she was not met. Then, as Martha said, "The Sanctified preacher carried her out. That was all she could get." Evidently Martha would walk rather than be carried by a Sanctified preacher. Martha had the job of feeding and entertaining the city visitor and was furious. She burst out, "I don't like no strangers in my house." She was already put out about sleeping arrangements, and refused when I offered to bring from Hawthorn Henry Jr. who stays with Estelle and Sam to go to school. She said there just was not room for him—and lo and behold, the visitor and the Sanctified preacher had brought Henry Jr. along with them. Martha said she would solve the bed problem by sleeping with Old Will until the unwelcome stranger left. That is evidently the height of inconvenience, and I can imagine that if Old Will doesn't behave, he will never know what hit him.

I begin to gather that Martha is not enjoying our domestic arrangements. She and Sissie used to be on the outs half the time, but I thought it was because Martha and Henry hated each other so. In the midst of her grumblings yesterday, Martha said she wouldn't be doing it for anybody but me. That would solve one angle of my problem if Idella wanted to come back, for I hadn't wanted to be unfair to Martha and Sissie. But if they aren't getting along in that small house, I should not have the same qualms. Sissie will do anything at all that she is *told*, and graciously, but if I don't "speak," nothing is done but the most routine cleaning-up. I am spoiled, and admit it, but I am inclined to blame part of my lethargy in not getting to work, on not being made comfortable. I don't eat properly when I have to stop and fix it myself, for one thing. It is all silly, when I should be grateful to have food to fix. The stories of starvation in Italy and India are appalling.

... I have been reading Jane Austen's novels for the first time. In a way, she is the Kathleen Norris[2] of the nineteenth century. Yet there is a shrewd and humorous knowledge of human nature. Matrimony is the sole preoccupation of all the "ladies," and marrying above or below one's "station" is sufficient material for a whole novel. Many of the tragedies come from lack of a "fortune" on which to marry, and the impoverished governess in love with the lord of the manor wrings your withers. The one I have just finished (while waiting for Smoky last night) is really a brilliant piece of characterization. But when all is resolved happily at the end, and Emma and Mr. Knightley of Donwell Abbey finally make the grade, "Emma, cannot you call me by my Christian name?" Emma, presumably passionately in love, "Ah, no, I shall always call you 'Mr. Knightley.'" ("And now, Mrs. Knightley, if you please.") One longs for a Hemingway to describe the "first nights"! The combination would be delicious. . . .

All my love,

1. J. T. "Jake" Glisson, son of Tom and Pearle Glisson.
2. Kathleen Norris (1880–1966), American writer, best known for her novel *Certain People of Importance* (Garden City, N.J.: Doubleday, Page, 1922). Jane Austen, *Emma* (London: Murray, 1816).

. . . .

(TLS, 1 p.)

[Cross Creek, Fla.]
Oct. 25? Monday, anyway
[1943]

Dearest:

... Henry's visiting daughter proved a dreadful loud-mouthed city creature but Sissie was delighted with her. How easily they corrupt one another. I kept Sissie only long enough to clean up, so that the poor thing could have her visit, and she came over in the afternoon to report on their plans with an air so different from her usual one. She had cake in both hands and just before she addressed me, she crammed her mouth full and began to talk from behind a great round ball of visible cake. It was the weirdest effect, and most revolting. I begin to doubt whether I can ever train her. She just doesn't have the touch. Repeated instructions about specific things do not register.

Have meant to tell you that I found out from Edith that Dr. Damon's charge of $1,000 was extremely reasonable for him. He usually gets $5,000 for seeing a woman through pregnancy and confinement, and charges as high as $10,000. I think Dr. Atchley's relatively high fee was because he was very much put out at me, when I was there after you left, for getting up and walking out while I was still having great pain. But I was going crazy in the room—could only see a bit of wall, like a prison—and felt sure the pain was only psychic. So it proved, for it stopped the moment I got out.

I am unusually well. Nancy Hale[1] is still ailing (or thinks she is) from the same operation I had. . . .

All my love,

1. Nancy Hale (1908–1988), American writer. MKR is referring to her hysterectomy.

. . . .

(TLS, 2 pp.)

[Cross Creek, Fla.]
Oct. 26, 1943

Dearest:

Your cable yesterday was almost as thrilling as the first one. You were *wonderful* to think of it. It gave me the grandest lift, especially after having no mail from you in so long. . . .

I had the loveliest dream last night, and felt so close to you. It was a little like my wandering dreams, but this time you were with me, and by God, we seemed to be headed for a definite and desired location! We were on a train and behaved rather scandalously—just scandalous enough, but not *too* scandalous—and I can still feel your lips.

. . . I went in to the Island Grove school-house yesterday to get our new ration books, and one of the workers was Zelma's most intimate friend—presumably my enemy along with Zelma. She was very cordial. . . . It made me feel that Zelma has disgusted even her own buddies, and if the case came to trial, that none of them would lie for her too dangerously. She, Zelma, is so unscrupulous, that my one fear in event of a trial, was that she would bribe or terrorize people to get up and lie. . . .

All my love, and you'll never know how many thanks for the cable.

. . . .

(TLS, 4 pp.)

[Cross Creek, Fla.]
[? October 1943]

Darling:

. . . Such strange weather! In the north, it would mean snow. Here, the fog-gray skies should mean rain, but it is very cold, and we just do not get rain without previous warmth. The rain is needed desperately. The leaves on the orange trees are curling, and it is impossible for the garden things to grow. They stay alive and that is all.

George Fairbanks is helping Jack to fix my fence near the lake, where Tom Glisson's hogs are getting into my cow pasture. They have all the grass uprooted, and the lack of forage is lessening Chrissie's milk and cream. The pasture has been tractored and is ready to plant to rye and rape as soon as I can go to St. Augustine and get the seed-planter I loaned you last year. So the hogs must be fenced out at any cost. Jack reported that they got the worst corner fixed tight— and this morning "someone" had opened it up and the hogs were in again. It looks as though Tom and I would lock horns yet. I told Jack that when they had the fence really fixed, I wanted to see it. Then if it was "opened," I wanted to see that immediately. Otherwise, Tom would only claim they did not do a good job. He is really sly and pretty terrible, but I understand him, and would like to continue friends. Mrs. Glisson paid what she must, may, have intended as a compliment—she said, "Now some people would say that Mrs. Rawlings was a mighty mean woman, but I think you're the best sport I've ever known." !!!!!!

I cannot break Martha of her trick of letting the feed get out, without mentioning it. The other day she said, "We ain't got enough cow-feed to last 'til the man comes again." The man was due in about ten days. It turned out that there wasn't enough to feed them that night. So with gas the way it is, I had to go clear to Citra, for Island Grove was "out." She did the same about hay. This morning the feed-truck delivered, and I went out to check. I asked her about meal for the new calf. She said, "We got some." I looked in the sack, and there was enough for no more than four meals—and the truck comes once a month. I think I will go nuts, and then it strikes me funny.

. . . Have finished all of Jane Austen, am stumped on "Ulysses," and am down to Boswell's Life of Johnson.¹ Will be driven to work yet. Think I can begin as soon as I get a tentative title that suits me. . . .

All my love,

1. James Boswell (1740–1795), *Life of Samuel Johnson* (London: Dilly, 1791).

. . . .

(TLS, 5 pp.)

[Cross Creek, Fla.]
Oct. 28, 1943

Dearest:

A gleam of hope for Sissie—. In leaving my room this morning, I told her to save my coffee, that I should want another cup, and instead of literally just saving it, or bringing the disordered tray, she brought in a small fresh tray. And when Martha announced with gloomy joy that I was out of staples, in the midst of fence-repairing, Sissie remembered seeing a large bag under the porch bench. I must admit that when she brought in a log for my fire, she spit tobacco juice three feet into the fireplace quite as a matter of course.

I had a note from A. J. Cronin¹ that he and his wife would stop overnight at the Castle next Thursday, ahead of the rest of their family, and invited me to dine with them. I was planning to go over soon in any case, so shall wait and go then. He said that they had decided they would like a house in St. Augustine, but the agents had not been encouraging. Perhaps when they see your place they will decide to settle there. Being Scotch, he is canny and may plan to look it over without committing himself. Said they would probably have to go further south.

I just don't know what to do about them [fan letters]. I am inclined to feel that anyone who would take offense at such a thing would not be at all sincere in "looking forward to your next book," as they write, but is simply an egotist who expects special attention. I have never written but one fan letter to a stranger, and that was years and years ago to Joseph Conrad.[2] I had no answer and expected none, but if I had received a note in his own handwriting, "Just to say Thank You—I am hard at work—" I should have treasured it, known my letter was read, and felt a participation in his work in his even mentioning it. Of course, Conrad is far out of my class, yet the people who write me pretend to be as admiring as I was. It is most depressing.

. . . The hammock at the back has grown up into the weirdest dense jungle you ever saw. A spooky place.

As Martha says, "boogerish". . . .

George[3] seems glad of the work, and the good dinner at noon. Told Sissie he lived mostly on cornbread when he cooked for himself. Had him give a coat of enamel to the two bath tubs, and when I led the poor creature into the back room, past his grandfather's antique bed, it gave me the queerest feeling of the ups and downs of this world. . . .

All my love,

1. A. J. Cronin (1896–1981), Scottish novelist.
2. Joseph Conrad (1857–1924), Polish-born British writer.
3. George Fairbanks.

. . . .

(TLS, 2 pp.)

[Cross Creek, Fla.]

Oct. 29, 1943

Dearest:

Had the usual trit-trot day in town, car repairs etc., came home with the car piled high with hay and feed and seed, and picked up at the florist's a gorgeous bunch of yellow chrysanthemums that the Lyons had ordered for me at my convenience. Am enjoying them so much, as flowers are scarce just now. A day like that tires me so, and I look so much like Harpo Marx[1] at the end of it, that I don't go to see the Tigerts or anyone. Also bought a batch of biddies to raise for quick fryers. Moe trembled all over but did not bother them. Their chirpings affected him about the way you would be affected these days if someone waved an open bottle of Barclay's in front of your nose. Only manners prevent the pounce.

Am a little depressed today, still tired for one thing, still grieved about the failure of the fan-mail effort—and yesterday dug out and read a short-book-length manuscript I wrote fifteen years ago—what was meant at the time as an objective study of my mother, told in the third person.[2] I remembered the thing, and thought there might be some details about my grandfather and his life that I wanted. There were, and it was interesting to me to notice how long ago he had impressed me as an effective character study. But there were so many unhappy details in the book, and the picture of my mother was one of such tragic futility, that it made me feel very badly. The *style* in which it was written made me almost literally ill. If I could ever have written that badly, I don't see how I was ever able to improve. And then I wonder, God, have I? Actually, it sounded so much like Jane Austen—though not as good, of course—. I haven't decided whether to burn it, or whether someday it might have the same amusement and interest for someone in the family that the old Michigan letters had for me. . . .

All my love,

1. Harpo Marx, vaudeville and film comedian.
2. *Blood of My Blood*, ed. Ann B. Meriwether (Gainesville: University Press of Florida, 2002), the autobiographical novel that MKR called "poor Jane Austen."

. . . .

(TLS, 2 pp.)

[Cross Creek, Fla.]
Oct. 30, 1943

Dearest:

Honey, if I don't quit telling you *everything*, you're going to begin to realize I'm peculiar. Yesterday afternoon was reasonable enough. It was calm and sunny and Martha and I picked up pecans together and gossiped. She told me about her childhood, of her father's hard work and prosperity, the barrels of syrup, the dozens of hams, the bales of cotton. "She was raised just as good as anybody, but it never made her foolish. . . ."

Well, I came in the house and started up the living room fire again, for the evening was turning cool, and I picked up the Bible. Somewhere in the back of my mind is a Biblical phrase that I might want for the title of my book. I couldn't find it where I thought it might be, but went on reading. There is simply no better literature in the world. And each time you come back to it after an absence, something fresh strikes you—what a mealy-mouthed hypocrite King David was, for instance—how wonderfully Job in his lamentations expressed all human torment in the face of the unknown—how passionate, even libidinous, overwhelmingly beautiful and quite out of place are the songs of Solomon—. Now I have been unable quite to get back on the wagon since my recent fall—I take a few drinks before supper—I am down to gin—. All of a sudden I thought, what a hell of a note—there I sit blissfully happy, with the gin bottle in one hand and the Bible in the other.

Eccentric though it may be, I can guarantee the pleasure of the combination.

From reading the New Testament through again, I was struck with a new theory about the Jews. It is utterly incredible that they should deny Jesus and his philosophy. Time and again he tells his disciples to pay no attention to the Gentiles, that their mission, and his, is to open the eyes of Israel to what nowadays we should simply call basic values. The doctrines of Jesus are irrefutable, except by a Hitler, for instance, or anyone with his own megalomania. However, the Jews have continued to deny these teachings—and amazingly, the despised Gentiles have taken them up, at least in theory. There is no question but that the standards of the Jews in general are materialistic—one of the fundamental sins against which Jesus preached. The Jews have occasioned a great measure of the dislike visited on them by their very graspingness. Now we have the anomaly of world horror, brought on to a great degree by the use of the Jew as a medium of hate by Hitler and similar thinkers—and the Gentile Christian world rising, and dying, to save the Jews! Of course, the fight is to save much more than the Jews, but as I said, Hitler used them as the spring-board. If my Methodist blood were a little stronger, I should certainly go out and preach solely to the Jews! They are outcast because they have not accepted the philosophy meant especially for them.

However, as the Old Boy said, there are damn few who understand what he's getting at, anyway.

Your loving fugitive from the nut-house,

. . . .

(TLS, 3 pp.)

[Cross Creek, Fla.]
Oct. 31, 1943

Dearest:

. . . Your letters have not been censored, except that you wrote the name of the town in the hills where your unit was headed, and naturally, the censor cut that out! Otherwise they have not been touched. I *want* to hear what you are doing. I can get the general war news from the papers! I'll probably know about the Burmese push long before you do!

I got a big kick out of your verses. I love your letters, anyway. They sound just as though you were talking to me, and that's what I want. I don't see that either of us wants any objective literary composition from the other—hell, read a good book.

Late yesterday, just before dark, I went out to the kitchen to fix a sandwich for supper. I walked out on the back porch, and outside the door stood a cute looking couple, the man in white middy uniform. We just stared at each other. Finally I said, "Hello," and they said "Hello" and just stood there. After minutes, it seemed, the man stammered, "We're just—a couple of——snoopy people." The girl said,

"We read————————the book," They tickled me, and after a couple of polite but cold questions, "How long had the man been in Service, where was he stationed, etc." (I was probably looking and sounding "formidable"), I decided I liked them, and as I was lonesome as the devil, invited them in for a drink. We had a very nice visit. The man turned out to be a former A.P. photographer, and knew Sigrid Arne, had worked with her on some of her Northwest stories, and knew a couple other newspaper friends of mine. They had a female English setter, named "Pretty," and the dumbest damn dog in the world, by their own admission. Moe fell terribly in love with her, and she hated it, and he chased her all over the house. The man asked me if I had many people like them, that came snooping around, and what did I do about it. I told him that I took a quick look and if they weren't attractive, I hid, and had the niggers run them off. They were pleased at being considered attractive and we separated with mutual esteem and were quite high.

I drove in to Citra then, to see if an old man was still alive with whom I left two saws to be sharpened two or three years ago! I also took along my best cross-cut saw for him to sharpen, if he was still on earth and in Citra. I had forgotten what a strange place he lived in. It was dark by that time, and there was apparently no light in the house. It is a vast three-storied wooden house, relic of 19th Century Florida wealth and style, set back under enormous live oaks. The porch is a menace to life and limb and I creaked over the boards and pushed open the front door. There must be all of thirty rooms in the house. Who lives there and why, I don't know. A crack of light showed under a door and I rapped on it. A very pregnant and rather pretty girl opened the door and said Mr. Hart[1] was not there, and to follow her. I felt as though I were in a dream, for the time I was there before, a very pregnant and rather pretty girl was sitting alone in a room, and said Mr. Hart was not there—and then led me to him! We went down pitch-black corridors, and past an occasional room with a dim kerosene light and queer-looking people just sitting. I said "Good evening" as we passed and no one ever answered. The pregnant girl led me out of the back door, and Mr. Hart loomed up out of the darkness. He looks like Charles Laughton,[2] older and a little larger, and walks with a cane, and he led me to his work-shed and took down my two saws from the wall, all shining and sharpened and ready for me,—after two or three years. He asked me three times to come in and have supper, and the time before he asked me three times to come in and have supper—and I wondered on both occasions, who, of the immobile people, would arise and welcome me and offer me supper, for there had been none in sight. It was as though no time at all had elapsed between my two calls, as though in fact it were all the same call. I should be inclined to think that I had repeated my peculiarly oblivious drunkenness of a couple of weeks ago, and had only dreamed my former visit over again, but in my car are two shiny, fresh-sharpened saws, and the cross-cut saw that was in the back of the car is not in the back of the car, and I know the fairies could not have lifted its weight, and that Mr. Hart and I together must have taken it out in the darkness. . . .

All my love—

1. Mr. Hart, not identified.
2. Charles Laughton, Anglo-American actor.

. . . .

(TLS, 2 pp.)

[Cross Creek, Fla.]
Nov. 1, 1943

Dearest:

I got back on the wagon yesterday and feel like the devil today. I think you and I *need* our toddy. Orchids live on air, which wouldn't raise most things, Sissie's children refuse almost any food but beans and cornbread, cows get along fine on just grass, dogs thrive on bones, robins eat worms and have the prettiest red breasts—and you and I would just get so puny if they took us off the bottle.

Old Will Woodward was found dead in his cabin—you remember the old fellow on the road to the river Styx—the one married to Liza, the awful old woman that Martha had a fight with. Liza claims she doesn't have a dime, though we all know she has been hoarding for years—she and Will together had old age pensions amounting to $25 a month, and gathered moss besides, and everyone knows it didn't cost them *all of that* big money to live. I know that's true, for Sissie feeds herself and children on $2 to $2.50 a week. So it is up to Henry Woodward, who was his much younger brother, to bury him, for Liza would just have turned him over to the buzzards. You might know, Henry came to see me if I'd make up any necessary difference. He said he hated to put the old fellow in the ground the way you would a dead hog—so of course I'm in for it.

Mrs. Glenn Bass—the pretty one, where we made the unfortunate deal for the chickens—came to me for ten dollars to get to Jacksonville to join her husband. After they bought the nice little place at Lochloosa, fishing got bad and he wasn't making enough to live on. So she has gone to Jax to be a welder—and after a week, Mrs. Glenn couldn't stand it. She is going to learn welding, too, and will probably be very good at it. Her mother has moved into their place and will take care of the three little boys. They will make easily $100 a week together when they finish their training. They are very much in love, and I told Mrs. Glenn she made me laugh, pining so for her husband after a week, when mine had already been away four months, and that I wished I was within ten dollars of you. I was eating dinner when she came, so had Sissie fix a plate for her. She is so pretty and sophisticated looking when she's dressed and fixed up, and then out she comes with her Crackerisms. She said of the roast lamb, "This meat taysess so good."

Tom Glisson just stopped by, and said Williams had given him until February to vacate the moot piece of property. Tom said laughingly that both their lawyers had told him and Williams they were being a pair of damn fools. No good will come of it—and I must go tippy-toe. If things get too hot, I can always be ill and go to bed and see nobody. As a matter of fact, I work well in bed, and shall retire with tray and typewriter if necessary. . . .

All my love,

. . . .

(TLS, 8 pp.)

[Cross Creek, Fla.]
Nov. 2, 1943

Dearest:

I am the laziest, most worthless creature in this county. Haven't done a darn thing today. . . .

I spent the whole morning reading a new book by a Negro, "New World A-Coming,"[1] that is causing a good deal of comment—favorable as far as I have seen in the Northern press—and of course the most rabid Southern objectors to progress for Negroes have never heard of it. It is a well-balanced book, and covers almost every angle of the situation, and it really lays the cards on the table. It comes down to the simple fact that Democracy is a farce if we hold a race as a subject people, segregated, denied self-respect, kept from participation in civic matters, and all the rest of it. The Negro who wrote the book agrees that it is up to the individual Negro to make of himself an acceptable citizen—but it is undeniable that artificial barriers should not be put in his way.

One angle he did not touch on, while admitting the importance and gravity of Southern prejudice, is [are] the reasons for that prejudice. He is probably unaware of them. To my notion, the basic one is that the South took a hell of a licking, and was impoverished in the process. While the Negro, and slavery, were not the sole reasons for the conflict, they were certainly fundamental. The beaten South has patched it up with the victorious North, but it still rankles, consciously or unconsciously, and when the Negro wants to make a step beyond what is still slavery, all the latent fury rises. A beaten people is obliged to retain a feeling of superiority in one way or another, and the die-hard Southerner does it by feeling superior to all Negroes, who caused him so much anguish. Of course the Negroes themselves did not cause the anguish—they were innocent victims of man's inhumanity to man—but they serve as the goat, and as the medium for the Southerner's asserting superiority. That is why he is so determined to "keep the nigger in his place."

The other psychological factor, which again this writer is probably unaware of, is that the Negro in the South still *is* an inferior person. The Southerner feels a natural horror at the thought of civic and social equality being given to the creatures that we see on Broadway in Ocala and on Saturdays in Union Springs. And association with them would undoubtedly be as repugnant to civilized and educated Negroes as it is to us. The moot question then comes in, as to whether they are hopeless. Well, a certain proportion of the masses will always be hopeless. But the theory of racial superiorities and racial inferiorities is pure Hitlerism, and it seems to me that it takes a great deal of arrogance to claim superiority because one's skin is pale. That again probably goes into the horrid aspect of human nature that makes a man wish to feel "superior"—to something. We of today are so recently descended from Goths and Vandals, from Huns—our American descent on the native Indians is so recent a scandal—that it ill becomes us to call ourselves "superior."

At any rate, it seems to me that all we can do is to open the gates to these people—and then it is up to them. Certainly the repulsive southern Negro will never be any better, if we go on as we have done. And think of the "white trash" that is unacceptable.

Giving the vote, eliminating Jim Crow in all its aspects, paying the same wages paid to Whites, allowing equal opportunity of education, living and advancement, is only the "democracy" of which we make such a fetish, is only basic human justice—and does not mean that anyone has to be buddies with anyone he does not care to.

This Negro writer makes that point at the end of his book. He writes:

"Whenever logic fails, inevitably the Southerner will ask the white man who supports this view (Equality) 'Do you want your daughter to marry a Negro?' Obviously this question obscures the real truth of the matter. For Negroes do not struggle for equal rights to marry white women. The question presumes, as well, that if a Negro is permitted to enter a polling place, a theater, a school, or a public conveyance, marriage between the races automatically follows. Listen to Langston Hughes:[2]

"Nobody sleeps with or eats with or dances with or marries anybody else except by mutual consent. Millions of people in New York, Chicago and Seattle go to the same polls and vote without ever cohabiting together. Why does the South think it would be otherwise with Negroes were they permitted to vote there? Or have a decent education? Or sit on a stool in a public place and eat a hamburger? Why they think simple civil rights would force a Southerner's daughter to marry a Negro in spite of herself, I have never been able to understand."

This is indubitable, isn't it?

. . . As to happenings at the Creek—. I had an answer from the man who had cut timber around the place where the Townsend family lives, and he informed me that he had sold his land there to Tom Glisson. I was so pleased, for I knew Tom would allow me to take wood from the cut pine tops, so told George Fairbanks about it, and arranged to have him come tomorrow to help Jack cut the wood. I went down to Glisson's last night, and asked permission, offering to pay the stumpage, and Tom almost fell over. The sale of that land was a carefully kept secret! I told him I had mentioned it to George and asked if George was a gossiper, and Tom very good-naturedly said, "Mrs. Rawlings, George is *it.*" Fortunately, he had consummated the sale, so I did no harm. Tom then confided to me that he is quietly buying up land the other side of the Creek, and plans to sell his place and move over. He said, of the Brice-Williams, "I aim just to get out of these people's way."

I feel he is being very sporting about it. . . .

All my love,

1. Roi Ottley (1906–1960), *New World A-Coming: Inside Black America* (Boston: Houghton Mifflin, 1943).
2. Langston Hughes (1902–1967), American writer.

. . . .

(ALS, 10 pp.)

[Crescent Beach, Fla.]
Nov. 5, 1943

Dearest:—

. . . I reached the Castle day before yesterday and first of all had a long talk with Doug. . . .

To make it as brief as possible, the Hustons have harried him as only the Hustons can harry people—and he doesn't have the stamina to take it. Both are at fault, the Huston's principally, of course—I know I couldn't work with them a week—but Doug is more neurotic and more of a sissy than I had any idea. I smoothed things over a couple of months ago. This time he wired me to 'phone him as soon as possible. I did so, from Gainesville, and he said that you had told him if he had to leave, to get in touch with Harris.[1] He (Doug) said, "Well, this is it. . . ." I am to talk with Doug again today and am going to talk with the Hustons and try to get them to be nicer to Doug, to keep him for your sake, and since Doug *seems* [underlined twice] in better shape since we talked and I sympathized, I am hoping it will blow over this time. But as I said, I don't know whether Doug has the guts to stay the year. The Hustons, over Doug's protests, insisted on having several more tables, set up permanently in the lobby, and are feeding *hordes.* And the food is *wonderful.* I had dinner night before last with the Cronins, and they were bowled over by it. I have never eaten a more delicious dinner. . . .

I imagine the place could be sold now at a very large profit, but that seems rather foolish, as I doubt whether you and I between us could possibly place the money in a better investment than the Castle. I do not believe that it will do badly after the war. When the tourist business is normal again, I think it will be full all the time. Doug has rented no. 16 for two months at $245 a month—the room *alone*, not the American plan.

I just can't advise your selling. No one knows what conditions will be, later, and it seems to me that income-bearing real estate is a damned good thing to hang onto. I may be wrong. . . . But I cannot see how the place could *ever* fail to return a decent living and a safe percentage on the money in it, and there are few things of which that can be said. However, I have a perfectly open mind and would gladly follow your judgment if it is otherwise. If you have been thinking of going into some other business after the war, that would enable us to work out a joint life better, a sale now might be advisable. I had always had it in the back of my mind, even before we bought the Castle, that we might work things out very happily if instead of the hotel, you bought and ran one of the local newspapers in Ocala or Gainesville, and we made our home, a real home, at the Creek. I feel you could have done that as successfully as building up a hotel. I often wish I had spoken of it before. . . . But I never spoke of this, as I felt the hotel business was what you *knew* and *liked.* And it seemed necessary at the time for you to become your own boss and be able to build up something of your own, to give us any chance of working out our relationship. The old situation was intolerable to me in several ways.

If you just get out of this mess, we can and will work things out. Don't worry about my not being here waiting for you and loving you. I have been through the mill, old dear, and you represent what I want, for I know your worth. You are tops with me, a conclusion I reached by trial and error!

. . . All of my love, and will write a *good* [underlined three times] letter this evening or tomorrow.

1. Harris P. Baskin, NSB's brother.

. . . .

(ALS, 10 pp.)

[Crescent Beach, Fla.]
Nov. 6, 1943

Dearest:—

. . . It has been so lonely at the cottage, simply divine weather, and I don't give a rap about going to the Creek—which I hated to leave! . . . You told me once that it was *places* I was attached to, and the feline instinct goes further, in not wanting to leave a place that I like. Actually, the combination of Creek and cottage is wonderful. I am happy in both places—then when the inevitable restlessness hits, I have only to move to the other to be perfectly happy again.

. . . The cottage is so easy to "keep" that I am better off here without a Sissie, as long as I can't have a Ruby or an Idella. Incidentally, Ruby is *not* with Jean. Which will make it even easier for her to come to me next summer, as she said she would like to do. I have decided to write Idella *once more* and offer her $20 a week for the duration. It would take 2 or 3 years to make anything of Sissie, and even then I am not sure it could be done. I have taught her to make a cream cheese and liver sandwich, but after telling her *three* [underlined twice] times to cut the sand-wiches in half, they still appear in truckman's style, big as a house and quite un-manageable. I really think that if Idella came back, I could go to work content-edly. But what is my deathless literature to Idella? What, answers Echo, is my deathless literature to anybody? *I* [underlined twice] certainly have no enthusi-asm for it!

. . . Tell your editor by all means to use Emily Post if the nausea isn't as revolt-ing as Julia thought, but not to use my home. Will write nice letter tomorrow.

All my love,

. . . .

(TLS, 7 pp.)

The Creek

Nov. 7, 1943

Dearest:

. . . A.J. is a perfect circus. He sticks the same sort of needles in you that Cabell does, but his humor is broader and he is gayer in general. His wife is an English Nettie Martin.[1] She was not prepossessing at first, but wears awfully well and has plenty of sense. . . . They were charmed with the Castle, and said that No. 22 which Doug gave them must be the bridal suite, it was so lovely. But as a matter of fact, it is a house and housekeeping they want. Price doesn't enter into it. In California they paid from $3,000 to $5,000 for the season for a house. He has made a hell of a lot more money out of his books than I have. He was furious at the price I got, and took, for movie rights to "The Yearling." He got $100,000 for "The Keys of the Kingdom"[2] which is just as peculiar to film as my story.

. . . Chet Crosby came by this morning and took Moe out with his dog for a practice run. When he brought him back, he said he had done very well, and has a wonderful nose. But I'm afraid poor Moe won't get properly trained, as shells just are not to be had—which is as it should be. It is much more important to shoot Germans and Japs than quail!

The Moscow conference[3] came out very well, with America, England and Rus-sia agreeing on basic principles. And the Senate voted, 85 to 5, to participate in a world arrangement after the war, with teeth in it.

In the recent state elections, there was a republican landslide. Dewey says he absolutely would not be a candidate in '44, so that leaves the field more to our friend Wendell.[4]

All my love,

1. Nettie Martin of Ocala, widow of Manny Martin.
2. A. J. Cronin, *The Keys of the Kingdom* (Boston: Little, Brown, 1941).
3. Moscow Conference, organized by Cordell Hull, secretary of state, to promote world peace.
4. Wendell Willkie.

(TLS, 2 pp.)

[Cross Creek, Fla.]
Nov. 8, 1943

Dearest:

We got our blessed rain at last. It began about sunset and rained most of the night, and sounded so wonderful on the shingles. I lay on the couch on the veranda and listened, and watched the lightning across the grove and palm trees to the east. The lightning played for an hour in the one place, and was so bright when it came that the moon seemed to be shining over the palms.

. . . Find I have been taken for $100 by the biggest crook in Island Grove. He told such a plausible story of needing it only until he had finished fattening his hogs for market, and offered the bill of sale on a tractor for security. His wife is a pretty little hunchback in Island Grove, and she and her nice mother were friends of Mrs. Rawlings, so I said, Sure. Mentioned it to Chet yesterday—find the man has no hogs at all—and the tractor in question he sold several months ago—and what money he gets he does not spend on his family, but on women in Ocala. I think I shall just have to stop lending money to *anybody* around here, as it is impossible, evidently, for me to separate the sheep from the goats. When an honest neighbor needs a little something to tide him over, there is no reason why I shouldn't help out, but I am tired of being "taken."

. . . Forgot to write you that Ruby has left Jean and has followed her beau to California. Jean says that is the end of her for either of us, for Fred reported domestic wages out there up to $50 a week. Jean is struggling with a girl about like Sissie—who won't even stay to get dinner at night. . . .

I *love* your letters.

. . . .

(TLS, 2 pp.)

[Cross Creek, Fla.]
Nov. 9, 1943

Dearest:

I woke up this morning to one of the usual Cross Creek jams. In fact, it began in the night. I had the trots, and Martha hadn't filled the water tank, and the water gave out. I have threatened to rout them out in the night the next time they did that to me—twice I've been covered with soap in the middle of a shower when the water quit. I woke up weak and cross and saw Dupree's[1] tractor drive in to go over my pasture so the winter rape and rye could be planted—and Jack hadn't showed up and hadn't finished cutting down some shrubs in the pasture. A cold blast came in yesterday evening, and I thought, Well, I'd have a good bedroom fire and my coffee and the world would look brighter—and Sissie announced that the bricks had caved in the floor of the fireplace, and a fire would burn up the house. I looked, and sure enough—. Sissie said, "I reckon the rats underminded it." I felt totally underminded myself.

. . . I had a gushy note from Arthur's Marjorie Lou.[2] She up and married her boy friend when he came home on a few days' furlough. I suppose she'll make poor Arthur a grandpappy as quickly as possible. . . .

At any rate, I realize how lucky I've been. I've had the best of everything, and if I should go through another windowpane for keeps,[3] mortal woman could not have had more than I have. Of course I'm greedy, and want the only remaining thing—a happy home life with you.

. . . Another Field Service book came out, "Ambulance in Africa,"[4] by Evans Thomas, and it gave me as unpleasant a feeling as Geer's book.[5] You men surely are individualists, in the most egotistical way. Thomas stressed this about *other* members of the Service, without realizing that he himself was as big an ass as any. He thought he was presenting a picture of himself as most modest, and was frank in giving his sensations of utter fear and dislike for the business—yet he means you to realize that he is a wonderful and grand person. I cannot see why either book should have been published. . . .

Your letter from Africa that arrived so late, in which you worried about my not waiting for you and loving you, because of your sins of omission, touched me very much. I do feel, and always did, that you could have given me a little more time away from the Castle, to be in the places and do the things that make me happy, but the situation was confused by my being the abnormal sort of person that I am, for the average woman could have adjusted herself to the life there very comfortably. I am old-fashioned enough to feel that the woman should follow the man—yet nothing could convince me that the hotel life was worth living. I could live in a hut with the man I loved, who was doing anything at all that I considered worth doing—but I should be miserable at the Waldorf! And I did feel that my need of you was so great when I was in the hospital in New York, that it mattered more than the damn George Washington ball. Aside from this, I have no complaints. You are everything I want, if we can work out a life that we can *both* live without frustration on either side.

All my love,

1. Talmadge DuPree.
2. Marjorie Lou Kinnan.
3. MKR might be alluding to Emily Dickinson (1830–1886), "I heard a Fly buzz—when I died" (c. 1862).
4. Evan W. Thomas (1920–), *Ambulance in Africa* (New York: Appleton-Century, 1943).
5. Andrew C. Geer, *Mercy in Hell: An American Ambulance Driver with the Eighth Army* (New York: Whittlesey, 1943).

(TLS, 2 pp.)

[Cross Creek, Fla.]

Nov. 10, 1943

Dearest:

I was so cross until about half an hour ago. . . . I *cannot* get to work, and it is nothing in the world but hound-dog laziness. And then I know that when I do kick myself into it, it will be out of the frying-pan and into the fire. I got a start on my pet at half past seven last night, when I had just settled down with Dostoyevsky's "Crime and Punishment"[1] and found it fascinating, and the damn Kohler just quit. I decided the gas was out, so beat the drums and Martha and Jack and Sissie flocked over and we put in ten gallons, and it would not start up again. I fiddled with this and I fiddled with that and Jack didn't know the first thing about it and Sissie leaned her head through the Kohler house window and rolled her eyes and Martha lit fat-wood torches and held them over the gasoline and nothing happened, so I had to go to bed. In the night Moe pushed out, banging three doors, and barked like everything, and a gun shot, and I thought, Oh God, some night hunter thought he was attacking and shot him, and I got up and saw flashlights, and Old Will had shot a 'possum. So I came back to the cold bed and hated the world. I damned myself for a selfish, worthless, lazy, schizophrenic, hypochondriac dipsomaniac, and I damned Mr. Kohler for inventing power plants, and I damned niggers that stand and watch while I fiddle with gadgets and stick their heads through windows. Then I felt better and went to sleep again. And this morning it was bitter cold and I couldn't have a fire in the bedroom and my coffee was horrible, and I rang the bell and hollered and Sissie didn't hear me, and after I decided to get up anyway, she popped the door open and said, "Did you rung?" No I did not rung but I thought I will ring your neck some day. Then Chet Crosby came to see about the tractoring—and fixed the Kohler—everything in the world was wrong, including perfectly dry batteries, after I had paid Yank Carlton twice recently to come out. Then I made a fresh pot of coffee myself and it was delicious, and Now I feel all right again, only it is so cold I can't get this big living room heated with the open fire, and Smoky and his full stomach insist on lying in my lap and I have to lean way over to reach the typewriter. He picks the most inconvenient times to be affectionate.

I was writing a letter to Idella just before the lights went out—had laid down Crime and Punishment to do it—and just have a hunch not to finish it. Something keeps telling me not to write her. But oh God I wish she was here. But having written her three times altogether, though I did not answer her last letter, I think she would come if she wanted to. She used to correspond now and then with the people in Palm Beach she worked for, and I think she does it just to get presents. They probably think she will be back some day, and send her money and silk nightgowns for Christmas.

I hired Sissie's Hettie Lou at 10¢ a day to keep the chickens off my fresh-planted rye grass, but Hettie Lou ignored the chickens and concentrated on me. She edged her way into the porch and asked ten thousand questions, beginning plaintively, "Mis' Rawlings?" She is cute as a bug's ear, and finally she corrected herself and said firmly, "Mis' *Baskin*." Then she looked up at me and said, "Martha calls herself Mis' Rawlings all the time." I have an uneasy feeling Martha can do a pretty good job of taking me off, too. She probably puts the tenant house in stitches "doing" Mis' Rawlings. Well, turn about is fair play.

. . . Was interrupted here to go across the grove to the pasture, in bedroom slippers and housecoat, to start the pasture planting, the tractor driver having ignored orders to do the rest of the grove first. Don't be surprised if my next letter mentions casually that I have shot, not a 'possum, but a 'coon.

I love you, even in my rages.

1. Fyodor M. Dostoyevsky (1821–1881), *Crime and Punishment* (1866).

. . . .

(TLS, 2 pp.)

[Cross Creek, Fla.]
Nov. 11, 1943

Dearest:

Happy Armistice Day. Would wish we were having a new one today, except that I think that the war will be wasted if we don't mop up on German and Jap home territory. The Japs will probably die to the last man, but the Germans will cry "Kamerad" the moment we touch the German border.

Yesterday became quite decent as the ball got rolling. We got the pasture planted, and there was a typical long Julia letter in the mail. I had not written Whitney Darrow, and he had sent me some books, so instead of the usual business letter (he had asked permission for a new cheap edition of "Golden Apples") I tried to write him a nice personal letter, for he is touchy and always feels left out. To fill up space, and because I knew it would please him to have anything so personal, as well as amusing, I quoted your health poem. It seems Julia was in the office when my letter arrived and he showed it to Dr. Atchley. He is still putting her through exhausting tests about the migraine headaches, and has discovered that while she is not diabetic, her blood does something wrong with the sugar intake, so he has her on vegetables and proteins. She was due to christen a ship in Baltimore, the day after she began her letter, named for her great-grandfather[1]—continued the letter the next day, and had such a headache she could not go. I think her headaches undoubtedly have *some* physical cause, but I think she uses them unconsciously for escape, too, for when she is safely and comfortably in bed with one, she does not have to go to Baltimore to christen ships, or talk with people (including family) she does not want to talk with, etc. I would copy her letter, but it is pages and pages of tinily written pencil hieroglyphics, and I almost put my eyes out deciphering it. I wish my two favorite correspondents, next to you, wrote more legibly and a little larger. And a lot of Julia's letter was thinking out loud about obscure French writers she has been reading, which meant nothing to me and would not to you.

I mentioned to Whitney that I had not written to Max, because I was too ashamed to let him know that I had not begun my book, and as I knew he would, he showed the letter to Max, who wrote me most consolingly, and reminded me that I go through this every time, "and it always comes out right in the end."[2] Max ended up with a typical Max qualm. He was so regretful that the day we were together in New York when it was so cold, and he had only a block to go, he had not insisted on lending you his overcoat instead of his thin raincoat! I doubt if Max ever thinks about himself, except to feel he should or should not do or have done something!

This is probably as good a time as any to pass on something that Max said. I wrote him excerpts from a couple of your first letters, about the torpedoes that proved to be the flushing of the toilet, the Hemingway language, etc., and he asked if you might perhaps be able to do a book along just those humorous lines. I didn't mention it, for two reasons: I thought, God! we can't have another writer in our already complicated montage; and I was afraid it would make you self-conscious about the "cute" things you say. It is one thing to be amusing in casual conversation or correspondence, and it is quite another to sit down to be deliberately funny, as you know from the woman who said to you, "Now be funny for Mother." And as the Old Hen said, "Tellin' is one thing and composin' is another." But I must not interfere with your career—. And heaven knows I could already make up a much more readable book from your letters, than those two awful Field Service books that have come out. But you might enjoy keeping a diary anyway, on the light side. Certainly "Look Here, Private Hargrove,"[3] is nothing at all, but people got a kick out of the amusing side of the present tragedy.

. . . You really have delicious ideas, but I don't know if you could do it on purpose. Anyway, I pass on Max's thought. You might have fun doing it in private when time hangs heavy.

Loads of love,

1. Charles Scribner I, the founder of Charles Scribner's and Sons.
2. Perkins's actual words were "because I know all will come out right in the end" (*Max and Marjorie*, 554).
3. Marion Hargrove (1919–), *See Here, Private Hargrove* (New York: Holt, 1942).

(TLS, 4 pp.)

[Cross Creek, Fla.]
Nov. 12, 1943
At night

Dearest:

. . . Finally caught a glimpse of a negro cabin where I had asked directions, exactly opposite from where it should have been, or I'd been looping the loop around those roads yet. That section seems to be my Waterloo. It is where Martha and I never found the wood man.

Reached home well before dark, and had just settled by the fire, when Martha reported plaintively that Jack did wish I felt like looking at the wood he and George got today. Since this was Jack's first enthusiastic gesture, I went out to admire, and it was really very handsome oak. The ceiling price on common wood is $20 a cord! Since Jack and George at $3 a day each can get from one to two cords a day, it is a great saving. I think we are in for a long hard winter. We have been having another cold snap, and yesterday the frost was so heavy it looked like a light snow. It was about 36 degrees. On the way to Gainesville I saw many fields of beans and egg-plants killed, and people were stripping the frosted sugar-cane so that it would not be sour.

. . . All of which reminds me that when I was telling you what Max wrote about your possibly doing a humorous book, I should have made the crack that another writer was all we needed to turn our ménage into a ménagerie. . . .

As you will see by the enclosed . . . Vera pinch-hit for Julia at the ship christening. I bet she ate it up, but it's too bad Julia wasn't able to go through with it. Vera is no kin to the Scribners!

The work on my book so far is wrong in an undiscoverable way. It is peculiarly *stiff*. It doesn't sound like me at all, and I feel as though I were trying to write for the first time in my life. Shall do a couple of chapters more and then send it to Max to see if he can put his finger on the trouble. But I shall do better to plug along and then perhaps begin all over again, than to sit and wait and have fits at not beginning. I hadn't meant particularly to make the older woman disagreeable, but with her first lines, she sprang into life as a completely horrid person. And she's no one I've ever known!

. . . I'll be glad when I finish "Crime and Punishment." I think it had a lot to do with my few days' depression. Spooky damn thing, as well as gloomy, too. The murderer is so much like neurotic boys we've all known, that it makes you feel that any college boy of your acquaintance is psychically capable of taking an axe to you. . . .

I have put in an awful two days' spell of missing you terribly, and tonight was the worst. It comes in waves. I get along a week or so quite well, then it hits me like a Notre Dame tackle.

Which reminds me (I am as bad as the Old Hen) Notre Dame is cleaning up this year. Licked Army. . . .

I love you so much.

. . . .

(TLS, 3 pp.)

[Cross Creek, Fla.]
Nov. 13, 1943

Dearest:

. . . A letter from Charlie Scribner said that he was reading Edith's new novel[1] in proofs, and is most enthusiastic, and believes it will have a very good sale. I am so happy about it and sent his letter on to Edith.

I accomplished my day's stint today, but it will have to be entirely re-written. On reading it over, I found I had just rambled on about things that interested me, but are utterly irrelevant to my story.

. . . I did break down and write Idella and offered her $20 a week, and felt so guilty afterward about poor Sissie. Now and then she does something right, and I get a glimmer of hope. And it seems awful to turn her over to the mercy of the Brices, who would pay her scandalously low—and not pay her at all when they didn't use her—and her children are nice enough to deserve help for the future. And if she marries again, it is bound to be a farmer—no danger of her going to New York with a colored college professor! I shall probably never hear from Idella, which will settle it, but I thought I would feel easier if she was at least definitely eliminated.

I STILL think there is something phony about Al-l-l-fred. . . .[2] He DOES NOT have that German accent for nothing.

. . . I heard from Mrs. Tigert, and Dr. John was away, and she had had all her children at home—and had no maid and was doing the cooking herself. I could have told her she couldn't hope to keep her cook at what she was paying her, but since it represented a raise over the old wages, she thought it was ample. There are going to be a lot of discontented domestics after the war. But what people used to pay in the South was a scandal, and I hope we never see such conditions again. It was worse than slavery. What is to be done about women, poor themselves, who need some help badly, I don't know.

I finished "Crime and Punishment" last night, and could wring the ghost of Dostoyevsky's neck for adding the epilogue, in which the villain, whose neurotic and egotistical psychology he had drawn as cleverly as any modern psychiatrist, was presumably headed for regeneration! Those birds just don't regenerate.

I just discovered that my Butane gas, which runs my refrigerator as well as stove and heaters, was completely out. Sent Jack into Island Grove to send a wire, and he was smarter than I, and telephoned them instead! They said they would get the truck out some time tonight. Jack is a wonderful worker, and I go on refusing to be enthusiastic or take him for granted, and he stays on, and I could ask for no one better. But sooner or later sex will raise its wooly head and he will marry something that Martha won't like and that will be the end of Jack at the Creek. Meantime, it is too good to be true to have a man on call. And with the wood pile he and George have managed, we women folk can manage this winter if he leaves. And George can be counted on for emergencies. Poor fellow, my hold on him is apple pie and such, each meal bringing reminiscences of his mother's cooking.

All my love,

1. Edith Pope, *Colcorton* (New York: Scribners, 1944).
2. Alfred Houston, a banker, whom MKR at first thought was a spy because of his German accent.

. . . .

(TLS, 2 pp.)

[Cross Creek, Fla.]
Nov. 14, 1943
(Sunday afternoon)

Dearest:

I've been listening to the Radio, trying to get a good symphony concert, but so far have had mostly trash. . . . Frank Sinatra had to spoil an otherwise good program, being introduced as "swoon-provoking Sinatra." I may not have heard the adjective correctly, for shortly after I had a superb bowel movement. Claude Pepper[1] was introduced, and I started to turn him off but did not, and was most agreeably surprised. He gave a splendid address on the new Senate resolution to participate in world affairs after the war, and on the Moscow conference. His accent, his diction, were beautiful and cultured, and I felt very proud of him.

Martha and Jack have gone to Micanopy to church, where Martha looks forward to consecutive sermons from 3 to 10 P.M. Jack, I presume, will be elsewhere. I begged Sissie to go but she would not. She said she had lived away from people so long she felt uncomfortable when she went out. Yet she looks as nice as anyone when she is dressed up. Martha will be exhausted tomorrow. I gave her your letter to mail, which will account for the Micanopy postmark.

Ah—Toscanini—[2]

. . . Had an hour of good music, including Debussy's[3] "Iberia." The program ended with Gershwin's[4] "An American in Paris," which I had never heard. The first part is the so-called "modern" music, like sur-realism in art, full of dissonances, and meaningless to me. Then it goes into a lovely dance tune (I suppose the American found a jook) and ends, except for the last few harsh bars, in a burst of pure jazz. It seemed an odd thing for the Maestro to be conducting.

Moe and I went for a walk, but he bounded off in the woods, lost track of me, decided to take no chances, and was waiting for me when I got home. Sissie and the three children[5] came plodding up the road. For entertainment, they had walked down to the Creek to look at their hog in the pen. The children were neatly dressed, but they all looked so pitiful. I feel so guilty about having written Idella, and almost hope nothing comes of it.

It occurred to me that when Hetty Lou said that "Martha" called herself Mrs. Rawlings all the time, she did not mean old Martha, but her little sister, about four years old—which is even funnier. Hetty Lou at least has decided that the bear I keep in the house is fiction, and I thinks she doubts seriously whether I eat little pickaninnies myself. She is almost too friendly, at least when I am working.

I am keeping myself on the job every morning while I am fresh. The work is still strangely bad, but at least it is getting begun.

. . . It is still cold, and dry again. The rain wasn't enough to sprout the rye on the lawn, and the chickens are having a field day. It was too cold to make Hetty Lou stand out and shoo them, and Moe and I have become discouraged.

All my love, darling.

1. Claude Pepper, then U.S. senator representing Florida.
2. Arturo Toscanini, Italian conductor.
3. Claude Debussy, French composer.
4. George Gershwin, American composer.
5. Hettie Lou, Little Martha, and David.

. . . .

(TLS, 2 pp.)

[Cross Creek, Fla.]
Nov. 15, 1943

Dearest:

. . . Sissie has learned to make a cream cheese and olive sandwich. As a result, if I decide to let her fix my supper and say, "Let's see, I'll have milk and some kind of sandwich," she says so hopefully, "Cream cheese and olive?" that that's what I usually have. I had it—again—and went for a walk. The air was cold and very still. The pasture adjoining Martha's house was beautifully tractored and is a smooth brown, and a ribbon of blue smoke from Martha's fire lay in a wavy line above the field, and someone was playing the guitar. It looked like one of Bob's paintings and was very sad.

. . . Sigrid Undset sent me a new small book of hers, a children's book again, and it is a fascinating thing of Norwegian medieval lore.[1] The publishers sent me Jesse Stuart's new book,[2] which I shall read, good or bad, as I am so low on new books, or unread ones. I tackled Boswell's Life of Johnson last night, and starved as I am, could not go it.

. . . We have a couple of hundred pounds of pecans gathered, but the squirrels must have eaten four times as many. I have had as high as 1200 lbs. The squirrels are so cute in the yard, and drink from the bird-bath, and I haven't had the heart to shoot them. . . .

All my love,

1. Sigrid Undset, *Happy Times in Norway* (New York: Knopf, 1942).
2. Jessie Stuart (1906–1984), *Taps for Private Tussie* (New York: Dutton, 1943).

. . . .

(TLS, 3 pp.)

[Cross Creek, Fla.]
Nov. 17, 1943

Dearest:

Now that I decided to begin my work all over again, I am stalling once more and have not worked for two days. Maybe I'd better ignore the bad beginning and just go on, then go back to the first awful chapters later. I think I wrote you that I finally wrote Idella, offering her $20 a week, and asking her to let me know whether she did or did not want to come back—and that immediately I had qualms about Sissie, for Sissie's pitiful sake, and also because I was balancing Sissie's *probable* faithfulness against Idella's perhaps temporary perfection. Well, I had an awfully nice letter from Idella this morning, and she said she would be happy to come back at $20—which made me wonder if the wage differential had something to do with her leaving in the first place. She also said that she would "expect" to have either Sundays or Saturdays off, which shows Northern influence, for I always gave her twice as much time off as the average maid gets, and many a time offered to take her to Reddick for the week-end and she said she didn't care about going.[1] I had written her that she must understand that while the war was on I could not guarantee to take her places as I used to, but that after the war I saw no reason why she should not have her own car. She wrote also, very nicely, that she knew we all had to do our part in the war, and on her days off if she could not hitch-hike home, she would not expect me to take her.

And she wrote, with great wisdom, asking me to make sure that Martha wanted her back and did not have her heart set on Sissie's staying, for she said that if Sissie's going did not suit Martha, Martha would make it so unpleasant that she would rather not come. She said that if I was sure the change was agreeable to Martha, she would leave New York Dec. 12, spend a little time with her mother, and come and take care of me as before. How I wish you were within advice-distance! If she ups and leaves me again, how I should wish I had stuck to the horrible, the incompetent, the reliable Sissie! Of course I may be fatuous in considering even Sissie reliable! If some dusky farmer from Babytown or Micanopy came courting her, and offered her and her children a home and living, she would be crazy not to go, and gratitude over my care of her and the children and Henry would last only so long, unless she is different—and then not TOO different! Yet Martha's daughter Hattie has worked for the same Baltimore family for fifteen years—I asked Martha why I hadn't been able to strike somebody as faithful as that. Martha said that the first year I was at the Creek, I baked a wedding cake for her, for Hattie's wedding, but I didn't remember. Hattie was married—her husband left, or she threw him out—but she has not missed a day in fifteen years with her rich Baltimore family.

Well, when Martha comes back from St. Petersburg Saturday, I'll have a talk with her and see how she feels about it. If Sissie's children are driving her crazy, she will give me the green light. If she only says that I must do what I want to do, I won't know how to take it. Or rather, I will know—and still won't know what to do. But Idella is right—if it doesn't please Martha for Idella to come and Sissie to go, there will be Hell to pay. I think Sissie probably should get some sort of pension. I myself would not want to turn her out to starve or depend on the Brice's low pay, but if she can get some sort of help for herself and the children, I think both Martha and I would feel all right about it. I was sitting on the toilet in the bathroom this morning, and Sissie KNEW I was on the toilet, for I had asked her to leave her cleaning there so I could go in—and she stood by the door and shouted a question at me about some newspapers on the floor. She is so hopeless about little things like that, as well as the cooking and general service. Damn (and bless) Martha, anyway.

. . . Another qualm about Idella and Sissie—. If there is, or was, a husband or a man in the case, who is in the Army, and Idella was not just working him for his allotment, she will undoubtedly clear out when he shows up again. Then I'll wish I'd stuck with Sissie. Or will I? I could begin all over again with no one worse than she, or more ignorant. And by then I may have given up the Creek—who can tell. I do love to plan ahead, to make a general pattern, and then live flexibly within the pattern. But I am miserable when I don't know where I'm going—or where I think I'm going!

The oranges are beginning to turn golden and are so lovely. Not sweet enough to eat yet, however. . . .

Hope to God I hear from you soon.

All my love,

1. See Idella Parker, *Idella Parker: From Reddick to Cross Creek* (Gainesville: University Press of Florida, 1999).

. . . .

(TLS, 3 pp.)

[Cross Creek. Fla.]
Nov. 18, 1943

Dearest:

I picked up pecans for two hours today, and if I had been doing it regularly, I would be built like a sylph—or would be in the hospital. . . .

This afternoon Sissie said suavely, "Did Momma tell you about the cow-feed?" Momma had naturally not, as Momma doesn't tell me even when she is here. There was not enough feed for the two cows even for tonight. I raged and fumed and asked why they couldn't get it in their heads that gasoline rationing did not permit of dashing to town whenever we were out of something, but Sissie passed the buck to Momma. So there was nothing for it but to go to Island Grove, which had no cow feed, and then on to Citra, which had none, either. I finally bought a sack of horse feed, and the Cracker store keeper said, "This won't harm your cows, but it might set 'em a-plowin.'"

As much for mischief as for anything else, when I went to Island Grove I took along a bottle of sherry and went to call on Mrs. Cason[1] for the hell of it, and out of pure curiosity as to how she would act. I think the old soul was tight as a tick, for she hiccuped all the time and immediately began telling me that she used snuff, but Zelma and Turner hated to have her do it and didn't want anybody to know. I have always enjoyed her, and we talk about our cows and the difficulty of getting a bull at the proper moment, and our gardens and the weather etc. We had the same sort of friendly and rural visit as we have always had, she was glad to see me, begged me not to go, thanked me profusely for the sherry, followed me to the car and said, "Come again." Neither of us mentioned her unnatural off-spring. It was really good clean fun.

I had a thank-you letter from Arthur's Marjorie Lou for the $300 I sent her for a wedding present, and she said she had sat down and cried when it came, and her mother had sat down and cried. The significance of mother's tears may be gauged by the fact that in the same mail there was a letter from the younger girl, Barbara,[2] whom I also met for one day when she was four or five years old. The gist of the letter was, and I quote, "You know Christmas will soon be here. What would you like me to send you?" Meaning, of course, "You came across for Marjorie Lou, now don't forget Mother and I are around, too. . . ." I can see why the woman would have made Arthur's flesh crawl. BUT WHY DID HE MARRY HER? And why did he marry the second one, a "good wife" in her way, but BORN to be a kept woman. It all goes back to the trait he had as a little boy, of wanting something, no matter how silly, and raising the roof to get it that very minute. Later would never do.

Marjorie Lou sounded as pitifully at sea as any kid I have ever heard of. . . . Arthur insists she has brains, but I doubt it. . . .

I *don't* know what to do about writing you letters like this. I *cannot* write, "It is seven o'clock in the morning, the sun is shining, it is a beautiful day," when it is really eleven o'clock and raining like hell!

Got back at my work again today, and it was a fraction less revolting.

I love you.

. . . I had a visit with Thelma. . . . Thelma said Sis had been up there, looking after Dessie's property, renting it etc. The Chancey's[3] are trying to sell their house on Davis Island and want to live at a hotel, one reason being, Sis told Thelma, that if they don't get out of a house by the time the war is over, Dessie will move right back in with them. Dessie and her friends almost drank and ate them out of house and home—evidently had done so, literally.

Still have not decided what to do about Idella and Sissie. I should never feel the same about Idella again, never trust her. It would be as though your mate had been unfaithful to you, and while you might technically forgive, and take him or her back, the affection and confidence would be gone. Think I will just be completely guided by Martha's reaction. She has said to me, of having to spend so much time with Sissie's children, "I wouldn't do it for anybody but you." She and Sissie always used to have quarrels, and if they are only heading for a blow-up in any case, and Martha herself wants Idella, I'll let her come.

Can you write me anything about the famine conditions in India? Your section seems to be one of the most afflicted places.

I am reading an absolutely fascinating book, a new one, but it reads like some wonderful old classic tale of travel, "The Land of the Great Image,"[4] which is, or was, Arakan, apparently on the border between India and Burma. The great image is a ten-foot one, presumably contemporary, of Buddha, and is now in a temple in Mandalay—if it wasn't destroyed when the Japs bombed Mandalay....

.   Lots of love,

1. Charity Cason.
2. Barbara Kinnan, MKR's niece.
3. Robert L. and Sis Chancey. The former took MKR on a memorable deer hunt in the Everglades (*Cross Creek*, 322).
4. Maurice Collins (1889–?), *The Land of the Great Image* (New York: Knopf, 1943).

. . . .

(TLS, 2 pp.)

[Cross Creek, Fla.]
Nov. 19, 1943

Dearest:

I had a wire today from Cliff and Gladys Lyons that they would come for Thanksgiving, bringing "four homeless officers." They said Thanksgiving was a regular work-day for them, so they would arrive about 4:30 P.M. and could only stay for dinner and the evening. But that will be pleasant, and I look forward to it. Will have Aunt Ida come over on the bus, then I'll take her back to St. Augustine over the week-end or the following Monday. I have a turkey ordered in Gainesville.

. . . I asked Aunt Ida for advice about Idella and Sissie, and she said by all means take Idella, even if it was not permanent, if Martha approved, as nothing was certain in any case. Think she is right. I have felt uneasy about a letter or two I wrote you that sounded as though I wanted you to give up or change your profession. I have done a lot of thinking aloud in writing you, and I was only weighing possibilities. You must never try to change what is necessary for you on my account. I don't think you ever would—but just don't think I ask it. One's personal integrity is too important, and I recognize it for others as quickly as for myself. If we only didn't miss each other so when we are apart, we could have two households so nicely, but it just doesn't satisfy, does it?

If I enlarge the cottage, I could put a work-room for me, with an extra bathroom, between, north of the big bedroom. A dining-room where the terrace is now, if a passage from the kitchen could be built, would make a real house of it. Well, we'll see. Nothing can be done about it now, for lack of both materials and labor.

I have an added hazard to the manuscript I am working on—Smoky lies on it and chews the edges. I shall probably end by using it for his pan, anyway. I don't know where I ever got the idea I could write.

. . . Jack and George continue to bring in beautiful wood. I think Chet Crosby forgot all about bringing the man from Citra to fix my under-minded bed-room fireplace, for I haven't seen him in two weeks.

All my love,

. . . .

(TLS, 4 pp.)

[Cross Creek, Fla.]
Nov. 21, 1943

Dearest:

It is a lovely Sunday morning. Black Jack is walking around through the grove playing his guitar as he goes. I don't know whether he is trying to charm the peacocks or whether he is practicing for a serenade under some brown gal's window. He sends and receives quantities of mail, and must express his love life that way, for he goes off only every two or three weeks for the week-end.

. . . Darling, the sapphire sounds too thrilling for words. I have always wanted one. But somehow or other, you must manage to have an expert pass on the relation of quality to price, or they will take your shirt. If the new book laid in India, "Indigo,"[1] reaches you in my last-mailed Christmas box, you will read there about the hoaxes in the native jewelry shops. . . . If good sapphires are too high, I understand moonstones are mined in India and are very reasonable, and I love them, too. But the sapphire would be wonderful.

. . . The New York papers are full of the liquor shortage, which is artificial, but I had been able to get what I needed in St. Augustine, Palatka or Ocala. So I wrote the Lyons, in wet Lake City, not to bring any liquor or let the other men bring any, as I would have plenty, expecting to stock up in Ocala yesterday. Well, the Brass Rail no longer sells packaged liquor. Goldman's was closed—I found out later, because they were sold out—and I ended up at a comparatively new bar on the corner of the Square opposite the old bus station and café, where an A&P used to be. The bar looked like old Temperance lithographs—filthy dirty, dimly lit, smoke-filled, with Boris Karloffs[2] by the dozen lounging at the counter. The bar-tender was out of a nightmare. A weird-looking man kept looking at me, and finally moved over and nudged me and asked if I was Mrs. Rawlings, begging my pardon, Mrs. Baskin. I was, of course, and saw no need to deny it, and then he asked if I'd seen Leonard Fiddia lately. . . . There was no Scotch, no rye, no Bourbon, no blends. Only domestic brandy and queer-looking wines and bad rum. I was questioning the Edgar Allan Poe bartender about the sherry, needing it for my Thanksgiving cooking and a terribly tough older soldier leaned up against me and said he knew the sherry and while it was a little sweet, it was all right for cooking. . . .

I happen to have one bottle of Haig and Haig, and several bottles of the best gin and some imported French Vermouth left over, so I can give my Thanksgiving company Martinis before dinner, and let them fight over the one bottle of Scotch. I know the domestic brandy won't be fit to drink.

. . . Cecil said that Tommy Sabin[3] was bored to death for several months in Syria and Africa, then went into the Italian campaign, where he is now. Cecil said that he writes that things now are too horrible for words. God, how I dread having you get into the same sort of mess. Not only because of the actual danger to you, but because, not being the hard-boiled type, the suffering you will see will tear you to pieces. The basic stupidity of the human race, in allowing war, crushes me. I think that is why the work I am doing now is bad. I simply cannot escape the ghastly reality of the moment. It would probably be better if I joined the WACS or worked as a nurse's aid in a hospital, anything at all immediately useful and practical. Dreams, literature, art, seem chimeras. The best that man has been able to think, to do creatively, has not been enough.

. . . I miss you horribly. 'Tain't funny McGee.

1. Christine Weston (1904–), *Indigo* (New York: Scribners, 1943).
2. Boris Karloff, Anglo-American actor, known for his macabre roles.
3. Tommy Sabin, son of Cecil and Dossie Sabin.

. . . .

(TLS, 3 pp.)

[Cross Creek, Fla.]
Nov. 21–22 [21], 1943
Sunday afternoon

Darling:

Since I have not worked today, and so should do double-duty tomorrow, I'll write your Monday letter today.

To begin with, after I finished my noon dinner, I told Sissie to ask Martha to come over. I waited until Martha and I were alone, then told her that Idella was ready to come back, and what should we do about it. As I hoped, she was tremendously pleased at the idea. Sissie's children are driving her crazy—she said, "I jest as soon deal with a bunch of convicts." And she told me that the Brice children had offered to put up from five to seven dollars a week for Sissie, if she could be induced to take care of the older Brices. Martha said, "You write Idella the door is jes' as wide open as when she went outen it." Martha does not think there is a man involved in Idella's leaving, but thinks, from things she overheard when she went to Idella's home at Reddick, that the sisters and two friends who were going to New York, talked her into making a try for the elegant life of Harlem. Idella uses the name of Miss Idella Thompson in writing from New York, and received her letters from me in that name, so it may all have been the wage differential, and her acceptance, pronto, of twenty a week, would seen to verify it. Anyway, Martha says go ahead, so I shall see the Brices today or tomorrow and make sure they will pay Sissie enough to live on, then write Idella to come. It is too good to be true.

... Dr. Cason and his mother stopped by for a visit, he, the bastard, in hunting clothes, having spent yesterday and today hunting with what I thought was my pal, Chet Crosby—who presumably had no shells, and had not offered to take me out the first day or the second of the season. I am furious at Chet, for it was Dr. Cason and Zelma who held him up on the quick-claim deed on his land—on which I gave him $1500, the full amount of the mortgage! Dr. Cason said "they" got 41 quail, and added, "You may know who shot the quail." Chet has told me that I am a better shot than Dr. Cason, bad as I am. Now WHY would he take that dog hunting and not ask me? Anyway, I had an ulterior motive in being nice to them, gave Turner a pound of butter and those pecans cost him plenty! For obviously, no member of a family can be too distressed by libel, if the rest of them accept your butter and your nuts!

I think Dr. Cason is just playing nice, in the event of Zelma's losing out. Selfishness is so obvious. He never asked about my health, about my work, or about you. And Nancy never asked about you when she wrote for a letter to my agent. You'd think those self-centered people looking for favors would be smart enough to ingratiate themselves. I can play a nasty game, too, when I have to, and once Zelma's suit is settled, I am going to tell Turner once and for all what I think of him. I tried to, when he ditched the poor girl with T.B. whose life he had ruined, but it never registered. But I think if I figure things out, I can manage to get under his skin.

Ross Allen sent me the two rattlesnake skins I sent him for dressing. The one from the Creek had not been properly salted, and is ruined. The one killed on my road just back of the cottage at the beach is a beauty. It is six feet long without head or rattles. ...

All my love,

. . . .

(TLS, 3 pp.)

[Cross Creek, Fla.]
Nov. 26, 1943

Dearest:

I didn't write you yesterday, Thanksgiving—the first day I've missed. I didn't have time to write a post-card to Santa Claus.

I met Aunt Ida at the bus in Gainesville the day before Thanksgiving, then we did the marketing. . . . I had written Aunt Ida about liquor, and Doug brought her a quart of Bourbon and a quart of Scotch for me. She was so cute, she got off the bus holding tight to her little satchel with the liquor in it and wouldn't let the porter touch it. She was really a great deal of help to me in the cooking, for Sissie was useful only to clean up. I cooked all day long.

The Lyons and three officers arrived about 5:30. We had an awfully good time, and dinner was delicious, if I do say so myself. I had baked sherried grapefruit, the turkey and dressing were wonderful, giblet gravy, mashed potatoes, candied yams, boiled onions, home-made cranberry jelly, pumpkin pie with whipped cream, salted pecans, stuffed dates, candied ginger, mints, etc., and a big fruit platter.

I had hoped for a bridge or even a poker game, but we got to talking and had such a good round of arguments that before we knew it, it was after one o'clock in the morning and they had to get back to Lake City. Aunt Ida was the belle of the ball. She was at her very best and at her cutest, and the men were crazy about her. I have enjoyed her very much.

As usual, I have forgotten all the funny things she has been saying. But in all seriousness, she calls the WACS the WHACS. Which is hard to improve on, though of course it is just her peculiar way of getting words wrong. . . .

We all talked about you, and several times Cliff said, "I wonder what Norton is doing at this minute." We missed you dreadfully, needless to say.

I had a very nice letter from your pal Paul Clark. . . . He wrote a crazy story about your being drunk together and your ending up taking a swing at the bartender, and the M.P.'s taking you both home. For a minute I believed it, then I realized he was just trying to be funny, for if you were really very high, you would be much more likely to kiss a nigger than to take a poke at *anybody*. And I have never known you to be so far gone that M.P.'s or anybody else had to take you home. . . .

Needless to say, I had a bit of a hangover this morning. Not so much from drinking, for we didn't really drink very much, but because of the tension of working so all day. I stayed in bed and feel better now and am up, in a housecoat.

The Brices chose yesterday to do their hog-killing and borrowed Martha and Jack, so that made it doubly busy for Sissie and me. I had my hog butchered along with theirs, and today we will make sausage and lard, when I can face the music. I let them use my truck to take the meat to storage, and am having the hams and bacon of my share sugar-cured and smoked and held there. My hog weighed 196 lbs. Dressed. . . .

All my love, darling.

(TLS, 2 pp.)

[Cross Creek, Fla.]
Nov. 27, 1943

Dearest:

. . . We made lard from my pig yesterday, and I have at least 20 lbs. I don't have so very much sausage, as I gave Martha and Sissie meat, and when I found that after Martha had spent two whole days working with the Brice-Williams on their meat they had not given her so much as a pig-tail, I gave her more meat. How can anyone be that tight?

Norman Berg sent me another Macmillan book that is a knock-out. "Arrival and Departure" by Arthur Koestler.[1] I don't see how I have missed the man. He has a couple of previous books that I saw well reviewed but some way it didn't register. . . .

. . . I noticed on the card Norman sent with the new book, "Southern Editor and Trade Manager," so he has evidently carried his point toward becoming a Max Perkins. I wish I knew what it is he is working on me toward. I'll be damned if he can ever get me to leave Scribner's.

. . . Aunt Ida has finished the sausage and is back, and there's just no use trying to type and listen at the same time. What she practices is a sort of mental rape. You are deep in typing or reading, and she invades you, violates you. . . .

The back bedroom looks fairly well with the new drapes and Bob's painting of the catastrophic crows, but it is on the dull side as to color. I brought the painting in to show it to the Thanksgiving guests and it is still on the living room mantel. I should really like it in here where I can see it, but I'm stuck now with expensive curtains that don't go with any others of my pictures. The Audubon in green tones I brought into the little room between the living room and bathroom and it looks very well. Some day I'll do something about that room. That obvious bed with Mother's lace spread is too depressing.

Sissie has popped in—Momma wants to know kin she git a onion. Momma kin. I kinnot write any longer to my love.

1. Arthur Koestler (1905–1983), *Arrival and Departure* (New York: Macmillan, 1943).

. . . .

(TLS, 2 pp.)

[Cross Creek, Fla.]
Sunday
Nov. 28, 1943

Dearest:

Chet really made it up to me about the hunting. He came by yesterday evening and asked me to go this morning. As I thought, he had gotten shells through the Jacksonville Gun Club, to which Dr. Cason belongs. I reached his house at 7 this morning and we hunted until 11:30. I have never put in more intensive shooting, and walking, and never saw more birds in so short a time. We [went] into the backwoods between Lochloosa and Hawthorn, and it was so wild that we saw a wild-cat kitten. We thought at first that it was a domestic cat, then realized what it was. The woods were beautiful. We have a great deal of color this fall. The black jack oaks and the sumac were bright red, and the wild grape vines were Chinese yellow. We got into four coveys, and one must have had forty birds in it. Chet did not miss his first ten shots—ten birds—then he said he got over-confident and only got two more after that. I got two altogether, but was very proud of that. Moe did abominably. So full of spirits he went perfectly wild. By the time the grass was too dry to hunt and Chet and his dog and I were tired, Moe had just slowed down so that Chet could do something with him. He said that the next time he took me, he'd like me to take Moe out the afternoon before and run him from the car and wear him out. It is good of him to bother with both of us, for his dog is splendid.

... The Patton[1] incident is creating a furor. I don't know whether it reached your section, but TIME said it was over southern Europe in about a week, although it was kept out of the papers until last week. It happened in August. He was inspecting a hospital after or during the Sicilian campaign, and found one soldier crying. He asked him what was the matter and the guy said he didn't know, that he could hear shells coming but couldn't hear them explode. Patton slapped him twice and cursed him, the nurse sprang at him to stop him, etc. etc. It turned out that the soldier had fought bravely through the campaign and had asked to be sent back from the hospital into action, but not only had genuine shell-shock but malaria with a high temperature. Eisenhower had Patton apologize publicly to all involved, but said Patton was too valuable as a soldier to do anything further about it. There is much talk pro and con, and the papers are full of it.

You may have heard that old Petain[2] got a bellyful and appealed to the French people to put up a fight for the old democratic way of life. The Germans kept him off the radio but his talk got circulated anyway....

All my love, darling.

1. George S. Patton, at this point commander of the Seventh Army. Patton's promotion was delayed because of this famous incident.
2. Henri P. Pétain, head of the Vichy government, had initially cooperated with the occupation forces of Germany. He was later convicted of treason, and his death sentence was commuted by Charles de Gaulle.

. . . .

(ALS, 10 pp.)

[Crescent Beach, Fla.]
At the cottage
Nov. 29, 1943

Dearest:—

... Darling, invite anyone you want to the Creek—just not the first week or two—don't come *home* with a bunch of house guests!

Aunt Ida and Moe and I drove over to St. Augustine yesterday afternoon. . . . I went up to see Jean. She was entertaining Wallie Bishop,[1] who was here, I think, when you were. He is Coast Guard, but drew a comic strip in private life, and still draws $100 a week from the syndicate. He is living in no. 12 at the Castle. . . . Then I went to the hotel and had a nice visit and drinks with Ruth. . . . Ruth and I had supper together. The tables were beautiful. The food is as good as ever. Spaghetti and meat balls were the main hot dish, and it was perfect.

. . . Ruth says there are rumors—and I heard them before—that in the spring the Coast Guard officers' schools will leave St. Augustine. . . . If that happens— and some of the Miami hotels have been vacated already—I am afraid there may be a rather lean period for St. Augustine until the war is over again. But I still cannot see selling the hotel. Suppose you sold it for $100,000. You cannot be sure of more than 4% interest on anything safe, which would be an income of only $4,000 a year—and I do not think after the war you could ever make as *low* a net profit as that, and it would usually range much higher—and you would still have the hotel. If we took the $100,000 and decided to travel and just use it up—$5,000 a year would last 20 years—and we might live for 40 years. And we couldn't travel on $5,000. And my steady income isn't much over $2,000.

. . . Well, I cannot kill off my friend and enemy, Dora, to please anyone. When she pops out of the den she shares with Medusa and Circe[2] and a few fish-wives and God knows whom else, she has to have her fling. I don't approve of her, but she disapproves even more of me, so there we are, cats with our tails tied together, and scratching and clawing in opposite directions. And if I ever became "all good," I think I should miss her. . . .

So much love, sweetheart.

1. Wallie Bishop, whose syndicated cartoon *Muggs and Skeeter* ran for forty-six years (1928– 1974).
2. Medusa, Greek Gorgon whose hair was made of serpents and whose hideous face turned the beholder to stone; Circe, a sorceress who turned Odysseus's companions into swine.

. . . .

(ALS, 6 pp.)

[Crescent Beach, Fla.]
Nov. 30, 1943

Dearest:—

The mail situation has me hanging on the ropes, not so much for myself as for you—and for the other men who just are not receiving their mail. . . . As I have said in many letters, I wrote two or three times a week up until the day I had your landing cable, Sept. 7—and from then on I have written *every single day*. What brought this on, was another letter from you that arrived yesterday. Mail from your base had come in after a month—and you had not begun to get one-tenth of my letters.

The situation also takes away my sense of freedom in writing a grousing letter if I feel like it, for the next letter is usually cheerio again—but you are likely to receive the one depressed letter all by itself and then not hear again for a month, which would give you an awful feeling. . . .

A Coast Guard officer who ate dinner with Ruth and Jean and Frank Howatt[1] and me at the hotel last night said the subs are still getting more boats of ours than is announced—which doubtless accounts for part of the mail. . . .

. . . The Cabells are back, and I went around to the Buckingham to see them. Priscilla has been suffering agonies with her arthritis, or neuritis. She can't comb her own hair or bathe herself. The other night James gave her her bath. I could see him trying to hold something in, then he chuckled and came out with it—he said "Percy" was so modest she made him turn the bathroom light out while he bathed her, and he wasn't able to do a very good job in the dark! I can't think of anything funnier or more ironic to happen to the author of "Jurgen"![2]

. . . It is so chilly this morning and I have a fire going in the fireplace. Now I must straighten things up and head back to the Creek to cook dinner for the Mays. As I have written before, Phil is bringing the brief in the lawsuit for me to see. Don't know what to do about drinks for them—could not buy Bourbon anywhere and forgot to ask Doug if he could spare a bottle. Am going home the back way. . . .

And I love you.

1. Frank Howatt, St. Augustine lawyer, cousin of Willard Howatt.
2. James Branch Cabell (1879–1958), *Jurgen: A Comedy of Justice* (New York: McBridge, 1919).

. . . .

(TLS, 2 pp.)

[Cross Creek, Fla.]
Dec. 1, 1943

Dearest:

. . . I am a bit tired out today, as yesterday was strenuous. After I wrote you from the cottage, I cleaned house, drove to the Creek, was rather late, found Sissie hadn't done a blessed thing, although I had told her our menu for dinner for the Mays, pitched in and cooked up a breeze, and just had time to powder my nose before the Mays arrived. Dinner was good, and Phil ate with satisfactory gusto. I had a turkey, and I have never seen a man make a worse botch of carving. Even Sissie, who at her own table would probably just pull the meat off with her hands, cut her eyes at me. Phil has more annoying physical and personal mannerisms than almost anyone I've ever known, and his perfectly nice wife is not far behind. They evidently don't bother each other, which is God's mercy. I think they are very happy. They brought their dog with them, a female toy Boston, a breed I don't care much for, but it is a cute little trick. She and Moe had the most glorious romp, and Moe fell fatuously in love with her. . . .

Phil has not received the Cason declaration, or whatever they call it, so cannot prepare a complete brief until he does. The enclosed is just the outline, based on his guesses as to what they are claiming. I really believe the matter will be thrown out at Tallahassee.

. . . I had a letter from Norman Berg, that crossed my thank-you letter for his books. When I saw him in the summer, he asked if I had ever thought of doing a strictly children's book, and I told him that I had done one some years ago, read it to a small boy-friend of mine, and the child cried so bitterly over it that I was appalled and called it all off. In his letter, he asked if I would let him see the manuscript, that it would be no violation of relations with Scribner for Macmillan to publish a child's book—and that it would be a good thing for me when I came to demand a straight 20% royalty on my next book! I am really much obliged to him for the tip, for I thought 15% was standard, but evidently it is not.

Phil brought me a pint of the pickled artichokes you are so crazy about and I shall save them for your return. They are in glass, so I couldn't send them to you.

Notre Dame took its first beating, after nine or ten straight wins, from the Great Lakes Naval Training Station (Navy), where W.D. is stationed, 19-14, and the sailors made a touch-down in the last few seconds of play, on a desperate pass. It must have been a wonderful game.

. . . I miss you consistently and dreadfully.

All my love.

. . . .

(TLS, 3 pp.)

[Cross Creek, Fla.]
Dec. 2, 1943

Dearest:

I just turned the peacocks out for the first time . . . and they are celebrating with the darndest noise. It sounds like a blast from a child's 10¢ Christmas horn. I can't tell which one makes the racket, or whether both do.

I have no qualms today about letting Sissie go, and am only hoping to God Idella doesn't fail me. The house is getting dirtier and dirtier and messier and messier.

. . . Jack and George Fairbanks are mounding the young orange trees, and I wondered why it was going so slowly, then decided that George will make the job last until the pumpkin pie and turkey give out. We finally got a good rain, and everything looks so much fresher. (Dept. of non sequitur.)

We had another cold spell, predicted to last 5 days, so last night I got tired of having no bedroom fire and moved to the back bedroom with Bob's crows and Smoky and Smoky's pan. Smoky hated the change and wet in the corner out of spite.

... Finally heard from Arthur, who will be in Alaska all winter, doing the same work. His engine broke down irrevocably and he thought maybe that would finish him, but the government evidently considered the work vital, for they gave him an AA-I priority *over* army supplies, for a new engine. Of course, he ate up all his profits, but he said he wouldn't be broke, even after paying for the new engine. There will be wonderful possibilities in Alaska after the war, for those who know how to pick them.

All my love.

. . . .

(TLS, 2 pp.)

[Cross Creek, Fla.]
Dec. 3, 1943

Dearest:

Add hazards of war: I realized all my underwear was ragged, and went into Akras in St. Augustine to stock up. I was allowed to buy only two slips, one brassiere, and two pairs of panties—and the panties were the dreadfully old-fashioned kind with draw-strings. I came back to the Creek, I put on the new panties, I go to the bathroom, (you know how it is, sometimes you sort of wait until the last minute) and there, instead of being able just to drop the drawers, I have to go through all the fumbling and untying the bow-knot without turning it into a hard knot, and not letting it slip back where I can never get it again—and oh, dear. It seems dreadful to have the Germans and the Japs mixed up with a lady's panties.

The peacocks slept last night on top of the duck pen, and the ducks raised hell all night. Tonight they are sleeping on top of the tenant house. Martha said they must be more used to colored people, as they had hung around her place all day. I said that it was amazing that peacocks would be that observing. It is true that a colored man took care of them at Gist's.

... I had a letter from Edie today, and Verle has finally been assigned to Combat Intelligence, and is being sent to Harrisburg, Pa. to school. Edie is going to the Poole's[1] farm in New York. I wrote you that Scribner's is terribly enthused about her book.

Such a racket is going on in the grove. I told Jack to shake the pecan trees, and he is high in the largest tree by the cow-lot, the pecans are rattling like hail on the tin roof of the barn, and Jack and Sissie are singing at the top of their voices. Jack is shouting, "Ain't we havin' a time." Jack tore his breeches and there were wild shrieks of laughter from Martha and Sissie with Hettie Lou giggling in falsetto. . . .

All my love,

1. Ralph and Kitty Forsythe Poole, from whom MKR bought the Crescent Beach cottage.

(TLS, 2 pp.)

Darling:

...I feel just as you do about writing. Many a day, when I have already mailed your letter, I feel like writing you again, and would, except that I have used up all the day's small news. Writing to you is really my greatest pleasure. I am just so afraid that you will receive some of the grouchy letters (never grouchy at you) and the nice ones or the gay ones will be the ones to go to the bottom of the sea. And it is beyond my power to affect sprightliness when I don't feel it. But I always love you, no matter how cross or depressed I may be. And there is never a day when the thought of seeing you again doesn't make my heart beat faster.

...Forgot to tell you that Aunt Ida is bearing down heavily these days on the use of the word "initiative," which she pronounces inn-ativ.

...Idella keeps her promise to come right after Christmas, I'll get along fine at the Creek and then the cottage, and we can get a fabulous rent for the apartment by the month if Ruth does leave. I shouldn't care to rent to transients, but anyone nice by the month would be all right.

Chet Crosby stopped by to report that he was still trying to get the man to come and fix my fireplace. I hoped he would ask Moe and me to hunt with him tomorrow, but he didn't. It is a treat to Moe and me, but none to Chet. He is in great demand as a hunting partner, because his dog and his shooting are so good, and he also knows where to find the birds.

Oh, did I tell you that Snow Slater is home on ten days' furlough and he and Ella May, with George Fairbanks trailing them like a happy dog, came over for a visit. Snow looks fine, is a private first class, is out of limited service but assigned to non-combat duty, as it seems he has no sight at all in his left eye. Which is amusing, as he has just made the Expert grade at marksmanship. . . .

All my love, sweet, and oh, what I would give to have you drive up to the gate!

. . . .

(TLS, 2 pp.)

Dearest:

I should welcome a friend, but am too tired to fool with strangers. Pleasantly and physically tired. Chet came by late yesterday and asked if I'd like to hunt this morning, after I had given up hope of being asked. He was taking out for its first lesson a puppy, litter-mate of the one he gave Norman Berg, and I suppose he figured it could make things no worse to take along Moe and me. Moe did much better today, and I think with one or two more lessons, would come close to being a hunter. The puppy was a little female he had turned over to a Negro to raise, and the Negro had named it "Ruth," no doubt after some very special brown gal, and of all darned names for a dog. It was a riot to hear Chet yelling "Ruth" across the piney-woods. She was totally undisciplined, and with the combination, even Chet's shooting was bad, and he only got three birds, and I shamefully shot a dove out of a tree. The woods were beautiful, and I enjoyed it regardless, but Chet really walked me down. Even he was tired when we quit at 12:30, and he said we had walked "at least" two miles *more* than we did last week. We were actually hunting on foot 3½ hours, at a fast pace most of the time, and the only times we even *paused* was when we lost sight of the dogs, so you may know we covered the ground. I must have lost pounds—but unfortunately, even after lunch, I am still hungry, and am toying with the idea of whipping up, not an upside down cake, but a chocolate layer one. I'll be a damn fool if I do.

... I have just read, for the first time, Thomas Wolfe's first book, "Look Homeward, Angel,"[1] and after those awful letters to and from his mother, and after meeting his horrible sister Mabel, it was a *ghastly* experience. It is so autobiographical, and his family, with the exception of a brother who died, is so unspeakable, that I'm amazed that in their greediness *they* didn't sue. After he made good, I suppose they decided they'd get as much out of him by being polite—as polite as such people could be. Have you read it? I am so sorry I didn't read it before—it is magnificent—when I could have taken it as a fictional work of art. Of course, it took genius to do it, even though there can hardly be a single incident and person (in spite of his denials) that wasn't taken straight from life.

I have been unable to begin my book again as yet. I have evidently tried to hurry it too much. My subject is too big for my capacities, and if I am to handle it all, I must let it grow as it will. I have realized that it really is not laziness or shirking or worthlessness that has held me up—I simply was not as ready as I thought. I had an amazing dream the other night, almost in the nature of a revelation, and pertinent to my subject, so I know the fermentation is going on. . . .

All my love,

1. Thomas Wolfe (1900–1938), *Look Homeward, Angel* (New York: Scribners, 1929); *Letters to His Mother.* (New York: Scribners, 1943). MKR's admiration of Wolfe is extensively documented in her letters to Perkins (see *Max and Marjorie*).

. . . .

(TLS, 3 pp.)

[Cross Creek, Fla.]
Dec. 6, 1943

Dearest:

The back bedroom, with a cozy fire going in the fireplace, is a damn hospital ward this morning. Moe and Smoky and I are here, all laid up. Smoky is still just as ill as a kitten can be. The milk of magnesia continues to work a little, and Sissie and I got a teaspoon of mineral oil down him last night, per Dr. Nichol's[1] orders, and I thought that would finish fixing him up. But he still tries to get rid of something at both ends and nothing happens. This is the third day he has eaten literally nothing, and the fifth that he has had only a few mouthfuls. . . .

Moe is "stove up" from his hard hunting yesterday and was too tired to eat breakfast, and is asleep in front of the fire. I am so stove up that getting out of bed to put a piece of wood on the fire almost kills me. I started out on the hunt yesterday morning with an already-broken back, for foolishly, the evening before, I had taken a two-mile walk with Moe on that rough graveled road in thin, high-heeled shoes. . . .

Thelma and R. J. Shortridge[2] came out yesterday afternoon, with a somewhat dubious proposition. R.J. wants to buy a new tractor, turning in his car on it. Tractors are scarce, and each dealer gets only a small allotment. Shaw and Keeter, in Gainesville, who are Thelma's buddies, had six come in. They are not willing to let R.J. have one, for the reason that they made a deal with the Ford agency in Ocala, allowing Ocala to sell Mercurys, and Gainesville to sell Ford tractors, with no poaching—and Mercurys—now I'm mixed up on the details, but what it amounts to is that Thelma is in Marion County and I am in Alachua, and if Shaw and Keeter sold her, from Marion, a tractor, Ocala would get the commission and they would not, and with tractors limited, they naturally are not willing to make her a present of several hundred dollars. So Thelma wants me to buy the tractor, and turn it over to them. There seems to be no government ruling involved, just a little County dirty work, so I can hardly refuse, but I don't like these evasive deals.

. . . I haven't heard from Idella since I wrote her to come ahead. She should have received my letter ten days ago, and I asked her to let me know the exact date of her coming, so we could all get straight out here. I have said nothing yet to Sissie. If Idella does not come, I am almost tempted to let the Brices have Sissie, if Martha thought she could straighten up for me every day. Sissie is beyond the pale. When she lights one of the bathroom heaters, perhaps using two or three matches, she just drops the burned matches on the floor. Nothing can be done with a 35-year-old woman with habits like that.

Thelma has just gotten the promise of someone who would have been ideal, I think, for me—a mature, what she called "Southern Yankee nigger." I asked her to explain that, and she said it was a southern Negro, trained in the North, who had come back to the South! This woman was born at Anthony, and her people still live there, which is always a pull. She lived and worked in Philadelphia for many years, and Thelma says, has a Yankee accent. The woman she worked for, a long time, moved to California and she did not care to go, so came back here, and is recently married to a decent country Negro who wants to do grove work! They will live in Citra. The woman made $22.50 a week in Phila., but is willing to work for less (it must be *much* less, for Thelma does not pay well), as she said she never had anything left up there by the time she paid her living expenses. Doesn't that sound like the couple I've been dreaming of? Of course, you come back, in the end, to Martha—. She would never stand for any outside pair. Especially since Jack is here—though I cannot believe he will stay. . . .

All my love, darling.

1. H. C. Nichols, a veterinarian.
2. R. J. Shortridge had a farm near Citra.

. . . .

(TLS, 3 pp.)

[Cross Creek, Fla.]
Dec. 7, 1943

Dearest:

I feel as though I should use the Dec. 15 cable to say to you, "Forget the sapphire," but it would certainly be interpreted as code! I too am amazed at the price of a good one, unless you picked out one as big as a robin's egg. . . . As I wrote you in the earlier letter, if you found sapphires too high, I would love a moonstone . . . . Jewelry has always seemed to me the last legitimate way of spending money one didn't know what to do with. Year after year I have thought I might treat myself to a decent diamond from a thousand to fifteen hundred, and year after year since I've been making money I have given away a thousand a year (it was more than that this year). . . .

I went to Citra yesterday afternoon to telephone Dr. Nichols about Smoky. He seemed to think it was just a matter of time until he got over the upset, but he is still a terribly sick kitten. . . .

Sissie had a wonderful break, poor thing, and I am so glad. I had taken her to the Welfare Boards in Gainesville, who sent her to the Red Cross, (after Henry's death) to see if she rated any help for the children. She filled out applications, and there was hope that the government itself would allow her $40 a month for the care of the children. It must have been allowed, for yesterday she received a U.S. Treasury check for $186, which figures out $40 a month since Henry's death. I can draw a free breath about her now, for she is independent of the Brice's slavery system and of my charity.

Martha has begin getting her old age pension, so with what I pay her and free rent, the whole family is doing well.

. . . Well, must make some sort of pretense at work.

All my love, darling.

. . . .

(TLS, 5 pp.)

[Cross Creek, Fla.]
Dec. 8, 1943

Darling:

. . . Once and for all, you don't need to worry about me and any human monkeys. I have been alone long enough and suffered enough to know that nobody else even looks good to me. I not only long for my Bonny who lies over the ocean, but I long only to lie with my Bonnie. And my Bonnie had damn well better Not be lieing [*sic*] over the ocean! I couldn't resist that bon mot—I don't worry about you one bit. You have a mental control over your emotions that I have always admired, and it will not fail you now.

. . . I was interested in your account of being persona non grata at the American Red Cross, for just the other day there was a story in the papers telling of how hurt and angry the English were, that in places where the only rest and recreation facilities are the Red Cross, the English are not admitted under any circumstances. There was even an editorial about it, but it said that since space and funds were not limitless, the line probably had to be drawn. But I think it is drawing a goddam fine one not to let in the AFS graciously. Think I shall write to someone about it.[1]

There are things I would like to write about the emotional angle of our separation, but even though the censor is as indifferent as Buddha, you just can't bring yourself to say some things. It amounts to—that I love you.

. . . Smoky is very much worse.

All my love,

1. Possibly the source for MKR's story "The Shell," *New Yorker* 20 (9 December 1944): 29–31, in which insensitive treatment by a Red Cross worker leads to a tragic death. NSB said later that "The Shell" was his favorite MKR story.

. . . .

(TLS, 3 pp.)

[Cross Creek, Fla.]
Dec. 9, 1943

Dearest:

The moonlight is almost bright enough to write by, if I took the typewriter out by the gate. Moe and I are just in from a long walk up the road. My back is still broken, but it seems to help it to exercise, and the evening was too lovely to miss in any case. As we set out, I heard Martha singing like Lily Pons.[1] I had never heard her voice so high or of such a sweet and un-nasal quality. The occasion for her song was her joy at my having brought her a hundred fine collard plants from Ocala, which she had just retrieved from the car. When we came back, Jack had Aunt Ida's old Victrola going full blast, and it sounded as though the tenant house were falling down, with the stamping. Martha told me Jack is a good dancer and is teaching Sissie to dance.

I took poor little Smoky in to Dr. Nichols this morning and left him, and Dr. Nichols said, as I knew, that he was a desperately sick kitten. . . .

I made several calls while I was in town. I had a bite of lunch at the Marion, and wretched stuff it was, too, and such a surly waitress. I went out and saw Christine.[2] Like most of the stories told by one's most intimate friends, John Clardy's story of their selling off their entire herd was anything but accurate. They just sold a few, relatively, keeping their best stock. When I drove up, a cow was standing by the barn, and for a minute I thought there was another cow standing beside her, but it was only Christine's butt. My God, it was enormous. You could have played backgammon on the shelf. Christine looked very neat, and looked well, but Ray was dirty and unshaven and generally ratty. . . .

. . . I also cannot find the interview with Lollie Pop Twitter, which Cabell keeps hounding me about, to make him a copy.[3] Tomorrow, if my back is better, I'll turn the house inside out once more. All my stuff is in the most ghastly confusion.

. . . A letter from Julia was waiting when I got back from Ocala. She wants to come down soon after the first of January, if that suits me. Since my work just isn't "going," it will certainly be all right.

I am reading Dickens' "Bleak House"[4] and it is wonderful. It simply cries to have us read it aloud together.

I stopped by Crosy-Wartman's yesterday to see Leonard and asked him to bring his family out for the day. He looked very thin and badly, and he said his mother would not live much longer. Uncle Enoch died a week ago, the one who hid the book out in the bushes and there come a little sprinkle of rain on it. I think I have never lived a more literally enchanting time than when I stayed in the Scrub with Piety, and we visited back and forth with Uncle Enoch.[5] Everything was so new and glamorous, and I have never liked a group of people better, or admired them more. We got up no later than 4 in the morning, and ate breakfast by the warm kitchen wood range, by a lamp, but before we had finished, the light was breaking through the fog, and the lovely hammock to the east emerged bit by bit. The hunting at night, the fishing, the prowling, the listening to old stories, were wonderful. I have never been happier. . . .

All my Love,

1. Lily Pons, French-American coloratura soprano.
2. Perhaps Christine Townsend Polk. The subsequent reference to "Ray" might be a mistake for Rob Roy Polk, Christine's husband.
3. Lolly Pop Twitter, a name MKR used to sign one copy of the N. C. Wyeth illustrated *The Yearling* (Tarr, *MKR: A Descriptive Bibliography*, 68).
4. Charles Dickens (1812–1870), *Bleak House* (1852–1853).
5. Leonard, Piety, and Uncle Enoch Fiddia.

. . . .

(TLS, 1 p.)

[Cross Creek, Fla.]
Dec. 10, 1943

Dearest:

Poor little Smoky died today. In spite of my vow not to, of course I have cried bitterly. The death of a cat, these days, almost comes under the head of humor, in relation to the pretty fix the human race is in—but I had made the mistake of becoming fatuously fond of him, and he could no longer hide it that he loved me, too. He was daily more interesting and adorable. Love of all sorts is such a trap.

You pour your affection into fragile vessels, and they slip and crash, and there is your heart's blood on the ground—and it is possible to lose quite a little from even a little cat-vessel. . . .

All my love,

. . . .

(TLS 1 p.)

[Cross Creek, Fla.]
Dec. 11, 1943

Dearest:

In the morning's mail I had a letter from Idella saying that she was leaving New York tomorrow and would spend the holidays with her mother, and would be ready to come back here the day after New Year's. She wrote, "Please don't be cross with me, for I know I have been a bad girl, but from now on I am the same Idella (smiles)." It made me feel so good, that in spite of my sorrow over Smoky, when I read Emily Post in today's paper, it set me off again. I think I may have to bring out a small volume, "Ask Emily Post," but would probably have libel sued to hell out of me.

I am both terribly superstitious and terribly Ralph Waldo Emersonian,[1] and I firmly believe in the law of compensations, and I feel that I have swapped my darling Smoky for Idella. I cast an evil eye on my poor loving Moe, and actually hope he will be run over, so that it will guarantee your returning safe and sound. You must not take offense at my grouping you with nigger gals and Siamese kittens and bird-dogs. Remember of what comfort to you the Huston's are, and I should swap them any day for a pair of nice full-venomed rattlesnakes. Comfort and affection are all relative. Just to make you feel like a human being. I can only say that I would swap everything else in the world that I care for, human, animal and pertaining to Nature, to have you back with me.

If you think the enclosed is funny, and if your paper wants to carry on the saga of Baskin vs. Post, they may use it—but without my name. . . .[2]

All my love,

1. Ralph Waldo Emerson (1803–1882), American Transcendental philosopher.
2. MKR apparently wrote humorous anecdotes to be published in a military war newspaper. These items have not been located. The specific reference here is to MKR's response to Emily Post.

. . . .

(TLS, 5 pp.)

[Cross Creek, Fla.]
Dec. 12, 1943

Dearest:

I was looking through my address book for addresses for Christmas oranges, and came across the newspaper picture taken when we were married, and just had to kiss your sweet little old broad smile. But shucks, it was only newspaper after all.

Am just back, Sunday afternoon, from eating dinner at Thelma Shortridge's. She won a turkey in a raffle! She has no maid—the Southern Yankee nigger decided she'd prefer Ocala, but she, Thelma, pitched in and cooked the usual big country dinner, and the rest of us washed the dishes. . . . We drove out to R.J.'s beautiful fields—English peas, cabbage and lettuce, acres and acres—and lovely green beans being plowed under because they aren't bringing enough to pay for picking and shipping. Isn't it criminal, with hungry millions in the world? The human race is so stupid, such a bad manager, that it hardly deserves to survive. I am taking Martha and Jack out to the field in the morning and we are going to pick several crates, and Quincey Sykes[1] will can them for me.

Well, we have gotten into just the sort of mess out here, anent Idella's return, that I was afraid of in my bones—only I didn't think it would happen this way, and certainly didn't think the Brices would do it just for spite. As I wrote you, about three weeks ago when Idella accepted my offer of $20 a week and said she would come right after Christmas, but wanted me to be sure it was OK with Martha, I talked with Martha, with whom it was more than all right, then went down and talked with Mr. Brice. I told him Idella was coming back, but before I told her to come ahead, did they want Sissie. I knew they did, and were probably sore because I was using her full time. He said they certainly did. I said I was paying her $7 a week, and what could they pay her. I knew that if I didn't make an agreement for her beforehand, they would pay her starvation wages—and with things as high as they are, God knows it takes a genius to raise four little children on seven dollars. Mr. Brice said that was a little high for them, but they would pay her six, and wouldn't need her much more than half a day every day. I said Idella would come right after Christmas, but if they needed Sissie for Christmas, it was all right and I'd have Christmas some place else. He said they would have no company and did not.

Yesterday noon comes Idella's letter saying she was leaving New York this morning, and would be on the job the day after the holidays. This morning Martha brings me a note the Brices sent Sissie, telling her to vacate the little house she and Henry lived in, (all her things were still in it) tomorrow! It said they were moving a colored family in there tomorrow. A day's notice, mind you, and today Sunday to boot.

I went right down and saw Mr. Brice and said that I thought we had it all arranged that Sissie was to move back to the little house and work for them. He said we had. At first he tried to hedge, and said the house belonged to Armour, and Armour was sending the family down, and he himself knew nothing about it until last night. I asked if the new woman was to work for them, and he said, "No." I asked if they still expected Sissie, and he burst out, just as ugly as could be, that he didn't want anybody he couldn't count on, that she might work a day or two and then not show up. (Which isn't Sissie at all—she is completely reliable.) He said, "I'm not interested in any nigger that doesn't work for me. That's the only reason I'd keep one around, is to work for me when I want it. That's what they were born for." I said that I was sorry I hadn't known earlier of their change of plans, as I probably would not have let Idella return. I said I didn't know what to do, as there was not room for them all in my tenant house, but I certainly was not going to turn Sissie out on the road. He said nothing, and I made a comment on the weather, and left.

I got to thinking about it, and realized two things that were back of it. One, when *he* got to thinking about it, he was damned if he was going to pay Sissie $6 a week. He has always paid darkies not only just by the day, but by the hour— uses them, at low pay, when he needs them, and they can shift for themselves the rest of the time. It is part of the most evil angle of the Negro situation—the determination of people like that to keep the Negroes still in a practical slavery. The other thing I had been afraid of, that he and the whole family were sore that I had preempted Sissie in the first place, and that Martha has attached herself to me, too. And from something he said, he is evidently still sore that I used poor dying Henry the last year or so of his life. But I always asked Henry first if Mr. Brice needed him—and they had never spoken for Sissie, during Henry's illness or after his death. I suppose they thought she would just be on hand for an occasional day's work.

After I had seen him, I talked it over with Martha, and she said she would not have told me otherwise, but this week Mr. Brice stopped Sissie on the road and told her he had a good mind to pitch her belongings out on the highway. And he told Martha that I had made fools out of all the niggers at the Creek, and of George Fairbanks, too, but I needn't think I was the only one with money—he had just as much as I did. Martha is inclined to blame the quarrelsome Williams influence—she says they can't bear it that I've gotten ahead. Isn't it sickening? They know how poor I have been, and what I have been through here. I was always hesitant about paying people here more than Mr. Brice did, for I didn't want to make it hard for him to get help, but as far as I know, I never employed anyone he would have used otherwise. Except Sissie.

I had Jack take the truck and move all Sissie's things up here today, and am sending them down to clean the shack and yard thoroughly. Mr. Brice said it was a mess, and I want it done so there can't be any criticism on that score. Martha reported just now, after I got back from Citra, that when she and Sissie followed the first truck-load back, Mr. Brice and Mr. Williams stopped them on the road, and Mr. Brice said to Sissie, "I want to get all this rigmarole straight. You don't have to move out."

I realized then that they had planned it just this way—to order Sissie out about the time Idella was due, just to upset me! I don't know how we will work out the living space—I told Martha that Idella would have to have her room, regardless—but we sure as the devil will manage some way. We'll crowd them in somehow, and I'll gladly give Sissie enough to live on, rather than have her at the mercy of such people. If it weren't for the small children, I could get her a good job anywhere, but we are nicely stuck. It really has not upset me, and rather amused me, for as Martha said, she believed the Brices would find they have cut off their nose to spite their face. I even doubt the existence of the family that is to move in tomorrow! I don't know whether they expected Sissie and me to beg them on bended black and white knees to let her stay in that hovel of theirs, or not, but they're sadly mistaken. . . .

An hour later:

Well, this is *one* letter in which I tell my problems, and then add the answer. Mr. Williams and a Brice son, Vincent, have just been here, hats in hand. Whether the occupation of Sissie's shack is true or no, they were having fits at the idea of losing Sissie! I held them sternly to terms, and they are to pay her the $6 originally agreed on. I shall tell her that the first time they try to beat her down on it, or try to charge her rent, just to tell them politely that she can make more in Gainesville, (which is, of course, true) and that she has to have that minimum to live on. I am so tickled about it all I don't know what to do. They were evidently never prepared for Sissie's moving out pronto. So, all's well that ends well. . . .

Just to be generous, since I had won my point with the Brices, I told them that once they got the house business straight, Sissie could come to them any time, and I'd manage with Martha until Idella got here. They were much pleased, and said they did need her right away. Little do they know that it will be a blessed relief to me. Poor sweet Sissie has driven me almost nuts. This settles a point in my mind about Christmas, which will not be happy anyway without you. . . .

I expect to get tight, and hope you can do the same, just as an anodyne.

All my love darling.

1. Quincey Sykes, Cross Creek neighbor.

. . . .

(TLS, 4 pp.)

[Crescent Beach, Fla.]
At the cottage
Dec. 15, 1943

Dearest:

. . . I think I wrote you that we got things fixed up between Sissie and the Brices. They wanted to move Henry Woodward's "things," and I guess Henry, too, to one side of the little house, and have Sissie move in on the other! The meek Griselda[1] had spunk enough to tell them nothing doing—when Henry was out, she went in and not before. She said to me, "I don't like Henry well enough for that."

The large fine sow that I took for my rent on the field back of Brices, had her pigs just before I left for St. Augustine. I asked Martha how many there were—she had broken out of the pen and made a bed in the hammock—and Martha said they hadn't been able to see them yet, that she had tried to count the sow's tits but couldn't get a good enough view. This is a brand new idea to me, that you can tell how many offspring there are just by counting the tits. According to that, every woman has twins. I suppose Martha thinks that the number of tits obviously in active employment indicates the number of piglets, but you know the mama pig does not engrave their initials on the different faucets, and if she did number them, the piglets would certainly cheat. And there must be plenty of times when there is not tit for tat.

. . . Oh dear God I wish you were here. You have been gone more than five months—it will be six by the time you receive this, and it gets worse every darn day. I thought I was going to be able to laugh off Christmas, but I'm not. I'll be so glad when it's over.

. . . I have absolutely nothing un-read here, to read, except Dostoyevsky's "The Idiot,"[2] and I have a hunch I'd better leave that alone, a day like this! . . .

All my love, darling.

1. Sissie is being compared to the celebrated patient Griselda in Chaucer's "The Clerk's Tale."
2. Fyodor Dostoyevsky, *The Idiot* (1868).

. . . .

(TLS, 3 pp.)

[Crescent Beach, Fla.]

Dec. 16, 1943

Dearest:

Here I am, still dug in at the cottage like a hibernating bear, just because it's abominable weather and I don't want to go home. Had fully intended to return yesterday. After the storm, it turned bitter cold, and is still dark and gray to boot, and the cottage is very cozy. If Leonard hasn't been to the Creek to repair the two underminded-bedroom fireplaces, I'll freeze to death over there. I haven't seen a newspaper for three days, am running out of cream and eggs and such, and don't care whether school keeps or not. Am figuring how long I could live on the stores of queer canned goods. I have green turtle soup, canned hearts of palm, stuffed olives and antipasto—guess I'd better go home.

The ocean is slate-gray, and is fair boiling. The high tide is roaring in at the foot of the sand dunes. I only stick my nose out to bring wood from the porch. Moe set out both last night and this morning to see his girl . . . and turned around and came back shivering. It was too cold and wet for friendship, let alone love.

. . . Why aren't you here, to live with me on green turtle soup and olives and love? Echo answers, "Why?"

I MUST clean up and go home!

(TLS, 4 pp.)

[Cross Creek, Fla.]
The Creek
Dec. 17, 1943

Dearest:

I wish to Heaven I had stayed at the cottage. As I wanted to do. Since you'll probably receive this a month ahead of the last two days' letters, will mention that I spent three days at the cottage, and it was storming, and turned bitter cold, and I was cozy there and hated to leave. Especially as both bedroom fireplaces at the Creek had caved in, so that I couldn't have a fire in either room without setting the house on fire. Leonard had promised to come and re-lay them the first day it rained. . . .

Well, to tell my tale of woe and get it over with. I reached home a little after six, and the temperature was dropping fast. To be brief, we had one of our genuine dandy freezes. I don't know how low it went, but at 9 A.M. it was exactly 32, and was still 32 at 10:30, and even the *ground* was frozen. Water pipes all frozen. I don't know about orange damage. Won't know until tomorrow's paper. I just went out to face my garden, but it was not hurt nearly as much as I expected. The rose bushes came through, the new tender foliage nipped a little, the narcissus came through (a mass of bloom) and evidently the calendulas, about to bloom, came through. Some of the ranunculas, which I supposed were very hardy, looked touched. I can't tell about them until later. Broccoli, lettuce, etc. not hurt. As I drove in, I realized we were in for it, and cut my poinsettias and burned the stems, and am enjoying them. Then I looked at my mail, and that cable upset me so that I never thought about another thing, and of course since I didn't tell them, Martha and Jack never thought about covering the plants, though they knew a freeze was coming. Leonard had not been here, so I couldn't have a bedroom fire, and was never warm all night long. Heating the big living room is impossible. Moe and I are practically in the fireplace, and still shivering.

. . . I have written you that Julia will be down early in January. I have heard from Arthur again, and there is a possibility that he will come down for a while, if he doesn't soon get the new engine for his boat. (Which I have written you about.) He wrote that he feels that he could do no more useful work than his transportation of defense workers, especially since three steamers have just quit the job, due to difficult conditions. The censor may not let the statement through, but it is *my own idea* that there is no question but that we are building bases in Alaska preparatory to bombing Japan from there. In a way, I want Art to come very much, and in a way I don't. I am in such a peculiar frame of mind, and feel as if I wanted to battle things through all alone. The book seems hopeless. Yet I can't sit back and do nothing—and am doing exactly that—except for an occasional requested piece of war propaganda for radio or magazine use. But I think I might be able to do Art some good. . . .

Well, darling, whatever you're doing and wherever you are, all the luck in the world, and all my love, *always.*

. . . .

(TLS, 2 pp.)

[Cross Creek, Fla.]
Dec. 17, 1943

Dearest:

When you wrote me that the Red Cross was anything but gracious to the AFS, it so happened I had just done, by request via Carl Brandt, an editorial bit for the Red Cross drive. I wrote Carl about your experience right away, and asked him to check with the proper person or persons. I enclose his answer, and I hope it means action, and that the Red Cross will soon receive orders to admit AFS members on the same basis as all other Americans. Carl is really wonderful about "coming across." The next time you want to go into a Red Cross Canteen, if orders have not reached them, you could mention that the matter is being taken up in Washington.

There are several bits in Bee McNeil's[1] letter that will interest you—especially the Negress in Maginn's! I have qualms every now and then about paying Idella $20, especially if I'm not going to earn it by getting work done on the book. Then I decide that $20 a week wouldn't be a darn bit of good to me if Sissie drove me into the nut-house, whither she has been pushing me step by step. I wonder why more of the Alabama Negroes don't migrate?

I meant to mention that it snowed in Pensacola, and no flurry either, but the real thing. . . .

All my love.

1. Beatrice Humiston McNeill, a close friend and classmate of MKR's at the University of Wisconsin.

. . . .

(TLS, 2 pp.)

[Cross Creek, Fla.]
Dec. 18, 1943

Dearest:

It was 32 degrees again this morning. The ice did not melt all day yesterday on the wash-pot. My garden came through very well, and we covered the plants last night, but the beautiful Turk's-cap bushes are frozen to a crisp, and patches of orange and tangerine leaves are curling. I still don't know about the fruit, though it can stand 32 a long time. This morning I had Sissie pour hot water in the frozen bird-bath, and in a few minutes two little doves were sitting all hunched over in it, warming their feet! . . .

All my love,

(Wire)

(CROSS CREEK, FL)

DECEMBER 19, 1943

DARLING IT WILL BE A BLUE CHRISTMAS WITHOUT YOU BUT HERE'S
BOTTOMS UP ANYWAY LOVE

. . . .

(TLS, 4 pp.)

[Cross Creek, Fla.]

Dec. 20, 1943

Dearest:

. . . I missed writing you yesterday. Cliff and Rebecca and the Dumas had accepted an invitation by 'phone Saturday to Sunday noon dinner, and of course I
had everything to do myself. Thought I'd get through in time to write you before
they arrived, but they came quite early. Rebecca did not come—although it was
Sunday, the beauty parlor was "fixing" her, the only time they could give her.
Probably getting her hair tinted poinsettia red for Christmas. Cliff was very
good-natured and seemed to enjoy himself. I had a big ham I had been saving,
and had him carve, and had to battle him to make him cut the slices out of the
middle, instead of at the scrappy leg end. I had ice cream for him, and after dinner he went to my room and slept for three hours, so he was happy. He is looking
very well. Kathleen is looking grand, and Charlie looks better than I expected,
knowing how ill he has been. He is terribly game. They are really both awfully
nice, and I'm very fond of them. They are staying with Rebecca until after Christmas, then going to Pompano on business, then will be ready for the cottage—and
the time element is not going to work out very well for me, as they will be just
about there while Julia is here. If Julia should happen to like them, we could of
course spend an occasional week-end with them at the beach, sharing the guest
room, but it would not be as pleasant. And if Julia took one of her dislikes to
Kathleen—who definitely has to be understood!—it would be just too bad.

. . . The Dumas' saw Louise Somervell recently and said she is simply skin and
bones. Brehon is a full Lt. General, and if Eisenhower is put in command of
forthcoming combined operations, Brehon has been mentioned as a candidate
for Chief of Staff. . . .[1]

In the enclosed by Steinbeck,[2] I think he had the praiseworthy motive of destroying any myth about the German superman—but the myth is long exploded
anyway, and I think he over-reached himself. He makes you so damn sorry for
the poor guy, so conscious of the common humanity of all stupid men, all dupes,
that you forget to be angry at Germany in general!

Black Jack put one over on me yesterday—that darn trouble-making truck. It
has been understood that he cannot take it joy-riding, both because he is too

young to be trusted and because I cannot skimp on my short gas rations and then let a young buck nigger use it to have a good time. But once in a while he can use it to take Martha to church and while she is there, he can visit his friends. I asked him Saturday if they wanted to go any place Sunday, and he said yes, to church, so I said all right. Whereupon he told Martha I had said he could take the truck, and he took off alone yesterday and got back some time in the late hours— after 1 A.M., I know, for I was awake until then. It is a proposition.

... This is the fourth morning of freeze in succession. It has been very trying, not being able to have a fire in the bedroom. And not even Smoky to keep my back or stomach warm. My, I do miss the little fellow. You will probably get this letter ahead of the others saying "A freeze came in last night," and you will think it is one freeze after another.

Although I am terribly nervous, I am wonderfully well. That operation did me an immense amount of good, and I begin to realize how the way I felt before, was getting me down. I stopped by to see Dr. Harris just to say hello, but he was out. Will try again. He said to let him know if I was unduly nervous, as he had something simple that was helpful, and I might as well take advantage. I think it is mostly mental, the nervous worry about you, not being able to work on the damn book, Sissie, etc. And of course when I do get to work again, I can expect the fidgets—so it doesn't bother me. I think only a damn fool would not be nervous, these days!

The 5th Army is making gains in Italy, but at high cost. The radio said yesterday that in the last successful action, all the officers of several companies had been killed or wounded....

Am biting off all my fingernails until I hear from you again.

I love you so much.

1. General Brehon Somervell and his wife, Louise. General Dwight D. Eisenhower, then supreme commander of the Allied Expeditionary Forces in Europe. Eisenhower chose General George Marshall instead of Somervell.
2. John Steinbeck (1902–1968), *The Moon Is Down* (1942).

. . . .

(TLS, 4 pp.)

[Cross Creek, Fla.]
Dec. 20, 1943

Dearest:

Three of the most gorgeous letters came from you today, actually six or seven, for they were doubles. They are wonderful, and make me feel so close to you, physically and inside of you. They were censored, however, with no great damage that I could determine, by a complete misanthrope, who gloomily snipped a bit here and a bit there just because he felt like snipping. I think he could tell that we loved each other, and I am sure his wife, if he has one, doesn't love him—so he stared off into space and hated the world and once in a while, snipped. He snipped out two of your dates at the tops of the letters—then paid no attention to "today was Thanksgiving". . . .

I wish you would not ever stop to think what my "mood" might be when I receive a letter. I have often told you that you could snap me out of a mood any time you cared to bother. And the worse my mood, the quicker I surge out of it when a letter comes from you. I hardly know which kind I love best—the humorous ones or the tender and rather sad ones. I love them all.

. . . I can't tell you how interested I was in your account of going into the cold private storehouse. If you have really never been in it before, I can tell you that yours is not the only one that is cold and empty—they all are—that's the hell of it. Mine is not a house, or a room, but a deep black pit. There is *never* anything in these places. Yet because they are isolated in time and space, they are almost the only places into which important things are free to enter. If you stay in long enough, you go mad, or blow your brains out—but if you wait patiently, you become aware of something that is like a cross between phenobarbital taking effect, and the first drink after a hard day. You become a tightly-strung instrument for the play of forces that are around and beyond us. Sometimes the tune is audible, so that you can seize on definite ideas or emotions— and anything good that a writer does, comes this way—and it is why a writer is obliged to go alone into this void. Sometimes there is nothing that can be expressed or identified, but you are left with a surge, a lift, that can come no other way, for the circumstances of daily living, the mass of people, make an impenetrable barrier to this so delicate thing that comes on velvet feet in the hush of solitude.

And as you have found, it is only one person you want when the sadness is too great. I think it was in "Golden Apples" that I said, "For to comfort any mortal against loneliness, one other is enough." And I think it is only in the happy relation of man and woman that the comfort is found. It has always seemed to me that the love of one's own child must be the strongest emotion possible, or at least I have wondered if it was not. Yet insensitive people are often violently maternal or paternal, and then it is only a primitive or entirely egotistic feeling. And apparently sensitive people are able to abandon their children if necessary to be with a certain man or a certain woman. But certainly the right man and the right woman together can fight the cosmic terror as can no other combination.

The completely gregarious are free of this torment, but they also miss "the power and the glory,"[1] and even if it saddens you, it is wonderful to me to have you go into this secret place and understand these things. For one selfish reason, I shall seem less "queer" to you! And we have shared so much, that even at the cost of pain to you, I am glad to have you learn to share the last cold but magnificent outpost. It is the core of life.

Your fear of want and poverty is truly an amazing counterpoint to my fear of homelessness. I have never had the slightest fear of going hungry, and I think this is because my rural living, and adaptability to it, have shown me how unnecessary it is to go hungry—-*in rural life*. Where one lives in a town or city, or is dependent on a job, starvation can stalk like one's shadow. On a piece of ground that one owns, it is almost literally impossible. Poverty is part of my background, too, but I fear of the homeless wandering and not the hungering. My life has been unstable, and I suppose it is because of that, that I have clung so to the shabby Creek. It has represented something tangible, something stable, something I could count on, when family, love and what-not came and went. I have been sure of your love for a long time, but the hotel represented two horrors to me: the entirely extrovert life, which as I just said, is a barrier to the secret and important things; and the transitory nature of it—the transitory people (A. J. Cronin said to me that one of the most awful words in American usage was "transients"). Oh darling, we should be able to work out such a wonderful life together. Just come back to me safe, even with a leg or an eye missing! And we can put up a front against all the devils in the universe.

. . . Yes, our demands on England about India are absurd. Especially, since we are still trying to keep the Negroes slaves. If you will ask for Eve Curie's book, "Journey Among Warriors,"[2] you will find a fine chapter on India. It seems that Cripps' offer[3] was practically, certainly eventually, that of complete independence, but the warring interior factions mistrusted one another and would not accept it. Yet much of England is very greedy and selfish, as witness Churchill's statement that he had not become prime minister in order to preside over the dissolution of the British Empire. There is no more reason why Britain should have an Empire, than Japan. Again, it is the Haves and the Have-Nots. And from a cosmic point of view, all this business of nations and empires is as archaic as tribal warfare. There are only, in the last analysis, human beings.

Darling, you can never say again that you only ride the wave. You are a truly big person, and you are your brother's keeper,[4] and doing a more practical job of it than I. In short, you are wonderful, and I love you terribly.

1. Perhaps an allusion to Graham Greene (1904–1991), *The Power and the Glory* (New York: Viking, 1940).
2. Eve Curie (1904–), *Journey Among Warriors* (New York: Doubleday, Doran, 1943).
3. Stafford Cripps, leader of the House of Commons, was sent by Winston Churchill with an offer to give India a leadership role in self-government. The offer was rejected.
4. Genesis 4:9, Cain's response to God, "am I my brother's keeper?"

. . . .

(TLS, 4 pp.)

[Cross Creek, Fla.]
Dec. 22, 1943

Dearest:

I have just had a most interesting experience—one I knew was coming sooner or later—that I had been dreading—and once it happened, there was no more dread—I am referring to an overnight visit of Zora Neale Hurston!

. . . Well, all that put me late, and I drove in home after seven o'clock, and here was a strange car up by the Kohler house. Sissie came over to fix supper and unload my car, and I said, "Whose car is that?" She said, "Somebody came from Daytona to see you." I said, "Do I know her?" and she said, yes. I thought of course it was Dessie and even as I asked if the visitor was in uniform, I remembered Dessie was in Texas. Sissie said, "She said she had a letter from you this morning." I said I hadn't written to anyone in Daytona, and asked where the visitor was. Sissie said, "She at the house with Mama. She colored." Then I clicked at once. I had thought of Zora, alone on her houseboat, and had dropped her a Christmas note and said if she would confirm her address, I'd like to send her oranges and pecans. As it came out, my note had sounded terribly depressed and blue, and I had spoken of making no progress on my book, etc.—and she had decided maybe she could help me or give me a lift, and had dropped her work and driven clear over here just to try to cheer me up. She had arrived a few minutes after I had left for Gainesville, and had been waiting.

Well, I had the most mixed emotions. I was so touched by her doing it, as I was touched by her offer to do my housekeeping while I worked—and it was suppertime, and it was night-time and bed-time—and dat old debbil prejudice fair stuck a needle in me. I was ashamed, and I was worried, and I thought this would probably be the evening Mrs. Glisson[1] would come up to ask me something, and the word would go out, and I would lose the law-suit!

Meantime, Martha and Sissie had fallen *fatuously* in love with Zora—and Zora herself had arranged things with such modest tact that I felt like a dog for having any qualms. Martha came over to say that she had supper ready for Zora. I said no, I wanted her to have supper with me. And I thought, "Watchman, what of the night?"——[2] and Zora had already been invited by Martha to spend the night there, and had taken her bags over there, and was taking it for granted that she would sleep there—and if I was a bitch about it, Zora would never have blinked an eyelash. It was all so quietly and gracefully done to spare me any embarrassment, if I proved the sort who needed sparing! And I thought of the tenant house already crowded to the rafters, and my empty house, and I thought, damn it, now is the time for all good men to come to the aid of a moral principle! So I said I didn't want to be selfish or disappoint Martha, but I had so much more room, and would Jack please bring her bags over here to the back guest room. And I have never in my life been so glad that I was not a coward. I had to hurdle an awfully wide ditch! I was amazed to find that my own prejudices were so deep. It has always surprised me that my thinking is so Southern. But I felt that if I ever was to prove my humanitarian and moral beliefs, even if it cost me the lawsuit I must do it then.

Well, from spending that time with Zora, who is a nigger, who is an artist, who is big and wonderful, I have advanced a long way, and she helped me in a way that she never thought of. She is entirely at home in both the white and the negro world, and any citizen of the cosmos should be so at home, and I am way ahead by the experience. We had a fine time, and by the time she left an hour ago, I had gone a long way.

She told me that in talking with Sissie before I came in, Sissie had said to her, "Mrs. Baskin is different from anybody I've ever known. She don't want you to be low and humble. She wants you to be up. There isn't anything in the world I wouldn't do for her." This made me feel good particularly in knowing that I had hid from Sissie my irritation with her. Zora also told me that Sissie said she would not work for "those people," (the slave-driving Brices) but was going to Hawthorn when Idella came. And as long as Sissie feels that she has a *choice*, and is not obliged to be knocked around here, I think that is fine. I have told her that she must educate her four very nice little children, so that they would not have to spend their lives working for the Brices at four dollars a week when the Brices felt like paying it.

And last night, after Zora was in the back room and I in the front bedroom, I had a nightmare. In the nightmare, I was taking a stand, and had gone to a negro football game where "high whites" were to be, and I was going with Negroes as a moral gesture. And it was going to cause me trouble in the lawsuit, and was going to make a pariah of me, and I hated it, but the die was cast. And when I reached the boxes, and a Negro came out and fervently welcomed me and I felt quite ruined, lo and behold, you were suddenly by my side, and were shaking hands with the Negro, and I had the most wonderful feeling of your standing by me. In the nightmare, you were a Dean of a college, and it was going to make trouble about your job, but you were there beside me, making the gesture with me. And I woke up.

Zora is much more conservative about the "Negro question" than I. She feels that it is up to the Negroes to prove themselves as human beings, but I feel that a fight must be made, human nature being as selfish as it is.

She drove off.

I read her an excerpt from one of your letters, and she said, "Why, that's literature." And so it was. But darling, if you can avoid it, please don't be another writer. Just go on being a wonderful and sensitive extrovert. . . .

All my love, darling.

1. Pearlee Josey Glisson.
2. Isaiah 21:11, the oracle: "Watchman, what of the night?"

[Cross Creek, Fla.]
Dec. 22, 1943

Dearest:

I am whipped down by three little nigger babies. After Zora Hurston left this morning about eleven, the truck set out with Mrs. Bernie Bass[1] driving, and Martha and Sissie, to go to Gainesville for Christmas shopping. At the last moment Martha asked if Jack might go. Jack was in disgrace, but since it was his one chance to Christmas-shop, I said all right. And it appeared that old Will had already gone to Gainesville with someone else, to Christmas shop. Sissie turned casually on departure and asked if I would mind keeping an eye on the children. This rather floored me, but everyone was dressed in their best bib and tucker, and I could not ask anyone to stay home to keep me from having to keep an eye on the children. So I said all right, but to tell them to stay put until I called them. The day was warm and Sissie assured me there was no fire in the house for them to fall into.

I wrote my letter to you about Zora's unexpected visit, I fixed myself a sandwich, and tried to decide on something to read until I should have gathered my strength to set out 170 flower plants I bought in Gainesville yesterday. I had counted on Jack's help in setting them out, but Christmas comes but once a year, thank God. I became aware of chirping like that of sparrows, and went back, and here sat Sissie's three little blackbirds on my back steps, waiting to be called. The oldest is Hattie Lou, aged 5, then comes Martha, aged 4, then David, very black and round, like a rich plum pudding, aged 2. It was all up then with gathering my strength. When I tried to return to the front of the house to read, they encircled the house like Indian fighters and called out, "Mis' Baskin?" until I gave in. I decided that the best way to kill three blackbirds with one stone was to go ahead and set out my 170 plants, and let them "help" me. The help was to consist of Hattie Lou's and Martha's taking turns at handing me a plant, one at a time, and keeping David out of the garden. This worked for the first dozen plants. Then they were all in there pitching, handing me plants. The Natural Gas man came, in answer to my frantic telegram saying that the refrigerator had gone out and food was being ruined. The Natural Gas man and I bent over the recalcitrant flame, and here were three little niggers bending over it too, breathing in my face. I felt something soft on my head, and it was Martha's little black paw, stroking me and feeling the, to her, strange texture of my hair. We returned to the garden. Hattie Lou, who has a deep bass voice that runs on like a stuck Victrola record, is a little sycophant. Whenever she realized that I was just about to throw them all out, she would say, "You sure does water good," or "You sure does set out plants good." When it came Martha's turn to hand me plants one at a time, she said, "I love you, Mis' Baskin." David, who had not opened the mouth in his black pudding face, announced stoutly, "I love you, too," grabbed up a plant to bring me, and trod straight down the row of delphinium I had just completed. I counted to ten, and said gently, "Don't step on the little plants, David." I was horrified to have David burst into a loud bawling and thought of course it was because he was hurt at being ordered off the delphinium. Not at all. It was just that nobody had thought to take David to the Mickens outhouse, and some sort of control having been urged upon him, catastrophe had overtaken him. He stood howling and peed on the delphinium.

I suggested that Hattie Lou and Martha take him home and change his breeches, but they said he had none to change to. I am sure he did, but they could not bear to leave the fascination of the new life. David was inconsolable over his accident, so Hattie Lou said she would give him a ride in the wheelbarrow. I agreed doubtfully and correctly, for where David's breeches had been only wet, they took up all the dirt from the wheelbarrow, so that he seemed soaked in ink. And of course Hattie Lou upset the wheelbarrow and pitched David out and he howled again and had to be allowed to pass plants to quiet him. David and I got along nicely and he only stepped on every other delphinium, and Hattie Lou found my mop and said she would wash it for me, and soaked herself from head to toe. About this time there came a queer high sound from Martha by the duck-pen. Hattie Lou said, "You know what that is, don't you?" I confessed I did not. Hattie Lou said, "She mockin' you. She bein' Mis' Baskin." And sure enough, it was recognizably and embarrassingly my voice, not only calling, "Jack! Martha! The gas is out!," but doing so in sickeningly dulcet tones plainly intended to take the curse off my routing them out at night to put gas in the Kohler tank. Every now and then through the nightmare that was the afternoon, Martha would suddenly "be" Mis' Baskin, and high saccharine notes would announce the dearth of wood or what-not.

Hattie Lou said, "We is to mind you just like you was our Mama, isn't we?" I said that was the general idea. She said, "You'll beat us if we don't mind you, won't you?" and I admitted accurately, by that time, that I would. Whereupon they decided to call me "Mama" and there seemed nothing I could do about it. Being Mama was stopped only by Martha's taking up the game that she and Hattie Lou evidently played together, "being" Mis' Baskin, for Martha suddenly ordered Hattie Lou to move the hose, and in the ritualistic way in which you play the Baskin game, "Who comes"?, Hattie Lou said, "Who is you?" and Martha said "I is Mis' Baskin," and Hattie Lou meekly moved the hose. This unfortunately attracted David's attention to the hose, and I looked up to see him with the nozzle half way down his throat, and about that time Martha turned the water on. I comforted David with apples—but alas, he was not sick of love, and still dogged me to hand me plants. Several times I told them to be very quiet for just a few minutes, and slipped in and lay down on the davenport to smoke a cigarette, but always the Indian war dance around the house began, and they called out to know what I was doing. I called back that I was resting, and Hattie Lou's Helen-Morgan[2] voice reported, "She restin,' her and old Moe." In between times they had chased Moe and he was worn out, too.

Dusk came, and the chickens and ducks and the peacocks began milling around, so I went into the barn to get feed for them. The chicken feed was low in the heavy metal barrel, so I held it tilted while Hattie Lou held the feed bucket and Martha up-ended into the barrel and passed out small handfuls of feed. David sat happily and wetly on a sack of cow-feed. Suddenly the barrel became very heavy and Martha had disappeared. She had just curled up inside it, and came out reluctantly. The cows were lowing, and the sow with the nine new pigs was squealing for her supper, and Hattie Lou inquired hopefully if I was going to milk, for they would help me, and it seemed to me I could not endure another particle of "help," and the blessed truck drove in. I cried out to Martha, "Thank God," and she said, "Is you had enough?" And I had had enough, but David had not, and was dragged off screaming. Hattie Lou looked back and said, "David don't want to go. He loves you." And if anybody wants the help or the love of three nigger babies, they may have my share.

My back is broken, to boot, for I stuck with the 170 plants so I could "keep my eye on the children. . . ."

Morning, Dec. 23

Exhausted as I was, I sat down last night to write you my own story of the tar babies, for I knew I'd never remember the details, as with the Old Hen, later. And I forgot a riotous incident, as it was. Everything was quiet once, and although it was heavenly relief, I decided I'd better check, as God knows silence was more ominous with them than activity. I found the three of them sitting like statues in the front seat of my car, and Moe sitting like a statue on the back seat. David was at the wheel, holding it about head-level with a firm grip. The three little pickaninnies and Moe were all staring ahead, and I realized they were all going at 60 miles an hour. I should have just left them there, but David's pants were so very very wet—.

Must get my Christmas boxes together. Mrs. Townsend sent over a note this morning, as she did years ago, saying that Jesse and Thelma[3] hoped I would bring Santa Claus. Damn it, I have never missed a year in taking them a box, and it certainly destroys all my pleasure.

All my love,

1. Theresa Bass, wife of Charles Bernie Bass. The Bass family is described in *Cross Creek* (137–39).
2. Helen Morgan, a "torch singer" during the Jazz Age, famous for sitting atop a piano and singing sad songs.
3. Jessie and Thelma Townsend. The Townsend family lived at Cow Hammock, south of MKR's house, before moving north of Cross Creek near Bear Gut Road.

(TLS, 2 pp.)

[Cross Creek, Fla.]
Dec. 24, 1943

Dearest:

Three fat letters from you yesterday, and the adorable silver pin shaped like the cutlass. That made all the Christmas I want. . . .

I had a jolly little old Christmas present yesterday—the threat of another lawsuit. A firm of Los Angeles lawyers wrote that a client of theirs had owned a pet deer which died last year, and in 1935 she had an article about it in some magazine I never heard of, and that there were so many points of similarity between her article and "The Yearling," that they believe they had a claim for damages, infringement of copyright, plagiarism etc. It is absurd, as I never heard of the article, and old Cal Long[1] told me the story of his pet deer in the fall of 1933. And a dozen people have written me since the book saying how much their pet deer was like Flag, etc. But it is all a nuisance. I suppose they too think I may pay something just to avoid trouble and possibly unfavorable publicity, but they're mistaken. I sent the letter on to Phil to answer, and when they find I'm not disturbed and have a lawyer, too, they may have sense enough to drop it—unless the Los A. lawyers are unscrupulous and plan just to milk the woman who once had a pet deer. . . .

All my love,

1. Calvin Long, the pioneer who lived on Pat's Island in the Big Scrub, from whom MKR got material for her fiction, among other things the inspiration for Jody and Flag in *The Yearling*. Long was the prototype for "Old man Paine" in *South Moon Under* (233). See also *Max and Marjorie* (234), where MKR spells his name "Payne."

. . . .

(ALS, 6 pp.)

[St. Augustine, Fla.]
Dec. 26, 1943
Sunday

Dearest:—

. . . Well, coming over here for Christmas worked out very happily. I was damned if I was going to be a sissy, so I drank like a fish and made myself have a good time. I had fought off some bad moments, with success, but just before Christmas dinner yesterday it hit too hard and too unexpectedly and I burst out crying. Jean and Wallie[1] were wonderful to me and I had a good brief cry, then took another drink and we all made wise-cracks and all was well again. It may have been then that for some reason an innocent question of mine put Jean in hysterics. I had been to the bathroom twice and there was no toilet paper anywhere in sight. I said, "There's no hurry, but since I'm spending the week-end, where the hell is the toilet paper." We had another good laugh when Bingy said,

"Moe knocked a ball off the Christmas tree with his tail," and I said, "Your mother did the same thing."

Moe has behaved very nicely.

. . . I have been to see Aunt Ida three times.

I am taking Jean and the kids to the Castle for dinner, then we are going to Freddie's in the evening for a party. Harry Evans[2] gets in today. You'll never know how I missed you and thought of you, I know you did me. Must leave and will write more tomorrow. Everybody including the kids sends love.

All of mine,

1. Jean Francis and Wallie Bishop, who MKR believes are having an affair.
2. Henry Evans, a Harvard University classmate of Maxwell Perkins (see *Max and Marjorie*, 518).

. . . .

(ALS, 10 pp.)

[St. Augustine, Fla.]
Dec. 27, 1943
Monday at Jean's

Dearest:—

Had expected to go back to the Creek this afternoon, but am held up by a couple of things. One, a cocktail party Marjorie Collins[1] is giving for the other half of the sister act. The other, Christmas afternoon I had a minor accident with my car, and since everyone was closed Christmas and yesterday too, I had to wait until today to take it to Thompson.[2] I had swung out in San Marco to make a right turn into Jean's drive, had looked back and saw no car—you know there are blind spots in a car—so did not make a signal for a turn. A soldier's car was behind me, coming way too fast, and decided when they saw my red brake lights go on, that I was making a left turn, so tried to pass me to the right. They were wrong and I was wrong, but since not giving a signal is the worst sin, I assumed all responsibility. . . . I tore up two of their fenders and damaged one tire, and they tore my front bumper off and mashed my front fender so the wheel had no play, so I had to have it fixed. Nobody was even jarred, so it's O.K. . . .

1. Marjorie Meeker Collins, a poet and wife of General Vivian Collins.
2. Thompson Motor Co.

. . . .

(TLS, 7 pp.)

[Cross Creek, Fla.]
The Creek
Dec. 29, 1943

Dearest:

I returned to the Creek yesterday evening from my pleasant Christmas in St. Augustine, to an old-timey Creek nightmare. I had donated Sissie to the Brices,

and planned to make out with Martha until Idella came. I found Martha droop-
ing in her gloomiest mood, and for once she had good reason. All three of the
Brices are in bed with the flu that is raging, and Mrs. Brice's condition is serious,
so Martha had been sitting up with them every night, giving Mrs. Brice her
medicine. The poor soul was worn out. This morning Sissie is sick in bed with
the flu and my gas is out, and Jack is leaving. It is cold and gray and generally
depressing. Jack was very nice about it. He is going to a contractor he worked for
before and of course will make much higher wages than would be reasonable for
me to pay here. He said he would really like to stay, that it isn't the wages in question, as he can save as much here, but just that Martha won't let him go off Saturday nights! He is staying long enough to cut more wood for me, as it has been so
consistently cold that my fine woodpile is already depleted. And my bedroom
fireplaces are still "under-minded." The Creek is horrible when things take a spell
of going this way. The peacocks got in my garden while I was gone and ate all the
leaves off my broccoli, and the calf went down to the lower, unfenced garden and
cleaned off lettuce, cabbage, rutabagas and beets. I decided to go on the wagon
yesterday, and did, and shall remain, but I wish I'd chosen some other time. . . .

. . . The Collins Sister Act cocktail party was better than I expected, for James
Cabell and I retired to a corner and talked. A good deal about you. I said I just did
not know what I should do if anything happened to you, and he patted my head
and said nothing would. I said well, if anything did, I was going to be awfully
mad at God, and he said he could well imagine Judgment's Day being held up for
several days while I was quieted. The Cabells are coming over soon to spend the
night. I don't know whether they are bringing Ballard[1] and I certainly did not
specify him, for having him under my roof would give me worse monkey nightmares than before. I received a Cabell Christmas card and thought at first James
was using old English or being funny, for it was "Sessions Greetings from the
Cabielles"—then I realized by God that they had let Ballard make them out. I
should love to see the epic poems that he said he "did."

General Collins[2] sent his best to you, and told me that you had given him such
a lift that he was still riding on it. He said when he spent most of his time battling
with selfish men and cowards who wanted deferments, in walks a man who says
"I have to go. Will you help me to make it?" He said he has never been so proud of
anyone.

. . . The mail has come, and the last blow has fallen in the moment's nightmare. Phil sent me a copy of Zelma's brief for the appeal to the Supreme Court,
and I must admit that it is an impressive document, especially if the members of
the court are of the customary backwood's politician type of mind. It seems to
me that we are fighting this war just to prevent people like me from doing such
things to people like Zelma. And at one point, it said that it was interesting to
note that Zelma came from a Georgia family. It did not carry further the imputa-
tion of my immigrant and Yankee character. As it happens, one of the aunts just

sent me a page from the publication of the Institute of American Genealogy, and it is interesting to note that I come from Virginia and South Carolina families. But there is no doubt that this brief is clever enough to have an effect on some people. I was right in my fears about Zora![3] But I think my shame is still secret.

I must spend the afternoon writing Phil and giving him some notes that occurred to me, so will stop. I have some more things to tell you about the St. Augustine visit etc. etc.

All my love,

1. Ballard Cabell.
2. Vivian Collins, then adjutant general of Florida.
3. Zora Neale Hurston.

. . . .

(TLS, 4 pp.)

[Cross Creek, Fla.]

Dec. 29, 1943

Dearest:

It is ten-thirty at night, and I have just finished work on some notes for Phil May in connection with his answer to Zelma's brief, and I should be tired, but am keyed up. The brief was 42 pages long, and my notes to Phil were eleven typewritten pages. Much of what I did for him will not be useable, but I wanted to relieve my mind by taking up various points. With no one to wait on me, I am fixing food for myself, and eating queer things, mostly peanut butter sandwiches, and part way through my notes I was sick as a pup. I decided it was no time to go on the wagon, so have dipped in the Barclay's and damned if I don't feel a lot better. Will try to go back on again tomorrow.

The last point in the brief was that I had been "unjustly enriched" by the book at Zelma's expense, her personality having "a substantial sale value," and so she should be repaid "to the extent of the enrichment." So I got out the goddamn book and counted up the characters, and there are 120 identified by name, and many of them occupied much more space than she did, and I figured for Phil that on a pro-rata basis she might possibly get as high as $25, but if we counted the Baptist and Methodist ancestors, whom I mentioned, and Hawaii which I said had lost much of its horticulture since 1910, because of the Mediterranean fruit fly, Zelma owed me money! I don't know whether a lawyer would answer such a charge in this way, but it seemed pertinent to me!

In spite of my determined attempts to ignore it, this case has done a good deal to shred my nerves. I can't blame all my confusion and disorganization and inability to work, on my love's absence. Phil sent me a copy of the letter he wrote to the people who wanted to start something about "The Yearling," and I was happy to see him dismiss it as nonsense. He wrote me that he could not understand a reputable firm of lawyers even considering such a case, and that he was sure neither lawyers nor clients would spend money on such a will-of-the-wisp. It is good to feel confidence in Phil's integrity, for you realize how unscrupulous lawyers could milk anyone.

A bright spot in the Cross Creek mess—in answer to my telegram today, my gasoline man in Micanopy dashed out and filled both truck and Kohler tanks, so I will have water with which to bathe, lights to go to bed by, and gas with which to use the truck to get wood. The gas man is trusting me for coupons, but I don't see how the Rationing Board can deny me gas for such basic uses. I am very careful about my gas here, use just a few inches of bath water, listen to the radio in the dark, go to bed usually at 9 o'clock, and only let the truck go out for necessities— and am losing Jack because he has no way to go off for a little occasional recreation. . . .

. . . .

(TLS, 5 pp.)

[Cross Creek, Fla.]
Dec. 30, 1943

Dearest:

Heavy, heavy hangs over my poor head. I mailed off my eleven pages of notes to Phil May, and on the same incoming mail was a letter from the income tax office trying to hold me up for the full total of the British tax of $1120 in 1941— which is money that never even reached this country! They said I should have had a receipt and filled out a special form, which has never been asked before. Ten days allowed to sign enclosed waiver! I don't believe the British government bothers with receipts for American tax payers, and ten days wouldn't get a letter one way across the Atlantic. I think perhaps a notarized statement or something from Carl Brandt should fix it up. But I feel as though the wolves were at the door.

Now get ready for hysterics. Quotes from a Christmas note from Aunt Wilmer:

"Marjorie dear one:

At Christmas time and again in June (my Father's birthday)—you just suddenly become to me 'Marjorie Peaches' or 'Goldie' as I see you running toward me across the meadow out at 'the farm' in Brookland (we never had a farm in Brookland)—and, as an associated picture that *will* always appear; the large number and to me terrifying beautiful tan and white cows and calves chasing after you. Just a beautiful girl of sixteen blowing wild in the summer breezes."

Do you want that notarized to believe it?

And Auntie Mabel[1] in Chicago writes to "dear little Marjorie away off in Florida" and hopes that all is going well and most happily with me and "the good man whom you have chosen as your 'traveling companion.'" They are all hell on quotes, and where in God's name do they get their phraseology? Auntie Mabel also wants a profile picture of me—she "doesn't care very much for the full front view which has been used a good deal." By the full front view I suppose she means the one with all the bust. I am a fool not to have saved the letters of these women. If I outlive them, I shall write about them, and I could never remember those breath-taking and dinner-taking turns of speech. Marjorie wrote again about Marjorie Lou's[2] marriage and wondered whether the young man would be able to support her after the war (he will probably be killed in it.) She wrote, "I understand he is a musician by trade."

I suppose when you analyze it, it is just pure Jane Austen. As to an 18-year boy's being anything at all "by trade"—. All I know is that he thought he would like to lead a band. How many 18-year boys can you name who don't think they would like to lead a band? Marjorie Lou wrote me from Sacramento that they were having a wonderful time, thanks to my gift, and though Arthur, the old fogey, disapproves, I think it's fine.

. . . When I came home from St. Augustine, I found Chet and Helen Crosby had been out and left me three huge cuts of venison. Martha said Helen told her Chet was so excited about it she almost had to wash his breeches. Chet came out today to say he was ready to begin picking my fruit, and to tell the story of his deer hunt, the first deer he ever got, and he says, it will be his last. He couldn't even eat any of the meat. He had taken Shorty Davidson duck-hunting, and Shorty took him deer-hunting in the Silver Springs preserve near the Oklawaha. He put Chet up a tree, and Chet said shooting the buck when it drifted in, feeding, was like shooting a tame hog. He said he was glad to have gotten one, just so his kids could tell about the time Papa came home with the deer, but he has had enough. He is taking Moe hunting Sunday, but my back is bothering me again so I sha'n't go.

I talked with Jack again about his leaving, and the trouble really seems to be that Martha treats him like a 10-year-old. I found he is 26—and she doesn't think he should go frogging around Saturday nights! I may still be able to work it out, if that is really all there is to it. I found he wouldn't make much more than $4 a day on the new job, as against $3 here, and with his expenses in a city, he is better off here if I can make Martha see reason.

. . . When the Thompson Motor Co. fixed my car after my minor wreck, I removed some things from the car before sending it to them, but some of the black brothers went off with the new pair of gorgeous cream suede gloves Ruthie[3] brought me from Nova Scotia. They paid no attention to Aunt Ida's gifts to me—handkerchiefs other people had sent her, and two padded coat hangers which I was glad to have, but which she assured me she had had a long time. I suppose when I'm 83 I'll be stingy, too. God grant I am never 83. Unless you are with me, when I think we would make a pair of very cute old bridge players.

Well, it's practically six months since you have been gone, and I only wish I could wake up one morning and find the whole year elapsed.

I love you, darling.

1. Mabel Traphagen, youngest sibling of MKR's mother.
2. Marjorie Lou Kinnan, MKR's niece.
3. Ruth Pickering.

. . . .

(TLS, 3 pp.)

Cross Creek, [Fla.]
Dec. 31, 1943

Dearest:

Two very funny and utterly infuriating things happened to me in the line of Christmas presents. Julia Scribner gave me a year's subscription to the food magazine, "Gourmet"—Nettie Martin gave me a year's subscription to it—and beyond the fact that I don't give a damn about the magazine anyway, they have had me on their free list for two years, for they want me to do some articles for them!

The final Yuletide cruelty came today. I had thought there was no reason for Marcia Davenport to send me anything at all, but if she did, I thought it would be some choice little New York item, chosen with great discrimination and care. Her gift arrives today—a box of celery from Denver, Colorado!!!!!!!!! Not only is celery, as you know, No. 1 Taboo on my diet, but Florida reeks with celery, being grown as close to home as Shands muck farm, and packed at a large packing plant in Island Grove. And I suppose Marcia paid the outlandish price for the damn stuff that people pay for oranges when they order them from specialty companies in Florida. It is all most brutal and really very funny.

. . . I just stopped to listen to the news on the radio, and there was an announcement of British and American action near the Bay of Bengal close to the Burmese border. Now that the time has come for you to get into action, my courage oozes. But there's nothing to do but take it—and refuse to be a coward about it. I think 1943 has been one of the worst of my life, and I am glad to see it go. I pray only that we will be together a year from tonight. I love you with all my heart.

1944

1944 was a year of repeated traumas. MKR devoted most of it to writing NSB and to answering the letters of servicepeople. The preparations for the Cason lawsuit continued as well. And, when she had a moment, she would attempt starts at the writing of *The Sojourner,* her "cosmic" novel. She had not realized how dependent she was on NSB until he left. Even her beloved Cross Creek seemed filled with trials. Julia Scribner, among others, visited her regularly in an attempt to bring cheer to her emotionally laden life. In April, the news came that NSB's unit had been cut off by the Japanese, but after a harrowing two weeks it was reported that he had escaped capture. In May, a fire at the Castle Warden killed two people, one of them, Ruth Pickering, a good friend of the Baskins. By June, the terms of the Cason lawsuit were set. Upon the ruling of the Florida Supreme Court, the complaint was changed from "libel" to "invasion of privacy." NSB contracted severe dysentery, and in early November was flown home to Miami and from there sent to New York to be treated. As soon as NSB was home safely and on the mend, MKR became concerned about the declining health of Maxwell Perkins. Her tense life continued and with it periodic attacks of diverticulosis. The year ended with yet another crippling event—Idella Parker, on whom MKR depended for so much, once again left.

. . . .

(TLS, 5 pp.)

[Cross Creek, Fla.]
Jan. 1, 1944

Dearest:

This doesn't at all seem like a new year. . . .

I left here at 8:30 and stopped by Idella's to take oranges, tangerines and pecans to the family and a small gift to her. I went in and sat down for half an hour, and the house was so immaculate, and not at all poor. Her father and mother are very light in color, with delicate features, and it must have been a blow to them to have their children revert so to type. He is a successful farmer, with land of his own. Idella and I were terribly happy to see each other and embraced warmly, and all was at once forgiven and forgotten, as with re-united lovers. Moe apparently did not remember her at all, which surprised me. But after all, it has been 8 months, almost half his life.

Idella told a funny story of the domestic job she had. Mrs. Mendelson,[1] the mistress, ordered broiled liver for dinner, and said it must not be too well done, that Mr. Mendelson liked it rare. Well, Idella and I never had broiled liver. I always preferred it quickly sautéed in butter. Idella was stumped. She just whisked it through the broiler, and when served, it was not rare, it was bloody raw. She took it away and put it in the oven for a few minutes, which of course only toughened it. She said that she didn't think a day passed without her mentioning me or the Creek. After the liver dinner, her mistress stormed into the kitchen in a fury and said sarcastically, "Will you please tell me just what you people ate at this Creek?"

Time passed and the Mendelsons were going to a supper party in one of the apartments at the Waldorf and were taking a baked ham. Mrs. Mendelson looked through cook books and fussed around and said she knew there was some way of simmering it first. Idella kept as still as a mouse. Finally Mrs. Mendelson asked her if she knew anything about it. Idella said yes, she knew how to do it, so she took charge, and turned out one of those beautiful glazed hams that we always have. It was the success of the supper party at the Waldorf and Mrs. Mendelson reported the enthusiasms next day. Idella said casually, "That's one of the little items we people used to eat at the Creek."

I think I see a little daylight here in Idella's willingness to come home. There are so many maids in a place like New York who are miles beyond Idella, and anyone who pays $35 a week expects perfection, and a gap in knowledge such as broiled liver would seem appalling. She seems genuinely glad to be back. This morning I gave Martha, who has been drooping and glooming around, fair warning. I told her that if Idella left again, I could not stay at the Creek, as I was too uncomfortable without someone who could take full charge, and I expected her to make Idella happy. I think when it came down to it, although Martha really is fond of Idella, she had hoped she would not come.

. . . I got tired of peanut butter sandwiches and had Martha kill me a chicken, and just went out to put on the fricassee. The kitchen is a nightmare. Empty tin cans sitting around, a pile of date pits on the porcelain table, left from the stuffed dates I fixed for Fred ten days ago, spoiled lemons and onions in the pantry, a pan too large in the new ice box, so that the inside door has a big dent in it—. I'm not going to touch a thing. I want Idella to see what she's put me through! The moment's mess is Martha's doing, and she at least knows better, but she is in that sulky state of inertia she goes into when things don't suit her.

. . . I have to sign off—when I finish a letter to you I feel more desolate than ever. As long as I keep rambling on, I am in touch with you. God, I wish I knew if you were in on that Burmese-border action. . . .

G'bye, darling, and a *lucky*, and satisfying New Year.

All my love.

1. Mrs. Mendelson is Mrs. Richards, according to Idella Parker (*From Reddick to Cross Creek*, 127–28).

. . . .

(TLS, 7 pp.)

[Cross Creek, Fla.]

Jan. 2, 1944

Dearest:

Between my anxiety about you, the damn lawsuit, and Martha, I got myself into a hell of a dither and of course brought on one of my attacks. But I lay in bed this morning and analyzed everything, and once I located the various sources of my nervous tension, it eased, and I feel better. I just have to *know*.

There is nothing I can do about you, so I might just as well accept it, reserving only a dirty look at God on the side to warn him that he'd better take care of you, or I shall go over to the side of the Devil and write wonderful books to corrupt the whole world. Of course pitting oneself against God or Destiny or whatever it is that meddles with us—or, perhaps worse, does *not* meddle with us—is risky and strenuous business. But being puny and helpless, except for the inner flame, there is a profound moral satisfaction in spitting back.

I remembered an incident that I have just written Phil May about, that I hope may be of some use to him in answering Zelma's brief, which goes to the Supreme Court tomorrow, our answer to follow within twenty days. In 1930 or 1931, when my first Florida sketches, "Cracker Chidlings," were published, Zelma and I were close friends. She herself had told me the stories I used in two of the sketches. There was a local furore on publication, the Ocala Banner saying that there were no such people, and I had maligned the state.[1] They later recanted and made a public apology. During the turmoil, Zelma was my staunch supporter. Not only that, but when Melie Ergles[2] took offense at my using her son's name and threatened me, it was Zelma who drove me in the Rawlings car to Melie's house, to propitiate her. Zelma assured her that I had meant no harm. This seemed to me pertinent. I feel better about the lawsuit since remembering this.

As to Martha, who has held a psychic black hand over me, I think I am on the road to getting that straight. You may not have received some of my earlier letters telling about Armour Brice ordering Sissie out of her house on a day's notice, at the very moment it was arranged for Idella to come back and for Sissie to work for the Brices, to the content and satisfaction of all at the Creek. Sissie and her three children, and Martha's grandson Jack, have all been crowded together in the tenant house during Sissie's unhappy attempt to do my work. With Idella's coming tomorrow, and no place for Sissie to go, there was not room in the tenant house for an extra dog, and that is what was upsetting Martha. To make room, she would have to sleep with old Will, and it appears that death is preferable. It also comes out that Jack's projected leaving was only to make room, so that Sissie would not have to go! Meantime, Sissie planned to move to Hawthorn and take a job there, and Martha would have let the useful Jack go irrevocably, for a week's difference in time! I have settled it temporarily by telling Martha to sleep in Aunt Ida's room, which she will do on Idella's arrival tomorrow. I am going to see the Brices today, for they told Sissie that the family that Armour moved into her house is leaving. They need Sissie badly, and if the other family is going anyway, it is up to the Brices to facilitate the move. Sissie has been sick with the flu for a week, and I had the most awful sense of guilt about the whole thing, for it did seem as though I was throwing her out with her offspring, just to make myself comfortable with Idella. The fact that I was paying the bills did not seem to mitigate my moral responsibility to human beings, even though very black. Then I decided that if Martha was raising all this hell because she was not willing to sleep with old Will, I should not burden myself with guilt because *I* want to be comfortable. You probably can't make sense out of all this—I hardly can, myself. How I damn my Methodist ancestors and my most unwilling sense of social responsibility! I had a violent argument with Cliff Lyons at Thanksgiving about this. He claimed that reasonable self-interest was the keynote of life, and I claimed that abnegation of self-interest was the keynote. Of course I am horribly selfish—but I have a sense of guilt about it—and make myself most uncomfortable trying to get away from it (from the selfishness). My theory and my practice are divergent. All the generous things I do, are in palliation of my selfishness. Just Dora and Marjorie fighting again—. How I should love to destroy one or the other—and I could, if I could ever agree with either, long enough!

As I wrote you, Chet Crosby was to take Moe hunting today on a training trip, and he asked me to take Moe on some of the Marion County back roads to run him down—Marion because it is open and there is less snake danger.

I went into Citra yesterday afternoon, (New Year's) to mail two letters to you and to get Thelma to ride with me while I turned Moe loose, so I wouldn't get lost. Thelma wasn't there, but most luckily Chet himself was at Boyt's[3] and said he could spare an hour, so we went in his truck, and it almost seemed as though Moe had already learned his lessons, for he pointed and held a big covey of quail—and nobody had a gun! Chet came out this morning and got him, and I did think this, and one more lesson at most, will make a real hunting dog of Moe. Chet said he never saw a dog with a better nose or more sense of hunting. Much good that does me, except that a bird-dog should be trained.

Martha just came in, and we had a drink together and a heart to heart talk, and I think all will work out, Jack will stay, etc. etc. She admitted that she was sending Jack away just for lack of room!

Again, how silly to write you these trivial Cross Creek matters across 10,000 miles. But the only alternative is to discuss the Cosmos! And that is even sillier, across 10,000 miles!

Well, I must gather my diverticulitus together and go down to the Brices and settle Sissie. Martha says Sissie will stay if they clear a house for her.

All this is probably "material" for a book, but nobody is going to trap me into writing another "Cross Creek." I often wish I had never heard of the place.

I told Martha about the possibility of your having already been in action and she was terribly disturbed.

"These are the times that try men's souls."[4]

I love you heaps.

1. MRK responded vigorously to the editorial (30 January 1931) critical of her portrayal of Crackers. See *Ocala Evening Star*, 2 February 1931, p. 2.
2. Melie Ergles, mother of Harry Barnes, whom MKR had unintentionally insulted in "Cracker Chidlings."
3. Boyt's Garage in Citra.
4. Thomas Paine, *The American Crisis*, no. 1 (December 1776).

. . . .

(TLS, 3 pp.)

[Cross Creek, Fla.]

Jan. 3, 1944

Dearest:

Not having eaten much yesterday, I was hungry this morning and asked Martha for a scrambled egg and piece of toast with my coffee. Since it is warmish for the first time, I said I'd have it on the breakfast tray instead of in the living room, as I have been doing. Martha brought in the tray, saying, "Haste makes waste." I asked what she had done, and she said she had burned the toast. I said, "Then what did you do, fix another piece?" No, she had brought it right along because the egg was done but would go and fix another, and sure enough when I turned the toast over, it was black as her face. She said, "You has always told me, jus' as soon as things is ready, to rush it to the bed."

You may think about that a minute. I not only never gave any such weird order, or at least did not mean to be taken so literally, but decided Martha was remembering something from her youth. We had a gorgeous rain in the night, and I expect my flowers to go to town. Unfortunately, the peacocks have taken to roosting on the platform on which rests the water tank. They would be very beautiful against the flame vine there, except that it's dark when they roost, and you wouldn't see the color of them or the flame vine—and anyway the flame vine is frozen. The reason they roost there is so they can drop down into the vegetable garden the first thing in the morning, where they have eaten off the multiplying onions and most of the broccoli leaves. . . .

My last few letters have dripped with laments over my anxiety about you, but I'm going to quit it right now. It is impossible not to worry, but I don't have to talk about it to you, who have a few troubles of your own. But don't think I'm callous when I go on with my trivial chit-chat of town and country.

I must go now and pick up Idella, whom I expect to swoon when she sees the house.

Last night I didn't think it would kill Martha to fix me a glass of orange juice and one of milk for my supper, while I took a walk. I told her to use the goblets in which we served water when we had company. I came home to thimblefuls of orange juice and milk in the smallest wine glasses. I suspect her of damn well knowing what she was doing—stupidity is her defense against doing what she doesn't want to do.

G'bye until tomorrow, darling. I love you terribly.

(over)

Sunday night is about the only time I listen to the radio. Last night Charlie McCarthy was very good. He was kidding Bergen about what Bergen didn't remember after a New Year's Tom and Jerry. Charlie said he drove Bergen home and put him to bed, but he told Bergen he kept throwing his clothes on the floor. Bergen asked why he didn't pick them up. Charlie said, "Well, you were in them."[1]

1. Edgar Bergen, a ventriloquist whose puppet was named Charlie McCarthy.

. . . .

(TL, 1 p. frag.)

[Cross Creek, Fla.]
Jan. 3, 1944

Dearest:

Idella was ready and waiting this morning—the only disturbing note being that she did not bring her trunk! But if she has a mental reservation, I think it was because of Martha et al. She pitched in on the awful kitchen and in a couple of hours turned it into a rural model for *Good Housekeeping*. She said, "I'm getting sorry for you," and when she hit my bedroom, I think she really was rueful.

I have the most peculiar fatigue tonight, and I think it is a let-down from the constant irritation and nervous tension of Martha and Sissie and their dirt and stupidity. Pray heaven Idella stays.

Phil May writes that he does not consider the Walton[1] brief a persuasive argument to the Supreme Court, which also makes me feel better. He said that it touched very sketchily on the only point where he felt they had a possible argument, I am to meet him here or in Jacksonville to go over his answer before it goes to the typist. It is good to feel confidence in Phil's integrity and friendship, for a lawyer out to make a lot out of me would have tried to impress me with the seriousness of the Walton brief. He said he had about decided to use as an exhibit the letter from the Los Angeles lawyers about the woman who had a pet deer before "The Yearling" appeared, "to show to what fantastic degree has extended the avarice which the news of Zelma's suit has evidently inspired." I am glad to have him work in some suggestion to hint at Zelma's greed, for a conviction of that would certainly influence a Court.

It has turned cold again after the rain, but Jack got back today and he and George Fairbanks will go at the job tomorrow of trying to fix my bedroom fireplaces so I can use them [remainder of letter missing]. . . .

1. Zelma Cason's attorney, J. V. Walton, who was assisted by his daughter, Kate Walton.

. . . .

(TLS, 4 pp.)

[Cross Creek, Fla.]
Jan. 5, 1944

Dearest:

. . . George and Jack finished the fireplaces, and while they have a dizzy list toward the chimney, so that you feel the ship must be rolling under you, they are at least safe to use. The boards the men took out, that the termites had eaten, were of the consistency of corn flakes. I imagine the next pound I put on will send me through one of the floors. This idea probably accounted for my dream last night, in which the Germans dropped a bomb on the house, and I said cheerfully as the walls and roof caved in, "The termites would soon have had it down anyway."

. . . Julia, bless her heart, sent me 2 boxes of 20 gauge shells and 2 of 12's, and I shall pass on the 12's to Chet, who has given me quail three times.

My Pinocchio rose bushes have caught up to some of the other bushes planted a month ahead of them. I can't wait to see how they do. If I find the peacocks snipping off any of those leaves, I shall have a dish I've always wondered about—peacocks' tongues. That will give Idella something to tell her Mrs. Mendelson.

Martha did not come over to sleep in the house here. I told Idella that probably just knowing she *could* get away from old Will, satisfied her.

I am enjoying the little silver knife pin you sent me.

Max sent Martha Gellhorn's new book, a novel, Liana,"[1] and it is simply fascinating. It is lush and tropical, and while I do not think it is "literature," it has also a great deal of wisdom and tenderness—and it is can't-put-it-down reading. Do ask for it, if you are having any time to read now. Also ask, as I told you before, for Arthur Koestler's "Arrival and Departure" and "Darkness at Noon."[2] Also ask for Gilbert's "The Landslide,"[3] sort of an adult fairy story, (Irish) and I *loved* it. . . .

All my love.

1. Martha Gellhorn (1908–1983), *Liana* (New York: Scribners, 1944). MKR liked the book, saying it was "a most exciting job," with a "Conradian quality" (*Max and Marjorie*, 559).
2. Arthur Koestler (1905–1983), *Arrival and Departure* (New York: Macmillan, 1943) and *Darkness at Noon* (New York: Macmillan, 1941).
3. Stephen Gilbert (1912–), *The Landslide* (New York: Knopf, 1944).

(TLS, 3 pp.)

[Cross Creek, Fla.]
Jan. 5, 1944

Dearest:

... I am sure I wrote you in the late summer, in a letter which is evidently one of the many you have not received (on your last report, you received 7 letters, where I wrote and mailed 21) that one of Caleb Milne's letters spoke of the suffering he went through in trying to spare the wounded the jolts of the road. I knew you would feel this way, and wanted you to know that any nervous tension you built up was the normal reaction of a sensitive man.

Your letters are so wonderful and so satisfying and so graphic, and I wish I always had engaging stories to pass on to you. One horror I have is that by some perversity you receive my despondent letters, or my stupid ones, and the ones with lively home tales are the ones not to reach you.

... (I saw a car full of people drive up, and they evidently tipped Martha generously, for she came in and was reluctant to have me refuse to see them. Finally she said, "Well, if you don't want to see them—," I said I didn't, and she said, "I'll just tell 'em you don't feel like foolin' with 'em." She probably knew exactly what she was doing, for to prevent such a statement, I went out).

... The stories of the native paratroopers and of the elephant sliding down the mountain on his behind are riots. The elephant story is one of those maddening ones, and you don't know whether your leg is being pulled, or whether the slide was accidental or the elephant was doing it on purpose!

I'll bet none of you could eat duck for his Christmas. Each one would be sure he had gotten the one that fell in the latrine. Your last letter was dated Dec. 1, making almost 5 weeks for delivery. I'm hoping you had a big batch of mail, and your packages, before Christmas.

Fancy your seeing sunrises! Odd things, aren't they?

The Brices have finally arranged to put Henry Woodward in the annex of their house, so Sissie can move into their tenant house, and we are all much relieved. Sissie is recovering from the prevalent flu, and now her three children are down with it, so that may delay the move. I hope not, as I am so afraid something else may happen, and I don't want Martha or Idella to lose patience. I have a very slight bronchial cough, but three packs of cigarettes a day would probably scratch kitten fur, to say nothing of the human throat. I am amused at your smoking, remembering your saying that you'd probably take it up when you hit a place where they were practically impossible to get. You can ask me for them, too, you know, I should imagine in any quantity (up to 5 lbs.) When your nerves get keyed to a certain pitch, I don't know anything to do but smoke, drink or scream....

Phil May was very much distressed by my last letter to him, in which I said that I did not see how I could go through a trial, as I was very nervous and could not work now. I think my subconscious intention, in sounding "pitiful," was to urge him to turn in such a good brief that the Supreme Court would throw the damn suit out, pronto. He promptly suggested some ways out, and I might as well enclose his letter. I should not consider for one moment either of the first two alternatives. The third, I wrote you about in one of the letters that probably did not reach you. Arthur Corcoran, former Pres. of the Wilson Cypress Co. at Palatka, told Phil that Russ McPherson, the present president, told him that Zelma's lawyer, Kate Walton, had been a patient of Riverside Hospital with something obscure, and T.Z. kept bringing in outside doctors just to look at her. She got sore, and when she left the hospital, threatened to bring suit against T.Z. for "invasion of privacy," which is the prime point in Zelma's case. Zelma having just decided to sue me, T.Z. was much interested on this point, and made a deal with Kate Walton to sue for Zelma on those very grounds. I wrote Phil that the Walton brief seemed to me to be trying her case as much as Zelma's, and that if the court made a precedent in her favor, she, Kate Walton, would pitch in and sue Hell out of Riverside. So I wrote Phil today that I would arrange to see Russ McPherson Monday on my way to Jacksonville, and if the story holds up under direct communication, I should be willing to have him blackmail T.Z. to stop the present suit, for it would give Zelma a good out, too. It may be that even this would not work, as if Walton would pitch in and sue T.Z. anyway, he would figure he might as well try it out this way, where Zelma might possibly make something. Anyway, it's worth trying. . . .

All my love, darling.

I am terribly proud of you.

. . . .

(TLS, 6 pp.)

[Cross Creek, Fla.]
Jan. 6, 1944

Dearest:

. . . I am just back from a day in Gainesville, struggling with the Rationing Board etc. Idella has been cleaning house more thoroughly in a day than Martha and Sissie would do in a year. This morning Idella said that she had not wanted to come back if there was going to be any trouble about it, and that she thought Sissie felt she was shoving her out. In that crowded tenant house, everyone can hear the others' whispers. She said that she heard Sissie say that she would not work for the Brices.

I had it out with Martha and Sissie once more, and I think they really do not have any feeling about it, but understand that I must have someone who can do everything and make me comfortable. I told them that if Idella left again, I should have to leave, and close down the whole place. Sissie has definitely determined not to work for the Brices and plans to move to Hawthorn. The Brices will be furious, and I only hope they will not decide I am to blame. I asked Sissie as a favor to me to stay with them through the winter, but she would not. How silly to write you all this local and domestic tripe—. Jack, I'm sure, is leaving Sunday, and I will never know why, whether it is because of a slightly better job, or because Martha makes so much fuss about his going off for a week-end, or whether she is sending him on, thinking Sissie will stay with her. I actually do not think she wants Sissie and the three brats. She is old and fussy and likes her peace.

George pain[t]ed the liv[i]ng room floor today, and I am marooned, writing now in the dusk on the porch in the cold.

Jan. 7

Dark overtook me on the porch last night. Idella and I have been cooking all day. Now she and Jack, in stocking feet, are settling the living room. The floor is still a little sticky. George was so proud of his paint-job, which is a mess, paint splashed up on the moldings, and dribbling over the edges of the French windows. Is it a dirty trick to give you my menus for the week-end? (In case you haven't received previous letters, Jean and Fred and Ruth and Bing[1] are coming this evening, Friday, to stay through Sunday.

Tonight:
Baked sherried grapefruit
Roast venison
Wild rice
Creamed scalloped celery
Braised onions
Wine jelly
Tangerine sherbet, fruit cake, coffee

Saturday breakfast
Orange juice
Country sausage and hot cakes
Maple syrup, honey, coffee

Saturday luncheon
Egg croquettes
Beets in orange sauce
Jellied tomato and artichoke salad
Biscuits
Utterly Deadly Pecan Pie

Saturday Night	Sunday breakfast
Consomme	Orange juice
Broiled chicken	Sautèed lamb-kidneys and mushrooms
Stuffed potatoes	Toast
Carrot souffle	Marmalade, coffee

Celery hearts
Cranberry jelly
Frozen custard and mangoes
Coffee

Sunday dinner
Tomato bouillon
Roast loin of Pork
Baked sweet potatoes
Succotash
Green beans
Spring onions
Corn muffins
Pumpkin pie with whipped cream, coffee

Idella said I should not send the menus, but I promised to tell you everything. God I wish you were here.

. . . Well, the St. Augustine family is nearly due, so had better go and fix up a bit. I turned on the radio while Jack and Idella were straightening the living room, and looked in to see Jack, in stocking feet, executing an elegant *pas seul*. Martha pretends to mourn that he is leaving, and remarked that he and Idella "got along so good," but I am sure she is back of his going for one reason or another. . . .

All my love, darling.

1. Jean Francis, Fred Francis, Ruth Pickering, and Bing "Bingy" Francis, the son of Jean Francis.

. . . .

(ALS, 6 pp.)

Hawthorn, [Fla.]
Jan. 8, 1944

Dearest:—

. . . Martha greeted me this morning, before I could even speak, with "O-ooh, I got such a crick in the back." I said a bit sharply, "Well, Martha, the whole world has a crick in its back." I gave her aspirin, and later whiskey, and she came in and sang for us, and again, words to "Come, Mary," that we never heard before, and very thrilling. It began to rain in the night and has *poured* almost all day—has just now begun again. . . .

Dear Heaven, if you were only here! All my love, darling.

(TLS, 4 pp.)

[Cross Creek, Fla.]
The Creek
Sunday evening
Jan. 9, 1944

Dearest:

The tumult and the shouting has died, Jean, Ruth, Fred and Bing have driven away, and I am alone on a cold raw gray Sunday evening. It is only 5:30, but is too dark to see to write. I have used the Kohler and gas so late for two nights, that I must retrench, so have a lighted candle on either side of the typewriter. The fire is red on the hearth, and if you were here we should snuggle up together on the davenport and take a nap.

We really had a grand long week-end, and I enjoyed it the most of anything I've done since you've been gone. But while I missed you terribly while they were here, you may know how bad it is now I am alone without you.

I am writing you as an alternative to a good cry.

... Jack left this morning, most amicably, and will drift back again someday, I am sure. He came in with a final armful of wood to get his pay. ...

Idella was superb. She earned her twenty twice over this week. I told her it was too good to be true to having her making everything so comfortable, and she said reassuringly, "It's true."

... I am driving to Jacksonville tomorrow to go over the brief with Phil May, going by way of Palatka to see Russ McPherson about the material I wrote you about. How I dread the trip. Will return tomorrow night if not too tired to drive. My bronchitis is infinitely better. Nothing lik[e] drinking and staying up all night playing bridge to cure a cold, say I. God, I miss you. Hate to sign off.

All my love.

. . . .

(TLS, 4 pp.)

[Cross Creek, Fla.]
Jan. 11, 1944

Dearest:

Ah! My first luxurious day in bed. A good fire on the hearth, two New Yorkers to read, and bouquets of flowers from the week-end that Idella just brought in to the bedroom as her own idea. It is still raw and cold outside, but very cozy in here. Moe is staying in bed, too. Idella is waiting on us graciously, keeping the fire going, and reading Jane Austen in the kitchen in between.

My day yesterday was so strenuous that I did not have a chance to write you. I drove to Palatka where I had a morning appointment with Russ McPherson. He was a little cagey at first, so when he invited me to go home with him for a drink and luncheon, I accepted, thinking he might talk more freely. I am sure he told the whole story, but it proved to be nothing Phil could make use of. Kate Walton was in the Riverside Hospital, and when Dr. Cason brought in other doctors, she told him—Russ was sure she meant it only jokingly—that he'd better be careful about broadcasting her case, or she'd sue him for invasion of privacy. T.Z. was much struck with the phrase, and when Walton returned to Palatka, Zelma appeared and asked her to take the lawsuit. Russ felt T.Z. was behind the whole thing. Anyway, it doesn't matter.

I drove on to Jacksonville, via Green Cove Springs, and worked with Phil on his brief. It seemed very convincing to me. It is filed Jan. 15, the enemy has five days to make an answer, then on Feb. 3 Phil and Walton have an oral argument before the Supreme Court, which gives its decision shortly. I am glad that matters will come to a head so soon. If the decision is in our favor, I'll get off a Feb. 15 cable to you. If you don't hear, don't be disturbed, as it may only mean some legal delay.

Anne Hill came in and had a drink with us in the office when we finished work. Her husband is on a submarine in Pacific waters and it will probably be a year before she sees him again. He saw the baby, a boy, on his last leave in October. Anne is staying with her mother for the duration. She has lost pounds and pounds and looked stunning. She sent her best to you. Phil's fat son has thinned out, too, and is in the service.[1]

Phil and Lillian had wanted me to spend the night at the beach with them, but I was anxious to get home. It was very cold and I was tired, and I drove at sixty for the first time since gas rationing. I got in at 8:30.

If the suit is settled favorably, now that Idella is here, I think I may come closer to getting myself out of my total mental disorganization.

. . . My seaman friend Jimmie Peters, the one on the "Lexington," sent me a string of South Sea shell beads at Christmas. I am way behind on my Service mail. Shall try to devote tomorrow to it.

I dreamed last night that I was the belle of the ball at a party where there were flocks of attractive men, all trying to make me, and even in the dream I decided not one was as nice as you and I should wait for you, and I spurned them sweetly and trailed out of the party in elegant blue velvet, and slim as a sylph. I must say it was an improvement on the monkey dreams, and much more reassuring to both my vanity and my self-respect. I must say that neither type of dream has had a parallel in real life!

All my love, darling.

1. Anne Hill and Philip May Jr., daughter and son of Philip May.

(TLS, 6 pp.)

[Cross Creek, Fla.]
Jan. 11, 1944

Dearest:

The end of my day in bed—and blessed if I'm not more tired than when I began it. It probably means that I've relaxed. I got bored and put on a coat over my pajamas and went out to look at my garden. It is all ready to pop into bloom, but has been stationary for weeks because of the continued cold. Those damn peacocks have entirely finished the leaves on the broccoli in the small garden. The edible buds are larger, however, than in the plants from which they have NOT eaten the leaves, so perhaps I have discovered something about broccoli. I offered the peacocks to Freddie and he refused with thanks. I sold the garden-eating calf to Tom Glisson.

The Gainesville rationing board is an unholy terror. Last Thursday when I was in town I applied for 17 gallons of special gas to make my trip to Palatka and Jacksonville about the lawsuit. I had to fill out a form in duplicate, tell how many coupons I had on hand, and describe the nature of the business. I did so in what seemed to me more than sufficient detail. I expected orange picking to begin this morning, and there was no possible way for me to make the trip in a day by busses and/or trains, and I so explained. The Board was to pass on such things that night. They also took my Registration Card. Saturday morning's mail brought no answer, but I was so sure they would grant so reasonable and necessary a request that I went ahead Monday morning and used up my regular coupons, which are none too much for my needs. As it is, I would not dream of going anywhere just because I am desperate with loneliness, but stick here like a good girl, never touch a drop of the farm gas for my personal use, etc. In this morning's mail comes a form card, request for special gas refused. God, it made me mad. Yet in writing the Board today to protest and give every darn detail of the trip, I had to hold my horses, as you can't afford to get them sore. I did say that since the lawsuit was one in which I was being sued for $100,000, it scarcely could be considered trivial business, and that I could assure them it had not been a pleasure trip. I said that since I knew special gas was given for just such emergencies, I could only assume that I had not given sufficient detail before, or the Board thought I was lying, and I offered to produce affidavits from Phil May and Russ McPherson. I shall appeal higher if they still refuse.

The petty bureaucracy that is running the country in all its details is simply insufferable. The most honest citizen is made to feel like a dodging criminal. I really think that the Republicans could garner most of the southern Democratic votes just by asking, "Do you want a perpetual rationing board?" Certain aspects of rationing in the time of war are certainly necessary, but the whole system is badly damaged. With Henry Adams, I am a believer in "conservative Christian anarchy."

I do so hope your Christmas boxes from me have reached you, solely because of the many good books in them. As I have written you before, pay no attention to thanking Martha and Aunt Ida for packages of books. "The Education of Henry Adams" was one of the good books.

Ask for "The Touch of Nutmeg" by John Collier,[1] a book of as weird short stories as were ever written. . . . I have suggested several books to you lately, to ask for, but I never know which letters you will receive. One was Jesse Stuart's "Taps for Private Tussie,"[2] which you will love.

How much we'll have to talk about when all this is over. Wars seem to me the recurrent nightmare of the world. And it is going to take an awfully expert job of psychoanalysis to cure them—and I doubt whether we have the brains or the willingness to face the facts and accept the treatment.

For God's sake, yes, come home when your year is up. You have done your share and more.

All my love,

1. John Collier (1901–1980) *The Touch of Nutmeg* (New York: Readers Club, 1943).
2. Jessie Stuart (1906–1984), *Taps for Private Tussie* (New York: Dutton, 1943).

. . . .

(TLS, 3 pp.)

[Cross Creek, Fla.]

Jan. 13, 1944

Dearest:

An OPA[1] letter to truck owners, even those who only have one truck, calling a meeting in Gainesville last night, seemed to hold a veiled threat, in that it said that attendance would be registered. At least 500 of us trekked to the Court House, and it must have taken at least 1,000 gallons of gasoline. A couple of Rotarian little pip-squeaks from Jacksonville took more than an hour to tell us that there were not going to be any tires for trucks, and we must make ours last, by immediate repairing or recapping when at all worn.

I stopped by the Glissons to see if we could double up on the trip, but Tom had already gone. Mrs. Glisson said she would enjoy riding with me. I had half an hour to spare, and had planned to stop by and see Mrs. Tigert. I did so anyway, and insisted on Mrs. Glisson's coming with me. Edith Tigert is an amazing diplomat. She got the whole picture, its overtones, placed Mrs. Glisson at once, even sensed the possible relation of the matter to the lawsuit, and when she told me how well I looked, turned to Mrs. Glisson and said, "You must be taking good care of her."

. . . Edith has a cook at last and is paying her $12 a week, which she considers terrific. Because I didn't want Mrs. Glisson to know, I couldn't tell her what Idella is drawing. . . .

I made a new beginning yesterday on the book, and while it is not as revolting as the first draft, it is still not right. I am still writing on the surface, and cannot seem to *give myself* to it. The result is a total lack of reality. Idella is the only star in my blue Heaven.

I'm hoping there may be mail from you today.

All my love.

1. Office of Price Administration.

. . . .

(TLS, 5 pp.)

[Cross Creek, Fla.]

Jan. 14, 1944

Dearest:

The peacocks are still eating my garden, and by diligent questioning, for Martha never offers any but the most useless and irrelevant information, I found why. When I assigned George Fairbanks to clip their wings, since he said he used to help his mother clip chickens' wings, he began on the hen. She did not act like a lady and fair ruined George's costume and he was so furious he would not finish her or touch the cock. Martha tried to reproduce his comments but was unable to, but I can well imagine that tie-tongued cussing was a treat to hear. I think I shall just have to sell them back to Gist for whatever he will give me. I should take them to the Castle, to be most ornamental around the grounds, but now that I have found that they eat the buds from rose bushes, that would not do, for Mrs. Huston put in a new rose-bed this year. The Chef would of course like nothing better than to serve roast peacock.

. . . I went in to Island Grove to the Red Derby last night to try to phone the Dumas. I heard from Julia yesterday and she is coming Feb. 5 or 9, so right now is a good time for the Dumas to use the cottage. I was unable to reach them. Mr. Gillis[1] asked to ride home with me. He is definitely the Tobacco Road type, and was quite rosy on beer that he could not or should not afford. He had a crocus sack of groceries over his shoulder. He used to live at the Creek, but is now at Cow Hammock. Do you remember Willie Gillis, the terribly cute tow-head that Rodenbaugh[2] took pictures of and was so crazy about? Willie is now 6, in his first year in school. Mr. Gillis thanked me for the Christmas box I left for the children, which surprised and pleased me, as he is the first person outside the Bass family even to acknowledge my efforts. He said that I was known as the poor folks' friend, that I was the only person to do things for them and "take Christmas" to the kids. He said that he was an old man with a young wife (he is 72) and couldn't do for his family much longer, and was making a sorry out of it now. He turned and said, "Wouldn't you like to have me give you Willie?" I murmured that Willie was certainly cute, and he said, "If you want a little wild boy—and I believe you do—with plenty of sense—Willie's the one for you."

He was perfectly serious about it, and having a little wild boy with plenty of sense sounds wonderful. But I have decided not to consider anything like that until you and I have the sort of home we want, and then we'll see. Idella is keen about the idea. She has been trying to get Sissie to give us little Martha, but no soap.

Sissie is still here, and I seem to be stuck. I can't throw her out. Martha is grumpy about something, but I can't tell whether it's because she wants Sissie to go or stay. It is still cold and raining. The most abominable winter I've seen in Florida. If I were a tourist, I'd be hollering for my money back.

... Julia wrote me that Scribner's considers Edith's book so good that they even have hopes of a Book of the Month selection. Isn't that wonderful, and wouldn't it be wonderful if it happened. . . .

One of the bad spells of missing you has slipped up on me. I love you.

1. Angus Gillis of Cross Creek, a fisherman.
2. Rodenbaugh, not identified.

. . . .

(TLS, 5 pp.)

[Cross Creek, Fla.]
Jan. 14, 1944

Dearest:

God damn to hell the mail service. Your cable has just been received about the hotel trouble—which I wrote you about MONTHS ago—and then when it was *settled* [underlined twice], sent you a cable saying "Ignore hotel trouble. Everything fine." Don't you pay attention to the dates on my letters, or didn't the cable ever reach you, or what? It is utterly maddening. You must have received a very old letter just recently, and either didn't get the cable, or, not having had the letter, didn't connect the cable with the belated letter. I'm sorry to have you upset at this late date. And God damn Doug, too, for getting things so upset. I do not now believe that he ever meant to leave, but he swore to God he couldn't take any more. Things are going beautifully now, and you'd think Doug had hatched the Castle from an egg he'd sat on, he is so paternal about it. And those God damn fiendish Hustons were evidently perfectly satisfied the minute they got Doug to the point of quitting, and me standing on my head. The last time I was over, Doug said they had been sweet as pie.

... I have tried to make a practice of writing you in the afternoon or evening and not sealing the letter. The next morning before the mailman comes, I read the letter, and if I have sounded too blue or something, I have a chance to tear it up and write a better letter.

... Anyway, all is fine and dandy at the hotel, I am well, Idella is here, Julia is coming in February, the lawsuit has its hearing Feb. 3 and I can't help but be optimistic about it, Smoky is dead, Moe is alive, very much so, and the peacocks have eaten my broccoli leaves.

The only good thing about your cable was the getting of immediate news that you are well, and the always welcome news that you love me.

And I love you, too. Heaps.

. . . .

(TLS, 9 pp.)

[Cross Creek, Fla.]
Jan. 15, 1944

Dearest:

. . . I owed Idella a full week-end, according to our new New York formality of "Saturday or Sunday off," because of her last week taking care of Fred and Jean and Ruth and Bing and me. I decided to kill two birds with one stone, so let her take the truck to go home, and sent her by way of Mackintosh to take the damn peacocks back to Gist. I told her to take whatever he would give for them. For some reason, Martha *hated* the peacocks. True, they wrecked my garden, but it was *my* garden, and she was not at all sore at the calf that ate up *her* garden. Anyway, we were all glad to see the last of them. . . .

I love you.

. . . .

(TLS, 6 pp.)

Hawthorn, Florida
Jan. 17, 1944

Dearest:

I drove into Citra yesterday, Sunday afternoon, to mail your letter. I was feeling unusually lonesome, so told Thelma Shortridge if she had the gas, I'd take her to the movie in Gainesville. Neither of us had been to one in so long we agreed we wouldn't know how to act.

The Old Hen[1] was at Thelma's, and pulled another monologue that would make somebody's fortune on the radio. I should have written you when I got home last night, but I am out of fatwood and the other wood is soaking wet from the rains, and I simply could not get a fire going in the living room. (Idella was having the week-end off). It was too cold to do anything but go to bed. Last night I might have remembered most of the stuff, but today it is gone. Its charm and weirdness are made up mostly of its irrelevancies, and that is why it is so hard to remember afterward.

She showed me a picture of Fred at about 22 in his Army uniform during the Spanish American war, and he really was fine looking. She said, "Oh honey, I had me the handsomest feller in six counties, look at him, honey, and his hair as black as coal and all that gold across the front of his teeth, and you may know I must have been somethin' turrible attractive, for he'd been around the world." How she got from one subject to another I'll never remember but in a minute she was talking about some woman-rumpus late in his life. Her psychology was and is the strangest I have ever known and what I figured out from this particular story was that she so hated to have other women think that Fred was putting anything over on her, that she turned all her fury, not even on the women he went with, but on the female gossips, and fought them violently for Fred's right to do as he pleased. At one point, Fred got caught up with by the gossips, and came home to the Old Hen and said he supposed they had told her he had been out with old lady Wilson. "And he said to me, "now you know I wouldn't ride with a woman as ugly as that, it was Mis Counts,"—you know, honey, that good-lookin' woman over near Ft. McCoy, the one killed a man—and I said to him, "Honey, don't you fret, I'll get 'em told, why they might know you wouldn't ride with a ugly woman. You just tell 'em all I know who you ride with and I don't care, and honey, you get in that old green Ford and you ride with any damn woman you want to, dear."

She ended up on the subject of Aunt Maggie, Fred's sister that I am so fond of. The Old Hen came back abruptly from a visit to Aunt Maggie on the east coast, and relations had evidently become strained, Aunt Maggie is a lady, used to be a school teacher, and the Old Hen must have driven her mad. Aunt Maggie was ill while the Old Hen was there. The Old Hen said, "There lay pore ol' Maggie, and she won't be here long, and the doctor had give her mineral oil and used a catheter. Maggie is the most cur'ous person I've ever knowed, Fred was cur'ous, the pore ol' feller, but Maggie was cur'ouser, and Fre[d] hisself said, "Wife, I don't understand Maggie." Now it wasn't me told it, it was Mis' Jenks, her boy used to think so much of Aunt Presh, has the sweetest little ol' wife and a couple of nice little ol' young uns, lives in Miami, and Maggie said to me, "Annie, it's just too much, it's just too much," she says, "it'll be all over Dade County that I'm constipated." Now facts is facts and Aunt Presh was so different, pore ol' soul, how she suffered, why, I could say to Presh any day of her life, "You goin' to have a baby tomorrow, or next week?" and she'd tell me and didn't care who knowed it. So I went over to Mis' Jenks and I no more than throwed the door open than she called out, "Has Maggie's bowels moved?" and I tossed my head and I said, "You'll have to ask her yourself. I ain't tellin.'"

Reading between the lines and knowing the Old Hen, it is plain to see that she was indeed making a saga of Aunt Maggie's bowel movement, and all Dade County was waiting for the news, as only the Old Hen could bring it.

Thelma and I enjoyed the double feature movie like any pair of yokels. Some kid soldiers behind us were as good as the show, with their comments. When they found they had an appreciative audience, they went to town and were very funny. Gainesville is packed with soldiers, partly from Blanding, partly from the nearby Air Base. After the show, "Petticoat Larceny" and "Minesweeper"[2] with Richard Arlen (which gives you a rough idea) we had a coke at the drug store. A terribly nice looking chap had evidently tried to date the cashier. She was as pretty a girl as I've seen in a long day, in such a *sweet* way, and obviously just as nice and lady-like as could be[.] She had refused him, I don't know on what grounds, but I heard her say, "I have an awfully nice girl friend who might," but he just stood sadly looking at her longingly. I have never seen a more wistful expression on a man's face in my life. His desire to go out with her was plainly not in the least wolfish. She was so darling and yet homey and he looked very decent, too, and it was either the dawn of real love on his part, probably more that he was just so damn homesick and lonesome, and *didn't* want a bitch, and maybe she reminded him of his own girl or his wife. And if you run into a nice girl like that, when you are lonesome, you tell her for me, like the Old Hen, "you ride with any damn woman you want to, dear." Just so she isn't so pretty and nice that she gets under your skin! There is a New Yorker story in that soldier and girl, if I could hit the key.[3]

... Idella reported that Gist took back the peacocks with no surprise, handed her the $25 I suggested as a fair rebate, and remarked sadly, "People never like peacocks when they get them home."

I was outraged that the typewriter ribbon got so pale, then realized that I have written you in letters about the equivalent of "Gone With the Wind."

I finally found a farmer willing to bring me a cord of fatwood, at $20, and he just brought the first load. When the fatwood gives out in Florida, as it is doing, we shall have to migrate to the South Seas. The weather continues unspeakable and unbelievable—cold, raw, gray. . . .

Oh, I do miss you so. When I came in from the movies yesterday just at dark, it was awful. Well, we are into your seventh month. For all its horrors, the time so far has gone quickly.

The Cabells want to come any time, now that Idella is here. She was delighted at the idea. One of the wonderful things about her is her genuine enjoyment of company. . . .

All my love,

1. The "Old Hen" is Annie Tompkins, wife of Fred Tompkins.
2. *Petticoat Larceny* (1943), starring Ruth Warrick; *Minesweeper* (1943), starring Richard Arlen.
3. MKR subsequently wrote a story on this subject, "Miss Moffatt Steps Out," *Liberty Magazine* 23 (16 February 1946): 31, 58–61.

. . . .

(TLS, 4 pp.)

[Cross Creek, Fla.]

Jan. 19, 1944

Dearest:

... Something in the back of my consciousness keeps telling me that I am on the wrong track. Certainly the forced quality of my style proves it, for when the material is right, the good style follows, or at least can be *made* to follow. I should rather do one good book every ten years, than a bad, even if saleable one, every year or two, so I think I shall be obliged to stop entirely, and try to reach out into the void after whatever it is I am trying to do, but am not succeeding in doing. When a literary war-horse, who loves to write even when it hurts, cannot do it, there is some good reason for balking at the sound of bugles. I thought the bugle had sounded, but it must not have been meant for my outfit.

A happy Lee's[1] birthday to you. It is a legal holiday in the South, banks closed, etc., but I don't know whether the federal government takes cognizance of it—in other words, whether or not the mailman will come today. . . .

I darted in and out of Gainesville yesterday, buying everything from bacon and a milk strainer to Noxema Cream for Idella's complexion. Which reminds me; she finished her shots in New York, and had a Nasserman when she returned to Florida, and proudly showed me the report with a big "Negative" stamped across it. This pleases me, too, as since her return she has used my china and silver for herself, which she did not do before. That is the only way in which Harlem has changed her, and she probably feels a little silly about that. I feel certain there was never a husband. According to Martha, she left for New York with two or three other ambitious girls from Reddick. They evidently had an apartment together in Harlem, for the new address reached Idella right along. When she gave me her new ration books, I noticed that the address on them was a Long Island suburb. The new books were issued shortly after you—and she—left, and since in the letter in which she told me she was making $35 a week, she also said that her mistress paid her railroad fare, I think she was working in the same domestic job all the time. There may have been two jobs, but I think the husband was a face-saving myth. Another reason I think so, is that when I brought her back from Reddick, she stopped by a colored home to pick up a dress, that she said one of the girls who had been in New York with her had packed in her trunk for her. Her first or second day back, she said with a spurious brightness, "Well, I had to choose between a job and a husband". . . . If it were not that I had read so many murder and psychological stories lately, I would tell her that if she stayed with me I should provide for her in my will, leaving her enough with which to buy a farm of her own, which is her dream, and since she is twenty years younger than I, the time element would presumably be just right. But after her deception of me, I think, "Now suppose that black mind began to brood on the fact that *when* I was gone, she would be independent—could it not gradually become an obsession?" Echo answers, "Yes." Anyway, all is wonderful from the domestic angle.

The situation as to Sissie is most peculiar. I seem to be stuck with her. She and the children have recovered from the flu, Mr. Williams has made two evidently fruitless trips to see her and urge her to come to them, as they have fixed a house for her, she still says she is going to Hawthorn—and does not budge. Martha has been rheumatic, or claims to be, and Sissie has been milking the cow and feeding the stock and fixed my breakfast while Idella was home for the week-end. Martha is getting her old age pension now, and I am wondering if in her subtle and obscure way she is trying to keep Sissie here and work her into Martha's old caretaking job. Yet everyone agrees that Sissie's children get on Martha's nerves—but you just can't tell. If they would only tell you the truth just once in a while. They tell you what they *think* you want to hear—then do as they have planned all along. I told Thelma Shortridge that Sissie still had not gone to Hawthorn and would not work for the Brices, and Thelma said she would like to have her, and is trying to find a house in Citra for Sissie, Sissie was not only enthused about the idea, but asked me yesterday if Mrs. Shortridge was ready for her, so I know from that, that she wants to go, for when they don't want to do a thing, they are the last to bring up the subject. I must try to pin Martha down. If the children don't bother Idella, and Martha wants Sissie to stay and do the stock work, it is certainly all right with me—but the Brices would be furious.

I stopped at Cicen's flower shop this side of Gainesville to pay my bill and get some flowers against the Cabell's possible coming, and some relatives of Mrs. Cicen's had just come in from Detroit, and proved to be avid Rawlings readers. I sometimes think that as a writer I am only the idiot's delight. The man said he would rather meet me than Roosevelt. As I left, he said musingly, "Nobody would think, to look at you, that you had such a wonderful mind. . . ."

Bernie Bass,[2] of all people, goes into the Army in a couple of days. Yet his family will receive about $200 a month, so certainly will not suffer. . . .

All my love, darling.

1. Robert E. Lee, general of the Confederate Army.
2. Bass went to training but was honorably discharged because he had four children (*The Creek*, 235).

. . . .

(TLS, 3 pp.)

[Cross Creek, Fla.]

Jan. 19, 1944

Dearest:

I was correct in feeling mail on the way, for Lee's birthday, uncelebrated by Uncle Sam, thank God, brought two letters from you, one a double feature. . . .

It is hideous that you evidently did not receive a single one of your Xmas packages. . . .

The mail situation is simply incredible. I don't know whether the trouble is general inefficiency, or more submarines on the loose than we are admitting. . . . I have put on a few more pounds, damn it, from sitting around and grieving and drinking and not working, but shall take them off and get all beautiful for you before you come home. There was a story in the paper today about a new WAC who was 30 lbs. overweight and so was refused a year ago. She went to work and took the pounds off, and the story writer said that since she had two brothers in the service, ready to die for their country, she thought she could diet for it.

I am so happy that there is no nonsense in your head about re-enlisting. You had to go—there were some subtle values involved, and I understand them—you were right to go—I, like you, should choose the same course again—but for the dear God's sake, if you get out of this, come on home. You will have done your share. You could have stayed out honorably to begin with, and you were wonderful to take part of the burden voluntarily. But the vast machinery for winning the thing "for our side" is in motion, and we shall win, of course, at the cost of hundreds of thousands of good young lives—but one man can only do so much. Even if you were not in it, I should be overcome with the horror, with the stupidity of mankind in general.

I have not done my share, yet I cannot see what I should do. I have written all the editorial and radio bits asked of me, have put all available funds in War Bonds, but have done nothing personal. . . . My one hope is that after all this is over, I can perhaps say some of the things that I know are important. I am at once blessed and cursed with an objective viewpoint toward the world and people. I have very few subjective and intimate contacts with human beings. When I do have one, as with you, it is a powerful one, and at the moment makes it impossible for me to be either objective or creative. I am living only for writing to you and in the hope of word from you. My letters to men in the service come next in my interest. There is not much left, after.

When shall we ever find time enough, when you come home, to talk about all the things we have been thinking about, and for which letters are inadequate? What you wrote, for instance, about the fine chaplain, who made you feel one should have some faith. "Faith" is such an inclusive word, and should be as broad as possible. I feel that it should be essentially open-minded and open-hearted, and here the Oriental mystics have something. Knowledge and understanding are floating about in the outer universe, and if one lays one's soul and mind bare, something comes through. Unfortunately, never enough. Wars will not end, poverty will not end, until the soul of man is able to put selfishness and hate behind. Sigrid Undset, for all her devout Catholicism, perhaps because of it, feels that this will never be; that man will never change; that each can only make his peace with what she calls God. This seems to me an utterly petty concept.

I had a great row with Cliff Lyons at Thanksgiving about this. He believes in "enlightened self-interest," while I held out for a complete abnegation of self-interest. But events are making me more and more cynical, and Cliff may be right.

Your letters are so wonderful, darling. I wish mine were half as good. And as I have said before, I am so afraid that all the dull and morose letters reach you, then, when I have an engaging tale to tell, that is the letter that does not get through

I love you so terribly much.

(TLS, 4 pp.)

[Cross Creek, Fla.]
Jan. 20, 1944

Dearest:

Another letter from you today. It is so wonderful to get the letters, and they make me feel so close to you, yet for that very reason I feel more lonesome for you than ever. It is bedtime, but I just have to begin a letter to you. I was glad to hear you had some relief from that dreadful post, though you may be back there by this time. Your letter was dated Jan. 1st.

... Maloney sounds like a most depressing case. Can you help him? Of course an inferiority complex is also an acute form of egoism. It is a morbid desire to be top-dog—is, in other words, a lack of perspective, of a sense of values. You might remind him that Lincoln, among others, didn't go to college, but did right well for himself. All a guy has to do to be "Intellectual" is to read and absorb what he reads. Because of that, and because you have a damn good mind anyway, naturally you are on the side of the intellectuals.

Next morning
Jan. 21

I became mercifully sleepy, and had a good night's sleep. I think I was about to say that I had thought the fetish of "a college education" was outworn. No man can become "educated" by so simple a process as sitting through four years of dull classes. The world of books, the world of thought, is available to everyone, and constitutes knowledge rather than wisdom. True education comes from within, from one's response to the world and to ideas. One of my pet characters, Dr. Albury in "Golden Apples," said, "Information can be passed from one to another, like a silver dollar. There's absolutely no wisdom except what you learn for yourself."

... A box of matches exploded in Idella's hand when she was lighting my bathroom heater this morning, and if it does not prove a bad burn, it is only because I had Butesin Picrate ointment handy. I saw the flare and knew at once what it was, though she never made a sound, and dashed out of bed and to the medicine cabinet and got the ointment on within a few seconds. Negroes are such stoics about pain. Her face was drawn but she did not make a murmur, where I should have screeched bloody murder. And she was upset when she found I had made my bed and tidied things up!

By great good luck, we are not having company that I had planned for. The Cabells had said they wanted to come over, so I wrote them early in the week, asking them for any day and night this week that suited them. I had ordered a turkey through Thelma Shortridge, from a countrywoman on her mail route, and the creature proved to be a 24-pounder when I got it!

... Well, I am stuck with 24 lbs. of turkey and a burned Idella! I wish you could bring in your unit to eat the turkey. I should gladly do the cooking. . . .
Oh I do so miss you and love you.

. . . .

(TLS, 2 pp.)

[Cross Creek, Fla.]
Jan. 22, 1944

Dearest:

I keep forgetting to send you messages. Margaret Mitchell and John sent you their love. . . .

Thirty-two degrees again this morning. It is incredible. The fruit is not hurt, is in fact improved, but I wish Chet would get it off. I understand the packing house is short-handed.

Idella's hand kept paining her after two applications of the Butesin Picrate, and I remembered the anaesthetic ointment the Riverside hospital gave me "to come home on" after that rectal operation. I decided that what wouldn't hurt a cut tail, wouldn't hurt a burn—and it was marvelous. She can use her hand to-day, and while there are places that are deeply seared, there are no blisters and no rawness.

It is impossible to heat the big living room [in] this weather with the fireplace, especially as the far door won't quite close! And Idella got out one of Aunt Ida's oil heaters and cleaned it up, and when I came out this morning there was a big fire blazing on the hearth and the heater going at the Arctic end of the room, and the place was as cozy as a hot mince pie.

Yesterday was George Fairbanks' "day" here. I have found that when George comes over to do some work, if it only takes him an hour or two hours, he considers it a day and expects his dinner and his three dollars just the same. Yesterday he put in six hours and reported that he was through, but I was hell-bent on his fertilizing the rose bushes and watering the new snapdragon plants, so asked him to do that. It would have been no more than a fifteen-minute job to do properly, but when I looked at the garden after he had gone, he had just whisked the hose across the plants and some of them didn't have a drop of moisture on them. I evidently made him sore by pushing him, even by a few minutes, for when I said, "Well, I'll expect you next Friday," he said, "If nothing don't keep me away," so I guess I have seen the last of George for a while.

Every now and then I stop to be amazed at how well I am. I am as good as anybody and better than most. The slight bronchitis has cleared up, too. Am laboriously climbing on the wagon today, and will probably feel like hell! But I must get some weight off before it becomes difficult to do. Had Idella put me on grapefruit juice and milk. I can get by when I have someone who will bring it to me regularly. I wrote you that she finished her shots in New York and is now Negative. . . .

All my love,

. . . .

(TLS, 3 pp.)

[Cross Creek, Fla.]
Jan. 22, 1944

Dearest:

I have discovered a most distressing reason for *not* being on the wagon. When the sun sets and the palm trunks are rosy and the red-birds are eating supper like mad in the bird-basket, I am cold sober. That, presumably, was the idea in hitch-hiking a ride on so generally unpleasant a vehicle. But I find I am left naked, with-out that delightful protective haze—and I miss you ten times as much. However, the sense of virtue and of will-power is terrific, so I shall stay with it. I had orange juice for lunch, and for supper fresh spinach with two poached eggs and a glass of V-8. I also took an hour's walk across the Creek with Moe and did a little garden work. Two weeks of it, and I could go back to the second notch on·my belt; a month, and I should be sending snapshots to the soldiers. That awful magazine, "Pic," wrote me that they had turned respectable and wanted to send a photogra-pher to do a couple of pages of pictures of me, and I thought to myself that I wouldn't let Arnold Genthe[1] photograph me right now for the Metropolitan Museum. I just ignored the letter!

When I passed Mr. Martin's house, I remembered that I had not told you the latest about his marital affairs. I had written you that in spite of his having thrown his wife out, announcing to her that she was divorced, she spent most week-ends with him, and that Martha commented, "Man and wife is a meculiar thing." It seems he re-married her a couple of times, although the opinion seems to be that they were pretty much commissary marriages. His last verdict to her is, that if he hasn't got someone else, she can come and live there, and he will give her her board and $5 a week, "But I'll be damned if I'll marry the woman again."

. . . I had a letter from Max Perkins today, and he had just had lunch with Edith. She is staying in New York for a month, while Verle takes his Combat Intelligence training at Harrisburg, Pa. Max said he tried to take Edith to a little French res-taurant, but found it so crowded he returned to the place he was avoiding on her account—his favorite, Cherio's—for the reason that Roi Ottley, a Negro who made quite a stir with his book, "New World A-Coming," has taken to frequent-ing it, and, Max said fretfully, spoiling it.[2] Ottley was there, and Max asked Edith if she minded. Of course she did not, and Max said she sounded sincere. They must think Southerners are amazing fanatics if they can't go into the same New York restaurant with an intelligent mulatto. However strong race prejudice may be in practice, when you think about it, it is pretty small and faded stuff. Humanity is so much more important—yet it is the basic element that is ignored—which is, of course, why we have wars.

. . . Well, I feel a little better for having written you. The second letter to you today. All my love, darling.

I think about you almost all the time.

1. Arnold Genthe, American photographer, known for his pictorialist style.
2. Perkins, in a letter dated 19 January, claimed that Roi Ottley's presence was "greatly hurting" Cherio's (*Max and Marjorie*, 560).

. . . .

(ALS, 4 pp.)

[Cross Creek, Fla.]
Sunday Jan. 23, 1944

Dearest:—

On one of the worst of our cold raw mornings, I went around singing a parody of the song from "Oklahoma,"[1] "Oh, what a lou-sy morning, Oh what a lou-sy day!" Today Idella said "you could sing the song right today, 'Oh, what a beautiful morning.'" And it has been one of those Florida dream days. It was crisp in the morning, so that I had fires, then the sun warmed the world, and the oranges looked like thousand-watt lights.

Moe and I walked down through the back of the grove and the doves went whistling out of the trees. I found a tree of Navel oranges I had forgotten, and they were delicious. And I found that a little palm tree has sprouted on the site of Pat's grave by the big magnolia. In the front yard I sampled that tree of very special mandarins, or tangerines, the pale ones that smell like sandalwood, and they were unbelievably sweet and exotic, almost like curaçao. A professional bee-and-honey man keeps hives in my grove, and the bees were lined up all around the edge of the bird-bath, drinking water, and apparently washing their wings. One enthusiast had fallen in and was drowning, but remembering the ingrate who stung me in the car when I was trying to save his life, I held a twig for this one to climb out on, instead of my finger. Tonight, just before sunset, there are *fourteen* red-birds in the feed-basket and at the bird-bath, and some of them are taking what I am sure is their first bath in weeks. I am sitting on the veranda, the first time I have been able to do so. But a chill is creeping in, and when I finish this, I shall have to go in the house and stir up the fire. . . .

Moe and I walked almost to Big Hammock and back, and it was just a fraction too much. I got back in time to hear the Leopold Stokowski symphony orchestra on the radio. They played Wagner's Prelude to "Lohengrin" and "Wotan's Farewell" and the Magic Fire music, and it was wonderful.[2] I am still on the wagon and on my reducing diet, and had poached eggs and hot milk for supper. I have invited Idella to come over about seven to listen to the radio, Jack Benny, Burns and Allen, Fred Allen, etc.[3]

... I had a funny experience with some "fans." A car stopped by the cattle-gap, and I was rather lonesome and decided I'd let them come in. When Moe went to greet them, they were very ugly to him, and I changed my mind, and when they backed up and blew their horn at the gate, I was all through with them, so hid. When I took my walk, a car stopped beside me, and I thought it was the same car. The man asked, "Is that Mrs. Rawlings' place back there?" "Yes." "How long ago was she there?" "Just recently." "Who is there now?" "Some of the colored people." "The ones she wrote about?" "Yes." "Do you live at Cross Creek?" "Part of the time." "Do you know Mrs. Rawlings?" "Yes. Nice day isn't it?" and I walked on. I was so sorry I didn't let them ask if I liked her, for I should have said sometimes I did and sometimes I didn't. Then the *offensive* [underlined twice] car stopped me, and the woman said, "Is this Katherine Rawlings?" And I said No!

1. *Oklahoma!* (1943), a musical by Richard Rodgers and Oscar Hammerstein.
2. Leopold Stokowski, conductor of the Philadelphia Symphony from 1912 to 1941; Richard Wagner, German composer, conductor, and author.
3. Comedians, especially known for their Sunday night radio shows.

· ·

(TLS, 3 pp.)

[Cross Creek, Fla.]
Jan. 24, 1944

Dearest:

I am tired tonight. Virtue is exhausting. I am on my fourth day at a thousand calories, (much less today) no liquor, and a daily three-mile walk, and I begin to feel it—as I should. I am getting all the vitamins I need, so it won't hurt me...

A howl is going up from the authorities that people are not using V-mail sufficiently. The threat was made in today's paper that if it is not used, other personal mail will be denied air mail. But you are so very far away, and need legible letters so badly, that I shall not use V-mail unless I have to.

I shall mail off the books to you tomorrow, probably in two or even three separate bundles. There will be Jesse Stuart's delicious "Taps for Private Tussie," Martha Gellhorn's "Liana," "Landslide" (an Irish adult fantasy), "The Land of the Great Image," a completely fascinating true story of Burma, and John Collier's evil and wonderful stories, "A Touch of the Nutmeg." I am not sending you either of the Arthur Koestler books, "Darkness at Noon" and "Arrival and Departure," as they are too morbid and gloomy and war-based. They are all right for us stay-at-homes, but God knows they would be no treat or hold no information for you.

I was able at Miss Terry's today to pick up a slightly used copy of a book Cliff and Gladys Lyons sent me for Christmas. I didn't want to send you my copy, as Cliff wrote an engaging verse to me in the front, and the book may not reach you—and you won't want to bother to drag any books back with you when you come home. The book is "The Screwtape Letters,"[1] by an Englishman, and

Screwtape is an elderly devil, high up, or, to use his reversal, low down in Hell, writing advice to his nephew, Wormwood, a young devil on earth who has been assigned to capture the soul of a young man who is in danger of becoming a Christian. It is everything delicious and witty, it is also shockingly profound, and hard reading, in a way, in that you have to keep your mind focussed on the fact that *everything* Screwtape says is from the devil's viewpoint! It is nothing to pick up in an idle moment, unless that moment can be very concentrated. I am sure that you will find it as exciting, even as disturbing, as I did. Some of the "intellectuals" in your group would be interested in it, and it makes grand material for spiritual and metaphysical argument. After reading it, I know for the first time who Dora is. She is the devil assigned to me. I must admit that the hellion has me going it nip and tuck. At the moment I am safely on the side of the angels, but she will know when to strike again. Unless she is a dismal failure, like the poor harassed Wormwood, who tries so hard, but seldom does the right thing—from the devil's angle. You become awfully sorry for Wormwood. Also, after reading it, I realize more than ever how truly noble you are. You have none of the sins that make Hell happiest.

I am still stuck with my 24-lb. Turkey. . . .

I took my truck to Citra a week ago to be gone over thoroughly (too bad you're not here to do it), and when I went for it on the appointed day, it hadn't been touched, as Raymond Boyt had come down with the mumps. Henry Boyt[2] said graphically, "He's got a head like a bull yearlin.'"

. . . The Mallards are so engaging now that the mating season is on. They are rather stodgy through the summer, but now they go around flapping their wings and standing on tiptoe and waggling their heads and tails. I sowed some more Italian rye seed on the lawn, and since no rain came to beat it into the earth, all my chickens and the Mallards and the red birds and doves are having a field day, and you never saw such a switching and sashaying and do-se-doing, between love-making and the first warm sunshine and all the Italian rye. It is worth losing the seed to see them all have such a good time.

All my love, darling.

1. C. S. Lewis (1898–1963), *The Screwtape Letters* (1942).
2. Raymond and Henry Boyt, owners of Boyts Garage in Citra.

. . . .

(ALS, 7 pp.)

[Cross Creek, Fla.]
Jan. 26, 1944

Darling:—

That simply magnificent Kashmir wool material arrived this morning and I fair swooned with surprise and delight. You hadn't said a word about sending me anything like that—or if you did, the letter was one that never arrived. The package, so cutely wrapped in cloth and sewed up, was dated Oct. 23. My dear, the stuff is *gorgeous* [underlined twice]—and those wonderful grayish shades that help me so much. If I weren't already working on my figure, I should be encouraged to begin at once. . . .

. . . All my love and more thanks than I can say for the gorgeous material.

. . . .

(TLS, 4 pp.)

[Cross Creek, Fla.]
Jan. 26, 1944

Dearest:

. . . Bernie Bass came to make a brief but formal farewell before going into the Army. He was terribly excited, and somehow I felt he was as pleased as Punch—he felt flattered that he was wanted and needed! We shook hands and I wished him luck, and he said, "I want to thank you for your friendship," which touched me very much.

. . . I have been worrying about my still unpicked fruit, as I expected Chet to show up with his crew three weeks ago but had not seen a sign of him. He came out today to say that he would get it off as soon as possible. They have only half a picking crew, and only eight packers in the packing house. Oranges are not paying enough to pay for the bother—$1.10 a box, way less than we got last year—yet a letter from A. J. Cronin yesterday said they were paying 5¢ apiece. That makes me furious. Aunt Wilmer said they were paying up to $1.10 a dozen. And all the packing houses have had trouble with the various kinds of workers and pickers striking for higher pay—and the grower already not getting enough to cover packing and shipping.   . . . I love you so very much. Goodnight, sweet,

. . . .

(TLS, 3 pp.)

[Cross Creek, Fla.]
Jan. 27, 1944

Dearest:

I have been trying out V-mail on letters to strange soldiers and sailors, and while it is wonderful for that purpose, as a few paragraphs fill the page, I sha'n't be able to use it for letters to you unless the increasingly fussy government makes an ultimatum of it. It just doesn't hold a mouthful.

I mailed off two parcels of good books to you. . . . I enclose the clipping about Veronica Lake,[1] for the principal reason that one of the books is "Victoria Grandolet,"[2] which I found fascinating. If and when you receive it, you can picture Veronica as Victoria—and I think she is fine for the part. To my notion, she can really act when she has a chance.

I enclose the story by Tregaskis,[3] as I thought it might help you a bit in handling the wounded. Unless your experience does not corroborate his theory—. They say the stomach and intestinal wounds are the worst. I think about it a good deal, and I tried to imagine the way I should have felt after my operation last spring without anaesthetics and morphine etc., and my imagination went so far and could go no further, for the agony I went through for several days, with all the help in the world, was unspeakable. I felt at the time that death would be much preferable to going through it again.

. . . Last night late I walked out in the yard and looked up at the stars, and wondered if you saw the same ones where you are. As well as I remember, the appearance of the Heavens is the same at the same latitudes, varying only according to longitude, but I can't be sure. You must be at about the same latitude as Florida.

. . . I am foolish enough to begin thinking about your coming home, but you have more than five grueling months ahead of you still. But it gives me a wonderful lift to think about all the happy things we'll do.

I love you so much.

1. Veronica Lake, actor.
2. Henry Bellamann (1882–1945), *Victoria Grandolet* (New York: Simon and Schuster, 1943).
3. Richard Tregaskis (1916–1973), *Guadalcanal Diary* (New York: Random 1943); *Invasion Diary* (New York: Random, 1944).

. . . .

(TLS, 2 pp.)

[Cross Creek, Fla.]
Jan. 28, 1944

Dearest:

. . . To my relief, George Fairbanks did show up today to work. I had him do a fifteen-minute job at the end of his day last week, that he did not want to do, and I was afraid I had scared him off. He is famous as the prima donna of Cross Creek, anyway. He was ready to quit today at 3:30, but agreed to pick up the trash in the yard, fallen oranges and palm leaves. I think that 4 P.M. is the time limit in his mind. And he does not arrive until 9 A.M.—but expects his full pay. But when I need him, I need him so badly, especially in cold weather to split kindling and bring in wood, that I gladly cater to him. It is also necessary to let him talk to me a few minutes, usually about his father or mother. And I must pay him personally, not through Idella. It is God's mercy that he doesn't mind eating alone in the kitchen.

I went through all your letters, sorting them into chronological order, and I am getting 9 to 10 letters a month, which is really wonderful, considering the distance and hazards etc. I have had three letters in January so far, so should have several in one mail any day now. . . .

All my love.

(TLS, 2 pp.)

[Cross Creek, Fla.]

Jan. 29, 1944

Dearest:

. . . That Italian campaign has been a terror. We are within twenty miles of Rome, but the Germans are fighting harder than ever.

I cut the first broccoli today, and diet or no diet, shall have it with Hollandaise.

This is an awful skimpy letter, and I might just as well have pleased the government and sent it V-mail! But there will be lots of news after I've been in St. Augustine for a day. Horrible news, held up for two years, was announced of Japanese atrocities. They murdered probably all of the people captured on Bataan and Corregidor, and presumably most the British taken at Singapore etc. The total murdered in cold blood after capture is supposed to be about 50,000. The reason given for not releasing the news when it became known to the Army and the State departments, was that they hoped to appease the Japanese into better treatment of prisoners by not making a public to-do about it. . . .

All my love.

. . . .

(TLS, 3 pp.)

[Crescent Beach, Fla.]

At the cottage

Sunday morning

Jan. 30, 1944

Honey:

Lordy, Lordy, how you would love it here this morning, and how I wish you were here. The weather cleared as Idella and Moe and I drove over yesterday, and we had a warm balmy Spring afternoon and evening. I was quite proud of my housekeeping when we came in the cottage, for it looked very trim and tidy. Perhaps Idella's lack of enthusiasm had been because she could picture a mess to clean up, after having just got the Creek straight, and having to haul wood up that steep flight of stairs. . . . She wandered from window to window, and said that when she reached either of the two places, here or the Creek, she thought she liked it best and wanted to stay. She said that when she walked in here, her first thought was, "Now why don't we just stay here?"

. . . Moe went down this morning to visit his girl again, Idella has the place spotless already, and it is a gorgeous sunny day. It was 41 degrees this morning, but must be warming up fast, and I'll go to the beach soon. There are hundreds of birds feeding at the edge of the water right in front of the cottage. A jolly fire is blazing on the hearth, Moe is sleeping in front of it, and it would be wonderful if only you were here to enjoy it with me. . . .

There are shrimp boats in close to shore, and planes going over—glad I don't have to go to the spotting post!

Oh darling—.

. . . .

(ALS, 6 pp.)

[Crescent Beach, Fla.]
At the cottage
Monday morning
Jan. 31, 1944

Dearest:—

The St. Augustine family and I had a very nice evening here yesterday—Jean, Ruth and Fred. I saved up calories for supper by eating just raw oysters and a couple of crackers for lunch, and taking almost a four-mile walk on the beach with Moe. They arrived at 6 P.M. Supper was all right, but nothing superb. We had cold turkey, scalloped oysters, fried stuffing patties, broccoli with Hollandaise, muffins, jelly, celery, radishes, onions, and banana ice cream and orange cake. The broccoli wasn't cooked enough and Idella didn't hit the Hollandaise quite right. It was Fred's unlucky night—he not only lost at bridge, but knocked a cup of coffee over on the white rug, and just as they were leaving, he knocked over the tall glass vase and soaked davenport, books and floor. I went for the mop and he went to the bathroom and got the bath-mat—and Jean, in putting on a new mouth, had evidently wiped the lipstick from her fingers on the back of the bath-mat, for where Fred swiped across the rug, there are two great smears of lipstick! We turned the rug (freshly laundered to boot) and nothing had gone through to the other side, so we are just hoping to avoid another accident before Julia comes, as I plan to bring her over here for a week when the weather is nice. This damn white rug is *fated* [underlined twice]. Nobody ever knocks anything over on that old green wreck at the Creek!

We played bridge until 1 A.M. I made some awful boners but won a little.

Ruth brought from the Castle a small package that had been lying there, and it was several copies of the U.S. Government Armed Services Edition of "Cross Creek."[1] I wondered if Phil would consider a copy helpful when he goes to Tallahassee for the oral argument before the Supreme Court, day after tomorrow so 'phoned him and he said he certainly did want it, so I am going in to St. Augustine earlier than I intended today, to mail a copy off to him. He said it might be a week or it might be *months* before the Supreme Court gives its decision! He reminded me that Judge Murphree[2] took from April to August for his. The long drawn-out angle of the thing is the very worst of it.

. . . I'm anxious to see Bonny the puppy—and needless to say, more than anxious to see Bonny the Boss.

All my love, darling.

1. The Armed Services Editions were cheap paper copies made available free of royalties to the servicepeople. Approximately 50,000 copies of *Cross Creek* were printed in this format (Tarr, *Descriptive Bibliography*, 111–12).
2. Judge John Murphree dismissed the libel case against MKR on 1 September 1943, but Kate Walton, Zelma Cason's attorney, filed a notice of appeal to the Florida State Supreme Court. The case, including various appeals, continued for more than five years, and the judgment was finally reversed. The court ordered MKR to pay the nominal damages of $1. For a complete history of the case, see Patricia Acton, *Invasion of Privacy* (1988).

. . . .

(TLS, 3 pp.)

[Crescent Beach, Fla.]
At the cottage
Feb. 1, 1944

Dearest:

. . . I picked Aunt Ida up and we went to the hotel, and I had a visit with Mrs. Huston and then one with the Chef. The Chef beamed on me with affection and spoke with unwonted tenderness—your cable to him had his heart fair dripping. Business keeps up, and they are short of help, of course, but not nearly as desperate as they have been. The Chef and Doug have each a quite good night boy. Mrs. Huston said that Doug was planning to drop the room prices a bit now. Some say the Coast Guard will soon be moving out, others say not. A whole flock of new barrack class-rooms has been built along the bay front, near the Marion Hotel, very ugly, but it must mean the Coast Guard is not nearly through with its work. The relatives of Coast Guardsmen who stay at the Castle have all been well-to-do and able to pay top rates without question, but some regular tourists are passing through, and Mrs. Huston said Doug thought it would be a good idea not to discourage them, with an eye to the future. Doug got some terrific prices through the winter for the more attractive rooms.

. . . I went to the Ration Board and talked with Esther Curtis, and was shocked at the news about Boo Tate's son Joe,[1] which I had not heard. He has been missing since Dec. 22. No one understands what could have happened to him. He was leader of the bomb squadron, and they had completed their mission and were returning to England, very high, and were over Holland. Suddenly Joe's plane just was not there. There were no enemy planes around, and he was apparently having no engine trouble or any trouble of any sort. Esther said that if he came down safely in enemy territory, it would be a couple of months before they heard, and if he came down in one of the few unoccupied countries, it would be several months. They were flying high enough so that if he was out of gas he could have glided down onto English soil. The uncertainty has Boo in pretty bad shape. She had been very ill before this happened. Esther said everyone tried to comfort her with the fact that the Germans undoubtedly see the writing on the wall and will not be abusing prisoners. And Joe was so expert a pilot that it is hard to believe he could not have brought his plane down without a bad crash, whatever was wrong. He was, of course, pushing his luck. He had completed his 50th bombing mission and rated a long furlough home, but felt as squadron leader he was needed, so kept on. The thought even occurred to me that he may have landed on purpose in Holland or one of the nearby occupied countries, commissioned secretly to do so, against the impending day of coastal invasion. It may be that parts of planes have been smuggled to the Underground, or dropped by parachute, and that a crew of trained men would be mighty handy to work with the Underground, to have local planes ready for our side when the invasion begins. I phoned Esther and told her to think about it as a possibility, and if it seemed to hold water, to pass the idea on to Boo.

I have lost 5 lbs. in 10 days, which is not bad. I have 15 more lbs. to go, and I can certainly hold out for a month. I could lose faster, but am comfortable at this rate. The Barclay's is no longer even a temptation. I don't even think about it. I feel simply wonderful. The four brisk miles on the beach seemed like nothing at all. . . .

All my love, angel.

1. Joseph H. Tate and son, Major Joseph Jr.

. . . .

(TLS, 5 pp.)

[Crescent Beach, Fla.]
At the cottage
Feb. 2, 1944

Honey dear:

. . . I left my car to be greased etc. and walked down to Aunt Ida's after my dental work. Idella had been to see her and Aunt Ida, with her usual tact, had jumped on her about her leaving. She said she did it jokingly, and I guess it was all right, for Idella also reported a pleasant visit. She asked Idella if she was going to be good now, and said Idella covered her face and nodded. Idella told her she loved me, and instead of saying that I thought a lot of Idella too, Aunt Ida bristled up and demanded, "Well, why wouldn't you love her?" Fortunately Idella seems to understand her and be amused by her.

Then I walked down to the Castle, where Ruth and Jean and Fred were having a drink in the bar. I had a small glass of dry sherry with them, but had no trouble avoiding other drinks. Ruth announced proudly that she had planned and ordered the dinner, and we all looked forward to very special things, and an abundance of it. She had the baked grapefruit, which sometimes people want and sometimes they don't, and clear beef consommé, which ditto, and which I despise under all circumstances. She had squab, which was very nice indeed, and I enjoyed mine immensely, but squab was on the menu anyway, and anyone could have ordered it that wanted it, and Fred was plainly broken-hearted that he couldn't have the roast beef he always wants at the Castle. There were four tee-ninesy [sic] new potatoes and three small whole boiled carrots, and the salad was just hard chunks of head lettuce. Fred asked "Did you order black-bottom pie for dessert?" and Ruth with the same pride as in her "planning," said we were to order our own. So Fred ordered sundaes for Jean and me and himself and ate all three.

... Did you hear the story of the two little mice who went to Hollywood? They were standing on Wiltshire Boulevard and a girl walked by, and one little mouse said, "Ah, those must be Betty Grable's legs." The other little mouse said, "Oh, no, I'm sure they're Dietrich's."[1] They had an awful argument, and then they saw an old looking mouse under a lamp-post, so they approached and asked if he lived in Hollywood. When he said he did, they asked him please to settle the argument and tell them whether the lovely legs that passed belonged to Grable or Dietrich. He said, "I wouldn't know, fellas. I'm a titmouse myself. . . ."

All my love,

1. Betty Grable and Marlene Dietrich, fabled film sirens. Grable's legs became an icon among the servicemen.

. . . .

(TLS, 3 pp.)

[Cross Creek, Fla.]
Feb. 3, 1944

Dearest:

... There was also a letter waiting from Arthur. His new engine arrived Dec. 4, just as he had about decided to come to Florida. The Shipyard that had promised to install it for him could not get help, and he could not get any, so he did the major part of the work entirely alone. He took out the old engine and appurtenances, tons, he said, and then the Shipyard was able to help. When they began to put in the new engine, they found that dry rot had set in, and a major repair job had to be done on the boat itself. He was most discouraged, as the unexpected repairs were so expensive that they will take most of the savings, on which he thought he was sitting pretty. A couple of thousand dollars is nothing when you get to fooling with a good-sized boat, and I expect the engine cost a couple of thousand easily. It seems to me that he is repeating Father's performance right over again, killing himself with overwork and nervous strain, to do the type of thing and live the type of life he wants to. I believe in living as one wants to, but not in killing oneself at it. However, as I wrote him, finding the dry rot now probably saved him a bad smash-up later, with perhaps loss of life.

Well, today was the day for the oral pleading in the law-suit before the Supreme Court. I hope Phil was able to bowl them over, and that they will decide *quickly* in our favor. I have stood all the strain I can, about it, and am just leaving it in the hands of the good Lord.

Phil told me over the 'phone that he had sent you by V-mail excerpts from his brief, and though I had to say that was very thoughtful of him, I felt it was the last thing in the world calculated to give you pleasure.

. . . I walked through my young grove today, looking for the bitter-sweet tree for oranges for marmalade, and the cold did quite a little damage there, after all. My fruit has not been picked, and is beginning to drop.

. . . I had a note from Norman Berg saying he would like to stop by one day next week. He has decided to enlist, and thinks he can get in the Marine Corps, on active duty. It certainly leaves Julie holding the bag, with somebody else's two little boys. I'm sorry he didn't come before Julia got here, for she doesn't like either him or Julie. Scribner's thinks he is not a friend to me, but I think that it's just that they don't like to have any of their authors friendly with a Macmillan man. . . .

All my love, sweetheart.

. . . .

(TLS, 4 pp.)

[Cross Creek, Fla.]
Feb. 4, 1944

Dearest:

. . . You said you had written of other tiring or upsetting trips, but I have not had any of those letters, except the one describing your first trip. None of your letters have mentioned the wounded or injured, since, and I imagined that the men are so thoroughly doped up when you get them that they can make the trip without undue pain. I should have thought you would carry morphine as part of your equipment, in case of some emergency. But I can testify that unless you are under ether, or a spinal anaesthetic, while morphine etc. help, you feel the pain right through it when things are bad. I suppose you are not allowed to mention the type of wounded you get. The only worse experience you could have than the Saunders one, aside from being hurt yourself, would be a similar trip with one of your own men badly wounded. Yet I doubt if much of anything is more painful than a compound fracture.

I had a letter from Lois today, and Ed is in Hawaii. I was surprised, as that means activity against the Japs, and his outfit is one of the strong ones, and I expected him to go wherever the push from Germany would come from. It is an encouraging sign, for it must mean that we already have sufficiently strong forces ready for the German invasion. . . .

She [Lois Hardy] also spoke of Chuck Rawlings' having married again—his third try—and some friend of hers had met the wife and did not like her. If she is a positive enough personality to be disliked by anyone, she won't stay very long with Chuck Rawlings. In the days when I worried about him, I wondered what the hell kind of woman *could* live with him, and decided it was only a nondescript mouse—and then her life would not be worth living. He has done some stunning articles for the Sat. Eve. Post from the S. Pacific, where he was their correspondent, so perhaps his over-sized ego is nourished enough so that he won't take out his inferiority complex in kicking a woman, mentally and physically.

My dear Julia arrives tomorrow morning. Idella has the back bedroom and bath spick and span, and I have pink snapdragon there, and some of the plum blossom. I have Bob's lovely sad crow-and-old-house painting over the mantel, and new draperies with a background of the same blue as his sky.

After Martha and I talked Sissie into working for the Brices this year, and they arranged for a carpenter to fix their shabby tenant house for her, Sissie has ostensibly gone to Campville to the doctor. Since she has been gone a week, and took the children with her, it seems certain that she has left the Creek for good. Martha thinks (or says) she will be back, but old Will says, "Sissie done gone." It is certainly all right with me, and having done my best for the Brices, they can't hold it against me now.

The Brice-Williams-Glisson row will soon flare into a battle. The Brices have fenced Tom off from access to the Creek, and Tom plans to go right ahead and use it. I suppose that means cutting their fences, and then a law-suit, which he and Williams both seem to be itching for.

I saw such a funny thing in the front yard this morning. The chickens come under the hanging bird feed basket for the feed the birds knocked out. Besides my regular game chickens, including several handsome young game roosters, I have a dozen fat gray "Dominickers" that I use just for eggs. There is a terrific caste system among them, and the games have nothing to do with the Dominickers. But this morning a gay young blade of a game rooster, elegant in iridescent green and red feathers, got tired of shooing off a waddly fat gray Dominick hen from the feeding ground, and "laid" her. It was exactly as though some beautiful cavalier had raped a fat old baker-woman. She was philosophical, and shook her feathers, and watched her chance to go back for a grain of corn. . . .

God speed the day. All my love, darling.

. . . .

(TLS, 3 pp.)

[Cross Creek, Fla.]
Feb. 5, 1944

Dear Honey:

Idella and I bustled around this morning to meet the 10:35 train at Island Grove—and it is 6½ hours late. Julia will be in a swivet. So we went on to Citra, where my truck was to be ready after extensive repairs, and Idella drove home in the truck for the week-end and I returned to the Creek. Idella had offered to give up her week-end, but since Julia will be here a month at least, I hope, I insisted on her taking her time off. Our arrangement is very satisfactory. Instead of the one day a week off, Saturday or Sunday, she takes the week-end twice a month. On one of her "off" week-ends, Julia and I will go to Pensacola to visit Bob. Idella left everything prepared for our meals—turkey a la king, egg croquettes, orange custard, fresh home-made bread, and a delicious salad Ruby taught me from one of Jean's recipes. You dissolve a package of plain gelatin in a cup of hot water, add the juice of a lemon and a small onion, grated fine, and a cup or so of cottage cheese, and then a tinge of green vegetable coloring, and let it set in individual molds. It has a delicious flavor and is very pretty. Through the summer, I used it in the center of a half of an avocado.

Idella's brother, your Edward,[1] is home this week-end on his last furlough before going overseas, so I wouldn't have had Idella stay here for anything. She is so sweet and dear, and I really do not think she will leave again. When we were driving back from St. Augustine the other day, I told her that I must make out a list of addresses and instructions for her in case anything happened to me. I told her where my will was, and about Arthur, and the AFS headquarters, etc., and said that I wanted to be cremated and the undertakers were not to be allowed to dash in and embalm me. I turned to her, and the tears were streaming down her face! I assured her that it was only common-sense to make plans against an accident, that if anything unexpected happened nobody would know what to do, and said I expected to live to be a very old lady, and only hoped I would be a nice old lady.

We talked about the Negro problem, and she told me about the Harlem riots, which were publicized as race riots. She saw them, and said that race had nothing to do with it, that the rioters were the lowest class of Negro hoodlums, who went wild and decided to "get theirs," and smashed in shop windows promiscuously and stole. They raided the grocery stores the Negroes dealt with, so that there was no food for anyone in Harlem, and when they stole from the dry cleaning and laundry establishments, they were stealing the clothes of colored people. She said that the better element was more distressed than the white people could possibly be, for they realized it reflected on, and set back, the whole Negro race.

There was very little that she liked in New York. Her rich Jewish mistress tried to break her of saying "Yes, Ma'am" and "No, Ma'am," and Idella said she could not change to save her, as she had been taught that the expressions were only courtesy, as of course they are. She said the Jewess would say, "Now you do not have to say 'Yes, Ma'am' to anybody. That's old Southern stuff," and Idella would say politely, "Yes, Ma'am." She said that the only thing she minded here was the people who seemed to hate Negroes and to try to humiliate them in such small and unnecessary ways. For instance, I loaned her my old Hamilton wrist-watch to use until you return, as I am wearing your watch. The strap had worn out and she went to Phinney's in St. Augustine to get a new strap put on. They said it would be ready at a certain time and when she went for it they had not touched it and said they could not do it, and were very ugly about it, and demanded to know where she got the watch, anyway, implying that she had stolen it. I told her that the was not one between the races, but one against the evil in human nature; that some people just had to high-hat it over anyone they thought they could.

I had engaged Martha to substitute for Idella over the week-end, and when I came back, she was waiting. I said, "The train is 6 ½ hours late," and Martha said brightly, "Miss Julia ain't come?" I have decided that she never listens to anything I say that she thinks is just social conversation. . . .

All my love, my sweet.

1. Edward Milton Thompson, "E.M.," a brother of Idella Parker, was a night doorman and bellhop at the Castle Warden. He was later killed in the war.

. . . .

(TLS, 3 pp.)

[Cross Creek, Fla.]

Feb. 7, 1944

Dearest:

Julia's train Saturday was 10 ½ hours late. She got in after 9 P.M. instead of 10:30 A.M. Fortunately the train left her off at Island Grove, where I was waiting. She said she was not unduly tired, so we kept a hunting date I had made with Chet Crosby for yesterday, Sunday. We left Chet's place at 8:30 and hunted until noon, then cooked quail in the woods in the Dutch oven. It was a lovely cool, day and we had such a good time. Before we went to our luncheon place, by the side of a small blue lake, with live oaks and palms at the edge, we stopped on a rickety bridge over a deep running stream to dress and wash the birds in the running water. Julia wanted to know the name of some wild flower and she stepped on the edge of a board to point, the board broke off and she simply sifted into water up to her arm-pits. We drove on to our camping place and Chet made a huge roaring fire, then went off and stayed in the woods while Julia stripped and I hung her clothes literally on a hickory limb. At the top, she put on a wool windbreaker of Chet's, miles too big, and around her nether regions she wrapped an old red blanket I had brought to sit on, like a sari, and I tied it with the clothes rope we were using to break Moe. She kept on her khaki hunting cap, and she was the funniest looking thing I have ever seen in my life. She looked like some half-gypsy, half-Cracker wild thing we had found living off in the woods and were giving a meal to. She had dressed as though for northern duck-hunting, and hung on limbs were her heavy duck hunting breeches, a pair of long woolen underdrawers, a pair of regular panties, a woolen undershirt, a white shirt, a sweater and her hunting jacket, also long wool socks. We ate lunch while they dried, and I said all we needed was some Cracker from Island Grove to see the array, and what a story

Zelma would have about the kind of hunting parties I went on. It really looked like the underwear for two women. Fortunately she never got at all chilled, and caught no cold. My, the lunch did taste so good, with quail gravy to dip the bread in, and the coffee perfect. We had hunted hard, and I really had had enough for the day, but at three o'clock we set out again and hunted until dark, and didn't get home until a quarter of eight. I had to fix supper, but it was a skimpy one, for I was too tired for fripperies. We feel fine this morning, but Moe is mighty quiet and has lost pounds. You have never seen a dog cover so much ground. By the end of the day, Chet had him pointing and holding and retrieving beautifully.

Julia looks fine and is happy to be here. She will stay a month at least. I am sure most of her illness is neurotic. If I had taken her to a tea party instead of in the woods, she would have had a headache, sure.

Idella was late getting back this morning, as the Boyts, while completely overhauling the truck, which she took direct from the garage to go home, had not done the one thing that was causing the trouble—cleaning out trash in the gas tank and gas line. She had to be pushed partway from Reddick to Boyts this morning, and Tom Glisson stopped on his way to the Creek, so she sent word what had happened, and Martha started breakfast and lit fires.

My fruit is to be picked this week, and I am much relieved, for it will soon be time for the orange bloom. Julia has never seen or smelled it, and now she is worried that the scent may be so strong it will make her sick! She's a funny kid, and if she doesn't get straightened out soon, is going to make an awfully eccentric old maid.

She reported that Verle passed his Combat Intelligence course very high in the class, after all his agonizing, and has just been sent to Pueblo, Colorado, where Edith will follow him, Julia didn't know whether he was to get more training and then sent overseas, as he wishes, or whether he will be stuck there for the duration. But she said Edith was in high spirits at the idea of so definite a change in locale. . . .

All my love, darling.

. . . .

(TLS, 2 pp.)

[Cross Creek, Fla.]
Feb. 8, 1944

Dearest:

Two letters from you yesterday, so I almost have my January quota now. The last letter was dated Jan. 18.

I had already sent you "Indigo,"[1] in your last Christmas box, and I decided that "Arrival and Departure" was too gloomy and morbid to send you, after all. I am having fits at your not having received all the books I sent.

Julia is doing a mechanic's job all over the place. She fixed the living room door that we never went out of, because it would not latch, and is now working on the light over the ice-box that had to be turned just-so to go on. As a matter of fact, she just now wrecked the light, but it was ready to quit anyway.

You did an odd thing—you used Dessie's name for two other women. You spoke of Dessie's law-suit. And in one of the last letters you said you hoped I did get to Dessie's for the week-end, and I haven't the faintest idea whom you meant.

I enjoyed your talk about the nature of the enemy! And agree with you.

Are you sure it is safe to sleep without the mosquito net even on a cold night? Sometimes on a bitter night, a mosquito shows up in my bedroom. Don't take any chances.

You must have felt horribly about the rat, after the night one chewed on your hair.

Can't you make little memoranda about the things you want to tell me about when you get back? Just a word written down that will recall an incident to your mind later.

There was an announcement over the radio that the Japs in north-west Burma made a surprise attack and re-took a village from the English. I get cold all over when I hear any such thing.

I got out all your letters yesterday and read excerpts to Julia and we had a wonderful time. She agreed with enthusiasm that it wasn't just my prejudice that made me think you expressed yourself vividly and wonderfully. She was fascinated. . . .

I love you so much.

1. Christine Weston (1904–), *Indigo* (New York: Scribners, 1943).

. . . .

(TLS, 2 pp.)

[Cross Creek, Fla.]

Feb. 9, 1944

Dear Honey:

My God, the commotion in this house on a rainy afternoon. Leonard arrived to work on the plumbing, Norman Berg drove in, I got bored and paid no attention to anyone and sat working cross-word puzzles, and just now went out to the back porch, where Leonard had to come in out of the rain, and here were Julia and Norman and Leonard with seven guns, and the benches on the porch emptied of a year's litter so they could hunt for shells and bullets etc., and Idella had had to leave her ironing and help them hunt for junk. I cleared out again in a hurry.

. . . Margaret Mitchell is all steamed up over christening another battleship. Medora Perkerson[1] is having trouble with her new detective mystery.

The rain didn't last. It has suddenly cleared, the sun is out and a good spring breeze is blowing. Am afraid Norman and Julia are going to bully me into going out with Moe for a short hunt and it doesn't appeal to me. They are shaking their heads together over the rust on my guns. Norman said it would be much more honorable for a man to beat his wife than to treat a good gun the way I treat mine. Julia shoots a gorgeous Belgian gun that belonged to her grandfather. She calls it her dowry! But wouldn't you hate to be married for your gun?

Leonard is almost through, so will get this ready for him to mail in Citra. God, Julia and Norman are back in the living room talking guns again—. I can't concentrate on my sweet at all.

All my love, dearest.

1. Medora Perkerson (1892–1960), writer and columnist, best known for *White Columns in Georgia* (New York: Rinehart, 1952), a history of antebellum homes.

. . . .

(TLS, 3 pp.)

[Cross Creek, Fla.]
Feb. 10, 1944

Dearest:

Norman Berg has come and gone, thank God. How he missed having Julia and me take him by the seat of the pants and throw him out, I do not know. After having invited himself down for the day, he said, "Did you invite me to spend the night?" I said, "I did not, but you may stay if you wish." (Julia interpolates here to say that in addition to a few other failings, Norman had the worst B.O. of anyone she's run into in a long time.) After having partaken of my hospitality, and eaten like a horse at luncheon and dinner, we sat in the living room in the evening and he suddenly lit into me. Out of a clear sky, and in such a vicious way, he accused me of not only disliking men, but of being the poorest judge of what he called "modern" men he had ever known. He was in that belligerent dead serious mood, and most offensive. He said that I was a good judge of simple characters like Chet Crosby and the men in the Yearling etc. etc., but when it came to a cultured man, he had "watched me react" and was appalled at my bad judgment. I tried to pin him down as to the vipers I had taken to my bosom, or on the other hand the saints I had snubbed, and finally he said that Bob Camp was one (in the beneath-notice class) and that I had been wrong about him and Julie! I had tried at the time not to express my opinion about Julie or about their proposed marriage, and the bastard had insisted on having my honest opinion, so by God I gave it, and he has held it against me ever since. He said that I said I could see what he saw in Julie but could not see what she saw in him! By which of course I meant that I could understand his being attracted to her sex appeal, especially since he hated his wife, but that since obviously all that Julie wanted was a virile man, I could not understand her being willing to marry an as yet undivorced man with two little children! He said, as though it were a great crime, that I had taken Lillian's side. It has stuck in his craw all these more than three years. He said with actual menace, "I'm just waiting to see you tackle the job of writing about a modern man." He evidently has never gotten over it that he never made the slightest impression on me. If he were not about to go into the Marine Corps and perhaps be killed, I swear I should ask him just to leave me off his route after this. He thinks he is going to be killed in the war and so does Julie. Wouldn't be surprised if she hoped to God he was. He is sure he can get in as combat correspondent, the man who sends back the secret official reports of battle action, but hopes to get in as a gunner, as he admits modestly that he is wonderful with guns. Julia's mild dislike of him reached the pitch you would expect. . . .

'Night, darling.

. . . .

(ALS, 4 pp.)

[Cross Creek, Fla.]

Feb. 10, 1944

Dearest:

She [Julia] and Chet had a good dove hunt yesterday evening. She proves to be no better shot than I, but Chet did some good shooting, she said, and gave her the doves, which she has never tasted. They didn't leave here until after 6 P.M. so Idella and I went ahead and had our supper and I had Idella leave a tray for Julia, cold birds, a salad etc. Julia got in about 8:30.

I am reading, have almost finished, the most fascinating book that is going to tear the state of Georgia into little bitsy pieces. I shall get it to you somehow. Julia knew all about the author—Lillian Smith, a white woman of a very good old Southern family, who has been publishing "The South Today"[1] from Clayton, Ga. Julia subscribes to it and it is liberal, even radical.

The book, "Strange Fruit," is so devastating and accurate a study of a Southern town and of the Negro—white relations, that you'll think you're back in Union Springs. There is even the telephone operator who knows and does everything. The book's written from the Negro point of view, and for a "white lady" to do that in Georgia is certainly exciting, and all hell is going to pop. I am tempted to order a copy for Miss Binney just to see what will happen. The book reads like all the tales you have told me.

All my love,

1. Lillian Smith (1897–1966), editor of the magazine *The South Today* and author of *Strange Fruit* (New York: Reynal and Hitchcock, 1944).

(TLS, 4 pp.)

[Cross Creek, Fla.]
Feb. 12, 1944

Dear Honey:

Lincoln's birthday, but to my surprise the rural mailman came today. However, he also came on Lee's birthday, so there was no unjust southern discrimination. Julia and I still have our colds, hers a head cold and mine the old bronchitis. We feel a little better today, but don't have much energy, so have just loafed around. Leonard came again yesterday to change the oil in the Kohler and put in new spark plugs, saving me in the nick of time from ruining the magneto, which means a job, formerly in Orlando, of re-winding the armature—and one cannot get the work done at all now. George Fairbanks came, and fertilized everything in the garden, and then a lovely heavy rain came, which I thought would be perfect and now one of our vicious cold spells is coming in tonight. It is due to be 26 degrees as far south as Lakeland and 22 to 24 degrees in this section. Martha and Julia and I put moss over all the garden plants, even including the rose bushes, which are covered with buds, and the ranunculas, which would have been ready to pick in a couple of days of warm weather. My oranges have not been picked, and the trees are covered with tiny tiny bud-blooms, so it is the usual old anxiety. Oranges aren't worth picking, as to price—yesterday they *dumped* carloads in New York—though people are still paying 40 to 60¢ a dozen—but if the new blossom is killed, we will have no crop at all next year.

Tomorrow is the last day of hunting season, and Chet came out to see if Julia and I wanted to go out, and of course we do. It may lay us up for a week afterward. But the last day—and the first—are hard to resist. Julia has made a terrific conquest of Chet, which pleases me immensely, both because it means he takes us hunting, and gives us the birds he shoots, and gives Julia a good time. There is so little I can do for her, with gas as it is, and she loves the hunting better than anything. When the weather warms, I hope he will also take us fishing. I am used to physical idleness, especially when I am trying to think, but I worried about Julia's being bored.

Martha's grandson Jack, who left me in January, is back in Mackintosh, and wrote Idella a letter, which gave me courage to suggest to Martha that perhaps he would come back for long enough to prune my young grove. Martha thought it extremely likely, so tomorrow we shall all either drive over in the afternoon to contact him, or I'll send Idella and Martha in the truck to do so. With my uncontrollable match-making instinct, I thought of course how nice it would be if Idella would marry a good grove man, but Jack just is not in her class. As a matter of fact, she said that she could not decipher his letter. It might have been a proposal of marriage for all she knew.

After losing five pounds before Julia came, I have not lost an ounce since. All I can hope to do, and be a good hostess, is to remain stationary, and then lose the rest after she leaves.

It's an odd thing, but I can't even concentrate on my letters to you with some-one else in the house. For one thing, Julia haunts my footsteps, and works or writes a few inches away from me. I am enjoying her, but it is definitely one of those periods suspended in time. But I feel all the time as though I were living in an eyrie at the top of a suspension bridge.

All my love.

. . . .

(TLS, 2 pp.)

[Cross Creek, Fla.]
Sunday Feb. 13, 1944

Dearest:

Well, it was 30 degrees this morning, and I still had my bronchial cough, so I could not see quail hunting, even though it was the last day of the season. Julia's cold was no better, either, but also no worse, so she decided she would go, and she and Moe drove off to meet Chet in the frosty dawn. The cold did no harm, but I left the moss on my garden plants, as tonight is due to be cold or colder. I stayed in bed all morning, then got up for dinner—lamb pot pie and pumpkin pie with whipped cream. We both ate too much.

Two gentleman of color just drove in, in a better car than mine, to call on Idella, one of them a beau from her Tampa days. I told her to feed them if she wished, but she said she didn't like them well enough to bother. She and Martha and Julia and Moe and I are driving to Mackintosh this afternoon to hunt up Jack, to prune my young orange grove.

Julia got back about one, and they did not even see a quail all morning, so I was glad I had not gone.

The sun is bright and it has warmed up to about 60, but the cold is just wait-ing to pounce as soon as the sun goes down again.

When I kidded Idella about her callers and not wishing to feed them, she said, "Well, you got the yard full of soldiers." I looked out and sure enough four were wandering around and Martha came in with her well-tipped smirk to ask if they might take pictures. Idella had a bad toothache today and it makes her cross and *very* niggery.

. . . Also forgot to tell you that Norman held Macmillan up, as he said he was going to, and they offered him the job of national sales manager. He said he wanted to be editor-in-chief. They have just put someone else in, in that job, but Norman said the man was ten years older than he, and he was willing to put in five or six years as sales manager, waiting, I suppose, for the editor to die—or be poisoned. My mistrust of him increases every time I think about it. Proving, of course, what a rotten judge of men I am.

All my love,

(TLS, 3 pp.)

[Cross Creek, Fla.]

Feb. 14, 1944

Dearest:

I intend firmly to ignore St. Valentine's day. The neglectful saint need expect no truck with me.

Martha and Julia and Moe and I took a lovely drive yesterday afternoon, hunting Jack. We went to Mackintosh by way of Citra and People's City, then came home over the River Styx. We found Jack on the highway with friends. He had on a zoot suit, gold-rimmed spectacles, and what, if a woman wore it, would be called a garden hat. He has been working at a packing house there. Seeing the good time he was having, I could not blame him for not wanting to be stuck at the Creek. He was glad to see me, and he and an equally elegant brown buddy, called, I am sure in irony, "Preacher," are coming tomorrow to do the job of pruning the young grove. I feel sure that after the war, when I can let him use the truck every week-end, he will be perfectly willing to stay here all the time. Martha was out of snuff, and we went up a side road off the highway to what the Negroes call "The Shop," and which, from the sounds emanating from a small gray box of a place, is a jook. Negroes were congregated outside, laughing and pushing, and since we were obviously there just for a moment, they paid no attention to us. Julia was fascinated. She said it was her first sight of Negroes really "at home."

I took Julia to the old Sampson house in the orange grove and we climbed to the tower for what to me is one of the loveliest and most exotic views in Florida. Julia was faintly cold to it, wishing no doubt that it was one of her damned New England hill-sides. We passed a gorgeous patch of English peas and I went to the nearby house to try to buy some, but the house-dweller did not own the patch. If Martha had not been along, I should certainly have stolen enough for a meal from a far corner that seemed invisible from the house, but it seemed a poor example to set to one who has probably spent sixty-five years trying very hard not to steal enough for a meal from pea patches.

On the way home we picked wild plum blossom sprays and it made me so lonesome for you.

When we drove in home, a sport car with the top down was in front of the gate and I heard the radio in the house going, and although it was a strange car, I said that it could only be brother Cecil, and so it was. He was on his way to Ocala to spend last night and today. He sold his old wreck for $500 cash, and bought this very nice 1941 roadster from an officer leaving the Air Base, for $700 cash. He had brought chicken livers to leave for me, but could not stay to supper, as Rebecca expected him at 6:30. He could not be sure I was at the Creek. He said Nancy had made a trip to Dayton but was due back last night. There is a dance in Ocala tonight, and he asked Julia and me to come in and be his guests at dinner and go to the dance, and we accepted, I with no enthusiasm, but glad to have some entertainment for Julia—though I am not at all sure she was enthused, either. We cannot either of us shake our colds, and will not, until we have warm sunny weather.

After supper, we just happened to talk about Negro church singing and Julia said she had never heard any and would love to, so we left Martha to do the supper dishes and Idella and Julia and I set out, looking for a Sanctified meeting in progress. There was none in Citra, but Idella said there would be one on in Reddick, so we drove over there. We went first to a very nice Negro church, Baptist, where Idella said they had good voices, but there was only a handful of people, so we left a dollar and slipped out. We found an old shack of a church where a Sanctified meeting was just beginning, and went in. The free-will offering had just been taken, and the leader was still pinning down the poor darkies with a gimlet eye to try to get a few more nickels out of them. I sent Idella up with three dollars and she murmured something to the leader, and I was horrified to have the leader announce that a lady had just given three dollars and would like to hear some real good singing. It seemed awful to walk into someone else's church and *buy* their songs. They did not really sing well, as the only two good voices were simply lost in mass shouting and clapping. They also used a tambourine and a pair of cymbals as big as cart-wheels. The "testifying" was definitely in the unknown tongue. They never really went to town, as we were parked up on a front bench and cramped their style. But it was new to Julia and she was fascinated, and the rhythm intrigued her enormously. With all her knowledge of music, she said she was unable to figure out the various rhythmic threads, or beats. Before she goes, Idella is going to take us to a Reddick church where she guarantees really good singing, and Martha says there is a Hawthorn church that turns out hot stuff, and she is going to find what nights they meet and take us.

. . . One of those strong waves of missing you has hit me. Some times are so much worse than others.

All my love.

. . . .

(TLS, 4 pp.)

[Cross Creek, Fla.]
Feb. 16, 1944

Dearest:

I missed on your letter yesterday—partly a hangover, partly bronchitis, partly because I was upset. Idella said not to write you about the capers I cut in Ocala, but I shall, as what's the use in writing to my sweet if I don't tell you what's on my mind. To make a long story short, I had been trying to hold in on the decision I have taken in my mind about the Negro question until after the lawsuit was settled. I began getting high at Mrs. Ax's for cocktails, and finished the job at

Rebecca's at a 9 P.M. cocktail party before the dance at the Legion Hall—and when someone at Mrs. Ax's made a typical southern and ugly anti-Negro remark, I found myself expounding moral principles for dear life, and when I got to Rebecca's I just kept it up. Everyone but Julia was against me—she feels as I do, and has for a long time—and I might as well have turned a rattlesnake loose, for the effect it had—especially on my popularity. Julia said yesterday that everything I said was true and right and needed saying, but I went at it the wrong way—too belligerently. As a matter of fact, it is fascinating to look back and see the revelation of character in our friends. Puny little Ray Horne amazed me by having a generous viewpoint and an open mind, and admitted to the truth of what I said, at least as theory. Frank Greene on the other hand, of Yankee ministerial stock, was as narrow as any Kentucky colonel, and as determined to keep Negroes in a complete slave status, taking the Nazi viewpoint that they are by nature an inferior race. Nancy did not agree with my conclusions, but agreed with the basic theories, and I think in time would be willing to accept the only justice possible in the matter, if one is not to be a hypocrite. Dorothy Greene would in time agree with me, from the Christian angle. Rebecca of course only murmured Fascist platitudes. Mrs. Anderson (and earlier, Miss Daisy, at Mrs. Ax's) almost swooned with shock.[1]

And the one complete horror—the only entirely shocking part of the whole thing—was the attitude of the so-called gentleman I have been kidding myself was one of my best friends—none other than our little pal Cecil. The time came for everyone to go to the dance, and Julia and I went to the dining room to the punch bowl for a last sip—no one else was in the room—and Cecil came out and stood on the other side of the table and glared at me as I have never been glared at. He said, as though I had committed some moral outrage, such as suggesting that Chinese babies should be eaten, "I am terribly disappointed in you." His eyes and expression were of such concentrated venom that I felt *sick*. I said, "Your heart is full of hate for me, isn't it?" and he said, "Yes." I said that there was no hate in my heart, that I felt only love for him and the colored people, and that that was the answer to the whole thing. He said, "You have never been hated in your life as you are hated here tonight." He meant, by everyone—and Julia and I with one accord just went upstairs where we changed to our evening dresses, packed our bag and went down the back stairs and drove home!

In many ways, Julia is older than I, certainly more cynical, and she asked, when I cried all the way home, why on earth I expected justice and love and common humanity of people.

I finally told Idella about it yesterday and said I didn't know whether [t]o write you about it or not, and she was terribly upset and gave me a real scolding. She said, "Please, don't ever do a thing like that again. You can't do any good, and it just isn't worth it."

I said I thought in the long run it all did some good, and that it was worth it, and that some of the people who didn't agree with me would do [a] lot of thinking.

The one unfortunate thing is that they can so easily fall back on calling me an outsider—and that is why the Georgia book by Lillian Smith, of Clayton, Georgia, is such a phenomenal thing. She is of an old Georgia family and "belongs," and it means something when she goes "all out" and fights. I'll manage to send you her book, "Strange Fruit."

. . . I do not see how I can ever feel the same toward Cecil again. This is the second time that his pure hate of me has surged from under his sycophantic suavity. Having been nothing but a petty parasite all his life, he is of course one of those whose only sense of superiority can come from being able to lord it over something or somebody—in this case, the natural butt, the Negro. The same sort of man, as an Englishman, would be one of the die-hards about the independence of India and the Indian caste system. It was such a satisfaction to him to be able to hate me and to tell me so, for he feels secure in the wall of social opinion behind him. He would not dare do it on his own.

Before Julia and I went to Rebecca's, we went and had a nice visit with Nettie.[2] Julia is an awfully good judge of people. In spite of Nettie's little hut of a house, Julia realized that Nettie was "somebody" and asked how she had never before met such a nice friend of mine. Poor Nettie—she told one of her incoherent stories of having come out to the Creek with John, when he went to his pasture on cattle business. They brought steaks etc. etc. planning to have supper with me, and she thought she passed my car on the road and I must not be home, etc. etc.—so they didn't come—and of course they never in God's world meant to go any place but the woods! As we left, Nettie took me aside and said she thought John and Francis[3] would be at Rebecca's and at the dance—as they were—and she didn't know whether John had mentioned it to Francis that they were going to the country, and it might be just as well if I didn't mention it, etc. etc. I could have wept for her. But anyway, as long as she feels that way about the bastard, I am damn glad he does stick by her, in his fashion, and give her an occasional outing. I arranged, very privately, with John to bring Nettie out next Wednesday, her day off, for the afternoon and supper. I had a hard time shaking Francis long enough to do it, too. She hung around me all evening. She looked very well and pretty and her glass eye really is not noticeable. . . .

All my love,

1. Dorothy U. Greene, wife of Frank R. Greene, a lawyer; Julia Ax; Mrs. Anderson, mother of Rebecca Camp.
2. Rebecca Camp and Nettie Martin.
3. John and Frances Clardy.

(ALS, 4 pp.)

[Ocala, Fla.]

Feb. 17, 1944

Dear Honey:—

. . . Chet was to take Julia hunting this afternoon. The season ended day before yesterday but he was so anxious to have her shoot one bird before she left Florida, so they are risking the game warden. I went to the RR station about a reservation for her the week of March 13, nearly a month away, and the agent was most gloomy about her prospects! . . .

. . . Tomorrow we go to Fred Francis's lodge[1] for the week end without enthusiasm. Julia tried to work up a sinus infection and I tried to work up a diverticulitis attack, but we both failed, so will have to go! She doesn't care to go to the cottage—likes the Creek better. . . .

All my love,

1. Hunta Hunta Hara.

. . . .

(TLS, 2 pp.)

[Cross Creek, Fla.]

Feb. 18, 1944

Dearest:

. . . Julia and Chet were just in from their illegal quail shoot, and had not only avoided the game warden, but had a bag of eleven birds, of which Julia had shot three. Chet was so pleased and proud that she had finally brought down quail in Florida. They left poor Moe behind, as their hunting was to be concentrated in a couple of fast and furious hours. He was very nice about it, and when I let Chet's dog in and fed him some of Moe's food with lots of milk on it, Moe was the most gracious host you ever saw. He sat down while Buddy ate, wagging his tail violently, and now and then looking back at me as though to say that he loved having company.

I found that I had missed the Tigerts by just a few minutes. Julia had not expected me home so early so discouraged them. I was sorry to miss them as it was the first time they had been able to get to the Creek.

Julia and I are balking on going to Freddie's today for the week-end, but the die is cast and we must go. And we'll probably have a very good time. I am disappointed that she doesn't want to go to the cottage, as that was one reason I accepted Fred's invitation, expecting to go from there to the cottage for a few days.

I'll have to miss mailing you a letter tomorrow and Sunday but will write them anyway and mail them Monday.

All my love, darling. (A newspaper item said that women should not write "nostalgic" letters to their men overseas. We are not to say, "I can't get along without you," or "When will you be home?" I intend to go right on saying it. I shouldn't think it would be very good for soldiers' morale to feel their wives and sweeties didn't give a damn!)

. . . .

(ALS, 8 pp.)

> [St. Augustine, Fla.]
> Sunday afternoon
> Feb. 20, 1944

Dearest:—

. . . Julia and I reached St. Augustine Friday at 5 P.M., saw Aunt Ida, had a drink with Ruth in the apartment, then drove out to Fred's lodge. Was surprised to find Ruth and Jean had been invited for last night for a party of ten or twelve, but not for the week-end. Fred has a wonderful cook. He also has a huge saddle and reins etc. made especially for his Palomino, in black embossed leather and silver, silver pommel etc. It stands in the dining end of the long room near the table silver.

He uses at least *300* gals. of gas a month in his Kohler—which makes my qualms over my necessary 400 a *year* seem very unnecessary.

I allowed myself to be talked into going riding with Fred, Julia and the ubiquitous Joe. Another "safe old nag" was promised me—just a short ride etc. I did want to see some of territory around here. All went well for about an hour, and we did go through a beautiful jungle swamp road, and I was beginning to get a little confidence, when, the last to go through a fairly deep stream, my "safe old nag" suddenly went perfectly crazy. Freddie looked back to see her going in mad circles in this narrow wooded place in deepish water, entirely out of control. She knocked me against saplings etc. and one foot came out of the stirrups and I did not see how I could ever stay on. I was in a pure panic and *furious* to boot. The explanation seemed to be that she had seen or felt a snake in the water and when *she* [underlined twice] got panicked I didn't know how to bring her out of it. Freddie dashed back and got hold of her bridle and finally managed to get her going in a straight line. And we rode more than 3 hours and I was exhausted, from the nervous shock and strain and just plain fatigue. Even Julia, a horse-show rider and jumper etc., was terribly tired, and was even more sore this morning than I. It is my last try at horse-back riding. There is no point in punishing myself so, when it doesn't mean a thing to me at best.

. . . Lordy, I wish you were here.

> All my love,

(TLS, 3 pp.)

[Cross Creek, Fla.]
Feb. 22, 1944

Dearest:

After I wrote you from Freddie's lodge Sunday afternoon, he and Julia and Joe came in from their long horseback ride, and Julia was beginning to be enthusiastic about Western saddles. Fred had let the cook off and fixed supper himself, including imported pate foie gras—and champagne. For himself, he brought out a quart of milk and Julia, a passionate milk-drinker, and an abhorrer of champagne unless it is the choicest, and even then it makes her sick, said, "Oh, I'd love milk," but Fred said firmly that the milk was for him and she must drink champagne. It goes to prove the value of tolerance and the fact that one man's champagne is another man's milk. It quite spoiled Julia's evening. We went at the Quiz books again, and Fred found some quizzes on which Edith Pope had gotten a 98 where Katharine Cornell got a 60, and where Julia and I TOGETHER only got a 55. It was a literary quiz, too—. We were so ashamed.

. . . We picked up Aunt Ida and had lunch at the Castle, hitting them just wrong, as there was a joint Rotary-Kiwanis luncheon meeting, at which Claude Pepper[1] was due to speak. Claude did not appear, so they ate promptly (probably as intimidated by the Hustons as I) and disbanded on the dot of two. At 2:10, Claude drove up. I spoke to him, and he was quite put out that they hadn't waited for him.

We got home at six o'clock, and Idella had prepared such a good dinner for us—quail, potatoes au gratin, broccoli, tomato aspic salad, hot biscuits, and the most delicious Black bottom pie I have ever tasted. It was a confection.

As we stopped in Hawthorn to buy groceries, I picked up Old Will, just off the bus from Palatka, where he goes every week or so to some quack doctor. After dinner, Martha asked mournfully if Idella could take *her* to the doctor (Dr. Strange) and I am sure that it was only because Old Will had had too much attention in general.

A wire came from Bob Camp today that he could not get us reservations at the hotel in Pensacola, but would be able to get a plane ride to Gainesville about March first and would see us then. Julia was plainly very much disappointed. One reason, I am sure, is that the man she has never gotten over being in love with, is in Pensacola, and she probably hoped to see him. He has married, but it hasn't cured her at all.

. . . Jean[2] had on a terrible new-style "short dinner dress," a sheath of black satin that ended at her knees or a fraction above, bare legs, black patent leather high heeled open-toed sandals, the top of the dress very low-cut and bare, with two tiny straps, and the sides cut out so deep that you could see her poor little brassiereless terribly flat and withered busts. Her hair was in a huge mane and she was the toughest, most whorish-looking thing I have ever seen. Fred said she looked like a hostess at a cheap dance hall and when she walked in his first impulse was to say, "I'll take a dollar's worth." Julia had met her several years ago when she and Fred were first married and said she remembered her as very sweet and pretty, but she thought now she was not only hard-looking but actually ugly. Very few women, if any, could wear such a dress, and it was certainly all wrong for Jean, who should avoid too-sophisticated clothes like the plague.

. . . My oranges are still unpicked, and we are going to drive in to Citra now to see Talmadge.[3] If he can't pick them, I think I shall call Shorty Davidson and see if he can. The bloom is almost out and the picking will ruin the trees for next year if not done immediately.

Jack and his friend failed again to come for the pruning. . . .

All my love, darling.

1. Claude Pepper, congressman from Florida.
2. Jean Francis.
3. Talmadge DuPree.

. . . .

(TLS, 2 pp.)

[Cross Creek, Fla.]

Feb. 23, 1944

Dearest:

. . . Yesterday afternoon Julia and I drove to Citra, through the Big Hammock groves, etc. and out to R.J.'s beautiful hammock farms. We came home with the car loaded with loot from the country-side—a soft-shell cooter, stolen roses and dogwood sprays, big heads of lettuce donated by R.J., and a whole crate of English peas—which I did pay for. Next week I plan to buy enough peas to have them canned.

We expect John Clardy and Nettie out for supper tonight, though it is not entirely definite. I found that Julia is mad about fried chicken and never gets it at home. And here I have been trying to think up ways to cook chicken, anything but fried. Tonight we'll have fried chicken, rice, lots of new peas, head lettuce with Russian dressing, and banana ice cream. For some reason, banana ice cream freezes more smoothly in the Electrolux than any other variety.

Did I write you that my pig-and-petunia pal Mr. Martin, died? A natural death, believe it or not. Swarms of children showed up from all over the south, and we found he had been married six times. That alone would wear a man down. I imagine that Tom Glisson will try to buy his fishing camp, as it would give him the outlet to the Creek that the Brice-Williams are refusing him.

Sissie is back here again with the children. Which may have something to do with Jack's not coming with his friend to do the pruning. Martha would manage it someway, without apparent communication, if she so desired. The Brices still have not prepared a place for Sissie, and now they say they do not intend to live at the Creek any more. Old Boss has been very ill.

. . . Cliff Lyons gave me coupons for ten gallons of gas to take Julia to Winter Park to hear the two-day Bach chorus sung, that she is so fond of, and in which a friend of hers comes every year from New York, to sing. Again, I am not enthused, but if Julia wants to go when the time comes—this week-end—I'll take her. We probably really couldn't get hotel reservations there, this time of year. Idella has made a date to take us to a colored church Sunday night where she guarantees good singing.

Saw Talmadge at the packing house yesterday and he said that picking the fruit late would not hurt the bloom at all. Also, the market price has suddenly gone a little higher, so I'll probably come out all right in the end.

. . . I think I miss you worse in lovely weather, like this!

All my love,

. . . .

(TLS, 2 pp.)

[Cross Creek, Fla.]
Feb. 24, 1944

Dearest:

Julia and I had just been called to lunch by Idella yesterday, when John and Nettie[1] drove in, hours before I expected them. Fortunately, I had a large meat loaf and plenty of vegetables and half a black bottom pie, so we "made out" very well. John had brought his outboard motor and fishing tackle, so we borrowed a boat of the Glissons and spent the afternoon, fruitlessly but pleasantly, on Lochloosa. We knew the speckled perch were biting, and wanted to fish for them if we got no bass. We stopped at the bank on the Creek where the commercial fisherman go out, to buy some shrimp for perch bait. The shrimp are infinitesimal duplicates of the sea shrimp, and live under the thick weeds at the edge of the Creek. Several of my Creek friends were on the bank and in a few minutes they had a large sieveful of tiny shrimp, and would take no pay. One of the two men who seined for them said nothing at all—just procured the shrimp, dropped them in our sieve, and went on down the Creek. One of the others, apparently apologizing for him, said that he talked to very few people. Our informant added thoughtfully, "He never spoke to his father."

John and I cast for bass while Nettie and Julia struggled with paddling the boat, as neither of them casts. Nettie was of course blissfully happy merely at being in John's shadow, and went into ecstasies over some of his long or accurate casts. John's bosom swelled with manly pride. He has a type of male coyness that could be endured only by a woman fatuously in love. When we finished fishing, quite without luck, except that I caught a sucker and a mudfish, he took us for a ride around Lochloosa. The evening was becoming windy, with a threat of rain, and John was not familiar with the channel, for returning, and Nettie and I both were a little uneasy. There was also a question as to whether his gas would hold out for the kicker. John took an infantile delight in going farther than Nettie and

I thought safe, and in recounting the various catastrophes that might overtake us. Nettie squealed, which pleased him no end, and when he brought us safely into the channel—about which Julia and Nettie were more accurate, within a mile, than John, Nettie said just the proper inflating things about his navigation and wisdom, and John was a happy man indeed.

We got in about 7:30 and Idella wisely had dinner about ready. We had no more than finished dinner and returned to the living room, than Nettie remarked that they would have to leave early, as they had *such* a long drive, and I was on pins and needles with her, wanting her to have time for a stop in the woods—and by God, John began talking horses, and Julia, also an addict, innocently of course and with almost equal delight, aided and abetted him—and once again, we had the History of the Horse. When he began, with a comment that he believed he had mentioned some of the principal facts to me, I said, "God, yes, and it took you an hour to tell it." John looked at me like a little boy who has had a lollipop snatched from his hands, but a query from Julia set him off, and we had it all over again. Even the patient Griselda[2] was bored and nodded off to sleep, looking the spitting image of Grandma. When John finally finished, she was so sleepy and it was so late, that I am afraid they had to drive straight home. On the lake, Nettie said, "Well, this is wonderful, if we don't do another thing." I thought, Shucks, I hoped maybe they'd stopped in the woods *first*.

Julia was crazy about Nettie. We plan another outing while Julia is here. I shall get them off early if I have to feign illness.

I follow the news from India and Burma avidly. And when the crossword puzzles use the names of places in either, I know them!

The latest from my poor Aunt Wilmer is a *long* letter, almost unreadable because of the handwriting. She had some serious accident to her hands—a bad burn, as well as I can figure it—and said she would tell me what happened when she was well enough to write about it—yet there were pages about other things! She is so unfortunate that I can only conclude that she does not amuse God as she amuses me. . . .

All my love,

1. John Clardy and Nettie Martin.
2. Patient Griselda in Chaucer's "The Clerk's Tale" from *The Canterbury Tales*.

. . . .

(TLS, 2 pp.)

[Cross Creek, Fla.]
Feb. 25, 1944

Dear Honey:

You should have seen Julia yesterday afternoon. She got restless and wanted a job of manual labor to do, so I turned her loose to hoe the front walk. She rolled up her slacks to her knees, put on her hunting cap, and worked like a dog. Idella said she looked "just like a little boy." After supper we both felt restless, so we set out in the car and ended up at the movies in Gainesville. A Rosalind Russell-Brian Aherne comedy[1] that amused us, probably because neither of us had been to the movies in ages.

The place is showing the effects of having no man. George has not come for three weeks, as the fishing is good. The grass needs cutting, the garden needs hoeing and working, and things look a bit seedy in general.

I'm certainly going to miss Julia when she goes. Have tried to persuade her just to stay on, but she says she can't stay away from her grandmother indefinitely. Of course, I'd *never* get any writing done if she did stay—but since none is in the offing, that wouldn't matter.

We have to go into Gainesville to market this morning. Am going to order a batch of books from Miss Terry. Am stuck with "Nicholas Nickleby"[2] and nothing else. . . .

Will write a better letter tomorrow.

All my love,

1. Perhaps *What a Woman!* (1943).
2. Charles Dickens (1812–1870), *Nicholas Nickleby* (1839).

. . . .

(TLS, 3 pp.)

[Cross Creek, Fla.]
Feb. 25, 1944

Darling:

One of the bad evenings of missing you—.

. . . Julia and I got in from a hard shopping grind in Gainesville about three this afternoon. Chet Crosby came out to see if we wanted to go fishing on Pee-Gee tomorrow morning (I think you know the place, to the right just before you turn off to Adela's camp). We could not, as Julia is under the weather and will be for several days. She has gone to bed and I am alone for the first time in three weeks, and do I feel it! It is almost hot this evening, and this part of the world is very lovely with the sun setting over the young grove and palms, and a dozen redbirds raising Cain in the feed-basket and bird bath. A squirrel just came to the bird bath for a drink of water. I can hear Martha *ping-ing* the milk into the pail in the cow-lot. My shabby little flower garden is beautiful—to me—with everything just about to pop into flower. The orange trees are loaded with bloom, ready to burst in a day or two. I'll try sending you an orange blossom in a piece of waxed paper. I picked one that was open, for Julia, the first she had ever seen or smelled. She was afraid she would not like the strong fragrance, but she did. I am enjoying her so much and shall miss her dreadfully when she goes.

I bought or ordered several books in Gainesville. . . . At Miss Terry's book shop (Miss Terry is a dear withered old maid who sticks a gun in people's ribs and makes them buy books). Miss Terry called Julia alternately and impartially, "Miss Scribner," "Miss Macmillan" and "Miss Harper." Julia said she didn't mind as long as she kept selling Scribner books.

. . . Boo Tate's son, Major Joe Tate, is still missing, and no word of any sort as to what might have happened to him. I wrote you that his plane simply disappeared over Holland after completing a bombing mission over Germany. He had given no indication to the others in the flight that anything was wrong, motors, gas, or himself.

Churchill and Roosevelt are saying that the war "may" last longer than 1944. But we are bombing Hell out of the German industrial and plane-producing cities, also out of Jap bases in the Pacific, and the collapse may be blessedly sudden. We are not doing too well in Italy, but my personal feeling is that it may be a clever delaying action, against the day of a continental invasion from the West, for the Germans are pulling divisions out of Russia to put into the Italian action. When we move from the West, everyone thinks we will move fast, for the time has been so long. In case you don't get any news, we have done more or less spectacular things against the Japs in the south Pacific—sunk many cruisers, destroyers, subs, carriers, etc., and downed huge numbers of planes. All that should help ease the pressure on your territory.

Willkie and Dewey are still battling for the Republican nomination, with a dark horse a possibility. Roosevelt has just lost prestige by having Congress override his veto on the new tax bill, and Senator Barkley[1] of Kentucky resigned as Democratic leader in protest against Roosevelt, and was unanimously re-elected. It may have a great influence on Roosevelt's running again. That female ass, Clare Luce,[2] announced that MacArthur[3] was the man for President.

Let me know *when* your term of service expires—whether your year dates from the time you left New York, or the time you arrived overseas. There are two months' difference, and to quote Wordsworth, "But Oh, the difference to me!"[4]

This is the kind of evening your little brown Dodge sports roadster used to drive up to the gate, and just about this time of evening. And of course, you wanted to drink first, and didn't care whether you ate or not, and I would be hungry—. I should so happily go without food tonight—.

All my love, angel.

I saw Mrs. Fox,[6] of "the little foxes," in Gainesville today. . . . She said she had taken up learning to play the violin to keep herself occupied, and recommended it to me, but with J.T. playing the cornet a hundred yards down the road, I might better take up tiddlely-winks—anything, as Aunt Ida would say, that doesn't show.

1. Alben William Barkley, Democratic leader in the Senate, later vice president under Harry Truman.
2. Clare Boothe Luce, writer who served two terms in Congress.

3. General Douglas MacArthur, war hero, later relieved of command by President Truman.
4. MKR is alluding to William Wordsworth's poem "She Dwelt Among the Untrodden Ways" (1800).
5. Estelle Fox. MKR is alluding to Lillian Hellman's *The Little Foxes*.

. . . .

(TLS, 3 pp.)

[Cross Creek, Fla.]
Sunday morning late
Feb. 27, 1944

Darling:

I am lonesome, yet happy, too, as I so often am on beautiful Sunday mornings. I have been lonesome most of the Sunday mornings I have known you, for you either "had" to go back to Ocala, or "had" to go down to the Castle desk. When you come home, I think I shall *demand* your Sunday mornings. But I have the feeling that I sha'n't even have to hint for them—.

The scent of the orange blossom is so deliciously heavy on the air. The bees are making a terrific fuss about it, and incidentally getting it well fertilized for next year's oranges. A duck has her head in an over-ripe fallen tangerine and is making the most revolting gulping sounds in the juice, like Phil May sloo-o-oo-ping his first taste of Bourbon highball. A squirrel who is making very bold in the yard these days is eating a fallen tangerine, too, holding it very daintily in his paws and taking neat little nibbles. I just picked a huge bunch of red stock and daisies and some ranunculas that matched exactly. I set out yesterday afternoon to hoe the weeds out of the garden, and Sissie was watching me and finally couldn't stand my clumsiness any longer and asked to finish the job, so I stopped joyfully.

I had the damnedest dreams about you last night. You had just come home from overseas, and of all weird ways to spend our time, we were at an Inter-racial meeting. There were elegant white people there, pale mulattos and very black Negroes. Someone called a black darkey "Sir" and a Southern white woman protested and you got up and with great formality shook the hand of the very black man and announced, "One says, 'Sir' to any man who behaves properly." Then you had a revulsion and said to me, "After all, I'm a Southerner." The white woman made a speech about the repulsiveness of black bodies. . . . We left the Inter-racial meeting and went to the apartment at the Castle, to spend our first night together. I undressed to get into bed, and noticed that the covers looked rather lumpy. When I turned them back, your nephew George was discovered under them, sleeping peacefully, and also just back from the Front. It posed a problem, as there was no other place in the apartment for him to sleep, and to my horror you said that you would go with George, since of course you could not put him out or leave him, to the home of one of your sisters, who seemed to be Mildred. You left me, and I crawled into bed, in one of my cold rages that it meant more to you to be with your "family" than with me. You had no sooner left than a bell-boy flung open the door of the apartment and ushered in a perfectly strange man, who promptly got into bed with me. I arose in a fury and called the hotel number and was answered by Mrs. Huston, and I wished her to call you at your sister's and ask you to do something about it. She said, "Oh, I'll call the Insurance Company. You know we have insurance against strangers."

This derived from an afternoon episode yesterday, just as Julia and I were driving out of the grove to go to Citra to mail some letters. A car had stopped, and the man and woman were in the yard. The woman seemed tongue-tied and the man explained that she had read "Cross Creek" five times. I said, "That's oftener than I've read it." The woman gulped passionately and said, "Oh, but you lived it." The man said he was an oil man from Texas, and had driven his wife all that way to see the Creek. He said, "You're leaving?" and I said that I had an errand. The woman said, "I'm coming back tomorrow, to orient myself." When Julia and I came back from Citra, I drove down to the Brices to complain about their hogs in my grove, and here was the Texas strangers' car. They had pounced on Hugh Williams, Mr. Brice's son-in-law, and he had been showing them all around. I have thought since, how wonderful it would really be, to have insurance against strangers.

. . . Julia has been in bed today, and I went into her room, and to amuse her, told her of my dreams. When I reached the part about your going off with George, I said, with a ghastly slip of the tongue, that you had gone off with him instead of spending the night *on* me—when of course I meant to say *with* me. She simply shrieked, and I blushed for the first time in many a year.

I have just read such a tender and lovely book, "A Bell for Adano,"[1] and shall either give you a list of books to write for, or get it to you somehow with a couple of other books.

The papers have had stories about the Jap encirclement of a British unit in north-west Burma, and the subsequent break-out and attack on the Japs, and I am afraid that not having heard from you means that you have been too hard at work since Feb. 7. I know you are all right, or I should have heard from A.F.S. headquarters.

All my love, sweetheart.

A story deriving from Admiral Nimitz,[2] but on which he could not be directly quoted, said that it was very possible that we would beat the Japs before we beat the Germans, and soon. We have been raising hell with their shipping and on their bases.

1. John Hersey (1914–1993), *A Bell for Adano* (New York: Knopf, 1944).
2. Chester W. Nimitz, commander of the Pacific Fleet.

(TLS, 2 pp.)

[Cross Creek, Fla.]
Feb. 28, 1944

Dear Honey:

Julia came somewhat to life yesterday evening, so after an early supper Idella took us to a colored church in Reddick for the singing. They didn't shout as the Sanctified-ers do, but some of it was very good. There was a sizeable congregation, and a choir of eight, and Idella's uncle played the piano. Her father also sang tenor in the choir. The choir sang quite respectable hymns from a book, but one of the preachers "lined out" some that are not in the books, and that is when everybody really went to town. Idella said they call that type of singing the long and short beat of hymn lining. They also call it long meter and short meter, and have a common meter as well. Julia was fascinated, and could not figure out just what they do. There was one most impressive older Negress in the congregation, slim and very erect, with the most delicate, finely chiseled features and bright sharp eyes, not at all like the usual large liquid bovine Negro eye. In the lining out, she came out with the most terrific deep voice you ever heard, with a strange pleasing harshness, like some great night-bird in the swamps.

Idella beckoned to a man, and said something to him, and the choir sang "The Old Rugged Cross" especially for me, as Idella remembered it was one of your favorites and you were always put out when nobody knew it. I could see you throwing your head back and acting sort of silly, but singing for dear life, so of course I sat with tears trickling down.

We didn't know until the last minute whether Julia would be up to going or not. Martha had planned to go with us if we went, and the damned cows chose that evening to refuse to come up, so we had to leave her behind. If Julia is able to, we'll go to a Hawthorn church tomorrow night, with Martha as guest of honor. We'll probably hear much more spontaneous singing there, too. Idella had told her friends the week before that we'd be there, and I think the choir thought we wanted to hear regular Baptist hymns. I whispered to Idella that it was very pretty, but I preferred the old-timey songs. She looked distressed and said, "Oh, you wanted Jubilee." At one point an old man let out a few weird bars and nobody came in with him, and Idella said, "He wanted to sing Jubilee." So I imagine that at Hawthorn we'll hear "Jubilee."

Bob's wire, that he could not get reservations for us at the hotel in Pensacola, but that he could get a plane ride to Gainesville around March first, also said, "Letter coming," and no letter has come, and the first is day after tomorrow. I shall be terribly embarrassed on Julia's account if he doesn't show up.

I have to go into Citra to see if Leonard can come out and check on the Kohler again. It has been fading, when started, worse than ever in its history. It took twenty minutes last night for it to get going, and it blew out two bulbs and made a peculiar sound. We went to bed by candle-light, as I was afraid of doing some serious damage. I have some books I bought for Leonard's little girl, who, I find, is being a very fine scholar in school and is a real book-worm. I gave her "Alice in Wonderland"[1] for Christmas, and Leonard said she was lost to the world. This time I got one of the Oz books, and Kipling's "Jungle Book,"[2] which Leonard himself will probably devour—and perhaps Elmer[3] when he is a little older.

. . . Julia is such a botanist that I have been surprised that flowers in the house don't mean to her what they do to me. She doesn't even care whether she has any in her bedroom. As a matter of fact, she doesn't enjoy bed as you and I do—doesn't like to read there, and unless she is really ill, wants to get up as soon as she awakens. She should really not have gotten up this morning, but she did, saying gloomily, "There's no future in bed."

Hettie Lou and little Martha are picking up the fallen oranges for me. Hettie Lou just holds the bucket and Martha does all the work. Idella and I long to keep our hands on Martha. She could wait on all of us in her old age, or ours!

All my love,

1. Lewis Carroll (1832–1898), *Alice in Wonderland* (1865).
2. Rudyard Kipling (1865–1936), *The Jungle Book* (1894).
3. Elmer Fiddia, son of Leonard Fiddia.

. . . .

(TLS, 3 pp.)

[Cross Creek, Fla.]
Feb. 29, 1944

Dearest:

Ah, Leap Year! Will you come and live with me and be my love?[1] Yes. Three letters from you yesterday. . . . The three letters told of what was evidently serious action. If it was the action I have been following in the papers, it came earlier than I thought. Thank Heaven you are safe.

. . . The censor raised a bit of hob with two of the three letters, and damned if the context would indicate anything that should not have been written. One story about a British officer was cut out, and it may possibly have been something of too critical a nature—I mean that you criticized him as a Britisher or something—for I understand the British are very touchy about such things. I can see that you are most careful about place names and locales.

There was every sign of rain this morning—and it is raining wonderfully now—and my garden needed fertilizing ahead of it, so I sent Idella to the tenant house to see if old Will or Sissie could do the job. Sissie was gone, trying to get a ride to Gainesville, and old Will was "in the bed." Now you or I could be "in the bed" and perfectly able to hop out and fertilize gardens, but when a darkey is in the bed, it is presumably serious, so I decided just to do the job myself. We keep the barn locked, where the fertilizer is, so I walked to the tenant house to ask Martha for the key. She was so damned sure I was going to ask *her* to fertilize the garden, that she came out bent almost double, and limping as though she had just broken a leg. I told Idella she should have saved her symptoms for some time when she was going to need them, and Idella said there hadn't been a thing the matter with her this morning. It did tickle me. I hoed the carrots and beets, and fertilized everything, and now the grand slow rain will give me a burst of bloom and of vegetables. I picked the first Pinocchio roses this morning. They are not as lovely a color as those Julia brought me in New York, being more pink and less salmon, but are still somehow exciting.

. . . She is going to have trouble getting home, as the papers announced that almost all train space was being taken over by the military, and that tourists in Florida were going to be stranded. No gas is being allowed, either, for them to drive home. She insists she must rejoin her grandmother, so I wrote Fred Francis, asking if he could pull his wires to get her a berth home.

I wrote Sigrid Undset, asking her again to come down, and asked to send her the round-trip ticket for the purpose. I was deathly afraid of offending her, but I had a beautiful long letter by return mail, and she was pleased at my asking to do it. She said that she did need a change and rest, but just could not leave now, when she must be in touch with all the news from Norway. I get more real sympathy and understanding from her about you, and my inability to do creative work at this time, than from anyone else. . . .

All my love.

1. Christopher Marlowe (1564–1593), "The Passionate Shepherd to His Love" (1599): "Come live with me and be my love."

. . . .

(TLS, 4 pp.)

[Cross Creek, Fla.]
March 1, 1944

Dearest:

The pictures arrived—all but the candid one. From your comment about being a pin-up boy for the "Whacks," I gather that the portrait was one of your bare rear. That sort of censorship makes me furious. It should not come under the head of sending obscenity through the mails for a man to send his loving and lonely wife a picture of his behind. There might be some objection to conveying a picture of his front, but behinds have always seemed to me both cute and modest. God knows the National Geographic depicts plenty of them, on savages, but I suppose a savage behind is considered as objective as that of a dog.

. . . Well, my running and hiding from strange cars at the gate proved a boomerang yesterday. One slowed down, obviously unfamiliar with the terrain, turned around down the road and came back and stopped, so I gathered up Julia and myself from the veranda, as I have been doing on such occasions, and we retired to my bedroom and went on with our reading. Julia peeked and reported a man walking up the path. He knocked, and we turned our book pages. I was so sure that a friend would call me by name, whereas this man only called "Is anybody home?" He probably heard Julia and me scurrying and whispering like mice. I also knew, or thought, that anyone hell-bent on seeing me would go to the tenant house for information. The car finally drove off—and under the screen door was the card, with a scribbled note, of a terribly nice man and his adorable old mother, whom I knew well through Bill Grinnell.[1] I felt dreadfully about it.

A little later, Mae DuPree[2] stopped by to see me, and I should have ducked her, too, not recognizing her car, except that I was now taking no chances. I had told Julia of Mae's statement that she intended if possible to send Talmadge out on the streets with a tin cup. I thought Mae looked very nice and seemed very pleasant, but Julia saw her cruelty underneath, and remarked that she should think a man would infinitely prefer being on the streets with a tin cup, to living with her. Julia is amazingly acute about people.

. . . Still no word from Bob, whose wire two weeks ago said he hoped to get a plane ride to Gainesville today, and a letter—which has never come—was following. Of course he may just walk in. If he does not, I shall feel awfully embarrassed on Julia's account. It may be only his dilatory ways, but I can't help thinking that he must have talked with Cecil on the 'phone and been persuaded that I was a dangerous person to know. Immediately after Cecil—emboldened only by feeling the weight of "society" behind him, told me he hated me, and everybody hated me, for my moral and Christian stand on the Negro question, Julia said not to bring up the subject, ever, with Bob, as she had talked with him about it and he was more violent than Cecil.

I have just read a fascinating new book by Ben Hecht, called "A Guide for the Bedevilled,"[3] on anti-Semitism, and it is a brilliant piece of work. He shows how such things as race prejudice and race hate are the product of the evil and actually murderous side of some (alas, too many) small human natures, and every place he uses the word "Jew" one could substitute "Negro" with complete accuracy. I feel that one should be *ashamed* to hate such people, and to derive a superior satisfaction from fighting to "keep them in their place." It is a sorry state if one's own "place" can be menaced by such unfortunates as the Negroes.

Martha, Idella, Moe, Julia and I went to Hawthorn last night to the Sanctified church for the singing. There was no preacher, and a small congregation, but they really did their stuff. At times the vibrations actually hurt my ear-drums. One of the Sister Deacons gave a reading from the Scriptures and Julia and I were both struck with her carriage and poise. My thought was that she was a natural actress, and Julia said that she used her arms like a dancer, supple and boneless and ineffably graceful. Among other songs, they sang "Just a closer walk with Thee," which is one of your favorites. You remember the beat of it—ju-ust a clo-o-o-ser (1-2-3) *walk* (accented) with The-e-e—. Early in the meeting everyone flopped on their knees for a shouted prayer, and they prayed for "the visitors." At the collection, I put in five dollars, and Martha, with a magnificent and superior gesture, put in two dollars, which was the equivalent of a hundred from me. Whereupon the next prayer said that because the church was sanctified, God had sent the visitors to help so nobly. One enormous black Negress made a really lovely talk, and said that "Singing is the coming of an angel." That is a hard phrase to beat in any language. Afterward, four "Sister Deacons" came up to us and welcomed us most graciously and Julia with equal grace shook hands with them all.

A weird mulatto girl named Denny, who used to come visiting at the Creek, came in during the meeting and sat next to Idella. Idella said that the girl poked her and said, "Hey, buddy, did them white folks testify?" Julia and I agreed that probably all we needed was time. Denny talked with us afterward and said she was coming to the Creek to see us and the boys. Martha snorted, "Huh, ain't no boys there now excusin' old Will. You welcome to him." I asked Martha if the girl were not Gullah, she talked so oddly, and Martha said, "Ain't nothin' but bein' crazy make Denny talk like that."

On the way home Idella told us tales of baptizing and converting etc. Her brother Edward was converted once, and at a meeting soon after was called on to pray, to his utter horror. He rolled his eyes at Idella and was obliged to stand up. The old sisters began shouting "Praise the Lord" and "Amen" and still Edward had not said a word. At last he moaned, "Lord help me!" and the sisters shouted, "Halleluja!" and for about ten minutes Edward stood suffering, crying out "Lord help me."

Today is Martha's birthday and we are having ice cream and cake for her, in which Julia and I shall share happily.

Julia has been cutting the grass and trimming the edges of the path, and has just come in with her cute little face filthy dirty. She seems so terribly young, but will be 26 this month. . . .

All my love, darling.

1. Bill Grinnell (Mrs. Oliver Grinnell), who brought Hemingway and MKR together at Bimini (*Max and Marjorie*, 244).
2. Mae DuPree, wife of Talmadge DuPree.
3. Ben Hecht (1893–1964), *A Guide for the Bedevilled* (New York: Scribners, 1944).

. . . .

(TLS, 2 pp.)

[Cross Creek, Fla.]

March 2, 1944

Dearest:

We went into Citra and Island Grove yesterday afternoon to arrange for having peas canned—English peas from R.J.'s farm. On the way back, I stopped at the unlived-in house in Island Grove where I steal pink roses—I think I told you that I found the house belongs to Bert and Melie Ergles (Melie being the woman who was going to whip me to death) and that every time I steal the roses, I lay myself liable to a load of buckshot from Melie, who lives in sight of the house— I noticed a man coming down the road whom I took to be the Island Grove gentleman who gipped me out of a hundred dollars with a phony tale of hogs he was not ready to sell and a tractor (which he never owned) on which he gave me a lien. I said smugly to Julia, "I think I'll have just a word with my friend." He stopped politely by the side of the car and I said sweetly, "Aren't you a little over-due?" He stared at me and I realized in the same instant it was not the right man! In the next instant, he said, "I'm awfully sorry. I've been meaning to return your disc harrow every day." I didn't even know—or had forgotten—that he *had* my disc harrow—. Julia made the comment that I could probably stop every other person in this vicinity and ask if they weren't a little overdue, and find by God they were.

Martha's birthday cake was on the scorched side, but the chocolate ice cream was delicious. We had her come in and cut the cake and sang "Happy birthday" to her. I forgot to offer her a drink, which she would have preferred to her other gifts.

Julia and I sat up until after midnight while she told me the story of her blighted love. She knows as well as anyone that the man is thoroughly self-cen-tered and would be hell to live with, but she can't get over it, regardless. The odd part is that it was the first—and last time—she has been in love. She said she had never even had any school girl palpitations. The man is at Pensacola and I am sure that is why she was so disappointed at not going over to see Bob—she hoped for a glimpse of the other bastard.

Will hold my letter to the one sheet so that I can enclose the interview with Tallulah.[1]

All my love,

1. Tallulah Bankhead, the actor.

. . . .

(TLS, 5 pp.)

[Cross Creek, Fla.]
March 3, 1944

Dear Honey:

A good letter from you today—dated Feb. 10. I am really faring very well....

... I hope the book missing from Martha's box was not "Indigo" (Christine Weston's wonderful book about India). I read it quick like a rabbit, so as to get it into your last box Oct. 15. Damn it, all the books I sent were so readable and I didn't want you to miss a one.

... Henry Heyl is evidently lying in bed working up a fit about Julia. She shows considerable interest in him, too, although I have assured her I should not pick him for a husband for her. I think her interest is mainly because he has a place in her beloved Vermont! It is such good news that he is getting better, and it would be fun to go with Julia to his place in the late summer or early fall. Perhaps we could still all go together in the late fall when you return.

The Cabells are afraid they are stuck indefinitely in St. Augustine, as *no* gas is being allowed tourists to return home. . . . Priscilla Cabell seems in permanently bad shape with her arthritis, and it is still out of the question for them to come over here as they planned.

Bee McNeil, who is a cat expert, said that Smoky undoubtedly died of enteritis, that she had known it to wipe out whole catteries. . . .

And speaking of unkindness—. Julia and I had breakfast together by the fire in the living room this morning, for the first time, and we had just finished (after the Hour With the Masters over the Gainesville radio station, 9 to 10 A.M.), when a large maroon car drove up to the gate and a man in uniform, on crutches, hobbled to the gate. Moe set upon him, barking horribly. Dogs are worse than anti-Semites and southern Ku-Kluxers in hating what they take to be alien. I felt I could not hide from a crippled soldier, so told Idella to welcome him in. Julia went to her room. The man was very nice, and from his insignia was apparently a Colonel. I asked him about his ailments, and he dismissed them as "an accident," so I don't know whether he was wounded in action or fell down some hotel steps chasing a whore. Anyway, he has been in Walter Reed Hospital for four months, and had read and pored over all my goddamn books. He said he had taken an aerial map and marked on it every place and incident I had mentioned, and was able to drive straight to my gate. He had been to Castle Warden for a meal, having been told about the place in Washington—and here is the horror—said that the librarian at Walter Reed had told him that ALL the recipes in my cook book came from the Chef at the Castle! Did I writhe! . . . The Colonel, or General, whatever he was, when I asked if he would soon be out of his crutches, said he would not, that he was supposed to be in London with Eisenhower now, but would be useless for some time to come. He didn't stay very long, and I rather resented not finding out more about him, when he knew so much about me.

Yesterday afternoon Julia and I went to Citra to get English peas for canning by my friend Mrs. Quincey Sykes (mother of Ivy).[1] As we left, we passed my pasture, which I had planted twice to rye and rape. Rape is a cow feed that re-seeds itself, and this is the first year I have tried it. I looked at the pasture as we drove by and said with satisfaction, "Rape coming up," Julia said, "H-m-m-m. Guess I won't try to go home."

This morning I dashed out of bed at eight o'clock to take Martha to Quincey Sykes to help with the pea canning. Mr. Sykes is a depressing-looking old guy, and he said with an air of mystery, "I want to speak to you before you leave." I thought, "Does he want ten dollars or a hundred, and what for?" I tried to slip off without talking with him, but he cornered me, and whispered, "You do a lot of traveling. I want to ask you to try to find me a Spitz dog. . . ."

All my love, darling. And when you call me "Peaches"—smile. But of course you do.

1. Quincey Sykes, wife of Moe Sykes, who on occasion did carpentry work for MKR.

. . . .

(TLS, 1 p.)

[Cross Creek, Fla.]
March 4, 1944

Dearest:

Idella is home for her week-end off, Julia is cutting the tough grass outside the fence, and Moe and I are being on the lazy side. Moe and I had such a worried night, and did not get our sleep. He got lost—. Julia and I went to Citra, then to Chet's house to leave some milk for Moe's mother, who has ten new puppies, then to Quincey Sykes' to get Martha and the canned peas. We both left the car to talk with Helen Crosby and Moe evidently jumped out there. When we reached home, he just was not there. We re-traced our steps and Helen said he had been there but would not let her catch him. We tried Citra, then I thought he might have set out for St. Augustine, as he did when I went to New York with you in July. We drove about twelve miles beyond Hawthorn. This morning Chet brought him out. He had gone back to Chet's place at one in the morning and Chet thought it was too late to bring him out, so kept him, much against his will, in the house. Moe and I had a happy reunion and he was allowed to lie on my bed while I had breakfast. He was *very* much upset about it all, as he felt it was all my fault for not having jumped out of the car, but I gladly took the blame, and he forgave me for my negligence. He is much nicer about my mistakes than Pat was.

. . . Chet just came out to see if Julia and I wanted to go fishing right away, so guess we had better accept, as we had to refuse last time he asked us, because of Julia's health. Will write a better letter tomorrow. It doesn't look like a very good fishing day to me, as it is gray and windy.

All my love, darling.

. . . .

(TLS, 3 pp.)

[Cross Creek, Fla.]
March 5, 1944
Sunday morning

Dearest:

Such a gorgeous morning. Not quite hot, bees going perfectly mad in the orange bloom, birds singing, and the house full of flowers from my garden. I have never seen such heavy orange blooms. Some of the boughs are so white and heavy with it that you'd think they were covered with a perfumed snow. If you were here, we might go to Silver Glen or to Magnesia Springs, or might just talk about it and decide no place could be nicer than this, and stay home. Moe is rolling on the smooth grass over which Julia toiled. . . .

I routed out poor Julia this morning before she had had her sleep out, as I heard the Kohler turn on and knew that Martha was making the toast. It also meant that the soft-boiling eggs were in the pot, Julia's tea cooling, and if nobody showed up to eat breakfast while it was hot, God knows Martha had done, ostentatiously and with disgusting virtue, her part. This is Idella's week-end off, and Julia and I feel like babes in the wood without her. There was a cartoon in the N.Y. Times I meant to send you, but the paper got thrown out. It showed a plump mistress lying at ease on a davenport, reading "The Joys of Cooking." Through the open door of the adjoining kitchen, one saw the maid, with her hair in her eyes, cooking up a breeze and *glaring* like nobody's business. Julia was brute enough to tell Idella to pin it up in the kitchen.

Julia and Chet Crosby and I had a grand fishing outing yesterday afternoon. I was entirely mistaken about the location of "Pee-Gee." I thought it was near Dessie's old cabin, but it is on the Citra side of Orange Lake. We reached it from the edge of Talmadge's grove, through a winding channel so narrow that the boat apparently was riding on dry land. The channel suddenly opened out into an enclosed arm or bay of Orange Lake, a mile or so each way. I caught two bass, one of them quite a nice size, three or four pounds, and Julia and Chet each caught one. Julia gets the hang of anything mechanical or manual in a hurry, and by the end of the outing she was casting very nicely. She had never done plug casting before. After she caught her fish, she was in raptures, and begged Chet to take us out again soon. Chet thinks she is the cutest and most wonderful creature he has ever seen, and stares at her dotingly, now and then nodding his head at me. Having him so intrigued by her has helped make her visit very pleasant, for he has made a great effort on her behalf with the hunting and fishing. And she takes to the life here as though she had been born to it.

When she was muffing her casting, she cursed worse than I do. She has so many of my characteristics—some of the better and alas, some of the worst—that it does seem as though she were my daughter, or at least closer kin than anyone in my own family. As a matter of fact, she is more vulgar than I, and uses words I should not dream of using. I picked her a choice navel orange the other day, and as she peeled it, she said gloomily, "A bird did something on it." I said Nonsense, and please to show me any such thing. We turned the peel over with our toes and there was no sign of anything unpleasant, and I said that in her usual ungracious way, she had imagined it or made it up. She simply shouted across the grove, "I guess I know bird shit when I see it!" At least I have the comfortable feeling that I could not possibly be a corrupting influence on her—.

I have put Martha at cooking us grits and frying the fish for our dinner. I am a bit afraid of consequences, as she has been definitely uncooperative this weekend. I wanted the fish when we got in last night, although it was rather late, as they are so much better when fresh out of the water, and I called loudly (and sweetly) to Martha as we came in. I don't see how she could have helped hearing me, but she never appeared. I fixed us a lobster salad for supper, and it gave Julia and me both weird amorous dreams. She dreamed that she was married to Bob and enjoying it thoroughly, and I dreamed that I was treading on thin ice with Wendell Willkie. I am sure that we should both, Julia and I! be equally disappointed—. . . .

Julia is in bad spirits today, saying she is on the verge of one of her headaches. It is only that she is bored, for I have proved this several times with her here, and I am trying to think up something, to amuse her. I am so certain that her ailments all come from sex frustration, but there is nothing I can do about it. I do wish Bob was more of a man, for I do think that if he were not so timid along those lines, he and Julia would have hit it off long before this. Maybe Henry Heyl will be a good bet after all. . . .

God, I wish you were here.

. . . .

(TLS, 4 pp.)

[Cross Creek, Fla.]
March 6, 1944

Dear Honey:

Another beautiful morning, and I am bursting with health and energy.

Julia's headache yesterday, or boredom, or whatever it is that's wrong with her, got too much for me. I couldn't cheer her up or think of anything that appealed to her. She was as cross as a pregnant cat, and I decided maybe we'd spent too much consecutive time together, and I must be getting on her nerves—or the place was, or something. She had said she was crazy about the Salt Springs crabs, but she didn't even want to ride over and see if we could get some, so I said I'd go off rambling alone. She sat sulking with the radio in her lap, and was still in the same position when I got home three hours later.

Moe and I enjoyed the outing very much. I wanted so badly to go on to Silver Glen and sit with the dogwood in full bloom in the sink-hole at Pat's Island, but I had already bought and loaded the crabs at Salt Springs, so decided I'd better get them on home and cook them. The scrub was very dry, and the road to Silver Glen might have been impassable. The fish-house had just two dozen crabs, big beauties, so I pounced on them. And I found the perfect carrier for them—a bean crate with wet moss top and bottom. There was almost no one at Salt Springs.

I stopped in Citra to mail your letter, and as I started up again, I saw Chet

Crosby's truck drive in behind me, with Chet and Dr. Cason in it. I stopped and they came over to my car and Dr. Cason fell all over me. When I got home, Martha about floored me by asking, "How's Miss Zelma?" It appeared that Zelma had been brought home Friday, seriously ill. Any news that Martha doesn't get isn't worth knowing. Needless to say, Turner had never mentioned Zelma. Idella said to me, "Now don't run in to see her and tell her how sorry you are." By that piece of sarcasm, she meant that she thinks I have been too soft with the whole family. She didn't approve of my letting Dr. Cason in the house the time he stopped by.

Julia went into the most appalling state of mind last night. She said she didn't want any supper and went off to bed. I had tea and a sandwich, and then lay on the couch on the porch. It was a heavenly evening, with soft moonlight. I drank in the orange blossom perfume, and heard the first whip-poor-will call in the hammock, and a night-bird cry as it flew over, and a wood-duck, and little black David first crying and then laughing. In an hour or two Julia came flouncing out with a quite unnecessary flashlight and said, "God, this is awful, brooding in the dark." I remarked mildly that I wasn't brooding, but was having a wonderful time, and I told her of all the lovely sounds I had heard. She snapped, "I didn't hear a damn think but mosquitoes, and rats in the wall." Earlier in the day she had lifted a curtain on the black depths of her mind and unhappiness, and I was *appalled*. She says she wishes *constantly* for a quick, painless death. She does not believe in suicide, however. She thinks that humanity and the state of the world are hopeless, and feels that life is not worth living for her. Heaven knows that the abyss of depression is familiar to me, but it is always a temporary thing, and even at its worst, I know that I will come out of it and life will seem glorious again.

Last night she really turned loose, and at times almost sounded a little mad. She talked a blue streak, and it was almost like a kettle boiling over, or a volcano erupting. She talked mostly about her childhood, and said that life was arranged all wrong, that one should be a child most of one's life, and have to go through only a short period of maturity. She fell silent and I thought she was through, and my thoughts wandered off, and I said, rather to myself, "I don't believe my N.Y. Tribune subscription has expired" (the paper didn't come for two days). She gave a short cry, and said, "What a mundane thought! How could you! I was playing with my childhood toys."

She had a recurrent dream as a child, and had it twice again in the last year, in which the walls of a room grow larger and larger and then recede, and she stands lost and frightened. Another recurrent dream is that she is driving a car and can't stop it. The theory that came to me is that her trouble is not so much a simple sex frustration after all, but is a morbid clinging to childhood and a refusal to become adult and take an adult and mature share in life, with its attendant responsibilities. The headaches are undoubtedly a secret subterfuge for not going out into the world. If my theory is true, it accounts for the sense of childishness I so often have about her, and for her looking about eighteen, when she will be twenty-six in a couple of weeks. Finding herself, in her maturity, so out of sympathy with her surroundings, is of course a factor. Her unfortunate love affair—in which the man never so much as kissed her!—has become also an excuse to herself for not participation in life. She is being, actually, a coward.

I dare not tell her what I think, for I may be wrong, and Dr. Atchley warned me, when I said I wanted so to help her, and felt she would talk to me more freely than to anyone else, that friendship and psychiatry don't mix—especially amateur psychiatry. I seem like a haven to her, and the risk of destroying her confidence in me would be great. I think I shall write him what I have written you. I believe that the reason she refuses to go in deep with a psychiatrist or anyone of that sort, is that in her heart she knows she is being a coward, and that she does not want to see daylight, and does not want to take the mental hurdle, which would bring with it responsibility and work and the breaking of the childish chain.

I thought perhaps she had had all she could stand of an environment so alien to her as the Creek, and this type of country, and told her that if she was fed up, not to hesitate to say so, as I understood perfectly and would not take it personally, and that we could either go to the cottage for a while, or she could manage to get back to New York on a day coach. She said that was not it, that she much preferred it here to the cottage, and that she had more and worse headaches in New York than she ever had here. She went her first three weeks here without a sign of a headache, the longest she said she had ever gone since she began having them. After she had rattled on for a couple of hours, working up to a strange crescendo, during which I said almost nothing, she suddenly said, "I think the headache's gone." We went to bed, and I heard her singing in her room, and sure enough, this morning, she has no headache. She is still depressed in a minor way, however, which she says is *habitual.*

I have begun to think twice about the desirability of her marrying, for unless she can correct her state of mind, sexual completion alone will not solve life for her—and I don't know what on earth a man would do with her. She is also such a rabid perfectionist, that I am wondering if any man on earth, in daily living, could hold up to her expectations. In the condition that she is in, the first minor disappointments in domestic life, which are inevitable, might floor her, and make her gloomier and more hopeless than ever. If love and marriage failed her, she would indeed be sure there was nothing to live for. I wanted to say, "Who the hell do you think you are, to be so critical of mankind and the world, especially when you don't lift a finger to help or to do a damn thing about it?"—but of course could not and would not. And she is also so depressed about herself, that she would be the first to admit that the fault was hers. It is beyond me. . . .

All my love,

. . . .

(TLS, 2 pp.)

[Cross Creek, Fla.]

March 7, 1944

Dearest:

By some amazing quirk, Julia got a reservation for a lower berth for March 13. . . .

It is probably a good thing that Julia will be able to go, for she admitted that she was unaccountably homesick for New York. I know the feeling—it hits without rhyme or reason, and when you gotta go, you gotta go. She said this morning that now she was due to go, and *could* go, she no longer felt an enthusiasm for leaving. But it is better this way, than for her to feel she was really stuck. And PERHAPS I can get down to work, now that I have frittered away the time for so long.

. . . Yesterday Idella and I picked out a great platter of crab meat, and Julia after saying she was crazy about it, so that I drove clear to Salt Springs to get crabs, hardly touched it. She is the most difficult guest I have ever had to feed, and Idella is worn out trying to please her.

It was 78 degrees when we went to bed last night, and in the night a thunderstorm came in. It is still storming—thunder and lightning, gusts of wind, and sudden downpours. Very exciting, and everything needed rain badly, and I am loving it. This morning I felt, not nervous, but restless and excited, and paced happily up and down the living room. I have on my red velvet housecoat and Julia began to laugh and said that I reminded her of "Tiger, tiger, burning bright."[1] If I had "work in progress," it would be the sort of day when I should work like mad. . . .

All my love,

1. MKR is alluding to William Blake (1757–1827), "Tyger" (1794): "Tyger! Tyger! burning bright."

. . . .

(TLS, 3 pp.)

[Cross Creek, Fla.]

March 8, 1944

Dear Honey:

Julia's reservation was safely ready for her in Ocala. Nobody will ever believe that she got it honestly. . . .

We went to a wonderful movie at the new theatre; "The Lodger," with Merle Oberon, George Saunders, and Laird Cregar.[1] It was the story of Jack the Ripper, and a bloody thing it was too. Julia clutched and poked me all the way through—verifying my theory of her childishness and delayed maturity. The movie was not so well done that anyone needed to get terrific creeps, but Julia, with her super-criticism of art and of people, gave into it like a ten-year-old. It was seven o'clock when we got out, and I planned to go to the hotel for dinner, to save poor Idella from having to cook for us so late, but the Coffee Shop is still closed on Tuesdays, so we had to come home and rout out Idella. We had cream of pea soup made from new peas, crab-meat au gratin, etc., and Idella popped up with chocolate pie with whipped cream for dessert.

Moe went away courting again last night and has not come back yet—eleven A.M. I'll give him a few hours more, then go hunting him. I'd rather he came home on his own account, as I'm not keen about having him trot off without a word to pursue his love life, then expect a taxi to call for him when he's through. . . .

All my love,

1. *The Lodger* (1944).

. . . .

(TLS, 2 pp.)

[Cross Creek, Fla.]
March 8, 1944
Evening

Darling:

Two grand fat letters from you today. The mail situation is really improving.

. . . I'll include "Strange Fruit" in the next package of books I send you. Also one of the loveliest books I have read in a long time, "Chronicle of Dawn," by a Spanish writer, Ramon Sender.[1]

The verses by Minnie Hite Moody[2] (you remember we met her in Atlanta) were in the N.Y. Times, and I found them most moving.

Moe went off courting again, and Chet brought him home yesterday noon. Again, he had gone to Chet's house at one in the morning. Chet felt, and said, smugly, that Moe wanted to "take up" with him, as he prides himself on being a dog seducer, but it was not that at all. Moe went to see a gal—Chet said the one in Citra had just gone out of heat—and Moe figured that going to Chet's was the quickest way of getting a ride home—and so it was—though Chet *detained* him over-night both times, and said that Moe tried very hard to get out again. Now that Moe has found that it's no soap as far as the lady is concerned, he hasn't left my sight for a moment. Chet is grieving over Julia's leaving, and is taking us fishing in the morning and again on Sunday. We are to meet him at 7:15 A.M., and I am kicking myself, and may send Julia off without me. Two in a small boat, casting, are really enough, anyway.

. . . For lunch, we are eating one of the young game roosters who was killed in fair combat. Martha arrived at the end of the fight, and when he fell dead, decided it was as good a way of killing a chicken as any, and dressed him and put him in the ice-box. It is possible that the fallen warrior will be immensely tough, but I think the winner would be tougher.

. . . James Boyd is dead; very suddenly, while speaking at Princeton. Neither he nor Benet can be spared.[3]

. . . I bought the first strawberries of the season, at 78¢ a quart, and shall make Julia some ice cream today.

All my love,

1. Ramón José Sender (1902–1982), *The Chronicle of Dawn* (New York: Doubleday, Doran, 1944).
2. Minny Hite Moody, writer and reviewer.
3. James Boyd, fiction writer, died in 1944, and Stephen Vincent Benét, poet and fiction writer, died in 1943.

. . . .

(TLS, 3 pp.)

[Cross Creek, Fla.]
March 10, 1944

Dear Honey:

Godamighty, what a morning! We are just in from a thoroughly uncomfortable fishing outing with Chet. I hated to get Idella up at 6 A.M., when all we wanted was tea and coffee, so told her just to set the table. I started to bed last night, and she had taken the alarm clock to the tenant house with her—. I also hated to rout them out so late, so just fixed it on my mind to awaken, and did so at 4:30 and didn't go to sleep again. When I went out to fix breakfast, there was a mouse, or a young rat, in the dining room and another in the kitchen. It was horribly cold and raw. We were almost to the arm of the Orange Lake known as Pee-Gee, reached by a mile-long winding channel from the Citra side of the lake, when Chet's outboard motor fell off into five feet of water. He finally got it up with a grappling hook, cutting his hand in the process. Of course the motor was temporarily ruined, until it can be taken apart and overhauled and cleaned, but we decided to paddle on out and fish anyway. We didn't get even a strike, and the cold wind swept across the lake, and the sky was gray, and it all made me wonder how I get myself into such jams. Chet and I paddled in, and a long hard pull it was. Partway, he asked us to let him out on a tussock and go on a few yards. Like so many countrymen, he is horribly modest and was plainly dying of shame. It wouldn't have bothered Julia or me, in the same situation, for a moment. . . .

Julia and I went to Gainesville yesterday afternoon to market. The night before, she said she felt delicate and wanted something digestible for her dinner. Naturally I suggested things like poached eggs. She was cool to everything and I finally asked her, if she were in her beloved goddamned New York and could get anything she wanted, what would it be. She said what she would really like would be a thick juicy steak—. She ended up by eating a hearty soup, jellied chicken and vegetables and a dessert. So I made up my mind I would get her a good steak if it harelipped Gainesville. As you can imagine, the good beef situation is a thousand times worse than before you left. But I went to Piggly Wiggly, where a young butcher is most accommodating. He was not there, but was expected. So we went on to the cold storage plant, where I left my hams and bacons to be sugar-cured and smoked, to take out a side of bacon. I had to wait more than an hour, and just as I was leaving, my nice butcher showed up, to take something out of storage. I told him what was on my mind, and he said he had a superb piece of beef in storage, that he was planning to take out in a day or so, and would take out then. A whole beef had to be carved up, finally, to get at the steaks—but God they were wonderful. We had a thick one for dinner, with baked Idaho potatoes, fresh raised rolls—and Dora's strawberry ice-cream. Even Julia was satisfied and thrilled. She has certainly been hard to cook for. She is used to two dinners a day, actually, with lots of courses, but everyone takes minute portions of each dish. When I visited at her home, I damn near starved to death. For the vegetable, I had new cabbage, which she said she liked, and when Idella and I were cooking, Idella asked if she should cut the cabbage in large sections, or in small strips. Since I couldn't eat the cabbage anyway, I told her to go and ask "Miss Julia" how she liked it. Idella came back, and I said, "What did she say?" Idella said demurely, and with a poker face, "She said, 'Hell I don't know.'"

Now that Julia is not stuck here indefinitely, she hates to leave. For two cents she would give up her reservation. I shall miss her very much when she goes.

. . . Last night as Julia and I sat together in the living room, she said, "There is one thing you do that upsets me terribly." I said, "*One* thing?" and bless her heart, she said there were very few things about me that upset her, and they were all minor, but this one thing really bothered her. I could not imagine which particular basic flaw in my character disturbed her. It proved to be the fact that on the typewriter I use a capital I for a one, instead of using the lower case l. !!!! I had been writing I944 and it should be 1944. Can you see enough difference to get in a swivel about?

She is a strange little person, and I love her dearly, but I shudder for her future. Thank Heaven, we are better friends than ever after her long visit. It takes real affection and sympathy to stand up under six weeks of being stuck in one place together.

All my love,

(TLS, 3 pp.)

[Cross Creek, Fla.]
March 11, 1944

Dearest:

It is six o'clock Saturday evening, and I haven't written yet today to my sweet my love.

. . . The Ben Hecht book on anti-Semitism was dreadfully disappointing after all. I didn't get disgusted until toward the end, but when Julia read it, she was outraged after a couple chapters. She is the most genuinely and unaffectedly liberal person I know, and has loathed anti-Semitism in the people she is thrown with, but she said that the book damn near made her a Jew hater herself. So I sha'n't send it to you.

I ordered, and have begun to read, a 2-vol. work by a Swedish sociologist Gunnar Myrdal, "An American Dilemma: The Negro Problem and Modern Democracy."[1] It is supposed to be definitive on the subject. As Julia says, it will at least give one ammunition.

Harper's Magazine has an article on our Wendell, called "Willkie, Man of Words," and it raises the very question that has been in my mind. I have felt, for all his terrific charm and appeal, that there may be a taint of insincerity about him. He is certainly out for Wendell, first and last. Yet he has a certain bigness, too. I could conceive of his going into the presidency and *becoming* big, once he had what he wanted and did not have to play poker any more, but without that, there is to me a certain suspicion of—I don't know what word I want—not quite hypocrisy, certainly—but also certainly not a *complete* integrity.

. . . Idella told me today that after Julia leaves Monday she thinks she will have to ask for a week off. This scared the pants off me. She said that her sister in Jacksonville,[2] the one married to the prosperous Negro doctor, had had a double operation and was very ill, and Idella's mother has been there running the household, but is not well and wanted Idella to come and relieve her. She wanted Idella this week, but Idella said she could not go as it was Julia's last few days. I was cheered up by Idella's saying that she hoped her sister would be well enough so that she would not have to go. She also said that she would like to take someone and train her at her own expense, so that on her bi-monthly long week-end off, I would not be high and dry. I don't know whether this means that she is preparing to get out from under again or not, but fatuously hope not. She has really been worked to death while Julia was here, as we have had three Ritz-Carlton meals a day, along with Julia's personal washing, and the terrific laundry of sheets, towels and table linens, for Idella is wonderful about having all linens changed oftener than most New York households do. . . .

All my love,

Charlie Scribner wrote Julia that advance readers of Edith's book[3] were so enthusiastic that they had put it into a second printing, making 10,000 copies before publication. Isn't that wonderful? He also said that I should be thanked for getting them all together, and that he should be thanked for not throwing the book out, as when it came in, it was impossible.

1. Gunnar Myrdal (1898–1987), *An American Dilemma: The Negro Problem and Modern American Democracy* (New York: Harper, 1944).
2. Hettie L. Thompson Mills.
3. Edith Pope, *Colcorton* (New York: Scribners, 1944).

. . . .

(TLS, 2 pp.)

[Cross Creek, Fla.]
March 12 [1944]
Sunday morning

Darling:

I went to bed last night a little before ten, and in a few minutes Moe slipped out and made off again. Julia, a firm believer in dog-beating, advised me to go after him at once and beat hell out of him when I caught him, as more efficacious than a beating when he returned, full of smugness. He is evidently on the verge of becoming a tramp, and I wouldn't give two cents for a dog of that ilk. I know what the trouble is, aside from his going courting, and it is that I have not been taking him walking and given him an outlet for his terrific energy. We set out in the car, and caught up with him just this side of Island Grove. I whipped him with a narrow red belt and brought him home and he has been properly cowed since. Julia also thinks she would like a man who beat her, figuratively at least. I could only tell her that once she had tried it, she would change her mind.[1]

Bob has never appeared, and I feel badly about it on Julia's account. I wrote him that she was leaving tomorrow, thinking it might spur him to wangle a day off and a plane ride to Gainesville, where I told him I could meet him. I hope he didn't interpret my note to mean that it was too late to come. I also hope that Cecil's row with me is not responsible for his having been so indifferent.

Poor Chet talked to Julia and me, and said he was suffering so about the war situation that he felt he should have to enlist. He is 39, and safe from the draft, but said it irked him to say, figuratively, to men who were in it, "Well, you fellows go ahead and clean up the mess and I'll be here when you get back—if you get back." He said that what was holding him back was the fact that he has just begun to get on his feet financially, and that if he went and came back in two or three years, he would be back where he started years ago. If he decides of his own accord to go, I shall of course tell him just to skip the payments on his mortgage to me. I asked him what his wife thought about it, and he said that part of the time she kidded him, saying that she knew he was bluffing, then when she realized he was serious, called him a damn fool. Talmadge DuPree also calls him a damn fool for considering it. Personally, I feel that he should go, for the sake of his own integrity, but I cannot take the responsibility of influencing him. He is an awfully decent chap, in a simple backwoods way. And he has certainly helped to give Julia a good time. We were to go fishing this morning if the weather was good, but it rained all morning. It has cleared now—noon—and I just went to Julia's room where she was packing, and told her not to dress, as Chet would probably call for us to go fishing this afternoon. Julia is snobbish in such unexpected ways. She said (in sweater and slacks), "Why would I dress?" I said, "For Sunday dinner." She said, "Still, why?" It reminded me of the time Bill Grinnell told me she had lovely silver for which she had no use, but of course I could not use it, because of the way I lived. Now anyone can use nice silver and china and furniture and linens. I choose to live simply, but I resent being classified with Crackers who *have* to live simply. That is where I am small—I should be above such things. But the Julia Scribners and the Bill Grinnells irk the——out of me. Poor darling Julia. I love her so deeply, and she loves me as profoundly, if not more so, for she needs me much more than I need her.

. . . When Chet came out last night to plan for Julia's fishing today (as I wrote you, he is most enamoured of her) the weather was bad, but it has cleared, so I suppose I shall have to sit in a wet rowboat all afternoon—.

I shall miss Julia terribly, but may settle down to work after she has gone.

All my love, darling,

1. MKR is alluding to her former marriage, occasionally violent, to Charles Rawlings.

. . . .

(TLS, 2 pp.)

[Cross Creek, Fla.]
March 13, 1944

Dear Honey:

Well, my beloved and half-batty Julia leaves me today. I don't know what I shall do without hearing "Oh, God damn it!" a hundred times a day, rushing to see what catastrophe has occurred, and finding that perhaps she has put her elbow in the whipped cream.

I came near killing her (by accident) or at least messing up her looks (again by accident) on the eve of her departure. After our Sunday dinner yesterday there was apparently no hope of good fishing weather, so we hopped in the car and headed for Gainesville to try a movie. Just around the sharp bend in the road toward the Creek, going fortunately at no more than twenty-five an hour, I saw one of the Brice mules galloping toward me in the middle of the road. He had run away, and was being driven home by Mr. Williams. I cut as far to the right as possible, the mule swerved into my path, I slammed on the brakes, but mule and car met, with utterly disastrous results to both. The mule simply piled up over the hood of the car, even crashing his hooves into the top of the car over our seats, and splintering the windshield on my side into frozen spray. The glass held, or consequences to me at least would have been serious. The whole front of the car is mashed to metal pulp. The poor mule was killed almost instantly. Mr. Williams, and J. T. Glisson, who was passing, both said it could not possibly have been avoided, and only the fact that I was driving so slowly kept us both from being killed. I am sure my insurance will cover the price of the mule, as well as all but $50 of my own bill. . . .

Ivy Sykes just walked in, looking like a new man in uniform, after nearly two years in the Army. It certainly straightens up the sloppy Cracker boys. He asked about you and sent his regards. The new draft is about cleaning up the able-bodied men and boys in this section. I think the groves will just have to shift for themselves.

I was about to finish my story when Ivy came. I didn't think the mule accident bothered me at all, but found I was a bit fidgety, so we took the truck and drove in to Chet's and got him to take us fishing. It finally cleared and was a beautiful afternoon and evening. We had only two rods and reels so they did the casting, and each caught a nice bass, which we are having for lunch today. I am certainly grateful to Chet for helping to entertain Julia, for without the hunting and fishing, and with her not being interested in going to the cottage, there would have been damn little to do here.

I kept Moe shut up in my room all night, and he paced up and down most of the time. This morning he headed out again. If it is only courting, he will settle down, but if he's taken to mere rambling, it will be a frightful nuisance. . . .

All my love,

. . . .

(TLS, 3 pp.)

[Cross Creek, Fla.]

March 14, 1944

Dear Honey;

. . . Several truck loads of soldiers came by, dragging a plow that cut a deep furrow right along the edge of the highway, raising hell with my grass. I went out and called to the driver, "I suppose there's a good reason for digging up my grass," and he said, "Yes, Ma'am, there is," so I said "O.K." and they went on digging it up. They stopped by the barn and I sent out and told them to help themselves to all the oranges they wanted. One of them said, "Oh gosh, it won't be any fun now. We were going to steal them."

Mrs. Glen Bass, the pretty one, came out to see me this morning. When she got out of the ca[r], I thought it was an elegant stranger and started to hide. She had on a gray flannel skirt and stunning sport jacket and looked like a million dollars. She and Glenn had been working at a Jacksonville shipyard for several months, making fabulous wages between them. Her mother stayed in their new house with the three little boys, but got tired of it, so they walked out of their jobs and came back with a pocketful of money and now Glenn is happily fishing on Lochloosa again. He was almost taken by the Army but was rejected on the last go-round because of bronchial asthma.

. . . I do think it is amazing that Julia and I, as peculiar as we both are (and of course she seems to me much more peculiar and difficult than I am—damn it, she *must* be!) got along so beautifully for so long, at such close quarters without a respite. I think we are more firmly attached than ever. Thank Heaven, Edith's book is going to make some money, so she can stay where she pleases. It may be New York, as she wanted to do some library research there.

. . . I bought two hundred tomato plants and Martha and I are going to set them out this afternoon, on shares. Old Will has gone to Palatka to see his quack doctor. . . .

All my love,

. . . .

(TLS, 2 pp.)

[Cross Creek, Fla.]
March 15, 1944

Dearest:

. . . Martha and I had just finished setting out tomato plants yesterday afternoon, and were panting and saying how glad we were we were through, when J. T. Glisson showed up and presented me with a handful of egg-plant and green pepper plants. We were glad to have them, but not right then.

Baby ducks have begun to hatch and they are so adorable. Evidently the foreign drakes were what was needed. It reminds me of a fascinating neighbor we had in the apartment house in Georgetown when I was going to high school. Her name was Mrs. Nolan,[1] and she was a spectacular blond with an ermine coat. She fancied herself as a high soprano and her voice, above the haphazard piano notes of her own striking, was as shrill as a hawk's. When she let loose, one of her parrots screamed with her, then, outclassed, shrieked, "What the hell! What the hell!" Mrs. Nolan kept large numbers of birds and we had a strong suspicion that large numbers of men kept Mrs. Nolan. There seemed no other way to account for men's voices late at night, through our bedroom wall which adjoined Mrs. Nolan's bedroom wall. There was a Mr. Nolan, very fat and inclined to drunkenness, who came home only occasionally. One day Mrs. Nolan, wrapped in the ermine coat, her hair freshly blondined and topped with a black velvet hat with an egret plume, was sweeping out to go down-town on her mysterious errand. She stopped to pass the time of day with Mother, to whom, for some strange reason, she was devoted, for there could not have been two more dissimilar women.

. . . Years later, I found among Mother's things one of those old fashioned photographs of post-card size, of Mrs. Nolan in the ermine coat and black velvet hat and egret plume. Across it was scrawled, "To my nearest and dearest neighbor." Studying the portrait with the eye of maturity, I knew for a fact that Mrs. Nolan had been our nearest and dearest whore.[1]

All my love,

1. The secretive Mrs. Nolan inspired MKR's story "Miriam's Houses," *New Yorker* 21 (24 November 1945): 29–31.

Martha and Will Mickens. By Permission of the University of Florida Libraries.

(ALS, 10 pp.)

[St. Augustine, Fla.]
March 18, 1944

Darling:—

. . . Idella and I drove in to town from the cottage yesterday afternoon and I brought her direct to the Castle to help prepare for the cocktail party. . . . In case previous letters are late, I gave a party for Edith to celebrate her new book. . . .

. . . Well, I might as well tell all—. I had had two or three highballs at the Drysdales, and through my party I tossed off Manhattans like water, out of pure absent-mindedness. Doug had room no. 6 for us to use, and all of a sudden— luckily when the party was almost over I walked in a trance to no. 6 and calmly went to bed. I woke up late in the night, and knew I wanted to go to the bathroom, and damned if I knew where I was. I had never expected to spend the night, and for a few minutes I was a trapped and disembodied spirit, feeling all the walls and trying to figure who the hell I was and where the hell I was—whoever I was. I finally placed myself, with infinite relief—and found the bathroom, ditto. I slept wonderfully, and awoke with a certain remorse for having walked out on my own party, but otherwise only agreeably frail and languid. . . .

I love you so much. . . .

. . . .

(TLS, 2 pp.)

[Crescent Beach, Fla.]
At the cottage
Sunday noon
March 19, 1944

Dearest:

It is the most divine day, and Moe and I are enjoying it thoroughly. We are just in from an hour's walk on the beach. The sun is hot, and good hot, and there is a cool March freshness in the air. The wind is strong, very spring like. I walked barefooted, part of the time in the water, and I really believe it would not be too cold to go in all over. I felt as though I were sailing along with no effort, and went nearly two miles north before turning back. When I did, I found why the going had been so easy. The high wind had been behind me, and had operated on my fanny as though it were a balloon. Facing into the wind, I had to fight every step of the way. . . .

Had a lovely dream about you last night, but it made me more lonesome for you than ever.

All my love,

(TLS, 3 pp.)

[Crescent Beach, Fla.]
At the cottage
Monday morning
March 20, 1944

Dearest:

This is "my day" with Aunt Ida, and there came a moment when I thought I should scream—then she suddenly struck me funny and all was well again. You know, she really improves on so many words. Her Mrs. Malapropisms are often most apropos. For instance, she informed me that her ex-landlord, Mr. Smith, died in "Catchahoochie." Now I know the insane asylum was named after the river, but they really should call it the Catchahoochie.

Well, Moe and I went in the rattle-trap truck yesterday afternoon to Boo Tate's and Esther Curtis'[1] cocktail party. It was an enormous party and all the town was there.... Boo Tate is being the most terrific soldier about Major Joe Tate's having disappeared over Holland in his plane, and believes, or says, that she believes, he is still alive....

I was horrified to have Alfred Houston say to me at the party, "We'll see you at dinner." I said, "When?" and he said, "Tonight." It was the first I knew of it. Then the Houston house-guest said, "We'll see you at dinner tonight." So I tackled Ruth Houston frankly and said that others seemed to think I had a date, and did I. She informed me that at my party for Edith, she had asked if I could come to dinner after Boo Tate's party, and I had assured her I should be delighted. I had to tell her that I had been in my cups and remembered nothing. As it happened, I was free, except for my date to pick up Aunt Ida, so went on over to the Houston place for dinner.... Ruth informed me that Alfred was the son of a young American who had gone to Chile from Maryland, and married a Chilean wife, whose parents were both French. She said, "Don't you think he looks terribly French?" With his German accent, I did not, but did not say so. I still cannot figure him out. I am retiring as president of the Library Association and Alfred is taking over. He is either a super-darling person—or a Nazi agent. Time will tell....

All my love,

1. Esther Curtis of the St. Augustine War Ration Board.

. . . .

(TLS, 2 pp.)

[Crescent Beach, Fla.]
March 21, 1944

Dearest:

Still at the cottage, but will go home in the morning. I've had a very pleasant time....

I stayed in bed all morning (Idella met me at Jean's last night) reading the damndest book, "The Lost Week-End,"[1] a superbly done study of a real drunk....

I love you so much.

1. Charles Jackson (1903–1968), *The Lost Weekend* (New York: Farrar and Rinehart, 1944).

. . . .

(TLS, 3 pp.)

[Cross Creek, Fla.]
March 24, 1944

Dearest:

It is dark, and Moe and I are just in from a walk, both panting from the heat. I made my social rounds in St. Augustine yesterday, in the truck, which looked even worse than before, thanks to a large gypsy bundle of laundry....

I saw the Cabells, and they will almost certainly not be able to come over before they go to Richmond, and I'm sorry, as with Priscilla's arthritis and the gas situation, I have the feeling they won't come down again. They sent their best love to you.

. . . We drove home with the menace of rain on bags and laundry, and just made it. The place had an abandoned feel at once, and it proved that Martha had gone to St. Petersburg, where Adrenna is or was ill. There wasn't a drop of water in the tank, and the birds were unfed and unwatered, but Sissie was doing the milking and feeding ducks and chickens. I have about 14 baby ducks so far—and only ate three of the old ones this winter! Sissie said contemptuously of Adrenna, "Tain't nothin' but the change o' life. She sure is old enough...."

Afraid Chrissie is drying up, and has not been bred again, and Dora I think is through forever. Think I shall just let the cow business go this summer, but it will kill me to buy and give points for butter.

Moe was gone all night and all day and I guess I have a tramp on my hands. He is tired but still acts restless tonight. I shan't let it worry me and will just hope he escapes cars on the highway....

Had a wire from Max Perkins[1] today asking if I had Edith's address, as it was important to communicate with her. He said there were to be wonderful reviews in the coming Sunday's N.Y. Times and Tribune. A letter was waiting from him here and he said they had printed 15,000 copies.

There were two good fat letters from you and I enjoyed the chief of the village, but was so sorry that you evidently did not get your leave. The news from India and Burma was good, then the news today is that there has been a Jap infiltration over the India border. Not a large or serious one.

. . . In TIME you will probably see the item about Charlie MacArthur. He won Helen Hayes' heart when he first met her, handing her a sack of peanuts and saying, "I wish they were emeralds." He is in Burma now and sent her an envelop of emeralds, with the note, "I wish they were peanuts...."[2]

All my love,

1. The wire is dated 22 March, and MKR responded on 23 March, saying, "Am utterly thrilled over high quality and success of book [*Colcorton*]" (*Max and Marjorie*, 561).

2. Charles MacArthur (1895–1956), playwright, was married to the actor Helen Hayes. He wrote a preface to *Letters to Mary: The Story of Helen Hayes* (New York: Random House, 1940).

. . . .

(TLS, 4 pp.)

[Cross Creek, Fla.]
Sunday morning
March 26, 1944

Dearest:

. . . The lawn grass has grown another inch over-night. I don't see how I can possibly cut it myself. Wonder if I couldn't stake out Chrissie and Dora and move them from patch to patch, to eat it off.

I feel wonderful and full of energy but so nervous I could literally scream. I can't do anything in moderation, so am off cigarettes and liquor at the same time, and reducing too. No love, no nothin.' What is there left? Just the goddamn spring flowers.

. . . The feed basket is full of infinitesimal gray birds with a touch of yellow, some sort of finches I suppose. The senior game rooster is standing underneath, picking up grains of feed as the little birds knock them out, and furious that I have so arranged the hanging basket that he can't quite fly into it. He is crowing his defiance. He is simply beautiful, in the most brilliant plumage, his bronze tail feathers lyre-shaped—God, I wish I were a hen.

I might have been resisting cutting loose on the subject of Julia again, but I might as well get it off my chest. For Heaven's sake don't round up any potential husbands for her—God help the man who does marry her. When I returned from St. Augustine to the Creek, there was a thick letter waiting from her. It was her bread-and-butter letter after nearly six weeks with me. It was the damndest hysterical tirade I have ever read—about my driving when I have a couple of drinks. At first I was so depressed—about myself—that I didn't know what to do. I thought, well, the drinking has slipped up on me and I am a besotted, danger-ous creature and just don't know it. Her letter, for all its high pitch, seemed aw-fully plausible. She said that when I had had a few drinks she had noticed that my reflexes were not normal and that she had never been more terrified in her life than when she rode with me. She said I would kill a child some day and remorse would ruin me, etc. etc. etc. She said that one time we set out from the Creek I "started out at terrific speed" and it gave her one of her headaches and she was madder at me than she hoped ever to be again, as she could picture herself in the hospital with something broken just because I was relieving my nerves by driving fast. She went on to talk about the mule accident and said that she could see the accident coming (so could I) and she was sure I did not put on the brakes until after I hit the mule, and it might just as well have been J. T. Glisson on his pony that I killed, etc. etc.

Then by God I got to thinking things over. I didn't want to rationalize and clear my own slate, just to be clearing it, if she was right and I had suddenly become a dangerous character behind the wheel. Well, I am not drinking any more heavily, not as much, as I have for twenty years—and I have never had an accident in my cups, and only two minor ones that were not entirely my fault, when I had not had a breath of a drink. We did not "start out" at "terrific speed," for I never do start out at high speed, but after a while I deliberately hit fifty, as we were going on a business errand for me and I knew that Julia would be bored, and I wanted to get it over with as soon as possible. Now you know fifty is not "terrific."

As to the mule accident, Hugh Williams, who saw it, said that I drew to one side and put on my brakes *before* the mule climbed into the car. I could see the thing about to happen, but thought at the time, that while one would have to stop dead for a cow or hog to make up its mind which way to cross, a horse or mule would *surely* keep its own path down the middle of the road. I was in perfect possession of my faculties and all this went through my mind at the time. I had two drinks before dinner, and then dinner, and was perfectly normal. Then I remembered the day Julia left, when I drove the truck and towed my car with Julia steering it. She was in an absolute panic when we reached Citra, where Chet Crosby was waiting to see if we were going to need help in getting to Ocala. I have steered a car that was being towed and knew that all one had to do was keep directly behind the car doing the towing, and trust *them* not to hit anything and not to drive too fast or to brake suddenly. But Julia said she would have to have signals, to know whether another car was coming on the left, and whether there was a mail-box or anything on the right, etc., and as I wrote you long before I got her weird letter, I indulged her and followed all the elaborate signals she devised, so that *she* would know about every dog on the road.

I began to realize that the letter was something hysterical on her part, but couldn't quite place it, and still thought maybe I was more of a drunk that I realized. . . .

Then something clicked in my mind, and I realized that Julia is afraid ALL THE TIME, both mentally and physically. Her "terror" at my "terrific speed" of 50 an hour (and I was cold sober then!), her fear that I would put her in the hospital, checked with her recurrent dream that I wrote you about, of her driving a car and being unable to stop it. Her constant morbid preoccupation with her health, refusing to eat the Salt Springs crab meat after I had driven over to get the crabs when she said she liked them, saying she was afraid they were too "rich." The car she cannot stop in her dreams is Life itself, and she is still a morbid and frightened child. There may also be something of that defensive and neurotic desire to slash out at people that I had before Dr. Atchley psycho-analyzed me in a mild way and have corrected to a large extent, for after her attack on me she has *deluged* me with loving letters, as though she realized she had done something that would take a lot of covering up.

The girl has me stumped. I cannot write her these things, for she is so on the defensive, so absorbed with herself, so critical of other people, that it would destroy all her confidence in me as one of the few people in her life who do not criticize *her*.

I shouldn't be writing you this trash and I may not mail it at all. I do like to write you every day and many days there would be nothing at all to write if I didn't tell you what I was *thinking*.

. . . Most of the time now I am living in a strange vacuum, not unhappy, enjoying the damn flowers and the pretty days etc., but now and then anxiety and just plain loneliness and longing for you stab like lightning through the comfortable wall of numbness.

All my love,

. . . .

(TLS, 2 pp.)

[Cross Creek, Fla.]
March 26, 1944

Darling:

. . . I haven't written your mother since hell began to pop in Burma, with Japs crossing to India, etc., for I know she is having fits, and I can't think of anything to say to her! Must get myself together and write her something gay.

. . . I heard they are using negro women in some of the groves to unmound orange trees, and it gave me an idea for my desperate situation out here. My young grove must be fertilized ahead of the unmounding (I have the fertilizer) and I believe Idella and Sissie and I together could do both jobs. The only trouble may be that the grove will be too wet to drive the truck through with the sacks of fertilizer.

Moe ran away again last night and is not back. The bond between us is certainly broken.

. . . Yesterday afternoon I suddenly got in a fury at myself about the cigarette smoking and hurled a whole new carton into the hearth-fire. I knew if I gave them away I should feel virtuous and promptly drive to Citra for another carton. I am counting on my Scotch blood to keep me from buying another until the time has at least elapsed that they would normally have lasted, and I'm hoping by that time I may be over the hump. Meantime I am about nuts. Dora and I are battling all over the mat. I say, "Damned if I'll be a slave to *anything*," and Dora says, "I *adore* being a slave." In the same rage I also poured a freshly opened quart of brandy down the drain. Dora has no words in which to express her horror at my folly. The Scotch blood still waves. . . .

I think about you all the time and love you so much.

(TLS, 1 p.)

[Cross Creek, Fla.]
March 29, 1944

Darling:

. . . I have visualized you in every possible contingency during the Burma evacuation. Sometimes you are plodding down the river bed, ducking into the banks when there are shots. Then I think of your poor feet, meant for dancing and putting under the cocktail table or bridge table! Not for two days down a river bed—. Then you are the one with "slight shrapnel wounds," and I almost hope you are, so you will be sent home—except that I know you would not want this. Then I picture the slight wounds, and you come home with a scar on your face and are still perfectly beautiful to me. I only hope you kept your hands over your doo-hickey—. (But you would still be beautiful.)

Then I see you as one of the men who was "presumed to have reached stronger British forces in an isolated forward position"—and sometimes you get there, and sometimes you are lost in the jungle and sometimes the Japs capture you, and I hope you will turn on the charm and cow-tow and salaam and they will think you are as lovely as I do. Then I go nuts—.

I am working hard physically so that I can sleep a little and get tired enough not to have to rush out on the Creek road screaming. I mowed a section of the over-grown lawn this morning and am still purple in the face. I'll have to do it in small installments, as it really is a man's job.

. . . Honey, if you *are* all right, this ends any nonsense about a sapphire. Put the same money in another A.F.S. ambulance, or some place where it will do a little human good. I feel as though I wanted to strip my life down to grits and collard greens. I love you with all my heart.

(Dora Rolley is Dead!)

. . . .

(TLS, 3 pp.)

[Cross Creek, Fla.]
March 30, 1944

Darling:

A wire from Mr. Galatti[1] yesterday afternoon said they had just had a cable saying all men were "presumed" to be safe. I'm not too enthused about that "presumed," as it would seem to indicate that the men who moved forward were not individually accounted for. He also said he would keep me advised. . . .

I had mowed one patch of lawn and found it really a bit too much for me, so dashed over to George Fairbanks' and persuaded him to come early today and cut the grass. He showed up, but has had to stop twice, for the rain. The grass looks nice for the first time, however, and is a gorgeous emerald green.

. . . With many chuckles, I had to write Julia a mortal blow, from Chet. He told

309

me that Julia and I were the only women he had gone hunting and fishing with, who didn't bother him. He said he'd just as soon have us along as a couple of boys or men. He was too bashful and modest to say just what he meant, but it was that it didn't quite slay him if he had to be put out on a tussock, and that we don't act or seem sexy. Knowing how Julia hated my calling her wholesome, it was with glee that I wrote her that Chet summed up his compliments to us by saying of Julia. "She has a good clean face." I added, "Sorry, pal," but was amused to death.

I have been too upset about you to tell you of a scare I had the day I went to Gainesville. I went to pay my taxes, and was informed at the tax collector's desk that the taxes had not been paid on my homestead piece, which is the section of grove that has the house on it, and that it had been sold!!! I almost fainted, for I could picture Zelma Cason out of meanness, or Tom Glisson out of slyness, paying up the taxes ahead of me and then buying it in. Then I found it had merely gone back to the County, and I was able to redeem it at slight cost over the taxes. It must really have been the fault of the tax office, for I go in every year and pay whatever bill they hand me. I pay no real estate taxes on the homestead piece, but have school and road taxes to pay, and these just had not been billed me since 1941. God, I was frightened.

It is too early to be hopeful, but I may be all set on getting caught up on the nightmare of unanswered correspondence, which has now reached two or three hundred letters. . . . I noticed that the Glisson daughter, Marjorie,[2] was at home, and a dim memory came to me that she had taken a business course and been a stenographer. I stopped by, and she was a typist at Blanding for two years and will be glad to try to do my work. She doesn't know short-hand, which I don't need anyway. The moot question will probably be the quality of the Cross Creek spelling. But if she is reasonably reliable on that, I am hoping she will be just what the doctor ordered, being right next door.

. . . Julia almost had hysterics when I told her about Edie's emerging from an hour and half in the bathroom to say, "You know sometimes I think that what I need is just time to dream." Julia has suffered from her, from her not keeping engagements in New York for luncheons, dinners, concerts, etc. She said Edie always showed up from one to three hours later and said she just couldn't help it.

I also had a note from Norman Berg from Parris Island, South Carolina, very proudly a private in the Marines. He said they really put them over the hurdles, probably on the theory that if they are going to crack, they had better do it now rather than overseas. He sent his best to you and signed himself "affectionately" so I guess he has forgiven me for the moment for not seeing what Julie saw in him! And saying so!

All my love, darling.

1. Stephen Galatti.
2. Marjorie Glisson, daughter of Tom Glisson.

[Cross Creek, Fla.]

March 31, 1944

Darling:

Well, I did have a letter from your mother. She had the A.F.S. notice about the supposed escape, but had not seen the more alarming newspaper story. I have done a good job of lying to her, saying that you could not possibly have reached the fighting front after your leave, in time to have been in on the catastrophe. In fact, I did such a convincing job that I have myself half-fooled and a little hopeful that it may be so! But I know there was time for you to have reached there. It boils down now to a question of whether, when you had been on active duty for so long, they put someone else on your ambulance for that particular piece of battle action in Burma.

. . . My walk at dusk last night was very lovely, typically Florida Spring. The road was covered with eager little frogs after the rains, and a soft stream was rising from everywhere, and through the pine woods, which someone had tried to burn, the fires had been put out by the rain, except that here and there a large tree still burned at the base where were the turpentine gashes. They looked like little house fires, intimate and cozy, and it was hard to realize there just are not any little houses in those woods. The weather cleared and it turned cold in the night. Today is brisk but beautifully sunny, and I have a comfortable fire on the living room hearth.

. . . I enclose the two fine reviews of Edith's book, in last Sunday's N.Y. Times and Tribune. One of them seemed to take something in the nature of a dirty crack at me, rather implying that my books were not at all spiritual and did not present the meaning of life! . . .

I wondered what Max meant when he told me that he thought my work had influenced Edith. When you read her book, I think you will agree with me that the only thing she may have learned from me was the tremendously effective use of a detailed natural background for your human characters. She had never done this before. But her style is certainly her own, and her substance. And even the nature angle I should consider how inevitable when she came to do such a story as hers. A writer would be a fool *not* to use it.

I have read over the two beginnings of the book I thought I wanted to do, and they are even worse than I remembered. I don't believe it is a book I should attempt. I *think* I know what I want to do, but have got to make awfully sure.

Martha and old Will are still in St. Petersburg with Adrenna, and I am wondering if it is Martha's solution of the crowded tenant house. Sissie has taken over Martha's routine of milking and stock feeding and butter-making, and it really doesn't make much difference to me if that's the way they want it, though I do miss Martha. And Sissie could hardly do dumber things in an emergency than Martha does. . . .

All my love,

(TLS, 2 pp.)

April 1, 1944

Dearest:

... Who should drive up yesterday, very handsome and snappy, but Dessie, on leave from Randolph Field at San Antonio. ... She is having fits at not being overseas, but said frankly the reason was that the WACS thought she was doing too good a job at recruiting. I said hell yes, when I thought of all the damn fool things she used to be able to talk people into, when she had a good cause to work with, a gal wouldn't have a chance. I think just to keep her hand in, she went to work on me, and only the fact that she was pressed for time kept Idella and me from being signed up, with Moe to go along as mascot. I had said laughingly, "Oh, I couldn't leave Idella and Moe," and she was all ready with the answers. I fully expect her to show up waving a paper, saying, "Well, kid, it's all fixed. The General has made a special rating for Moe."

She said to tell you to keep your eyes open for her, that she'll be along directly!

She said she has been seeing a lot of casualties, especially from the South Pacific, and a high percentage are mental casualties. She said they just sit and stare into space. She said, truly and wisely, that the American people simply are not conditioned for war. And a damn good thing in the long run, I say. Somebody has to think war is folly. I hope you can manage not to let it get you.

... I wish Martha would get on home. Baby chicks and ducklings are hatching and Sissie doesn't keep up with them, and I don't know how to take care of them when things go wrong, and we are losing them. I found a baby chick wandering alone by the front steps and he was so glad to see somebody and be picked up and have his cold feet warmed. Martha would have known where he came from and to whom he belonged. For the first time Sissie mentioned the fact that two or three other lone chicks had showed up, and had died. She found the mother of one and said casually, "She had her head bit off. But wa'n't nothin' else wrong with her." In other words, asides from having no head, the hen was in perfect condition.

Little black Martha is on a fair way to becoming like old Martha. She came over to the house and I said, "How are you?" She said, "Sick." I said, "What's the matter," and she said, "Nothin.'"

Last night Moe and I came in from our walk, and I heard Aunt Ida's old Victrola going full blast in the tenant house, and I was so darned lonesome, I went over and sat in Idella's best chair and listened to records, the most intriguing of which was "Dead cat on the line". ...

All my love, darling.

(TLS, 2 pp.)

[Cross Creek, Fla.]

April 3, 1944

Dear Honey:

... I have put in a most gloomy week-end. It rained most of yesterday, Sunday, and all last night, and is still pouring today. Sissie was supposed to look after me while Idella was off, and I pay her well for it, but I have had to build my own fires last night and this morning. Between rains I took Moe for a four-mile walk, and it was chilly and depressing when we came in, so I made a fire in the bedroom and went to bed with a strange, complicated and fascinating book, "The Conspiracy of the Carpenters."[1] What is so aggravating about Martha and Sissie both, is the way they disappear without even asking you if there's anything you want. I didn't stay in bed late after coffee this morning, and when I got up and found out how vile and raw the weather was, wanted a fire in the living room and Sissie had vanished. And of course had not done as Idella would do if there was any chance of needing one, put wood in the basket. I called Sissie but could not make her hear me. There were three large logs on the back porch and I managed to pull off enough splinters to get a fire going, using about four N.Y. newspapers in the process. There is no earthly reason why I shouldn't build my own fire, but you hate to over-pay anyone for things they don't do!

The Glisson daughter Marjorie, who was a typist for two years, is coming up this afternoon to see if she can handle my work. I am very hopeful. Hugh Williams and his wife dropped in yesterday on what I foolishly thought was a social call, as they brought a copy of Cross Creek for me to sign. But it was to check on my insurance payment for the mule; to get me to work on Sissie again, who is holding back now they finally have a house for her; and to inform me that the row with Tom Glisson will undoubtedly reach the courts soon, and they are calling me as a witness.

James Colee in St. Augustine wrote that Judge Gray owns the south half of the lot at the beach that he thinks adjoins my land, to the north, and asked if I was interested in buying it, at approximately $350. I certainly am, as I have always wanted to be protected from anyone's building too close to me. Also, if I ever enlarge the cottage, it would be fine to have more room to the north, as I'd like another bathroom there, and a work-room for me. So much of my paper-confusion would be saved if I had a private room for all the muss, with regular filing cabinets and enough desk space etc. I don't know why I have put up, all these years, with working any old place both here at the Creek and at the cottage, and having no place for business papers and manuscripts etc. There is no proper room that could be converted at the Creek, as the two small not-much-used rooms are dark and unattractive. ...

All my love,

1. Hermann Borchardt (1888–1943?), *The Conspiracy of the Carpenters* (New York: Simon and Schuster, 1943).

[Cross Creek, Fla.]
April 4, 1944

Dear Honey

No news yesterday. It was tough going.

Between you, and the war in general, and the cross-word puzzles, I have the Atlas in my lap most of the time. I got to studying the coast line of Europe and decided we were certainly not planning the invasion against the French coast, which we know is fortified to the hilt. I decided that if I were doing it, I should go in across the Netherlands, where we can absolutely count on the population, and which we know has not been fortified as heavily as France. Well, the Germans must have figured the same way, for a few days later it was announced that they had opened the dikes and flooded a large part of Holland, and were ready to flood half or more of the country—incidentally ruining land and cities that have taken centuries to build.

The very heavy book I have been reading, "The Conspiracy of the Carpenters," by a refugee German, is an amazing study of the mental processes of such people as Hitler and Nazis. It establishes the type of mind and spirit, not as Satanic, for the author shows that in the "old days" when people believed in both God and the Devil, Satan himself was the acknowledged foe of God, and by such acknowledgment, established the reality of God, but as the Anti-Christ, which is infinitely more dangerous, for to this type of mind God simply does not exist. The author also develops one of my own pet theories, namely that the machine age is not "progress" at all, but has a stultifying effect on the human mind and spirit. Unless you get desperate for reading, I sha'n't send the book, for it is such hard going. For a couple of hundred pages, nothing much is dealt with but abstractions. Then suddenly the most fascinating human beings emerge, tied in with the abstractions, and you follow both breathlessly. But it is hardly for reading in the midst of the Burma campaign.

The campaign against the Japs in the south Pacific is going nobly, and we are wiping out all sorts of enemy installations, ships, planes, men, airfields, etc. The Burma campaign, from reports we get, is as desperate as the campaign in Italy. People *hope* that the Italian campaign is a stalling action, to divert German divisions from both the Russian front and the coming invasion. But there is no such reason for the Burma battle. Much concern is being expressed over the joining with the Japs, against India, of Sandrha (sp.?) Bhose,[1] with some Indian divisions. Bhose is called a traitor by everyone, but he is probably only misguided, because of his hate and mistrust of Britain, not realizing that Jap masters would be worse than British. The same applies to Ireland, against which England and the U.S. have been obliged to set up an embargo of all supplies, as De Valera[2] has refused outright to oust the German and Japanese embassies and spies there. Ireland too, in its hate of England, does not realize that Germany would be so much more vicious a ruler—and ruler it would be—that it is cutting off its nose to spite its face. . .

I had a letter from the duck boy, Neal Smith, still in the south Pacific. He wrote that he saw an ordinary sailor doubled up in concentration over the reading of Neal's copy of "The Yearling," and thought, "Ah, yes, youngster, it's good that you're learning that all yearlings must grow up." Whereupon the sailor looked up and said, "Oh, look, Mr. Smith, what I got on the mail trip to the beach," and pulled out of his pocket for admiration an ear he had hacked from a very dead Jap body—.

Neal also wrote that he had seen King Vidor[3] in Hollywood, who told him an amusing story. Several months after the filming of "The Yearling" had been dropped, Vidor was walking around the M.G.M. lot and came across a workman carefully watering 30,000 more cans of corn. Nobody had remembered to stop raising corn for Flag.

The Sunday Jacksonville Times Union had a *snide* review of Edith's book, saying it sounded as though written by a northern tourist, although the author "claimed" to be a Floridian. It also mentioned that Edith had written other books, including "Not Magnolia"[4] (that monstrosity that she regretted!) under her maiden name of Edith Taylor. At first I thought the review was by the type of Southern woman who could not stomach Edith's theme and charitableness, then decided the reviewing of the book had been given to her because she was to write a letter to the book department of the Times-Union, expressing astonishment that an understanding review was not given to a superb and nationally applauded book.

Margie Glisson did not show up yesterday to type letters for me, but is supposed to come this afternoon. . . .

All my love,

1. Subhas Chandra Bhose, the leader of the Indian Nazi Party, who collaborated with the Germans and the Japanese in World War II with the aim of ousting the British from India.
2. Eamon De Valera, Irish statesman who declared Ireland neutral during World War II.
3. King Vidor, Hollywood film director.
4. Edith Taylor [Pope] *Not Magnolia* (New York: Dutton, 1928).

. . . .

(TLS, 6 pp.)

[Cross Creek, Fla.]
April 5, 1944

Dearest:

I had written Lois Hardy what I knew about the Burma trouble, and she wrote back immediately. She had seen or called the Mark Ethridges, who received the same word from headquarters that I did. They got Washington on the 'phone, including the British embassy, who evidently did some cabling for them, for they found that young Mark was *not* one of the five men who reached the lines on foot. The British embassy told them soothingly that the isolated advanced British post that the other A.F.S. men are "presumed" to have reached, was really a very strong one, and they were sure everything was all right. This still does not let us know whether those men reached the forward post safely. You have spoken of young Mark so often lately, that I think you may have been wherever he was—though after your leave, everything may have been changed for you. I thought of pulling some wires to get information, but decided it would be wasting valuable time for other hard-pressed people, and that Stephen Galatti would have definite news as quickly as anyone. I decided to get to work only if I found you were "missing" or had definitely been captured, and then I was going to move Heaven and earth.

... Margie Glisson came to do letters yesterday afternoon, and it went as well, or better, than I dared hope for. ... I have been correcting and signing the letters this morning, and some of her mistakes were pretty weird. scotch, english, american, chamber of commerce, were all lower case, just like that—in fact the only proper name, or rather, place name, that she capitalized was Florida. Then on the other hand she had it Very Sincerely, with a most superfluous second capital. She spelled some words that I thought were simple, as a Cracker would pronounce them, so litany came out litney, while ancestry came out ancestery. One man wrote for information about the Pearce family (my grandmother Kinnan's family) and he was plainly related, so I answered his questions. I said that my brother was named Arthur Liston Kinnan, changing the Liston to Houston—and saw to my horror that my brother was named *Author* Liston Kinnan. Authors really are never *born*! ...

The first thing that interrupted me when I was writing you yesterday, was Cecil driving up to the gate! I forgot all my hard feelings, ran out to meet him, fell on his bosom, saying, "You don't hate me!" and he sobbed, "I could never hate you!" and we both wept and wept! Peace, it's wonderful! The poor devil said he started to write me after the row, but felt he just had to see me instead. We had a drink and he stayed to lunch, very backwoodsy, of fried ham and scrambled eggs and cornbread etc., then he had to get back to Jacksonville. I don't know whether I'm right to be such a softie, after people have been nasty—but of course I'm right. To quote Eleanor's[1] probably apocryphal remark, "Everybody must love everybody." It is after all the only answer. And what I have been kicking about in relation to the Negro question, was the lack of love, in the broadest sense. Anyway, I'm glad Cecil and I "made up." And when he left, I handed him a copy of the moot "The Races of Mankind," which I sent you, and asked him, without indicating its contents, if he'd read it as a favor to me, and he said he would, "with pleasure"—and now he probably wants to cut my throat all over again!

Well, Cecil was just leaving as Margie came to type again, and we had worked about two hours, when a car drove up to the gate, and I said, "Damn! Maybe they'll just go away." And out stepped Nettie and Bob! . . .

Bob looked grand. I was so glad your pal Mr. Goldman had let me have liquor, for Bob drank the Scotch and Nettie and I drank the Bourbon, and we all warmed up and Bob told wonderful stories. At Pensacola they have several men, officers and enlisted men both, who were on Guadalcanal and such hot spots. One amusing story is that when planes would land in the Polynesians and Melanesians etc., the native girls and women, clad in skirts only, would rush in, crying, "Push-push? Push-push for cigarette!" The story was that the officers felt it necessary to hold aloof, but the enlisted men went in heavily for push-push. Probably like my buying of the peacocks, push-push for a cigarette seemed an irresistible bargain! On one small cruiser, the enlisted men were below with native girls, and one chap came up on deck to the officer who is now at Pensacola, saluted smartly and said courteously, "I'd advise you to go below, sir. There's some mighty good push-push there."

. . . Well, as the afternoon wore on and we got mellower and mellower, it came out that Bob had deliberately kept Julia and me from coming to Pensacola, not because Cecil had told him things were not as they should be, but because Bob was determined not to get involved with Julia! I almost fell over. He began telling me things about Julia's character, including her snobbishness that crops out so horrifyingly now and then, her dislike of the tropics, etc., and in defending her, I said that she was unhappy in her milieu, and was a great liberal. Bob said she was not as liberal as he was. Being on the way to being high, I said, "All right. How do you stand on the Negro question?" And Bob lit into me with all four feet, saying that he had been painting Negroes with loving sympathy before I scarcely knew they existed, and that when he first began showing me his drawings of Negroes and Negro houses, I turned up my nose. He pointed to the still-life over the mantel of cannas etc., and said as contemptuously as though the artist were an enemy instead of himself, "But you preferred stuff like that!" I was speechless!

Finally I told him that I had asked him that question, because Julia, after the Ocala row, had said to me, "Don't ever bring up the question with Bob. He's worse than Cecil." And Bob, with amazing perspicuity, said that Julia's liberalism was meaningless, as she did nothing about it, and did not intend to disrupt her easy and parasitical life to do anything helpful to mankind—a conclusion I had come to about her since her revelation of herself in the long weeks she spent here! I said to Bob that I was astonished that in his short periods of knowing Julia, he had seen taints that it had taken me so long to discover, whereupon Bob said I was the poorest judge of human nature he had ever known—and he could cite other instances where I misjudged people—and remembering Norman Berg's accusation of the same thing, mentioning Bob as one of the men I was wrong about, I almost had hysterics, which Bob fortunately attributed just to good nature!

I think our Bob may have become a man. He made some crack about women and I said, "You're getting cynical," and he said, "No, I'm just getting to be like everybody else." He went on to say that he planned to marry (which is certainly an encouraging sign) and was "looking around very carefully," had considered Julia and rejected her, whether or not she would be interested, because of her family's snobbishness and her own, her parasitical way of life, her super-criticism of everything and everybody (which I remember I wrote you irked me!) and her refusal to do anything about the things she criticizes. He said, very truly, "If she's such a liberal about Negroes, why doesn't she go up into Harlem and help them where they are dying like flies of tuberculosis?" But, he continued, again truly, she won't as she doesn't mean to do a thing but sit around and "appreciate" music and art and criticize other people.

Bob has not influenced me in the least, but while I got over the awful session I put in with her the night she talked about her childhood, I have not been able to get over her unwarranted attack on me for what she called my lack of control when driving after a few drinks. I told Bob I felt she needed help, which was past my power to give, and he said she didn't *want* help—and I had come to the same conclusion already. It is dreadful to have your opinion of your friends, your feeling for them, fluctuate so. I suppose you are immune from that. . . .

All my love,

1. Perhaps Eleanor Roosevelt.

. . . .

(TLS, 2 pp.)

[Cross Creek, Fla.]
April 7, 1944

Dearest:

. . . Margie Glisson came earlier than I expected, to type, and by working until 5:30 we finished up, all but some letters I just have to do myself. . . .

While we were working Thelma Shortridge came dashing out, and finally said she had to see me alone, so we went into the bedroom where she informed me that she just had to tell someone that she was going to have a baby. I am quite sure that she covered most of Alachua and Marion Counties with the same secret news. However, she is terribly pleased, as it will give her an excuse nobody, not even R.J., can deny, to talk about her health (she is as neurotic that way, and as attention-craving as Biscuit) and to coddle herself. She plans to go to Safety Harbor to "relax" so there will not be an accident. She also said that if all goes well, it will make her marriage seem not as impossible as it has—she is 36, and has been unhappily married to the dour R.J. for 19 years. She seemed to want something of me, so I asked what I could do, and she said just hold her hand, and would I promise to take the baby if anything happened to her. I said surely, blithely. As a matter of fact, I should not be at all surprised if it proved a false alarm (like the time I killed the rabbits) and proved to be something she et [ate], no doubt.

. . . Chet came out to have the grove fertilized, and is using a truck-load of Negro women. George Fairbanks worked on my garden, so household matters are smooth, for a while anyway.

. . . Oh, don't think I told you that when Bob was jumping on me, about being way behind him on the Negro matter, and by not seeing the seamy side of Julia, he said loftily, "You are the poorest judge of human nature I've ever known." Coming on the heels of Norman Berg's saying those exact words, and citing Bob as an instance of my bad judgment, I had hysterics, which I could not explain!

All my love,

. . . .

(TLS, 3 pp.)

[Cross Creek, Fla.]
April 8, 1944

Dearest:

I bragged too soon about Margie Glisson's improvement as a typist. Her own air of confidence fooled me. When I came to correct the last batch of letters, they were unbelievable. I did think a native Floridian would know how to spell "grapefruit"—but it came out three times as "greatfruit."

I reached Christine's¹ rather early, as after I finished my business with Turnip-seed, it was just the wrong hour to go calling. I was obliged to stay sober, as she had only been able to get some incredibly bad rum to drink. . . .

We had a pleasant old-timey evening, but toward the end Bob and Ray cut loose on the subject of Jews. They brought out all the old shibboleths, the Jews had a strangle-hold on everything, including the publishing business, they ruled the government, etc. etc. I am no Jew-lover, God knows, but I know how danger-ous anti-Semitism is, as is nigger-hating, just because it is an outlet for the evil tendency in mankind that seems to have become worse lately, and that ends in either Fascism or revolution. I decided to keep my mouth shut this time, as it was too soon after the other row, but I suffered. Bob is tainted by Rebecca, who is rabid on the subject, but Rebecca is a born hater, and almost thoroughly evil. She said once, "I wish we did the way South Americans do, spit on people. I've always wanted to spit on people." She giggled, but she meant it. Ray finally said, "Ger-many had to throw out the Jews, and we've got to do something about them, too. They had a strangle-hold on Germany." I said mildly, my only remark, that if they were so strong there, it was odd that the Nazis had been able to throw them out so easily. The answer was that, oh, they weren't strong in a military way. And after crying out how menacing they were because of their strength, Ray and Bob

319

ended up by saying that they were weaklings, just weaklings. It is all such nasty business.

... Mr. And Mrs. William Mickens sent word to their daughter Sissie please to have Idella or Mrs. Baskin meet them in Gainesville today, as they were returning home. Period. I asked Sissie if they were coming by train or bus, and when. She said they always came by train, and she thought it reached Gainesville around four or five the afternoon. Inquiry in Ocala revealed that the train arrives at 3:12. I have to do my marketing, so shall call for them in state. I'm glad Martha is coming back, as Sissie has been letting my baby ducks and chickens die in droves.

I use your name shamelessly ... to get liquor, and have no trouble getting all I need of good stuff, including Scotch for guests. .... There is a new 20% tax on liquor, many luxuries, cosmetics, etc., which is as it should be. ...

All my love,

1. Perhaps Christine Townsend Polk.

. . . .

(TLS, 2 pp.)

[Cross Creek, Fla.]
April 9, 1944

Dearest:

My God, the agony I went through about you. And you reached the Front after it was all over. Two welcome letters from you yesterday—and I'm so sorry food poisoning spoiled your leave—and one letter said that on your return you found "plenty of excitement." Now darling, since we have had news dispatches about the narrow escape of the A.F.S. in Burma, since we know that the Japs have crossed the Imphal-Mainpur highway, and hell's a-poppin,' your mild statement that you found plenty of excitement was anti-climactic, to say the least. Do tell your censor that in this country we know everything that is going on, except that we don't know the exact location of the troops and ambulance units within, say, a hundred miles. Otherwise, there are no secrets. ...

... Well, I went to Gainesville yesterday. Mr. and Mrs. William Mickens arrived by train on time, we did our marketing and reached home at 5:30 P.M. At 6 P.M. Sissie came over and asked if Idella would take David to the doctor. I was furious for two reasons: if the child was ill enough to be taken to the doctor, she should have known it before I left for Gainesville, and taken him to a doctor then; and Idella had worked like a dog all day, not only cleaning my house from top to bottom in preparation for Monday's company, but had raked the tenant house yard etc, to get it neat for Martha's return—while Sissie sat on her hunkers and told Idella she'd kill herself working if she didn't watch out. I did not see why Idella should be the goat for Sissie, so I said that as soon as I had my supper I'd take them to the doctor myself. A good thing I did. Asking at Boyt's garage, I found out that Dr. Strange did not keep office hours Saturday night. I asked if Dr. Strickland at Citra were by any chance sober, and found he had been so all week. When he is himself, there is not a better plain doctor. He announced that David had an advanced case of bronchial pneumonia and also had an abdominal condition caused either by the pneumonia or very probably acute appendicitis and even peritonitis. He said it was an emergency case calling for hospitalization, so I went over to Boyt's and called the Gainesville hospital and they were wonderful about it and said they would accept it as a charity case. We drove to Gainesville and had to wait until after 11 P.M. for the doctor to come in (who proved to be Dr. Tillman, the best in town) and he corroborated everything Dr. Strickland had said. The child's condition was critical—as a matter of fact, it was Martha who, on walking in the place, said he was "bad off" and must go to a doctor—Sissie didn't have sense enough to know it—and the hospital said that Sissie had better stay there all night. I got home after midnight. "Lady in the Dark,"[1] in technicolor, with Ginger Rogers, and the reviews say it is grand, is at the movie house in Gainesville, so I am going in now to the first show, 1 P.M., and will then go to the hospital.

David was such a brat that it might be a good thing if he did not pull through, but at the age of two, it is too early to determine character, so I hope he is all right. . . .

All my love,

Don't think I remembered to tell you that Wendell Willkie took a terrific beating in the Wisconsin primaries, which were a test case—and withdrew as a candidate for the presidency. If the Republicans nominate that little pip-squeak of a Dewey, I shall stump doubtful States, for Roosevelt.

1. *Lady in the Dark* (1944), starring Ginger Rogers and Ray Milland.

. . . .

(TLS, 2 pp.)

[Cross Creek, Fla.]
April 10, 1944

Dearest:

I don't know how far I'll get, as Ruth and the Langston Moffatt's are due in half an hour. He is hell bent on doing an interview for the *Record*, and since I have given him fair warning that there just is not a story, it is his grief. I don't remember whether I wrote you that I heard from Sigrid Arne, living in New York now, still Associated Press. She said her story on me was turned down, only her second flop in all her newspaper years. Thank God, eh? I wired Ruth to spend two or three days if she could.

I drove in to the movie, "Lady in the Dark," in Gainesville, in pouring Easter rain. It was striking in color, but I was very much disappointed. I had anticipated it keenly—perhaps that was the trouble. But I was *bored to death* for at least two-thirds of it.

I went out to the hospital, and found David the brat unfortunately greatly improved. There was no appendicitis, just the bronchial pneumonia, and his breathing was very different. In fact, he lay in state in a white bed, clean for the first time in his life, in a room of his own, playing with an Easter basket someone brought him. He was also, for the first time in his life, getting as much attention as he wanted. I hope Martha gets a chance to work on him, otherwise he will certainly grow up to be lynched.

. . . Also forgot to pass on a story Nettie told at Christine's.[1] About once in two years she comes out with a killer, like "Twa'n't Elmer," and I wonder where she gets them—perhaps from Shorty Davidson. Well, a man went into a country store and asked the buxom widow-lady storekeeper for a dime box of raisins. The raisins were on the top shelf near the ceiling, and she climbed, most revealingly, up a ladder to get them. When she came down, the man said, "I believe I'll take another." So she climbed up again and he really got his money's worth. She looked down from the top of the ladder, and saw that an old gray-beard had come in and was staring up at her. She said, "Is you're a raisin, too?" "No'm," he said, "just tremblin.'"

All my love.

1. Nettie Martin and Christine Townsend Polk.

. . . .

(TLS, 3 pp.)

[Cross Creek, Fla.]
April 11, 1944

Dearest:

. . . A second letter from Sigrid Arne, in answer to mine, in which I spoke of my anxiety when the A.F.S. had the road cut off behind them, etc. etc., also gave me a good laugh. She was all sympathy and distress, and had dashed to Dewitt McKenzie, of the Associated Press, who has known India since his cub days, and was at what is now the Burma front a year ago. He reported:

1. Nature there is more cruel than the Jap.
2. Any man who has done fishing and hunting through the Florida swamps has a good chance of coming through because of knowing how to trail, hide and eat off the land.

Ah, I have such a vivid memory of Bear-foot Baskin trailing, hiding and eating off the land! He was desperate, but sly as a panther. I saw him find the trail. His eyes shone and he motioned me to silence. He tracked silently for hours. Suddenly there was an alarm in the cypress swamp. A squirrel crashed through the underbrush and Baskin threw himself prone, invisible to all, except that his butt made a mound like the week's washing. When the danger was passed, he rose, brushed off his breeches, said "Nuts to that!" and pounced on the nourishment his woodsman's instinct told him was at hand. It was a keg of moonshine, half-full, and his keen nose had informed him it had not been more than four miles away. He held the open bung over my parched lips and said, "Follow me, and you'll never have to do without."

Dear Jesus, if your survival depends on the trailing, hiding and eating off the land that you've done on the home gridiron, you're a gone gosling! If you only had Leonard and Chef Huston with you, you'd stand a pretty good chance.

What about my sending you the Japanese edition of "The Yearling"?[1] You could point to the name that you said they spelled wrong, if you are captured, and bow from the waist. However, your captor might be a critic who would hand you a sword with which to commit hari-kari—.

All nonsense aside, I happen to know you are in a tight spot. I take some comfort in Max's peculiarly Max-like comment in a recent letter, "Don't you think humorous people like Norton are always lucky?"[2] As a matter of fact, I have a strong feeling that your luck will hold. Just try not to let it *get* you, psychologically. After all, look at the punishment I'm taking, worrying about you, and I'm not crazy yet. (I hope, I hope, I hope.)

. . . I had a letter from Charlie Scribner, saying Julia had asked him to write me for her. She has been and still is quite ill with the measles, and thank God she could only have caught them AFTER she left Florida. Charlie said he hoped his child had not over-stayed her welcome. As a matter of fact, she did, not because she bothered me or because I didn't enjoy her, but because she was so damn fussy and critical, and it whipped both Idella and me, trying fruitlessly to please her.

Charlie said that Edith's book had actually sold 10,000, 5,000 more were in stock, and another 5,000 was about to go to press. Edith rather shocked me in writing that Scribner's had sold some sort of minor serial rights to the book— after getting her O.K., of course—for $2,000, "Scribner's taking $1,000 while I get the other thousand. I am glad to have it, but I feel I want it *all*." That is the standard agreement between author and publisher, and was in her contract, as in everyone's—the publisher even takes in half of the Book of the Month payments—and after Edith would have been grateful to get a thousand dollars ALTOGETHER out of the book. . . . If the book sells the 20,000, she will get a cold $8700 out of it, as it is priced at $2.75 and I told her to have a clause put in her contract that she should get 15% instead of the usual 10% if the book sold over a certain small amount. I suppose Verle will come back broke from the war and will pocket her earnings, and then make dirty remarks about her always needing editing. . . .

All my love,

1. There were five different translations of *The Yearling* in the years 1939–1940, but none during the war (Tarr, *A Descriptive Bibliography*, 252).
2. Perkins wrote, on 19 January 1944, "I can only hope that all goes well with Norton, and don't you think that humorous people are lucky in these kind of things?" (*Max and Marjorie*, 560).

. . . .

(TLS, 3 pp.)

[Cross Creek, Fla.]

April 12, 1944

Dearest:

. . . I have been reading a delightful cookbook, done in the personal vein of mine, "Clementine in the Kitchen,"[1] about a wonderful French cook, with many grand French recipes. Almost every one uses onions or shallots or garlic, and wine, and I get tired of the high flavor, but some of the dishes I mean to pounce on. There are some lovely simple desserts.

Sissie was home for the day, and had to go back to the hospital, where the black David is having his ups and downs, and by the grace of God, George Fairbanks had come to cut the grass etc., and was willing to drive her to Gainesville in the truck. It would have been most inconvenient for either Idella or me to take her in.

I had two more letters from Edith yesterday. Again, I was utterly shocked by a grasping, mercenary streak that she is suddenly showing. I wrote you about her kicking about Scribner's taking half of the $2,000 paid for some minor serial rights to her book. In one letter yesterday, she raised Cain because they weren't advertising the book. She said they had done much better by Martha Gellhorn's "Liana"[2] (which I sent you), and she couldn't see that "Liana" was any better book than hers, and after the reviews "Colcorton" had received, she did think it was too awful for Scribner's to let it "wither on the vine." And since this is her very first break, and since the book would have been thrown out on its ear if I hadn't asked Max to work with her on it, and while the credit is certainly hers for doing a good book, still, Max's work and the prestige of being with Scribner's are more luck than most writers have. I think it is distinctly poor judgment and bad taste on her part to make any kicks. Charlie Scribner wrote me that their advertising space is rationed, as is their paper, and since all books, he said, good or bad, are selling, they cannot do much more for any one book than for another.

I mentioned this to Ruth, and in her timid way, she said, "Don't you suppose that's Verle's influence?" It had not occurred to me—and of course it is! I also wrote you how hoity-toity he had been about the book, and about her, Edith, and I'll bet my bottom dollar he is acting just the way that bastardly Chuck Rawlings did about my first book.[3] Chuck egged me on to raise Cain with Scribner's, just because he could not endure, not only any trace of success, but my having pleasant relations with my publisher, and I'm afraid Verle is cut off the same piece of shoddy cloth. I don't think it would have occurred to Edith, left to herself, to be anything but delighted over having the book do so well and make what it is making. . . .

All my love,

1. Samuel Chamberlain (1895–1975), *Clementine in the Kitchen* (New York: Hastings House, 1943).
2. Martha Gellhorn (1908–1998), *Liana* (New York: Scribners, 1944).
3. *South Moon Under* (New York: Scribners, 1933). MKR was especially upset over the foreign rights and royalties, writing to Maxwell Perkins in 7 March 1933: "I think Mr. Scribner rode rough-shod over everyone—including me—and I don't like it at all." Perkins took the blame for any misunderstanding, even though it was MKR who was mistaken about the issue of rights and royalties (*Max and Marjorie*, 97–99).

. . . .

(TLS, 3 pp.)

[Cross Creek, Fla.]
April 13, 1944

Dearest:

A gorgeous morning, golden and windy, and definitely cool. Martha and Idella are washing, Moe is chasing squirrels, and the ducks are starting nests, and setting, all over the place. Martha said reverently, "Them's good drakes."

. . . I dreamed about the lawsuit last night, so perhaps the Court is working on it. Two of their decisions in other matters were announced yesterday, so sooner or later they'll reach Zelma. I seem to detect an upward swing in my luck just lately, and if the decision is favorable, I'll know that I'm out of the woods again, for a while. It would also encourage me to work. There has been a heavy hand pressing on me, and it seems to have lightened.

. . . So many writers have died in the last two or three months: James Boyd, Major Thomason, Irvin Cobb, Hendrick Van Loon, John Peale Bishop,[1] and a couple of more I forget at the moment. Well, it will make room for some of the new ones!

I had a letter from Roderick Peattie (brother of Donald Culross Peattie)[2] from Macmillan's, saying they were planning a series of books, The Epic of America, and wanted me to do Florida. The River Series probably set them off on the idea. Some of the books will cover sections rather than individual states, and they want them done in a way, though historically accurate, that will reveal the spiritual and psychological regionalism." It is a little bit tempting, as Florida has never been "done" to suit me. I have two qualms about it; one, that if I get into a piece of fiction, it will irk me to have a commission hanging over me, though they say there is no hurry. The other, Florida is so diversified that I do not know whether it is possible [to] do a book about it that would have any artistic unity. But I think I may accept, as it would be a wonderful job to take on some time when I was unable to do creative work. It would have been perfect for these past almost ten months that you have been gone. Right now, I really think I am ready to go to work on my own book.[3]

I also mistrust anything that sets itself up as an EPIC! Epics are accidents, their epic quality established only over a long period of time and it is fatuous impudence for any group of writers to say solemnly, "We shall now sit down and write masterpieces for the ages."

Macmillan probably meant only that the series of books would reveal the epic quality of the United States itself (does it have one?), but it still sounds most pretentious to me.

Although I loved Cabell's "St. John's" (did I send you a copy?) I should have adored doing it myself, and in one or two ways, could have done a better job than he did. That is, I could have given more of the feel of the river itself. On the other hand, I could not have managed the delightful human interest that he did.

... I agree with Bob, in his griping about Julia, that you just couldn't think of living with anyone who didn't love the South, and Florida, as we do. ...

All my love, darling.

And did I remember to tell you that "Strange Fruit" has been banned in Boston, because of "obscenity"?

1. James Boyd (1888–1944), famous for his novels about the frontier; John W. Thomason (1893–1944), known for his illustrations; Hendrik Van Loon (1882–1944), journalist and historian; Irvin S. Cobb (1876–1944), novelist and humorist; and John Peale Bishop (1892–1944), poet and fiction writer.
2. Donald Culross Peattie, novelist, also known for his books on nature and those devoted to it. Roderick Peattie, an editor at Macmillan. MKR later changed her mind. Perkins was pleased by her decision and wrote to her on 27 July 1944, "I am glad you have given up the Florida book, for if you did that, it should be entirely your own book and not in a series" (*Max and Marjorie*, 573).
3. *The Sojourner.*

. . . .

(TLS, 4 pp.)

[Cross Creek, Fla.]
April 14, 1944

Honey dear:

... I took Ruthie[1] to the bus at Hawthorn, and was genuinely sorry to have her go. She would have liked to stay longer, too, and left with tears in her eyes. She is a lonelier soul than I have ever been in my worst moments, for no matter how low I might get, how frightened, I always had a certain impudence, knowing that I could go out and haul in some sort of man, while Ruthie can't—unless you count Pickering! But she has a basic strength, and I admire her and am very fond of her. She wears wonderfully. ...

I shall shoot any of the gang who try to meet you at the boat with me, or barge in with champagne and fireworks at once. I had the loveliest dream last night.

You had returned, and ah me, I went to a rack of beautiful clothes and selected the most elegant and seductive blue night-gown, but was in such a tremble when I started to put it on that my quivers woke me up and I found, mundanely, that it had turned cooler and what I really needed at the moment was to pull up another blanket—. But I shall haunt the shops to find the duplicate of that blue nightgown. The only flaw in the dream, aside from waking up too soon, was that I was embarrassed at not having taken off the pounds I plan to take off before your return. There I stood, naked as a jay, conscious of your eyes on my ample rear, like the awful time at the apartment, when I had been concealing my too-fat legs from you, and as we left to go down to a formal dinner, the skirt of that damned mustard-colored evening dress was caught up under the edge of my girdle—revealing all.

. . . After Ruthie left, loneliness overtook me, but I walked off the worst of it, doing a good four miles with Moe. Several times on the road I have run into a delightful Island Grove character, Pheifer Prince, who was the man, I forget the name I used, in "A Crop of Beans."[2] Pheifer had stopped to ask if anything was wrong, or if I was on foot on purpose. He passed me last night, halfway to Island Grove, and stopped to say, "Miss Marge, dogged if I ain't decided you like to walk."

When I got back, Idella had lighted a fire on the hearth, and that was cozy, and I got through all right until I could go to sleep. I feel faintly lousy, and hope Edith doesn't show up for a few days. Idella and I have to go in to Cecil Bryant this afternoon to work out OUR income taxes, and when that is done, I should like to spend a day or so in bed. A notice in the paper said that farm workers and domestics had to pay income tax if their income was over $500 a year, and for employers please to inform them to that effect. Idella's income will be $1040, and she almost fell over when I told her she was supposed to come across. She said, "I'll be awfully glad to pay, but I always thought income taxes were just for rich people."

I have discovered that Martha is better off financially than Aunt Ida. She gets $5 a week from the old age pensions, I pay her $5 a week, and Will gets $5.25, and they live rent-free, with fuel, milk, eggs, etc., provided. Aunt Ida only has $10 a week!

Sissie is still in Gainesville, where David the black brat is improving, but cannot leave the hospital until next week. Sissie, with friends, came out at eleven o'clock last night and went back at twelve. The car drove in over my cattle-gap, waking up me and Moe both ways, and I shall have to tell them that I put in the cattle gap for my own convenience, as I drive in at night alone, and it was too much trouble for me to open and close that barn gate alone, especially in the rain.

I have told Idella that she could get by without declaring on an income tax, as no one could ever catch up with her, but she said if it was right, she wanted to do it. I told her frankly that after Zelma's lawsuit is over, I mean to go all out on the question of Negro rights and it will be a talking point, that if a citizen is called on to pay taxes, he should have the right to vote, and should have all the other privileges of any tax-paying citizen.

Ruth had to change a bill in Hawthorn, and gave me $5 to give to Idella, and Idella was terribly upset and did not want to accept it. She said she was not only well paid for her work, but enjoyed having company and making them happy, and she would rather have our guests just say "Thank you" and not *pay* for something that was part of her job and that she was pleased in any case to do. Such an attitude SHOULD make many white people feel very small—they want to feel big. Idella said she would write Ruth and thank her, and tell her we hoped she would come again, and must not do such a thing again.

Edith's daily letter yesterday asked me to forget the letter she wrote about "Colcorton" not getting the proper advertising etc. I am glad that she realized the implications. In the same mail, Max wrote me that Katharine Cornell was terribly enthused about "Colcorton" and was having someone put it in play form, and had asked Scribner's not to dispose of the dramatic rights until she had a chance at them. Max wrote wistfully that Edith's letters were very good, but he was having an awful time tracking her down, and she just must communicate with him, to say whom she wanted for an agent for such things as Katherine Cornell's drama-interest.[3]

Max also wrote that though he had only met you once, he thought of you as a friend, and please to keep him in touch about you.

Another thing about the Negro's civic responsibilities, aside from their being taxed (and you will remember that we fought England because of "taxation without representation") is that Negro men are drafted for the Army. You cannot force men into military service for their country, without giving them the same rights as anyone else. . . .

All my love, darling.

1. Ruth Pickering.
2. The character's name is Lige Gentry in "A Crop of Beans," *Scribner's Magazine* 91 (May 1932): 283–90.
3. Perkins writes in a letter dated 10 April 1944, "Katharine Cornell is very excited about the book and has asked us not to dispose of the dramatic rights until we hear definitely from her. She is having someone put the book into play form" (*Max and Marjorie*, 563).

. . . .

(TLS, 3 pp.)

[Cross Creek, Fla.]
April 15, 1944

Darling:

I dreamed about you all night. In one, you came home, and I forgot the blue nightgown. In the other dream, I set out for Burma to find you! I took one of my nightmare train trips, and got off at the end of the line, which was none other than the Burma jungle. I walked for miles through mountainous jungle, and stopped to drink from a stream of almost black water. There were strange thick clusters of algae that I had to keep pushing away, to drink. The trunks of the trees were black. I walked out into a clearing, and it was a town. The town was one I knew I had passed through before, but it was only when I woke up that I realized it was a town I have driven through in other dreams! My dress was ragged and I carried a paper sack of food for you. The town was civilized, somewhat modern and had a very simple monument in the town square, not much more than what I think is called an odelisk [*sic*]. The jungle, and a deep ravine, were on one side, and on the other it opened up into mountains, not too densely wooded. People stared at me, and I asked politely, "Is this Imphal?" I realized they thought I was a spy, popping out of the woods that way, and no one would answer. I said, "I've come a long way, and I'm lost, but this should be Imphal." Then I saw the A.F.S group walking down a side street, in khaki shorts, most of them very young. I ran a long way and finally found you!

. . . I had a letter from Henry Heyl, saying he continued to improve, and had every reason now to believe he would live to a ripe and ornery old age. . . .

He inquired tenderly again about Julia. I had thought I had better tell him for God's sake to lay off any serious thoughts about her, as he would really have a problem child on his hands if anything came of it, then decided to keep my big mouth shut and let things take a natural course. The chances are nothing will ever happen anyway. If they did interest each other, it would be time enough to tell him, as a physician, something about her. I was awfully sore at her after her perfectly insane letter about my driving, but am getting over it, and shall write her as soon as I can do so without going off on a tangent as wild as her own.

Henry said he had thought a good deal about you, and about me, during these bad Burma days.

Cecil Bryant fixed me up on my 1944 income tax—at which I can only guess— in a few minutes yesterday. Mr. Jones' price was not worth it to me. He didn't know a thing about the foreign taxes and got me in a mess and I had to come across with an extra two thousand. Cecil only charged me $5, but I gave him 10! I don't know whether I did the right or the wrong thing about Idella. I didn't take her in with me. When he figured it up, on her $1040, she would owe $98, and I simply could not see it. He said the lowest rate now on any income tax is 22%— about $500 of her income would not be taxable. Domestics do not have the benefit of Social Security, and anything she puts away for her future would have to be saved in her next few years. She gets no benefits from living under a caste system, has no voice in government, and is a pariah in public places, and I saw no reason why she should fork over so high a percentage of her pay. So I told him just to forget it. He advised me, wisely, not to tell her any of this, but just to tell her that when we got to figuring the deductions, she didn't have to pay. Perhaps I'll have her pay some year when I am ready to make an issue of the voting etc. Cecil almost fell over when I told him what I was paying her, so evidently domestic wages have not risen very much in Ocala.

The only trouble with her high wages, as I told her, is that it shouldn't take her very long to save enough for the farm, and home of her own, that she wants, and then she'll leave me! She says she isn't saving nearly as much as she should be. I imagine her family gets into her a bit.

I didn't stay in Ocala. When we got home, found orange boxes dumped for picking and they have begun this morning. Haven't seen Chet in some time, but the last I heard, juice fruit was bringing $2.16 a box, which is wonderful.

Am missing you horribly, but the weeks do manage to slip by.

All my love.

. . . .

(TLS, 3 pp.)

[Cross Creek, Fla.]
April 16, 1944

Darling:

The news from Burma has me hanging on the ropes, and nothing can be done about it. Mountbatten's announcements continue suave, with assurances that there is nothing to be alarmed about, but the implacable news dispatches report the British and Indian forces cut off from supplies by every medium except the air. Stilwell's[1] forces sound in better shape, except that if the Ledo road is cut off, the whole campaign to and through China is shot to hell. All reports say that India is swarming with American troops—I hope they'll throw them in and brighten the corner where you are! You probably are not even getting mail, and getting none out.

I am mailing you a parcel of good books . . . and hope they reach you to tide you through the monsoon period, which will probably be more depressing than battle. I hate to think of those huge ambulances slewing around in the mud on mountain curves.

It is another lonely Sunday, half sunny, half inclined to rain. Martha went through a long rigmarole about Henry Woodward's accusing Sissie of having done something mysterious and illegal with Martha's dish-pan, but Henry, the black scamp, is the one what got it. Patient inquiry as to where I came in on it, finally revealed that Henry has moved to Palatka, bag and baggage, including the dish-pan, and Martha wanted me to write Henry a letter. Writing a letter, I gather, is more deadly than a crack with a lighter'd knot. Recovering the dish-pan did not seem to be the moot point, but crushing Henry to earth, as he crushed Truth. I asked Martha since when she needed anyone's help to handle Henry, and she said if the low-down black rascal was here, she wouldn't have to call on nobody—but the great distance, when one cannot write one's own letter, is a decided handicap. I concocted this letter, and submitted it to her for additions:

Dear Henry:

Martha wishes me to inform you that you stole her dish-pan, and you don't need to think she doesn't know it.

Martha said with satisfaction, "Don't need to say another thing. That's *hit*."

I remember that the last letter I wrote, was for Henry himself, protesting to the Gainesville undertaker who laid out old Will Woodward, Henry's brother, that the undertaker had robbed Henry of five bucks. We never heard from the undertaker, and I am sure that Henry did not expect to any more than I did, but Honor was served. It is precisely the same reason that elderly Englishmen, incapable of hitting people with lighter'd knots, write their famous letters to the London *Times*.

There has been immense activity round about, on this otherwise calm and dull Sunday morning. Hattie Lou discovered an enormous chicken snake invading one of the nests where a duck is setting, and there was a great to-do while it was killed. Three game hens were setting in the loft on the same nest, and four biddies hatched. They would certainly have been tramped to death under the impact of triple mother love, so we removed the four biddies and one hen, leaving the other two feathered Madonnas to fight it out over the remaining fourteen unhatched eggs. My sow got tired of waiting for me to find her a boar—dear knows I had done my best—and made a break for it through the fence, her nine pigs trailing her, wishing, I suppose, to watch. We let her go, for she may know about somebody I don't know about. Dora and Chrissie seem doomed to widowhood. There isn't a bull at the Creek.

I heard Lex Green[2] over the radio last night. He is running for governor, and I had thought I might possibly vote for him, since Upchurch[3] of St. Augustine is a famous ass, and I don't know any of the other candidates. Well, Tom Glisson would be an equally suitable governor, perhaps more so. Lex used the evangelist's whine, thanked the people for "being so good to him" all the twenty unaccountable years they sent him to Congress, and asked them to be just a little better to him this time, as he considered the governorship of Florida a much bigger job than that of the presidency of the U.S.A., for the simple reason that there were no finer folks in the world than in Florida. Apropos of what, I would not know, he then gave statistics on war production. I had to shut off the radio, as my stomach was getting queasy. And I should not be at all surprised to see him make it.

I have been a Claude Pepper[4] supporter, in spite of his patent demagoguery, for the reason that he has taken a courageous stand on many unpopular questions. Well, the Supreme Court of the United States, as I think I wrote you, ruled that Negroes must not only be allowed to vote, but to vote if they wished, in the

Democratic primaries. It created a terrific stir in the South, and there were threats from various quarters, and Claude, who is being hard pushed for re-election to the Senate, came out with the statement that Florida would find a way "to maintain white supremacy." Probably Claude's opponents are as great demagogues as he, but I mean to investigate. Actually, I think that once Claude was safely in again, he would be liberal, for he always has been, and has fought the poll tax laws. He is fighting for his political life—and of course I am being just as cowardly, in holding my horses on the Negro question until the law-suit is settled.

Do you get tired of having me say, God, I wish you were here!?

All my love.

1. General Joseph W. "Vinegar" Stilwell, commander of the U.S. forces in the India-Burma-China theater.
2. Robert Alexis Green served in the House of Representatives from 1925 to 1944.
3. Frank D. Upchurch, a St. Augustine lawyer.
4. Claude Pepper, then U.S. senator.

. . . .

(TLS, 4 pp.)

[Cross Creek, Fla.]
April 17, 1944

Dear Honey:

. . . I had a time getting in my walk with Moe yesterday. We set out, and half a mile from home rain overtook us, and we dashed back. I fixed an early supper, and Moe convinced me that we hadn't walked nearly far enough for my health and his pleasure, so out we went again. Around the bend, Moe called my attention to something against the fence, and it was a huge heavy turtle. I waded through poison ivy and picked it up and took it back to Martha, and since the walk still seemed incomplete, made a third jaunt, I must have done a good five miles altogether, for I was stiff this morning, and it takes a lot of walking to bother me. I did not acquire any poison ivy, as when I took my shower before going to bed, early, I soaped my legs and arms and let it dry.

We killed another big chicken snake, invading a setting duck's nest, and as we gathered for the social ceremony, I stared at little black Martha, wondering what was so damn peculiar and so familiar. She was wearing an old white turban of mine that you may remember, for I think you never liked my toques (I had a blue one and a white one) and I wore them until they were beyond the pale. The turban was amply large for me, and on little Martha, worn far forward, it drooped over her eyes and ears so that she looked like a small black mushroom with a large white top. . . .

I am deep in a fascinating two-volume book that is also hard, intensive reading, "An America Dilemma—The Negro Problem and Modern Democracy," by a Swedish social economist, who is economic adviser to the Swedish government. I wish I thought I could get you to read it—actually, I have to read it as slowly as you read—but it is necessary to keep the footnotes open at one side while you read, and it is so long and scientific, that only a preconceived determination to learn as much as possible about the subject could keep one at it. It is considered the definitive tome on the whole matter.

While revealing pitilessly and dispassionately both the totally unfounded irrationality of American behavior to and judgment of the Negro, and the amazing rationalizations made to attempt to cover up the irrationality, the book is also extremely generous to the American nature, saying that the American Creed is a noble ideal genuinely imbedded in American thought and action, destined to be of ultimate inestimable value to the world's thought and action. The author shows that the very discrepancy between the American Creed and the actual treatment of the Negro, including the mental reservations and discriminations, accounts for the violence with which the most prejudiced defend their stand, as it is natural, psychologically, to be most on the defensive, and most violent in one's rationalization, when one knows, in one's secret and unadmitted conscience, that one is wrong, or at least knows in secret that one is acting contrary to one's highest ideals.

Of course, the trouble is, that those who need to read such a book will be the last to read it. Take for instance, the fight put up successfully by Southerners to bar from the USO the pamphlet I sent you, "The Races of Mankind,"[1] which merely states the scientific findings of reliable and disinterested anthropologists! Where such a book is helpful, is in giving scientific ammunition to liberals, so that when they persist in discussing the question, they need not rely on counter-prejudice or emotional argument, as I did in Ocala, but can present quiet facts that sooner or later will have an effect.

The author shows that the admitted inferiority of the mass of Negroes is a vicious circle. Low wages, bad housing, bad food and health conditions, lack of education, lack of participation in social responsibility, a lower standard of culture, of morals and manners, keep the Negro despised by the majority of whites, who for selfish economic and hidden psychological reasons *prefer* and choose to keep him inferior, so that the whites are unwilling, and say it is of no use, to improve wages, housing, health and social conditions. The Negro consequently has no opportunity, as a mass group, to improve. He quotes George Bernard Shaw,[2] who said in one of his plays, "The proud American nation forces the Negro to black its shoes—and then looks down on him *because* he is a shoeblack."

The author presents scientific data which have more and more denied the ancient biological theories of heredity and inherited intelligence and characteristics, and accepted the thesis that there is practically no difference, allowing for differences in individuals everywhere, in mental capacity and moral capacity, in any human beings who start from scratch together, that the whole thing is a matter of environment and training and opportunity.

And the whites' hidden psychological reasons for mulattoes,' or anyone with a trace of Negro blood, being considered Negro, to the simple facts that during slavery, and long before the civil war, it was desirable to increase one's slave holdings, and designating any child born of a slave mother, regardless of its white or black or mulatto paternity, a Negro, automatically made it another slave; also, in this way, legal or marital responsibility was avoided! . . .

All my love.

1. Ruth Benedict (1887–1948), *The Races of Mankind* (New York: Public Affairs Committee, 1943).
2. George Bernard Shaw (1856–1950), British (Irish-born) playwright.

. . . .

(TLS, 2 pp.)

[Cross Creek, Fla.]
April 18, 1944

Dearest:

Everyone is talking politics, including the village clown at Island Grove who sits in the shade on the steps of the post-office or Mrs. Copeland's general store. I told him yesterday the Army would catch him if they caught him sitting there, and he said he was trying his best to tempt them. To my surprise, this section is cold to Lex Green for Governor. I thought that after sending him to Congress for twenty years, they would automatically vote for him, but the clown said "No, I've voted for him all my life, and a man has to have a little variety."

Willkie's withdrawal has increased his prestige, and those who were out to "stop Willkie" are left looking very foolish.

. . . The orange-picking is still going on, so I must have a good crop, although the comparatively small size of the picking crew is undoubtedly responsible for the time it is taking. The colored pickers are all mad about my game roosters, and are going to buy the young ones. I am glad to get them off the yard, as they fight all day long, and don't have enough hens to go around, and have gotten too tough to eat.

I went to Citra especially to mail your box of books, and found it too heavy. When I divide it up today into two packages, I shall include another book I finished yesterday, "Nine Lives with Grandfather,"[1] which is delicious.

The courts of Montgomery, Alabama, have done something that I presume is giving great satisfaction to the stalwart battlers for white supremacy. A Negro lawyer has been disbarred from practice, by the invoking of some forgotten statute that a lawyer cannot defend anyone who has not employed him. The man's offense was that he carried to court the case for sixteen Negroes who had been refused the right to cast their votes. It seems that four of the sixteen had not made technical arrangements with him. We supreme whites are wonderful and noble people, and by God I guess we can find more ways than one to keep the damn nigger in his place. People as sick and smart as we are, by God, we ought to be supreme. . . .

All my love, darling.

1. Stephen Longstreet (1907–2002). *Nine Lives with Grandfather* (New York: Messner, 1944).

. . . .

(TLS, 4 pp.)

[Cross Creek, Fla.]
April 19, 1944

Dearest:

You might know that any public conveyance on which Edie traveled would have weird things happen to it—. It was due in Gainesville from Tallahassee at 9:30 P.M. and never arrived, for the reasons that it had two blow-outs and caught on fire. Another bus had to be sent from Jacksonville and the passengers transferred at Bradford, and Edie arrived, big-eyed, at nearly 1:30 in the morning. I put in my own saga, waiting for her. I had to reach the market before closing time, then went to the hospital to see Sissie's little black David, who is improving and living like a pig in clover. Then I went to the first movie.[1] It proved an engaging affair, with Joe E. Brown and June Havoc, and to my surprise I found the big-mouth Joe a delightful comedian. June Havoc was as tough as the burlesque show that made up most of the movie, very good-looking with a wonderful pair of legs, and a perfect riot. I got out just in time for the 9:30 bus, only to be told it would be a couple of hours late. I was in no mood for sociability, so decided against calling on the Tigerts, and went back uptown to the second-rate movie! I caught the feature just starting for the last show. When I saw that it contained Don Ameche, I winced—and then sat and cried through the picture for nearly two hours. It was a very simple affair, almost an "Our Town" from the war angle. It began with Don Ameche and Francis Dee as a middle-aged father and mother of one son, the announcement of whose death in the south Pacific comes at the very beginning of the picture. The father is a druggist in a small town, and it is all most nostalgic, remembering the intimate drug-stores of one's youth. The father cannot accept the fact of the son's death, and retreats into silent bitterness, and the ex-glamorous Ameche does a beautiful and sensitive job. The locale Reverend fails to reach him. Then the father's own grandfather, played by Harry Carey, materializes and goes over the dead son's happy life, and that makes the bulk of the picture. Some of it is gently poetic, as when Harry Carey says that as long as there is a "Happy Land"[2] (the name of the picture), where little American boys can play Indian in the corn, it is a land worth dying for. The picture was directed by Irving Pichel. Wasn't he one of Elise's countless-as-the-sands-of-the-sea husbands? I came out mopping my eyes, and felt a little better to see very young female chits also mopping theirs. The idiocy of *dying* for a happy land did not occur to me until later.

Back to the bus station, and no more news of Edie's equipage. I parked on what is not much more than an alley, turned on the radio, smoked innumerable cigarettes, and waited. And darn near had a pick-up beau on my hands. He was a dreadful-looking person, six feet tall, with one of those vast bellies developed by fifty years of cornbread and white bacon, coat-less, with suspenders, a broad-brimmed Stetson, and what appeared to be the badge of a deputy sheriff on his left bosom. It was because I thought he was a sheriff that I smiled and answered politely when he came up and said, "Good-lookin' dog you got there," as it is always pleasant in my hazardous life to stay on the right side of the Law. He continued, "Bet he bites, don't he?," and warned by an obscure instinct, I said heartily that he certainly did. He asked where I lived, and so on, and finally, all in one breath, asked, "You in the timber business? Your—husband—in the timber business? You married?" I understood then that a sheriff doesn't ask those particular questions, and I said, "What's the badge?" "Oh, that's my picture. I'm at Camp Blanding." (Evidently in charge of a gang of ditch-diggers.) A bus came in that was not Edie's, but it gave me a chance to get away, saying to Moe as I left, "Guard the car," (whereupon Moe wagged his tail and looked for a face to lick) and my pal disappeared.

. . . Sitting in the car in the shadowy alley at midnight was like watching a Saroyan play. To the right was the dark bus shed, where a group of Negro boys was waiting. Every now and then, as at cue, they came out into the light of the one street-lamp and danced and sang, and then faded back into the obscurity. To the left was a little hole-in-the-wall all-night café. It was painted a Robert Camp blue inside, and the outside brick wall was the soft oyster-white, with gray shadings, that he uses so much. Soldiers went in and out, and had beer or cokes, and sometimes a single lonely soldier would stand at the door and look in and then go away, as though being with others without being a part of them would make him lonelier than before.

A very young girl with a mane of yellow hair, in a white sweater and short blue skirt, came out and stood against the wall and was joined by a young man with a visored cap. He was a taxi driver, or a bus starter, or something of the sort. He was slim and moved with indolent grace. He was wise and understood the stirring in the girl and was impassive and aloof, either from indifference or because she was still so young. She was graceful, too, and like a butterfly with a golden head and white body and blue wings, and she fluttered toward him, and away, and pirouetted, and the instinct she did not quite understand made her wish to entice him. She did little dance steps, and they did not seem to be saying anything, and he leaned against the white wall with his cap over his eyes, and sometimes as she whirled around she trailed her fingers across his arm. He began to play with her, lazily, and caught her and swung her back and forth, and it was as rhythmic as a dance. She turned her back to him and leaned against him, and he put his arms around her waist and put his face in her neck, and I heard her laugh. He turned her toward him with one arm under her shoulders and the other across her body, and bent her far back, as in an Apache dance, and kissed her. It was a more beautiful kiss, and he held her with more grace, than Charles Boyer ever managed with Greta Garbo.[3] After a long time she fluttered away from him, and ran away down a dark alley, and he strolled away in the opposite direction.

The orange picking continues, and it is really an exciting time, the end of the long year of growth and labor. Very young boys are working this year, and there are two colored women among the pickers. One weighs well over two hundred pounds, and wears a red bandanna, and when I watch her vast butt sway up the thirty-foot ladder against the fragile limbs, I shudder both for her and for the orange tree. The crop is turning out amazingly. There will be between fifteen hundred and two thousand boxes.

One colored boy asked to buy one of my young game roosters, and Martha caught it for him yesterday. Today when I walked through the grove he asked how much he owed me. I said fifty cents would be enough, and asked what he was going to do with the rooster, did he intend to raise from it. He said, "Yessum, just use him for a yard rooster." Then he added, (which I had hoped, for that is what they are born for) "I kind of figured on maybe fightin' him jest a little." I said, "I hoped you picked a good one." He said, "I noticed him the minute I come on the place. He sure can fight."

The pecan trees are in full leaf, and the oleanders along the fence are a mass of white bloom. It is a good time of year, and I do so love the life. I should be *entirely* desperate without you, any other place. But the cottage and the sea will soon seem good, too. When the flowers are gone in my garden, and the heat lies like fog, I shall be ready to go.

. . . The news from Burma yesterday and today is better, both as to Imphal and Kohima. I can't tell which is your base. Mountbatten's moving his headquarters to Kandy on Ceylon is being taken by the papers to mean that naval attacks will also soon be made against the Japs.

I love you, darling.

1. *Pin-Up Girl* (1944), starring Betty Grable and Martha Raye.
2. *Happy Land* (1943). *Our Town* (1940), starring William Holden and Martha Scott.
3. Charles Boyer and Greta Garbo, actors. MKR may be thinking of the film *Conquest* (1932).

. . . .

(TLS, 2 pp.)

[Cross Creek, Fla.]
April 20, 1944

Darling:

. . . Such a cute, nice little colored boy, who doesn't look over fourteen, is doing a man's work with the orange pickers, lifting the heavy boxes and moving them on a little hand-cart. He said yesterday he understood I had a job here for a "steady man" and he'd like it! This morning he stopped to admire my flowers and said his flower garden would soon be almost as pretty. I asked him what he had, and he said zinnias, petunias, roses and lilies! I am giving some consideration to it, though as I told Idella, unless Martha "adopted" him, it would be no use. She said she thought he might possibly be kin to the Mickens, as Martha had been very friendly with him. Of course, this time of year, at least after the orange trees are hoed, I can get along without a "steady man" better than any time. Though I have never had a man on the place who didn't find enough to do to keep busy five days a week.

Edith's habits, of which of course she is totally unconscious—aren't we all?—do amuse me. It took her an hour and a half to eat her dinner last night, as she was telling me someone's life history. There were ten sentences to every small bite of food. Idella was so puzzled and kept peeking in, sure that we must be through. Edith said last night she'd like to get on a better schedule, and begin waking up earlier in the mornings, so that she wouldn't stay up and read all night, as she had found most people didn't do that. We agreed on nine o'clock for her breakfast to be brought, and at 9:40 Idella had to appeal to me as to whether to wake her up by fair means or foul, or leave her alone and fix another breakfast. I said to wake her, and it took us both to do it! I went back to my room, and noticed Idella had not returned. I looked out, and Idella said Edith had said to wait just a minute while she brushed her teeth. Idella had already been standing with the tray about fifteen minutes, and I told her for goodness sake to take it in and put it on the bed, as Mrs. Pope was sitting on the toilet dreaming. Idella almost had hysterics.

. . . Sissie is moving down to the Brice's at last, and I am so glad, as the crowding, and Sissie's dirt, were too much in the tenant house. I found the reason for Sissie's total incompetency when she was trying to do my work. Idella said she is just naturally filthy dirty and utterly lazy. Each of the children gets one dress a week, and that is all. . . .

All my love,

. . . .

(TLS, 3 pp.)

[Cross Creek, Fla.]
April 21, 1944

Dearest:

Edith and I talked until eleven o'clock last night, and I mean talked. The subject of the advertising, or non-advertising, of "Colcorton" came up, and I gave her both barrels. The full choke barrel was of course that without Max Perkins, there wouldn't have been any "Colcorton." Any price she pays because of Scribner's conservatism is more than worth it. And I pointed out that 20,000 in the first month is nothing at which a hitherto unknown and not quite competent writer could turn up her nose. Then the truth came out, as funny little Ruthie had sensed at once: Verle was back of her complaints. After insisting for years that "Colcorton" had no possibilities, and Edith would never get anywhere as a writer, Verle was the one who raged at Scribner's when they didn't have full-page ads. It was Chuck Rawlings' performance all over again. And *intended* to make Edith dissatisfied with her phenomenal break in luck, and in her tangible accomplishment. I put it gently that Verle had a streak of what I call old-fashioned maleness (by which I really meant a terrific inferiority complex, which expresses itself in sadism) that was more or less inevitable in a virile man with an attractive and clever wife, and as long as she recognized it for what it was, it need not bother her, but she should not let it give her false values.

Whereupon Edith informed me that Verle had always had an inferiority complex, and very much so about her! I think she really loves him very much, and finds him satisfactory as a male and as a mate—and in a way she has allowed his virility and positiveness to intimidate her and hypnotize her—but she sees him as clearly as—well, as I have wondered if she did! Under all her moon-struck dreaminess she does not miss a thing, and it is a fine augury for her future work in fictional characterization. She spoke, with all kindness and understanding, of Verle's peculiar background of the deaf-mute parents, the total lack of cultural and social background, of which he was the first to be conscious. She said exactly what Ruth had said to me, in almost the same words, that when she married Verle she *built him up,* both to himself and to other people. Then she pulled her punches and said that Verle "really" considered her only a lovable moron. I said that he "really" did no such thing, that he knew perfectly well that she had a brilliant mind and great artistic capabilities, but it was part of the "old-fashioned maleness" (!!!!!!) not to admit or recognize it. She apologized for her apparent greediness in wanting Scribner's to push "Colcorton" to gigantic sales by saying that money meant nothing to her (as I knew it did not) but that she wanted to have a sizeable capital for Verle to work with when he returns from the war! I lapsed into silence, for what was in my mind was the question whether Edith will find it possible to live with Verle as time goes on, if she continues her artistic success, and if he is *small* about it.

Ruth told me a story that Edith has never breathed to me. There was a time, rather early in their marriage, when she all but divorced Verle. She had even been to a lawyer about it. Ruth said that Verle neglected Edith shamefully, and humiliated her, and was not kind to her. The matter was precipitated when Ilya Tolstoi[1] appeared on the scene, and Edith was swept off her feet and decided (without Ilya's having had any such thought himself!) that here was her man and her destiny. It was Ilya himself who persuaded her out of it! I think the fact that he was Tolstoi's grandson had a great deal to do with it, and the matter never reached the status of an "affair." But if Verle ever pushes her too far, I think he will find that he does not have on his hands a lovable moron, but a woman of cold steely perception. Verle will be unfaithful to her while he is away, and I am wondering what that will do to his attitude to her when he returns. I cannot decide whether he has already been unfaithful or not. At one time, as I told you, I thought he was being so. Then I thought perhaps it was only talk. Last summer she told me of their being in New York together, and going to a cocktail party at the Benet's,[2] when Verle got very drunk. They took a taxi, and Verle made love to her as though she were a strange woman. He said, in his cups, "Why don't you break down and have a little fun, Baby? Don't you know your husband is running around with blondes?" Edith laughed it off as an amusing incident of Verle in a rare inebriation, but I wonder if underneath, she *knew*. Now that I am aware of her keen realism, I am more convinced than ever of her potential genius, for that had been the only quality that seemed to me to be holding her back from full literary expression.

I had told her that I was on short rations as to gasoline for the Kohler, and so we could not stay up too late, or read in bed too late, burning the lights, and she understood. But last night after we went to bed I dozed off, woke up with a start, and realized the Kohler was still running. I went near her door, and she was blissfully reading. And she read and read and read, using gallons of gasoline—. It was not that she was deliberately selfish, but only that she has even less time-sense than I do. If I mentioned it, she would say, I am sure, that she had read "a few minutes" before going to sleep. I have decided that she is a dangerous person to have around. She attracts too-lively forces. Her bus catches on fire——Yesterday afternoon I was typing on the veranda, and I heard her sweet and gentle voice drawling, "Ma—a-a-rjor—ie, what kind of snake has red and yellow and black bands? Gosh it's pre-e-e-tty."

I said as casually, "Probably a ribbon, or garter snake. If it has a black nose, it's a coral snake." I felt very certain that it was *not* a coral snake, as none has been seen around the place for four or five years. But I went out, under the Mandarin orange tree, and here was Edie, near-sighted as the devil, with her face practically in the face of—a coral snake! It was just about as large as coral snakes ever grow, twenty-four inches, and it had the black nose by which Ross Allen taught me to identify the species, "black for death." I sent her for Idella to bring my gun and to hold Moe, and shot it. But it really was very pre-e-e-tty. . . .

All my love,

1. Ilya Tolstoy, grandson of the author Leo Tolstoy.
2. William Rose Benét, poet and critic, and Elinor Wylie, poet.

. . . .

(TLS, 3 pp.)

[Cross Creek, Fla.]
April 22, 1944

Dearest:

After supper last night Edith, Moe and I went for a walk, and were almost home again, just about dark, when Chet drove by and said he was on his way to a political meeting at Citra, where a famous half-wit who is running for County Commissioner was to speak, and it should be a treat and didn't we want to go, and having nothing in God's world to do, we piled in and put Moe in the back of the truck among the orange boxes and off we went to the rally. It was certainly backwoods democracy in full swing. The meeting was in the school-house, and the candidates were all holding their stomachs from being previously gorged by the Citra ladies on chicken pilau. . . .

We got a big kick out of it.

. . . Edith hasn't a word from Verle, so we feel sure that his outfit moved right on shipboard and went right out. She is being very philosophical about it, and said there is even a certain relief in having him definitely headed for the thing he has wanted to do, as they went through protracted farewells every day for a month, until their nerves were wracked. The most important part of his job is the assembling of all information when his bomber squadron returns from an attack, and coordinating it in a secret report to headquarters. It sounds very important, too. . . .

All my love.

Must tell you about one of Aunt Ida's rare letters. She wrote, "Everything is very quiet here. The old gentleman died, after lying in a semi-comma for over a week."

I said to Edie that we could sympathize, as I was sure we had both lain in a semi-comma for over a week, and it was truly deadly.

. . . .

(TLS, 3 pp.)

[Cross Creek, Fla.]

April 23, 1944

Darling:

Four *wonderful* letters came from you yesterday and I was so thrilled. . . . I'll send new copies of A Tree Grows in Brooklyn,[1] for you would love it, and perhaps the Portrait of the Artist,[2] though the latter can wait for reading any time.

. . . I was especially happy that you are evidently in such good spirits in the midst of the cataclysm. Having confidence and pride in your outfit in general probably helps a lot.

Yesterday afternoon a terrific storm came in, and if you get any more water in a vertical position than we did then, I'll know what a monsoon is. You could not see across the road to the other fence and grove. It began coming at an angle, and the corner of the veranda where the table is was four inches deep in water, and so was the corner of the living room by the little red sofa. The door on that side doesn't quite close, and through the crack of half an inch enough rain came in to make a lake in that corner of the room. I heard this morning that one of Mr.

Brice's huge oak trees crashed, falling across the shed in which he kept his car, and crushing the car to junk. And he had no insurance.

This morning is a gorgeous sunny one after the storm, and Edith and I got up for a waffle breakfast on the veranda. It was so peaceful and beautiful, with the red birds in the feed basket, and the palm leaves shining, and a bouquet of pink roses and snapdragon and lavender fluffy-ruffle petunias on the table, and Edith said that she wondered, when you came back, whether it would seem like a dream to you, and Burma and India a reality, or vice versa.

After dinner we are going into Gainesville to a dog-and-little-boy movie, "Lassie Come Home,"[3] and I know we will weep buckets. . . .

You asked me if I still love you! I've been a-tellin' you and a-tellin' you that I do! I love you more than anybody in the world.

1. Betty Smith (1896–1972), *A Tree Grows in Brooklyn* (New York: Harper, 1943).
2. James Joyce (1882–1941), *Portrait of the Artist as a Young Man* (New York: Huebsch, 1916).
3. *Lassie Come Home* (1943), starring Roddy McDowell and Elizabeth Taylor.

. . . .

(TLS, 7 pp.)

[Crescent Beach, Fla.]
April 24, 1944
At the cottage

My dear:

This is perhaps the most distressing duty I have ever had to perform. My judgment, and that of others I have consulted, is to give the news to you, instead of trying to withhold it, for fear it might reach you in a roundabout and incomplete way and disturb you even more than the truth.

Ruth Pickering died yesterday morning in a fire at the Castle Warden.

The facts are these, as far as determined:

At nine o'clock yesterday, Sunday morning, a woman checked in who told someone she had had a quarrel with her family and run away. At the desk they said they smelled liquor on her breath. The theory is that she fell asleep in a drunken stupor, perhaps even from just ordinary exhaustion, with a lighted cigarette. She was in No. 17, the only available room. Doug was downtown working with Oliver Lawton on the books. The fire definitely started in 17. The people in the two rooms directly under the apartment had gone out, by the grace of God. There was no one in that part of the building on the third floor except a woman asleep in a room catty-cornered from 17, and Chef or Robert awakened her and she grabbed her clothes and dressed out on the balcony.

The maid discovered the fire at 11:15 and by that time it was in full sweep from No. 17, across the hall and up the stairs to the apartment. The woman in 17 had made the bathroom across the hall and collapsed there, and was also dead.

Now about Ruth. I have decided I might as well give you the works, and you can just brace yourself and get the whole thing faced at once. I'll say first, however, that the one and only thing that makes it endurable, is that the doctors say that both women *unquestionably* were overcome by smoke and passed out and died before the flames reached them. I don't know about the other woman, but Ruth was not too much burned, and they *know* she died before she could have felt any pain.

Driving out yesterday, without any details, I was sure that the fire must have happened in the late Saturday night and that Ruthie slept right through it. The tragic truth is that she aroused and knew. It *seems* as though she could have gotten out, and it also seems as though she either lost her head or was in a complete daze, but that is perhaps impossible to determine, as it is difficult to get an accurate check on the time element. She kept the door of the apartment closed all the time night and day. Whether she did not even think of the roof and fire escape, or whether she opened the door and there was too much smoke and flame to cross, or she *thought* there was, we do not know. There *seems* to have been an unaccounted-for time element that she could have utilized. She had put on a dressing gown and bedroom slippers of two different kinds, and stopping to put on anything at all was of course madness.

Doug returned to the hotel at evidently about the moment the fire department got there, nearly 11:30. He ran up the fire escape and across the roof to the apartment outer door, that is, the roof door, and the apartment door itself was closed. He said the smoke was then so black and thick and acrid that it did not seem possible to cross those few steps to the apartment. He called to Ruth, and says that if he had been positive she was still in there, he would have made a dash across even if it cost him his life, but by that time the fire department was working on the corner of the building involved, and when he got no answer from Ruth, it seemed possible the fire department had already gotten her out of an apartment window. I do not remember whether he said the flames were up the apartment stairs then or not. At any rate, they must have followed the thick billowing smoke by a few seconds. He ran back and called down to have the firemen send him up a gas mask, and was going to cross to the apartment, but no one sent up a mask and he was driven back by the smoke and flames.

In the meantime, Ruth had gone to that tiny bathroom window and called for help. The fire department seems, offhand, to have bungled badly. They had a ladder up by that time, but it reached only to the third floor. Ruth called to bring a longer ladder or to hold a net for her. Neither of these things was done. It is probable that at about that moment she was overcome by smoke, for the bathroom, next to the stairs, was the worst trap. The flames from the stairs cut through that wooden set of shelves where we kept towels and toilet articles, and I can only presume that when she disappeared from the window the fire department concentrated on getting water in. She was found on the floor by the toilet. Her feet and hands were burned, and her dressing gown was burned only about twelve inches up from the bottom, so the doctors know that it was the smoke that killed her and not the fire itself. And they say that death from being overcome by smoke is quick and painless. Some sort of poisonous gas is generated and it produces a drugged stupor even before the suffocation comes. Her face was in bad shape but they said it was not from actual burns but from the intense heat that followed.

Friday night Ruth sat up all night until 7:30 in the morning with Emmy Isaacs,[1] drinking and talking, and did not get much sleep Saturday. Saturday night she was out with Jean and a couple of others and did not get to bed very early and said then she was utterly exhausted. Ordinarily, Jean said, she, Ruth, would have slept most of the day Sunday. When she was aroused, she evidently wandered in utter confusion and was incapable of cool or quick thinking. Jean said she was always very hard to get going in the morning under the most normal conditions. When her father died at 5:30 in the morning, and the nurse called them, Jean got on the 'phone at once, and she said it was half an hour or more before Ruth seemed to know what was going on. It *seems* that she had time to throw that big bedspread around her and make a dash for the roof, but of course we cannot be sure. She had been using the roof for sun baths so should have known what a quick exit could have been made that way.

All the windows in the living room were closed, and it seems as though she could have saved herself by merely opening one of those large windows and just hanging far out so that she could get away from the smoke and breath fresh air. The bedroom was the least damaged and least *smoked* part of the apartment, and it seems too as though she could have knotted sheets together (extra ones are always kept in the drawers in the room) and gotten out of the bedroom window. It wouldn't have taken much longer than putting on a dressing gown and hunting for slippers. If she didn't have time, she didn't have time. If she did, it is easy to picture her in an accentuation of what is almost her normal haziness, waiting for someone else to do something.

I always felt that apartment was a fire-trap, and had planned what I should do if trapped— either bolt for the roof with a wet towel over the face and the bedspread wrapped around—or tie sheets to the foot of the bed and drop the last story if necessary.

Chef and Robert were heroes. They grabbed fire extinguishers and one went up one stairs and one up the others and tried to put out the fire. Robert was trying to put out enough [of] a path to get through to the apartment. But the thing had gone too far for any of that.

I think there will never be trouble between Doug and Chef again. Sobbing, Doug pointed to Chef and said, "You'll never know how wonderful that man is." Doug is in a state of extreme shock, but in spite of it is doing an efficient job of attending to necessary details. Next to you, I feel sorrier for him than for anyone. He was *devoted* to Ruthie, and also feels responsibility, and also feels that possibly he *could* have gotten across, although the fire department said no one could have made it and lived. He said, "Don't you suppose the Little Boss can come home?" I told him No, that you had a job to do and were too much needed where you are; that there is nothing you can do about it here now, and that you are saving valuable lives every day.

You will probably have more of a sense of proportion about it than I am able to achieve, for you are seeing so much of death and of pain, and from an objective viewpoint, the destruction of the men there is infinitely more tragic than the ending of poor little Ruthie's never-happy life. It just comes so damn close home.

As to the damage to the hotel, the fire was halted in that wing, and except for water damage on that side of the building, only that third floor corner and the apartment stairs and apartment bathroom are actually gone. The apartment stairs are *charcoal*, and you can see daylight through them. I must tell Doug and the police guards today to be very careful about letting anyone go up them. The apartment living room is completely blackened by the smoke and there is some water damage. Also, the extreme heat did queer things to the walls and ceiling. The bedroom is not so badly blackened. The fire department evidently did a good job at least in confining the fire to a comparatively small portion of the building.

Willard Howatt[2] was right on the job and assured us that you are thoroughly covered as to insurance for everything, even the possibility of liability suits. I feel sure Ruth's sister will not do anything of the sort, but the family of the woman who evidently started the fire may, as they are apparently of not too good a class. But Willard told Doug he would not have to give even a thought to that angle, that the insurance companies have their own lawyers etc. Doug said the books and everything were in perfect shape within two or three days, everything paid up, mortgage, interest, policies. The only financial loss will come in loss of revenue while the place is being prepared for operation. Doug checked out all the guests at once, and had them all sign statements, as no one lost any personal belongings. For all the dreadful shape he is in, he really used his head. And Chef was a regular old Rock of Ages. I don't think I can ever be cross at him again, either.

Ruth's sister in New York was reached by phone and will get down as soon as possible, but was unable to get on a train or plane yesterday. It seems as though she could have gotten a seat on the stream-liner, but Jean rather indicated that the sister is not the sort who would sit up all night for anything or anybody. She wired Jean full authority to make all arrangements and take care of everything. Jean is almost killed, as I am, but is being wonderful, and staunch. She and Alfred Houston and Frank Harrold went to the apartment shortly after I got in, and got Ruth's keys and papers and put her valuables in a bag, which Frank Harrold took to the bank. Her deposit box will be opened this morning. They know she had a will, and hope that she specifies cremation in it, for she had told Jean she wished that.

I shall probably have to endorse your power of attorney, as Willard said I shall have to sign a great many papers.

I had given Doug the name of Boyt's garage in case of an emergency if he could not reach me by wire or phone at Island Grove. He phoned there and at 12:30 Henry Boyt drove out to the Creek, but the message was only that there had been a fire, and for me to call Doug just as soon as possible. It did not sound too awful, and if it was only a minor fire calling only for insurance details there was no point in going over until today. We had planned to go to Gainesville anyway, so had a hurried lunch and drove in. I had told Idella to stand by. As soon as I talked to Doug I told him I would be right over. We turned back to the Creek, picked up our bags and Idella, and reached St. Augustine about 4:30.

Jean was out on a sail-boat, but a drag-net was put out for her and she was finally reached, and she got to the hotel about three-quarters of an hour after I did. The Alfred Houstons were splendid, too, and offered Edith and me the use of their apartment (Edith's old one) in town. To add to the nightmare, when we reached the cottage about ten o'clock last night, neither lights nor water would turn on. Junko found the trouble this morning.

Doug had been planning to close the hotel for two weeks in May, to do some painting and repairing and give the Hustons a vital vacation, so that period is being merely advanced. I shall write you every day, of course, but for the moment that seems to cover the details. I would give anything in the world to spare you this, but the announcement went over the radio all afternoon and evening, and will be in the papers, and I felt, as did those I consulted, Frank Harrold and Willard Howatt etc., that the chance was too strong that someone else would write you something about it that would be dangerously confusing.

I could even imagine someone's, DeVene Harrold, any casual correspondent, writing, "So sorry about the awful tragedy at the hotel," and you would even picture the whole thing burned down and perhaps even think Doug, or the Hustons, or I, was involved. So I feel I can't do a thing but give you the blow below the belt, knowing you can manage to take it. I even thought of sending this in care of Lt. Patrick, to give you at a time that might be more opportune than when you were just setting out on a difficult drive, for instance, but that seemed sissy business, too, and I felt you wouldn't want it done that way.

Edith said one helpful thing—that you had given Ruthie more happiness in her two years at the Castle than she had ever had in her life.

All my love, my darling, and I wish to God we were together to comfort each other.

1. Emily Isaacs of St. Louis, who wintered in St. Augustine.
2. E. Willard Howatt Jr., St. Augustine lawyer, cousin of Frank Howatt, also a St. Augustine lawyer.

[Crescent Beach, Fla.]
April 25, 1944
At the cottage

Darling:—

After the suggestion was made by Caroline Spades[1] to Jean, we decided to have Ruth's funeral services at the Castle Warden. In spite of the circumstances, everyone felt that was what Ruth would have wanted. We have had "universal approval" of the plans. Ruth was rabid on the subject of no church services and no preacher ranting around, but as a sop to Ruth's older conservative friends, and not to leave God quite out of it, God's having already apparently had quite a hand in things, we engaged the Episcopal minister to read a psalm and then give a brief prayer and the brief committal. We also engaged the Florida Normal Choir to sing. It is impossible for Judge Jackson[2] to make the brief friendly talk we wanted, as he is obliged to hold court in Deland. Langston Moffatt agreed to do this. He asked me to meet him this morning to help him with his tribute, and since it is a difficult thing to do—so must hurry this letter.

. . . Clint Jackson said to me yesterday, "I wonder if Norton will ever know how much he did for Ruth?" and others have said the same thing, that you gave her more understanding and comfort than she had ever had, and that she had been happier her two years at the Castle than ever in her life.

I had a brief talk with Doug and Willard Howatt about the insurance and re-building angle, and Doug said he wanted to have the necessary repairs made, stairs, beams, floors, that sort of thing, but just close off that section of the building, not refurnish or anything like that. He said that whole third floor corner was a natural fire-trap. He wants just to bank the rest of the insurance money, as Willard said the company would undoubtedly pay right off when the estimates were made, and let you do as you wish when you return—put in a rear fire-escape, or whatever you want to do. He said he would not need the rooms through the summer, anyway. I O.K.'d this plan. Willard said that at a rough guess, he would say it would take $15,000 to repair the damage.

Doug was in much better shape yesterday, and is being very efficient.

I feel like the woman who stands up against a board and had knives thrown around her outline. The mule accident proved a bit of a shock, and the two weeks when I didn't know about you had me almost down, and this seems like the knife that finally hit.

There was nothing in the Jacksonville paper about Ruth's death or the fire. The woman who started the fire proved to be a Jacksonville beauty parlor operator, and her family proved to have considerable influence and kept the whole thing out of the Times-Union. They evidently did not want it known she was in

St. Augustine, where she evidently had no business. I am even wondering, after we found that out, if she set the fire deliberately, to commit suicide that way.

I don't have time to write any more.

All my love,

1. Caroline Spades, wife of the Cyril Cox Spades who served on the St. Augustine Free Public Library Association with MKR.
2. Judge George and Clint Jackson of St. Augustine.

. . . .

(TLS, 3 pp.)

[Cross Creek, Fla.]
April 26, 1944

My dearest dear:

All I can do is plod along and tell you details. Much as I hated it, it seems definitely best now, to have told you, for while the Richardson family kept the story out of the Jacksonville Times-Union, it was in the Journal, and the Associated Press sent it all over the country, and Jean had wires from New York and Chicago.

I am rather non compos mentis this morning, but will just talk on and tell you about the services etc. Ruth's sister Jean Dell arrived about 1:30, very calm and collected, and seems like a very sweet person, looks a good deal like Ruth, a larger and prettier and more vital Ruth. The services were at 4.

. . . The whole ceremony only took about fifteen minutes. The choir sang Rock of Ages, softly, the Episcopal minister said the 23d Psalm, Langston Moffatt made the most *perfect* talk of four or five minutes, in such a sincere and natural voice— a *strong*, good, unhesitating voice, too,—in exquisite taste, saying "Ruthie would not want this to be a sad occasion. She would want us to think of it more as a farewell party" and went on to speak of her kindness and goodness, of how she was totally without malice and had never been known to say an unkind thing.

. . . The minister said the Lord's prayer and gave the very brief committal, ashes to ashes, etc., and as the casket was carried out and then we left, the choir sang Swing Low, Sweet Chariot, very very softly and kept singing it until it finally faded away, and of course we were most of us almost killed.

I am emotionally and nervously exhausted, but am all right.

. . . I love you so much, and am grieving so for you, and everyone says the same thing and wishes you could be spared this, but hopes you know how much you did for Ruth and meant to her. . . .

(TLS 2 pp.)

[Crescent Beach, Fla.]
April 27, 1944

Darling:

I am still pretty well floored but in much better mental shape—thanks mostly to Ruth's *wonderful* sister, Jean Dell. She and Jean Frances came down to the cottage to dinner last night, and Jean Dell and I went into *our* bedroom and talked and talked. It ended up with *her* comforting *me*. She and Ruthie had become very close, but only after Jack Pickering left the picture for Jean and her husband loathed him.

I am not in very good shape to write about it, for while I really needed to spend the day in bed, I have been working on a few paragraphs about Ruth for Langston Moffatt to use in his Sunday column. But anyway, Jean Dell and I went deep into everything, Ruth's frustrations, the accident itself, the sense of moral guilt that I feel about that apartment fire-trap. Which I know you will feel too, and so forth. Jean herself said that almost anyone else could probably have gotten out, but Ruth was always slow to arouse, was deaf, and had no sense of smell. She said too that she felt Ruth had come to a turn in the road, after a desperately unhappy life, had had two happy years, thanks mostly to you, and was probably destined, if this had not happened, to a lonely old ladyhood, more and more alcoholic. In other words, she feels everything is all right. . . .

All my love,

. . . .

(TLS, 2 pp.)

[Cross Creek, Fla.]
April 29, 1944

Dear Norton:

I'll be glad when the world looks reasonably normal again, and I can enjoy writing to you once more. Writing you, all this week, has been only a painful duty, and I hate it. I mean I hate having it feel that way. I have felt as though every letter has been just another blow below the belt for you. If I find that no one else mentioned the catastrophe to you, I won't be able to forgive myself for doing so. . . .Of course, our joy in your return just cannot be the same now. But I am still inclined to think it is better for you to make your mental adjustment now, for if you got the whole thing as you got off the boat, say, you'd wish you hadn't come home at all. Everyone I saw in Jacksonville yesterday spoke of the fire, and I am sure someone will mention it in writing to you. Well, I did the best I could, I mean what seemed best.

. . . I am perfectly all right, just still feel as though a steam roller had gone over me and I hadn't sat up yet.

All my love,

(TLS, 4 pp.)

[Crescent Beach, Fla.]
April 30, 1944
May 1

Dearest:—

... Dinner at Mrs. White's was rather an odd affair. The only guest left besides Aunt Ida is Mr. Mears, and I never heard an old guy make so much racket with his rations. . . . Afterward, Aunt Ida and I went to the movies. It was a technicolor, "The Gang's All Here,"[1] with Carmen Miranda and Alice Faye and Edward Everett Horton, and was so much better than the much-touted "Lady in the Dark"[2] there was no comparison. It was terribly funny, and Carmen Miranda was a *riot*. It was also beautiful, and they did revolutionary things with pattern and color.

Idella met me and we came to the cottage, and she is now cleaning up. We will go back to the Creek late this morning. . . .

All my love,

1. *The Gang's All Here* (1943).
2. *Lady in the Dark.* See letter of 9 April 1944.

. . . .

(TLS, 3 pp.)

[Cross Creek, Fla.]
Back at the Creek
May 2, 1944

Dear Honey:

We were all three glad to reach the Creek yesterday afternoon. . . .

We found Martha sulking, to the extent that she hasn't come to speak to me since we got back. My flower garden was almost dead for lack of watering. She had had Mrs. Guthrie[1] "take her to the doctor," which is her way of expressing herself when she feels put-upon. Old Will was in a rage, and said he was going back to talk to me, but has not come near me. It seems that while I was in St. Augustine, a son of theirs, with wife and child, was due to arrive, and Old Will asked Chet to let him have someone to drive my truck to meet them. I hadn't had time, or in fact hadn't thought of it, to speak to Chet when we rushed to St. A., but Chet quite properly told them that with me away, the truck could not go out except for something like serious illness. I suppose it hurt their prestige with the son. And just now Idella came over giggling with fifty cents to say that the son would like me to get him some Hava-Tampa cigars when I went in to Island Grove to vote. It doesn't set very well, but I'll do it—but if he pulls anything else, a few sparks will fly. The damn son, or Old Will, could have watered the garden if Martha really felt badly. And Julia had sent me a large box of fresh asparagus, and it must have been noticeably damp when it arrived, and Martha parked it on Aunt Ida's antique square mahogany table, and the table is *ruined*. The top is veneer, like most good mahogany tables, and the veneer has lifted in ridges and is cracked. Martha probably pictured us as having a whale of a good time, which was why we stayed away so long. I suppose the pensions she and Will are getting are having their effect. Together, they have been getting well over $15 a week, and I understand it has been raised lately, and they live rent-free, use my wood for fuel, and get milk and such things, garden seed and space, without a cent of cost. They are much better off than Aunt Ida. Such things of course play into the hands of those who say, "See what happens when they get independent," but people who have *never* had any sort of security cannot be held responsible for their reactions.

Had a letter from Louise Somervell[2]—I'll send it along. Also one from Phil May, saying he knew I was uneasy about not hearing from Tallahassee, and so was he, as the delay made the outcome seem rather ominous. But he said his partner John Crawford said he felt it meant the Court had reached a favorable decision already, and the judge writing it out was trying to turn out a literary masterpiece in keeping with the literary tone of the suit! But that could just as well apply to a literary masterpiece that went agin us! I have to laugh at my writing you that the heavy hand over me seemed to have lifted a little.

Phil and Lillian have bought a piece of land near the mouth of the St. John's and will build after the war. To be nearer it while they begin work on the grounds they have taken a cottage at Mandarin.

. . . Forgot to tell you that Doug has said both TIME and LIFE had phoned him from New York about the fire, and wanted all sorts of details about you and me, and he was very cold and said he didn't know, to most of their questions. It occurred to me that the calls may really have been from Ham Basso on TIME and Russell Davenport on LIFE,[3] just to make sure you and I were all right. . . .

I love you so much.

Had a typically Dessie letter, in one of her noble and philosophical moods. She said I was failing in my duty—not to the country, but to literature! She pointed out that I had written understanding books about Florida and Crackers only because I had actually lived among them and shared their lives, and now it was my duty to get into the war and see it at first hand so I could write about it. If she means the WACS, don't believe they see any more of it than I do.

1. Mary Guthrie.
2. Louise Somervell, wife of General Brehon Somervell.
3. Hamilton Basso and Russell Davenport, the former a novelist who chronicled southern society, the latter the husband of Marcia Davenport and in 1940 the campaign manager for Wendell Willkie, Republican candidate for president.

(TLS, 3 pp.)

[Cross Creek, Fla.]
May 3, 1944

Dearest Norton:

. . . Martha is still sulking and still has not come near me. She is sort of a black Aunt Ida. Idella said she finally gave in and sympathized with Martha over the state of her health, and Martha has forgiven her and *they* are friends again. But I am out in the cold. It may go back to some sarcasm of mine that I couldn't be sure registered at the time. As I threw bags in the car to go to St. Augustine, I told her what had happened. She recoiled with shock, followed me to the door and said, "Oh, my back hurt me so all night." I said, "Well, that's just *too* bad"—and I guess she "got" it. Her visiting son, who is no doubt making comments on the horrors of life at Cross Creek, just strolled down the road all in white linen, with a large white Banama [*sic*] hat. No Hava-tampa, however, as neither Citra nor Island Grove had any cigars at all.

Julia still deluges me with letters and I still haven't been able to write her, though I really should thank her for the decayed asparagus that ruined the mahogany table. She wrote that she saw Ernest Hemingway in the Scribner office and he sent regards to me, from under or over a *long* almost *white* beard and a huge pot-belly. Julia wondered how the glamorous Martha,[1] now in England, will react, when she sees him so adorned. Ernest was never an Adonis, to my notion, though he fancied himself as such. His high thin voice always threw me off, to say nothing of the fact that while talking he keeps scratching his chest. This may be an unconscious effort to impress one and all with the idea that he has so *much* hair on his chest that it is inhabited.

. . . Sissie's David, I am afraid unfortunately, recovered, and is home. When Sissie leaves the Creek, as she is bound to do, I am going to make an earnest effort to get little Martha for Idella and me, not to make a slavery [*sic*] of her, but to give her a chance. Idella told Edith that she would just have to get a puppy or kitten of her own, or a child, as whenever I left the premises my animals had to go with me, or, if left behind, did nothing but watch the road, until I returned.

I do think she means to stay with me. She also told Edith that her people kid her about me, and say I am her true Mama. I think I shall tell her about my plan to leave her money for a farm, the amount graded according to her time of service to me. If I don't get around to putting a codicil in my will, remember this. If the time should be short, just a few hundred dollars will do, but if the years rock on, I'd like her to have from one to two thousand, accordingly.

The news from Burma is so good these past few days that I am drawing a breath again. The European invasion is expected momentarily, and Major George Fielding Eliot, who is usually a bit of an ass, pointed out that we will probably throw off the Germans' planning by more or less ignoring their well-fortified coasts, and land everything by gliders far inland. He said that our success in doing this in Burma showed how potent such a plan could be. Stalin has just called for a joint closing-in on Germany from east and west.

Dewey, who will undoubtedly be the Republican candidate, and whom I have despised, has just made such an intelligent address that I am about to be won over. He said, in effect, that everyone with any sense realizes that the United States must cooperate internationally, must go in strongly for a world organization, backed by force, and must cooperate on international trade after the war, that there is no question about such an attitude's being necessary. And he said that the point at the moment seemed to be that we do not know how "personally and privately" post-war negotiations are being carried on by Roosevelt, and that it is dangerous to have such things handled secretly by one man. He is quite right, to my notion.

. . . Voting the Democratic ticket, I voted in the primaries yesterday for the ticket committed to Sen. Harry Byrd of Virginia. But if Dewey continues to show more perspicuity than I gave him credit for, I shall certainly vote, and work, for a change of regime.

All my love,

1. Martha Gellhorn.

. . . .

(TLS, 4 pp.)

[Cross Creek, Fla.]
May 4, 1944

My sweet, my love:

So help me God, I shall quit you if you come home writing stories. It is hellish enough to carry around my own delusion that I can write, without your bringing off the boat with you, like a rat carrying the Bubonic plague, the delusion that *you* can write. You are a born narrator. Your letters have carried over this quality, thank Heaven, and have sounded just the way you talk. But it is not one out of a million who has this gift, who is worth a damn when he becomes self-conscious and tries to put his tale in formal prose. The Old Hen's "Tellin' is one thing and composin' is another," takes on new wisdom in my mind every day.

Your story about the ambulance trip when you kept picking up flute-players, was quite good, except that you didn't know what to do about a tag-line for the ending. But the same story would have been a hundred times better and more vivid if you had merely written it to me as you have written of other incidents.

The little boy in Georgia story was probably a psychological release for you. How you ever grew up sane and balanced, I'll never know. Your childhood seems to have been utterly hideous. I should not speak brutally of an exercise that you would be the first to say was only that. I realized from this why, on second thought, the New Yorker never used the story you told me—both stories are just too *dated*. Threatening a wife with going to a Negress is a part of southern Victorianism. I suppose there are husbands who still say, "All right, I'll get some-one else," but the general set-up in both those stories is distinctly "period." The first part of your story was not too badly written, though full of clichés (the common fault of the amateur) but the end was downright embarrassing. "Diphtheria had claimed another victim." That sort of writing always sounds like a parody. Also, the story was not truly a story, but was like that affair Edith read to us, something of personal interest.

What did interest me about it, aside from having it make me wonder why you don't bite your finger-nails and hide in corners when company comes, is its relation to the whole race problem. Gunnar Myrdal, in his scholarly two-volume, "An American Dilemma," said that it is important for the sociologists to trace down from case records, almost impossible to get in any number, the moments when whites are first imbued with prejudice against the blacks, and the moments when black children first become aware of their pariah status. This particular episode was evidently such a moment for you, perhaps the second one, after the other you told me. It also shows how the prejudice is tied in with the sex angle, and with the general sense of sex-guilt.

A few Negroes tried to vote in the Democratic primaries the other day, and there was an interesting report on the results. In most places, a sheriff or deputy sheriff stood outside the polls, armed, and told the occasional Negro who showed up that it was a white man's Primary. A woman school teacher was turned away in Tallahassee. In other precincts in Tallahassee the few Negroes who came were allowed to vote. . . .

It is evidently snake-time all over the tropics or sub-tropics. Yesterday on my evening walk I *just* missed stepping on a huge cottonmouth. I must not walk so late in the evening. I know I don't need to warn you to look into your bed for cobras and what-not—you will!

All my love,

. . . .

(TLS, 3 pp.)

[Cross Creek, Fla.]
May 5, 1944

Dearest Norton:

I always thought the expression, "Once in a blue moon," was sheer fancy—but yesterday evening the moon *was* blue. It was about half full at eight o'clock. The sunset had faded, but there was still light, and the sky—and the moon—were a positive blue. I kept looking away and looking back, thinking I was carrying over the color of the sky in my imagination, but there was no question about it. It stayed that way about half an hour, then turned whitish silver, then took on a more golden cast. Some phenomenon should have occurred simultaneously, but there was none.

Yesterday afternoon Thelma Shortridge came dashing out, to announce the result of her pregnancy test as positive. She was immensely excited, both because it makes her a legitimate center of attention, and because she is genuinely pleased at the prospect. Her regret is that Fred[1] did not live longer, as he would have adored a grand-child. I still miss him dreadfully, and she will never get over it. I made her favorite drink, Alexanders, to celebrate, and Idella had a sip with us. Martha appeared at the barn and Thelma shouted across some hundreds of yards, "Martha, I'm going to have a baby." Thelma repeated in front of Idella her insistence that I must promise to take the baby if anything happens to her, and there was an unholy glint in Idella's eye.

Thelma drove me out to Shands prairie to look at the vast celery fields, ready for cutting, or digging, whatever they call it, in a few days. It covers the prairie in two directions almost as far as the eye can see, and lies in beautiful broad bands of varying shades of green, I suppose according to the times of planting. Old Shands is dead, you know, but a son of his is raising the crop in collaboration with some new people, the Bells, from Sarasota, who built the celery packing house in Island Grove. They also bought the little house at the corner where Mother Rawlings and the boys lived when the boys were going to make a fortune in the boom. They have made a completely modern, if in bad taste, house of it, are awfully jolly plain people, past middle age, and most desirable adjuncts to the village. . . . I was most pleased to hear that Dr. Cason had made enemies of them! Before they fixed over the little house, just to be near the packing plant, they lived during the season in a trailer next to Chet Crosby's new place. I may have told you at the time, but Dr. Cason descended on them and ordered them off! They replied that the land belonged to the Seaboard Railway, with which they were completely en rapport. Dr. Cason said, "Well, you're nothing but squatters anyway." He thought they were just poor folks who could be bullied, and it is a joke on him that they could buy his damn hospital as a fertilizer store-house if they wanted to.

. . . I am reading a fascinating book, a translation, new, of a Brazilian classic, "Rebellion in the Backlands."[2] The backlands correspond to our scrub country, but infinitely more desolate and difficult, and at variance with the Brazilian lushness—which exists in other parts of the country. The descriptions of landscape, flora and fauna are right up my alley. . . .

Claude Pepper goes in again as Senator, without a run-off. . . .

Had my checks from Talmadge DuPree on the house grove, and made a net of about $1800. Just looked up to the young grove across the road and see smoke from a forest fire drifting through the back. It is painfully dry, but there seems a promise of rain. . . .

I love you heaps.

1. Fred Tompkins.
2. Euclydes da Cunha (1866–1909), *Rebellion in the Backlands,* trans. Samuel Putnam (Chicago: University of Chicago Press, 1944).

. . . .

(TLS, 2 pp.)

[Cross Creek, Fla.]
May 6, 1944

Dear Honey:

The yard outside my bedroom, where Edie almost kissed the coral snake, has turned into a damned jungle. Last night I was reading in bed and Moe began to bark and I heard a rustling sound. I turned the flashlight on the yard, and in the alcove by the spider lilies a simply enormous turtle was trying to find his way around. It was ten o'clock and I decided not to call Martha, though I knew she wouldn't forgive me if she lost a kettle of turtle stew. I thought it would probably hang around the yard and lay and we could track it in the morning. I went back to bed, heard another commotion, and a mother duck began squawking and Moe made a terrific fuss. Again I swung the flashlight around, and Moe insisted the trouble was under the north Turk's cap, and there was a possum eating the duck eggs. This time I did call Martha and she and Idella brought my gun. It was the biggest possum any of us had ever seen, as Martha said, "a ole bull possum." He weighed all of 20 lbs. Martha tucked the turtle under one arm and the possum by the tail in the other hand, and went off humming. I doubt if they can eat the possum. His flesh would probably be very strong. Though since he has cleaned out three duck's nests in as many days, dear knows he has been daintily fed.

. . . Hope "Colcorton" reaches you. There is a wonderful dog in it, "Hongry." You asked me what "Colcorton" meant. It is the name of the plantation where the action takes place, and Edith borrowed it from the name of one of her grandfather's places in England. Some people at Scribner's said the name didn't mean anything, and Max answered, "Well, Pendennis[1] did all right." Personally, I like that sort of name.

Idella just reported that the possum is in the pot.

Also, the elegant Mickens son, who dresses in white linens and smokes Hava-tampa cigars, reverted to type. She said he was as excited as a kid last night when Martha showed up with all her edible loot, and said he wished it wasn't so late, as he would certainly get up and cook that cooter right then. Then he said if he had enough wood, he'd get up and cook it anyway. She said she didn't know how early he did get up this morning, but it was no later than four o'clock, and she said by the time she came over to work, the cooter was *eaten* and the pot scrubbed and the possum cooking.

. . . Old Boss Brice, very white-haired and wizened, walked in to use the truck to go to town. Think I told you a storm blew a big oak down on his car shed, crushing his car. (Never am sure what vital Creek statistics I remember to pass on!)

All my love,

1. William Makepeace Thackeray (1811–63), *The History of Pendennis* (1850).

. . . .

(TLS, 2 pp.)

[Cross Creek, Fla.]
May 7, 1944

Dear Norton:

For no known reason, I am cross as a bear this morning, and it's a beautiful cool sunny Sunday morning, too, with hot gingerbread for breakfast. Think I began getting sore last night. The moon was almost full, and was gorgeous, the goddamn whippoorwills were singing, and a silver julep cup of gardenias I had stolen, reeked like hell. It was like the balcony without Romeo and Juliet. I . . . just suddenly feel like an old maid. This morning I discovered that the front of my hair has turned very gray. None of my people get gray hair—my grandfather at 82, my mother at 54, had chestnut brown hair, and on the Kinnan side the hair stays black to the bitter end. It made me furious. I am mad at Life in general. Of course, I undoubtedly make a mistake in thinking of Life as an enemy instead of a friend, and I also make the mistake of tilting at windmills. But how I wish there was something tangible I could tackle and kick the daylights out of. The answer, as I know, is work. I suppose I'll turn out another sappy sweetness-and-light book.

I snapped at Idella this morning, something I do no oftener than twice a year. When I showed her the gray hair, she was as upset as I, and I apologized for my crossness. It was not serious—one of my garters was lost, and I said it was her fault! Silly—. I have thought that when I wrote you that Dora was dead, you probably thought I meant the cow. I meant my alter ego, and of course she is no more dead than the Phoenix.[1] When I was upset about you, I made all sorts of promises to God or Fate or what-have-you, to be a good girl. "When the devil was sick, the devil a monk would be. When the devil was well, the devil a monk was he." Dora was behind the bushes all the time, thumbing her nose. And quite right she is, too. Dora has more sense than I do. With no self-pity at all, I have gone over the nasty things that have happened in the last year or so; the law-suit; the operation, which was more ghastly than I have ever admitted; having you go; the horrible worry about you in March; the mule accident; the fire and Ruthie. Only a nitwit or a saint would think the last year had been cute. Again, it is asinine to yap about things across 10,000 miles, and I should wait to write you until I feel angelic again, but if [I] was sweet and gentle for eighteen months, you would know damn well I was lying, or was going to bed with somebody, or was cold-out crazy.

Moe is sore, too, because I wouldn't let him sleep on the bed last night.

I am sure that I was right in my conjecture that the long distance calls from TIME and LIFE were Ham Basso and Russell Davenport checking up on you and me personally, for Max wrote me in distress, saying that Ham had given him the news,[2] and Marcia Davenport wrote me in even greater distress, urging me to come to New York and take a vacation with her.

The game rooster has lost his control over his flock. The only hens who pay any attention to him are two brown ones that I kept shut up a long time, intending to eat them as fryers, and when they outgrew the skillet, turned them a-loose. When he clucks to announce the discovery of food, they are the only ones to run to him. He is sore, too.

The Gainesville paper has been throwing out copies at my gate, as samples, and I find that "Jane Eyre"[3] with Orson Welles and Joan Fontaine, is in Gainesville today, so shall go in to the movie, hoping it will improve my disposition.

. . . Parents do so much damage. My nightmare homeless dreams persist, and my mother usually appears in them. From a nightmare last night, I awoke to realize that I had depended on my mother for a certain spurious sort of *approval*, which I have never had from anyone since. Everyone is crazy except thee and me, and sometimes I think thee is a little queer—.

Still and all, I love you.

1. In Persian myth, the Phoenix self-immolates every five hundred (or one thousand) years and is reborn from its ashes.
2. Perkins wrote to MKR on 2 May 1944: "I just now heard from Hamilton Basso of that terrible fire, and I know how it must trouble you. I want to say how deeply sorry I am. It will grieve Norton too, but in a way I am glad he was not there when it happened" (*Max and Marjorie*, 565).
3. *Jane Eyre* (1944), a film based upon Charlotte Brontë's novel.

. . . .

(TLS, 2 pp.)

[Cross Creek, Fla.]

May 8, 1944

[D]ear Honey:

The Burma news is bad again—heavy offenses by the Japs against Kohima. I suppose your letters about now will say, "Things are fairly active. There is a little bird outside the window, something like our tom-tit, known as a snooperoo." I don't mean that I don't adore your nature notes—I simply eat them up—but I mean that it irks me to know that hell is popping and the censor has you bullied into writing as though you were taking a tour through the Museum of Natural History.

For the first time this morning I feel that Dr. Harris' hormones are easing my jangled nerves. I was rather discouraged last week, especially as I was still so nerve-wracked that I was totally unable to cut down on the liquor and cigarettes as per orders. I felt so wonderful for a long time through the winter, then the unbearable two weeks of anxiety about you, and Ruth and the fire, all but had me a candidate for a strait-jacket. I really feel swell this morning. It is gorgeously cool, almost cold, which is amazing in May. George Fairbanks came to work on the garden and the yard, and perhaps with some of the weeds cut down, the snakes and animals won't be so sure I am holding Open House.

. . . The movie, "Jane Eyre," was perfectly wonderful. It was interesting to notice the absorption of the hoi-polloi in the old classic. They didn't even laugh at the old-fashioned touches. Orson Welles over-acted, but was terribly impressive just the same, and Joan Fontaine was as wonderful as in "Rebecca". . . .[1]

I love you so much.

1. *Rebecca* (1940), starring Laurence Olivier and Joan Fontaine.

. . . .

(TL, 5 pp.)

[Cross Creek, Fla.]

May 10, 1944

Dearest:

. . . The building damage [the result of the Castle Warden fire] was a little over $10,000, the furniture a little over $6,000 with the furniture insurance $5,000. The total claim of something over $15,000 will be paid promptly. A good deal of it will be banked for you to finish up with as you wish when you return. . . .

Julia, guilt-ridden, I am sure, after her attack, is still deluging me with things. A box of books was here from her when I returned yesterday. I still have not been able to write her. I am terribly sorry for her, but my entirely sympathetic love is gone, I am afraid, forever. Not because I can't take being jumped on, justly or unjustly, but because she has proved such a coward.

Idella was frankly sorry to have me return too soon, as she planned house-cleaning and was deep in it. She found that either termites or the larvae of carpet beetles, I can't be sure which, had gotten into a corner of my choicest books, including some first editions of old English books that were dear to me, Peter Scott's wonderful wild fowl book.[1] Etc. I had been handling the books no more than two weeks ago, but some of them are simply gone. Life is sometimes a discouraging battle in the sub-tropics. In the north, of course, one battles the weather. There are moments when I am so damned tired of fighting this, that or 'tother, that I am ready to quit, but I know I won't. . . .

All my love.

1. Michael Bratby and Peter Scott, *Through the Air: Adventures with Wild Fowl* (London: Country Life, 1941).

(TLS, Ip.)

[Cross Creek, Fla.]
May 11, 1944

Darling:

. . . I have written Ham Basso, and I was evidently right in thinking that the long distance calls to Doug from TIME and LIFE were our personal friends checking up on us, as Max reported that Ham had informed him of the tragedy. Did I tell you that Marcia Davenport begged me to come up and stay with her? I shall not go, as I really think I can get down to work at any minute.

George Fairbanks has been working on the yard and garden, very slowly, evidently getting in as many dinners as possible.

. . . I wrote Henry Heyl, and decided to warn him that Julia was a problem child. He can't help falling for her, and I felt he should know she was a neurotic of the first order. It may be just a challenge to his medical knowledge, but he is certain to like her, and so—. I had more books and more letters from her. She said she almost fell over when her brother,[1] whom she had considered a snob and a Fascist, along with the rest of her family, stood up to them on the Negro and Jew questions, and almost walked out of the family home in protest against their lack of liberalism. This has melted me, and I shall write her tenderly. . . .

So much love, darling.

1. Charles Scribner Jr.

. . . .

(TLS, Ip.)

[Cross Creek, Fla.]
May 12, 1944

Darling:

Another awful wave of missing you—. Funny, how you get along pretty well for a while, and then all of a sudden you get so lonesome for 'tother, you think you'll bust. Some music, for instance, I just can't take. I don't use the radio much, but took it to bed with me last night, and played it early this morning, and they picked on some of our favorite songs, and it hurt my heart.

. . . Idella took advantage of my getting out early this morning to spring-clean my room, and how it held so much stuff I don't know.

. . . Julia sent me some pictures she took while here, and think I'll send you a couple. One is of me on that goddamned horse. They are a little large for distance mailing, however.

As well as I feel this morning, should be able to write you a dandy letter, but haven't a thought in my head. All I can think about is picnics and wishing we could go to Silver Glen for crabs.

I love you heaps.

. . . Have had returned, two letters to James Still. He must have moved, but I am rather anxious about him. Though he was not in actual combat, I am sure. Haven't heard from that scamp of an Arthur, but know he is working like a fool. He sure does things the hard way.

. . . .

(TLS, 2 pp.)

[Cross Creek, Fla.]
May 13, 1944

Honey Dear:

Still in the awful spasm of missing you. The reason such spells come and sort of go, is that you couldn't *stand* feeling this way all the time. I miss you constantly, but the bad waves, thank Heaven, are periodic.

The evening was clear when Moe and I set out for our walk yesterday, but a mile down the road a sudden rain squall overtook us and we were soaked. I kept thinking Idella would come after me in the car, and she said she thought of it but it seemed sort of silly since she thought I'd show up any minute. There was no point in dressing again, so took a shower and went to bed with a book I wish I'd read years ago, "Counter-Attack in Spain,"[1] pub. 1937, by Ramon Sender who wrote that lovely little book I sent you—shucks, can't remember the name— something about dawn.[2] I really never knew what the Spanish Civil War was all about, but the rest of the world seems to have been just as dumb. It was part of the beginning of the general retroactive sweep, which, if it had succeeded all over the world, would have set us back a thousand years. And the battle won't be won when we lick the Japs and the Germans. That same element, with the same type of thinking, is strong in this country. It is all part of the age-old fight between good and evil. It seems as though it almost kills people to be good! The Negro question—and India—are part of it.

Julia wrote me that she was knocked flat with delight when her brother young Charlie, on leave at home, fought the family along the lines of tolerance and liberalism, for she had been afraid he was going to fall into the selfish and Fascist mold of the rest of them. Things got so tense that he almost walked out and spent the night in town. If she would only get out and *do* something, instead of taking it all out in futile talk.

The Writers' War Board keeps wishing off apparently silly jobs on me, but I can only do them, on the outside chance that they know what they're up to. They have asked me to do an article on Florida for a magazine, TRANSATLANTIC,[3] published in England, for the purpose of giving Britishers an understanding of the U.S.A. and its mental workings. The copy of the magazine that they sent me seemed to me the height of banality. They say it goes to 50,000 of the more intellectual Britishers, but I'm damned if I believe they read it. I shouldn't.

They have also asked me to do a short article "on any war or post-war theme," as part of a series to be syndicated in newspapers. Can't think of any subject but the Negro question that I should even have any right to pipe up on. Writers' platitudes are even worse than those of politicians. They are only sublimated ads for Post Toasties. They all remind me of Bruce Barton's god-awful "The Man Nobody Knows,"[4] in which he made Jesus out a damn good Rotarian and a super-salesman.

Chet Crosby came out yesterday to say he had found someone to do my tractoring, (also, I think, to talk, for he has a good mind of its limited type, and doesn't seem to have anyone really to talk to.) He amused me so about Edith, who was certainly a new specimen to him. He said, "Miss Marge, there was something about her I liked. But you know, at first, it seemed to me she was deaf and dumb. Just something in the way she looked at me." That was of course her big myopic eyes, and the quality that makes Verle consider her "a lovable moron"— and after spending some time with her I almost feel the same way, and have to keep reminding myself of her great creative ability.

. . . This is Idella's week-end off, and she has gone, and I feel abandoned. I said "Good-bye" sadly and she laughed and said, "Now you like to tell Moe when you go off for two days, 'I'll be back in a minute.' . . ."

All my love,

1. Ramón José Sender (1901–1982), *Counter-attack in Spain* (Boston: Houghton Mifflin, 1937).
2. *The Chronicle of Dawn* (Garden City, N.Y.: Doubleday, Doran, 1944).
3. "Florida: a Land of Contrasts," *Transatlantic* 14 (October 1944): 12–17.
4. Bruce Barton (1886–1967), *The Man Nobody Knows* (New York: Grosset and Dunlap, 1925).

. . . .

(TL, 1 p.)

[Cross Creek, Fla.]
Sunday May 15, 1944

Dearest:

I am up a little early for Sunday morning, but Martha is giving her life's blood to me while Idella has her week-end off, and I could picture her sitting gloomily on the back bench waiting for the unappreciative Queen of the May to arise. So I routed myself out and had my second cup of coffee on the veranda. I gave Martha an extra five bucks yesterday and thought it would entitle me to a hot dinner this noon, but Martha just finished in the bedroom and bathroom and commented, with a downward inflection that meant I was a dog if I questioned it, "You won't need me until tonight." I said No. I guess I know my place.

. . . When Moe and I took our walk, he came down twice on the prettiest point on quail, and didn't stir. I think he will finish training very easily this fall.

(TLS, 3 pp.)

[Cross Creek, Fla.]

Monday May 15, [1944]

Honey:

. . . I fixed some lunch, then drove in to Gainesville to the movie. I thought I was getting myself a big treat, Ginger Rogers in "Tender Comrade,"[1] but it proved a waste of time and precious gas and forty cents. I have seldom seen a worse picture, just tripe. At the end, Ginger receives a telegram that her husband has been killed in action, and she goes upstairs to the baby's crib and makes a speech to the two-months' old baby about the meaning of the war. The photographer really abused her, too, and she was positively ugly.

I set out for the other movie, and that proved to be "The Son of Dracula,"[2] and I couldn't quite see that, so drove on home and listened to the radio. . . .

Martha reported that three panthers are living over this side of the River Styx. George Balknight[3] says he saw one, very close, and someone else saw the tracks and said they were unmistakable. They are believed to be a grown male and female and a young one. I doubt it very much, as I know of no wild territory nearer than Gulf Hammock from which they could or would have come. However, I suppose it is possible. If it is true, they will turn up outside my bedroom window.

Martha said demurely, "I hope Will don't mention it to 'Della. She so scary." Which amused me greatly, as Idella does things you wouldn't catch a one of the Mickens doing without a police force around.

I finished "Counter-Attack in Spain," and it is "For Whom the Bell Tolls"[4] without love in a sleeping-bag. It is a true narrative and is very wonderful.

. . . Time is certainly moving on. I feel so ashamed of the way I have wasted this year. I think I have never had a year that was such a total loss. I just don't know what's the matter with me.

Did I remember to tell you—I think not—that I am buying the lot north of the cottage, a hundred feet, at $550, which I think is a good investment. I do want to be able to control any building adjacent. . . . Enlarging the cottage is probably the temporary answer to our living arrangements. And when I get starved for real country and woods, perhaps we could take summer vacations elsewhere.

. . . Our successful offensive in Italy seems to bear out the theory that we were deliberately tying up the Germans there until we were ready to move fast everywhere. But the invasion is going to be a bloody and heart-breaking business at best.

All my love, sweet.

1. *Tender Comrade* (1943), starring Ginger Rogers and Robert Ryan.
2. *The Son of Dracula* (1943), starring Lon Chaney Jr. and Robert Paige.
3. George Bauknight. The Bauknight family was among the original settlers at Cross Creek. The homestead was approximately two miles west of the bridge (Glisson, *The Creek*, 232).
4. Ernest Hemingway (1898–1961), *For Whom the Bell Tolls* (New York: Scribners, 1940).

(TLS, 3 pp.)

[Cross Creek, Fla.]
May 16, 1944

Dearest:

Early morning is wonderful, isn't it. I'd enjoy knowing it better if it weren't so much trouble meeting it half-way. After going to bed early last night, feeling like the devil, I woke up early, and after one cup of coffee I took a long walk across the Creek. Moe couldn't believe his luck. The early sun lay through the hammock in such lovely slanting bars. The magnolias are in full bloom. The Creek itself was deserted, not a soul in sight, man, woman, nor, with all the rafts of young uns, child. They were all, including the new-born babies, on the lake fishing. The Creek was still and dark, and the cypresses are in full new leaf. And the second cup of coffee just now tasted so good.

I had a visitation yesterday afternoon of Ella Mae Slater[1] and Mrs. Bass and the four little Basses[2] and the little Basses' little white dog, who loves Moe. The children were ordered to by hand stay out, but one by one they infiltrated into the house. The visit was purely social, and its main purpose was to show me a luridly tinted portrait of Bernie in his uniform. The baby had sat on the portrait and the glass was broken, but Bernie looked very rosy and very elegant. He never had that much color in his face in all his life. (I was somehow much amused to read in the paper that poor old Mahatmas Gandhi,[3] along with his other ills, has hookworm.) Snow and Bernie have both been deprived of all their teeth by the Army, and new sets are being furnished free, "mighty good ones, I hear tell," Mrs. Bass reported, "and powerful pretty." Snow has won more marksmanship medals and Bernie is already a private first class. I enjoy such visits very much, if only they didn't stay so damn long.

When they finally left, I drove over to Citra to mail some papers to Doug, and to go to the grocery store, and I ran into Leonard. We were alone in the grocery store and he brought in a bottle of whiskey, which was passed around impartially to us, including the storekeeper, and we all shared cozily the chaser of 7-Up. I bought a beautiful Swift's Premium ham, and some of the best country sausage I have ever eaten, which Idella and I had for supper with new potatoes. Leonard said, "Not meanin' to nose into your business, but have you settled your law-suit with Zelma?" I informed him of the status of the suit and he laughed and said he had felt sure Zelma was lying—that she is going around saying that she has already gotten $10,000 out of me! I hope it does not come to trial for the simple reason that I believe I am dealing with a crazy woman—one demented with her own venom. I quoted to Leonard my statement to Phil May of "millions for defense but not one cent for tribute," and knowing Leonard's cosmic interests, started telling him the source of the quotation, in connection with the Barbary pirates, and Leonard picked up the tale and finished it and informed me that it was the first time in our history that we sent troops overseas! I do not think he has forgotten one word of anything he has ever heard or read.

... The bass season opened yesterday, and I'm hoping Chet will ask me to go fishing.

I am beginning to get soldiers' mail from the overseas editions of The Yearling and Cross Creek, and bet I am in for it. . . .

Heaps of love,

1. Ella May Townsend Slater, wife of "Snow" Slater.
2. Teresa Bass, wife of Bernie Bass, ran a fish camp and café at Lochloosa. The four Bass children: William Alfred, Bernie Lee, Bernice, and Roy. A fifth Bass child, Alton, died at five years of age.
3. Mohandas Gandhi, Hindu nationalist and spiritual leader, known for the use of passive resistance as a political tool against the British in India.

. . . .

(TLS, 3 pp.)

[Cross Creek, Fla.]
May 17, 1944

Dear Honey:

I am groggy this morning after an all-night losing bout with some sort of varmint. Moe and I both kept hearing it, once on the porch, and he would dash out with that damned blast of a bark of his and around the bushes and we'd come back in the house and doze off, then it would begin all over again. And each time we went in or out a flock of mosquitoes would come in and I battled them all night. I am cross as a bear just from lack of sleep.

Yesterday afternoon Martha and Idella and I, and Tom and J. T. Glisson and a Vet., all battled my nine shoats to get them what Martha calls noxinated. I thought noxinated, noxinated, that ought to be a perfectly good word, what's the matter with it. Then I realized it was a combination of vaccinated and inoculated. The nine shoats were goddamned if they were going to be noxinated and they fair tore the barn down, and kept popping out as fast as we could pen them. We had it around and around the house and through the grove. When the job was finally done, Martha said, "Folks say they don't know where the devil is. Huh, I know. He in hogs." We are having an awful time with them in general, and I don't know whether I can stick it out until hog-killing time next fall.

After selling and giving away game roosters, I still have three. There is the head man, then the second man—and the loser. The loser is the most comical creature I have ever seen, with lots of personality. I keep hoping that some day he'll turn and beat hell out of the other two. He is only about half their size, with the longest, skinniest legs you ever saw, and a long lean neck with the feathers off it, and long feathers sticking wildly out of wings and tail as a consequence of his flights. He looks exactly like the pictures of Cuban and Haitian fighting cocks. Although he always loses, he never gives up, and his head is constantly bloody but unbowed.

I was walking along the road with Moe yesterday evening and noticed the blueberries are thick this year, and ripe, and very large. I can't eat them, but I picked my handkerchief full for Idella. Fresh blueberry pie would be hard to beat, as a dessert. While I was prowling among the bushes, I discovered what has been smelling overwhelmingly sweet along the road. It was the most delicious fragrance and I couldn't place it, no magnolias around, the bay trees not yet in bloom. I found it was the scrub, or saw, palmettos, blooming. They are so dense and low the flower spikes weren't noticeable.

I had such a sweet letter yesterday from W.D.[1] He said, "We all wants to return home but this job out here is got to be done and done write this time for keeps. If you could see how every body is working together it would make you proud to be in here pitching too. With God help and his will we will win this great fight and return home in a peaceful world once again."

"Be nice," with God help and will, did the W.D.'s find a little *fairer* world to return to. A paragraph like the above makes "White supremacy" sound like the ravings of an idiot.

I also had, from the South Pacific, as nice a letter as I have ever had, from a man who had just read Cross Creek and The Yearling in the overseas editions. He mentioned that he was a writer, though he had made only the pulp magazines, but hoped to do creative work eventually. At the end, he spoke of Martha, and said, "I am colored, too, but instead of hindering me, it spurs me." I noticed his Navy rating was Steward, 1/c.

. . . The pre-invasion news from Italy continues wonderful. We have pushed the Germans back to the Hitler line and are giving them hell.

It seems definitely Dewey and Roosevelt for presidential candidates. Each has enough pledged delegates to carry their respective conventions. In that case I think I shall be obliged to vote for Roosevelt again. Claude Pepper somewhat exonerated himself from his forced political statements about "white supremacy" by putting up a fine fight against the poll-tax. A minority group of southern Senators was able to defeat it again, however, by threatening a filibuster. I think the liberals should simply start a fund to *pay* the poll-taxes for Negroes who can't afford it, and let the fight go on from there.

All my love,

1. W. D. Williams had been a porter at the Castle Warden.

(TLS, 3 pp.)

[Cross Creek. Fla.]
May 18, 1944

Dear Honey:

. . . I am still struggling to get the damn thing [book] read—it is by a Roosevelt-hater, John Flynn,[1] and sets out, by tracing the rise of Fascism in Italy and Germany, to show that we are following that same pattern. It is incredibly dull, and the hell of it is, I shall have to read it through to be perfectly certain that I disagree with Mr. Flynn! I believe what it will come down to, is Roosevelt's *motives*—and with all his vanity, and love of personal power, and politicking, I still believe him to be a genuine idealist. If so, he will in the end have done more good than harm. If he is an opportunist, and really longs to be a dictator, as I believe Mr. Flynn is working up to trying to prove, he is of course dangerous. But I do not believe it. . . .

I am beginning to get ready in my mind to move to the cottage. The heat descended yesterday, and the mosquitoes are bad, I can hardly scrap a bouquet from the garden, and the vegetation and snakes begin to seem ominous and creepy. It is impossible to take a walk without seeing at least one snake. Last time, I had to call Moe off a small cottonmouth. He is very cautious about snakes, however.

. . . I am wondering what your life will be like when the monsoons begin. The reports would indicate that most battle activity will have to stop, but I suppose the little rising sons of b's will keep on creeping through the wet jungle just the same. I dreamed last night that the monsoons came and they decided none of you A.F.S. men need stay through the summer, so I came over to help you pack to leave! If your summer proves rather idle, be sure and keep out of mischief. I'll admit I have had very little opportunity or temptation not to be a good girl, but still, I *am* being such a good girl, and *hating* it, that I should cut the throat of any nurse or WAC or what-not that you even looked cross-eyed at.

You are so strongly in my mind, and seem so *near* to me, that I feel you have had the unspeakable St. Augustine news, and are reaching out to me. Your mother wrote that she had not mentioned the fire to you, as she wanted to be sure you received first, my letters giving the complete story. She is such a dear, and one of those who always thinks of the other fellow first. . . .

Edith's book is in its fourth printing. She is not only now satisfied, but is overwhelmed by Scribner's good advertising, and said she wrote Charlie that she was terrified, as now, if "Colcorton" didn't sell a lot, she would know it was her own fault.

. . . Oh my dear, I do long for you so. The next four or five months will seem like as many years.

All my love,

1. John T. Flynn (1883–1964), *A Country Squire in the White House* (New York: Doubleday, Doran, 1940).

(TLS, 2 pp.)

[Cross Creek, Fla.]
May 19, 1944

Dear Honey:

The one and only Leonard showed up yesterday evening to do some odd jobs, including putting new oil in the Kohler and checking it, and a dozen minor things that were out of order are running smoothly again. He said it was definitely termites that ate my books, and he found several boards in the living room that they have devoured from within. He knows a small saw-mill where he can get good lumber, and is coming out soon to check over the house, then he and Daniel[1] will come and make repairs. I don't think there is a door in the place that closes properly, and in some cases it is because the termites have eaten the frames, and the hinges won't hold.

Leonard informed me that young Elmer[2] is impossibly "mean." I said, "Won't they take it out of him when he begins going to school?" He said, "They will, if they can get some help." Elmer has taken to running away, and it seems an old red-boned hound is to blame! The hound had been ranging off by himself, running deer, and Leonard noticed that his absences often coincide with Elmer's. He watched them one day, and followed down the sandy road, and found that the hound led the way, stopped to look over his shoulder to see if Elmer was coming, waited for Elmer to almost catch up with him, set off again, and kept luring Elmer on that way. Elmer is probably only another Leonard, for Leonard didn't learn all he knows about the woods from sitting home by the fire.

. . . Idella was *so* put out with me this morning. Today being Friday, and the Lyons and three officers coming Sunday, she decided to do her big housecleaning today, and her cooking tomorrow. I didn't think anything about it, woke up feeling good, and restless, dashed out of bed and took my coffee to the veranda, turned on the radio, and walked into Idella bringing in the scrub-bucket. I said something gay and cheery and got no answer. I said, "Why Idella, you don't want me," and she said, "I said to myself, of all mornings, I hope Mrs. Baskin doesn't get up." I promised to keep out of her way, and even pitched in and sorted magazines and papers, and she forgave me.

. . . I sent Phil a clipping from the N.Y. paper that will amuse him. You probably know of Arthur Train's fictitious lawyer, Ephraim Tutt, in stories in the Saturday Post. A Philadelphia lawyer is suing Arthur Train, and Scribner's because he bought Train's "Ephraim Tutt: the Autobiography of a Yankee Lawyer,"[3] thinking it was non-fiction, and found that Tutt was fictitious and the book a literary hoax. He is suing for the price of the book, $3.50, and also tried to bring an injunction against Scribner's to prevent further sale of the book. I typed across the top of the clipping, "This guy is sore because 'TAIN'T true!" The article quoted Max Perkins, who said it would be a tragedy if the Phila. lawyer won the suit, as there would be no more literary hoaxes, which were always great fun. Arthur Train said

the book was not a hoax, but was a legitimate way of bringing a fictional character to life, as of course it is. The guy is probably just like Zelma—jealous of Train's
success. His case seems infinitely more ridiculous than Zelma's, and of course
Train's book will now be bought by people who never heard of it before. An actual suit with Zelma would pay me, financially, but it would not be worthwhile in
the strain on my nerves, and the setting of neighbor against neighbor.

All my love, sweet.

1. Daniel Fiddia.
2. Elmer Fiddia.
3. Arthur Train (1875–1945), *Yankee Laywer: The Autobiography of Ephraim Tutt* (New York:
   Scribners, 1943).

. . . .

(TLS, 2 pp.)

[Cross Creek, Fla.]
May 20, 1944

Dear Honey:

I had the usual love-fest with Mr. N. Goldman[1] and came out with nearly fifty
dollars' worth of good liquor, even some vat 69, in case any of the Lyons' friends
are Scotch addicts. I must say the addicts of Scotch and a lot of other things are
getting glad to take what is offered. I thought I would make mint juleps tomorrow. The menu at the moment stands at baked ham, candied sweet potatoes,
corn muffins, egg-plant souffle, squash, tomato aspic salad, home-made strawberry ice-cream and angel food for dinner. For supper, cold ham and jellied
tongue, egg croquettes, rolls, cottage cheese salad, and black bottom pie. Good,
huh? The strawberry season for some reason has been poor, very few berries, and
sky high, 30¢ a *pint*. It took 90¢ worth for my ice cream but it will probably be the
last call. I almost choke when I eat egg croquettes, wishing so that you were having some with me. I am getting lots of eggs and don't go to the market very often,
and it suddenly dawned on me that we didn't have to wait for company to have
egg croquettes, so Idella and I have had them several times. She dreads them less
each time!

I told her yesterday about planning to leave her enough for a farm of her own
if she sticks with me. She was very much touched and said, politely that she
hoped she went first. I told her she had jolly well better not.

I don't have all the details, but it seems that an escaped colored convict came
to the Creek, as far as the Glissons, and Tom suspected him and held him, and
sure enough. Glad he didn't get one house further, as I am so desperate for help
I should have fallen on his neck and put him to work. Of course, an escaped
Negro convict is likely to be guilty of nothing more serious than stealing his
grandmother's harmonica. But when they escape, they are rather apt to be the
killers. . . .

... We are still battling our own hogs, and this morning the old sow broke the bottom of my gate and slipped the latch. Old Will mended it most ingeniously with an old broomstick, in place of the iron rod! ...

So much love,

1. N. Goldman, the Baskins' favorite source for alcohol.

. . . .

(TLS, 2 pp.)

[Cross Creek, Fla.]
May 21, 1944

Dear Honey:

... Ridiculous people are doing everything possible to help "Strange Fruit." It was banned in Boston, for obscenity, and is in the courts there now. The federal post-office banned it, then lifted the ban—with the result that tens of thousands are having their attention called to it. I don't know whether the charge of obscenity is an alibi, or not—I don't remember anything objectionable—except that when Tracy tried to make love to Nollie when he was drunk, things got a bit rough—but most convincing.

... Martha talked Idella into taking her to Citra last night to a barbecue. Sissie was to go, too. Idella was not enthused, but agreed. When she asked Martha if she thought Sissie was ready, Martha said, Oh, Sissie was long gone. So off they went in the truck, and in a few minutes Hettie Lou came up, saying Mama wanted to know if they were coming for her. Poor Sissie. She might have caught herself a beau at a Citra barbecue. Don't think Idella had a good time. She said they are a pretty rough crowd over there.

... Forgot to tell you of the lovely inscription Edith wrote in "Colcorton"— "For my revered friend, Marjorie Kinnan Rawlings, And for Margie, whom I love. Edith."

Another "Zelma" has popped up with just the same sort of libel suit. A cousin of Betty Smith ("A Tree Grows in Brooklyn") has upped the anty to $250,000, claiming that she suffered "public scandal, infamy and disgrace" through being identified as the prototype of a character in the book, Aunt Sissie. Guess I shall have to try to send you another copy of the "Tree." It is so adorable. As I remember, Aunt Sissie was just as cute as bug's ear, a bit on the rough side, but lots of fun.

... You spoke of the three books I sent you that the Japs are presumably now using for toilet paper, and mentioned "Westward Ho."[1] I don't believe I sent you that. As far as I know, I've never read it myself.

... I hate to sign off, as I feel so forlorn when I do. We must learn to get the very most out of life when you return. You have always done that, and I do it when I'm on the crest of the wave. Nobody has a better time than I when I'm "in the mood." I must learn to keep the mood. . . .

All my love, darling.

1. NSB meant Stephen Vincent Benét, *Western Star* (New York: Farrar, Rinehart, 1943). See letter of 29 May 1944.

. . . .

(TLS, 5 pp.)

[Cross Creek, Fla.]
May 22, 1944

Dearest:

. . . The day with the Lyons and friends was a little disappointing. To begin with, they came hours later than I expected them. . . . At three o'clock they drove in—having pulled a Baskin and dallied with friends in Gainesville! They had had two o'clock dinner in mind and felt they were only an hour late.

. . . You know, I think a good name for that weight around the middle is The Chastity Belt. I am so conscious of the superfluous pounds that I couldn't possibly look coyly or sweetly at a man. It would be too much like Sigrid Undset in "For Whom the Bell."[1]

. . . The radio said your monsoons begin in a few days now. It spoke of a place that I can't spell, but sounded like Metchina, that is in Stilwell's hands, and is a useable base for action even through the flooded period. That may be a good deal north of where you are.

. . . The bee man came to get the honey from his hives in my grove, and gave me a yard-long comb of orange blossom honey from my bloom this spring, and he said it had the finest flavor he had ever had. I took a taste and it is out of this world. Maybe I can save it for you. (Along with the charm.) I'll guarantee saving the charm, but the honey may turn to sugar if the summer is unduly hot.

True to form, I no sooner got high last night than I turned to the tall thin dull man and asked, "And how do you stand on the Negro question?" He stared at me, and, I realize now, a bit glassy-eyed himself, asked, "How do you stand on the freight differential?" This seemed mad and irrelevant, but we finally got together and what he was getting at, was the alleged necessity of keeping Negro wages low in the South, because the White South is poor, due to the freight differential! The New Orleans magnolia had as open a mind as possible under the circumstances, and I made some headway. I find I can appeal to people's snobbishness by remarking that of course opening the gates to true opportunity for the Negro is the responsibility of southern aristocrats, who can afford to be fair. She made one unanswerable point (though there must be an answer) (continued on the back of page 2) as to what would happen if the vote were given at this stage to Negroes in sections like hers, and like parts of Mississippi and Alabama, where great hordes

371

of the worst type predominate as to numbers. She said it would mean the worst types of Negroes in all the civil offices, and the whites would just have to move out. She says she believes in education and health and good wages etc., and then doing the other things when the Negroes are really ready. All I could say was, that when it comes down to it, we just do *not* improve their education and so forth, and have kept using that as an alibi too long. I also said that I believed opening the gates would be exactly like the granting of women's suffrage. I can remember all the same talk, that women would take over the world, would run men out of their jobs, and the world would be ruined—that women were definitely inferior to men and had to be by hand kept in their place! Well, the gates were suddenly opened wide to women, and my God, they don't even bother to vote most of the time. Babies continue to be born, men continue to have jobs, and the only apparent difference is that it's a woman's own fault these days if a man beats her!

Which reminds me that Idella was telling me about her great-grandmother, her mother's grandmother, who was a rare character around Reddick and lived to be nearly a hundred and told everyone, black or white, what she thought. The Bishops are an influential farming family there, and there were two brothers, one living in sin, the other given to beating his wife. Aunt Milly ran into one of them in the store and said, "You nasty dirty stinking thing, I want to talk to you." The man said, "Aunt Milly, you've got the wrong Bishop. I'm Frank." She peered at him and said, "Well, you beat your wife. You're a nasty dirty stinking thing, too."

Lots of love,

1. Ernest Hemingway, *For Whom the Bell Tolls* (New York: Scribners, 1940).

. . . .

(TLS, 3 pp.)

[Cross Creek, Fla.]

May 23 (I think) 1944

Dearest:

. . . She [Edith Pope] was "accepted" for the MacDowell Colony in New Hampshire—where I would not be caught dead—and is much pleased about it. . . .

The sulphur dusting crew dusted my grove this morning, believe it or not, at two o'clock in the morning! It seems it has to be done, to be efficacious, while there is still dew, and before there is any wind. So unless they have finished by eight o'clock, when a little wind always stirs and the hot sun dries the trees, they might as well not bother. I fully expected Moe to tear the place down when they began—and he slept right through the whole racket! Some watch dog. The sow also broke in and I heard her outside the window eating something with an awful racket, that may have been fallen tangerines—or may have been duck eggs. Moe slept through that, too, and I was too lazy to bother.

I had the most elegant dream about you. You were returning, and we were going to be married all over again in a church ceremony. You were to come directly to the church without seeing me first. Mrs. Wendell Willkie dressed me, in a white satin brocade with train, one long bright blue glove, and a little bunched veil like the kind Italian kids wear for their confirmation. Frankly, I looked like hell. Here you were in front of the church, and you looked so beautiful. You had on a brilliant electric blue silk shirt, and I decided you must just have washed your hair, for it stood up in a great wavy bush. You didn't recognize me for a minute, and then the loveliest look came over your face and I had to go and wake up before you reached me. Of course then I got to thinking about the nightmare of our actual marriage so-called ceremony, and the Popes' insistence on the wedding supper, where they had such a good time they couldn't break it up, and Aunt Ida was in clover, too, using her eating implements as though she were directing a symphony orchestra. Toscanini might get some wonderful effects if he could study the flourish she can manage with a salad fork. . . .

So much love,

. . . .

(TLS, 4 pp.)

[Cross Creek, Fla.]
May 24, 1944

Dearest:

. . . It is also going to be hot as the devil any minute. I am just back from driving over to see if George could come and fix the fence where the Hamon[1] cows broke it down. George was on the lake, but I left a message, hopefully and no doubt futilely. . . .

Last night Moe and I got ourselves another possum. It was such an ungodly hour, two or three in the morning, that I didn't have the heart to call anyone. Moe kept him cornered under a Turk's-cap bush while I went for my gun and shells, and then I had the problem, calling for at least three hands, of holding the light on the possum, shooting with some degree of accuracy, and keeping Moe out of gun-fire range. The creature was close against the house, and I didn't want to destroy the meat for Martha and also didn't want to set the house on fire, for the wood in that old porch is just tinder. I finally managed a head shot, and Moe and I went back to bed very much pleased with ourselves. I think we are having so much trouble with varmints because the grove has not been tractored, and the weeds are so dense that everything in the woods feels perfectly at home.

Late yesterday afternoon I sat, very lonely, waiting for a storm to come in, and Rex Withers[2] drove up. She was on her way to Green Cove Springs from Ocala, and at Island Grove turned off impulsively to say hello and see how I was doing and get first hand news of you. Rex and I have always liked each other a lot, without ever having been close friends at all, and I think she was astonished at the warmth of her welcome! I was certainly glad to see her. We had drinks and I asked her to stay to supper, and when she was sure she was really wanted, she did so gladly. I had good "scraps" left from the Lyons week-end, cold sliced ham and jellied tongue loaf, etc., and strawberry ice cream and cake. I never saw Rex looking better. She is almost a beauty, I think, and has such quiet poise and dignity and sweetness. We had a really grand time, and good gossip as far as Rex's niceness permits her to gossip! I'll pass on as much as I can remember.

...No mail from you yesterday, and it is getting bad. Over three weeks now....

All my love.

1. Hoyt Hayman owned Cow Hammock, south of MKR's property.
2. Rex Withers, not identified.

. . . .

(TLS, 3 pp.)

[Cross Creek, Fla.]
May 25, 1944

Darling:

Two letters from you yesterday, practically saving my life. And how I regret the two that blew out of your hat! I need every one and every word. The mail service has certainly gone hay-wire again and I wonder why. I have written you every day, and there seems no reason for a two-week gap....

Your account of the air battle was fascinating, and the censor took out only the numbers of planes the R.A.F. shot down.

...A good letter from Henry Heyl, and I think I'll just send it along. I think I told you at the time that I finally decided to write him that Julia was a problem child, and since he was pretty certain to fall for her if he met her, I felt he should know it. I can hear her saying bitterly, "There goes another of your good jobs of picking a man for me."

... Getting my British royalties is a farce, and I still can't see how the British and American governments between them manage to absorb almost all of them, but they do. Out of about $2500 British royalties last year, I ended up with a net of a couple hundred. The Cronins' oldest son will be with the invasion forces, and the son who was at Princeton has gone to Canada into the Air Force, and A.J. is feeling as low as a doodle-bug, all around. He said he had been looking forward to enjoying the publication of "The Green Years,"[1] as he thought it was the best work he has done, but he said the joy is out of everything. He also said he wondered whether the income tax descent came from the exaggerated reports of his earnings, so evidently those huge sums I read of were not correct.

... He [Dr. Atchley] recommended the same stuff, I am sure, that Dr. Harris is giving me. The stuff isn't working any miracles, but I am not giving it a fair chance, as I can't seem to leave the Sunnybrook alone. I wrote some difficult letters yesterday afternoon, got terribly nervous and almost unconsciously nipped along as I worked, and all of the sudden, about supper-time, realized I was over the rim, and piled into bed where Idella discovered me, puzzled that I hadn't called for supper. I was dimly conscious of her using the spray-gun in the room, and when I came to along in the night, she had damn near finished me with it. The air was reeking so that I was almost choked. The mosquitoes are very bad just now.

. . . Collier's has hired Hemingway to cover the western invasion from England. Martha is in England, also writing for Collier's.[2]

. . . Am so anxious to have "Colcorton" reach you and know what you think of it. I am reading it again, as I read Verle's copy very hurriedly in St. A., and finding it a beautiful job indeed. Max had her take out a lot of Clement Johnson (Sinclair Lewis) but there is still too much of him, and still too much child-birth, of which Max also made her take out reams, to her distress. She still wishes it had all been left in, for she thought, "Doctors are going to love this part." It is the same old problem of a writer's not having a sense of proportion in using personal-history material. It was all so fascinating to Edie that she couldn't see why everyone else wouldn't want to go through every pang and clinical symptom. Am afraid she may always have trouble that way. . . .

All my love,

1. A. J. Cronin, *The Green Years* (Boston: Little, Brown, 1945).
2. Both Ernest Hemingway and Martha Gellhorn were a part of the 6 June D-Day invasion, Hemingway in a landing craft and Gellhorn aboard a hospital ship. She managed to get ashore; he did not.

. . . .

(TLS, 2 pp.)

[Cross Creek, Fla.]

May 26, 1944

Dearest:

Bright Taylor . . .[1] came out yesterday afternoon with the insurance check on my car, and another paper to sign before Mr. Brice can get his mule money. . . .

At just this minute Bright came out again this morning, bringing also the mule adjuster. I convinced him that $250 was not too much for the Brice mule, and he went down and paid it. I also had Bright check over my farmhouse here as to coverage. There is an awful lot of wood in the rambling old place, a lot of roof area, and it could not be reproduced for the price of a compact little bungalow.

. . . Your two sentry stories are a riot. Bright said to tell you he was simply itching to hear your tales when you come back. I said we'd have to have a big party, give you a couple of drinks, put you up on a box, and all of us sit on the floor and make you tell us everything.

This is an awfully dull letter, but it just can't be helped.

I love you so much.

1. Bright Taylor, manager of Ocala Insurance and Investment Co.

(TLS, 4 pp.)

[Cross Creek, Fla.]
May 27, 1944

Darling:

. . . And one reason the book[1] has been no-go, I am sure, is that after I have written my heart out to you every day, there doesn't seem anything left, even though my letters have not been creative, like Katherine Mansfield's. I mentioned to Edith that I kept being surprised when my typewriter ribbon grew wan and pale, but figured up that since you had been gone I had written you nearly 250,000 words, and Edith laughed and said, "There's your book!" I don't mean that I begrudge the time and the words, for there are other more potent reasons why I have been prostrate but not creative, but I do mean that I resent not having you receive every one of the 250,000!

. . . Your Mother . . . could never figure exactly where you were, but we knew you were wherever the British-Indian forces were fighting the Japs in eastern India and north-west Burma and all we had to do was follow the news dispatches, and as I wrote you in one rage at not being told *anything*, we knew within a hundred miles where you were, and within a few days of what you were doing. One reason your censorship was eased was because the American correspondents raised pure hell and even went on strike; said they would send no more India-Burma dispatches until they were allowed to tell a fragment of the very stuff the Army itself released. Also, things have been going so much better, that the Japs themselves know to their sorrow where you all are!

. . . Isn't Hemingway's accident ironic! Everyone was thinking how brave he was to cover the first wave of the western invasion—and he gets seriously conked riding with a doctor in an ordinary automobile![2]

. . . Martha came up with another convict scare last night. Three white convicts escaped from Gainesville. She begged me to lock my doors last night and keep my gun in my room, so I did, to satisfy her. She said she has been uneasy about me since the other negro convict showed up out here, and just didn't sleep nights, waiting for me to call. Which is the biggest piece of black blarney possible, for when I struggled alone the other night to restrain Moe and handle a flashlight and a gun, all at once, to shoot the possum, nobody ever peeped from the tenant house after the gun fired! For all Martha knew, it was a murder or a suicide, instead of possum in the pot. Of course I totally forgot I had latched the doors, and when Moe had to go out in the night, we were both puzzled that he couldn't seem to get out. This morning I had to let Idella in, and when she saw the gun, she laughed and said, "Moe, she's slipping."

Moe and I had a grand long walk yesterday evening, halfway to town and back. I gathered a big bunch of tar-flowers, which are just beginning to bloom, you remember those palest pink star-shaped sticky flowers. The blueberries in those gallberry flats along the road are so thick that in places you get a blue sheen, as of a patch of blue flowers, and they are unusually large this year. If I didn't think Edith would attract all the rattlesnakes in the county, I'd go in and pick some for canning while she is here. I may leave her behind early some morning and slip in and do it anyway. . . .

I love you so much, darling.

1. *The Sojourner*, which was not finished until the fall of 1952.
2. On 25 May 1944, Hemingway was involved in an automobile accident in London, which required a four-day stay in the London Clinic.

. . . .

(TLS, 6 pp.)

[Cross Creek, Fla.]

May [27] 28, 1944

Darling:

Well, thanks to the mail service, the hellish thing happened that I prayed would not—you received only partial information about Ruth and the fire, without having had my long letter giving the complete story. One reason I wrote you was for fear someone else would pass on the same casual items. Just in case the April 24 letter never does reach you, I might repeat briefly: At 9 o'clock Sunday morning Apr. 23, a Miss Betty Richeson from Jacksonville, a beauty shop operator, checked in and was given the only empty room, No. 17. It seems probable she had been drinking, at any rate was upset. The girl on the desk said she smelled liquor. She was also talkative and said she had had a quarrel with her family and had run away. At 11:15 a.m., there being no one in that wing except this woman, and Ruth sleeping late as usual in the apartment, the maid went up to clean and saw the smoke and flames and called. Chef and Robert ran with fire extinguishers, and approached the fire from both staircases—one reason certainly why the fire did not spread any further than it did. Doug was down-town working with Oliver Lawton on the books. He returned at about the time the fire department got there, about 11:25. He ran up the fire escape and across the roof and the black smoke was so dense up the apartment stairs that he did not dare cross unless he knew Ruth was there. The apartment door was closed—she kept it closed all the time. He called and got no answer, ran back to the roof and called for a gas mask, to cross, and no one paid any attention in the excitement, and by the time he ran back again, the flames were insurmountable.

. . . Anyway, the Richeson woman is believed to have fallen asleep with a cigarette. She was found in the bathroom across the hall—may have gone over there to be ill or something and collapsed, leaving a lighted cigarette in the room behind her. Several of us have even wondered if she was the cock-eyed sort who might deliberately have set fire to the room, thinking she'd make her family "sorry," and then have passed out in the bathroom.

Everyone feels that almost anyone but Ruth could have gotten out. Unfortunately she did not sleep through it, as I too hoped when I first got the word at 2 that afternoon, but aroused—we don't know the time element there—and seems to have shut herself in the bathroom, which after the stairs, caught the worst of it, and was the one sure trap in the place. The bedroom and living room were absolutely black with smoke, but were not burned at all. Ruth had time to call the firemen from the bathroom window, that tiny little slot, then was evidently overcome by smoke immediately after. At any rate, she died from the smoke, *definitely*. All the living room windows were found closed, and if she could not get to the roof, it seems she could have opened one of those big windows and just hung out it, getting enough fresh air to last until a ladder could be put up. It seems as though by putting a wet bath towel over her face and grabbing up "the blue elephant" and wrapping it around her, she could have made it to the roof, even if she collapsed after getting there. Or the window ledge outside the bedroom window was broad enough for her to have stood on until rescued. Of course, the smoke and flames were in the rooms underneath, and we just don't know. The interior of that wing, down to the second floor lounge, was pretty well destroyed. Actual building damage about $10,000—covered by insurance—furniture and equipment damage, something over $6,000—and you had $5,000. Smoke and water of course did a good deal of that. Every inch of the whole place was black and greasy from the smoke. The hotel commission wrote Doug—of course I have written you complete details in other letters—said they were never satisfied about the apartment and would not allow it to be used for anything but storage—no one, not even owner, can live there again. . . .

Your letter almost broke my heart all over again. I knew it would hit you that way. And I knew you would feel a sense of blame about it. I know I did. It just seems too much for you to have to bear such a burden, when you have your hands full where you are.

My dear, I am wonderfully well physically, and not too badly off nervously, though for a time it was almost impossible going, and you must not feel that you have done anything to me. No man can lose his own integrity to keep some fool woman from going to pieces. And under everything I have such a basic resilience and just plain stubbornness, that I am being an ass in the nick of time. You *had* to go. Things important to you were involved, beyond, over or under the rather obvious duty call, and I have been aware of those elements right along, and agreed with you. I think Ruth's death is too high a price to pay, and if anything happens to you, it will not have been worth while, but short of that, the sacrifice we have both made is a minor matter compared with the things that mattered. . . .

As I wrote you before this happened, I believe you could sell now at a good profit, for hotels in Miami, Palm Beach and on the West Coast have sold lately at fabulous prices, in anticipation of a post-war flood of pleasure. But you would be at loose ends when you came back, and I still think that even if Doug ran it, we should get, over the years, a higher return on our investment than from anything else we could put our money in.

Of course, as I keep harping, until I know you are sick of it, I worry about our working out a joint life. Something is wrong with me, I know, to be so set in my ways, but I should have to choose to die, rather than live in any hotel, under any circumstances. You are a born hotel man, and there is no reason for you to deny your nature any more than I should deny mine. I know we can work it out, for after admitting your gregariousness and my need of rural living, little brick walls in both of us, (that may prove to be bricks made of straw!) we want to be together more than we want anything in the world. With that understanding, which I am sure has grown on both of us, though we knew it and it did not really need any growth, we'll manage something. If you sold the Castle, you might want to develop something within commuting distance of the Creek. But the Castle seemed so perfect for you, and you have been and will be able to give people so much through its medium, that it requires more than serious thought, to consider giving it up, even at a big profit. I just don't know. Perhaps I should be psychiatrized [sic] first, to find out whether my clinging to the Creek is a reasonable thing, or a morbid clinging to something unreasonable! It does seem such a perfect, simple home, if your business were near-by. I know so *precisely* what *I* want. The Creek for home, for headquarters; you with a business that took you away all day, while I either lolled or worked; you coming home toward evenings alone together; (and after I have either worked or lolled all day, you'd be surprised how sociable I am, and how ready to go, or have people in, come sunset!); real days off together, picnicking, fishing, rambling; real vacations together—and the Creek to come to after the ramblings. To me, it sounds like Heaven. The alternative, if you keep the Castle, is probably a similar place in the country near St. Augustine, and if that seemed feasible, I think I could go that far on a compromise. The Creek suits me in its isolation, its utter rurality (is there such a word?) and in its *simplicity*. It is perfectly possible that after the war the traffic will be so heavy on this road (it was beginning to bother me) that I should *welcome* getting away from it. We will almost certainly get a power line out here (which I want and need) and the poles down the road in front of the grove would irk me to death! I cannot tell whether it is the peculiarities of the place itself, so consonant with my peculiarities, that please me, or whether I should be equally happy in any simple place truly in the country. I *think* the latter.

I have been here *sixteen* years—the longest period I have ever spent in any one place in my whole life, counting my childhood. My life has been confused (aren't they all!) and through many phases, desperate. I have been tormented here—and it is still home. But as I say, being still the subject of obscure fears and frustrations, my clinging to it may be morbid and perverse, and a similar place in a more convenient location might solve *everything*. I have no enthusiasm for my writing, but I *have* to write—but that in itself, fortunately, need not trouble us. I also *have* to be with you—so surely we can work it out.

Darling, don't ever say to me that you "will always be a little man." You are big, and always have been, and have been getting bigger right along. And how can anyone react to the world, if not subjectively? Subjectivity is one thing, selfish egotism and smallness quite another. One does have to learn that one's subjectivity is not the core of the universe, but you have always known that, much better than I, except in my transcendent moments.

I am so ignorant that sometimes I feel illiterate. Searching for something to read yesterday, I took up Thoreau's "Walden,"[1] which I had never read. It is completely enchanting and I shall send it to you, and you must read it slowly, word by word. Thoreau says, "All men want, not something to *do with*, but something to *do*, or rather something to *be*."

That is your particular triumph, so much higher than being United States Senator or Ernest Hemingway—-*being* such a *luminous* person that everyone who comes within range warms his hands at your lovely flame. God knows I have warmed myself at your fire, and I feel insolent when I put any conditions on it, such as saying that I cannot live in any hotel, and so forth. I have felt often with you that Bread was being offered me and I have insisted on having a stone. I only know, aside from that, that I droop and die away from rural living.

Oh darling, come back to me.

1. Henry David Thoreau (1817–1862), *Walden* (1854). MKR's claim that she had never read *Walden* seems hard to believe, especially since much of its philosophy is in *Cross Creek*. Yet she persists in this claim in later letters.

. . . .

(TLS, 4 pp.)

[Cross Creek, Fla.]
May 29, 1944

Darling:

. . . I shall make myself work on the Florida article for *Transatlantic*,[1] that OWI sponsored British magazine I wrote you about. . . .

Martha, who is filling in for Idella on the latter's week-end off, is, I think, deliberately doing everything possible to cure me of having her fill in. I pay her well for the extra help, but it is still an overwhelming favor on her part. I suppose most of it really is plain stupidity, but she does seem to go out of her way. Last night our main dish was jellied chicken, and Martha heated the dinner plates to a crisp. Then Edith's scrambled eggs for breakfast this morning, and her toast, were served on clammy cold plates. This morning at 8:30 nothing had happened, though Martha comes over every morning with Idella and knows I have my orange juice and coffee between 7:30 and 8:15. I put on a housecoat and went out, and here sat Martha on the bench, Patience on a monument, "waiting to see what you-all wanted." The coffee was made, but only enough for one, the two glasses of orange juice sitting out in the heat. The front porch and living room had not been cleaned and straightened, as she "didn't want to 'sturb you-all." It was so late that Edith got up and came out, dressed, so I had Martha serve her on the porch. Edith dawdled as always, and I had another cup of coffee, and long after, I looked out, and here sat Martha. She hadn't been to clean the bedrooms and bathrooms in the hour and half, as she was "waitin' to get the dishes." She is so damned ostentatious in her waiting to serve at the moment desired, that I cannot help suspecting her motives.

It is almost noon-dinner time and I made us a Tom Collins. We both gagged at the first sip. The sugar was salt! And it turned out Edith's breakfast sugar had been salt, from the same bowl that Martha had filled, and Edith thought it didn't taste like the usual Cross Creek coffee but was too polite to say so! Martha showed me the sugar-jar, which I had used yesterday to make banana ice-cream, which was certainly all right, from which she filled the bowl, but I still think she slipped in some salt as part of the curing process.

. . . In the letter from your mother yesterday, in which she asked if I had had news from you, she remarked that she had sent you a clipping from LIFE, showing Negroes registering to vote, and said, "We haven't had *that* here yet," and went on to tell a tale of a Negro knocking over some sacks of flour, the clerk ordering him to put them back, the Negro saying, "Put them back yourself and the hell with you," and the clerk beating up the Negro. Your mother is too old and frail for me ever to breathe a word of the way I feel, but the true Negro problem comes in the relation evinced there. There are certainly two sides to it in such an Alabama community where the backward Negroes out-number the whites. Why wouldn't the Negroes say, "and the hell with you?" One the other hand, with hate having been built up over so long a time (even though that hate is the fault of the whites), there is certainly a perfectly respectable fear on the part of the whites, if the backward Negroes came into power in such a section. Of course they are backward because we have held them back, but the immediate problem is serious. In general, I am sure I know the answers, but for communities like that, I don't. White evil has gone on too long, and now for them there is a perfectly definite black evil, and it is a genuine one.

After dinner

. . . It dawned on me, when you said one of the books I sent you that you lost was "Westward Ho," that you meant "Western Star," Stephen Vincent Benet's post-humous and unfinished book.

Martha and Sissie and I plan to go early in the morning to pick wild blueberries for canning. Will leave Edith sleeping, and a note for Idella. I told Martha to bring me coffee early, and I expect by God I'll *get* it early. Four A.M. wouldn't surprise me in the least. It seems the blueberries are easier to see when the sun is not bright. Also, the snakes will not be active.

. . . I have always been afraid that some time or other you would grow a mustache—. . . . I have always loathed mustaches, but have never lived with one, so can't be sure. But I do think it would be safer if you looked the way I think of you when you first show up again. I remember when I was still Arthur's darling little Peaches, when Father went away on his month's vacation with a flowing mustache-cup mustache, and came home with a small clipped one, and I burst into tears and wouldn't and couldn't kiss him. Not that the clipped item was not certainly a great improvement on the walrus whiskers—it was just that he came back *different*.

> Now it is Monday morning
> May 29
> really and truly

Martha and I have gone wild and there will be no work this morning. She and I were out at seven this morning, picking blueberries. I shut Moe up, as I did not want him tearing through the palmettos and gallberry bushes in what we know is rattlesnake Heaven. I left Edith asleep for the same reason! Martha and I cut under the cattle fence and worked first up the old sand road. Then we began seeing berries farther and farther out in the open flats and keeping working out until we heard something in the bushes, and since the sun was getting a sting in it, we called quits and came home. She had picked just twice as many as I had. Imagine we got about six quarts. I'll can them this morning. Then we will all drive over to the turn to Snow's place where there is a wild plum thicket, as the plums may be ripe. They were beginning to turn when I was there a week ago.

. . . Edith and I talked until 12:30 last night about our parents! I think she was pumping me, which was alright. I think neither you nor I has anything in the family cupboard to touch her father. He was a complete skunk.

> All my love, darling.

1. "Florida: A Land of Contrast." See letter of 13 May 1944.

. . . .

(TLS, 3 pp.)

> [Cross Creek, Fla.]
> May 30, 1944

Dearest:

Martha and I have been giving the woods fits. Idella and Edith asked to go wild-plumming with us yesterday morning, and of course Moe had to go, too, as it was safer territory, so we all piled in the car and set out. The plums were still not ripe at the turn to Snow's place, so I drove on across the River Styx. It was covered with water hyacinths in bloom and was alive with white ibis. Still no plums. Martha directed me to an old clearing where Aunt Delphie lived many years ago—and here were plums so thick that we filled our baskets in no time.

Martha led us back farther in the pine woods, and here was another abandoned clearing with an enormous pear tree loaded with pears that will be ripe in July—and an *apricot* tree. I did not even know apricots could be grown in Florida. Martha said the apricot tree was as old as she was. It too was loaded with Fruit, which will ripen in the early fall. She said when the apricots are ripe, you can smell them for half a mile. In the clearing was an old white Scuppernong vine, and next January or February I am going to dig it up and try to move it here. We located several fine patches of wild grapes, which will be ready about August. We had a heavenly time, and I wished for you all morning.

Yesterday afternoon Martha and Sissie went off blueberrying again, and Martha reported finding a very abundant patch and asked if I cared to go again. I said I'd go this morning and she was delighted. We arranged for her to bring me orange juice at 6:30 this morning, and I put on the red pants you hate so and we set out just as the sun was coming up. The mist lay over the pine woods and the gallberry flats and everything was cool and dewy and lovely. I had asked Martha if we needed to take the car, and she said not unless *I* didn't care to walk, and I thought it was probably only around the bend anyway. Well, we walked and we walked and we walked, until we had gone even farther than I go when I take my Marathons. Martha pointed to a road and said that was it, and we cut off into the flats. It was an old unused road, thickly grown over—and not a blueberry bush in sight. Martha said, "There's due to be another road here somewhere." We kept getting into wilder and wilder country, and Martha said, "Must be the road's done growed over." A thought struck me, and I asked her when she had last picked blueberries there. She said, "When Mrs. Whitman[1] lived at the Creek. Me and her used to come here." Mrs. Whitman moved from the Creek all of ten years ago—. What on earth possessed Martha to drag me off to a place she hadn't been to in years, when she knew of a thick patch near home, I'll never know. It was not that she was saving the other patch for herself, for both times she has offered me her pickings. We turned back and began investigating, and stumbled on blueberries so thick that we didn't know where to begin. The bushes were sometimes weighted to the ground. The terrain was not too spooky, though we know rattlers are there, but we could see what we were doing. When we started, Martha cast her eyes to Heaven and said, "Now Lord, lead us where the danger ain't." A bobwhite seemed to be calling, "Are they sweet? Are they sweet?" and Martha yelled back, "Course they're sweet!" I have made part of the plums into jelly, a beautiful ruby red, and canned the blueberries, and feel as though I had done the first constructive work of the year! And I am covered with redbugs. Both times I tried to let the soap dry on me in the shower, but evidently did not wait long enough or did not use strong enough soap.

. . . Idella has the problem of fattening Edith and reducing me at the same table. It seems Edith did gain five pound in the five days she was here before, and I think I did, too! This time, I do not eat desserts when she does, she has rich milk where I have vegetable juice, I leave the butter alone and I'll swear she eats a quarter of a pound at a meal. And she has appropriated my pet couch on the porch and lies there while I sit up, so we both ought to achieve the desired results.

Our luncheon menu included fresh corn souffle and fried okra. Edith will have a blueberry tart with whipped cream which I shall forego. . . .

All my love,

1. Mrs. Whitman, not identified.

. . . .

(TLS, 2 pp.)

[Cross Creek, Fla.]

May 31, 1944

Dearest:

I have decided not to send you Thoreau's "Walden," but to save it to read aloud when you return. It is too delicious not to be shared. I had conceived of it all my life as a stuffy if not insane compendium of nature notes done in an antique stilted style—and E. B. White[1] at his best never turned a neater or a more riotous phrase. If I had read "Walden" before, I should not have written "Cross Creek," for "Walden" is precisely the type of book I had hoped to do, and of course did and could not.

. . . I have been on the wagon over a week and feel grand, but a little woozy from my low-calorie diet. I have had Idella bringing me grapefruit juice in mid-morning and afternoon, and it tides me over. I told her yesterday that when I had it regularly, I didn't even want a drink, and she said, "I'll strip the trees."

I am also a little woozy from three nights of interrupted sleep, coupled with the very early rising. A horrid razor-back hog breaks in the yard at night, and five or six times a night Moe dashes out and chases it off, barking like Cerberus.[2] Or is Cerberus silent? Anyway, he barks like hell.

My own sow and nine pigs break in, and nine little pigs of Glissons. The other day I sent Martha to Tom to ask him to get them out, along with his razor-back, and he remarked coldly that when my pigs broke in his yard he drove them out without sending for me. So now we have to do the best we can without a man. . . .

All my love, darling.

1. E. B. White (1899–1985), humorist and wit, who made famous "The Talk of the Town" column in *The New Yorker* and "One's Meat" for *Harper's*. Later he became well known for the children's classic *Charlotte's Web* (1952).
2. Cerberus, the three-headed dog that guarded the entrance of Hades.

(TLS, 3 pp.)

[Cross Creek, Fla.]
June 1, 1944

Dearest:

... Every evening just as Idella began to bring things out to serve dinner, Edith has given a darting glance like a startled fawn, torn off to her room—necessitating Idella's taking the hot dishes back to the kitchen—and reappeared in a change of costume. Twice, including last night, she has worn a depressing number, a cross between a dinner dress and a housecoat, that I am sure someone gave her and she had dyed. It is a gloomy shade of spoiled mulberries, but she trails out happily in it. Last night when she ran to dress—while Idella took everything back again—by golly, I slipped on the old mustard affair of mine, and we ate a rather frugal supper in unattractive glory. Something at Edith's bosom kept catching my eye. She had on no brassiere, and her flat breasts were almost hanging out, for she loves decollete, and in between her breasts was what looked like a black ravine. I thought my God her chest had cracked open and I was looking at her lungs, liver and lights. It was her *comb*. A common black barber's *comb*.

... Alas, a sad ending to the story of the blonde biddy that Martha and I gave to the hen who had twelve black biddies. She pecked it to death. It is evidently one of the more hideous of primitive traits to want to kill anything that is *different* or anything that is not one's *very* own. That is one reason I have so little "family feeling"—it seems to me a form of savage egoism.

... The man who has been working on turning Edith's book into a play for Katharine Cornell reported that he talked it over with Guthrie McClintoc,[1] who was still interested, but said in the form it was now, he could not see it as a *play*. So the man is going at it again.

The news dispatches report a recent heavy Jap offensive against your sector, said to be repulsed. Your weather is also evidently bad. Stephen Galatti is back in New York after inspecting the A.F.S. in Italy and the Central Mediterranean. I wonder why he didn't go on to India and Burma. I suppose it would be too hard to get him in and out.

... Phil May is very much upset that the Supreme Court has not given a decision. It is nearly four months now. If the judges don't do something soon, they will all be on their vacations and it will be fall before we hear.

... I really long to strip myself down to essentials, for there lies the only true freedom. Reading "Walden" has brought back all my ancient desire for an attractive *hut* somewhere in a beautiful spot. I shouldn't even need, and be dependent on, any Idella. I should even feel a lot better if I stirred around and did my own simple work. But of course the Creek is a good compromise between comfort and sophistication, and genuine simplicity. ...

All my love, darling.

1. Guthrie McClintoc, a producer.

(TLS, 2 pp.)

[Cross Creek, Fla.]
June 2, 1944

Dear Honey:

Life began very early at the Creek this morning. I awoke early in anxiety, for Moe had run away the night before after I told him it was too hot to take a walk. I didn't know whether to go after him or give him time to get it out of his system. Lo and behold, he came home soon after sun-up, and I arose to greet him. He is utterly exhausted, and while it may be from love, I think it more likely that he and Chet's dog hunted all night in the moonlight. Edith awakened early and came out to join us, so we had breakfast together on the veranda, in housecoats, and now it is about the time Edith usually wakes up, and breakfast is over, the house cleaned and we have settled down to work.

. . . Tom Glisson insisted on giving me fish without charge yesterday, and I really should not mind, as his use without rent of my corner of land at the Creek is all that enables him to have a fish business at all. He was chuckling over a terribly funny circumstance and told me about it. As you know, he is a large employer of illegal fishermen. He now has about eight fishing families renting shacks from him at the Creek, and I think he sets them up with their seines and boats. They net the fish illicitly and he pays them so many cents a pound, then re-sells to the wholesale dealers at a high profit. He is getting really rich and has bought hundreds and hundreds of acres across the Creek. Well, night before last the game wardens got several seines and 600 lbs. of fish—and they sold the fish to Tom! He said he was afraid the fishermen might be sore at him, but he had convinced the game wardens that it was better for the fish to reach the market to feed people than to be wasted. They sometimes try to deliver the captured fish to the poor house etc., but without ice for the transportation, it usually spoils. Whether the game wardens will turn the money in to the county or pocket it, deponent sayeth not. I am sure the fishermen *will* be sore at Tom, for they are the only losers. And Tom almost certainly paid the game wardens less than he pays the fishermen.

. . . Being on the wagon makes me so provoked, for while I feel better in general, my insides do not behave as well. I think it is because the liquor keeps me relaxed. However, I shall try to stick it out for the sake of reducing.

We are still battling pigs, my own and the neighbors! I should get rid of mine except that if I am to be over-run with other people's, my own might as well be feeding in here, too. . . .

All my love,

(TLS, 2 pp.)

[Cross Creek, Fla.]

June 3, 1944

Dearest:

. . . I simply do not understand Edith's attitude about the advertising of her book. She said it would take several years to do her next book, and she wanted to talk to Scribner's to see what they were going to do about it. I didn't get what she meant, and then she asked if I thought it would be a good idea to talk with Whitney Darrow[1] instead of Max or Charlie. I said, "My God, don't try to talk to Whitney about a *book*." She said, "Oh, I meant what he planned to do for the book, how much they would spend on advertising it, and so forth." I was horrified and remarked that a book would first have to be written before any publisher would know whether it was worth spending *anything* on. She persisted, and I said there probably weren't more than two or three writers in the country who could dictate to the publishers on business angles, and that I for one had never questioned anything like that, that it was to the publisher's interest to sell a book anyway. But she kept on, that she had known some people with Farrar and Rinehart who "pinned them down" beforehand. I was so angry I was trembling. I had thought she was humble and modest about her work, but I have begun to feel she may have that same queer *vanity* about it that she does about watching her own face in the mirror. And this thing I think is her own idea—I don't think its Verle's. I suggested that she might prefer publishing with someone besides Scribner's, and if she is going to act that way, I wish she would. She toyed with the idea, basing it all on what a publisher would "guarantee" to spend on the book. I point out to her that it would be ethical for her to talk over the book with Max beforehand, as she plans to do, and still publish with anyone else, but it would not be ethical to put him through another hellish editing job—and then publish with someone else. It is simply beyond me, since Colcorton would not have been worth reading without Max. She is evidently assuming that her next book will be a masterpiece. I am so *disappointed.* . . .

All my love,

1. Whitney Darrow, sales manager for Scribners.

. . . .

(TLS, 5 pp.)

[Cross Creek, Fla.]

June 4, 1944

Dearest:

"They" keep urging us to send light-weight mail, and thin air mail envelopes, except for the huge business size, are simply unobtainable. Of course "they" want us to use V-mail, and I suspect them of keeping the air mail envelopes from us, the way Mother used to hide the candy. "They" have publicly apologized for a two-week gap in mail coming from England, and say increased censorship and lack of transportation, both due to the coming invasion, are responsible.

. . . . I didn't get home [from Ocala] until seven o'clock, and Idella said Moe had howled like a mad dog all afternoon. I couldn't take him, as parking in the heat would have been impossible. Yet an hour or so after I got home, Moe went off again and was gone all night, coming in just at daylight. Idella and I agreed that he was a old-fashioned male. He resents *my* going off, but once I am safely home, he thinks it is all right for him to ramble. I'd love to know what he is doing.

. . . A radio item said the Chindits[1] in your area were doing fine, then gave out of ammunition. . . .

All my love,

1. Chindwits, natives named after the Chindwin River in Burma.

. . . .

(TLS, 3 pp.)

[Cross Creek, Fla.]

June 5, 1944

Dear Honey:

By actual count, twenty-one pigs are living in the house grove and it isn't their fault they're not living in the house. There is my sow, who lifts up fences as she pleases; her nine pigs, who are quite sizeable now; a stray red barrow with a hernia, which is depressing; an enormous steel-gray razor-back boar with large white ears, to whom I have taken the most violent personal dislike and who turns the ducks out of the pen every night; and nine baby piglets of Glissons who are still small enough to be cute. It is the over-ripe fallen oranges that attract them all. Yesterday I saw each little pig with an orange in its mouth. They ran off in a line, and all that was lacking was a liveried footman holding a salver under each one.

. . . Martha and Idella have just finished the washing and are taking the truck to go across the Creek and get more wild plums. I am tempted to go, too, but have some checks I really should mail out this morning.

Last night was the first time in weeks I have taken a notion to use the lights at night for reading, and of course the damn Kohler had to cut up. . . . At last I gave up, toted the radio and heavy farm battery to the bedroom to listen in the dark, though reception was poor because of the atmosphere—and the moment I got set, the lights behaved perfectly. I resent the animosity shown me by the mechanical things around here.

How much news do you get of the war on other fronts? The Italian news is wonderful, Rome in our hands without a fight there, thank Heaven, and the Germans in full retreat across the Tiber. I imagine the western invasion will come at any moment, to coincide with this. That damn Pope, after making no complaints about German occupation of Italy, rared back on his dew-claws and said the Papal guards were ready to fight anyone who bothered the Vatican, presumably meaning us. The Catholic Church has certainly played pals with Fascism in Italy and Spain. . . .

All my love,

. . . .

(TLS, 3 pp.)

[Cross Creek, Fla.]
June 6, 1944

Dear Honey:

Any time you get tired of Moe and Idella and me, just say so. I can always copy excerpts from the classics—.

Moe is working on the night shift. About ten o'clock at night a sly look comes over his face and he eases out of the back screen door with much less banging than usual. Then he shows up in the morning on the dot of the seven o'clock whistle, when Martha and Idella are stirring. I really think he believes that no one knows he has been out all night. I can understand his slipping off, but I do not understand the regular hours. It is almost as though he made a certain bus.

I have been doing so well on the wagon, and reducing, that I felt free to ask Idella to give me a massage this morning, and it was wonderful. I don't mind asking her when I am cooperating, but I can't expect her to do all the work for me.

Yesterday evening Martha started into the pump house to start the Kohler to water the garden, and she and Idella let out whoops and called me to bring my gun, that there was a rattlesnake under the pump. It proved to be only a large king snake, and while Martha said they were fine to have around, to catch rats, she wouldn't go in to start the motor and I had to do it. They do look just as creepy as though they were poisonous.

. . . I made some more wild plum jelly yesterday, and this time did it the way the old-fashioned experts used to—didn't squeeze the pulp, strained the juice a second time, skimmed it carefully, and this batch looks like liquid rubies.

. . . The tractor has just come to cultivate the grove and I am certainly glad. The place had begun to feel a little too primaeval. Hope Chet follows it out, as I want to find out if he knows anything about Moe's peculiar disappearances.

Am so anxious to hear whether you can go to Kashmir.

All my love,

(TLS, 5 pp.)

[Cross Creek, Fla.]
June 9, 1944

Dearest:

. . . Found I had lost five pounds, and Idella really went to town this morning on a massage. Then she insisted on giving me a facial and I squirmed and got fidgety and she had to skip a few "movements." They teach them the silliest systems of dribbling their fingers over the customer's puss, and Idella did it just the way the high-priced operators do in New York, and it drives me perfectly nuts.

Well honey, you'd better hurry home or there won't be room for you in the car. Your family now consists of me, Moe, Idella and little Martha. Sissie is letting us take Martha for the summer, with the understanding that in the fall she will decide whether we keep her. I am sure by that time she will be willing. Idella is so thrilled, and Martha is all agog. Idella will make a wonderful mother. I told her I'd give her money to buy clothes for Martha in Ocala, and she said she would only get a couple of things, then would buy materials, as dresses are expensive and shoddy at the same time, and she'd rather make her things. Martha is only four, and can count to fifteen. David's hair had been neglected, so Martha took it on herself to cut most of it off, then turned the scissors on her own kinks.

Moe ran away again last night, but came home very early, along in the middle of the night, and this morning, for some reason is sore at me. He wags his tail when Idella speaks to him, but turns his head away when I do. Am afraid he is going to be as neurotic as Pat was.

I have continued reading Thoreau with infinite delight. Some of his sentences are gems. One is, "Most men lead lives of quiet desperation." And he wrote, "We have nothing to fear from our foes; God keeps a standing army for that purpose; but we have no ally against our friends, those ruthless vandals."

. . . When you come home, I mean to jump all over you about this "education" business. I am afraid you don't know what education is. You are so much better "educated" than most college graduates that it isn't funny. Education is not something that is automatically garnered by the paying of tuition, the living in a dormitory, and the listening to facts from the rostrum. Education is first of all, reading—and beyond all, absorbing into oneself the wisdom of others and the developing of wisdom for oneself. My own "education" is a puny thing, for I am woefully ignorant of many of the greatest classics, and if you are game when you come home, we'll read them together.

Incidentally, Idella is reading Dostoievksy's "Crime and Punishment". . . .

All my love, darling.

(AL, TLS, 6 pp.)

[Lake City, Fla.]
Blanche Hotel
Sunday A.M. June 11 [1944]

Dearest:

. . . After dinner, Cliff[1] showed me the high points of the base, and took me into the Celestial Navigation Trainer and had the boys on duty put on a show for me. The Trainer has been in use about two years, was very secret at first, but there is nothing hush-hush about it now. There was even an article in Readers' Digest about it called "Bombing Berlin from Binghamton." The cock-pit of a plane is complete as to all instruments, simulates conditions of flight, winds, etc., and is set under a most amazing dome which simulates the stars, and the men are taught celestial navigation that way. The Navy is very proud of its pilots, for every pilot has to be a navigator as well. The youngster who was at the controls of the Trainer told me flying was a cinch—it was only navigation that was difficult.

The Naval Air Base here is a comparatively small one, not in a class with Jacksonville or Pensacola, but they do intensive advanced work here, and have a good many expert pilots return from overseas for refresher courses. It is built out in the pine woods, like Blanding, but is [written portion ends].

[Continues in typescript] Under the trainer plane they move huge photographs taken from the air at 10,000 feet, at the same speed at which the ground would move from a plane going at a certain speed, with certain speed of wind. The miniature gadgets are all so arranged that when they release the bombs, they can see where they hit, just as from a real plane. It has saved many lives, as the pilots get a chance to correct their errors without having to go through actual flights to do it.

Back home at the Creek
Monday morning June 12, 1944

. . . Sunday morning Gladys thoughtfully ordered breakfast for me in my room, and that was my one respite, and I had just finished and started to write you, when I was stopped again. We had dinner and spent the afternoon at the Commandant's, and I liked all the people I met tremendously. Of course I had to tell all your tales, even the one about the dish-pan hands, and everybody wants to meet Norton. One of the nicest men there is the chaplain, Bert Copper. . . .[2]

Women are of course not allowed in the Navy planes, but at Pensacola some of the men would let their wives or girls come out the field, and if there were no instructors or superior officers in sight, would slip their gals in the planes for a ride with them. One chap did this, taking a girl up with him, and when he came down to land, some sort of landing test was in progress and an instructor stood there by a rope stretched across. The guy didn't dare land with the girl, so eased up again and flew around and came back again, but the instructor was still there.

He did this several times until his gas was almost gone, and he knew they would begin to think he was in difficulty and would contact him. In desperation, with his last gas, he flew out over the Gulf and simply bailed out.

I asked, all agog, "But what about the girl?"

The answer: "Oh, she was an old bat. She just flew home."

Cliff said sometimes nobody asks about the girl, and then the narrator is really stuck!

Cliff and Glad send their love.

A letter from Edith, in New York, was waiting here. She was to have lunch with Guthrie McClintoc last Saturday. It seems Katharine Cornell wants very much to play Abby, but McClintoc is not at all keen about her playing a mulatto!

A letter from Max Perkins said Hemingway was not badly hurt in the accident in England and was in the hospital only two days and cabled Max he was back on the job, and Max said he was sure he was in time for the first wave of the invasion. Max said his gray beard is "magnificent" and makes him look like Bluebeard. Max said he did not grow it for foolishness, but as protection against sun and wind burn in the work he has been doing in the Caribbean. I suppose now he is enchanted with the effect it produces on everyone. But I still think it is an added hazard with Martha.[3]

Martha handed me notes from three sets of callers whom I missed Sunday.... Also a note from Mr. (Petunia) Martin's widow, who was here with her lawyer, calmly telling me to go to Gainesville today or tomorrow to see him, where he would explain everything. She had to go back to Tampa. I know she is trying to get what property he had, and probably wants me to testify that old Martin acknowledged her as his wife, for I have serious doubts as to their having been actually married. I shall certainly not get mixed up in anything like that.

Idella shopped in Ocala for things for little Martha, and they are certainly cute, especially the postage-stamp-sized bathing suit.

Willie Snow [Ethridge] was crazy about "Colcorton." She and Mark both liked it much better than "Strange Fruit"....

Darling, we must begin to make plans about meeting etc. It takes so long for us to make contact. Do you want me to meet you in New York and have some time playing around there, perhaps going to Henry Heyl's in Vermont? (I sent you his letter announcing his recovery, his marriage and his removal to his new farm.) Or would you rather come straight home to Florida and have me meet you here? Whatever appeals to you is all right with me. And if you want me to meet you in New York, do you want me to bring any of your clothes, or would you rather wear your uniform until you get back to Florida? And if I meet you in New York, can you contact me, perhaps by cable, so that I won't have to wait too long there? I can use a couple of weeks up there, but would not want to get stuck for a month....

All my love, darling.

1. Cliff and Gladys Lyons.
2. MKR and Bertram Cooper were to become close friends, as she wrote to Norman Berg, 18 July 1945: "[He] is a good friend of mine, a scholar, a profound thinker. He was in love, in a soul-saving way, with Julia Scribner, wanting to make her happy and take her out of her dreadful environment" (*Selected Letters,* 268). Julia Scribner instead married Thomas Bigham, also an Episcopalian minister.
3. In his 8 June 1944 letter, Perkins does not mention Bluebeard, but does say that the accident gave Hemingway "another scar,—and he looks better for his scars" (*Max and Marjorie,* 568).

. . . .

(TLS, 3 pp.)

[Cross Creek, Fla.]

June 13, 1944

Dear Honey:

. . . I finally heard from Arthur, and after all these months, his boat is still not ready for the defense type of work, though he has been taking private passengers to keep the pot boiling. The type of work he was doing has ended in southern Alaska, but he thinks he may still be needed for the same thing in the far north, toward the Aleutians. If so, he will do that this summer. If not, he will go into the Navy.

. . . The Glen Basses (the ones you know) came by yesterday on what was ostensibly the friendliest of social calls, then just as they were leaving, oh by the way, would I lend them some money. This time I refused, saying I didn't have it to spare, which was pretty well true, but actually it irked me to have them do it that way. Also, there is no reason for them to be out of money. They left their high-paying jobs in a Jacksonville ship-yard, where they were needed, because they prefer the idle life of the fisherman. Now the fishing has gotten poor. . . .

He is in a bit of trouble, but if the story he told me is straight, should have no trouble getting out of it. When he moved to Lochloosa and began fishing there (illegal trapping) he divided the sale of his catch between the two dealers there. One of them was sore because Glen didn't sell him all his fish. The game warden made a big haul of traps, and Glen now believes this man tipped off the warden out of spite. Anyway, Glen saw the game warden driving off with a huge load of traps and wondered if his were among them. He saw the dealer in question driving down the road and says he only wanted to ask him if he knew whether the warden had got Glen's traps, ran out to the car calling, "I want to see you," and the dealer, with what he thinks, or says, is bad conscience, thought Glen had found out he had tipped off the warden, pulled out a gun and threatened to blow Glen's head off. Glen said he saw red and reached in the car to try to get the gun away and pull the man out, intending to beat him up, but succeeded only in twisting the man's arm, when people ran and broke it up. The dealer got the sheriff and had Glen arrested for assault and battery, and his trial comes up in about a month. He says his wife and her mother and father saw the affair and saw the other man pull out a gun, so I should think he would be all right.

On my long walk yesterday evening I passed a car of Negroes who were gathering blueberries. Someone hailed me, and it was old Beatrice.[1] She must weigh 200 lbs. She said she has no husband now. "They ain't any of 'em goin' to do you right, and I figured I'd do better alone. That Leroy ain't no good." From which I gathered she had tried Leroy once again. She is still in Jacksonville, cooking at a restaurant. She was more alarming looking than ever. Now that she is so big and fat, her blind eye is almost shut and she has a new scar across her nose, and I'd hate to have her take out after me with a razor! She thought I looked fine, and said, "Ain't you never goin' to get old?" She wanted a copy of Cross Creek, which I shall send her. . . .

So much love,

1. Beatrice, MKR's former maid.

. . . .

(TLS, 3 pp.)

[Crescent Beach, Fla.]
June 14, 1944
At the cottage

Darling:

Well, we are just settled at the cottage. . . .

As we set off, Idella said, "Now when Mr. Baskin comes home, we'll have to get a trailer." The car was loaded to the gills, Moe in the back seat, and Idella and little Martha and me on the front seat. Moe was so afraid he would be left that he spent the morning in the car, and little Martha was so afraid of the same thing that she wouldn't eat any breakfast, and simply dogged Idella's foot-steps. All the way over she stood up with the sun beating in on her little black head, so that she could see everything. And never said a word. I think we will enjoy her a lot.

On Wednesday all the towns close in the afternoon, so I had to stop in Palatka to shop for night-gowns for Mrs. Glisson! She went to the hospital in Gainesville yesterday for an operation, I think the same one I had, and needed thin cotton nightgowns and hadn't been able to get any, and asked me to get some for her. Believe it or not, night-gowns are a war casualty, though I can't imagine the women's underwear factories making bombs. I combed Palatka, knowing I would be too late in St. Augustine, then mailed my scant findings from there.

. . . When we reached the cottage, we almost fell over. The Hustons, as I have written you, were to use the cottage for their vacation—and how they ever found time to take the dogs on the beach, I cannot imagine. The place was so much more immaculate than Idella and I have ever left it, that we could have died of chagrin. On the mahogany coffee table in front of the davenport were two bottles of choice Old Crow Bourbon. On one bottle was written, "Thanks, Mrs. Baskin. We enjoyed every minute of our stay. Chef." On the other was written, "We truly thank you for your kindness. The only thing that was not perfect was having to leave and I wept all the way to St. Augustine, Peggy Huston. . . ."

All my love, dearest, and God, I wish you were driving in!!!!

. . . .

(TL, 2 pp.)

[Crescent Beach, Fla.]

June 15, 1944

Dear Honey:

. . . After supper last night, the whole family went for a walk on the beach. Sissie had insisted that little Martha was afraid of the water, but I told Idella it was the kind that comes in a wash basin, and she had not seen enough of that to know whether she was afraid or not. The little thing was enchanted, and walked boldly along several feet out in the ocean.

. . . I woke up early this morning, and Moe and I went for a long walk, then I had a swim. It was not rough, but there were some breakers, and it is rather creepy going out alone beyond the last breaker to get a smooth place to swim. And then you put your feet down and can't touch bottom, I just don't like it when there isn't another soul in sight. Moe didn't help a bit, for he sat on the sand and howled like the death watch. The water was a divine temperature, just cold enough. There are signs of donacs,[1] but we haven't hit the tide right yet.

I have got to settle down to real work on my Florida article for the Office of War Information, for use in a British magazine called *Transatlantic*. It has to be in New York five days from now, so I have to quit fooling around.

1. Donac or donax, a mollusk.

. . . .

(TLS, 1 p.)

[Crescent Beach, Fla.]

June 16, 1944

Dear Honey:

Idella and I have been up and at it since 6:30 this morning. I have almost finished my dull article on Florida for the British magazine, and am a bit tight, since the work was so unpleasant that I seemed to need fortification. It is hot as hell, and any work that isn't done early in the day, just has to go over until the next day.

Yesterday afternoon Doug came down, bringing assorted mail and wanted to talk. He and the Hustons have become entirely *en rapport* since the fire. He was even able to talk the Chef into having cold plate luncheons, with only a couple of hot dishes, to keep him from wearing himself out over the range. The room business has been slow since the re-opening, and the regular dining-room business, but the Sunday night buffet suppers are going strong, about 150, and the rest will follow. Things would naturally fall off somewhat this time of year, in any case.

... Norman Berg writes that he will probably go overseas with the Marines within a month, as classification specialist. When Marines are killed, he will have the job of replacing them with men suitable for various types of work. . . .

All my love,

. . . .

(TLS, 3 pp.)

[Crescent Beach, Fla.]

June 17, 1944

Dear Honey:

I am so distressed about the persisting diarrhea. Did you forget the beginning of your masterpiece, "Of uncooked foods be ever wary, Avoid exhausting dysentery"? I gather that you have had no green foods, uncooked or otherwise. But I do hope you have been careful in that strange and unsanitary land. . . .

Little black Martha is very happy, and contrary to Sissie's insistence to me that her children all refused any food except those awful boiled dried beans, white bacon and cornbread, eats everything, including vegetables, that Idella puts before her. Last night I got ready for bed early and had just gotten into my nightgown when Idella came up. She was dressed in that black and white plaid house coat of mine, and said, "I'm sorry, but our child seems to be sick." I got the strangest feeling. It was as though I were looking at a black replica of myself, and calling it "our child" accentuated the uncanny feeling of being somebody else. "Our child" I decided after questioning was only constipated, as was to be expected after Sissie's raising them on castor oil. I prescribed and doled out milk of magnesia, and this morning she is all right, and is happily eating bran cereal.

I am so absurdly keyed that moving over seemed to upset me, and every time I have spasms of pain, I think of you driving an ambulance in the heat and stench in the same and worse agony. I do hope you get leave and go to Kashmir. . . .

All my love,

Yesterday, two days after arriving here, I received over the phone a wire from Martha. "My baby Hettie died in Salisbury Maryland. Please come at once." Now what good I could do at Cross Creek with baby Hettie (aged about 50) dead in Maryland, I do not know. I wired Chet to check and lend Martha money for anything that made sense.

(TLS 2 pp.)

[Crescent Beach, Fla.]
Sunday morning
June 18, 1944

Dear Honey:

"Wings over Jordan"[1] is on the radio, and it is a hot Sunday morning, the surf with that steely look it gets sometimes in the sun. The heat is so nearly insufferable here, I can't imagine what it is elsewhere. The actual temperature is not so high, strangely.

. . . I finished my article for the War Board, and guess I will go into town today to mail it, as "Mme. Curie"[2] is at the movies, with Greer Garson and Walter Pidgeon.

. . . I had a letter from Julia, and they have been having the Far Hills place full for week-ends. Julia said one night she had to sleep on a couch, and it upset her ordered life badly and she spent a sleepless night. By Heaven, she *is* an old maid.

. . . My insides are much better after a mild attack, and I believe the strain of doing that article was what was bothering me.

Little Martha has been asking Idella when we were going to the Creek, and she thought she was getting homesick—but it turned out she only wants to inform Hettie Lou[3] of all the wonders! Idella said she heard her reciting, to herself, an account of our trip over, and she hadn't missed a thing.

Aunt Ida is in fine shape, mentally and physically. She said she was grateful for her home, and she believes Mrs. White likes her! . . .

. . . Well, if you were here, we would go for a swim, but I have no incentive to go down in the sun alone. Idella gave me a good massage and I had a cool bath so will let it go at that.

All my love,

1. Wings Over Jordan, a gospel singing choir.
2. *Madame Curie* (1943).
3. Hettie Lou Mickens Fountain.

. . . .

(TLS, 2 pp.)

[Crescent Beach, Fla.]
June 19, 1944

Dearest:

. . . I did not go to town yesterday after all. I was going almost entirely to mail my article to Clifton Fadiman for the War Board. I used to make Sunday trips to mail your daily letter, but the way you don't get them discouraged me, so now I don't use the gas for that purpose. I really needed to go to the bank today and did not want to make two trips. So when Idella's sister Thelma[1] and some friends came down from the Florida Normal College, I gave her my article and your letter to mail for me, and think she is reliable.

I feel a great sense of relief with the article off my hands, but have the embarrassing feeling that I do my writing with my intestines instead of my brain, for I am still having trouble.

I have one other chore to do, a long letter to the Atlantic Monthly that I have already done twice but must do again. A famous naturalist, Dr. Thomas Barbour, director of the Agassiz Museum at Harvard University, has done a naturalist's book on Florida and parts of it are running serially in the Atlantic. He seems to have something of a chip on his shoulder about me (perhaps because "Cross Creek" beat him to the gun!) and in the May issue disagreed with me on something that was purely a matter of personal opinion. In the June issue, he quoted that unfortunate error in the Saturday Evening Post that had the frog and crab etc. pictures, in which the text writer pounced on my mention of limpkins and announced that I habitually killed and ate them at Cross Creek. To begin with, there are no limpkins in the Cross Creek section, which Dr. Barbour should have known. And in "Cross Creek" I said specifically that years ago I killed and cooked and ate and enjoyed two limpkins when I stayed with the Fiddias on the Oklawaha, "Then I heard of their vanishing history and would not shoot another." But Dr. Barbour said I should be ashamed of myself and that it was criminal to advertise the edibility of a fast-disappearing rare bird. I want to make my point, but not to be disagreeable. One point is that it is scarcely scientific for a naturalist to take the Sunday Evening Post for gospel, while ignoring my own statements on the matter!

...All my love, and I do hope the dysentery is not the dangerous kind and you are better and are on leave.

1. Thelma Thompson Brown.

. . . .

(TLS, 4 pp.)

[Crescent Beach, Fla.]
June 20, 1944

Dearest:

...I saw James Colee about the beach land adjoining mine, and after the owners of the 100 feet north of me said they would have to have $500, and would not pay any commission (they are evidently very ignorant almost illiterate people in Palatka), I agreed to pay $550, which would take care of the commission, they announced they would have to have $500 for each of the 50 feet! So I told Colee just to drop it. Judge Gray who owns 50 feet between our cottage and the Dupont's, will take $200, but can only give me a tax deed, so will have to get Willard Howatt's opinion as to whether there is any safety in that or not.

Doug took me through [the Castle Warden] and showed me what they have done. The rooms, with the floors done over, fresh curtains and new coverings on the chairs, etc., look lovely. They had an awful time getting materials, and the sixth choice they took for covering the two large davenports down in the lobby is to my eye God-awful. I was hesitant in my praise and found they all think it is wonderful so had to cover my tracks in a hurry. They covered two of Edith's Victorian chairs, the piano stool and something else, in the same stuff and I think it is an eyesore, but may be wrong. All the place is in running order except the part that was actually burned and Doug is making some very sensible changes there that are costing no more, sometimes less, than mere replacement of the status quo. I can't describe it very well, but in room 17 he worked it some way to put in a bathroom, a small one, took out the tub in the bathroom on the second floor used as the Ladies' Room (for it was never used), which gave him room for a closet in the bedroom adjoining, etc. etc. He wants to make a change in the staircase to the apartment and is waiting for someone to make a sketch, and think I will ask him to submit it to you before going ahead. I wrote you some time ago that the Hotel Commission has refused permission for the apartment ever to be lived in again.

On the third floor, where the wall tapestry was burned, Doug wanted to take the tapestry off the walls of the private dining room and move it up there, but I dissuaded him, as I have the feeling some day you may want to make one large room again of those two. He paneled the two stretches on the third floor and it really is not noticeable.

I have never spoken of damage to our own things in the apartment, but it was very slight. Bob's water-color of the River Styx is ruined, as the combination of water and heat made it steam and the colors ran, but Doug has it on a dark wall on the third floor and the effect is good. All but one of the Audubons came through with damage only to the frames, and the other one is by no means ruined. . . .

Business came back with a bang, 160, I think it was, for Sunday buffet supper, over 200 in all fed on Sunday, the rooms *full*. The burned wing is not ready. In No. 3, they put the bed from our apartment, including the blue elephant and the blue boudoir chair, both of which, while water streaked to some extent, cleaned up so that they look all right. I beg your pardon, they have Bob's water color over that bed, and the light is such you don't notice the damage. The mauve settees are by the fireplace in that room, a marble-topped dresser and antique mirror that Edith sent there recently, and it makes a stunning bridal suite. Doug charges $9 for fresh-married soldiers and $12 to civilians in the same condition.

. . . I signed the insurance check, $15,000 and some hundreds, and Doug and Mrs. Huston are saving you several thousands out of it. Doug and I feel we rooked the insurance examiner horribly.

The Hustons fell in love with my cottage and asked if I would give them first chance if I ever sold it.

I ran into Jean[1] down-town and I asked her and the boys to go to the movie with me, and she asked me to come for early supper. . . . I went down to the movie to tell Idella. I started up the rear entrance and the cutest, toughest little red-headed freckled Dead End kid dashed out of the alley and said, "Hey, Lady, you're makin' a mistake. That there is for the niggers. . . ."

All my love,

1. Jean Francis.

. . . .

(TLS, 3 pp.)

[Crescent Beach, Fla.]
June 21, 1944

Darling:

. . . Your extreme loss of weight is alarming in a way, but wonderful in another, though I think you can well carry more than 137 pounds. . . . I shall pitch in harder than ever now on my own reducing, as if you are able to return an Apollo, I can try to approximate Venus instead of Hebe. As a matter of fact, the Venus de Milo[1] herself is about in my class, but those were the good old days when the boys wanted as much gal as possible. When Idella is pummeling me and I am eating a frugal meal of lean meat and vegetable juice, I think sadly how Rubens[2] and I would have enjoyed knowing each other. The high lights, the shadows, he could have attained on a butt like mine!

. . . The movie last night, "Madame Curie," was a sad Hollywood mess, to my notion. They did their best to make it scientific and impressive and simple, but "simple" by Hollywood standards is still unseemly melodrama. And I am afraid I have had enough of my erstwhile favorite Greer Garson to last me the rest of my life. In her own effort to achieve "simplicity," she wore the same face all through the thing, with practically no expression at all. Someone truly simple and *unknown* should do a job like that. It was *most* unconvincing to have Greer Garson discovering radium and fair swooning over it, and Walter Pidgeon loving her, scientifically and impressively and simply, almost to death. . . .

June 21 (actually)

We walked on the beach yesterday evening, all of us simply exhausted by the day's heat. Moe had not been out all day, just lay panting. . . .

. . . I am more puzzled than ever about the status of the law suit. The paper announced that the Florida Supreme Court had begun its new 6-months' session, told the number of cases, several hundred, they had passed on from the last session, how many had had personal opinions written at length and how many were decided just by noncommittal vote—and not a word has been heard about Cason Vs. Baskin. It is a nightmare, though I have been pretty well able to put it in the back of my mind. . . .

All my love,

1. *Venus de Milo*, a sculpture, now at the Louvre in Paris.
2. Peter Paul Rubens, seventeenth-century Flemish painter and greatest representative of baroque art.

. . . .

(TLS, 4 pp.)

[Crescent Beach, Fla.]
June 22, 1944

Dear Honey:

I was most terribly lonesome last night. Moe and I walked almost four miles on the beach and got back at 8:30. I had literally nothing to read, and the radio is in town being fixed, so I lay listening to the surf and wishing you were here. . . .

June 23

I was horribly depressed, for no good reason, and could not finish your letter yesterday. I have gotten over it, but have a strange turbulence of mind. I shall have to go to work.

. . . Idella went down on the beach yesterday evening ahead of me (she had taken the hint from the evening before when I went down alone. Sometimes I am glad to have her walk with me, but usually I like to walk fast and far alone, thinking.) She sent little Martha back to tell me the donacs were there if I wanted to come. They were boiling up by the billions, very small, so that it was almost wrong to gather them, yet there are so many they will not be missed. We got nearly a dish-pan full and I made two quarts of wonderful strong broth.

. . . This morning I went on the beach early, and found a turtle crawl and nest. I dug and I dug but I could not find the eggs. I am sure no one had been ahead of me, though there is a car that goes up the beach every morning at seven, and I am sure it is two Minorcan fishermen looking for turtle eggs. They used to go at night, but now cannot go on the beach until after sunrise. But the turtle could not have been a large one, and if they happened not to be noticing at just that moment, the turtle crawl would have looked only like the masses of sand the sand crabs turn up every night. The crabs feed at night by chewing masses of sand for microscopic nourishment, then spitting out the sand, and in the morning the beach is covered with little series of mounds. There were no tracks near the turtle nest, and I did not dig deep enough, or in the right direction—and it is always possible that the turtle did not actually lay. If the tide now coming in does not cover the nest. I may go back and dig again, if I can find a spade or something other than my finger nails.

...How and why such tales start is beyond me. Idella told me that the last time she was at Reddick, the Mayor there, Judge Comardie,[1] told her that Tom Glisson had told him that Idella and I were drunk together all the time, and the only reason I kept Idella was because she would get drunk with me. The Judge said if it was true, Idella had learned to drink at the Creek, for he knew none of the Thompsons drank. Idella assured him that she did not drink at all, and though I enjoyed a drink, in all the years she had been with me she had never seen me drunk. Of course I knew Tom was infinitely more treacherous than a rattlesnake, but it saddens me, when I thought we were getting along nicely, to find him so vicious and spreading absolute lies. I understand that it enrages him and his wife, and probably enrages the Brices, too, that I can keep a good maid when they can't keep anybody. . . .

Idella finds she has a good deal of work to do on little Martha. For one thing, she tells stories, not imaginatively, but just to get out of things. The other morning she came up for breakfast and I thought her face looked mighty streaked, and I asked her if she had washed it. She said, "Yes, Ma'am." Idella took one look at her and knew she had not and sent her down to wash it. At lunch, Idella told her she could not have her dessert unless she finished her vegetables, left the kitchen for something, came back and said, "Did you eat your vegetables?" "Yes, Ma'am." Her plate was clean so Idella gave her the dessert. Later, she found the vegetables dumped in Moe's pan! All of that, and her dirtiness, is Sissie's fault, for Sissie is so lazy she lets the children take the easiest way out. I am glad we are having a trial period this summer, for Idella may have enough of it by that time.

All my love,

1. Dickson Sloan Cromartie.

. . . .

(TLS, 3 pp.)

[Crescent Beach, Fla.]
June 23, 1944

Darling:

Western Union just phoned from St. Augustine and read me your cable saying you were better in every way and it made me much happier. The cable also said you would not send mail for a few days and I hope that means you were setting out for Kashmir. . . .

I had a letter from Edith from New York, all agog over her meetings with theatrical folk about the matter of making a play from "Colcorton." After reading the play form as it stands, she did not like it at all and thinks Guthrie McClintoc was wise not to commit himself. Someone else will probably try the job of writing it. Edith is to be on Orville Prescott's[1] program over NBC tomorrow afternoon. . . .

A swim would be wonderful, but there are still high rollers from yesterday's north-east wind, and I am thoroughly unhappy in them by myself.

My vague sense of despair was not helped by a letter from Phil May, which I enclose. It is horrible to think there may be several judges on the court who have the same sense of resentment that Zelma has and think, "By God, let her pay." If it were not that such ghastly things have kept happening to me that I have no confidence in my luck, I should feel that all was going to be well, but just sheer misfortune can do anything these days. Not that I am at all crushed—I am getting angry, as I always do when things are piled on too thick.

I was also infuriated by another letter, not actually a letter, in my mail. I sent Clifton Fadiman the 2500-word article on Florida for the British magazine that he requested, so that it would reach him by his deadline, June 20. I received a typewritten "acknowledgment" from a secretary, even her name typewritten, saying the regional article I had submitted had been received, and she had turned it over to the Editorial Committee, and I would no doubt hear from them! I typed under it, "What the devil is this piece of condescension? Clifton Fadiman *asked* me to do this job. He wrote me last week reminding me the deadline was June 20. Better give it to him." Some dumb bunny just assumed I had sent it in of my own free will.

I am terribly fed up with the Writers' War Board anyway. They keep sending out all sorts of long statements of policy, national and international, for writers' signatures, and they are all just so much hot air. The last one was a statement on what American writers think should be done about Germany after the war. I don't feel capable of passing judgment on the fate of Germany, so did nothing about it. Today comes a passionate letter from Lewis Gannett, on the N.Y. Herald-Tribune, begging me not to sign it, as it cast aspersions on a previous statement made by the Council on Democracy—. And none of these statements of "policy" remotely touches the roots of things—ordinary greed, ordinary human evil and human hate, all accentuated by the fetish of "national integrity."

The government has just banned, or barred, from those Armed Services editions of books, four utterly harmless ones—I forget two, but one is a new life of Justine Holmes nothing but the facts, and one is E. B. White's rustic and innocuous "One Man's Meat."!!!![2] The defense is that they contain "political" ideas.

I also had a go-round with the Writers' War Board, though it was not their fault. Christopher La Farge[3] asked me to do a 150-word bit (seems to me I wrote you about this) as one of a projected series to be run by the newspaper syndicate NEA, on war or post-war themes. "Something close to your heart." So obligingly I sent in a brief account of a true experience. On the diner of the train going to Michigan last summer, a handsome colored lieutenant came in amiably with two white lieutenants and they all sat down at a table together. A soldier, a sergeant, was sitting next to me, and impulsively I asked him how the men in the Services felt about fraternizing with Negroes. He said, "Lady, I'm from the South myself, but all I can say is, if a man's good enough to die for his country, he's good enough to live with it." I called the item, "The Southern Soldier and the Negro."

La Farge wrote me that NEA had rejected the item as "too controversial." He said the incident made them almost abandon the project, but they decided to give it another try, and would I please send something else on a war theme, again "close to my heart." I wrote back that I could not provide any starry-eyed platitudes, as the stand we were taking on the Negro to me invalidated the whole war, for there was nothing of the noble crusade in setting out to stop other nations from doing precisely what we intended to keep on doing to the Negro. I cannot wait to hear what you think about India, and the British, but I imagine such subjects are taboo by mail. I know they would be from your end.

I tank I open a bottle—. Wish you were here. I should snap and growl, and you would laugh at me, and we'd go swimming, and come in and get high and have donac broth and salad about ten o'clock.

All my love,

Editor's note: MKR types at the bottom of the page of the May letter: "The rest of Phil's letter would not interest you, as it is about the death of a cousin of his, Fontaine.[4] Fontaine was the charming Old School tobacco grower at Quincey of whom I told you an engaging incident. We were looking at wild flowers in the west Florida woods and Fontaine broke a spray of those lovely Silver Bells and gave them to me. I said, 'But won't they die?' and he said, 'Yes, Ma'am, but they'll die in yo' hand.'"

1. Orville Prescott, book reviewer.
2. E. B. White, *One Man's Meat* (New York: Harper and Row, 1944).
3. Christopher La Farge, a novelist and member of the Writers' War Board. The MKR manuscript has not been located.
4. Fount May.

. . . .

(TLS, 3 pp.)

[Crescent Beach, Fla.]
June 24 [1944]

It was *unbelievably* hot last night, and Doug phoned and asked if he and his wife could come down for a swim. Think he figured I might be lonely, too. As I was. It was too rough to swim, and we were cool only while we were actually in the water. The crabs were thick and Doug and I both got bitten, enough to draw blood, and a wave knocked Verne down so that she skinned her knee. I took them to the turtle nest and we dug up yards of sand but still found no eggs. After we returned to the cottage and dressed, we were as hot as before. It didn't cool off at all until after midnight, and Idella said her little apartment was stifling and she didn't go to sleep until after one. . . .

All my love,

(TLS, 4 pp.)

[Crescent Beach, Fla.]

June 25, 1944

Darling:

The mild intestinal attack I have been having just did not leave me, so I stayed in bed all day today, Sunday. I should probably have done so earlier and gotten it over with, if I had had a good book to read. I read, alas, too fast as usual, Somerset Maugham's new novel, "The Razor's Edge."[1] It is fascinating. The man is a terrific story-teller. At one point, it seems as though the book will go to great heights, but it becomes peculiarly frivolous at the end, and one realizes the author is, after all, only a superb narrator. But I was grateful for that much.

. . . Among the books from Miss Terry in Gainesville that I had ordered, was Willie Snow Ethridge's "This Little Pig Stayed Home."[2] I read that yesterday afternoon, and it is delightful. . . .

. . . Idella has reflected the peculiar depression I have been in, and we are far apart, all of which is my fault. When I go off into distant places and leave her behind, she becomes pure nigger, and when I snap out of it, I have to make a great effort to make her happy again. . . .

Yesterday was one of the hottest days in Florida history.

. . . Having been ensconced here only two weeks, with no intention of returning to the Creek so soon, I found that this coming week Idella has to be a delegate at some church conference, at Hawthorn, of all places, and is taking her time off next week instead of this. She is hoping frankly that I will go back then, as it means easy transportation for her, and being able to park little Martha while she is a delegate. But I don't think I shall go. I decidedly do not want to, and would not on my own account. And if having to tote little Martha everywhere with her, as I have to tote Moe, and warning her about it, if she gets fed up, it will be best for her to find it out before we have made a permanent arrangement. (That sentence lacks a verb somewhere, but it is too hot to go back and hunt for it.) Moe is panting, but still wants to go on the beach, but I don't think I shall do that, either. I wish the radio were not snarling so. . . .

June 28

. . . It is going to be another scorcher of a day. It is nine in the morning, and is already 84 inside the usually cool cottage.

Idella is having a certain amount of trouble with little Martha. A poor mother can do almost irreparable damage in four years. She gobbles her meat, all Idella will give her, and bread, and refuses the vegetables. When Idella insists, she cries for hours and refuses to touch any food at all. Of course lazy Sissie just gives in. I told Idella to stick it out and to call me any time things got too thick.

I am in a better frame of mind this morning and Idella's spirits have picked up in consequence.

. . . Which reminds me of one of the many cute things in Maugham's new book. A marvelous old snob is about to die and is rather looking forward to it, having been distressed by the deterioration of society on earth. He said, "There'll be none of this damned equality in Heaven." Another cute one, which I am afraid is not new, was, "American women expect a perfection of their husbands that English women expect only of their butlers." That sounded vaguely familiar to me....

All my love,

1. Somerset Maugham (1874–1965), *The Razor's Edge* (London: Heinemann, 1944).
2. Willie Snow Ethridge, *This Little Pig Stayed Home* (New York: Vanguard, 1944).

· ·

(TLS, 3 pp.)

[Crescent Beach, Fla.]
June 27, 1944

Dear Honey:

... I had an amazingly sprightly letter from Max Perkins. He remarked that you seemed to have a gift for adventure, and he hoped you did get to the Vale of Kashmir, which had always sounded to him more desirable than Paradise. I think I wrote you that Edith wrote me that he had had a physical check-up at last, and they found he was very sound, but was getting most of his nourishment from alcohol. He wrote me that it was not that he was getting too much alcohol, but was not getting enough food. He said that he liked to drink because, with life moving so fast, alcohol slowed everything down, and you had the feeling of there being no hurry. He said that if he lived to be old, he thought he should take up hashish, so that he would have the feeling of moving in eternity![1]

He is not at all worried about my book, and said that my suffering was all to the good, as what was right would come out of it.

I haven't listened to the radio today, but that little pip-squeak of a Dewey seems to have the Republican nomination sewed up. I wonder, if Wendell had played hard to get, if he might have stood a better chance. Probably not, as the Old Guard hated him with an unholy passion.

Speaking of hate, it is astonishing to find that we have a genuine enemy in Argentina. I read an article in the Atlantic a few months ago, by an Argentinian who likes us and understands us, saying that Argentina has built up a picture of us as aggressive imperialists who are a menace to the whole American continent, and has also built up a picture of herself as the U.S. of South America, and a hell of a lot better than we are—a peculiar, aggressive inferiority complex. I was shocked to see a back-page item in the N.Y. paper the other day saying that Argentina had jailed flocks of French, British and American citizens. I don't like the sound of it all....

All my love,

1. MKR uses much of the language from Perkins's remarkable confession (*Max and Marjorie*, 570–71).

(TLS, 3 pp.)

[Crescent Beach, Fla.]

June 28, 1944

Dear Honey:

... The Harrolds[1] said one of the fishing Pomars[2] said he had been seeing lots of sharks in front of my cottage! That finishes my going in alone!

DeVine is even more all-out on the Negro question than I, which interested me no end. It is a matter of moral principle with me, but she says she actually would just as soon have a colored room-mate as a white one. She did not mean a Beatrice or Adrenna, of course! I still have to fight a lingering prejudice, and when little black Martha touches me, as she loves to do, I cringe. But if one recognized it for prejudice and a hang-over from one's prejudiced training, it will pass. DeVine followed me to the car and said, "Any time you want to start a race riot, just let me know." I said that was exactly what I wanted to stop.

All my love,

1. Frank and DeVene Harrold.
2. Harold and Dorothy Pomar, owners of a bar and convenience store near Crescent Beach.

. . . .

(TLS, 3 pp.)

[Crescent Beach, Fla.]

June 29, 1944

Darling:

... I don't know when St. Augustine has seemed as charming to me as it did this morning. So early in the morning there was very little activity, and the town was sunk in oleanders and hibiscus and flowering vines and sleepiness. The little streets seemed so engaging, and the few people I ran into, and knew, smiled with such a leisurely friendliness. . . .

Yesterday afternoon I turned on the radio and heard all the state delegation at the Republican Convention casting unanimous votes for Gov. John Bricker of Ohio, and I thought an upset had occurred and they were voting for him for president and I literally shed tears of joy, for he seemed so much preferable to Dewey. I thought, "They licked the little bastard." When it was over, I found they had already nominated Dewey as the Presidential candidate and were only nominating Bricker unanimously for Vice-president. It seemed he had made a spectacular and sporting renunciation that morning of any claim on the presidential nomination. Dewey flew to Chicago and made his acceptance speech at ten o'clock last night. I listened intently. His voice was much better than I remembered it, deep and strong, and the whole speech was forceful and telling. He made many undeniable points against the Roosevelt administration, such as the "one-man government," the confusion and disagreements within the Administration, saying it had become "old and tired and quarrelsome." He said if elected he would have a cabinet of strong, young, expert men, and that their departments would be left to their judgment and management. He said there could be no possible criticism of the military management of the war, and if there had been no civilian interference with the military, there would be none with a change of government, but if there *had* been (and of course we know Roosevelt has had his finger in every pie), it would stop at once. He said there could be no question of the need of our cooperation with the rest of the world for peace, and that all agreements toward that end would no longer be accomplished by stealth, private conferences and "the magic of high-sounding phrases." He spoke of unemployment and the need for disposing of it through free play for industry and business and the natural abundance of the country. He asked, to great effect, 'Do we have to have war to have jobs?'" All this was to the good, and I was much impressed. Then he ended on a note that sickened and frightened me. I really do not believe he realized how it would sound to other nations, but all the time I was listening to him, I did so not only with my own reaction, but with that of Willkie for one, of Roosevelt—and of other nations. He said that the old, tired, quarrelsome present government seemed to take it for granted that the United States was also old and tired and finished, but that actually we were still so powerful and vigorous that "there is no limit to our horizons." Now that will verify all the fears other nations have had about us, that we are imperialistic and greedy. It was most unwise and unfortunate.

Bricker will unquestionably strengthen the ticket. I met him when I gave a talk in Columbus, Ohio, for the women's journalistic society. The day after my talk they had a luncheon, with Bricker the only man present, and I sat next to him and liked him very much. He is conservative, but not unduly so.

Like everyone else, I have not yet made up my mind. Roosevelt may still have a surprise up his sleeve and refuse to run again. If a liberal Democrat, without Roosevelt's egotism and bureaucracy, should be nominated, I should prefer him to any return to anything approximating pre-war capitalism, which is doomed. If a "practical" administration (which is desirable) did not work out, we should have revolution—and I should be in the fore-front!

All my love,

. . . .

(TLS, 2 pp.)

[Crescent Beach, Fla.]
June 30, 1944

Dearest:

. . . I dreamed that you came home—and was it a lovely kiss—and we were considering buying Grandfather's farm to live on. . . . I have just gotten the Star Route Mailman trained, and now a stranger is going to take over this route. Either Mrs. Rawlings or Mrs. Baskin is going to have to fight like hell to get her mail, and Miss Thompson[1] probably won't get hers at all.

. . . Sissie wrote Idella that they brought Hettie's body to Florida and buried her at Macintosh. I don't know whether Martha went to Maryland or not. Imagine not. Old Will, the gadder, probably went. He keeps the highway hot. . . .

All my love,

1. The maiden name of Idella Parker.

. . . .

(TLS, 2 pp.)

[Crescent Beach, Fla.]
July 1, 1944

Dearest:

The ocean is strange this morning. It is smooth and calm, like gray oil, but there is something ominously alive in the slow surf. Huge breakers roll up, very slowly, hang for what seems minutes, so that you seem to be looking into long dark caves, then collapse like cliffs falling. Yesterday evening I went for a walk on the beach. The sea oats are tall and thick, and I pushed through almost a little forest of them. It was exciting, and I seemed to be passing through into another world. And when I went out on the bare lonely beach I was very conscious that it is not my world. I suppose there are people who really love the sea. But there must certainly always be fear, too.

The book[1] balked again and I have been wasting my time, but enjoying myself. I enjoy an occasional vacation even from my comfort-creating Idella, and when I am entirely alone, have a delicious sense of playing hooky, of escaping something. It doesn't take time for this to pass!

I wasted yesterday afternoon and evening reading a book that is utter tripe. Aunt Ida loaned me a couple of Miss Dryce's books, as I was entirely out, and this one, "Dragonwyck,"[2] is widely advertised and high on the best-seller list. It is impossibly bad. I tried to figure out why it would be a best-seller, and realized, of course, that women will lap up any book in which the hero "threw her roughly on the bed." It is the dream of every plain and mousey woman to have a man so "mad with passion" that he would throw her roughly on the bed and go to town, and the poor souls don't realize that they should be utterly disgusted and outraged. Rape is the mirage toward which the dry and thirsty female pants in her dreams. . . .

Today I am wasting time on a Ben Ames Williams[3] best-seller, which is also tripe, but much more entertaining. In this one, it appears as though the heroine were working up to throwing the hero roughly on the bed. At the moment, the hero is trying hard to escape, but the gal has him in a New Mexican cloud-burst under an over-hanging rock and his chances are slim. I am sure she is about to do something obvious, such as letting her silk blouse fall open, revealing the pearly breasts. I am going ahead with it, as from the first flash-back chapter, I gather that while she got her man, by God, he murdered her, and that is certainly worth building up to.

I had a letter from the nice Episcopalian chaplain[4] at the Naval Air Base at Lake City, and he said he would like to come over some day. I think maybe *he* would be a good person for Julia, for he would, or should, have Christian fortitude to handle her! ...

All my love,

1. MKR is referring to her writing of *The Sojourner.*
2. Anya Seton (1906–1990), *Dragonwyck* (New York: Houghton Mifflin, 1944).
3. Ben Ames Williams (1889–1953), *Leave Her to Heaven* (Boston: Houghton Mifflin, 1944).
4. Bertram Cooper.

. . . .

(TLS, 2 pp.)

[Crescent Beach, Fla.]

July 2, 1944

Dear Honey:

... I had a long letter from Edith, completely happy and completely worn out after several weeks in New York. She said when she went to school at Columbia for one year, it took her five years to get over it. She said her legs get muscled like a ballet dancer's from miles of walking, while the rest of her fades to skin and bones. She said it was a good thing I didn't love the place, as it is pure dynamite for a writer. She said the most devastating angle was the literary teas, and it seems as though people write only in order to be able to go to them, paying as it were in a literary coin, which becomes smaller and smaller. Of course it is insane to try to go to the teas in the first place, but Edie doesn't want to miss anything.

... I enclose a couple of clippings. Hemingway at last looks as he has always longed to——*distinguished.* If he can get his squeaky voice down a couple of octaves and stop scratching his stomach, he will be most impressive.

I was surprised to read about Sam Byrd,[1] as I thought he had, by choice, a cushy job, aide to a land-locked Admiral or something. Sam puts on an awful lot of front, but under it there is really quite a decent little guy. ...

All my love,

1. Sam Byrd, the actor, once tried to convince MKR to write a dramatization of *South Moon Under.*

. . . .

(TLS, 5 pp.)

[Crescent Beach, Fla.]

July 3, 1944

Dear Honey:

I had a scare last night—I thought Idella had walked out on me again. Once upon a time I should only have been concerned about *her,* but a burnt child kills two birds with one stone, you know, and I was certain she was gone. She was not on the 7:20 P.M. bus, the only one from Hawthorn, and I came gloomily home to the cottage in a sad rain and brooded. I put down a half-pint of brandy and decided not to let it get me this time, that I'd be better off doing the very easy housework here myself, and even almost decided to get gas somehow and drive out to Michigan and spend the rest of the summer incognito at a farmhouse near my grandfather's old place. I knew just the place, and near it is a small very old red brick abandoned house with a fireplace, and I was going to fix that up for a workshop, and even got as far as wondering whether to take my card-table in the car or trust getting a work table out there! I was really very gay about it. As a matter of fact, I am in such better physical shape now that I could have weathered what would once have been catastrophe. At the time it happened a year ago, I just was in too low a physical condition to stand being abandoned by everybody.

...At seven-thirty this morning a car drove in, and here came poor Idella and her big suit-case (the size of which was one thing that made me decide she was gone) and little Martha, trailing wearily up the steps. What had happened was something that should have occurred to me—there was a mob of Negroes to get on the bus at Hawthorn, (Sunday evening), some of them just from short stops along the way, and the bus driver took as many as he could, filling the aisles even, and said he just could not take any more!

Idella knew I would be in town but also knew it would be almost impossible to reach me and the poor thing had fits. She finally found a colored man who lived in St. Augustine and was driving over at 4:30 this morning, with his car already full to the roof. She begged so hard that he said he would take her, and charged her $5. There were nine in the car!! The next bus left Hawthorn at 9 this morning and that meant reaching the cottage about noon—which would have been perfectly all right if I had known—but Idella said she had been away so long she felt she just had to be here this morning in time to get my breakfast and straighten things up.

She didn't get to the Creek, but Martha came Sunday to the church conference, and the poor soul really had needed me badly for comfort. Her daughter had died after an operation for appendicitis. Chet helped take care of arrangements and Hettie's employer sent the body to Florida. Adrenna came up from St. Petersburg and is still at the Creek. It seems that Hettie was already dead when we left the Creek. There were two wires, and no attempt made to deliver them....

All my love,

. . . .

(TLS, 3 pp.)

[Crescent Beach, Fla.]
July 4, 1944

Dearest:

... I wrote you about the Macmillan proposition to do Florida in their projected "Epic of America" series, and that I wrote them I thought the scheme asinine, bombastic, juvenile and futile, but if time was no object, I should rather bungle it myself than have somebody else bungle it. I had a long letter from the president today, saying he had not known they were calling it a series of "Epics," and he was as horrified as I was. Meantime, I had a letter from Max saying that he thought it would be a mistake for me to do it. As any time I wanted to do a generalized book on Florida it would be better to be entirely free from the restrictions of a "series," but that I must do as I wished.[1] I had asked Macmillan, or rather just told them, that while I did not want an advance, I should expect a straight 20% royalty (which stemmed back to Norman Berg's no doubt subversive remark that on my next book I should insist with Scribner's on 20%!!!) The Macmillan president said that 20% just was not paid, and also said that since they planned the series to be chronological, Florida should be the first book. That gives me a clear out, and I shall refuse the whole thing, recommending Edwin Granberry or A. J. Hanna[2] to do the job. The Macmillan man begged me to do the book, saying no one else could or should do it, but unless I could do it as an old lady when I had nothing better to do, I could not be tied down. I feel much relieved, and only hope they don't turn it over to a complete ass. . . .

All my love,

1. Perkins wrote that the series would not be of an advantage to someone of her stature (*Max and Marjorie*, 570). MKR subsequently declined Macmillan's proposition.
2. Edwin Granberry (1897–1988) had published the novel, set on the Florida coast, *The Erl King* (New York: Macaulay, 1930), and Hanna and Cabell had published *The St. Johns*.

. . . .

(TLS, 2 pp.)

[Crescent Beach, Fla.]
July 5, 1944

Dear Honey:

. . . [W]ent to the movies, George Sanders, whom I like, and Virginia Brice, in a pretty good substitute for a Saturday night Western, "Action in Arabia."[1] It had races between airplanes and Rolls-Royces over the desert, native tribes and camels and knives in the back and everything.

All my love,

1. *Action in Arabia* (1944). The actress is Virginia Bruce, not Brice.

. . . .

(TLS, 4 pp.)

[Crescent Beach, Fla.]
July 6, 1944

Dearest:

. . . Well, Mrs. White is kicking Aunt Ida out. Just that. That is certainly her privilege, as there is no reason for her to run a charitable institution, and Aunt Ida is not her responsibility, but the way she did it is needlessly cruel. She should have told *me* she did not want her, and I could have cooked up something in such a way as to spare Aunt Ida's feelings, but she simply told her bluntly last night she would have to arrange to go. Not at once, but still—.

. . . I then phoned Mrs. White . . . and then she announced that she could not keep Mrs. Tarrant, that anyone that old was too much responsibility, that she paid the summer maid almost as much as Aunt Ida paid her, and if Aunt Ida were not there she would not have to have a maid at all. I said that I knew Aunt Ida would be glad to fix her own meals, and she snapped, "Have you ever seen her trying to do anything?" and went on to say that she and Aunt Ida could never keep house together. She said, "Our way of living is just too different," which is the very high-hat sort of thing Aunt Ida has been conscious of, all along, poor thing. She said she thought Aunt Ida would be happier if she went back to Ohio to live, that she was always talking about it and regretting she had not bought a little house there and kept a roomer to help out. She said Aunt Ida did not have to leave any time soon, that we might even be able to "arrange" for her to stay another year, meaning of course that she would expect me to up the ante.

I assured her that I would move Aunt Ida as soon as possible, and that she was certainly not her responsibility.

Evidently, Aunt Ida finished the job of getting on her nerves, for Mrs. White sounded almost hysterical (she said that Aunt Ida's "help" in getting their supper after the maid had gone, consisted of pouring the ice water!) and I know exactly how she feels, for nobody gets me to the screaming point as Aunt Ida can do. But what I do resent is her telling an old woman of 84 she was not wanted, instead of letting me handle it tactfully.

I went at once to Idella, who was hoeing the walk, and she was so indignant that she said she did not think I should even let Aunt Ida stay there while I made arrangements. I had already decided that I had better bring her here for the time being, and Idella said we must pack her up and move her here right away, and make her feel really welcome. The Negroes are not always kind to one another, but they have a great gift for compassion—perhaps because it has been their history to be ruthlessly kicked out when not wanted.

What I can do, God knows. Places to live, of any sort, are at a premium. I do think that if I can find a little apartment, near a grocery store, Aunt Ida would be better off keeping house, and even if the over-work kills her, she would be happier than dragging out a longer life under such circumstances as she has been in. I have no question but that the shock of this will shorten her life sharply. It seems pretty rotten, after the hard life she has had, to get a kick like this at 84.

Understand, I do not blame Mrs. White one bit, and even sympathize with her, but she didn't have to do it that way.

I am going in this afternoon to see Aunt Ida and tell her to begin packing up, and Idella and I will go in and help her and move her. Will finish my letter tomorrow.

Oh boy, the whirlwind. Idella and I went in after lunch yesterday and Aunt Ida is a wonderful sport about this, but was just sort of numb and crushed. Mrs. White had simply floored her. I saw no reason for her to spend another night under a roof where she was not wanted, so we went to work. Her wardrobe trunk was in the attic and Idella and I carried it down with no difficulty. When I get mad in the cold way I was then, I have the strength of ten. A pure heart isn't in it with a calm sort of rage! I arranged for a trucker to come tomorrow morning to take things out, and we filled the car with suitcases and smaller things, slapped Aunt Ida's over-night things in a hand-bag and a hat on her head and brought her back to the cottage. I left an envelope for Mrs. White with a check for a hundred in it. . . .

I am not going to let this disturb me at all. As you know, I hate it, but there is no reason to get upset. And I am so damn sorry for Aunt Ida that any irritation or inconvenience to me does not matter, and we are doing everything to make her feel welcome. I have told her just to relax and enjoy her vacation. She can stay as much of the summer as necessary until I find the solution. I am going to make every effort to find a tiny apartment near a grocery, and wish I had done that when she first came to St. Augustine. But actually, she is in much better shape than she was then.

We will go in after lunch again and finish packing. The amount of junk she has saved is incredible.

. . . I wanted to take a long walk last night to do some thinking and get myself together, and though the tide was almost to the dunes, I thought it was going out, so Moe and I set out. Actually, it was coming in, and by the time we turned around a mile and a half from home, it came in with that sudden surge and by God, we had to take to the dunes. It was almost dark and it was rather spooky. But I had myself licked into shape by the time we got in, and all is well. My really very firm moral principles are at odds with my natural selfishness, and sometimes I have to shake myself until my teeth rattle. Dora would walk all over me if I'd let her, but the old girl is black and blue this morning.

Don't worry, because I am not.

All my love,

. . . .

(TLS, 3 pp.)

[Crescent Beach, Fla.]

July 7, 1944

Dear Honey:

I should never believe that bad luck could turn to good so rapidly. I have solved Aunt Ida's problem (and mine!) so easily that we still can't believe it is true.

After three years of suffering at Mrs. White's, she will be where she would have been happy from the beginning. We have taken for her Mrs. Bugbee's[1] apartment on the second floor over the florist shop, and it is *exactly* what she wants. It is her kind of place and she fell in love with it at once, and it will make her the coziest little nest in the world. She didn't have a single fault to find, and is in Seventh Heaven.

. . . Miss Grace very tentatively asked forty dollars a month, but agreed to thirty without hesitation. She is to pay for gas and electricity for the time being, but if Aunt Ida's being there uses enough more to matter, we will take care of that. As you know, the place is just a few steps from Weinstein's[2] and the bakery and the A & P and all the commotion of St. George that Aunt Ida loves so. I think she will be blissfully happy, and she has already asked Doug and his wife to dinner, and Mrs. White also! Aunt Ida said what of course I thought but could not say, "Mrs. Bugbee and I are both just queer enough so I think we'll get along dandy."

At Aunt Ida's instigation, I was nice to Mrs. White, and am glad now I didn't say any of the ugly things I felt. When we reached Aunt Ida's room yesterday afternoon to pack, Mrs. White was lurking there waiting for us, and I almost think had been standing outside the door listening (fortunately we talked only about the packing!) For she suddenly appeared in the room. She was in a manufactured blazing rage about our clearing out that way so suddenly, and was all set to "make something" out of our going into her attic to get the wardrobe trunk. If Aunt Ida hadn't asked me beforehand to try to keep her as a friend instead of making an enemy of her, I should certainly have given her the works, but as it was, I was peaches and cream and she calmed down at once. I realized that having a guilty conscience about it and about having hurt Aunt Ida, she was all set to take the offensive and try to put us in the wrong if we were sore—as our getting out that way would indicate. It worked out very nicely and today she kissed us both when we left, and told Aunt Ida she must still think of her place as home.

Idella worked like a trooper and did all the dirty work of packing. . . .

All my love,

1. Grace Bugbee ran a florist shop in St. Augustine.
2. Weinsteins, a popular grocery.

. . . .

(TLS, 4 pp.)

[Crescent Beach, Fla.]
July 8, 1944

Dear Honey:

. . . I have lost ten pounds and think the other ten will follow comfortably. I didn't realize I had lost that much, as I had been being only careful, without making any strenuous effort, but got on the scales and there it was. I announced it to Idella and Aunt Ida and they said it was so obvious they thought I knew. Aunt Ida said, "I've been noticing it all week, but I didn't say anything, as I didn't know whether you'd like to have me." Ye Gods, anything I should be so *pleased* to have noticed! . . . The first night she was here I felt so sorry for her and was so anxious to make up for the hurt that had been given her, that I kissed her good-night affectionately, and since then, like a child you have encouraged, every night at bed-time she rushes to me and envelops me and plants a wet kiss smack on my face and I almost DIE. I have always hated to have women touch me. Even women I am terribly fond of, Edith and Lois and Bee and Julia, I get over the necessary embrace on arrival and departure as quickly as possible. I suppose it may go back to the physical revulsion I felt for my mother.

I am making myself get over the creeps when little black Martha touches me. Now and then she sidles up to me and puts her hand very quickly on my arm, then takes it away as quickly. It feels like a soft little kitten's paw, and I tell myself that I should like it if it were an animal! I love to touch cats and dogs, any animal whose fur isn't too rough. . . .

I had a long letter from Edith from the MacDowell Colony, and she is crazy about it. Each person has a studio like a little chalet, all by itself in the woods, out of sight or sound of anyone, with a fireplace, tea set and tea arrangements, and a toilet. People sleep in Mrs. MacDowell's large house (which I should hate) and Edith has the Florida room, and she said it made her feel like an inmate of the deaf and dumb home! People eat together, and I should hate that, too, but Edith is completely happy. She is trying to do a play outline of Colcorton for Guthrie McClintoc, and if it suits, an experienced playwright will take over from there. The man who did the play before turned it into cheap melodrama. She said she also did the review of Caroline Miller's new book for the N.Y. Times, not wanting to, but not wishing to refuse, as the Times had been so generous with her book. It is Caroline Miller's first book since "Lamb in his Bosom" in 1933, and Edith was terribly embarrassed, as she said the book is pretty bad and just does not come off and she hated to have to say so, knowing how much Caroline Miller has been through and how much the second book must mean to her future.[1]

. . . Julia sent me some more asparagus, and it had been a whole week on the way, and like the other, was an appalling box of wet mush. I think perhaps I had better tell her so this time, as she will just keep sending asparagus, and evidently it can't stand the trip without icing. . . .

All my love,

1. Caroline P. Miller (1903–1992), *Lebanon* (New York: Doubleday, Doran, 1944); *Lamb in His Bosom* (New York: Harper, 1933).

(TLS, 2 pp.)

[Crescent Beach, Fla.]
July 9, 1944
Sunday morning

Dear Honey:

The family has just listened to "Wings Over Jordan," Idella scraping carrots in the kitchen, Moe on his back with his legs in the air, little Martha sliding around on the floor in her clean pants, inching as close into the living room as she dares, and Aunt Ida interrupting at the soprano's high notes to tell of various other choirs she has listened to in a long and vaguely attentive life. Tears come to her eyes when the Rev. Glenn T. Settle mentions God, and her eyebrows lift a little at mention of Jesus. Aunt Ida has always rather resented Jesus. God is very real and close, and some day he will keep me from smoking and drinking and cursing, and Aunt Ida says, "When we have God, why do we have to have a son? Why do we have to worship two Gods?" And of course Aunt Ida does not.

. . . I think we'll go into the movie this evening "Gaslight,"[1] with Charles Boyer and Ingrid Bergman. Boyer is a villain for the first time, and I think I may prefer him that way.

I feel wonderful, but don't know what to do with my energy. The ocean is calm enough for me to swim, but I can't forget those sharks Pomar reported. There is no one else on the beach.

July 10

. . . After thinking I was going to hit the movie just right, we arrived right in the middle, and it was the sort you really should see from the beginning. I was so disgusted. If a picture makes any pretense at artistry, I like to get the feel of it as a unit, to watch it build up step by step. Unless it is just comedy or trash, I get no pleasure from merely watching people walk across the screen. The picture was beautifully done, and Boyer and Bergman were superb. The roles really gave them something to get their teeth into.

Idella met, and brought home with her, her youngest sister[2] who is in training at the Jacksonville Negro hospital, a very nice and pretty girl. And was the car packed. The three colored females took up the back seat, so Moe had to ride in front with Aunt Ida and me, and he resented it to no end. . . .

All my love,

1. *Gaslight* (1944).
2. Dorothy Thompson Harris.

(TLS, 3 pp.)

[Crescent Beach, Fla.]

July 11, 1944

Darling:

. . . I am terribly disturbed about you, as I thought you would be getting over both your physical and mental troubles, as soon as you got away from the Base. Of course, the ice-cold trash you put in a sick stomach at the Red Cross canteen could even have knocked you out if you were normal. The complete idiocy with which you often eat has always puzzled me, and when you do it, I wonder if you can possibly be simple-minded.

It is more than a month now, and it is dreadful not to know how you came out. You might even have had to go to the hospital, for I should think two hundred miles in a crowded bus would have finished you. But I am hoping you felt better when you reached the cool mountains in that lovely place, and were sensible, and had your river trip.

. . . I am a little snappish this morning, as you can probably tell, because I am worried about you, because the mail is so maddening, because after feeling superbly I am having another go-round with my insides (very minor, but annoying) and because Aunt Ida is driving me nuts. If I did not have things arranged for her, and so satisfactorily, I should swim out into the ocean and whistle for the sharks. I lay in bed after breakfast, trying to relax from the pain, and she came in and for a solid hour told me the most trivial details of Mrs. White's household, all of which I had heard many times before. She is reading "Grapes of Wrath," and she looked up and said, "This is a wonderful book for anyone to read that's moving. . . ."[1]

All my love,

1. John Steinbeck (1902–1968), *The Grapes of Wrath* (New York: Viking, 1939). MKR reported this same malapropism to Maxwell Perkins, 10 July 1944 (*Max and Marjorie*, 572).

. . . .

(TLS, 4 pp.)

[Crescent Beach, Fla.]

July 12, 1944

Dear Honey:

Aunt Ida———.

. . . Her appetite is almost as astonishing as Nettie's Grandma's, though Grandma was in a class by herself when it came to a mess of cow-peas. Every dish, every item, brings forth a comparison with either similar or dissimilar dishes at Mis' White's, usually, I am glad to say, in my favor. She is especially pleased to be returning to a life where one is offered second helpings. I have noticed one angle that helps to account for Mrs. White's suddenly reaching the breaking point— Aunt Ida's peculiar, since embarrassingly *enthusiastic*, table manners. With the table full, one pays little attention, but sitting alone with her, one has the sensation of dining with an avid old diving bird. We had cold cuts for supper, beautifully arranged, with the proper large fork and meat-server. Aunt Ida ignored these very practical helps and used her own fork, not only for the meats, which were remotely manageable, but for the tomato aspic salads arranged around the meats. When Idella passed the bread, again she used her fork to spear it, from a great height, swooping down like a water-turkey. When she comes to the last inch or so of a glass of iced tea or milk, she lifts the glass and swirls the remaining liquid round and round. She does not *stir* iced tea, she attacks it, using that particular diving motion to send the iced tea spoon to the bottom of the glass, beating at the helpless lemon. A sherbet glass or fruit cup at dessert is lifted high and in front, where it is turned upside down for the last remnants and examined as a scientist examines a test tube. I have tried having Idella serve her larger and larger portions of dessert, so that she will be obliged to leave a little and I will not have to bear the weight of that last straw, but to no avail. The final fragment is scoured out, and the silver arranged or disarranged with a last happy gusty clatter.

. . . Aunt Ida just dashed over and stuck a finger in my shoulder and said, "Do you know that sometimes women go into stores to try on dresses and they don't have a stitch on underneath?" I told her I had heard vague reports of this distressing habit.

I really should have made notes down the years of her malapropisms, for a side-splitting story could be made of them, though no one would believe a word of it. One does not rinse anything—one rinches it. My teeth still click when she speaks of a gray big rose or of putting on a nigh-gown. She is dear and admirable, but she is *common*, as Mrs. Fiddia, for instance, is not.

I have written Martha that we will be home for the week-end, and in great detail asked her to kill a chicken if there was one of suitable size or fitting destructibility. This, to keep her from slaughtering an infinitesimal fryer or the best laying hen, just because "you told me to kill a chicken." I should really eat some of the over-populous ducks, but my excuse now is that duck meat is too rich for the summer. My feed bill is at least a dollar a day, sometimes more. . . .

All my love,

. . . (Little black Martha came in to tell me something, and Aunt Ida, who pokes me at the slightest provocation, said sternly, "Don't bother Mis' Baskin.")

. . . .

(TLS, 3 pp.)

[Crescent Beach, Fla.]
July 13, 1944

Dear Honey:

Damn, I hunted all over for my cigarettes, and found I was lying on them. It is my last pack, and they are flat as pancakes. . . . I wrote you about having to do an article on Florida for a British magazine, via the Office of War Information (you know, hands across the sea), and I was disgusted with the results, for as I wrote Clifton Fadiman, it was almost impossible to cover the ground he wanted covered in 2500 words without having it sound like a dry listing of facts. He wrote back that they liked the article, and I must remember that what seemed trite to me, would seem entirely exotic to our broad A brothers. The article was a bit short, and he suggested that I do another page or two about the Florida I am most interested in personally. Whether this was to make me happier or to fill up space, I wouldn't know, but probably the latter. I dilly-dallied and did not answer, and a wire came over the phone last night asking if the material was on its way. So I pitched in this morning and did a rather lush addition—and am happier.

. . . Something is wrong with Idella, physical or emotional, to such an extent that Aunt Ida remarked on it. I should be quaking in my boots, except that I have resolved never again to be so at the mercy of a servant that I was overly disturbed by her leaving. Now that I am feeling so much better, it would not be calamity. I tried to sound her out, and of course she denied there being anything wrong. I told her again that if she stuck with me, she would find herself well provided for.

I have just finished a delightful English book that you will enjoy, Sir Osbert Sitwell's (of the famous Sitwell writing family) first volume of his autobiography.[1] There is one delicious and cutting section in which he describes the descent of the "poor relations," sometimes married couples but mostly unmarried women, who move from country house to country house, welcome because they are (deliberately) "such fun". . . .

All my love, darling.

1. Osbert Sitwell (1892–1969), *Left Hand, Right Hand* (Boston: Little, Brown, 1944).

. . . .

(ALS, 2 pp.)

[Cross Creek, Fla.]
At the Creek
July 15, 1944

Dear Honey:

My it seems good to be here. We got in yesterday afternoon about four and Martha had cut spider lilies and had the place dusted. Everything looks lovely. The grove is in wonderful shape and had been tractored recently and Chet had sent someone to cut the lawn grass.

Martha had simply abandoned my garden, and the weeds and grasses are so tall that you wouldn't be surprised to find a lion in them. The rose-bushes have been smothered, almost literally to death, and I don't know whether I can save any of them or not. Also, either the poor quality of the feed we buy now, or some neglect on Martha's part, perhaps both, has cut down the amount of milk and cream, and the small amount of cream is very thin. Chrissie should give the best milk in the county, with Dora and Ferdinand for parents. Nothing here will ever really be right until I get a good man on the place again. But how I love it—. I shed tears of joy at being here.

Martha has plenty of fryers for me, and I have got to eat some ducks. . . .

All my love, and wish you were here.

. . . .

(ALS, 6 pp.)

> [Cross Creek, Fla.]
> At the Creek
> Sunday July 17 [1944]

Dear Honey:—

With all my feelings of genuine tenderness for her, all my insistence to myself on toleration, Aunt Ida has literally driven me to drink the last two days. I simply cannot figure out why she gets on my nerves so. Even getting to the bottle presents its difficulties, for she trails me so, and if she knew how much I was drinking in my ready-to-scream despair, it would only bring on a moral treatise. She has me blocked now. We were on the porch, and since her *physical nearness* bothers me so, I went into the living room to read. I took a chair at the book-case side of the room, by the front door—and bless Katy if she didn't follow me in with her book, and sit down on the uncomfortable red velvet sofa, the closest seat to mine in the room. I suppose I should be touched by it, as I am by Moe under my feet, but there is an element there beyond my control or my understanding. And now I can't get to my Sunnybrook [whiskey]—. Will have to wait until near enough dinner time so that she won't be shocked.

When we got in from Gainesville yesterday, I was ready to whoop and thought of course she'd go to the bathroom so I could get a drink. I said, "You can use my bathroom. You don't need to go all the way back to yours." She said, "Oh, I don't have to go," and there she stayed. I suppose it is a funny picture, my having to dodge a funny old lady in order to get tight as an anodyne against her—.

. . . Dear Jesus, now she has come out to the porch again—.

. . . I think she [Aunt Ida] will be able to move into Miss Grace's apartment a week from tomorrow. I may leave for Chatahoochie[1] the same day—. . . .

> All my love,

1. Chattahoochee, where the Florida state mental institution is located.

(ALS, 4 pp.)

[Cross Creek, Fla.]
At the Creek
July 17 (I guess)
1944

Dear Honey:—

. . . I was so worried this morning—Idella was due back with the truck from her week-end at 7:30 A.M., and she didn't get in until 10. She had had a blow-out, and all the men had gone to work, and she and another woman put on the spare. Am sure the story is straight, as she stopped at Boyt's to have the tire repaired, but you may imagine that Martha went around with a very smug air. Martha did her damndest over the week-end to break me of calling on her for anything extra. The water gave out, although she had two days' notice of my coming, and she said with that righteous air that infuriates me, "I never pump up water when you isn't here 'ceptin' to fill the duck ponds." Of course all the time she is using water at her house from the faucet I had put over there! Also, the gas gave out, although Chet had told her to put more in. She put in what the law called for, 5 gallons only. Etc. etc. etc.

After dinner yesterday we drove over to check up on the pear and apricot trees, and the pear tree had been stripped, although the pears must have been grass-green. She said it wasn't nothin' but them nasty old stinkin' turpentine niggers what stole them and of course they had just as much right to them as we did! There were only a few green apricots left.

Leonard came Saturday afternoon with a trailer load of lumber for my minor repairs, and he and David will come in about two weeks to fix odds and ends. One thing Aunt Ida does that bothers me, and it bothered Mrs. White, she points out things that need doing as though you were both blind and utterly stupid. "Marge" (and I hate to be called Marge), "You must get this chair fixed. It'll tear somebody's dress. Marge, there's a hole in this screen. The mosquitoes will come in. Marge, this door sticks. You want to get it fixed." It was a satisfaction to be able to answer to *everything* [underlined twice], "Yes, Leonard has that on his list."

It will be interesting to see whether little Martha is anxious to go back with us or not. She stayed with Sissie while Idella was gone, complaining to big Martha that "Miss Idella went off and left me." Sissie said she "had" to whip her already, because she and Hettie Lou didn't get along. If we keep her, the less she has to do with the rest of them, the better.

I ordered fish for today from Mr. Martin's heirs and assigns, who are running his camp. Tom Morrison[1] has left the Creek so that he won't have to testify in the suit between the children and the so-called Mrs. Martin, for possession of the property. Must drive over now and get the fish.

Old Will is weeding my garden with infinite condescension—.

All my love,

1. Tom Morrison, the self-proclaimed naturalist of Cross Creek, once suggested introducing manatees to help unclog the local waterways. The plan was rejected (Glisson, *The Creek*, 231).

. . . .

(TLS, 4 pp.)

> [Crescent Beach, Fla.]
> Back at the cottage
> July 19, 1944

Darling:

. . . I had a bit of bread upon the waters. In the spring three doctors from South Carolina stopped by the Creek and I was pleasant, and told them to get oranges from the grove. One of them wrote asking for the proper express address, as he is sending me a box of Carolina peaches. Will be glad to have them, as peaches are sky-high and we do not get the best ones down here. Prices are terrific on most food stuffs. The price ceiling seems like a barrage balloon that has had hell shot out of it. Am getting braced for Aunt Ida's squawks when she begins shopping.

I expect Aunt Ida will go into another decline when I get her settled and then "neglect" her.

We were reading the huge accumulation of newspapers and Aunt Ida was working on a N.Y. Tribune. She cried out, "Oh my, Dr. Kingsland dies, skin specialist." She sounded as though it came very close home, but added, "There's so few of them."

. . . Had a nice letter from Wray Rawlings[1] in Los Angeles, where he is a naval architect, saying that you might come home from the East, and if I joined you, to call him and his wife and use their place, as conditions were crowded. Should not do so, of course, but it was nice of him. Golly, if you do come home that way, don't know whether I could get to the Coast or not. The Military is using everything. . . .

> All my love,

1. Wray Rawlings, brother of Charles Rawlings, MKR's first husband.

. . . .

(TLS, 3 pp.)

> [Crescent Beach, Fla.]
> July 20, 1944

Darling:

Three fat letters from you in the mail yesterday. . . .

Now I'm damned if I'm going to speak of "My husband, the Sergeant." I just cannot picture you with stripes. Darling, you aren't changing your *nature*, are you? You are itching to get back to the battle line—. Love, don't come home and try to beat me.

I am terribly distressed about what you have been through physically. I was hoping the dysentery was not the bacillic [*sic*] type. I suppose your mess had a dirty native cook. If you are sensible on the boat coming home, and don't drink too much and eat rationally, it should do you a lot of good. . . .

All my love,

. . . .

(TLS, 3 pp.)

[Crescent Beach, Fla.]

July 21, 1944

Darling:

Two more letters from you yesterday. It is either a feast or a famine. . . .

The two letters told of your time in the hospital, and it is a damn shame. As you say, it is especially depressing to have it hit at the end of your time. I really don't think you would have gotten in such shape except for the fire. As I wrote you at the time, I felt as though I had been steam-rollered, and if there was something wrong, like the dysentery, to start with, it would take forever to get over it. I suppose the doctors have warned you that if you are not careful now, you will have prolonged effects from it. It wasn't *amoebic* dysentery was it? I hope to God not.

. . . No, the diverticulitis has given me less trouble than I have ever had, and I don't understand it, as I have never been so disturbed and so highly-keyed as this past year. Having so little trouble is probably because I have kept away from people so much. I think the undue eremitism was an animal instinct, to hide out when my system required quiet.

. . . The combination of Miss Grace and Aunt Ida is either going to keep me away entirely, or put me in hysterics. Probably first one and then the other. It is going to be just about the weirdest combination in St. Augustine. . . .

All my love,

. . . .

(TLS, 3 pp.)

[Crescent Beach, Fla.]

July 22, 1944

Dear Honey:

Well, I have spanked a child for the first time in my life. Little Martha is both hard-headed and a bit sly, and Idella has been having some rounds with her. Yesterday morning, working on Aunt Ida's apartment, it got pretty hot, so I told her she could get out of the car and come upstairs with us. Moe was already lying on Miss Grace's cool tile floor and she said she didn't mind and really didn't seem to. The old painter-carpenter was doing some work for her, the phone kept ringing, and I didn't want to add a scrap more confusion, so told Martha that she must not go downstairs. The first thing I knew, she had slipped down. When she came up, I turned her over my knee and gave it to her briefly but I think unforgettably. I was rather shocked to find that it came as naturally as though I had been spanking brats all my life. Who was it advised, "Never strike a child except in anger?" I really think it is more healthy than the sinister way I used to get spanked. I seemed to manage to commit my crimes in the morning, and the promise of the spanking was held over me all day, while I coaxed and cajoled my mother not to tell my father. She devoured my hypocritical and fawning pleadings, would finally agree not to tell on me, and would turn down my panties and wallop me about six in the evening. She probably told, anyway.

. . . The Democrats nominated Senator Harry Truman of Missouri for vice president to run with Roosevelt. I don't know a thing about him, except that he is acceptable to the Deep South, which Wallace[1] was not. Texas, Mississippi and Louisiana have been threatening a bolt from the Democratic party over the Negro question, but the Missouri nominee fixes that. . . .

All my love,

1. Henry A. Wallace, vice president of the United States (1941–1945).

. . . .

(TLS, 2 pp.)

[Crescent Beach, Fla.]

Sunday July 23, 1944

Dearest:

I *guess* I can stick out the four more days until Aunt Ida moves on Wednesday. But I am thanking Heaven for my good fortune in having found a place for her the moment she was kicked out. What should I have done if everything were indefinitely indefinite! I should have lived through it, of course. . . .

I feel a perfectly wild restlessness this morning, and even the monotonous chanting of little Martha, which usually registers no more than the recurrent note of a tree-frog, sticks little needles in me. I asked myself what I should really like to do, and I should really like to ride a broom-stick over the ocean. Since that is impractical, I have just had a drink of brandy instead. . . .

All my love,

. . . .

(TLS, 2 pp.)

[Crescent Beach, Fla.]

July 24, 1944

Dear Honey:

I walked off my fidgetiness yesterday, Moe and I doing six miles. . . .

For the first time, Moe was willing to go on the beach alone with little Martha, who quite naturally is timid about going by herself. I can see them from the windows, and he isn't running, as he does with me, but stays with her, taking a good deal of punishment, I should say. She tried to get on his back to ride him and when he just lay down, or collapsed, she went head over heels against the sand dune.

... If you can give me, from your end, some idea within two or three weeks of when you should arrive, I can just go on to New York, and might visit Skip and Betty Clark[1] in Darien, Conn., for a few days, perhaps spend a couple of days with Bill Grinnell, and if it doesn't seem feasible or you don't care, to go up to Henry Heyl's in Vermont, Julia and I could go up there for a few days. I could leave my address and phone number with Scribner's—better make it Whitney Darrow, as he is there late and early and on Saturdays—and you could radio him from the ship when allowed and he could notify me in time to get back to New York. . . .

There *must* be a hotel in New York to my taste, but I have not yet found it. I thought that high corner room at the Gotham looking down Fifth Avenue was attractive, but I don't like the Gotham itself. I get claustrophobia at the Barbizon. I despise the St. Regis. The St. Moritz overlooks the Mallard ducks in Central Park and used to have good coffee, but it is rather out of the way. Jean[2] raves about the Little Hotel, but I have a prejudice against little hotels, and it isn't high enough to get a good New York view. And of course I should be miserable at the Waldorf. One place I'd love to have you take me for dinner is the Bossart Marine Roof in Brooklyn. It was closed for a year but is now open Saturdays and Sundays. I was there once, twenty-five years ago, and it has the most heavenly view in all New York.

I may put Julia at the job of finding a hotel I would like. Of course, if you don't want to spend more than a couple of days in New York, the hotel really doesn't matter.

All my love,

1. Skip Clark, a friend from the University of Wisconsin days.
2. Jean Francis.

. . . .

(TLS, 3 pp.)

[Crescent Beach, Fla.]
July 25, 1944

Dear Honey:

... My escape flights are good for my figure, for Moe and I walk much farther then we used to. Last night the sky was gorgeous, and we walked and walked, and it was dark when we came in. Aunt Ida had been out on the coquina trying to sight me, and was peering anxiously out of the window, "worrying." I felt as though I had carried her on my back the whole five miles. We move her finally tomorrow. . . .

At the very end of the sunset, a huge pale pink V appeared in the west, with a silver sliver of moon right in the center, and it seemed a fine omen. . . .

All my love,

. . . .

(TLS, 5 pp.)

[Crescent Beach, Fla.]

July 26, 1944

Really in the afternoon of the 25th

Darling:

. . . Bob has been made a full lieutenant. (How Cecil laughed when I told him by God you were a sergeant.) Bob will either be given some sort of Navy artist's job in Washington, or at sea, and he is pulling wires to get the latter. How he will manage to paint little nigger houses on the ocean, I don't know.

. . . I loved your poem about the svelte pelt. You have my approval to be a light rhymster.

. . . Strange Fruit is not in the St. Augustine library and Miss Akin refuses to stock it! Some time when I am feeling no pain I must tackle Miss Akin—. . . .

So much love, darling.

. . . .

(TLS, 5 pp.)

[Crescent Beach, Fla.]

July 27, 1944

Dear Honey:

A communication from Galatti[1] yesterday, saying "I regret very much but there will be no way of letting you know regarding Norton's arrival here. I will be able to let you know when I receive word that he has left the other side. I know that you will realize that all matters pertaining to shipping are entirely secret."

. . . I do think we'd love a little time together in New York, as after that we probably won't go any farther than Silver Glen until after the war.

. . . Cecil said they were having shark trouble at Ponte Vedra. The Red Cross in Jacksonville brings down war convalescents every day in groups. Three men went in swimming and a shark attacked one of them. . . . And another man was attacked there by a barracuda. Ordinarily it is too far north here for barracudas, and for most sharks, but imagine you can guess the reason. Don't think I'd enjoy going now even in water knee-deep. . . .

Love,

1. Stephen Galatti, director general, American Field Service, New York.

(TLS, 2 pp.)

[Crescent Beach, Fla.]

July 29, 1944

Darling:

. . . This is Saturday and I told Aunt Ida I'd be in this morning. Idella doesn't care about taking her week-end off and will just go visiting in town as long as I am in. I decided we'd go in this afternoon instead and stay for the first evening movie. It is "Double Indemnity"[1] with Barbara Stanwyck and Fred MacMurray and Edw. G. Robinson, and is supposed to be a fascinating crime picture, with Barbara and Fred as the criminals. The movies have been poor and I haven't tried to go. "Four Jills in a Jeep"[2] over Sunday, and TIME said that in the Pacific, much as the men love movies, they all walked out on the picture. I can understand how they would despise most of the civilian tripe about the war.

All my love,

1. *Double Indemnity* (1944).
2. *Four Jills in a Jeep* (1944), starring Kay Francis and Martha Raye.

. . . .

(TLS, 1 p.)

Crescent Beach, Florida

August 1, 1944

Dear Honey:

. . . I saw and advertisement for turkeys on the Mill Creek Road and ordered one and will drive out with Aunt Ida this afternoon to get it. Then I shall go to the movie "Lifeboat"[1] with Tallulah Bankhead. I am leaving all my family behind for a change.

Max Perkins wrote me that he was obliged to take two weeks off and would have to take some more in the fall. He blames it on changing his habits, and quotes Arthur Train as saying, "Never change your habits."[2]

All my love,

1. *Lifeboat* (1944), starring Tallulah Bankhead and William Bendix.
2. Maxwell Perkins wrote to MKR on 27 July 1944: "I did get myself laid up, but not with anything painful, or apparently serious. [. . .] This that I had was due to fatigue, although I wasn't conscious of fatigue. I suspect that it was largely due to the doctor's inducing me to change my habits" (*Max and Marjorie*, 573).

. . . .

(TLS, 1 p.)

Crescent Beach, Florida

Aug. 2, 1944

Dearest:

If we had been forced to use V-mail as threatened, I think I would have written you once a week instead of every day. It takes the heart out of you. The daily news seems too trivial to be photostated! . . .

I suffered through supper with Aunt Ida, tried to ditch her for the movie but couldn't get away with it, so we went to LIFEBOAT with Tallulah Bankhead and it was wonderful. It was the sort of movie you want to talk over with someone afterward, full of subtle points and bits of stage business, and Tallulah was grand. She has more sheer personality than any other actress I can think of. The audience was unusually moronic and infuriated me, as they shrieked with laughter over the things that were light only on the surface but with utterly tragic implications. A Jewish boy on my left ate peanuts in my ear and Aunt Ida nudged me on the right, and I hope I can see it again with you. . . .

All my love,

. . . .

(TLS, 1 p.)

Crescent Beach, Florida
Aug. 4, 1944

Dearest:

I think this will perhaps be the last letter I'll try to send. No point sending out my carrier pigeons to starve to death. You probably will not receive my last few letters anyway. The radio this morning said the combined British, American and Chinese forces in Burma had taken Mitikyina, and that work could now go forward on the Lodo Road. It said the Japs fought to the end, and I can't help wishing you were Sergeant-ing at base instead of driving an ambulance this last month. Night before last I distinctly heard your voice say my name. You said it quickly and sharply, and it was not particularly a call of distress, though there was alarm in it, but it sounded more as though you were warning me, as one speaks sharply to another when a car is approaching unseen.

All my love, and I'll be seeing you!

. . . .

(TLS, 7 pp.)

[Crescent Beach, Fla.]
Aug. 7, 1944

Darling:

. . . When I stopped writing you, I had to do something, and wrote two short stories, which I thought were wonderful as I finished them. Now the oftener I read them, the lousier they get, so I shall re-write them. One is already almost indecipherable from editing, and each change seems for the worse.

. . . James[1] said I had been in his thoughts a great deal, "I mean in chief on account of Norton, who is a person so much nicer than and superior to you and me in every respectable respect." He said he felt like a bigamist, as Percie had suddenly lost every trace of her arthritis and was a different woman. And he said he would "value all news of Norton." He is sweet, too, like a rose with a bumble-bee in it!

429

I am glad the Strange Fruit finally reached you. Esther Curtis told me of being in Sally's shop when an Army officer asked for it and was told she did not stock it. He said he trusted it was not because of race prejudice, and she backed up and said no, of course not, and she could order it for him. We have just had a shameful thing in Philadelphia. Eight Negroes in Philadelphia were promoted to "platform" jobs, whatever that is, in some part of the transportation system, and a strike was called of the whole transport system of the city, in protest. Philadelphia is the second city in the country in importance of war plants, and the workers were unable to get to their jobs for nearly a week. The Army had to take over. I am only glad that it did not happen in the South.

I shall celebrate my birthday tomorrow, though no one will know it, by the dubious method of entertaining Fred Francis and the Frank Howatt's at bridge and dinner. As I wrote you, I have not met Virginia Howatt and am prepared to dislike her, as the story goes that she left poor mousy Frank and her two children and was Dr. Vernon Lockwood's mistress, kept by him in Jacksonville, returning to Frank recently. Yet God knows he is so dull that I may end up by urging her to walk out for good. Though I cannot see how any woman could leave her children. . . .

All my love,

Aug. 8 [1944]

Darling:

. . .I read Idella what James Cabell wrote about the mangoes, and on my breakfast tray this morning was a carefully printed communication, "Happy Birthday to Mrs. Baskin. Happy Birthday to the one who can be good and sweet when she want to be. And may you have as many happy days in the Future as you have had in the Past. Your Maid Idella." I told her that I had always been allowed to do whatever I wanted on my birthday, and I chose to pretend that I was good and sweet all the time and she laughed like hell. People must be conscious of a *suppressed* violence, for I swear I seldom really blow up or do anything overt.

1. James Branch and Priscilla Cabell.

. . . .

(TLS, 3 pp.)

[Crescent Beach, Fla.]

Aug. 9, 1944

Dear Honey:

. . .A letter from Phil May said the Supreme Court had adjourned until Sept. 5, announcing there were eight cases on the docket undisposed of, and he said Cason vs. Baskin must certainly be the oldest. He said a decision now could not come before Sept. 15, and he has to plead a case in Tallahassee Oct. 4, and if there is no decision by then, he will inquire tactfully what is holding it up. It looks pretty ominous to me. Phil told me long ago that there is one old duffer on the bench who would certainly think a woman's cussing was so awful that it would be libel to mention it, and he may be holding out for a trial. Dear God. Well, I'm in better shape to go through with it if it should come. And if it does, you'll be here to hold my hand and get up on the stand and look pitiful.

. . . And your cable of course was the high spot, even though signed Orton Buskin. I think Orton and Dora Rolley might enjoy knowing each other. . . .

All my love,

. . . .

(TLS, 3 pp.)

[Crescent Beach, Fla.]
Aug. 12, 1944

Dearest:

. . . She [Aunt Ida] is having peculiar difficulties with Miss Grace. I knew there were likely to be difficulties of some sort, and being Miss Grace's they could be nothing but peculiar. Miss Grace has simply taken over and Aunt Ida can hardly call her soul her own. Miss Grace has decided they can live more economically by sharing all foods. Without asking Aunt Ida whether she wants half a chicken, Miss Grace buys and cooks a chicken and divides it carefully in half and tells Aunt Ida her half comes to so much. Aunt Ida has to eat what Miss Grace plans, and at the hours Miss Grace thinks she should eat it. She said ruefully, "I never did get a chance to make a pie from those apples you gave me." Aunt Ida is more flabbergasted than upset, at present, but I told her she would simply have to divide things with Miss Grace when she wanted to and not when she didn't. She said it was hard to handle, and said, "I never knew anybody as good at that as you are. When somebody suggests something you don't want to do, you have the most wonderful way of just ignoring it."

Miss Grace said to me, "I've just read Mr. Wendell's 'Around the World,'[1] and it's all right, but my, the President looked so tired in the movies." Incidentally, it looks as though Roosevelt were about to pull one of the slickest political tricks in history. It is understood that he has invited Willkie to confer with him on foreign affairs! Since Dewey and his gang have ignored Willkie from beginning to end, it is pretty cute. Russell Davenport has announced that he cannot possibly support Dewey. He was speaking for himself and not for Willkie. Many of the papers are clamoring about the folly of the Republicans in ignoring Willkie, and the Tribune said it looked as though Dewey was afraid of greatness. I should like to see some practical executive ability in charge of government, which he could certainly contribute, but I can't see that little smart Alec dealing with great foreign powers after the war. He is apparently not much more than a Boy Scout who made good.

And one reason I don't want to see you with a little mustache, is because with the same dark coloring and the same way of lifting your heads when interested, I was afraid you might look like Thomas E. Dewey.

... That is a disgraceful story that got out about Merrill's Marauders.[2] Even if promises to them were not kept, they should have been glad to get to work again when so desperately needed. Personally, I have been sorry for many reasons that we did not have general conscription. I should have liked nothing better than being assigned to Dishpan No. 1 or Pastry Board No. 2. Just on my own, I couldn't seem to think of a suitable useful niche. . . .

All my love,

1. Wendell Willkie (1892–1944), *One World* (New York: Simon and Schuster, 1943).
2. General Frank D. Merrill. Merrill's Marauders, an advance combat unit, were famous for their penetration into Burma.

. . . .

(TLS, 4 pp.)

[Crescent Beach, Fla.]

Aug. 14, 1944

Dearest:

. . . Carl Brandt will have received my two short stories[1] by this morning, and I am all a-squirm and wish to Heaven I hadn't sent them in. I thought of one dreadful flaw in one particularly. They are both *queer*, anyway, and I wrote him that I didn't know whether they had something or whether I was going slightly nuts, and alas, the answer has come to me.

The contract went through for a Spanish edition of "Golden Apples."[2] As a matter of fact, the book has more of a Latin point of view than my others and the cad-hero will probably seem all right in Spain, whereas England and the U.S. lifted their eyebrows.

Idella discovered that my bedroom and the hall are *alive* with ticks, and I mean alive, walls, floor, rugs, bed, chaise longue. Moe has evidently been bringing them back a few at a time from his early morning jaunts and they have been breeding up a breeze. She has killed and sprayed, and still they creep out, and it seems to call for professional handling. . . . Thank God Julia is not visiting at Crawlings-by-the-Sea.!

. . . I took the family in to the movies last night, picking up Aunt Ida also. It was Deanna Durbin in a Somerset Maugham story, "Christmas Holiday"[3] and was a top-notch job. The man was Gene Kelly, whom I had never seen, and should have avoided him ordinarily, as somehow I got the idea he was a comedian and a tap dancer—and he is a superb actor. He plays the part of a New Orleans aristocrat of the usual impoverished (except for the family mansion) family, weak, and utterly charming, actually a more vicious Pat Anderson. Deanna has developed amazingly, sings only two songs, and then in a muted torch-style, and is as good an actress as any of them, and has become perfectly beautiful. It's another picture I'd like to see again, and with you. . . .

All my love,

1. "The Shell," *New Yorker* 20 (9 December 1944): 29–31; and "Miriam's Houses," *New Yorker* 21 (24 November 1945): 29–31.

2. *Manzanas de Oro*, trans. Jorge Garzolini (Barcelona: Caralt, 1945).

3. *Christmas Holiday* (1944).

. . . .

(TLS, 7 pp.)

[Crescent Beach, Fla.]
The Cottage
Oct. 5, 1944

Darling:—

. . . I was so happy over the "Health improved. . . ." Then early yesterday afternoon came Galatti's wire, saying you were ill with an undiagnosed fever. I gathered that the customary cable had been sent him, notifying him of the departure of the men who were waiting with you—and that permission to leave had been refused you because of the "undiagnosed fever." I wept bitter tears, not so much for my own disappointment, as for you, knowing how bitter it must be to be detained in that hell-hole. . . . What I don't know is whether you were held up because an undiagnosed fever would possibly be contagious or infectious for others, or because the medicos at your hospital would not release a man for a long sea trip, with an undiagnosed fever. Anyway, I cabled you at once, and wired Galatti asking if he could possibly arrange to have you flown to New York, for diagnosis and proper treatment. If you are held up because of the fear of contagion, it is of no use, but if it is for your own sake, God knows you would be better off to go through a couple of days of discomfort, perhaps even having to change plans, but ending up at that wonderful Harkness Pavilion, with the wonderful Dr. Atchley calling in the world's foremost experts on tropical fevers—and me to soothe your fevered brow. If the situation is the latter, I intend to move Heaven and earth to get plane transportation for you. In my wire to Galatti, I told him that General Brehon Somervell and his wife were our friends, and should I pull Army wires, or could he handle it better. If he can't do anything, I shall telephone Louise, and if it is possible, I know things will be managed. I can even appeal to my ex-hostess Eleanor Roosevelt for assistance. She loves to meddle in such things. . . . If I do appeal to Mrs. Roosevelt, to get you out of the Black Hole of Calcutta, I shall do so through my good friend, her secretary, Miss Thompson, and shall explain that I now understand Mrs. R's cracks.

. . . I did finish a couple of short stories, and one was accepted by the NEW YORKER. And Carl Brandt is still stuck with the other. He sent me the letter of rejection from the COSMOPOLITAN—and I could kill him for submitting it to such people—saying that they loved it, but it was too far outside their ken, and would "shock the already sagging girdles off our matrons." Actually, the story was extremely moral and literally God-fearing. . . .

The Lyons spent a week-end with me not long ago, and are coming again this week-end, bringing a delightful Episcopal minister who is now a Navy chaplain.[1] He leaves shortly for duty in Hawaii. I should warn you, Love, that I have become most religious. I have known for years that it would happen. It is in my blood. I still hang short of what I believe is known as "conversion" or "acceptance of Christ," though I have accepted the doctrines of Christ for a long time, since there is no other answer to the mess of the world. . . .

More tomorrow, and all my love,

1. Bertram Cooper.

. . . .

(TLS, 4 pp.)

[Crescent Beach, Fla.]
At the cottage
Oct. 6, 1944

Darling:

. . . Galatti had cabled your Calcutta headquarters asking if the medicos will release you from the hospital if I can arrange plane passage for you. I get the cold creeps to think that might reach you as you were about to board a ship, and you would decide to wait for a plane——and then Brehon Somervell would be in Timbuctoo and could not be reached, or perhaps could not do anything about it anyway, and you would have to wait two more months for a ship. Dear Jesus, I am about crazy. If it weren't for the Goddammed oceans, I know you would be setting out to walk home.

One reason I don't want to be stuck in New York too long before you come, is that I am afraid of Idella's getting restless. I am giving her two weeks' vacation with pay, then she is supposed to go to the Creek and clean house thoroughly. She says she won't mind being there alone while she is cleaning, but if she has to sit and wait she will go as wild as Moe does when I abandon him. I am afraid she might just walk off. . . .

All my love,

. . . .

(TLS, 1 p.)

[Crescent Beach, Fla.]
The cottage
Oct. 7, 1944

Darling:

. . . I took Aunt Ida to the movie of "Dragon Seed"[1] last night. It was effective, though I imagine the Chinese would have Oriental hysterics over Hollywood Chinamen. . . .

All my love,

1. *Dragon Seed* (1944), starring Katharine Hepburn and Walter Huston.

. . . .

(TLS, 3 pp.)

[Crescent Beach, Fla.]

The cottage

Oct. 11, 1944

Darling:

    . . . I'll have to be my own cook, as Idella told me yesterday I'd have to get someone else to work for me. She says it will be just temporary but I don't feel I can ever trust her again. I knew she had what was diagnosed as gall-bladder trouble when she came back from New York, and got her prescription for medicine filled from New York. She has really not looked well lately, drawn and pale, and says she has an acute pain in the diaphragm that keeps her awake at night. She said they thought it might be liver, and it sounded like the kind of pain you had. Anyway, she wants to go to the negro hospital in Jacksonville for X-rays, and an operation if necessary. If it is all straight, I told her I'd rather she went now and was back when you returned, as I can keep house at the cottage very easily. And if I find you have left by boat, I can always go to New York. Well, time will tell. I refuse to have fits over trifles.

    I had a delightful week-end with the Lyons and Bert Cooper, the chaplain who is leaving for Hawaii. We did nothing but eat and drink and swim—and play "the game". . . .

    Wendell Willkie died suddenly three days ago. Edie went by the church to see him "lying in state"—. Edie would—.

    All my love, angel, and goddamn it, GET ON HOME!

. . . .

(TLS, 4 pp.)

[Crescent Beach, Fla.]

At the cottage

Oct. 12, 1944

Darling:

    . . . Edith had fabulous stories to tell of her summer at the MacDowell Colony, where many of the artistic great and near-great have stayed. Apropos of Thornton Wilder, who wrote "The Bridge of San Luis Rey" and "Our Town"[1] there, she said she was told of a trip he took for the purpose of re-virginizing Ruth Gordon.[2] It seemed Ruth Gordon had been Jed Harris'[3] mistress for years and had a child by him, but was to be married to a nice man. She did not want to plunge from a life of sin directly into respectable life, so took several weeks' trip through New England with Thornton Wilder and his sister, and at the end, was presumed to be again a pure and honest woman.

... Oh darling, my heart is just about broken over the mess you are in. Pray Heaven I get the green light on trying to get you home quickly.

All my love,

1. Thornton Wilder (1897–1975), *The Bridge of San Luis Rey* (New York: Boni, 1927) and *Our Town* (New York: Coward-McCann, 1938).
2. Ruth Gordon, the actress, was married to Garson Kanin.
3. Jed Harris, writer and producer.

. . . .

(TLS, 4 pp.)

[Crescent Beach, Fla.]
At the cottage
Oct. 13, 1944

Darling:

Here goes on another letter, just in case. The prospects of your getting home, and by plane, look much brighter. I feel much more encouraged about everything. Galatti sent me a copy of a letter written by AFS headquarters in Calcutta, saying about Oct. 14 if all went well, you would be strong enough to fly home and they were working on it, and also about Oct. 14 British and Yank doctors would confer to see if a flight was "available." Well, that was all I needed, and I went to work, and I hope I have done the right thing. My meddling so often turns out to be just the wrong thing, but in this case I thought it could do only good and could not possibly do harm.

Anyway, I called got Louise's[1] number in Washington, and had Louise on the phone in about ten minutes. She was sweet as always and most distressed that you were ill, and said she would get hold of the General right away to ask him to arrange priority, or a definite order, whatever is the required process, for you to fly back, and she is to telephone me as soon as she has definite news. If plane passage is already arranged at your end, well and good. If not, Somervell can and will do it, I am sure. And even if passage is arranged for you at your end, an order or what-have-you from Somervell would only expedite things. I just felt I couldn't fool around and take any more chances on its being muffed in Calcutta. I gave Louise the name of the Pan-American Airways vice-president that I talked to on the phone the other day, as once Somervell gives the green light, they can take care of such details as indicating what planes are leaving and when, and *how* it will all be worked.

The last I knew, your folks did not know you had been really ill, and I only mentioned that you had had some stomach trouble. I wired them just now that a letter from headquarters indicated a good chance of your flying home soon and I would keep them informed. I thought the bit of lift would be good for them, even if it takes some time for things to work out.

... If Louise gets passage arranged for you today or in the morning, I think we will go to the Creek for the week-end. Idella goes to the hospital in Jacksonville

Monday for a check-up and has the problem of parking little Martha, so if I get things straight, we might as well go to the Creek for everybody's benefit.

...All my love, sweetheart, and here's hoping things move fast from now on.

1. Louise Somervell, wife of General Brehon Somervell.

. . . .

(TLS, 2 pp.)

[Crescent Beach, Fla.]
At the cottage
Oct. 14, 1944

Happy birthday, darling!

...She [Louise Somervell] read me a copy of the cable General Somervell had just sent to the commanding general of the China, Burma, India theatre, saying he would appreciate his making inquiries and making arrangements for immediate plane priority for Norton Baskin., AFS, ill in 47 British General Hospital, Calcutta—that he had been advised you could travel after Oct. 14—and to advise him of the time and place of your arrival. Louise said the commanding general would receive the cable last night. As soon as Brehon gets the return cable, she will wire me, and I shall meet your plane if it arrives on the east coast. If it is the west coast, you will probably just go on to New York by plane and I'll meet you here and you can go to Harkness or not, according to your condition.

...I couldn't possibly get the wire from Louise before Monday—this is Saturday—so all of us, including Edith, are going to the Creek in a few minutes, where we shall park little Martha so that Idella can go to the hospital in Jacksonville Monday to find out what is wrong. I am sure she means to come back. She was very ill yesterday—acute pain in the diaphragm.

I am on tenter-hooks, but feel happy and encouraged for the first time in many weeks.

All my love,

. . . .

(ALS, 4 pp.)

[Cross Creek, Fla.]
At the Creek
Sunday Oct. 15 [1944]

Darling:

Edith, Idella, little Martha, Moe and I got in to the Creek yesterday afternoon, and will go back to the cottage tomorrow morning—minus Idella and Martha. Idella has to go to the hospital.

I came to the Creek with such a happy lift, and nine times out of ten, am depressed at once by things going wrong. Idella confided to Edith that Mrs. Baskin always got upset by something when she came back to the Creek.

The moment we got out of the car, Martha announced happily that the Kohler wasn't working, and of course I cursed badly. Idella turned to Edith and said, "You see?" Edith pulled a book out of the book-case and it fell apart in her hands—termites! They have eaten a lot of my books, including "John Brown's Body."[1] I remarked that the insects would about certainly win their war against Man—and probably a damn good thing, too.

Monday morning discovered the termites had completely destroyed my precious Bartram's Travels.[2]

Took Idella home, as she said she had to draw out money for the hospital, and would go on to Jacksonville from Ocala. I am terribly suspicious, as she had a postal savings account in St. Augustine. . . .

All my love,

1. Steven Vincent Benét (1898–1943), *John Brown's Body* (New York: Doubleday, Doran, 1928).
2. William Bartram (1739–1823), *Travels* (1791).

. . . .

NORTON ARRIVED HOME FROM INDIA
ON 29 OCTOBER 1944

. . . .

Norton and Marjorie. By Permission of the University of Florida Libraries.

1945

1945 was a year of certain relief. NSB had recovered to the point that he could assume his management duties at the Castle Warden. MKR made public appearances on behalf of the war effort. She began to spend more time at Crescent Beach in order to be near NSB. Her letters to servicepeople continued unabated. In May, MGM began filming *The Yearling*, this time starring Gregory Peck and Jane Wyman. In June, Julia Scribner married the Reverend Thomas Bigham. Throughout the summer, MKR stayed at Crescent Beach, but not without frequent trips to Cross Creek, where Martha Mickens had established herself as the matriarch. Progress on *The Sojourner* was almost nonexistent, although not for the want of trying. MGM offered a movie contract, which MKR had to decline for she knew that as yet she did not even have a story much less a viable manuscript. Still, to have NSB back and to enjoy his company and the company of close friends offered its compensations.

. . . .

(TLS, 4 pp.)

Hawthorn, Florida
Tuesday morning
[20 March 1945]

Dear honey:

. . . The news at the Creek is almost entirely of the wild life, including Mr. Bowen. His daughter-in-law cracked him over the head with a hammer when he threatened to kill the long-suffering Mrs. Bowen.[1] When I passed his house, I saw my truck there, and stopped. He came out to my car so drunk he could scarcely talk. He thrust his hand into the car with the bills for the wire etc. he got for me in Gainesville, and when I took them, left his hand most obtrusively across my arm and against my front. Old Will reports that he has another man lined up to finish the carpenter work, so I shall have Mr. Bowen get the rest of the lumber owing me at the Citra mill, and send him packing.

Two rattlesnakes appeared, one at the front corner of our yard, and was taken alive, the other further down the fence line, which was killed.

One of the gilts I had penned for killing, proved to be enceinte, and last night Will asked permission to release her. When he did so this morning, she headed for the woods and began making a bed, and little ones are expected before evening. Motherhood seems to take Will and Martha completely by surprise. Chrissie produced her last calf after their telling me that she had never even been bred.

Martha asked if I still meant to butcher the small pig in the pen and was crushed when I said I did. She said, "It's a pure picture, and so womanish." I suppose this may be a mild hint that it is enceinte, too.

She asked if I had heard from Idella, and when I said not a word, she remarked, "Well, it never too late for a raccoon to wear a ruffle-bosom shirt." This seems most cryptic to me as I don't know whether she means that Idella is acting unduly uppity, or that she may still be expected to appear. . . .

All my love,

1. The destitute Bowens asked for MKR's help when they were starving. See letter of 21 February 1950.

. . . .

(TLS, 2 pp.)

Hawthorn, Florida
Wednesday
[21 March 1945]

Dear honey:

. . . It's the thyroid, and I am in for another battle with the flesh. The world and the devil are on their own for a while.

Mr. Bowen and I came to the parting of the ways. He not only wanted to take my truck in last night, but wanted my gas for it. Since he said he had finished hauling the lumber, it didn't make sense. I told him he was going to push me too far any minute, and asked why he wanted to take the truck. He started a cock-and-bull story about having new fenders put on the truck, and since he is supposed to be finishing the duck pen, it was obvious he wanted it to go for liquor. I cut him short and said I would drive him in. Had Martha go with me, and as he got out of the car he murmured to her that he was quitting. I told Martha that I could be nice just so far, and then when too great advantage was taken—she interrupted to finish, "they just courtin' death." Oh God, why do I go places.

Love.

(TLS, 2 pp.)

Hawthorn, Florida
Thursday morning
[22 March 1945]

Dear honey:

...Am tired but blissfully relaxed after yesterday's ordeal. The two talks to two such different audiences were a bit thick. I talked over the heads of the women and under the heads of the kids, but the kid talk went better. I shall not consider another talk anywhere for less than a thousand dollars and then shall probably refuse. It is a form of prostitution and I'm like the woman who would do it for a million but not for five. The horrible women didn't give a damn about what I had to say yet I really gave it some thought. Guess I'll talk to niggers and kids for free! ...

All my love,

. . . .

(TLS, 3 pp.)

Hawthorn, Florida
Friday morning
[23 March 1945]

Darling:

I had a nice little visit with your mother yesterday afternoon. She looks perfectly grand, years younger, her face nice and rosy, instead of so pale. . . .

Damn, when I accepted Nancy's and Cecil's[1] invitation for dinner, it didn't register that Nancy said she was doing the cooking. She made very good spaghetti, but we didn't have it until nine o'clock. I began to get high, so at eight o'clock I slipped off down-town in the car and had a hamburg.

Nancy has the most awful black eye I have ever seen in my life, and it was five days old then. Sally Anderson's son Dave, 23, a pilot, wounded three times, is home and out of the service, and has a bad case of battle shock. He was at loose ends before he went in the service. Well, Walter Winchell came on the radio (this was at the party Sunday) and Dave got the idea that John Maloney was Walter Winchell, and suddenly stood up and swung at John. (He, John, will learn to dodge the Camp-Andersons!) He landed a couple, and Nancy rushed in to try to stop him, and he swung on her!

...I asked Cliff about Dorothy May,[2] and at first he didn't remember her, then I mentioned the crippled boy and he recalled her—and she never did any sort of work for the Camps,[3] let alone cook for them! . . .

All my love,

1. Nancy and Cecil Clarke.
2. Dorothy May, maid at Crescent Beach.
3. Robert Clifton Camp Sr. and Rebecca Camp, parents of the artist Robert Camp Jr. The elder Robert Camp was the head of Florida Power.

(TLS, 3 pp.)

Hawthorn, Florida
Wednesday
[11 April 1945]

Dear honey:

A typical return to the Creek—. Will reported with unhidden joy that a wild-cat caught a game rooster and hen out of an orange tree near the house, the very night we left. Also something had eaten the head quite off one of the ducks. The only creature I know of that does that is a weasel. It bites off the head and sucks the blood, like Dracula. Two ducks nests had been broken up. Leonard had come, so we had water, but it will have to run indefinitely on the pressure pump, as Leonard reported the big water tank is past repair. As far as I know, it is impossible to get one now. I was busy until late with the Atlanta Journal people, and Martha prepared dinner most unwillingly and unhappily, and got her revenge by not touching Araminta's[1] room——so of course when I discovered it at ten o'clock, I had to pitch in. I woke up in the night mumbling, "Chaos! Chaos!" The world looks better this morning, as always.

The talk at the Hawthorn high school apparently went off all right. The youngsters kept me nearly an hour altogether, asking questions after I talked about twenty five minutes. I was horrified to find that some of the town beldames came, too, but I just ignored them.—...

All my love,

1. Araminta Rankin, old friend of MKR's from Rochester, New York.

. . . .

(TLS, 3 pp.)

Hawthorn, Florida
April 12, 1945

Dear honey:

The presence of my guest is having the salutary effect for which I hoped. I got vast quantities of correspondence done yesterday, and took an hour's walk with Moe after dinner. Escape serves its purposes.

... Martha is definitely sulking. When she finds out in another day or so that Mrs. Rankin is not making a bit more trouble for her, she'll cheer up.

I am enjoying the Elliot Paul[1] detective stories. But I should think that writing them would ruin his style for his more serious work.

I had an affectionate letter from the Widow Slater, saying that she and Rodney[2] were enjoying the book, and that I was their favorite writer. She told me of some of their triumphs and troubles, and said, "I tell you this because I know you understand our condition better than anyone." I was relieved and touched to find her friendship was genuine.

I must write Max, alibi-ing once again for not being at work.[3]

All my love,

1. Elliot Paul (1891–1958), Massachusetts-born expatriate, wrote satirical mystery novels.
2. Rodney Slater, the crippled son of the Widow Slater, was one of the prototypes for Fodderwing in *The Yearling.*
3. On *The Sojourner*, not published until 1953.

. . . .

(TLS, 3 pp.)

Hawthorn, Florida

Apr. 13, 1945

Dear honey:

What a blow about Roosevelt—.[1] Last night about nine o'clock Martha came to tell us that the Brice's had sent little Martha up with the news, which they had just heard over the radio. The only people who will be happy about it are the Japs and Germans and Westbrook Pegler[2] and Aunt Ida—. I don't know what the rest of us will do. Four years of that mediocrity, Truman! Perhaps he will recognize his limitation and turn things over to the best men. But who is there wise and experienced enough? It seems as inopportune as the death of Lincoln.

I had a heart-breaking letter from my chaplain friend, Bert Cooper. Someone had sent him the clipping of Julia's engagement, and she had written him, too, and it seems that Bert really had hoped to marry her and was very much in love. He said the mail reached him one night after the worst day he had, when the last of the Iwo Jima casualties were taken aboard his ship, and he was exhausted physically and emotionally. He wrote five long pages, saying he just had to pour it out, and that he needed a chaplain himself!

Also, which distresses me infinitely more, Bert said that Bigham is "one of the wettest blankets that ever embraced the cloth." Also, "he's an intelligent, damned intelligent, fish, well versed in the social graces—pompous, smug, and—the stiff-est test of all—I don't think you'll like him." He said that Julia did not sound to him as happy as she should be. I am worried no end and am glad I don't know the man, for I wouldn't dare lift a finger to interfere.

I shot an enormous chicken snake in the yard yesterday, and that is evidently what broke up the duck nest. Another duck showed up yesterday from no one knows where, with five little ducklings. Martha and I ran and opened one of the doors in the new duck pen and she walked right straight in with her brood and went in the little house. It was too cute for words. She seemed to know at once that it was a safe shelter. . . .

Love,

1. President Franklin Roosevelt died suddenly on 12 April.
2. Westbrook Pegler, a columnist.

(TLS, 5 pp.)

Hawthorn, Florida
Saturday
[14 April 1945]

Dearest:

As I think about it, there is no special point in your coming over while Mrs. Rankin is here. She is dull even to me. . . .

When we reached Gainesville yesterday, the movie proved to [be] the "The Princess and the Pirate,"[1] and I wasn't keen about seeing it twice, and Araminta didn't care about it, so we came on home after my marketing. . . .

I picked up at Miss Terry's "Apartment in Athens" by Glenway Wescott,[2] and it is a beautiful piece of work. You will like it.

I had a nice letter from Bobby Jones, saying Golenpaul[3] had sent a check for $500, as the Governor's and my contribution to the Red Cross. . . .

Talmadge DuPree came by yesterday to give me my Big Hammock check—a *net* of over $2,000. That makes about $5,000 in all on my groves, for this year. That is wonderful. Of course it won't keep up, but still I can afford to keep the place no matter how little I am here. Though again, I want to be here winters. It is still terribly dry, but my fruit has not begun to drop yet, though groves on higher ground are losing much of the crop.

All my love,

1. *The Princess and the Pirate* (1944), starring Bob Hope and Virginia Mayo.
2. Glenway Wescott (1901–1987), *Apartment in Athens* (New York: Harper, 1945).
3. Bobby Jones, the famed golfer. Dan Golenpaul, responsible for the radio program *Information Please.*

. . . .

(TLS, 3 pp.)

Hawthorn, Florida
Sunday
[15 April 1945]

Dear honey:

. . . Good old Martha is having company today and when I found, on inquiry, that she planned to make biscuits, told her I'd give her lard and flour and to make me a pan when she made hers. She came over just now and is making mine here—found Will brought rolls from town yesterday and she didn't need biscuits, but left her dinner to make them for us.

I asked her about Adrenna, as she hadn't said anything, and she said had hoped to hear from her yesterday. We agreed that Adrenna would not want to be alone at the cottage, but maybe she would come to me here next winter. I'd just as soon have her as Idella. Don't know whether to write Idella again or not. Guess I'd better. . . .

Will put her [Araminta Rankin] on the bus Wednesday, or Thursday if I can take it that long. She is really a dear, it is just that I am such a fool and get up set when I am disturbed at work. Louisa Alcott[1] wrote with dozens of children screaming and tugging at her skirts, and she will out-last me.

Love,

1. Louisa May Alcott (1832–1888), American novelist.

. . . .

(TLS, 3 pp.)

Hawthorn, Florida
Monday
[16 April 1945]

Dear honey:

Lots of news. Yesterday I drove to Citra to see if I could get word of Thelma. Mrs. Rankin said she would go along for the ride. R.J.[1] was not there, but Raymond Boyt said Thelma has had the second operation and was sitting up a little, still at Duke hospital. R.J. has never tried to phone her, to say nothing of going to see her! When a toughie like one of the Boyt's is shocked, you have something right amazing. . . .

Love,

1. R. J. and Thelma Shortridge.

. . . .

(TLS, 4 pp.)

Hawthorn, Florida
Tuesday
[24 April 1945]

Dear honey:

A little to my surprise, old Will got off the train, and not at all to my surprise, Adrenna did not. He got in my car quite as though it were a taxi he had ordered, and made no reference to the missing offspring. After a bit I inquired casually about her, and he said, "Oh, she kind of tied up down there. She be home in two or three weeks." So that's that. Martha showed no surprise when we drove in, and I realized that she had come as close as she cared to letting me know there would be no Adrenna, by advising me not to go to town if I didn't feel well. I made no comment, and she said, "Wish we could set the clock back fifteen or twenty years. Us wouldn't need King George for a daddy." Yet she knew all along Adrenna was not coming. I sometimes wonder where we get the idea that we are the superior race, when they take us in and make fools of us any time they want to. What I minded was being used for transportation for old Will! I just barely felt well enough to drive in, and it could easily have been a great hardship. He can always get a ride to the Creek. . . .

As it turned out, it was great good luck that I did go in. I went to Mr. Mixon[1] at Baird's to inquire, with little hope, about fence wire. He said, "How did you know we got in, an hour ago, the first fencing we've had in several months?" It is always gone in a day, so I got my application signed, and am going back with the truck this morning to get it. He also told me of a man who was getting out cypress fence posts, near Fairbanks. Old Will said Yes indeed, he knew where Fairbanks was, just two miles on the road to Waldo. It turned out to be seven—. . . . I know I sound like Miss Grace or Mrs. Nickleby,[2] and by God, that's the way I feel. . . .

Love,

1. Samuel Mixon of Baird's Hardware, Gainesville.
2. Grace Bugbee, the St. Augustine florist; Mrs. Nickleby from Charles Dickens's *Nicholas Nickleby* (1839).

. . . .

(TLS, 5 pp.)

Hawthorn, Florida

Apr. 25, 1945

Dearest:

. . . Believe it or not, I had a letter from Idella, and a very nice one—probably the sort that she writes all her ex-mistresses. She said My, she was glad to hear from me (!) and she had not written as she had been waiting for developments from day to day. Anyway, she is still "needed" at home, and made a plausible, if too comprehensive, story of it all. They had word two weeks ago that Edward was killed.[1] She ended, "I can never say that I don't want to work for you again and tell the truth (I should much prefer her to have said she did want to work for me again!) but it's just, I can't, not now anyway. I do hope you will get one of those persons and even though they aren't what you want, try and use them until the way is clearer for me. Hope Mr. Baskin don't over work and worry at the hotel too much."

I really think she will drift back some day, perhaps in the fall, and meantime I shall continue as though she were *not* going to drift back.

I took Moe to the Gainesville vet and described the worm I had seen, and he pronounced it tapeworm, and gave me medicine—I mean medicine for Moe— Moe and I are not that close. Moe passed it, and there must have been thirty feet of it. . . .

The grove has been fertilized and cultivated, and the crew is now cutting out sour orange sprouts. The grove looks fine, though we have not had enough rain. We didn't get the downpour I drove through.

. . . The Gertrude Stein[2] is simply wonderful. Don't know when I've enjoyed anything so. . . .

Lots of love,

1. Edward "E.M." Thompson, Idella's brother, was killed in World War II.
2. Gertrude Stein (1874–1946), *Wars I Have Seen* (New York: Random House, 1945).

(TLS, 3 pp.)

Hawthorn, Florida
<April 28>, 1945
May? [3 May 1945]

Dear honey:

Martha . . . gives as good as she gets. She was just as sore at me when I drove in as I was at her when I drove away. She was in the kitchen and ignored my very presence. I walked in and said Hello and she half-turned and said coldly, "Oh, you here?" Needless to say, her back is fair killing her. That was our only conversation, except for her fractional appearance at the door of the porch to remark that I didn't want anything, did I. I wouldn't have dared want anything, and unpacked the car and fixed supper alone. This morning she said again that her back was destroying her and she had been to doctors and the witch woman and nothing did any good, and she wanted a talk with me when I got up. Old Will is raking the yard, and when she finished this morning she said she would talk to me later, when there was no one around. A hundred to one that she and Will intend to move to St. Petersburg with Adrenna—. I seem to see the pieces of that particular jig-saw puzzle dropping into place.

Old Will told me that Mr. Williams[1] told him to tell me not to think hard of him for not calling me in the Glisson law suit! It seems he is "saving" me for the end.

Miss Terry had sent two books, "The Ballad and the Source,"[2] which I began last night, and it is delightful; also the collected short stories of Katherine Mansfield[3] which I ordered two years ago, a grand thick volume. . . .

Love,

1. Hugh Williams and Tom Glisson were disputing ownership of land.
2. Rosamond Lehmann (1901–1990), *The Ballad and the Source* (New York: Reynal and Hitchcock, 1945). Miss Terry, owner of a bookshop in Gainesville.
3. Katherine Mansfield (1888–1923), *Short Stories* (New York: Knopf, 1945).

. . . .

(TLS, 4 pp.)

Hawthorn, Florida
Friday
[4 May 1945]

Dear honey:

. . . I was right about Martha. We had our talk, and she said, "What about me going off?". . . I said of course she must go if she wanted to, but that if or when she did, I should also of course have to close up the place entirely and not come back, and sell the cows and pigs and ducks and chickens. She gave a little start and said, well, she'd just rock on a while and maybe she would feel better. I think she was tired of waiting on me, especially if I was going to get cross at her, and thought I was here indefinitely. So I told her I was moving to the cottage Monday to stay for the summer and had a good woman to help me. I gave her a back rub and am taking her to Dr. Hook this afternoon, and this morning she seemed gay and normal. However, that was certainly what was back of the Adrenna business. I think she wanted to come *here* to move *them.* Some day a poor innocent nigger is going to tell the truth—and nobody will believe him.

It might be a good thing if Martha did leave the Creek. I think she is my greatest tie here.

You will love "The Ballad and the Source," although it makes your blood run cold. The woman in it is a ghastly cross between me and the Biscuit,[1] with something so much more evil added that she is really a dilly.

I put up the Audubon, and noticed, as I should have before, that it is not a genuine one, only a chromolithograph done in 1860. That is why the Old Print Shop sent it so casually wrapped and rolled. It is not valuable at all, and I am much relieved, as I didn't want A.J.[2] sending anything as expensive as the original would have been. The picture simply dwarfs the dining-room, and the other pictures look like finger-prints on the wall. I shall probably have to put it in the back room, to be put up only if the Cronins visit us.

I had a letter from Margaret Mitchell and she said she had to restrain Evie Robert by force from saddling the horses for them to ride down and see me. Margaret said she told Evie she believed in waiting to be asked. . . .

Love,

1. Harriette Bigelow.
2. A. J. Cronin.

. . . .

(TLS, 3 pp.)

May 6, 1945

[Postmark: 5 May 1945]

Dear honey:

I don't believe Annie Carter's[1] tale for a moment. Husbands appear from Oklahoma, without notice, at the crucial moment, only in nigger women's alibis. I learned that lesson from Idella. Think I shall have to suggest to Mrs. Bethune[2] that she give a course in truth-telling. The only question is whether she means to come at all or not. If she does not, the story on May 16 would be that her husband wants her to go back with him—. . . .

I shall have to go to the cottage anyway, because I told Martha I was going, and she has reached the end of her tether, too. However, when I took her to Dr. Hook yesterday, we spoke of our myriads of pigs and Martha said firmly, "I'm going to stay right here and take care of them." I think when I was cross at her her reaction was the same as mine when I was a little girl. I would be in disfavor and decide that since nobody loved or wanted me, I should run away. And I often did, sometimes for as long as two hours—.

I enclose the perfectly incredible item from the N.Y. paper. Evidently Nettie was not joking about Ingrid Bergman's being considered for Ma Baxter! What ARE those asses up to? I am sure in the picture Twink Weatherby will do a strip tease while the Forresters break into full orchestra. . . .[3]

Love,

1. Annie Carter, a maid suggested for MKR by the Owen D. Youngs.
2. Mary Bethune, black educator, founder of what is now Bethune-Cookman College in Daytona Beach, Florida.
3. Ingrid Bergman, Swedish actor. The film alluded to is *The Yearling* (1946). Jane Wyman played Ma Baxter.

. . . .

(TLS, 2 pp.)

[Cross Creek, Fla.]
[6–9? May 1945]

Dear honey:

. . . Heard from Arthur who is in Seattle for a month or two. He may sell his boat on the high market and charter something else, for he says he has a lot of business signed up. If he doesn't get his price, he will have some renovations done in Seattle. He had brought his boat down from Alaska single-handed, al-most non-stop, the fool. If you think I am an idiot about taking care of myself, you should know Art better. He said he was a little punch-drunk—.

Am enjoying the Katherine Mansfield no end. Will bring it over when I come. Am also steadily plugging away on the correspondence, but it is like the fairy story where you have to eat your way through a village of soup. There seems no end.

. . . I wrote Annie Carter asking her to let me know for sure whether or not she intends to come May 16, that I should much rather know now if she is not com-ing. . . . Martha and I are love-birds again—.

. . . .

(*Selected Letters*, MS not seen)

[Cross Creek, Fla.]
Friday Evening
[September 1945]

Dear Honey:—

. . . Now honey, feeling that our love for each other is a tragedy is putting it too strong, and I didn't mean to go that far. But as far as I am concerned, it is a mis-fortune and a hell of a nuisance that I have exactly the man I want—and can't accept his way of life.

But if you are willing just to make allowances for my eccentricities—and to admit that a large part of my objection to your way of life isn't eccentric at all—

and will go on being sweet and patient and let me come in to roost when I feel like it and take off again when I feel like it, I still think we can work it out.

We are no worse off, and I think a lot better off, than in the last couple of years before we were married, when we saw a lot of each other in the winter and you could only come to the cottage every 3 or 4 weeks in the summer. As soon as the gas rationing is over there will be no problem at all.

When I see you next, I want to go into all this very thoroughly. We never have. You take an aggrieved attitude, and dismiss me as just plain nuts, and I get completely inarticulate.

I have "read a book," and found out the KIND of nut I am. It isn't as bad as it might be! And I am not completely nuts, and there is some excuse for me!

Anyway, I am extremely fond of you, and nobody else can have you. I mean to keep our lives together in some way.

All my love,

. . . .

(TLS, 4 pp.)

[Cross Creek, Fla.]
Monday Evening
[19 November 1945]

Dear Honey:

If I ever write a sequel to "Cross Creek"—which God forbid—it will certainly be titled "Chaos at the Creek." Perhaps the first volume should have been so named. Anyway, another time I shouldn't glorify a goddamn thing. After fretting and stewing all day as to whether the black painter of white walls would return at all, Martha murmured just now that Little Will had told her that Wilson had told him that he suspected a man of slippin' aroun' his house, and he was fixin' to lay up and catch *him*. Martha said, with her customary *infuriating* demureness, "I reckon that why he taken today off. He figure Monday a fine day to catch a man." I am sure she knew this all the time. I hope he caught his man and gets it all over with.

Also, this morning, Martha reported that Buddy wanted to see me, to know what he should work at. I asked her if he and Little Will didn't have their work mapped out together, and she said, yes, but he just wanted to ask me. Ast me. I trotted to the back door, and said that unless they had something more important planned, it seemed to me that they should continue getting in wood. He made vague objections, and after infinite backing and filling, said, "Little Will jes' ain't up to workin' today." Now Martha knew THAT when she called me!!! Little Will does really have hay fever, but he probably also has a Monday hangover. And Martha, bless her old utterly maddening soul, is standing by like a Trojan and we have accomplished today the work of ten, even though our hearts may not be pure.

After I phoned you from Boyt's today, again my car would not start. They worked on it two and a half hours. Finally got it going, deciding that the condenser had been at fault—and when I drove in at the Creek, clouds of black smoke were rising from the motor—.

Margie Glisson, the Tom Glisson's ewe lamb, who married soldier boy early in the war, and from whom she has been separated unavoidably for two years, while he was in the Pacific, was six months pregnant when he walked in last week. He took one look at her stomach and walked out again.

Have had in mind Phil May's request that I query casually various of the "characters" in "Cross Creek" as to whether they had objected to my mentioning them. In Baird's Hardware Saturday morning, ran into old Joe McKay,[1] one of those about whom I had been a bit dubious. We chatted amiably, and I finally said, "You didn't mind my mentioning you in The Book, did you?" He said no, indeed, he was glad of it. He said, "That book really has been sold all over." Thinking of Africa and Spain and Brazil and Finland etc., privately I agreed. He said, "Why, Ma'am, they've even heard of that book up around McClenny."

Then he added that he'd never read it! So I said I should leave him a copy as soon as I could get one. In cleaning out the book-shelves, I found a copy I didn't know I had, inscribed it tenderly to a Good Neighbor, and went by to leave it. He was not there, but Tom Morrison[2] was. Now Tom was the one who went to Scruggs after Zelma filed her suit, wanting to file one, too. I said to Tom that I wondered if he'd read the book, or would like a copy, and said, "You didn't mind my mentioning you, did you?" and he mumbled, "Oh, no." (I do think that pure *cowardice* would keep two or three of his ilk from appearing against me.) I asked again if he'd like a copy of the book, and he said, "No'm, he'd read that one [*Cross Creek*], old man Martin loaned it to him, and he'd much rather have a copy he'd seen in a window in Jacksonville, but the store was closed, *Cross Creek Cooking* [*Cookery*]!!!!! I fair RUSHED my own copy to him, inscribed to a Good Friend of Many Years' Standing.

Sunday morning I went by to see the Townsends. After a long chit-chat, I asked if they'd minded me writing about them, and Mrs. Townsend said, "Why, no, they'd enjoyed it a heap." She said, "You wrote so nice about our little party."

God, these people are really so *sweet*.

George Fairbanks was there, and if I wrote unkindly about anyone at the Creek, it was about him, and gritting my teeth, I asked George if he'd minded, and he said, "No, Ma'am, it was all right." That clears up all the people about whom I was even remotely ungenerous.

Stopped by to see Thelma one evening, and she asked me to go over and see her mother, who had gone back alone to her little shack. Went by, and the place was dark, although it was only a little after nine, and I hesitated, but decided not to call or knock for two reasons: one, that Mrs. Tompkins, if asleep, should not be disturbed; two, that in her condition she was quite capable of turning one of

Fred's ancient fire-arms on me. The next time I stopped to see Thelma, she didn't even ask if I'd seen her mother, but told me that Mrs. Tompkins had turned violently against me because I had gone to see her at Chatahoochie and hadn't brought her home!!!!!!

Love,

1. Joe McKay, the oldest resident of Cross Creek.
2. Tom Morrison, a Spanish-American War veteran and resident of Cross Creek.

. . . .

(TLS, 2 pp.)

Hawthorn, Florida
Tuesday Afternoon
[20 November 1945]

Dear Honey:

Things are going better. Martha, instead of being crushed by work, is cheerful and reported this morning that she felt SO much better. The painter came today, and volunteered the services of his wife, beginning tomorrow, to help Martha and me. (Except, presumably, to entertain the man who'd been slipping around.) Little Will and Buddy have gotten in a grand pile of wood. . . .

Met a former resident of Island Grove in town and she said, "What's happened to your weight? You look so poor and old." I said I'd worked hard to get it off, and she said it was a pity, as I looked so much younger when I was fat. I slunk away.

When Martha was washing dishes from the china cupboard she threw away the rose-petal contents of a Chinese rose jar my mother started long before I was born. It has always kept its fragrance. To Martha, it was just dead leaves. Really don't know why I had any sentiment about it, but I did, but told Martha it didn't matter at all. As hard as she's worked the past week, she could throw out anything but Moe or the Wyeth cranes,[1] and I shouldn't peep. . . .

Much love,

1. N. C. Wyeth's cranes, from his illustration for the "Pulitzer Prize Edition" of *The Yearling* (Tarr, *Descriptive Bibliography*, 62–74).

. . . .

(TLS, 1 p.)

Hawthorn, Florida
[10 December 1945][1]

Honey:

We are sorry we missed you, you gad-a-bout. Red and I (Red Vines) played golf this afternoon and then we were taken suddenly dronk. Decided to come up and have dinner with you not because we were dronk but because we wanted to see you. When we got there the cupboard was full but where in the hell was

Mother Hubbard. Adrena said you would be back suddenly so we decided to wait—and waiting we decided to cook so that mama would have a nice hot dinner when she got home from work—but hell it look like mama doesn't come home from work. So we ate the food—very bad and now we have to go home as somebody has to protect the dignity (or is it the sanctity) of the home by being in the right place at the right time. We would like you to come in and have dinner and bridge with us tomorrow night. If you like you can mess up my kitchen. I have to clean up just like you do. Let me know if you can come and what time so that I can get a fourth. Hope you don't mind our making ourselves at home.

Love

KO.

1. The date of this letter is suspect. The envelope accompanying it is postmarked 10 December 1945, but its facetious content—MKR is inebriated—does not match the letter following it. Also Adrenna Mickens was not with MKR in 1945. However, in the absence of other evidence, this intriguing letter is placed here.

. . . .

(TLS, 2 pp.)

[Cross Creek. Fla.]

Thursday morning

[11 December 1945]

Dear honey:

. . . Idella was just bringing out my baked potato and broiled steak for an early supper yesterday, when two cars drove up at the gate. She groaned and I cussed. It proved to be Nettie[1] and John Maloney and Bob Camp! Also a young man named Aristotle Rommelle, and a Marine recently home from three and a half years in a Jap prison camp. He had wanted to tell me of reading "Cross Creek" there etc., and knew pages by heart.

. . . As we were drinking on the porch, Tom Glisson came by. . . . I asked him in for a drink and to my surprise he accepted and had two, and was the life of the party.

He announced how much he and his wife[2] loved me, and what a wonderful woman I was, and that in all the years he'd known me, this was the first time I'd ever asked him in for a drink.

Much love,

1. Nettie Camp or Nettie Martin, most likely the latter.
2. Pearlee Josey Glisson.

1946

1946 was a year of two major trials. The first came in March, when NSB decided to sell the Castle Warden Hotel. It was not an easy decision, and directly involved MKR, who owned an interest in the hotel. NSB decided to seize the opportunity of managing the two restaurants at Marineland. The second trial had even greater impact. In May, Zelma Cason's "invasion of privacy" lawsuit came to trial. It proved to be a sensation. Witness after witness was brought forward, finally MKR herself. The tension of the trial was often broken by moments of humor. In the end, the jury found MKR innocent of all charges. Cason's attorneys, J. V. Walton and his daughter, Kate Walton, filed an appeal before the Florida Supreme Court. Both MKR and NSB were grateful that the trial was over, but the Cason appeal created renewed tension. MKR returned to the writing of *The Sojourner*, but with little success. In September, she began to expand her "boy-and-dog" story, then titled *A Family for Jock*, for MGM. In November, Maxwell Perkins recommended that it not be turned into a book. To make matters worse, NSB found himself in disagreement with the owners of Marineland.

. . . .

(ALS, 6 pp.)

> [Cross Creek, Fla.]
> Tuesday P.M.
> [15? January 1946]
> I wouldn't know
> what time, as I forgot to
> bring the Dali watch,
> and yours chose this
> moment to go on the blink.

Dear Honey:—

I am *not* [underlined twice] tight, but can no longer be intelligible with a pen, let alone a wobbly Parker pencil. Oh, God, the confusion. When things are like this at the Creek, I would give my entire patrimony (anything short of my matrimony) to have a *complete* household at the beach.

Planned to leave for Ocala this morning at 9, having a comfortable breakfast and reading the New Yorker. I asked Martha what the two men were doing, and she said proudly, "Sugar, when you home, nobody don't *move* [underlined twice] 'til you comes outen that room and tells 'em what to do." Since I am paying the waiting pair $52 a week, and I found they did *nothing* last week after I left, I arose and put them to work.

Wilson, the painter and carpenter announced firmly to the Mickens that he would not return until after the holidays. It seems the sheriff for whom he is working now gave him permission to shoot the man hanging around his (Wilson's) wife, so Wilson can't pass up a chance like that.... Exchanged my Olds this morning for a '41 Ford, very rattly, but will probably *keep running* [underlined twice] until my new car comes.

Picked up Idella on the way home. Bettyrine[1] is now scraping paint from the windows, Martha pressing draperies. It is so cold, we can only work in the rooms with heat.

... It was announced to me when I reached home yesterday that both tanks were entirely out of gas. Phoned the Standard Oil car at Micanopy this morning, but when I returned from Ocala, the truck had not come. We had to have the Kohler for the electric iron for the draperies. I gave Buddy money and sent him in to the new Island Grove place to fill the truck with gas and bring 5 gals. In a can, ethyl preferred but the regular would do. Buddy never got past Caren's beer place! Reporting happily that since they didn't have ethyl, he filled the truck but brought back the can for the Kohler empty. Sent him back and he returned with 5 gals. Of ethyl....

Love,

1. Bettyrene, companion of "Little Will" Mickens.

. . . .

(TLS, 2 pp.)

[Cross Creek, Fla.]
Tuesday afternoon
[29 January 1946]

Dear Mister Honey:

There was the usual backing and filling, milling and mauling, over the hog-killing, getting help etc., and it finally came out that Martha thinks it is the wrong time of the moon and the lard will waste away to nothing. After a supreme psychological effort on my part, we got help and killed only two of the four large hogs. One of the others I am giving to Martha and I guess she thought I would or should give her both, because she wanted to buy the fourth one, knowing damn well that I never let her pay for anything like that. This time I balked and said no, I wanted the hams and bacon myself. I had already given her the best of our two remaining sows, etc. anyway, I got the two into the storage plant for curing and smoking. When I got back three hours later, Little Will was SITTING WAITING FOR ME TO TELL HIM WHERE I WANTED THE MEAT ODDS AND ENDS. He DID fool around the day he drove to the cottage. I suppose he got in a panic, for after wiring me he sent word to Chet Crosby that he was in trouble, and Chet made two trips to Hawthorn, and never did find him. The truck had been repaired and Will had left the garage before noon, he found. It is useless to try to use one of the black brothers unless you can stand over him all or most of the time.

Chet said he picked 1780 boxes of oranges here and 180 boxes of grapefruit, and I still have several hundred boxes of Valencias and June bloom left. I was surprised and pleased. . . .

My mood lightened and I am cheery again. That is the advantage in being really and truly a bitch. Things don't get you down for long. If you were really and truly nice, you see, you would be *crushed* by the various bits of perfidy, black and white. Hurray for bitchiness.

I wrote Charlie Scribner. Suggested, after inviting them for lunch or dinner, and explaining about not enough bathrooms to ask them for over-night, that it might make up their extra mileage if they spent that night in Ocala instead of going back to St. A., but said that is they didn't feel they could take time out to come to the Creek, you would have a reservation for them at the Castle. Really don't think they will come by the Creek, for there is no love lost between Vera and me, but I have done my duty. . . .

Will now go back to my busy bitching.

Love from your busy-bitch-Baskin.

. . . .

(TLS, I p.)

[Cross Creek, Fla.]
Wednesday afternoon
[30 January 1946]

Dear Honey:

. . . Martha made the lard today, and I am making scrapple now. Will wait until we butcher again next week to make the good imitation pate de foie gras. . . .

It is simply wonderful here, and I hope the grand weather will last while you and the Hardys[1] are here.

. . . Lois said not to make any plans, but it does seem as though we should have at least one dinner party for them. But whom to ask, who wouldn't bore the pants off them? The Tigerts are stuffy unless you happen to be fond of them as I am, the Camps are worse, Nettie is grand but I think John Maloney would bore them. Any ideas? Verle and Edie? . . .[2]

Much love, darling.

1. Ed and Lois Hardy, friends from Louisville.
2. John J. and Edith Tigert; Robert Camp Sr. and his wife, Rebecca Camp; Nettie Camp, wife of Clarence Camp; John Maloney; and Verle and Edith Pope.

. . . .

(TLS, I p.)

[Cross Creek, Fla.]
Tuesday morning March 5,
[1946]

Dear Honey:

. . . An old colored man with a hare-lip and no nose is grafting Parson Brown buds on the sour orange stock through the grove. I ran into him on my way to the back vegetable garden to pull carrots and my hair stood on end. Was glad it was daylight—though in the dark of course I wouldn't have seen that he didn't have any nose. The sour orange trees are all laid low, *covered* with bloom, and I brought in a big armful for the house. Wish I could get a truck-load of them to you.

Phil May and Lillian were here yesterday afternoon and evening. He went over Zelma's answers to her Interrogatories with me, and one of them was a gold mine for us. He asked if I had changed my opinion about Interrogatories and I said they were wonderful. He was almost as surprised as Kate Walton[1] and Zelma will be at the total amount that came in from "Cross Creek"—$67,780.35. I pointed out that while that covers the four years since publication, most of it came within a two-year period and so was subject to very high income tax, and about $30,000 of it went to the government, that I put $25,000 in War Bonds and had used the rest to live on and didn't know how much longer it would be before I had additional income come in, if at all. He still wants to talk with T.Z.,[2] but I am against it.

The people bringing out the Mansfield collection liked the introduction,[3] and I was pleased and relieved. It seemed terrible to me. Have to do something for a Norwegian magazine on Sigrid Undset in America, and thought *that* would be easy. My error. . . .

. . . I wrote Carl "No" on the MGM contract.[4] Expect he will be disgusted with me. . . .

Much love,

1. Kate Walton, an attorney for Zelma Cason.
2. T. Z. Cason, once MKR's physician, was the brother of Zelma Cason.
3. MKR wrote the introduction for Katherine Mansfield, *Stories* (Cleveland: World, 1946).
4. MGM was seeking an advance contract on *The Family for Jock*. See letter of 2 April 1946.

(TLS, 2 pp.)

Hawthorn, Florida
March 6, 1946

Dearest:

Wrote Langston[1] telling him to use the cottage if he wants to, and get the key from you. Said he could leave his papers there in between, and it was all right even when I would be coming over for a week-end. I feel so sorry for him, trying to work on the most important thing in his life, in that tiny house with Lady Claudia, the Duchess mother-in-law, and two boys who play the drums, the trombone, the saxophone and what-not. It seems to me that sooner or later that great, elephantine patience of his will blow up and he'll run amok, and I shall be obliged to cheer.

I MUST investigate the Peabody system. Wrote some letters in my cups late yesterday afternoon, and sent a batch to be mailed in Citra by Little Will as he took Wilson home. This morning I hunted around and thought, "You fool, SURELY you didn't mail that thing to Stanley Rinehart"——but I had—. . . .[2]

The Stanley Rinehart thing was really something. He had written that he was sending me a book by a Florida author, Charles Baker,[3] didn't know whether I remembered "Charlie" (I did not), thought the book was grand and would I send a comment. The book came and it is simply horrible. If I had written it, I would be run out of Alachua County. It is worse than "Tobacco Road,"[4] and the same sort of evil, perverted thing. Hervey Allen,[5] on the jacket, vouched for the "authenticity" and Charlie, also on the jacket, said there wasn't any nature-faking in *this* book, by jiminy.

. . . Leonard is working on the Kohler, bless his heart. Will be interested to get the dirt from him about the Yearling film.[6]

. . . I don't see how I can come over for a while, darling. Phil wants me to ask different friends to testify, and I must make the approaches gradually. Will ask Leonard while he is here. Know you can't get away, either, but I can always come over for a day and night, or a week-end, if you will have any time free at all. . . .

All my love, darling.

1. Langston and Claudia Moffett; the former was working on *Devil by the Tale* (Philadelphia: Lippincott, 1947), for which MKR wrote a blurb (see Tarr, *Descriptive Bibliography*, 240).
2. Stanley Rinehart, a publisher.
3. Charles H. Baker (1895–?), *Blood of the Lamb* (New York: Rinehart, 1946).
4. Erskine Caldwell (1903–1987), *Tobacco Road* (New York: Scribners, 1932).
5. Hervey Allen (1889–1949), American novelist.
6. *The Yearling* (1946), starring Gregory Peck and Jane Wyman.

(TLS, 2 pp.)

Hawthorn, Florida
March 7, 1946

Dear Honey:

Well, I think you are insane, but each of us had to head for the asylum in his own way. If you will be happier not owing anybody anything, more power to you, and maybe you'll be a little more fun, too. And am I cured of putting my nose in your business! You can run a whore-house and I sha'n't try to deflect you. . . .[1]

A wire from the Lyons[2] asked us to come to dinner tomorrow with Robert Frost. I may have to go in the truck but will go. I haven't been off the place. . . .

Ivy[3] came out to see me just now. He's another of the G.I.'s who liked the Germans!

Snow came by to pay off his back interest. He will gladly testify in the suit. Said "any of the people over there will." Leonard said he would testify. Leonard, Snow, Ross Allen, Nettie, Dessie, think they will probably be more effective than anything we can say. May ask Bernie Bass and one of the Townsends, possibly John Clardy. Think it might be cute if John said Yes, he took it as a compliment to be written about, but there was one thing in it he objected to. Q. What was that? A. She didn't get the names of my dogs right.

. . . Idella could not be better-natured, and has been scrubbing up a breeze. She was O.K. when she got in from her week-end. I told her she should be ashamed of herself for acting as if, or thinking, I would try to gyp her. . . .

Love,

1. NSB is negotiating the sale of the Castle Warden Hotel.
2. Clifford and Gladys Lyons; the former was the head of the English Department at the University of Florida.
3. Ivy Sykes.

. . . .

(TLS, 4 pp.)

Cross Creek, [Fla.]
March 15, 1946

Darling:

. . . The Jacksonville day was hell, and I smoked five or six packs of cigarettes. . . . [T]he Revenue office was just as nice and helpful as could be, and gave me the figures we needed. What Phil had to do, was not only, in justice to me, to take off the income tax I paid from my gross returns, but in justice to abstract honor, to estimate what portion of my income taxes and what surtax had come from "Cross Creek" alone. It worked out that up to Jan. 8, 1943, less than the first year after publication, the book paid me net $30,000, and since Jan. 8, 1943 to date, three whole years, my net returns were $18,000. I suppose Kate Walton will refuse to believe it, and we shall have to prove it, but that should be much simpler than working out the calculations in the first place. Phil thinks Kate and Zelma will faint when their belief in millions to be gone after is deflated to that $48,000.

We did a lot of work on the apparently simple interrogatories. One question to be answered was whether or not I wrote the things about plaintiff quoted in their declaration, and I pointed out to Phil that it was not fair to us to have to answer that with a simple "Yes," when Walton had taken out of context only about a dozen sentences of the less kindly order.

Phil consulted with John Crawford,[1] who said, "Why, that's simple. Merely say, 'In answer to interrogatory No. 2, I exhibit and put on file a copy of the book Cross Creek, written by me and published etc. etc. with my knowledge and consent." As a matter of fact, this answer covered interrogatories 2 and 3, 3 being whether the book was "caused" to be published by me, some rather subtle such expression that had an overtone of my presumed malice and general evil. By answering that way, the jury is obliged to read the whole chapter and the whole book, and Phil had been trying to find a way to make that allowed and required!

We didn't finish until nearly six o'clock, and meantime Phil had announced that they would not take No for an answer, to my going out to Mandarin for dinner at their place. I have refused every time I've been in Jax and when they insisted, and on Aunt Ida's necessarily going, too, I agreed. As a result, we didn't reach the Creek until 11:30 at night, and I was *exhausted*.

The May temporary home is charming. Lillian has exquisite taste and is accumulating some beautiful stuff. And she cooked, alone, one of the most delicious dinners I have ever eaten; superb onion soup, lamb curry, etc. etc., marvelous green salad, and what Aunt Ida said was the best lemon pie she's ever put a fork in (waving her fork as she spoke.)

Little Will and Bettyrene were back when I got here—. It seems he "thought he told me" he was taking Bettyrene to visit her folks for a couple of days—. Probably Bettyrene's folks told them they didn't know when they were well off, and packed them back again. Meantime, that black bitch of a Martha had taken down their bed and piled it in the new bedroom that hadn't been painted yet, and dumped every bit of their stuff, personal small belongings, pots, pans etc. in what is to be the new kitchen, not even sealed yet, and Wilson is having a hell of a time doing his work while avoiding the bed, springs, mattress, kettles, slop-jar, suit-cases etc. Martha did it while Idella was home, too, knowing damn well Idella would have advised her to wait for me to say the word. It was just pure cussedness, to make Bettyrene mad. I realize now, too, that it means that Martha knew all along they were *coming back*. Otherwise, she would have moved in HER stuff, to beat Idella to it. She is keeping away from me, but when I saw her when I went to inspect the work-in-progress, she was as demure and saintly as a chocolate Madonna. I have just finished consoling Bettyrene, who was not killing-mad, as I should have been, but "bad hurted." What "hurted" her worst was that in the surreptitious moving, Martha managed to break off a castor on the new bed.

I had a long letter from Arthur that all but broke my heart. I'll save it for you to see. He is not just waiting for the Alaska season to open, as I thought, but is working like a dog on his boat to get it ready, doing most of it himself to save the money. I had deliberately made it sound, when I wrote him last week that I wished he would come down for a month or so, that I needed him for moral support during the law-suit, that I was lonesome to see him, etc., rather than scaring him off by telling the truth, which is, that I hadn't liked the depressed sound of his previous letter, both as to health and spirits, and felt that coming here would do him a world of good at perhaps a critical moment. Well, I did too good a job. If he came, it would mean either spending several thousand dollars to have the work done in the ship-yards, which he can't afford, and he will not borrow—OR giving up his summer bookings—and this he is planning to do!!! He said that he read my letter again and again for any trace of concern on my part for his welfare, and there wasn't a word, and it was the first time I had ever asked or suggested anything for my own welfare. To be sure he hadn't missed anything, he showed my letter to a friend, who said, "Art, your sister needs you." That was the impression (with my usual sly plotting) I intended to convey, never dreaming it would make him plan to throw over all he has worked for, for ten years! And Carl Brandt called me an honest woman—. I am wiring Art that I completely misunderstood about his activities and thought he was waiting idly and I am doing wonderfully. There is so much more in his letter, and he isn't off the beam at all, as I feared, but only harassed to death for several good and valid reasons. . . .

1. John Crawford, attorney partner of Philip May.

. . . .

(TL, 3 pp.)

> Hawthorn, Florida
> Sunday morning
> [17 March 1946]

Darling:

Tony [cat] and I crowded into the little bed next to the bathroom. The room across the hall, back of the living room, was totally uninhabitable, thanks to heavy rains that came through that part of the roof as though there was no roof at all. I had hoped that one of the aunties[1] would insist on using the little bed, but Gracie tucked herself happily into the far bedroom with private bath, and the red bedroom is just right for Wilmer, as there is room in it for her to keep and ride her stationary bicycle. Wilmer doesn't have to go to the bathroom in the night, and gets around wonderfully on the crutches, so my hope that the step down into the bathroom would keep that room for me (as Gracie is too short to reach the clothes rod in the closet) went glimmering. Gracie sized up the situation at a glance, and said, "You mustn't put yourself out. Just give me the little room. It will be quite all right." Her tone was that of one who knew, patiently, all along, that she would be the goat. There was of course nothing for it then but to fix them up as I could see the rooms appealing to them.

. . . I think there is no question but that they will be glad to go to Marineland[2] at the end of their visit. If you have a chance to come over (you could sleep on the porch) would love to have you, and really, you should see them in a Kinnan habitat. They will, I am sure, strike you as perfectly normal people. The Kinnan battiness is of a most subtle sort and is not noticed by many. I don't know why I am so cynical and nasty about it. I just never have been crazy about Kinnans. Marjorie the second included.

I gave Martha hell, and brought up the two tricks she had pulled on me, then, having made my point, or so I thought, we once again swore undying fealty and had a drink together. Yesterday afternoon when Idella was resting, Martha came to me and said, "Who does you want to help you with the company, me or Bettyrene? Either way is all right, I just want to know." Having realized that a large part of the trouble came from her having been wildly jealous when we used Bettyrene when the Hardys were here, think it would suit Martha to a T, there was only one answer. I said that Idella probably would not need any help, as we didn't plan to give them the rich and varied foods we sometimes have for "company," but if and when she needed help, we would love to have Martha, if she felt well, and if not, to tell me. She floored Idella, at dinner-time, by showing up in best working bib and tucker saying, "*Mrs. Baskin told me to help you.*" It gave Idella the feeling that I didn't trust her to turn out a simple dinner alone!

Patrick Kinnan was the first Kinnan in this country, about 1660. "He was Scotch-Irish, from just over the border, and in this country he had large farms." Which makes me positive that Patrick was Irish as Paddy's pig and was probably somebody's stable hand. Gracie is not on the trail of proving one line of descent from Edward Kinnan, who was "a drummer-boy in the American Revolution," which is worked out to mean that when Edward was about 12, he followed the Army with his mother's dish-pan and tin spoon for sound effects. Gracie finally got to see the original Kinnan silver, belonging to a Mrs. Edward Kinnan, I think it is, in Westchester. "At first she didn't want to let me in, but she ended up by asking me to tea." Gracie stayed to tea.

Am I not *horrid.* . . .

All my love.

Memo on Luncheon Conversation

Wilmer: This is such a *big* plate of the hearts of palm. I wonder if maybe it isn't too concentrated, like eating that many walnuts or something.

Me: Oh, no, it's more of a vegetable, not a nut at all. It has berries.

Wilmer: Berries? What color are they?

Me: Nearly black.

Wilmer: How big are they? (Before I can speak) As big as cherries?

Me: About as big as cherries.

Wilmer: What size cherries? Big cherries or little cherries?

Me: (desperately) Medium-sized cherries.

Wilmer: I still think it's probably too concentrated, like nuts.

Me: Oh, no, it's full of iron and vitamins and valuable things. It has a very slight laxative effect.

Gracie: It does indeed have a little nutty flavor.

Wilmer: What color did you say the berries were?

Gracie: She said "Nearly black," darling.

Me: (In anguish) You'll have to excuse my hair done up in curlers under the turban. I'm just between permanents. I don't want to get another until I have some hot oil treatments.

Wilmer: That's perfectly right. And what really worries me is the way all the great civilizations collapse. Sooner or later, Peaches, every single civilization has collapsed.

Me: (Ringing the table bell, very faintly) Idella, may I have some more water—.

1. Grace and Wilmer Kinnan.
2. NSB sold the Castle Warden in March and then took charge of the restaurants and bar at Marineland, south of Crescent Beach.

. . . .

(TLS, 4 pp.)

[Cross Creek, Fla.]
March 19, 1946

Dear Honey:

. . . Had to advance Wilson $30 yesterday, bond for his wife. He told me tenderly that it wasn't her fault, she was obliged to hit a man over the head with a jug. Wilson was at home at the time—. And speaking of bond, Mr. Neil[1] brings out telegrams and pockets his dollar and never mentions the loan. The last time he came, he came in and sat on the porch some minutes and seemed to want to say something, but never did. I'm certain he has gambled away the $250.

. . . How they [the aunts] go for their glass of Dubonnet before meals. And how I misled Idella when I told her they wouldn't eat much! But except for moments when I want to scream, either with laughter or irritation, I am enjoying them and they are apparently having the time of their lives. Gracie began reading a Ben Ames Williams[2] book Idella had urged on me. She found a soiled page and remarked on it, and that she hadn't done it, turned it over, and said, (it was pub-

463

lished in 1941) "Why, isn't this an *old* book?" She put the book down and said, "I make it a rule never to read a book more than three years old."

They had never heard of Robert Frost, which amazed me in Wilmer. Then I realized, for all her college degree, she is peculiarly ignorant and is not in the least intellectual, for all her emphasis on the mind....

Love,

1. Mr. Neil, husband of the postmistress, owed MKR for a loan.
2. Ben Ames Williams (1889–1953), *The Strange Woman* (Boston: Houghton Mifflin, 1941).

. . . .

(TLS, 2 pp.)

[Cross Creek, Fla.]
Saturday afternoon
[23 March 1946]

Dear Honey:

... The evening with the Lyons was lovely and Cliff and Gladys were so sweet, and yesterday's luncheon with Mrs. Tigert and Mrs. Weaver[1] was most pleasant. Tuesday afternoon we are going in for Mrs. Tigert to drive us around the campus and have tea at her house, and Wilmer is dubious about this. She gets so exhausted, and when tired, in pain, that she wanted to rest before starting on their return trek.

Phil May and Lillian will be here for dinner Monday night. He goes to the pretrial hearing early Tuesday morning in Gainesville....

Much love.

1. Alice Rossing Walden Weaver, wife of Rudolf Weaver, founder of the School of Architecture at the University of Florida.

. . . .

(TLS, 3 pp.)

Hawthorn, Florida
April 2, 1946

Dear Honey:

A strange man and woman are prowling around the front yard and have been all around the house, but since they have not addressed me, I am typing away as fast as possible, hoping they'll just go away—. We seem to have no actual existence for one another, and it is an odd, disembodied feeling.

Such a nice note from Carl Brandt, after I wired I could not sign the MGM contracts until after a fresh start on the book.[1] He said he understood, and it was all right, and to sign them whenever I felt like it.

Little Will came mumbling to the door last night as I was eating a late supper. I told Idella to ask him if it could not wait until this morning and he said not, so

I left my lamb chop and went out. He was quite drunk, and apparently wanted to start out for Tallahassee to bring back one or two of his girls to cook and wash and iron for him, as Bettyrene has had a bellyful and will not be back. I can't quite see his real wife's letting her now-useful girls go to take care of him, after carrying their burden alone for so long. I told him we'd have to talk it over today. He had not cut the grass, which should have been done Saturday. He is in the same mental state as when Alberta left him. I really wish he would just move on. He cannot be trusted alone through the summer.

. . . As soon as I can screw up my courage, I feel I *must* write you about the food at the Dolphin.[2] It is not right, Norton. Besides the poor quality, it is not served attractively. My combination sea food platter was stone cold, from the plate itself to all the items on it. The stuffed crab was almost entirely bread crumbs. If you don't want to use the individual wooden salad bowls, something should be done about the serving of the salad. A small amount is just dumped or sprawled on an over-sized plate and it looks depressing, though the flavor is good. At least a large lettuce leaf under the salad would help. The onion rings I have had there were only half-cooked, and were cold, too. I thought that when the Chef could charge a little more, and had a chance to do things right, that he would serve truly memorable food, and now I wonder if he is capable of it. Also, the flowers have been half dead most of the time I was there. I think the Hustons[3] have gone half-wild with the idea of making lots of money, for you, of course, and are turning every possible corner, and I do not believe it will pay in the end. Lots of people tell you things were wonderful, I know, but I think they are only carried away with the charm and uniqueness of the place itself, and perhaps with your personal charm, too. Don't just take my word for this. Ask some others, candidly. . . .

. . . It is the same old Castle Warden menu, of even lower quality, at a higher price. The Chef had been cutting quality constantly at the Castle. . . .

I am not being "ugly," as you thought when I blurted out that the food was mediocre. For your sake, I want you to make a success d'estime of this thing. . . .

Much love,

1. Variously titled, *A Family for Jock* never reached book length and was instead published as a serial in the *Saturday Evening Post* under the title "Mountain Prelude." Often referred to as the last Lassie story, the work was an expansion of the famous story "A Mother in Mannville." The story, significantly altered, was eventually made into a movie, *The Sun Comes Up* (1948), which highlighted the musical talents of the star Jeanette MacDonald. MKR was given screen credit but had little to do with the script (Tarr, *Descriptive Bibliography*, 267).
2. The Dolphin was the restaurant at Marineland.
3. NSB had taken the Hustons with him from the Castle Warden.

(TLS, 2 pp.)

Hawthorn, Florida

Apr. 4, 1946

Dear Honey:

I was sorry you could not come with the folks yesterday, for Keith and Fanny McHugh proved to be the same sweet, plain people I had known in school, and in New York when they were living on $35 a week. . . . I enjoyed them so much, and it made me feel good to find they were anything in the world but the stuffed shirts I had feared. The Middle West way of life and of thought, to which I was exposed for four years, is a sound and honest one, and the only fault I have found with it, is that it sent out its men . . . with the avowed purpose of "being a success." Yet I think that was the curse of the generation, and the two or three before it, rather than of a section.

. . . I am free to go to the Kentucky Derby!!!! What about you?????? I might *threaten* to go without you, but actually, I would not enjoy it if you were not there. . . . You have owed me some fun for a long time. Early May should be an in-between season at Marineland.

Little Will's trip to Tallahassee (he showed up yesterday afternoon) proved to be for the purpose of getting his actual wife, Fanny, to come back, and he said she is arriving Friday! Time will tell. If it is so, she might be a stabilizing influence, and if he will really work, I can afford to keep him on. He hasn't earned his salt the last few weeks.

Martha rounded up Sissie, and Little Will was back, and Idella had a boy-friend visiting, Timothy, with a nice voice, so we had a good quartet to sing. Timothy knew "Come, Mary," and it was the best I've ever heard it, for on the most enchanting off-beats, he would come in with a deep, hushed whisper, "Tone the bell." You can imagine how effective it was. We ended up all singing like hell together, just the plain old hymns.

All my love,

. . . .

(TLS, 2 pp.)

Hawthorn, Florida

April 6, 1946

Darling:

Phil May is due in half an hour, to work all day, and Scruggs[1] an hour or so later. And I have, at last, a bellyful of Cross Creek intrigue. It's too tough a game for me, and they play for keeps. Too involved to go into, but Mrs. Williams[2] told me that Zelma and Dr. Cason had spent more than two hours at Tom Glisson's on Thursday morning. I had talked with Tom *previously* to the talk with Mrs. Williams, thank Heavens, and while he did not mention their having been there, I really do think all is well. He said he would take the highest pleasure in testify-ing that he and his family felt complimented by my writing of them. He said,

"You've done more for Florida than the Chamber of Commerce." As many of the Townsends as I want will testify, and unless Phil wants more, we agreed on Mr. Townsend and Dorsey.[3] They were so sweet about it. Mrs. Williams jumped at the suggestion that Vincent Brice[4] testify for their family, and said they all knew how pleased I had made their father and mother, and she was sure Vincent would stand up and say so, but I am to see him on his next trip here.

Chet is balking like everything! He is perfectly frank about it, said it would hurt him in a business way, and Talmadge would be terribly sore at him if it made them lose Dr. Cason's business. I asked if it wouldn't take care of things if he was just subpoenaed unwillingly, then he'd have to answer questions truthfully, and he said it wouldn't help a bit. He groaned, "Oh my God, Miss Marge, can't you get me out of it?" Told him I'd talk it over with Phil and see him at 12:30. Mr. Dyess'[5] asking about possible trouble with Tom had nothing to do with me! They have rented their store and he is going in the fish, alligator and snake business, whole-sale, and they think Tom is sore at their encroaching on his territory, and just *hoped* I wasn't friendly with Tom!!!

I am all in.

I don't see how I dare try to go to the Derby. I think I'd better stay right on the pot and play it close to the chest. . . .

Much love.

1. Sigsbee Lee Scruggs, MKR's Gainesville attorney.
2. Grace Flora Williams, wife of Hugh Williams.
3. Samuel J. Townsend and his son Dorsey.
4. Vincent Brice, son of "Old Boss" Brice.
5. Carey Dyess, proprietor of the "juke joint" on Zelma's Island Grove rental property (Acton, 94).

. . . .

(TLS, 2 pp.)

Hawthorn, Florida
Saturday afternoon
[6 April 1946]

Darling:

. . . Phil and Scruggs and I had a most satisfactory session and are well satisfied with everything. We had completed our business and were having late lunch (such a good lunch, superb steaks from Mr. Gay, broccoli etc.) when in walked the Ed Hardy's child[1] from Rollins, with another girl and two U. of F. boys, headed for a formal dance at Gainesville. The steaks were wrecked but I had Idella fix them bacon and eggs and we had a nice visit.

. . . [T]he Derby is May 4, and Phil thinks I need to get away, and should go. Told him I could not go unless you could, and I felt you needed a break in things much more than I do. He and Phil Jr., on furlough from the hospital, are going to Marineland Thursday, and at the same time Phil is taking some St. Augustine testimony, and he is going to try to persuade you to go to Kentucky.

Scruggs talked with Tom Glisson today, and Tom assured him we could count on his fullest support. Scruggs also talked with Chet, who told him frankly that while T.Z. might act as if it was O.K. if Chet was subpoenaed and testified, that Dr. Cason was the most vindictive man in the world, and would certainly not only withdraw his business from DuPree,[2] but would try to get Chet thrown out. . . . None of Little Will's true family showed up yesterday, and he has gone off for the week-end, to Bettyrene, I am sure. Poor black devil.

God, I'm lonesome. Would set out for the beach now, but know you'd only have to excuse yourself to get ice or help or something! . . .

All my love,

The Youngs'[3] barbecue is 1 P.M. Saturday, so save a few hours then.

1. Jean Hardy, who was attending Rollins College in Winter Park, Fla.
2. Talmadge DuPree.
3. Owen D. Young and Louise Young owned "Washington Oaks," once a plantation, now a state park, which is three miles south of Marineland.

. . . .

(TLS, 3 pp.)

Hawthorn, Florida
April 9, 1946

Dear honey:

Up betimes, be Jesus. Little Will has not been seen since Saturday afternoon. Said then, he'd be back Sunday evening. One of the sands-of-the-sea Mickens, Fred, is visiting from Miami with wife and child, and was to help Will and Wilson finally raise Martha's roof—the simple project for which began the whole damn building. I took Idella home yesterday for a party for her newly married sister, and told Martha that if Little Will got in last night, he could collect Idella and Wilson this morning. If not, she could bring me my coffee early, as I'd have to go for them. Never say "early" to Martha if you don't mean it. She was clattering pots and pans in the kitchen at five o'clock, and I had coffee at six. She says Will is a pukey buzzard. And I say the whole thing is her fault. . . .

This ends Little Will, even if he shows up again.

I don't feel too well, just nervous exhaustion. The fluffy-ruffles are blooming, which is some compensation. The new roses not doing very well, need the proper spraying etc. One definite job I gave Will to do last week, was to walk back and forth across grove and pasture, pulling up any deadly night-shade. Walked through the back of the grove yesterday and found it *full* of night-shade. Pulled up dozens of bushes until I got tired. He hadn't even tried. (Had to stop and kill a chicken snake with the fireplace shovel). . . .

Chicken snake not dead, must go and pound some more.

Love,

(TLS, 4 pp.)

Hawthorn, Florida
Apr. 10, 1946

Dear Honey:

... Mae DuPree whom I ran into in Citra after I had taken Wilson home, came home for dinner and the evening with me. Would give anything if she would testify, but she says she simply cannot afford to, with her own suit still pending and in a mess. Dr. Cason is still her doctor, as he is Talmadge's, and he has not taken sides between them, as I have not, and I can see that if she went to bat for me, Dr. Cason might pitch in against her in her suit. Anyway, she gave me some choice bits. Said she was not at liberty to give me details, but indicated that she knows T.Z. is back of the whole thing. Advised me not to pull any punches. The best item, was the fact that Zelma said to her, "Marge paid off everybody in the book but me, and I'm going to get mine." Along with Aunt Ida's report on "I'm going to get some of that easy money," this would seem to establish greed rather than modesty as the seat of Zelma's pain. Mae also told me that in the days when she and Zelma were really intimate, Zelma used to run around Mae's house, in front of Talmadge, in nothing but a brassiere and very thin, short silk panties. Mae said "It is impossible to invade Zelma's privacy. It is impossible to embarrass her." She said, "Why don't you ask Talmadge to speak up about Zelma?" I said I knew he would refuse, as he would figure it would cost him T.Z.'s grove account. Don't remember whether I told you that Scruggs talked with Chet after Chet had begged me to let him off, and Chet said T.Z. was the most vindictive man in the world. The amusing thought occurred to me that I could do a bit of intimidating myself, by threatening to take away MY grove account! Or actually doing so! But they know I wouldn't stoop to it. Doug Whidden would rejoice to have my account and would probably even be honest for a couple of years. . . .

... Wish I could get you on the phone. If the cottage is wet with paint, I might even come over for the Young's party and a visit with you. . . . Haven't talked with Idella about going over. She is acting ugly this morning, possibly because their roof was off last night and the mosquitoes must have made sleep impossible, as I had some in my room. I also sent her in to pick up Wilson this morning, which she seemed to resent, though surely she should realize, as Little Will did not, that it is their goddam comfort I am spending so much money on. . . .

Much love,

· ·

(TLS, 2 pp.)

Hawthorn, Florida
April 18, 1946

Dear Honey:

... Kentucky at that time, at any time, as a matter of fact, can lay you absolutely low with parties. Ed and Lois will have all kinds of invitations, and we can let them accept as many or as few for us as you say. Lois always has a so-called breakfast before the Derby. You get looping by noon, eat Kentucky ham and beaten biscuits, and reel in to the Derby at two. Also say whether you want to go to the races Thursday and Friday before the Derby. I do think it would be nice to save a little time for bridge and just being with Ed and Lois. . . .

It was a horrid cold day yesterday but the Youngs and Cases[1] seemed to have a good time. "Dick" turned out to be Mr. Young's son,[2] in his late twenties, I'd guess. Not impressive.

. . . Phil May convinced Willard[3] the girl's name need not be brought in. Phil said they could have a conference with the judge beforehand to make sure of it. Willard wants to be subpoenaed, and will testify, "reluctantly". . . .

Love, and DO answer my questions.

1. Everett Case, president of Colgate University, and Josephine Young Case.
2. Richard Young, son of Owen D. Young, whom MKR was later to regard with affection.
3. Willard Howatt, a St. Augustine lawyer.

. . . .

(TLS, 3 pp.)

> Hawthorn, Florida
> Monday afternoon
> [22 April 1946]

Dearest:

I went in alone to Gainesville Saturday night to see a movie and happened to hit "The Lost Week-End."[1] I didn't think it was so wonderful. The fixed-up happy ending seemed pretty sloppy to me. Saturday I had all kinds of company. . . . Sunday, I sat here alone the whole blessed day, and not a soul came! So in the evening I went in to the movie in Gainesville *again*, a perfectly lousy thing with Betty Field, "The Southerner."[2]

Had a wire from Phil to phone him, urgent, and went in and called over Doug Whidden's wire. Doug was not there but I left a thank-you note for him. Phil wants me to meet him tomorrow in Palatka to make the Green Sheet visit. He had had my letter telling of our perfectly amazing drink and call, and was so tickled he said he'd never get over it. He said nobody but the Baskins would have handled it that way, and with such aplomb.

While I was in Island Grove, I went by to see Mrs. Cason, and said I heard she had been ill. She turned the subject and we had a visit, chatting about other things. I remembered that I had a bottle of sherry and one of Gordon's gin in a box in the car, from the flock of stuff I had gotten in Ocala for the two luncheons, so I took the gin in to her and told her to keep still about it. She said she'd put it in her cupboard where nobody would find it. She said, "Marge, I really like gin," and I said I did, too, especially in hot weather. She is a cute old gal and I see no reason why she shouldn't have her toddy.

. . . It turns out that Thelma has an enemy, too, but we don't know yet who it is. Someone wrote in to the Post Office Department in Washington, claiming all sorts of absurd things, that she took time out from her job to do other things, none of it true, but the First Ass't. Postmaster General wrote that her permanent appointment could not be confirmed unless she could clear the charges. I have written him, and have written Joe Henricks.[3] Her health is improving rapidly, and she runs the Citra office with complete efficiency. . . .

Ran into Chet at the Island Grove store today, and asked him if he remembered a school teacher named Mary Swan Martin.[4] He said he wasn't sure ————. ????????? Can't think who else to ask, to find out whether she is the one that Zelma got run off. Guess I'd better just write Miss Martin direct.

Well, could chat on, but it is five o'clock and Wilson is ready for me to take him home. Don't dare let Idella tote him too often, for fear that jug-swinging wife of his will pop her one.

Much love, darling.

1. *The Lost Weekend* (1945), starring Ray Milland and Jane Wyman.
2. *The Southerner* (1945), starring Zachary Scott and Betty Field.
3. Joe Hendricks, Ocala postmaster.
4. Mary Swan Martin once taught school in Island Grove.

. . . .

(TLS, 3 pp.)

Hawthorn, Florida
May 8, 1946

Darling:

. . . Idella has been having a high old nigger time. She had not done a scrap of house cleaning, and said impudently that I told her not to do any! She said she had washed the blankets—which I had told her to send to the laundry, leaving money for that purpose. I think she probably got scared after a week of gayety and had not sent the blankets, so pitched in and washed them herself to cover some of her tracks. Two colored men and a colored woman were here. One car drove in just ahead of me, with fishing poles. It is most discouraging.

The yard is a jungle. One of the guests killed a small cottonmouth by the mailbox, where I had just passed.

. . . Don't know what time Phil is coming. There was a letter from him saying Dessie had phoned him and had made arrangements to be here in person for the trial, which made me feel good. He has located the girl Zelma persecuted, in West Palm Beach, and a friend of his there is to see her.

Also a letter from Wilmer, worrying about the trial, saying she thought we out to have Scribner's lawyer come down, as not matter how good Phil might be, the case is unusual and out of line with all his past experience, which is true. But I laughed when she said that she was sure Scribner's would be glad to send him at no expense to me, as they had made so much from my books! Can't you see Whitney Darrow putting out a thousand or more? . . .

Much love, and I do kiss [miss] you so much.

. . . .

(TLS, 1 p.)

[Cross Creek, Fla.]
May 10, 1946

Dear Honey:

I went to Dr. Hook this morning and he gave me wonderful relief. He said the cervix (sp.?) is out of place, and also there is a good deal of inflammation with a fancy name. Anyway, I am much eased. . . .

The Lord sent me the perfect witness this morning. Too long a story to tell now, as I want to get this mailed in Citra when I take Wilson home. Anyway, she has known Zelma all her life, and as chairman of the State Welfare Board, was obliged to flunk Zelma on her first merit examination, and Zelma had it in for her. She will tell all.

Mae DuPree will testify. Chet is in agony. Phil May and Scruggs spent all yesterday here and we saw many of the witnesses, most of whom, especially Snow, will be fine. A letter today from Snow's mother said she wants to help, and having read all my books, cannot see how anyone depicted could take any offense.

Wilson is waiting, so must stop. (Old Will came home.)

Love,

. . . .

(ALS, 4 pp.)

[Cross Creek, Fla.]
Monday A.M.
[13 May 1946]

Honey:

. . . Thelma came out yesterday to report that she had found the missing link in the teacher—Zelma incident, and of all people, it is *Chet's brother.*[1] He took around the petition to brief the teacher, etc. etc. He went to Thelma and said he didn't want to butt in, and maybe I didn't need the testimony but he'd like to be called if I wanted him.

If I wanted him!!!

I'll phone Phil from Ocala today.

Norman Berg came out while she was here, and stayed until after 8, and ate practically a whole fried chicken. I was so glad to see him again and hear about Japan. He reported on his celebration with you, and I said I didn't see why he and I couldn't celebrate too! So we did, but very mildly.

Oh, Thelma gave me an angle on why Chet is in such a state. Dr. Cason has something on him, and I can see how Chet might have visions of his whole life collapsing. Will tell you about it. . . .

All my love,

1. Marvin Crosby.

. . . .

(TLS, 3 pp.)

Hawthorn, Florida

May 31, 1946

Darling:

. . . I had the Glissons to supper with me last night. I wired Nettie and Henry[1] to come to supper last night or tonight if they could, no notice necessary, and as they did not come last night, will sort of look for them tonight.

. . . Noel Moore's[2] wife died last night of a heart attack. I'll go in there today, too, and will go to the funeral Sunday. It will be in the little old-fashioned cemetery near the turpentine still opposite Lochloosa. Incidentally, Zelma always wanted me to go to one of the "cemetery-workings," which she considered riotously funny, and I would not, knowing I would be too tempted, (though I think such a story would have been more poignant than anything else) because I knew it could only offend.

I went to see Marvin Crosby, and he wasn't home, but I had a long visit with his mother. She asked me in confidence if I *had* paid off everyone but Zelma—. She also said information had been spread (I am sure she meant Zelma said it) that Mrs. Slater was dead! She said, "'Twas even told what she died of."

Thelma was in bed yesterday, not only drunk, but am sure she had taken some kind of drug. There was an off odor. She is asking her pound of flesh in payment, and there is absolutely nothing I can do but pay gracefully. . . . Don't think I told you of Dessie's pound of flesh. She asked me to take a bird-dog for the summer, one of Chester's[3] that he can't have wherever he is, as it is near a railroad and the dog howls for an hour after each train, a dog Dessie will hunt this winter. I said I couldn't keep him with Moe, as I had found I could not control two dogs together, and she said it would be OK to leave him with Martha. I didn't expect to begin paying back my debts so quickly—.

Oh yes, I called on Mrs. Abstein,[4] the one who owed me money, and wrote me the note during the trial. She said that while she was a good friend of Zelma and Mrs. Cason, she had been pulling for me, "like everybody else." She said she had never forgotten how good I had been to her.

Have been taking a good big meal once a day to the Basses. Bernie was darning the kids' socks and the place was neat as a pin. Think part of Mrs. Bass' weakness was lack of food. Her mother works, and while she stayed there, she had no one to do anything for her but a sorry sister in law who, she said, wouldn't cook for herself, let alone anyone else. Mrs. Bass said that if there was a can of soup in the house, the sister in law opened it for her, if not, she just didn't have anything at all to eat.

Saw Mrs. Baker[5] in Hawthorn. Bought a crate of Fordhooks and am enjoying them so much. Bought the stove in Citra that Leonard found for me, $50, practically new, just the right size. The Williams' man and his grown son[6] will bring it for me. Had a long visit with Mae DuPree. She told me in the strictest confidence, so please don't tell a soul, that she has seen Clayton,[7] her lawyer, since the trial ended, and he told her "they" paid him $1,000 outright, and for five weeks' work, he felt he couldn't turn it down. He told her he admired me so much, and would she bring him out to meet me! She asked if she could, and I said I'd have to think about it, that it seemed to me he played dirtier pool than was called for.

. . . Everyone says they feel Zelma has had a much-needed and over-due lesson and may be a changed person, and that they think she would welcome my friendship.

. . . And am still eating ham—. And mighty glad it isn't crow.

All my love, darling. . . .

1. Nettie Martin and her son Emanuel Henry.
2. Noel Moore, deputy sheriff of Island Grove.
3. J. C. Vinson, MKR's friend and physician from Tampa.
4. Mrs. Abstein, not identified.
5. Mrs. Baker delivered mail from Hawthorne.
6. Hugh Williams and his son, George H. Williams Jr.
7. E. A. Clayton, associate counsel for Zelma Cason.

. . . .

(TLS, 2 pp.)

Hawthorn, Florida
June 6, 1946

Darling:

. . . Have written a story that is no good, but think I can do it over again and make something of it. Also still think that the book I tore up so often is the one I have to do.

Had a letter from James Branch Cabell. He followed the trial through the St. Augustine Record, and said at first it made him furious, then he decided it was something past Lewis Carroll's wildest fancies and was riotously funny, and hoped I felt that, too, as of course I do.

Will stop, as Idella is going in to Citra to get things for Martha, and am sending a note to Thelma.[1]

1. Thelma Shortridge.

(TLS, 5 pp.)

Blowing Rock, N.C.
Saturday
[15 September 1946]

Darling:

I've missed you just as much as I knew I would. Was glad to hear that you and Idella met in Boone! She said the bus was ready to start, when she saw you, and she called to the driver, "Oh please, let me speak to my boss." She said, "That's the first time I've ever called Mr. Baskin my boss."

She is crazy about it here, and shudders to think she might have gone all her life without seeing the mountains.

. . . Boone has a sizeable colored population, most of them mulattos, with a mountain cast of features! There is a Coloredtown, with four churches, one Methodist, one Holiness Baptist, one Missionary Baptist, and one Sanctified.

The rain has cleared and the sun heats the work-room where I am now, but the valley is full of mist. The heater reaches to just inside the little-room door, and is very cozy. I'll take tomorrow off, and get down to real work on Monday. . . .

All my love, and hurry back.

. . . .

(TLS, 4 pp.)

[Blowing Rock, N.C.]
Sunday morning 11:30
[16 September 1946]

Darling:

. . . The mountains have not been clear since you left. The sun was bright all morning, but it is now cloudy, and the valley obscured entirely.

Idella can go in the balcony at the movie, and we will go to the 3 P.M. show today. The only other show is 9 P.M.! I'm sorry it is closing Wednesday. Will check on Boone, but imagine they have nothing there but Westerns. Asheville comes in very well on the radio.

All my love,

. . . .

(TLS, 4 pp.)

Blowing Rock, N.C.
Sept. 16, 1946
Sept. 17

Darling:

. . . I looked idly at the kitchen memorandum just now, and thought it was Idella who had written, "Write Mr. Baskin," then I recognized your handwriting!

We went Sunday afternoon to see Danny Kaye in "The Kid from Brooklyn"[1] and I laughed my head off, but Idella came down from the balcony with a newly acquired colored lady friend and was very lofty about the "silliest" picture she'd ever seen. The girl rode home with us, and she and Idella busted a gut trying to out-high-hat each other. We went last night to "The Bells of St. Mary's"[2] and of course anyone but Bing and Ingrid would have turned your stomach. Remembering the turtle story, it seemed on the rough side when the housekeeper asked Bing if he'd ever been up to his neck in nuns—.

. . . I started to write to Phil May at Gatlinburg, but stopped myself in the nick of time. Sha'n't even write him at his office, until it is too late for them to forward to him while he's within two hundred miles! I am anxious to know whether the case was appealed. . . .

I got well over my average of work done yesterday. From now on the story interests me, and I hope to go to town. The Charlotte Sunday paper had a movie column that said I was under contract to write a story for Lassie, and gave the terms.[3] I was quite upset, both because I would not have set out to write a story for Lassie, and because I don't want either Phil May or the Florida Supreme Court to know that that much money will be coming in!!!! It only goes to show you that you should never do anything of which you are ashamed. . . .

My love,

1. *The Kid from Brooklyn* (1946), starring Danny Kaye and Virginia Mayo.
2. *The Bells of St. Mary's* (1945), starring Bing Crosby and Ingrid Bergman.
3. "Mountain Prelude." MKR was to receive $30,000 upon delivery of the manuscript, an additional $30,000 at the beginning of filming, with contingent compensation not to exceed $150,000. See letter of 2 April 1946.

. . . .

(TLS, 2 pp.)

[Blowing Rock, N.C.]
Sept. 18, [1946]

Darling:

. . . I found the road to the valley. It is dirt and rock, and I was advised not to try to drive it in wet weather. I walked down it yesterday afternoon after I finished my work, and must have gone a mile and a half, perhaps two. It was extremely steep, very beautiful, and Moe and I were having such a grand time, when I realized I was tired—then had to climb UP again. I expected to be stiff and sore, but am not at all. There is a settlement in the valley named "Globe," and it is 8 miles by road. It rained last night, but as soon as things are dry, I'll drive down.

. . . You remember the chestnut-bark house below us, where the women's voices were so loud? It belongs to one of my favorite high school teachers, Miss Alice Wood. . . .

My love,

(TLS, 2 pp.)

[Blowing Rock, N.C.]
Sept. 19, 1946

Darling:

. . . When I finished my work in the late afternoon, we drove into the valley so low, and finally found Globe. It was a beautiful and exciting drive, not as scary as the one up Grandfather's Mt. or from Banner Elk to Boone, but plenty steep and winding. We bought fresh eggs and saw a saw-mill—I should probably say, seen a saw-mill—where I think we can get kindling. The man who owns the new house won't sell his scrap wood, as he has one of those little stoves himself. It is 8 miles to Globe, but the round trip took nearly an hour and a half.

. . . We went to the last movie of the year last night, a ghastly thing, Margaret O'Brien and fairies,[1] and left the front door ajar, the keys inside, Moe ditto. When we got home, Moe had banged the door shut and locked. By luck, Idella had not latched the back door. . . .

My love,

1. *Our Vines Have Tender Grapes* (1945), starring Edward G. Robinson and Margaret O'Brien.

. . . .

(TLS, 1 p.)

[Blowing Rock, N.C.]
Sept. 20, 1946

Darling:

We have had a slow mountain rain since last evening. The sound on the roof is lovely. The valley and the mountains are invisible. The world ends with the trees that are just across the road. . . .

I am so anxious to know whether the suit was appealed. The Florida paper began coming yesterday, dated Sept. 17, so I have no clue. I think it will be safe to write Phil today!

The story goes rapidly, awful tripe, but I think all right for M.G.M. . . .

My love,

. . . .

(TLS, 2 pp.)

[Blowing Rock, N.C.]
Sept. 21, 1946

Darling:

. . . Yesterday afternoon I took a long walk (down the road below us, which eventually joins the road into the valley and Globe). . . .

The mountain people here at least talk exactly like country Floridians, "git," "kin," "shore," "I be dogged" etc. . . .

My old school teacher Miss Wood came up and spoke to me in the store. Don't know who told her I was here. . . .

My love,

. . . .

(TLS, I p.)

[Blowing Rock, N.C.]
Sept. 22, 1946

Darling:

. . . It looks as though I may have to make a trip to Asheville to run down my two folk songs. Cliff Lyons wrote me that the U. of N.C. experts told him that THE authority on mountain music is there. He also gave me the name of the definitive collection of mountain songs, which he said should be in the library at Asheville. I have written a book store in Asheville to see if they can get the book for me. If they can, and it has what I want, I can get along without making the trip. Imagine Idella would be afraid to stay here alone, and I don't see how I could make the trip both ways and do the work, without an over-night stop.

. . . I have been suffering terribly for a drink. Got along fine for a week, and since, my tongue has been fair hanging out. . . .

My love,

. . . .

(TLS, 2 pp.)

[Blowing Rock, N.C.]
Sept. 24, 1946

Darling:

. . . I had a cheery letter from Julia, in spite of depressing news. Her nausea continues so extreme, that after what she called a cycle of it, she becomes dehydrated and literally starved, and has to go to the hospital in an ambulance for intravenous feedings. She has spent 8 and 5 days at a time in Medical Center. Dr. Damon and Dr. Atchley have given up on her and say she'll just have to spend at least one out of every three days in bed, straight through. There seems to be no danger of losing the baby. She remarked with her customary *pleased* gloom, that the wan and weary mother would no doubt produce a healthy bouncing enormous child.

She simply floored me by saying that she was thrilled that I wanted to be [the] godmother. I had said no such thing, in fact, it had never occurred to me! But I wrote back that it would please me no end, and would probably save hard feelings among all her many friends and relatives up there. She begged me to come to New York this fall.

She also wrote that Charlie[1] had had a wire from Verle, saying Edith was very ill, too ill even to sign her contracts. Please check on this and let me know.

I am still puzzled that you have not asked about the law-suit and informed me. . . .

My love,

Had wanted very much to drive to Boone yesterday to see the movie of Anna and the King of Siam,[2] but told Idella I wouldn't drive that mountain road in that fog to see the premiere of the Yearling.

1. Charles Scribner Jr.
2. *Anna and the King of Siam* (1946), starring Irene Dunne and Rex Harrison.

. . . .

(TLS, 1 p.)

[Blowing Rock, N.C.]
Sept. 25, 1946

Darling:

Woke up cross as a bear this morning, with no idea why. I worked hard yesterday, about 3500 words, and may have overdone it. But when I *can* go to town, I like to make up for the days when 1,000 words about kills me. God, why I am fooling with this tripe—. Yes, yes, I know damn well why. The more shame to me.

Expect my school teacher Miss Wood for dinner tonight. She was the prettiest teacher I ever had, soft brown hair and the most beautiful big blue eyes, gray-blue, and lovely skin, quite young, and I was sure she would marry. She is now a very large very dull lady with white hair. . . .

My love,

. . . .

(TLS, 2 pp.)

[Blowing Rock, N.C.]
Sept. 25, 1946

Darling:

There was a good thick letter from you in the box when I walked down yesterday afternoon.

Well, you wouldn't have been able to find out anything about the law-suit in any case, unless you'd 'phoned Scruggs and Carmichael![1] A letter from Phil May dated Sept. 23 said a letter came from the Scruggs office Sept. 21, informing him that Zelma and the Waltons appealed, on Sept. 14. Phil said there was evidently no notice of it in the papers, and he was most put out with Scruggs for taking that long to notify him.

I think they deliberately waited as long as possible—the deadline of the 16th came on a Monday—hoping it would fret me. I can hear Zelma saying, "Let 'er sweat." And from now on, I refuse to give it more than a passing thought.

. . . Since you said you were dining at Edie's Monday night, I have decided that she just wasn't ready to sign her contract, and said, "Oh, Verlie, please wire Charlie Scribner I'm sick." And Verlie did a good job of it. . . .

My love,

Let's see if I can estimate about when I'll have finished my job—. Have done 75 of the required 150 pages. Have been working out from 5 to 8 pages a day, very occasionally as high as 10. If anything slowed me down to an average of 5, that would make it 17 more days, if my short division hasn't failed me. My God, it has—it's 15 more days. . . .

middle of October.

1. Sigsbee Scruggs and Parks Carmichael, law partners.

. . . .

(TLS, 2 pp.)

[Blowing Rock, N.C.]
Sept. 28, [1946]

Darling:

. . . I take it all back about my old teacher Miss Wood. She is anything but dull, and we had an awfully nice time yesterday evening here. She has kept up with lots of the high school kids who were my friends, and had news of everyone. She is also a great liberal, and in Blowing Rock finds herself a lamb among wolves, although the old conservatives of course think it's the other way around. I don't know whether she has a mortgage on her house or not, but she lives on a pension of $103 a month—.

. . . The story has suddenly turned into the most awful chore. I am practically 2/3 through and have kept up to schedule, know where I'm going from now on, and see where I can make it stretch, and am all but nauseated. It was impossible to do it with Lassie in mind, and give it any literary quality at all.

My love,

. . . .

(TLS, 2 pp.)

[Blowing Rock, N.C.]
Sept. 30, [1946]

Darling:

Well, the cold has finally caught up with us. It is gorgeously bright and sunny this morning, but all of a sudden Idella and I realized we were freezing. I lit the fire in the fire-place, and we have one heater going, and Idella stoked up the kitchen stove, and it is getting cozy. . . .

My love,

Marjorie Kinnan Rawlings. By Permission of the University of Florida Libraries.

. . . .

(TLS, 2 pp.)

[Blowing Rock, N.C.]
Oct. 2, 1946

Darling:

. . . I believe I will have the first draft of my story finished by Monday or Tuesday Oct. 7 or 8. At least, by working hard, I can have it finished then. If you would really enjoy coming up, what do you say you leave next Monday morning Oct. 7, which would put you here Tuesday the 8th. Then we'd have the rest of the week here, for walks and drives, and if you *would* read the terribly dull and uneventful MSS. and give me ideas for things to *happen*, I could get the revision clear in my mind and plunge right into it when we get home. I want to get the damn thing over with and get disinfected—. . . .

My love,

. . . .

(TLS, 2 pp.)

Waldorf-Astoria Hotel
New York, [N.Y.]
Sunday
[1 December 1946]

Darling:

Am so glad I caught you this morning before you left the cottage. I checked with the mail desk, and two letters had gone to the other suite, and they delivered them promptly. This morning I got Deborah Kerr's[1] mail.

Forgot to tell you I slipped away yesterday afternoon and went to the matinee of Katherine Dunham's "Bal Negre."[2] It was one of the most exciting things I've ever seen. The woman is a great American artist. Some of the mulatto girls were so much more beautiful than any white woman I've ever seen! And two of the male ballet dancers were more blond than our friend Cecil—. I sent a note backstage impulsively, and Miss Dunham recognized my name, and I went back for few minutes. It seemed "The Yearling" is her mother's favorite book. She knows Zora Neale Hurston, too. Miss Dunham has the sweetest, *saddest* face. I had a deep feeling of love for her.

Am having dinner tomorrow night with Sidney Franklin[3] and his wife, and we are going to the Helen Hayes show,[4] my very last choice of all, for the play is lousy. Will wait to see if you can get away, and if not, I'll take in Henry V and Harvey.[5] If you don't come, I'll probably leave Friday instead of Saturday. MGM will have to get me reservations home. I understand traffic south is terrific.

I talked to Carl Brandt last night about that Rawlings woman, and she had shown him my letter, too. He said she is not only an utter fool, but he thinks she is actually cold-out crazy. He says they are not divorced. I said that she certainly sounded like the worst possible woman for Chuck,[6] and he said it didn't matter what kind of wife Chuck had, no woman, nobody, could help him. He said he has given up the struggle to get work out of Chuck. It seems Carl nursed him through every story and article, and it was Carl's doings to have him go to the Pacific for the Post, and Carl says he cannot give any one person that much time and energy. Carl looks ten years older than when we saw him. He has been on the wagon for a year.

Let me know if you get an idea for a good title for my story. Mr. Sisk[7] is not going to use the name "Lassie" in the title. He said he finally won the battle to have the dog listed like any of the actors, so that Jock will just be played by Lassie. He and the Post both want another title and don't like "Mountain Prelude."

. . . Well, must bathe and dress to go to Mrs. Scribner's.

Am having dinner Thursday with Charlie and Vera.

All my love,

1. Deborah Kerr, film and stage actor.
2. Catherine Dunham, choreographer and dancer, especially known her combining of African and Caribbean rhythms into modern dance.
3. Sidney Franklin, bullfighter.
4. Helen Hayes, film and stage actor.
5. Mary C. Chase (1907–1981), *Harvey* (1944), awarded the Pulitzer Prize for drama.
6. Charles Rawlings, MKR's first husband.
7. Robert Sisk, producer of *The Sun Comes Up* (1949).

. . . .

(TLS, 3 pp.)

[Cross Creek, Fla.]
Sunday morning
[? December 1946]

Dear Honey:

I am having the most divine morning in bed, with only Tony for company. Even Moe is off prowling. I suppose Old Will is on the road, or perhaps fishing, though it is cold and windy, Martha is in St. Pete, Idella flounced off yesterday for a week-end that I don't think she had coming, Little Will and Betty-Rene went off last night to get drunk, more or less with permission, and came to this morning just long enough to stagger to the pens and let out the ducks and chickens, milk the cow and strain the milk, wash my supper dishes, I shudder to think how, and staggered back again to sleep it off. Peace, it's wonderful. I told them last night to have a good time, as long as they didn't get in jail, wreck the truck, and were able to take care of the stock. By God, they just did make it, which is perfectly all right. I do like to be taken literally.

Idella sulked all morning yesterday and I wondered what was wrong. Toward noon, I said sweetly that I didn't dare use the Ford, and she and the junior Mickenses could agree about what they wanted to do and where go in the truck, and she could get away that evening or Sunday, whichever she'd prefer. She *snapped* at me, *simply all nigger*, "This is my week-end off." I said mildly that I thought she was a week-end ahead, and she had been off all last Sunday. She snapped, "'hat was just something extra you said I could have. This is my week-end." I snapped right back, "Well, take it." You would think she had to fight me all the time to get her *rights. . . .*

Ross Allen stopped by yesterday evening and invited me to go on a week's trip with a scientific group south of Clewiston to explore a set of newly discovered

Indian mounds of most unusual type. Also said that if you wanted to go, we could take an extra Glades buggy, I think they call them. This will be in April and I said it would depend on the time and length of the trial, and did not think you could go in any case. . . .

I told him about Dessie's Alaska project and he thought it would be wonderful but foolish. Said we absolutely should not consider it without a radio set that would send and receive, in contact always with the nearest help. He had with him an awfully nice young chap, just back from the war as a big bomber pilot, whom he is training in the rattlesnake business! I said I could understand how a man who had been doing such safe work would want another cushy job. Smiles. This chap said he was a radio expert and would make a set for Dessie and me if we went. Also said, "If you don't go with her, I can go!" Said I'd introduce them when Dessie came for the trial. It might be a good idea at that. Ross also said the movie company that has just finished filming "Gator Bait"[1] at the Springs, is going in April or early May to the most remote wilds of Alaska to do a nature film there, and he thought between us we could get them to take Dessie along. I wrote her last night about it and it is probably the answer for her, though God help the movie company. Ross is anxious to testify in the suit, though it probably wouldn't be very helpful, as it is so obvious that any and all publicity helps him and he would naturally *prefer* to be written about. However, I do think it might be effective to have as many possible of the people written about say they were glad and proud to be included. Ross said, damn it, why hadn't he ever thought to ask me to pose at the Springs with one of his snakes. What did he mean, "pose with," and with which one and which kind of one of his snakes? Why, *holding* one of his rattlesnakes. I said it was a deal if he would let me name it Zelma. . . .

Love,

1. *Gator Bait* apparently was not released.

1947

1947 was a year of great loss for MKR. Maxwell Perkins's rejection of *A Family for Jock* hurt deeply. Yet there were also constructive moments, as Perkins and MKR plotted out a children's book to be called *The Secret River*. MKR was also delighted to learn that her good friend Zora Neale Hurston was coming to Scribners. "Mountain Prelude," a rewrite of *A Family for Jock*, was beginning to be serialized in the *Saturday Evening Post*. Then, in May, the Florida Supreme Court reversed the lower court's judgment and awarded damages to Zelma Cason in her "invasion of privacy" lawsuit. MKR was ordered to pay one dollar in damages plus court costs. Perkins immediately wrote, expressing his sympathy and distress. It proved to be his last letter to MKR. He died suddenly on 17 June. The telegram was delivered to her at her new summer home in Van Hornesville, New York. Perkins's death was an incalculable loss to MKR. She had lost a source of inspiration, a trusted editor, and, most important, a best friend. She spent the remainder of the year trying to get her literary and personal life in order. The family of Owen D. Young played an important role in helping her deal with the "unspeakable grief." Through all of this, NSB remained her source of strength.

. . . .

(ALS, 4 pp.)

[Cross Creek, Fla.]
Sunday
[16? February 1947?]

Dear Honey:

... My typewriter is broken, the water gave out again, and the battery is dead in my car, and Idella in Reddick with the truck! However, I had a good bath last night *before* the [eye] glasses capsized; Martha ran into Chet Crosby on the road and stopped him, and he will prime the pump when he returns from fishing, and Idella can push me with the truck tomorrow, to go to Gainesville to have glasses and typewriter repaired. Meantime, I am enjoying a most heavenly day here....

My love,

(TLS, 2 pp.)

Hawthorne, Florida
Feb. 21, 1947

Darling:

Before I forget it, do you happen to know the whereabouts of Lamar Josey? He is a nephew of Mrs. Glisson.[1] She said he knew you in India, helped you with your ambulance or something, was crazy about you, and during September, was a baker for you at Marineland. He visited her at the Creek in your station wagon, which must be news to you. She implied that he was a pretty wild drunk. Her father died a week ago, in Georgia, and left quite a bit of property. Certain papers have to be signed, and Lamar's signature is needed. No one has seen him since his visit to Cross Creek last fall. If you can suggest any way of tracing him, it will be appreciated.

... Phil and Lillian didn't get in until after 9. ... We were all too tired to talk much business, but they are coming in fairly early this afternoon to go over things. Phil did say that the Waltons had weakened their case by their false claim that the Supreme Court meant that my admission of having written and published the Zelma material automatically established invasion of privacy.

I can certainly report to the querulous Mr. Berg that my status in the neighborhood is unchanged. Have already been embraced by Mrs. Glisson, Mrs. Carey Dyess, and Mae Dupree, with joy that I am here for a while, all hoping you will be over often. And greeted affectionately by the Hugh Williams.

All my love,

1. Pearlee Josey Glisson, wife of Tom Glisson.

. . . .

(TLS, 2 pp.)

[Cross Creek, Fla.]
Sunday morning
[9 March 1947]

Dear honey:

... Well, I am making some progress. Yesterday afternoon I finished the first draft of the child's book to go with Bob's pictures.[1] I'll work it over just once again, and send it on to Max. He can then tell whether I should simplify it further, for juvenile reading, or expand it into something more adult. As it is, I have fallen between two stools—in fact, tripped the hell over three or four! The story is neither one thing or another, but Max will know which way I should swing it. I could even pare it down to a very basic text to go with the pictures, and use some of the elements in a regular story, though I should prefer to make it, for juvenile use, just as good as possible. I shall never forget something I read when I was writing advertising copy—"Never try to *save* an idea. *Use* it, and a new one will spring up, like a phoenix from the ashes."

I shall hold up the story until I get to the cottage and can have the pictures crated and sent to Scribner's. I feel they should examine text pictures *together*. If the thing goes over, I shall insist that Bob have a royalty, instead of a low flat payment as on the cook book. I am writing Bob to ask how to have the pictures sent, whether framed or not.

Sunday night

. . . They began picking my fruit Friday, and will continue tomorrow, taking everything, valencias and all. Chet and the picking foreman said they had never known the orange bloom to be so late—hardly a sign of it. Just as well, I guess, if it's going to stay so cold.

All my love,

1. *The Secret River* (New York: Scribners, 1955). The Robert Camp illustrations liked by both MKR and Maxwell Perkins were never used. The illustrations were done by Leonard Weisgard.

. . . .

(TLS, 4 pp.)

Van Hornesville, N.Y.
June 22, 1947

Dear Norton:

I have had a hectic Sunday morning. Up betimes, and finding it quite chilly, put on the coffee pot and then laid a fire. I laid two of the long logs on top, and they not only filled the fireplace, but were too far forward, and jammed, and I couldn't move them. All of the sudden *billows* of smoke began pouring out, and in the low-ceilinged house, even throwing the doors wide didn't help, and in a few moments the place was so smoke-filled I had to dash out of doors. For an hour I kept dashing in and out, with my handkerchief over my nose, getting one window open at a time, and trying futilely to push the logs farther back. My bedroom was so thick with smoke that I couldn't see the windows. I finally got one open from the top, and eventually risked hurrying upstairs and opening a window there, and was choking by the time I got outside again.

I thought surely I had ruined Brown's Hollow,[1] but now that everything is clear again, I find no damage done. The smoke was so *clean* that a thorough floor-mopping and dusting will take care of it. . . .

Whoever left the old-fashioned pot-pot in the lower bedroom knew what he or she was doing. I use it joyously, rather than cope with the stairs at night. But getting up the stairs with the pot takes a bit of doing! Be prepared to hear of a *gruesome* accident—.

Yesterday afternoon Louise came down and took me driving around her farms. The houses she has done are amazing. . . .

The Young's insisted on my coming to dinner last night, and I am to go to lunch today, before the Commencement exercises. It seems like an imposition, but the invitations are certainly genuine, and I had a fine time. Josephine and Everett Case were there. . . .

. . . Mr. Young is especially wonderful with his grown children around him, and they openly adore him. When Charles, who must be over 40, accepted brandy after dinner, Mr. Young said, "What a way to raise my children," and gave him an enormous slug.

With all my love,

1. Brown's Hollow, a small farmhouse restored by Louise Young, wife of Owen D. Young, and occupied by MKR for the first two summers she spent in Van Hornesville.

. . . .

(TLS, 2 pp.)

Van Hornesville, N.Y.
June 24, 1947

Dearest Norton:

. . . Louise drove me to Cooperstown yesterday afternoon. She has started me on my reducing diet, and had me stock up with meat. The meat market is swanky enough to live in, and is run by people who have a big cattle farm and dress and age their own meat. The steaks and roasts are superb. One feels all but *stuffed* on the diet, feels well and strong. If you get serious about your pouch, I'll send it on to you. No point in wasting time and letter paper if you're going right ahead eating rolls and potatoes and drinking. The diet takes off at least three pounds a week in complete comfort, and after one is where one wants to be, reasonable caution should keep one trim. . . .

Much love,

. . . .

(TLS, 2 pp.)

Van Hornesville, N.Y.
June 25, 1947

Dear Honey:

. . . I foresee that instead of living this summer off the fat of the land, I am doomed to live off my own fat. I weighed today—. It is incredible to have so crept up on myself. If Louise's rate of 3 lbs. a week loss works out for me, by fall I may feel safe in nibbling a few hickory nuts. I really think I will lose faster than that, as cutting off the liquor makes so much difference to me. I have eaten steak two and a half days, mounds of lettuce with only lemon juice, spinach and asparagus ditto, grapefruit, no salt at all, and tomorrow will be a big day, as I get a hard boiled egg on my lettuce. The next day I have a piece of broiled fish, and I am all excitement.

. . . I almost finished today my article for the Book of Knowledge.[1] It has an August 1 deadline in any case, and I wanted it out of the way.

I was happy to hear from Phil May that the Supreme Court turned down the petition for a re-hearing. Phil thinks the Waltons will try to go to the U.S. Supreme Court but does not believe they can. As long as I failed to make the point for which I was fighting, I rather wish the case could end with Zelma's feeling *she* had won a moral victory. It would save me a lot of annoyance as long as she lives.

I am entirely contented here. Only on a rainy evening like this, I wish you could walk in. You'd have to join me on my diet, and there isn't a *drop* of liquor in the house. I shall keep it that way. My problem will be afternoons when I drop in at the Young's and he is home, and wants someone to take a drink with him. I can probably just sit back and let Louise fight the battle for me.

All my love,

1. "If You Want to Be a Writer." *Book of Knowledge* (New York: Grolier Club, 1948), 247–49.

. . . .

(TLS, 2 pp.)

Van Hornesville, [N.Y.]
July 3, 1947

Dear Honey:

With great self-control, I save my N.Y. paper each day to have with my next morning's breakfast. Breakfast is the only meal I look forward to and enjoy, for in spite of the black coffee, I have a piece of dry toast with a spoonful of strawberry jam. I think I have been taking off the weight almost too fast. Yesterday I had lost a pound and a quarter since the day before, and this morning I feel rather queer and wobbly. . . .

I do think I am going to have a problem in tact when I get down to my book. I thought I had stopped Louise from coming between 10:30 and 11 with my mail, by saying I would pick it up each afternoon when I go to weigh, but she comes regularly. I have become terribly fond of her and enjoy seeing her. This morning she brought with her, her daughter,[1] who is staying with her for a week, most attractive and nice, and an artist. When Virginia saw my papers around the typewriter, a light over it, etc., she insisted they should not come at that time of day, and Louise said, "Oh, *I* don't bother her." I thought it was a good time to get in a hint, so I said it was all right, that I wasn't into hard work yet and when I was, I'd holler.

I found I was suddenly about forty letters behind again—they still keep coming on about the story in the Post. . . .[2]

All my love,

1. Virginia Brown Greene, Louise Young's daughter from her first marriage, was an artist and designer.
2. "Mountain Prelude."

(TLS, 2 pp.)

Van Hornesville, N.Y.

Sunday night July 6 (?) [1947]

Dear Honey:

... The active Youngs have me whipped down today. I took Virginia rambling in the car, and we ended up picking wild strawberries. The next morning Louise took me to her garden strawberry beds to pick for me to make jam. Yesterday morning I made the jam, and if Louise hadn't helped me with the hulling when she brought my mail, I'd have been doing it yet. I didn't wash dishes for three days, and have spent all today cleaning up. I made 24 glasses of regular strawberry jam, and eight little cute jars of the wild strawberry.

The night of the Fourth the Everett Case's had a huge family picnic on top of a hill where they have a cabin, looking over the whole Mohawk valley. Mr. Young's three sons, and Josephine, with all *their* countless children ... were there.[1] The children had prepared an enormous bonfire, and as soon as it was dark, lit it, and everyone sat around and sang. You would have loved it. ...

I am waiting to hear from Charlie Scribner as to whether he wants me to finish the child's book before I do at the other.[2]

The Young's are a marvelous family. I am enjoying being a part of it.

Since he was 9, Dick has "published" a family "magazine" called "The Dumpling," usually only about twice a year. Some of Josephine's poetry has been in it that later went to the Atlantic Monthly, and there is some extremely good stuff in it. Dick told me he world consider a contribution from me. Mr. Young remarked, "What a temptation to reject." I said it certainly would not be anything exclusive if he did, as I had been rejected by the best people. I couldn't resist writing "The Use of the Sitz-bath,"[3] and he used it. I'll send a copy. ...

My love,

1. Phillip, Richard, and Charles Young, and Josephine Young Case.
2. *The Secret River* and *The Sojourner*.
3. "The Use of the Sitz-Bath," *Dumpling Magazine* 11, no. 2 (6 July 1947): 3–7. MKR contributed five pieces to the magazine (see Tarr, *Descriptive Bibliography*, 234–35).

. . . .

(TLS, 3 pp.)

Van Hornesville, N.Y.

July 9, 1947

Darling:

... I think it is grand that you are *liberated* from Mr. Huston. I know how painful the break was for you, but he had bullied and harassed you too long.

Edith[1] has never answered my letter, which isn't like her. How are they behaving about Mion? And do you ever suspect the *faintest* taint of treachery in them towards both of us?

... I wrote Martha that you would go to the Creek as soon as you could, to see how they were. I thought it might help to keep them on their toes about the grass etc. if they expected you to drop in.

... Yes, I read Rebecca West[2] on the Greenville trial without looking at the signature, and half-way through, thought, "Only Rebecca West could do a job like this." Her perceptions are indeed amazing.

All my love,

1. Edith Pope.
2. Rebecca West (1892–1983), *The Meaning of Treason* (New York: Viking, 1947), an account of treason trials following World War II.

. . . .

(TLS, 2 pp.)

Van Hornesville, N.Y.
July 11, 1947

Dear Honey:

... I had a nice letter from Idella, and she said she longed to be here with me and Moe and Benny. She said it was awful, not having anything to do. . . .

All my love,

. . . .

(TLS, 2 pp.)

Van Hornesville, N.Y.
July 14, 1947

Darling:

... I have now lost 8 lbs. Am probably losing too fast, but I can't help it. Without the toddy, I simply have no appetite, and it's the most awful chore to cook my frugal meals, and I eat only about half of what I am supposed to. I have a couple of drinks with the Young's on occasional late afternoons, but it doesn't seem to hurt.

... Norman Berg sent me a copy of the Ida Tarbell biography[1] and it does look dreadful.

The cottage must be ghastly with all that dirty work going on. But it should be fun when they get into the actual building. Don't make the terrace so big that you'll push my studio right on top of the Duponts![2]

Charlie Scribner wrote me that they are going to get out a book of Max Perkins' letters. . . .[3]

Much love,

1. Ida M. Tarbell (1857–1944) was known as the "muckraker" for her sensational articles and exposés. Perhaps MKR is referring to Tarbell's autobiography, *All in a Day's Work* (New York: Macmillan, 1939).

2. The DuPont family owned property next door to MKR's Crescent Beach cottage, which was being remodeled.
3. Maxwell Perkins had died suddenly in June. The book referred to is *Editor to Author: The Letters of Maxwell Perkins*, ed. John Hall Wheelock (New York: Scribners, 1950).

. . . .

(TLS, 2 pp.)

Van Hornesville, N.Y.
July 14, 1947 (night)

Darling:

. . . I have bought a place here! Now wait, now wait, until you hear about it.

. . . The place is the most enchanting little old Colonial house (Mr. Young is going to find the exact date, but it is not much later than Revolutionary at the latest) with several acres of land, the most divine view, and the house is in wonderful condition. I paid $1250 for the whole thing, which included the lawyer's fees for title research etc. I can't describe the house—you'll simply have to *see* it. It is *adorable*. From Louise's many projects, she says that it will not cost one cent more than $2,000 to put in the partial new roof, plumbing, electricity, new plastering etc. Allowing for furniture, picked up here and there, the place will not total more than $4500.

It will make a marvelous vacation place for us, and a work place for me for, say, six weeks, September and half of October, when it is nicest here.

The deal has just gone through, and I *had* to tell you. You will love it as much as I do when you see it.

. . . There are two fireplaces to go in, and while I should rather have liked the local field-stone, that is expensive, and I am having brick, painted white. There are two clumps of peonies in the front yard, lilies of the valley by the door-step, Sweet William gone wild all over, lovely rose-bushes, currant and raspberry bushes, an old hop-house, some beautiful woods that go with the property, a fine well, etc, etc. It is all too good to be true, especially at the price.

The place was so choice that when an enterprising young farmer bought the adjacent farms from a cousin of Mr. Young, he and Louise went to a great deal of trouble and expense to have this place set aside. . . .

I hate to tell you, but it is going to cost so much less to make a little gem of this than to add on to the cottage, that it isn't funny. So when the cottage is well along, come on up and help me find furniture. I *know* you will be absolutely thrilled.

. . . Get your work done and COME ON UP!

All my love,

(TLS, 2 pp.)

[Van Hornesville, N.Y.]

July 16, [1947]

Darling:

I am just back from a trip to our third home. A terribly nice young farming couple owns the land adjoining ours (it was when they bought that Mr. and Mrs. Young got the little old house and some land set aside) and they had some antique things in the house that had belonged to the last owner and resident. There was a lovely old piano, two beds, a spinning wheel, and odds and ends, and I bought them today of [from] the young Fredericks,[1] for a most modest price.

The Fredericks and I are buddies already. They have a registered Holstein dairy herd, milking 75 cows, two hired men, (I don't mean that they milk the hired men) live in the ugliest farm-house, have a gorgeous Palomino riding horse, and are an odd combination. They have two vicious black Spit dogs and a pleasant black mongrel dog, and while the dogs accept me when I get out and go in, I don't know whether Moe will survive or not.

. . . I have begun my book.[2] It does not please me, but the style is more what I have had in mind.

My love,

1. Ellis J. and Lilian Fredericks.
2. *The Sojourner.*

. . . .

(TLS, 2 pp.)

[Van Hornesville, N.Y.]

July 17, [1947]

Dear Honey:

. . . Now Honey, don't let time slip up on you at the cottage about having some of the furniture re-finished. The dressing table and the chest of drawers in our big bedroom need doing over. Also, the dressing table in the guest room and the two small tables with one drawer on which Leonard just slapped some sort of white-wash, need doing in a pickled pine finish. The wood in them is a good maple, and can be finished off nicely. . . .

You seem to be in a hell of a mess as to the Dolphin, so I suppose you won't be able to come up during August as I had hoped. . . .

My beginning of the book proves today, once again, no good at all—.

"Sometimes I sit in front of my typewriter for eight hours, and produce only one line worth publishing——."

I did not find that one line—.

My love,

Editor's note: Enclosed is a drawing in MKR's hand of the Van Hornesville house.

(TLS, 1 p.)

Van Hornesville, [N.Y.]
July 18, [1947]

Dear Honey:

Another love letter from Idella today, and if she gave me an accurate report, that wretched little Aunt Ida is not using the $5 weekly credit I established at Weinstein the way I intended. Idella said that each week Mrs. Tarrant gives her *her list*, and the next week she gets the stuff on her way, and she said $5 doesn't go very far and she often has to put things back after she gets them checked at the desk. If this is the way it sounds, instead of getting good meats and fresh fruits etc. that she has been too stingy to buy, Aunt Ida is simply using my $5 to pay for her bread and flour and coffee etc, staples she can perfectly well afford to pay for herself. I don't know what to do about her. . . .

My love,

. . . .

(TLS, 5 pp.)

Van Hornesville, [N.Y.]
July 19, 1947

Darling:

I guess I'll gloom right back at you. To my notion, a book that won't go is really worse than help that is all too ready to! Mr. Young plied me with his terribly strong drinks night before last, and in my cups I ended up doing what I hate to do—told him my title and my theme. However, after Max Perkins, I think he is the one person I *could* talk to about it. He seemed genuinely enchanted and said it was a beautiful theme, and he saw just what I want to do. He urged me not to bother with style at the moment, but to get it going. I told him I'd rather tear up a few pages at a time than a whole quarter of a book, and that it had to sound right from the very first word—which it does not.

I have just read Josephine Young Case's first book, a long narrative poem that is *magnificent*.[1] I think it rates along with "John Brown's Body." Perhaps you will let me read it aloud to you some time.

I can't see why the breezeway has to be of those dreadful cement blocks. It is covered now with good coquina, and unless you are making a regular Italian pergola of it, a little more coquina, taken if necessary from the walk around the cottage, would finish it. The coquina could have cement in between to make a solid floor. If there was some valid reason against the coquina, for God's sake, use brick.

July 23 [1947]

Did not get to finish and mail you letter Saturday, and on Monday I found myself an orphan at the mercy of the Christians. I woke up Monday morning with as bad a diverticulitis attack as I've had in many a long day. It has happened before when I dieted and didn't get enough bulk. . . .

You are a sweet lamb not to mind my buying the little old place. You will find it just as irresistible as I did.

. . . I had a letter from Martha, and Adrenna is at the Creek, but evidently is not interested in coming back to us, as "she can't give you a definite answer now about working for you because of her work in St. Petersburg." I call that a magnificently specific turn-down from a black sister. Both of Martha's letters have been typed, by whom I have no idea, but presume it is a white person. This letter says, "I know a woman who can do your work as good as Idella, she is very dependable and is middle aged and healthy. She has her health card and can come at any time to work, just let me know when you want her and I will have her here when you get here, you can try her out and if you aren't satisfied with her work she can go back home. She is no stranger to the white folks in Micanopy, her name is Annie Evans."

This is weird, coming from Martha, who has never lifted a hand to get me anyone before, let alone promise someone! . . .

All my love,

---

1. Josephine Young Case (1907–1990), *At Midnight on the 31st of March* (Boston: Houghton Mifflin, 1938).

. . . .

(TLS, 3 pp.)

[Van Hornesville, N.Y.]
July 27, is it? anyway, Friday
[25 July 1947]

Darling:

. . . I feel all right again, but faintly wobbly. To add insult to stomach ache, I didn't lose an ounce during the days I ate practically nothing. . . .

Stuie Crocker[1] and his bride are to spend the night at the Young's. . . . The bride is a daughter of Dr. Barbour[2] the naturalist, with whom I had some correspondence. Mr. Young has been to Washington for the first conference of the citizens' committee on our world loans. It will be wonderful to hear him, if he doesn't talk himself out on the drive up. I am to go in to dinner.

Louise is unbelievably kind to me. I really don't mean to sound querulous when I fuss about her bossing me. Her daughter Virginia said to me, "Let me warn you not to let my family run you, especially Mother. You just have to take a firm stand when it really matters. . . ."

I am working, but it is still bad. . . .

All my love,

---

1. Stuart M. Crocker, vice president of United Electrical Securities and General Electric, and later CEO of Columbia Gas System.
2. Thomas Barbour wrote extensively about Florida natural life.

(TLS, 2 pp.)

June [July] 28, 1947
Van Hornesville, [N.Y.]

Dear Norton:

. . . Do you have the book "Mr. Blandings Builds His Dream House"?[1] I thought I saw it at the cottage. By all means read it. It is riotous, but also scares the pants off you about building. What started out to be his $10,000 house ended up as a $40,000 one! Louise still insists that $7,000 is absurd for the small additions to the cottage. Some of the lovely old places around here can be bought for about $1200, which includes some acreage, and she had been fixing up her places for from $2,000 to $3,000. I may come back owning a third home—. I *love* it here. . . .

All my love,

1. Eric Hodgins (1899–?), *Mr. Blandings Builds His Dream House* (New York: Simon and Schuster, 1946).

. . . .

(TLS, 2 pp.)

[Van Hornesville, N.Y.]
Wednesday morning
[30 July 1947]

Darling:

No wonder I haven't been able to get you on the phone! This is the first I knew that you were sleeping at Marineland. I might have known, with the mess going on at the cottage, but you hadn't mentioned it. . . .

I have lost 10½ lbs., but have just hung there for over a week. Every time Louise makes me stay for a meal, she has such rich and irresistible food that three days of starvation no more than keep me even. I feel grand, and Louise says I look like a different person.

I had the Youngs and Mrs. Powis[1] for supper Monday night. I got a bottle of Hennessey from the hotel for flavoring my mangoes for dessert, and the next day I nobly took it in and left it at the Youngs so that I wouldn't drink it. Louise said she must compliment me. I told her my liquor battle had become serious. . . .

All my love,

1. Julia Powis, the mother of Louise Young.

(TLS, 1 p.)

[Van Hornesville, N.Y.]

July 31, 1947

Darling:

I had a letter from Martha Gellhorn,[1] in Mexico, saying that of course I wouldn't remember her, but she had stopped by our cottage one evening—which struck me funny, as she knows well no one could possibly forget her. She said she wanted to finish a book in the States this winter, and did I know of a house on the beach she could rent. She didn't say what she was willing to pay, whether she would have a car, or whether she would keep house (I imagine so) or take her meals out. . . . I think it would be fun to have her around, and hope we can find something for her. I think perhaps she hoped she could have our cottage, but I only said that we would be in it all winter. I am sure she would want a house with some isolation, at least enough for work. And she spoke of our lovely beach. I don't think she would want to be right in town—unless she has no car.

All my love,

1. Martha E. Gellhorn, a journalist, married Ernest Hemingway in 1940 and was divorced from him in 1945. MKR entertained Gellhorn and Hemingway at the Crescent Beach cottage in September 1940, after a chance encounter at Marineland. MKR "liked Martha immensely" (*Max and Marjorie*, 469).

. . . .

(TLS, 2 pp.)

Van Hornesville, N.Y.

Aug. 2, 1947

Darling:

. . . I had written Julia Scribner saying "Wouldn't you like to run up for a week with me?" and yesterday to my utter horror she replied, asking if by "You" I meant her alone, or herself and Tom, if the latter, they could come from Aug. 8 to 13 inclusive. She begged me to be frank, but of course it is impossible! I said by all means bring Tom if she was sure he would like such a quiet place. I warned her about the Sitz bath. . . . But I am terribly disappointed, and hope it still works out that Julia will come alone. It is hard for me to think of her as a pair.

. . . Aunt Ida doesn't need to squinge [*sic*]. Half the time she calls Roosevelt, "that bastard, excuse me, I just can't help it."

Louise will be away three days this week, and a little later she and Mr. Young will spend a week in Hanover where he has called the next meeting of the Citizens' Committee. PERHAPS I can get my book going then.

. . . Louise has not had too easy a role as the second Mrs. Owen D. Young. A lot of his old friends high-hatted her for years. . . . No woman could have made him a more wonderful wife.

All my love,

(TLS, 1 p.)

Van Hornesville, N.Y.

Aug. 5, 1947

Darling:

... Why are people so *anxious* to have us "separated"? I think it's horrid.
... Have lost 11½ lbs.—....

All my love,

. . . .

(TLS, 1 p.)

Van Hornesville, [N.Y.]

Aug. 6, 1947

Darling:

... I too hope that the cottage will eventually seem like home to me, too. I shall do my very best about it. But something about it has always left me un-satisfied after a certain length of time, and I think it is because my feet are not on the earth there, and I don't see trees around me. If you would let me spend five months up here each year, I think I might be able to wean myself away from the Creek, and spend the other eight months at the cottage with you. I have not been so happy in years as I am here. And this in spite of Louise's activities interfering with my work—.

... I didn't have the expected letter from Julia, so last night I tried to telephone her from the Youngs, and finally talked to Vera Scribner, who said that Julia and Tom had gone off on a five-day fishing trip. This irked me, as I still don't know whether Julia and her Tom plan to come at the end of the week. Oh, well.

All my love,

. . . .

(TLS, 2 pp.)

Van Hornesville, N.Y.

Aug. 11, [1947]

Darling:

... Julia and Tom Bigham arrive this afternoon, Tom to stay through Wednesday, Julia a little longer. They said Sitz bath or no, they'd rather stay with me....

All my love and thanks for my birthday present and wire!

. . . .

(TLS, 3 pp.)

Van Hornesville, N.Y.

Aug. 14, 1947

Darling:

It has been 90 here this afternoon, and Julia and I are just back from lying in the pool in the brook below the cottage. The water is like ice, and at first I thought it would kill me, but we are certainly much more comfortable now. . . .

Tom returned to New York by train this morning, and Julia will drive the car to Far Hills on Saturday. . . . Tom is the slowest man in the bathroom, a regular Grandpa Traphagen. . . .[1]

Tom is really just as nice as can be, and I like him, and think he is really all right for Julia.

. . . The first night, Monday, that Julia and Tom were here, Julia battled all night with Benny. She doesn't care for cats, and Benny of course, when he came in about 1 A.M., headed upstairs to their room.

She chased him from bed to bed and under beds and he never had such a good time. Finally she caught him and threw him out and closed the bedroom door, which opens inside and is not tight, and her story is that it took all her weight to keep him from opening the door, as he hurled himself at it.

I heard a commotion up there and didn't know whether the Bighams were fighting or making love, but felt it was none of my business in either case. The second night all slept soundly, and Benny realized he wasn't wanted or admired upstairs, and then last night Julia had hysterics because she found a beautiful jade-green Katydid in the room. She doesn't mind snakes, but has a phobia about any sort of insect. . . .

All my love,

1. Abram Traphagen.

. . . .

(TLS, 2 pp.)

[Van Hornesville, N.Y.]
[15 August 1947]

Dear Honey:

I sat down and wrote Edie a long letter, giving my reasons, as it seemed to an affectionate outsider, why she should not take this child or any other. Now I have decided that I cannot mail it. It is too personal and important a matter for me even to express an opinion. I am convinced that it would be a ghastly mistake for her to keep the little girl. From what you said, I don't think Verle really wants to adopt *any* child.

. . . Marcia Davenport wrote me from Prague and will be in New York, I have promised Whitney Darrow[1] and his Alice an evening, and so on. Whitney is the great hypocrisy in my life. But I happen to know the terrific difference it makes to writers if they are in his good graces. He wrote me so happily the other day that while they were having to increase the price on one edition of one of my books, they were not asking me to take a cut in royalty, as they were doing with most of their writers. I have nothing tangible against him, and certainly don't actually dislike him. I am merely nicer to him than I would be if he didn't control the Scribner advertising purse-strings—shame on me.

I have ordered Walter's book,[2] and am delighted at your report of it.

(Horrible thought: probably Whitney is nicer to me than he would be if I hadn't had some good sales!)

All my love,

1. Whitney and Alice Darrow, the former a vice president at Scribners.
2. Walter Gilkyson, *Toward What Bright Land* (New York: Scribners, 1947).

. . . .

(TLS, 1 p.)

Van Hornesville, N.Y.

Aug. 16, 1947

Darling:

Julia left this morning, and we both grieved. She is going to come up later for a week, when Tom "makes a retreat" or whatever it is. He is so High Church that he is almost Catholic. She is itching to get back to her photography, and we agreed that even if I was at work, which I hope and expect to be, it would be fine, for she could take my car through the day and go off prowling in search of subjects. . . .

All my love,

. . . .

(TLS, 2 pp.)

[Van Hornesville, N.Y.]

Aug. 18, 1947

Sweetheart:

I'm so sorry I depressed you with my perpetual fussing about Cross Creek. As a matter of fact, I have always been able to work at the cottage, and I think the new studio with its isolation will be the answer to everything.

. . . It is getting mighty lonesome without you. Don't dare begin writing me *notes*. I always feel your letters before I open them, hoping they'll be thick. . . .

All my love, darling, and please don't get so down.

. . . .

(TLS, 1 p.)

[Van Hornesville, N.Y.]

Aug. 20, 1947

Darling:

. . . Aunt Wilmer has enough choice antique furniture in storage for a whole house, and I rather hoped she would offer me the use of it, as she had complained about paying storage, but she only wrote that she knew how thrilled I was in hunting for the right things. . . .

Didn't I write you that Arthur says he will have to give up his expedition business, as he cannot make money at it? He said to be prepared to hear of drastic changes. I am so worried about him. . . .

All my love,

. . . .

(TLS, 1p.)

[Van Hornesville, N.Y.]
Aug. 25, 1947

Dear Honey:

It's only 11:30 in the morning, and the temperature is 86 already. Louise apologizes for the weather as we do in Florida—. "Most unusual." I picked two quarts of blackberries from around the Yankee house, and am burning up. . . .

I saw a notice in the Sunday N.Y. paper about the publication of Walter Gilkyson's book. How I pray that it is good. I'd like to have them here for a few days—they said they'd love to come—but will have to wait and see when Julia is coming.

I have been writing verse—.

Verle[1] just wrote that he is sure he can find a place for "anyone as attractive as Martha Gellhorn" if she will "fix her sights" at around $110 a month. She had written me again that she would go as high as $150, but would like to pay less. . . .

All my love,
Mrs. Norton Baskin

1. Verle Pope was a state senator and a real-estate agent in St. Augustine.

. . . .

(TLS, 1 p.)

[Van Hornesville, N.Y.]
Sept. 4, 1947

Dear Honey:

A gorgeous morning! I was up at 7 and walked down to the brook and found the pears getting ripe. I was so hungry when I got back that I added another scrambled egg to Benny's, and divided with him. Moe ate dog biscuit, looking most abused.

. . . Bee McNeil evidently is not coming at this time. Julia will be here soon.

Do you still think the studio should be the same egg-plant color as the living room at the cottage? I have seen a lovely shade of blue-green up here that would be good if I could match it. With the picture windows, the eggplant might be too much of a contrast. Just how far along are things?

All my love,

(TLS, 2 pp.)

[Van Hornesville, N.Y.]
Sept. 8, [1947]

Dear Honey:

... Idella wrote me, asking me to lend her $25 to pay you back! She said she'd feel better about owing me, than you. It sounds queer to me. I've been such an easy fool with her, she probably thinks she can talk poor-mouth and I'll make her a present of it—as I've done so often before. My soft days with her are over. She wrote that she was getting along "fair," but it was a pity she had to marry a poor man;[1] that she had always dreamed of her own house with a white fence, and now she guessed she'd never have it. She'd have had it if she'd stuck with me. I understand her as little as anyone I've ever known, even including Martha!

I had been doing some drinking again, and my weight slipped up three pounds, so Saturday I took my total stock in and turned it in at the Young's. I had had quite a bit left over from my party. Thought I wouldn't go in at the cocktail hour yesterday, Sunday, both by way of will-power, and not to wear out my welcome there, but I got so suddenly lonesome that I went in, and found everyone else with the blues, and glad to see me. Even Mr. Young was sitting alone in his study, half-listening to the radio, with a sad expression on his beautiful face—the first time I've ever seen him that way. He said that it had been a depressing day but did not know why.

His heavy responsibilities are making a mark on him.

I have begun reading Northrop's "The Meeting of East and West,"[2] which Norman gave me in Norcross. It is heavy going, but as fascinating as Toynbee. . . .[3]

All my love,

1. Bernard Young, Idella's first husband.
2. F.S.C. Northrop (1893–1992), *The Meeting of East and West* (New York: Macmillan, 1946).
3. Arnold J. Toynbee (1889–1975) was in the midst of his twelve-volume *Study of History.*

. . . .

(TLS, I p.)

[Van Hornesville, N.Y.]
Sept. 11, [1947]

Dear Honey:

... Carl Brandt, the dog, wrote me, "And how is the book coming?"

... I am getting my weight back down again, and feel a bit queer.

All my love,

(TLS, 1 p.)

[Van Hornesville, N.Y.]
Sept. 16, [1947]

Darling:

Julia is coming this Thursday to spend a week. Mr. Young and Louise are leaving today, to be gone about ten days, so I'll be doubly glad to have Julia here.

We got water yesterday, at 207 feet—I only have to pay for 189, as part was the depth of the old well—and it is a fine steady flow of 8 gallons a minute, well above the average, they say. The water is ice-cold, and when they finished pumping, it was running clear enough to drink. Getting water and making jelly seem so much more constructive than writing! ...

This is only a Hello, with my love.

. . . .

(TLS, 1 p.)

[Van Hornesville, N.Y.]
Sept. 18, 1947

Darling:

... Have been having a good time with some short stories. Funny, how I suffer over a book, and love doing short stories. If I ever finish this next book, will stop punishing myself and just do stories and verse.

All my love,

. . . .

(TLS, 1 p.)

[Van Hornesville, N.Y.]
Tuesday morning
[23 September 1947]

Dear Honey:

It is a magnificent sparkling day, but my God, it was exactly 32 when I got up this morning. I must say, Julia thrives on catastrophes. Her cold is much better and she is extremely cheerful. I think she would be most disappointed if she couldn't go home and tell about the hell she had gone through in the course of her visit to me. I gave her the electric heater I bought, for her upstairs bedroom, and my electric pad, and I was up early building a roaring fire in the fireplace. A little more water has come into the well here, and we are getting along all right. We both had baths at the Young house yesterday, and Halvor[1] brought down milk cans of spring water for drinking and cooking. Did I write you that I found out that Julia had simply been turning on a faucet in the bathroom and letting it run all the time she fooled around, sometimes an hour at a time? Anyway, thank God for my beautiful 207-foot well at my own house, with its wonderful steady stream of good water.

... Was so glad to have your letter yesterday about the hurricane. I can't help wishing I'd been there, to see the real thing on the coast. Too bad the cottage wasn't ready, so that all the Baskins could have gone there. It is so darned *low* at Marineland, that I was afraid of a tidal wave....

All my love,

1. Halvor Sandvold, caretaker for the Youngs' houses and grounds, who also took care of MKR's gardens.

. . . .

(TLS, 3 pp.)

[Van Hornesville, N.Y.]
Sept. 24, 1947

Darling:

... Your good long letter came today. I read it twice while Julia was taking her bath at the Young's. I don't know when the World's Series is on, but do you think that after you get *here*, and we decide then how we want to divide the time between here and N.Y., will be time to phone a N.Y. hotel, perhaps, and make our reservations? Any hotel where you can get us in, is all right with me. I am so revived, that I enjoy almost everything, and really look forward to the Big City.

I wrote Walter[1] about his book, which I loved, too, and he answered. They do not know whether they will be in Florida this winter or not. When I know more about Arthur's plans, I would be tempted to offer them Cross Creek. If Art is going to spend a long time with us, I'll put him to work at the Creek, a new fence, plantings, etc. If he is making a short visit, we could still take him to the Creek for a few days if the Gilkysons were there....

As I wrote you before, you may attend a Carl-Carol Brandt and Marcia Davenport dinner or not. I must, and want to, do it. Also I want a few hours alone with Marcia. By not having separate time in N.Y., I don't see how I can spare you from spending an evening with Whitney and Alice Darrow. That would be the only chore in which you would have to join me. Julia begs me to go to the antique shops there, as she thinks the prices are much lower than around here.

She leaves tomorrow. We have had an awfully good time, in spite of everything. Yesterday we rode for miles and she took lots of pictures....

I gathered a huge lovely puff-ball from the meadow, and will eat it after Julia goes, as she says it looks like a skull and refuses to have anything to do with it. At least, I am reasonably certain it is a puff-ball—. A large member of the mushroom family, you know. They are delicious sliced thinly and sauteed in butter. If it is NOT a puff-ball, give Benny to Bernice Gilkyson, Moe to Chet Crosby, and look out for yourself—.

All my love,

1. Walter Gilkyson.

(TLS, 1 p.)

Sept. 27, 1947

Dearest Norton:

Now listen, dear, just how livable will the cottage be when we get back Oct. 20? And will the maid's quarters be ready? I had another love letter from Idella, but she didn't say a word about helping me this winter, and I don't think I can consider approaching her. She is such a trickster that I hate to get mixed up with her again, if I can get anyone else. I have no idea about the woman that Martha recommended, in someone else's hand-writing. The old aunt died who was living with Annie Carter and Martha Williams,[1] and I think one of them might come, though I don't know whether for the whole winter. Adrenna is out of the picture. If the maid's rooms aren't ready, I might have to ask Idella to come every day on the bus, damn her soul.

My love,

1. Annie Carter and Martha Williams, whom MKR was considering hiring as maids.

. . . .

(TLS, 2 pp.)

[Van Hornesville, N.Y.]
Sept. 27, 1947

Darling:

. . . I don't know which mother-of-a-son showed up at Ernest's place in Cuba. It was probably Pauline, the mother of his two sons by her. Pauline was the one who took him away from his first wife, her best friend, while living in their house. He had a son by the first wife, too. I imagine that Ernest takes-away very easily ——. . . .[1]

All my love,

1. Pauline Pfeiffer married Hemingway in 1927, and they divorced in 1940. Hemingway's first wife was Hadley Richardson; they married in 1920 and divorced in 1927. MKR is responding to a letter from NSB dated "Wednesday" [24 September 1947]: "When I came in Monday Mr. Hemingway was waiting to say hello. It was too early for lunch but we decided to have a small cut or two and he stayed for the two o[']clock buffet. I enjoyed him very much but should never try drinking with him. He walked out in fine shape and I was left talking to myself. He asked about you and your work and I told him that you were up there and had not been able to get into your book. He asked me if you were afraid of it and I told him I did not think so. He said[,] 'You know when you have done a tremendous job like Marjorie has you sometimes get scared and think you can't——you can't——. You tell her that.'" Norton then reports that Hemingway was worried about his oldest son, Patrick, who was suffering in Cuba from the effects of an automobile wreck in Miami, which is what MKR is referring to in her response.

(TLS, 2 pp.)

[Van Hornesville, N.Y.]

Oct. 1, 1947

Darling:

I'll write you a note, to try to calm my shattered nerves. This is really and positively the last time I shall ever agree to speak in public. I have suffered more over the Colgate commitment than usual, because I don't want to let down Dr. Case. . . .[1]

My love,

1. Everett N. Case, president of Colgate University, 1942–1962.

. . . .

(TLS, 3 pp.)

[Van Hornesville, N.Y.]

Oct. 3, 1947

Dearest Norton:

. . . The morning talk went off all right. The chapel was full, a thousand or more, and it was a grand audience, mostly G.I.'s. Dr. Case had been a little anxious that I might not have very many people. I should love to have gone into my real song and dance, telling Leonard's stories, etc., but the chapel, and organ music beforehand, cramped my style. But I worked in some good clean fun, and the boys broke into applause now and then. Josephine[1] had a big luncheon party, and in the afternoon I had an intimate session with the boys interested in writing— no faculty allowed. The faculty arrived at the end, and there was tea, and I took it as a compliment when the boys groaned as the Dean came in to say that we had used up our time. Boys, my eye, they are men of the world, and I am sure I got more stimulation out of the session than they did. They floored me with many a question. There were about 25 there, and three or four, I am sure, really have something.

. . . The Case's invited us to the Cornell-Colgate football game, played at Colgate a week from tomorrow, Oct. 11. But I suppose you would have to make your pay-roll first. You would love the place, if you can arrive by then. . . .

My love,

1. Josephine Young Case.

(TLS, 2 pp.)

[Van Hornesville, N.Y.]
Oct. 4, 1947

Dearest Norton:

. . . The coloring this autumn is not going to be spectacular, as the sudden *freezes* when the sap was high in the trees, froze the leaves of many varieties, and it will be mostly the maples with color, against a background of brown trees.

. . . Darling, I do think we should call the new beach mansion *your* house. After all, I have two more houses, and you have put more into the cottage than I. If it is your house, you might be home oftener for dinner!

I wrote Martha, as I think I told you, about checking with the colored woman she had recommended. I received the following pencil-written letter yesterday, done, I am sure, by Old Will, and I'll copy it for you and then give you the translation.

October the 10/1/1947

Mrs. Basket i have receve you letter an glad to hear from you an Mr basket we an so well at the tim Presen but i hop you both ar well an the woman i tell you about she is nam annie even an she is a nise woman an the cow is jumpin the fence an i dun al i can to keep them out an i tell the Hamon a bout them an the an don nothen about it yeat i do wosh you was hear Nothen more to say from

Martha Micken

Translation

Mrs. Baskin, I have received your letter and glad to hear from you and Mr. Baskin. We ain't so well at the time present, but I hope you both are well.

Shucks, you can translate the language as well or better than I. . . .

My love,

. . . .

(ALS, 4 pp.)

[Harkness Pavilion]
[New York, N.Y.]
Friday Nov. 14, [1947]

Darling:-

I'll 'phone you tomorrow afternoon as planned, and will have definite word by then. At the moment it appears that the week's checks and tests are wasted time and money, and that the original plans for operation will have to go ahead. The doctor who finished up the intestinal X-rays etc. etc. with the examination in which you stand on your head and have a locomotive run up your rectum with the headlights on told me that while there are slight scars etc. from previous diverticulitis, that part of me is now in wonderful shape, the lump in my side has nothing to do with the intestines. . . .

Today was unpleasant, with so much blood being taken for tests that the intern had to switch from one arm to the other, nothing but coffee for breakfast, consommé and tea for lunch, and *four* enemas before the final examination. I wrote a sonnet between enemas.

I still don't think I care to do anything over the week-end. It is bitter-cold and windy and the world is not nearly so friendly a place as this comfortable room with Charlie's white orchid sprays, the river view and the nice nurses. The luxury is insupportable, but I am bearing up bravely. When I came back from the tail-probing two nurses were scurrying around bringing me tea and sandwiches, though it was nearly dinner-time, so afraid I'd be *hungry.* I felt so guilty about it all.

. . . Marcia Davenport also came to see me last night, bringing an armful of new magazines. . . . I still think there is no point in your coming up, unless possibly to take me home. I am adjusted, and it would only make me lonesome to have you come and then go away, and I know you couldn't stay for ten days or more. Dr. Atchley would let you know if I got desperate and sissified.

All my love,

. . . .

(ALS, 2 pp.)

Harkness Pavilion
[New York, N.Y.]
Monday Nov. 17, 1947

Darling:

. . . Julia came yesterday afternoon and we went to the Italian movie "Shoe Shine"—heart-breaking. . . .[1]

All my love,

Editor's note: Written at the top of page 1: "I don't want Idella and Bernard being too free with my car, but if they go to Reddick they could bring back the butter. Get the pkgs. or have Idella get them for the butter and put it in deep freeze. It does not keep in ordinary box."

1. *Sciuscià* (1946), directed by Vittorio De Sica.

. . . .

(ALS, 4 pp.)

[Harkness Pavilion]
[New York, N.Y.]
Sunday afternoon
Nov. 23, 1947

Darling:

I was so happy to have you call this morning. Just now and then your voice would sound far away and I would miss a few words. . . .

Vera Scribner sent me the most spectacular flower arrangement—2 purple orchids, with lavender spikes behind them, some japonica twigs, and in the foreground forget-me-nots and pink rose-buds. A nice note with them asked me to "convalesce" at Far Hills before going home. Marcia also asked me back, and Gladys Lyons wrote begging me to take the plane to Durham and convalesce with them. You can imagine how wretched I should be anywhere but home.

. . . I do wish I could give you a definite day right now. One reason I cannot, is a complication that popped up out of the blue. I decided not to tell you about it over the 'phone, as you would worry *needlessly*, and I will be perfectly comfortable by the time you get this. We discovered a small cyst in each breast just *yesterday*, and they will have to come out (the cysts.) Dr. Atchley says it is "nothing at all," not much more than a surface incision, almost no scar. . . . The surgeon says it may not delay me at all, and in any case, probably no more than another couple of days. Dec. 2 would be the *minimum* 14 days in which they would let me out, so Dec. 2 to 6 will probably be about the time. You can understand why it is impossible to set a definite day right now. They will do the word on the cysts Tues. or Wed. I'll know tomorrow. I won't have to have much anesthetic and it only takes a few minutes.

I must admit I was floored by the *belated* discovery of this, after a solid week of tests and X-rays etc, but it seems they would not have considered doing the two operations at the same time, anyway. I'd much rather have the harder one behind me. And I told Dr. Atchley this morning that by God, we *knew* these weren't diverticuli.

There seems nothing left on which the boys can conceivably whittle. Julia said "*Surely* they'll discover hemorrhoids just as you're leaving."

Also have meant to tell you that everyone at the Scribner's week-end with the exception of the Colonel was crazy about you. But if Vera thinks I'm going to convalesce there so she and her pals can have another good time (with you), she's crazy. Anyway, I was glad to have my own feeling corroborated that you have been *most entertaining* not *at all* objectionable, as you feared.

My nurse is wonderful, and sort of breaks my heart. She is middle-aged and so dumpy and ugly and trots home each evening to her solitary tiny apartment, where the first thing she does after she puts her supper on to cook, is to go down to the basement and divide a can of cat-food among 3 alley cats that are waiting for her every day. When the war ended she went down to Times Square all alone and watched the crowds. A big treat is to take the Subway down to Macy's and spend an hour just looking. A nurse, she says, that brings a cold bed-pan oughtn't to be a nurse. She heard "the wedding" over the radio. "The Princess' tararrah [*sic*] was all shining."[1]

All my love,

1. On 20 November 1947, Princess Elizabeth, now Elizabeth II, married Philip Mountbatten, now the duke of Edinburgh.

(ALS, 4 pp.)

[Harkness Pavilion]
[New York, N.Y.]
Friday Nov. ?
Day after Thanksgiving
[28 November 1947]

Darling:

I suddenly *relaxed* yesterday afternoon for the first time. I had as usual been minding everything more than I let on. Now that my worries are definitely over, I shall make quick work of the rest of the convalescence.

They took the stitches out of the abdomen this morning, and the scar etc. is fine. The breast stitches come out next Tuesday. If the healing has not gone fast enough there, there would still be time to wire or 'phone you and have you post-pone the reservations home. But that part will probably be all right, too. I *could* move a lot more than I am allowed to at present, but Dr. Haagensen in anxious to keep the breast scars as inconspicuous as possible. I have really taken a bit of punishment through not having a night nurse, except for the first night after the breast operation. It makes me rather cross at our beloved Harkness, for the other hospitals don't have any trouble in getting special nurses right around the clock. . . . Thank Heaven for Miss Rogers—8 to 4.

I had asked Dr. Atchley whether to tell you in advance about the breast opera-tions, and while he usually believes in telling everybody everything, he said in this case he considered it better not to upset you ahead of time. He was afraid you would think "This is *too* much" and would take a 'plane up, not be able to do me a bit of good right then, etc., and he felt it was more important for you to be here to take me home.

The operation took longer than expected, but they kept me under pretty light anesthesia anyway, so much so that Miss Rogers said I kept up a running conver-sation with the anesthetist most of the time. What they thought a small cyst in the left breast proved to be large and deeply embedded, and that took 50 minutes, and the larger one on the right breast was at the surface and only took 20 min-utes. As I told you, I had a cup of broth that noon and ate a light supper that night. I do remember coming out of the anesthesia back in bed and yelling "My titties hurt!" but Miss Rogers says only Dr. Atchley was here, so it was O.K. . . .

Am enjoying "The Root and the Flower[1] so much. . . .

Well, a week from today! I have had enough Harkness for once!

All my love,

1. L. H. Myers (1881–1944), *The Root and the Flower* (London: Cape, 1935).

1948

1948 was a year of foment. It began with MKR once again taking up the plight of blacks. Her recognition of her own racist tendencies and those of her friends plagued her. She found herself engaged in frequent arguments, once with the governor of Florida. In April, she accepted an invitation to speak at Fisk University, which was then a black institution, and made the point of staying in the home of its president. During this period, she wrote another "Lassie" screenplay for MGM, with the working title *A Bad Name Dog*. The screenplay was rejected by both MGM and the *Saturday Evening Post*. MKR continued to work on *The Sojourner*, again without much success, and in September she had another bout of diverticulosis. In November, she considered writing a sequel to *Cross Creek*, but that project was quickly shelved. NSB managed to cheer her up during the holidays with thoughtful gifts and much-needed attention.

. . . .

(ALS, 4 pp.)

> [Van Hornesville, N.Y.]
> Sunday Noon
> [13 June 1948]

Honeybunch:

. . . I am sitting by the fire and doing the Sunday puzzles—very faintly, so that I can rub them out for Mr. Young to do while he sits on the john, which the totally irreverent Louise informs me is his morning habit.

That Louise!!! She says *proudly* [underlined twice] that she is no housekeeper, which is the grossest understatement. For three days I have been unable to use the cream in my coffee, because of the most putrid taste and odor. Everything in the Frigidaire has been all but unusable. . . .

No laundry had been done since Louise reached here. . . .

Betty and I went through the house gathering up the washing, and I was appalled when we reached the two Young beds (left un-made) which I thought they used separately. But no!!! Never say *again* [underlined twice] that Moe is spoiled in being allowed to use a couch.

. . . Owen D. and Louise share a 3/4-width bed with a stone-hard, lumpy old mattress——and dirty bed-clothing——.

They eat on a dirty cloth in the kitchen——. We have had dinner twice in the dining-room, once when Miss Freeman[1] was here. Louise glories in her cooking, which is really very good. I can assure you that you will not be imposing on her if we both stay here for the two probable days of your visit to Van Hornesville. She wants praise and appreciation, that is all—and *loves* [underlined twice] company that will give it.

. . . Miss Freeman told me *fascinating* [underlined twice] things about the Cabells—. . . .[2]

My love,

1. Margaret Freeman, later the second wife of James Branch Cabell.
2. James Branch and his first wife, Priscilla Cabell.

. . . .

(ALS, 2 pp.)

[Van Hornesville, N.Y.]
Monday Morning
[14 June 1948]

Darling:

. . . I 'phoned Julia's apartment yesterday, and Edith[1] answered. She plans to leave for Florida this Tuesday, disgusted by not having had any fun in New York. After a *long* [underlined twice] chat, she said casually "Julia's here. Would you like to speak to her?" This rather floored me, as my original intention had been to speak to Julia—

Henry Heyl 'phoned here yesterday, from Amsterdam, N.Y. I have no idea how he reached me or knew I was here—he said he had a hunch I was "in residence." He begged us to "run over" to Vermont to spend some time with them this summer or fall. I was very stupid and did not realize until later that Amsterdam is only about 40 miles away, and I could easily have asked him, or them, to come here and then have taken them to the Sportsmen's Tavern for dinner.

Miss Freeman is a Virginian "Lillian May,"[2] particularly with other people. . . .

I woke up in the night, and my book suddenly appeared in complete focus. So I shall tell Carl Brandt that I can't be bothered with going to bed for 50 or 60 thousand dollars, and I cannot wait to get to work. I shall probably be more impossible than ever for some time.

My love,

1. Edith Pope.
2. Lillian May, wife of Philip May.

(TLS, 3 pp.)

Van Hornesville, New York

Aug. 27, 1948

Dear Honey:

. . . Idella is crazy about it here. She said she couldn't understand how I could bear to leave it. And has she worked.

. . . Idella says please tell Bernard[1] she has been too busy to write him, but she will do so as soon as possible.

Wish you were here. You would have a heavenly time.

Much love,

A frantic cable was here from Marcia,[2] saying by no means to allow mention of Masaryk[3] at Cross Creek, and to cable her the address of the Czech translator. Of course, I left that at the cottage, so wired Carl to take care of things.

1. Bernard Young, Idella's husband.
2. Marcia Davenport.
3. Jan Masaryk, Czechoslovakian foreign minister, about whom MKR said, "[He] has one of the most magnificent minds and spirits I have ever met" (*Selected Letters*, 291).

. . . .

(ALS, 2 pp.)

Van Hornesville, New York

Monday 9:15 A.M.

Aug. 30, 1948

Dear Honey:-

. . . Could not have managed without Miss Freeman, but will be so glad when she leaves tomorrow. She just happens to get on my nerves terribly.

. . . Carl Brandt 'phoned me at Louise's and said not to worry about Marcia and the Czech translator, that she gets upset these days about everything.

Much love,

. . . .

(TLS, 2 pp.)

[Van Hornesville, N.Y.]

Sept. 2 [1948]

Darling:

. . . At 6 yesterday evening all the clan gathered at the Everett Case's house for their annual exhibit of work done in 1947, prizes being awarded. Some of the work was serious and important, other pieces were silly or touching. I entered a minute jar of wild strawberry jam, with the notation, "Total Work Accomplished for 1947."

... Idella's husband Bernard was to go to an Army hospital for treatment of his stomach ulcers. This would perhaps explain her tackling you for $25.

I have made absolutely no provision for maid's quarters at the Yankee house, as even if Idella and I get together for the winter, colored help up here would be out of the question, and I plan just to have someone from the neighborhood come in to clean up when we are here.

All my love,

. . . .

(TLS, 2 pp.)

Van Hornesville, New York
Sept. 2, 1948

Dear Honey:

I knew it was Norman and Julie who are all out for Wallace.[1]

I had the most violent intestinal attack the morning I took Miss Freeman to the train. Did not see how I could possibly drive the car. It vanished (the attack, not the car) half an hour after her train pulled out—.

Bee McNeil and her friend arrived that afternoon. They had rented a car in Boston. We had a perfectly lovely time together but they had to leave this morning, too short a time. Bee has aged but is her wonderful gay self.

... It turned cool while Bee was here and Idella had kept lovely fires going.

... Idella is all right here. Mary Sickler brought her entire family to call one evening, and they all became great buddies with Idella.

Oh, it is divine here. . . .

All my love,

1. Norman and Julie Berg. Henry A. Wallace in 1948 launched the Progressive Party to oppose Harry S. Truman, whom Wallace blamed for starting the Cold War.

. . . .

(TLS, 1 p.)

Van Hornesville, New York
Sept. 3, 1948

Dear Honey:

It is wonderful to be alone here. Today I finished a bit of verse that I began last summer, and tomorrow I shall get down to real work. . . .

Much love,

(TLS, 4 pp.)

Van Hornesville, New York
Sept. 4, 1948

Darling:

I thought I *did* write you what looks well at the house, and what doesn't. You would have been wild with joy to be here for the big arranging—and if you had been at the two-day auction, would have bid on everything in sight.

. . . The day I was gone so long at the auction, Idella reported she thought she would die of lonesomeness. Mary Sickler told me this morning that Idella . . . was lonesome. Mary said "I hope she gets good and lonesome and goes home, and then I can come back to you." However, am sure I wrote that the Sicklers all liked Idella very much. The Egans[1] invited her to come down and spend an evening with them. There is evidently no color prejudice.

My God—Louise has just been here . . . has simply torn my place apart. . . . It will take Idella and me an hour to get things straight again. She has taken Idella off to show her Van Hornesville, and I am to follow. Idella said dubiously to me, "Please don't be too long, Mrs. Baskin."

Yes, the Hodding Carter[2] articles have been good. . . .

My love,

1. Margaret and Martin Egan. The former served as a nursemaid for the Youngs and later as a maid for MKR, and the latter was a contractor who did most of the restorations on MKR's home.
2. (William) Hodding Carter II, southern journalist whose editorial efforts to combat racial inequity earned him the Pulitzer Prize in 1947.

. . . .

(TLS, 2 pp.)

Van Hornesville, New York
Sept. 6, 1948

Dear Honey:

. . . I went to the Phillip Young's picnic but did not stay for the dance—slipped away, I thought, quietly. Louise discovered me gone and raised a great hullabaloo. As Faith said coldly yesterday, "No one would have missed you otherwise." Louise and Mr. Young drove up here just as I had started undressing for bed. I brought out the bottles and lit all the candles and we had a lovely private house-warming.

Yesterday Idella took the older two Sickler children to the movies in Fort Plain, and I played bridge at Louise's, then we went to the Family show. Louise had me stay to dinner afterward, and as Idella was waiting, she was invited, too, and helped Gertie,[1] the occasional cook. Idella waited on table very nicely and washed the dishes. Idella and Gertie are together cozily.

Louise has a strange artist friend staying with her, Mrs. Leonabelle Jacobs.[2] She is stout and wears spectacular Hawaiian prints and large costume jewelry and her hair is marigold-color. She says she knows you, but you wouldn't remember her. She may have stayed at the Castle Warden. She plays good bridge. And she can really paint.

. . . Now darling, please come up here at the time that suits you best. The movie story[3] is the sort that can be taken up and put down, with no damage done. I do want to stay into November, and as I said, you would hate the trip with Uki yowling so.

All my love,

1. Gertrude Sandvold, wife of Halvor Sandvold, was also a cook for the Youngs.
2. Leonebel Jacobs, a portrait painter.
3. *A Bad Name Dog*, which was later rejected by both MGM and the *Saturday Evening Post* (Tarr, *Descriptive Bibliography*, 267).

. . . .

(TLS, 2 pp.)

Van Hornesville, New York
Sept. 7, 1948

Dear Honey:

. . . Josephine and Everett Case and 9 assorted children came yesterday for the viewing. They were wild about the house, and Everett played the most enchanting Bach and Mozart on the old piano. I said of the first piece, wisely, "Ah, Mozart!" and of the second, "Ah, Bach!" Everett said, "You have the composers right, but just reversed."

I am sending you a wonderful issue of the ATLANTIC. Don't miss a thing in it. An article against Wallace, and an answer to it in the front part, a story by Martha Gellhorn, and several other fine things.

Did I tell you I read aloud to Bee and Ada, most of "At Midnight on the Thirty-first of March?"[1] They wouldn't let me stop. Bee is so emotional, and was on the edge of her chair. . . . Josephine was pleased when I told her.

All my love,

1. A poem by Josephine Young Case.

. . . .

(TLS, 1 p.)

Van Hornesville, New York
Sept. 9, 1948

Dear Honey:

A handsome and extremely cross young man installed my telephone yesterday afternoon, all alone, in exactly four hours, including having to cut off large tree limbs for passage of the wire. I should have made my first call to you, but knew you would be on the Creek trip. The number of Mrs. Norton Baskin, Res. Van Hornesville, is Richfield Springs, N.Y., 337 F 2.

I made my first call to Mr. Young.

Charlie Scribner writes that he agrees thoroughly about eliminating Zelma entirely from "Cross Creek" and substituting another character in the next and subsequent editions. Whitney agreed, too.[1]

Carl Brandt passes on a snappish note from Mr. Sisk,[2] saying that they have been waiting for the Lassie story, and don't even know what it is to be about, and if they don't get something soon, will have to go into production on something else. I shall really try desperately to get it finished within a month.

. . . Much love, and if you don't hear from me so often, it will mean that I am getting work done—and you can 'phone me. Early morning or late at night would always catch me.

1. No such alteration of *Cross Creek* was done.
2. Robert Sisk, a producer at MGM.

. . . .

(TLS, 2 pp.)

Van Hornesville, New York
Sept. 11, 1948

Dear Norton:

Leonabelle and I have become friends, after what she reported the other night had been a most unpropitious beginning. It seems that when I was first introduced to her, I told her she looked exactly like a parrot. Of this, I had no memory, only a dim sense that I had done something wrong. I thought Mr. Young would have convulsions. He took a startled look at Leonabelle, and I suppose realized, as I did, that I could not have been more accurate if I had studied her for four weeks.

Louise invited Idella and me for dinner last night, and told Mary Sickler she wouldn't need to come to help Gertie the cook with the dishes, as she has been doing. She said Mary burst into tears! There were ten of us at table (Louise upstairs in bed, of course) and Idella served with style and service plates and hauteur, in her best gray uniform and white organdy apron. . . .

My love,

. . . .

(TLS, 2 pp.)

Van Hornesville, New York
Sept. 13, I think [1948]

Dear Honey:

Idella is beginning to be a little anxious about getting home. I finally made contacts for her yesterday, with the very nice colored servants of Sen. and Mrs. Stokes.[1] Louise told me to go right ahead and barge in. I had forgotten that I had met them at her formal dinner last year. I 'phoned, and they were waiting for me, most cordial. I had a pleasant visit with them on their fabulous pillared piazza, while Idella did her visiting.

... I do want to finish my movie story before she [Idella] leaves and before you come. I am working steadily on it every day, and two weeks more should see the first draft finished. Possibly even less, if I hit a burst of speed, as I did in Carolina. Then a week more for revision and copying.

By that time, the foliage should have at least begun to turn.

Once the story is out of the way, I'll feel more independent about everything.

... Will work just as fast as I can. ....

All my love,

1. State Senator Walter W. Stokes and Hannah Stokes of Cooperstown.

. . . .

(TLS, 4 pp.)

[Van Hornesville, N.Y.]
Sept. 17, 1948

Dear Honey:

... Louise came to life when Mrs. Ambrose Clarke[1] asked us for luncheon and bridge yesterday. Said she could go if I would do the driving. .... She warned me that Mr. Clark(e?) out-Britished the British. Mrs. Clark is cute as can be (played bridge with her last summer) and I like her immensely. Louise said they have so much money they can't begin to spend the income. (Clark Thread and Singer Sewing Machine.) I asked what they did about income tax, and she said they probably didn't have any—everything is in tax-exempt bonds. A bit annoying, eh, what? ...

All my love,

1. The Clarks were among the most prominent citizens of Cooperstown, supporting everything from the Baseball Hall of Fame to the Glimmerglass Opera.

. . . .

(TLS, 2 pp.)

[Van Hornesville, N.Y.]
Sept.? Anyway, Friday evening
[24 September 1948]

Dearest:

I have been in the most amusing mess all week. I just had to wait for Idella to leave, to have an old-fashioned intestinal attack, the kind for which I used to go to the Riverside Hospital. ....

I do think I could have worked on my long story yesterday or today, in spite of everything, but the research material I asked Carl Brandt to have done for me, on the un-training of war-dogs, and which he wrote he had sent three or four days ago, simply has not come. ....

I had reached a point in my plot where I needed to be accurate.

I do want to get the beastly thing done in a hurry.

. . . I imagine that Idella will be at the cottage at least long enough to go to bed with Bernard. Please—no, how silly, you won't receive this until after she has come and gone—if she was sincere in saying that she wanted to come back here for another month. . . .

. . . Should not write you about my troubles, as they are bound to be over and done with by the time you receive the tale of my woes.

Anyway, wrote what may be a good bit of verse while I have been under the weather. And I swear to God, no more POST or Hollywood stories—.

My love,

. . . .

(TLS, 3 pp.)

[Van Hornesville, N.Y.]
Sept. 28, 1948

Dear Norton:

After your welcome call last night, I went to bed with a book. Idella planned to retire early, too. Uki[1] had not come in. Idella called him again and again. I decided he was punishing her, as he had me, for leaving him. So a little before ten, when I was ready to go to sleep, I went down myself. I had on bedroom slippers, a thin silk bed-jacket, and my very best pink satin nightgown, which is as long as an evening dress. I called Uki from the back, then walked around to the front of the house and called again. He answered at once, in his loudest and most anguished voice—and from a great distance. I thought at first he had gotten caught among the boards where the old barn was taken down, and I walked that way, calling. He answered every time, and I realized he was farther away than that. I went back to get the flash-light, and Moe,[2] and had to wake up Idella, as I couldn't find the flash. Its light was faint, so we added matches and candles and all got in the car and started down the road that leads up Mt. Tom. I stopped every few feet and called, and as Uki answered, it became clear that he was somewhere up the Mount. I took the flash and set out alone, but Idella insisted on coming with me (she in corduroy house-coat). Moe, the sissy, stayed in the car, wanting none of it, but I made him come, to help track down Uki. Well, there are the remains of barbed wire and an old stone wall between the road and the big field at the foot of Mt. Tom, and I have had to get through cautiously in daylight, and in heavy shoes. The lower part of the field had not been cut, and it was a mass of thistles. We worked our way to the foot of the Mt., until we seemed to be on a line with Uki's voice. Idella stayed in the field with a candle, and I started climbing, Moe following reluctantly.

Let me make excuses for myself right here. Of course, Uki *always* sounds abused, but he was more distressed than ever. I have worried about his running

519

around since I had his claws clipped, as he has little protection against an enemy, cannot do much climbing or get a good purchase. (Damage to the upholstery has stopped.) I was afraid a wood-chuck had attacked and hurt him (they fight dogs terrifically, you know) or that he had gotten into something he couldn't get out of.

I am sure I couldn't have climbed that hill in the daytime. It goes up at about a 45-degree angle. From the icestorm of two years ago, and timber-cutting at the top, it is a mass of fallen boughs and tree-limbs. Under these are rocks of all sizes, some slick with moss, some loose and rolling down the moment I touched them. Occasional deep wet holes. Very few small trees to hold to or pull up by. At one point it got so steep that I simply did not think I could go higher. Then Uki wailed tragically and sounded a little closer, and I worked on up, on my knees, digging in with one hand, and holding to the flashlight with the other. The flash wavered uncertainly, quite dim. Moe began sliding and slipping back down the Mt. and I had to force him to stay with it. I got as far as I could, to an over-hang I could not cope with, Idella's candle the faintest of glimmers far below, and finally picked out Uki's eyes with the flash. He was up a tree, in a crotch. I simply could not get closer, and set to work to coax him down. He was still some distance away, and up. Moe set to work like a good fellow, and reached the tree. I swung the light on him, and I think the sight of him assured Uki. I heard a little crash, which was Uki jumping down, and then he made his way to me. He was thoroughly frightened, quite unhurt, and awfully glad to be with me. He stayed right behind me as I struggled down again. Moe slid down ahead of us. Without much to hang on to, I simply could not walk or creep down, and did most of it on my bare rear. The bedroom slippers caught in the brush, the train of the night-gown got caught in my heels and the flash got fainter and fainter. It was eleven when we got to the field, I panting with exertion and Uki with terror.

I really don't know how I did it. I feel good about it, though, as I have let myself go so soft, and I am glad to know that I *can* do a difficult physical thing when necessary. I changed nightgowns and got into bed quickly, as I didn't want to catch more cold. I looked at the mountain gown this morning, torn, muddy and draggled, of course, and it has blood all across the back, so I imagine my behind must be a pretty sight. Otherwise no damage, and Uki stayed out this morning only half an hour, and is back in bed with me. And I thought there was no trouble here he could get into! Something must have chased him. He does practically all his prowling around the hop-house, for the tiny field mice.

Still have not received my research material from Carl Brandt, and must phone him.

All my love,

1. MKR's Siamese cat.
2. MKR's pointer dog.

(TLS, 4 pp.)

[Van Hornesville, N.Y.]

[29 September 1948]

Darling:

. . . Louise came in yesterday afternoon late as I was writing you. Mr. Young is in New York. I asked her to stay for dinner with me and she was delighted to. I bathed and put on a housecoat and we chatted in the "parlor" while Idella whipped up quite a formal dinner. We had a good start, as I had ordered steak and had already had Idella put in the oven a Japanese persimmon pudding, of Louise's Fla. persimmons, by Bee NcNeil's recipe. It was really delicious. Idella used a white damask cloth and served formally. I spoiled everything by saying, "Gosh, a big white tablecloth. We mustn't spill anything on it." Idella could have killed me.

I think it gave Louise something to think about, I mean the nice serving etc. that I have obviously even when alone.

I couldn't resist saying casually to her, "I climbed Mt. Tom last night in my best nightgown." She said, "Why, what did you do that for?" . . .

All my love,

. . . .

(TLS, I p.)

[Van Hornesville, N.Y.]

Oct. 4, 1948

Dear Honey:

. . . Mr. Young and Louise and Dick came for drinks and supper last night. . . .

The Youngs were almost as upset as I that you say you can't come now. Idella was nice about it and said she would stay as long as possibly could. It would make a great difference to our comfort to have her here when you are, but I can't detain her when she is ready to go. She was stretching it to stay quite late. I hate to have you make the trip home with the animals, also. It spoils it for you, while I don't mind at all.

Well, you are so sweet about letting me work out my destiny, that I can't interfere with yours. . . .

Must finish my story now. . . .

All my love,

. . . .

(TLS, I p.)

[Van Hornesville, N.Y.]

Oct. 7, 1948

Dear Honey:

Damn it, I had a day and a half free from pain and thought I was all right, then I was right back up to my ears in it again. I have watched everything carefully for some time, diet, liquor, even cigarettes. I must be tense as hell about something, and I can't figure it out.

Carl Brandt reached here in time for dinner Tuesday. . . .

He liked the story, and his suggestions were just what I needed. I rather look forward to the re-writing, as I know just where I'm going.

Please phone Aunt Ida for me. I planned to write her a long letter, and just cannot do it. . . .

All my love,

. . . .

(TLS, 2 pp.)

[Van Hornesville, N.Y.]

Oct. 8, 1948

Dearest Norton:

I am so happy and relieved that you have been suffering. Now is the time for you to read Lecomte de Nouy's "Of Human Destiny."[1] You will realize why you are dissatisfied with yourself.

Circumstances, combined with your sensitivity, have tended to muffle your *constructive* self. I have always been so certain that you *had* something. This true and deeper self emerged when you plunged deliberately into the ambulance service. It has depressed me more than I can say to see you slipping into a form of vegetativeness. It has had a paralyzing and stagnating effect on me, and I have been totally unable to help you, have probably even made it worse, both because you cannot endure anything from me but complete approval, even sometimes imagine disapproval when it is not there, and because I myself am not well-enough adjusted to give you a sense of security with me, let alone have any emotional or mental strength left to spare, to share with you.

I hope you will go right on suffering until you work it out. I am only afraid that when you do, you will suddenly, with no warning to me, do, much as you did in the war, something noble and exotic, such as announcing that you will be leaving the next day for South America, to raise chincona bark to make free quinine for India——.

In the meantime, I should think that you would look on the Dolphin, the Periwinkle and the Penguin Bar, as a fine way to make quite a bit of money quickly—to be used eventually for a purpose—toward a goal. I shouldn't be surprised if something of the sort were not already stirring in the back of your mind.

All my love and cheers for the good fight,

1. Lecomte du Nouy (1883–1947), *Of Human Destiny* (London: Longmans, Green, 1947)

[Van Hornesville, N.Y.]
Oct. 9, [1948]

Dearest:

. . . Yes, better send me the books from the Creek, if not too awfully much trouble. I have been reduced to borrowing mystery stories from Mr. Young. Charlie Scribner sent me a fat box, including Martha's and Zora's books.[1] (I also have Nora Beckham, Bridie Steen and Three Roads to Valhalla here.)[2] Have devoured everything, being in bed so long. Carl Brandt picked up Martha's book to read in bed, and asked if he could take it home to finish it, and would send it back. Told him of course to keep it. But he is to send me James Gould Cozzens' new book.[3]

It's a pity you have already sent your mother a couple of Zora's books. It would be wonderful to spring this one on her, and afterward inform her it was by a "nigger."

Among Mr. Young's books was Constance Rourke's "Audubon,"[4] which fascinated me. . . .

Yesterday was a marvelous day of rain. It swept in steadily almost all day, much needed, and the fog was so thick that the bedroom seemed like a lighthouse. Could not see past the horse-chestnut tree from the front window. Saw a cock pheasant slip into the corn-field at the back. Idella kept the room toasty warm and I was cozy and actually "enjoyed poor health." Then last night and this morning the fiend hit again, and no amount of Phenobarbitol helped. It felt as though a handful of ground glass (not too finely ground, either) had *stuck* amidships. I have had worse attacks, but never a bad one that lasted so long—three weeks now. Bought equipment and have gone back to the hot oil retention enemas, which will eventually smooth things out. I had forgotten how awkward and humiliating they are!

Also read a book of Mr. Young's, "Road to Survival,"[5] that has stirred me deeply. It is both stimulating and terrifying. Not because of the atom bomb, but because of the whole world's destruction of its natural resources, soil erosion, destruction of water-sheds, so that the world's water level is dropping perilously, along with almost general over-population, so that if things continue as they are going, in a few decades, there will not be a sufficient food or water supply for the whole earth. The author of the book suggests practical remedies, and I must say they are drastic. They include urging us to use part of the Marshall plan[6] money for contraceptives! He writes that 2 billion dollars were spent on the development of the atomic bomb, and that it would be well worth the same amount of money for scientists to develop a simple contraceptive to be used by women that would be practical in countries such as India and China, which are without sanitary or water facilities.

I can't wait to ask Mr. Young if he finished the book (while it has an introduction by Bernard Baruch,[7] it gives hell to the big companies) and what he thinks of it. From my own trek through the South in doing my forestry article,[8] from seeing the devastation of the land there, from seeing the same thing when Julia and I drove through New Hampshire and Vermont, from seeing it in upper Michigan, and in places, in Alaska, I have been remotely aware of what was happening (even the floods are caused by the denuding of high forests) but I never thought of associating it with over-population, or the wars that follow, as in the ease of Japan, terribly over-populated. But this is only part of it, and you must read the book for yourself.

All my love,

Oct. 11

Might as well make a manuscript of this! If I am up to it, hope to re-write my story this week, and won't be able to do much else.

Am still fighting the attack. Severe pain yesterday afternoon but it seems a bit lighter this morning.

As I said on the phone, after getting high with Mr. Young, I slept better than for many nights, and felt grand in the morning. They came for noon dinner, and are coming to dinner again tonight. Louise must be fed up with cooking, and probably Mr. Young with the confusion, or they would not have accepted gladly for twice in succession.

. . . I think you imagined it that Dr. Atchley wanted to see me during one of these attacks. He saw me in one for a week when you went over-seas. I remember the pain while they were taking the barium X-rays once again, and the doctors remarking on actually seeing the spasms. However, if I am not all right within two more days, I'll take the train down to N.Y.

Saturday evening while Louise was out of the room, I told Mr. Young about your letter to me telling of your depression about yourself. I told him what I had written you, and said I hoped it would be encouraging and stimulating, and would not seem harsh. Then he told me something that I imagine he has told very few people—certainly not Louise! He said that any man worth anything, was obliged to go through that experience, perhaps again and again. He confided to me that there had been times when he was so depressed about himself, that he had considered suicide. Don't let him know I told you this, although he would have done so himself under the same circumstances.

1. Zora Neale Hurston (1903–1960), *Seraph on the Suwanee* (New York: Scribners, 1948); Martha Gellhorn (1908–1983), *The Wine of Astonishment* (New York: Scribners, 1948).
2. Joseph Stanley Pennell (1908–1963), *The History of Nora Beckham: A Museum of Home Life* (New York: Scribners, 1948); Anne Crone (1915–1972), *Bridie Steen* (New York: Scribner, 1948); and Catherine P. Stewart, *Three Roads to Valhalla* (New York: Scribners, 1948).
3. James G. Cozzens (1903–1978), *Guard of Honor* (New York: Harcourt and Brace, 1948).
4. Constance Rourke (1885–1941), *Audubon* (New York: Harcourt Brace, 1936). John James Audubon (1785–1851), perhaps best known for his *The Birds of America* (1827–38).

5. William Vogt (1902–?), *Road to Survival* (New York: Sloane, 1948).

6. The Marshall Plan, named after Secretary of State George C. Marshall, was enacted to help rehabilitate Europe after World War II.

7. Bernard M. Baruch, American businessman and statesman, was appointed to the United Nations Atomic Energy Commission in 1946.

8. "Trees for Tomorrow." *Collier's Magazine* 117 (8 May 1943): 14–15, 24–25.

. . . .

(TLS, 1 p.)

[Van Hornesville, N.Y.]

Oct. 13, 1948

Dear Honey:

. . . Yesterday was bad, and I could not work, but got off some necessary correspondence. Late in the afternoon I was ready to yell, and had Idella take me (us) for a drive. This morning things are reasonably comfortable.

I will be doing awfully well if I get my long story re-written and off to Carl before you come. There can be no question of my staying on alone later to try to work seriously. This month-long illness has put the fear of God in me.

My love,

. . . .

(TLS, 2 pp.)

[Van Hornesville, N.Y.]

Oct. 14, 1948

Happy birthday, darling:

Will try to phone you later today.

O.K., have a stomach ache instead of a moral awakening—they are probably all the same thing anyway.

It is news to me that you called yourself a son of a bitch by mail, and that I agreed with you. I merely pictured you in "the depths of some divine despair" and thought it was wonderful. Now it turns out to have been only sour cream sauce.

However, I have to blame my vegetativeness on something (I couldn't possibly blame it on *me*) and you might be gentleman enough to take the rap.

I had a marvelous day yesterday, entirely free from pain. Then woke up at 5 A.M. today in agony again. It has eased off and now, 2 P.M., is not so bad. The one good day is encouraging and I'll give myself another day before doing anything drastic. It occurred to me that since the Cooperstown hospital is now tied in with Medical Center, I could phone Dr. Atchley and have him make arrangements for me at Cooperstown. They would have to take another set of barium X-rays, and could either send them to N.Y. for comparison with the ones on file there, or vice versa.

But I have been through all that so often, and it always proves so utterly futile, and they do *nothing* for me that I can't do for myself at home. They would want to stick that prostoscope [*sic*] or whatever they call it (I am sure it's what the veterinarians use for delivering calves) up my rear, and either they wouldn't be able to get it up because of the soreness at the sigmoid, or they'd say, yes, the area was swollen and inflamed, and give me a shot of dope. And the damn thing eventually passes off of its own accord. It is only that it has lasted so very long.

. . . Practically all of Idella's letters from Bernard are on Dolphin Tavern stationery, and without my glasses, I always think they're from you. Don't know how expensive the stationery is, or whether he uses it for everyone.

She has turned cheerful again, and has been very sweet to me. . . .

All my love,

. . . .

(TL, 1 p.)

[Van Hornesville, N.Y.]
Oct. 15, 1948

Dear Honey:

We should really never discuss serious subjects by mail. I agree with you. Started to tear up the letter I wrote yesterday, for fear you wouldn't realize I was being flippant.

Got well into the revisions on my story yesterday afternoon. Feel a great deal better this morning. Enough so, at least, to be sure that nothing out of the ordinary has happened to my insides. . . .

. . . .

(TLS, 2 pp.)

[Van Hornesville, N.Y.]
Oct. 17, [1948]
Sunday afternoon

Dear Honey:

. . . The New Yorker turned down the story that was my pride and joy. They not only did not "get" it, but gave it the most astonishing interpretation, which made sense, but had never occurred to me. . . . That is three rejections out of the four stories I did last summer. And I am supposed to tell Tom, Dick and Harry how to break into print—. The story[1] the Post took, should be out soon. I hoped the New Yorker would use it, but Carl sent it direct to the Post. I had to ruin the ending for them, but can put the original one back again when I get enough "queer" stories for a volume.

1. "The Friendship," *Saturday Evening Post* 221 (1 January 1949): 14–15, 44. MKR published no more short fiction after this story.

1949

1949 was a year of little consolation. MKR was dispirited, despondent, even suicidal. NSB seemed unable to cheer her up. She began to drink more heavily and became increasingly concerned about her weight. In May, she left Cross Creek for Van Hornesville; in June, NSB came for a long visit. She spent a great deal of her time tending to the restoration of the house and to the planting of flowers. Owen D. Young remained her inspiration. She listened awestruck to his analyses of world events. In July, she visited Julia Scribner in New York. By the end of the summer, she had completed the opening chapters of *The Sojourner*, but they did not satisfy her. Perkins was dead; she had no one to advise her. Norman Berg, the Macmillan editor, tried, but he could not replace Perkins. NSB came to get her in the fall, after her recurrent bouts of illness, and she spent the rest of the year moving between Crescent Beach and Cross Creek, the former keeping her closer to NSB, the latter keeping her closer to her writing. Christmas was "dreary."

. . . .

(TLS, 2 pp.)

[Van Hornesville, N.Y.]

May 11, 1949

Dear Honey:

. . . I know you intended to send Mr. Cabell's book[1] to your mother yourself. And evidently Miss Binney didn't even notice the dedication.

This morning my bedroom windows were thick inside with steam that was almost frost. When Idella brought coffee, I said it must be quite cold. She said in disgust that it wasn't cold at all. She was going by the inside of the house, which was delightful. . . .

I realized why I have always had such a strange reluctance about bringing Idella here. It is because she's ALWAYS here. At the other places, she was away in her own place at least half the day, and even at her work, was usually at a distance. That is unconsciously why I began using the typewriter up in the bedroom, although I prefer the dark in the dining room. . . .

Much love,

1. James Branch Cabell, *The Devil's Own Dear Son* (New York: Farrar and Straus, 1949), which was dedicated to NSB.

(TLS, 2 pp.)

[Van Hornesville, N.Y.]
May 14, 1949

Dear Honey:

... I have been desperate for reading matter. A book came from Norman Berg, "The Hunter's Horn,"[1] that he mentioned to us, and it was fascinating and tided me over for a few evenings. .... The book came this morning from Gene Baroff that he had promised, Thomas Mann's collected stories,[2] a good thick volume that will hold me a while. My large order from Scribner's has never come and I wrote them today. The box is probably sitting at the Creek.

I made a rhubarb pie yesterday, my first in many years, so good, but Idella had never tasted rhubarb and didn't like it. Today I made hot gingerbread to have with rhubarb sauce for lunch. I have lost several pounds of weight, although my appetite is fabulous.

Much love,

1. Harriette Arnow (1908–1986), *Hunter's Horn* (New York: Macmillan, 1949).
2. Thomas Mann (1875–1955), *Stories of Three Decades* (New York: Knopf, 1936).

. . . .

(TLS, 3 pp.)

[Van Hornesville, N.Y.]
May 17, 1949

Dear Honey:

... The "feel" of the book seems to be coming. The only "writing" I've done was what started out to be a lyric verse, and ended up as a study in madness. I am charmed with it, which almost certainly means it's no good.

... No, dear, I was in fine shape after the first night. Idella spelled me one hour the first day, two the second, and that was all. She was willing, but she *slept* all the time, and she was so nervous when she did drive that she didn't make the steady mileage necessary to get here. Another time, I think Savannah should be the first stop, then an easy jaunt to Chapel Hill the next day. The rest isn't so bad.

... Did I write you that a letter from Walter[1] said that when they returned to the Creek, Bernice had a miscarriage, having been two months pregnant? I seriously question whether it was a miscarriage, for they evidently kept to their schedule. But Martha had told her she was pregnant! As Walter said, "That old midwife!"

... Bernard[2] phoned Idella Sunday evening. I said she was in Cooperstown, and he wanted to know where he could reach her there. .... She met a young colored woman that day, and they all went to the ball-game. She was so happy and amazed that they were allowed to go—. She said her friends asked how long she would be here, and she said to keep their fingers crossed, she might be here until August. ...

Julia phoned me Sunday, and will come up about the end of this month. . . .

Much love,

1. Walter and Bernice Gilkyson.
2. Bernard Young, Idella's husband.

. . . .

(TLS, 2 pp.)

[Van Hornesville, N.Y.]

May 19, 1949

Dear Norton:

My box of books came from Scribner's yesterday, a feast. They have also found me another first edition of Bartram's Travels. . . .[1]

1. William Bartram (1739–1823), *Travels Through North and South Carolina* (1791). MKR's original copy had been eaten by termites at Cross Creek.

. . . .

(TL, 2 pp.)

[Van Hornesville, N.Y.]

May 23, 1949

Dear Honey:

Idella horrified me by coming in while I was still having breakfast, with lilacs and iris which I assumed she had plucked from my own bush and bulb. I was even more horrified when she told me proudly that she had begged them of Mrs. Redjives,[1] the worthy neighbor I have not even met, because she had so *many*. I informed her that the country women up here raised *yard flowers*, never intended for house or vase, and that what she had done was the equivalent of asking for an armful of flowers from a Southern woman's porch plants, also never meant for cutting or interior decoration. This she understood.

1. Ruth and Johnnie Redjives, a prosperous farm family who lived close to MKR.

. . . .

(TL, 3 pp.)

[Van Hornesville, N.Y.]

May 26, 1949

Dear Norton:

It has been raw and rainy all week, bad for the crops, but probably a boon for me, for I am staying quite faithfully with the typewriter. Yesterday I wrote thirteen words and this morning X-ed out five of them. It was still a hard day's work—. How I dread Louise's return, and her cheery, "Have you been a good girl? How many pages have you done since Mama left you?"

I really think that from now on when anyone asks, "Are you writing?" or

"What are you writing?" I shall fall back in return on Peggy's[1] question, "Have you had intercourse lately?" It seems to me that one activity should be as private as the other. How embarrassing to have to *tell* people when you do it!

This is Idella's afternoon and evening in Cooperstown, and it is good to have the house empty. Peggy Egan took her to Mohawk the other day, with Mrs. Hemenway[2] and the wife of the post-master, all quite naturally. Two white maids were with the colored group last Sunday, and Idella said that everyone had such a good time together, with fried chicken and singing, "Why, Mrs. Baskin, you didn't stop to think those other girls were *white*." It is odd to realize that we seem just as different and fearsome to them, as they do to those of us who have not had a chance to be with them on uninhibited terms. I refer of course to the cloistered, segregated whites and negroes. I don't know how Idella thinks of me, but apparently I am rather without color or race of any sort, for her to have told me that. . . .

1. Margaret Mitchell.
2. MKR may mean Mollie Hemenway, wife of Frank Hemenway, who was the head cattleman for Owen Young's prize Holstein cattle.

. . . .

(TLS, 3 pp.)

[Van Hornesville, N.Y.]

June 1, 1949

Dear Norton:

Hah, our great hunter, our cat! There have been mouse-signs on both living room davenports and all over the kitchen. Of course, I have to keep my bedroom doors shut at night, or Moe comes downstairs and has himself a couch. Also thinks he wants to go out. So, I planned everything for Uki to catch the mouse or mice. Idella was to shut her bedroom door, so that Uki wouldn't bed down with her and sleep through everything. My doors were to be shut, Moe inside, Uki out. Uki's pan was to be in Idella's bathroom, with a formal introduction. Uki was to have the run of the house and the run of the mice. So, I go to bed and read. Idella takes her bath and goes to bed. Terrible, heart-broken yowls at my door. A desperate scratching, which keeps up. I realize *that* isn't going to work. I get up and call Idella and we start all over again.

The safari begins with a new direction, great vigor. The hall door to the dining room is to be closed, and Uki is to intercept the game before it gets to the living room. His pan is moved to the kitchen. But he must have a bed of some sort for in between mice. I get my blue Guatemalan jacket from the closet, and bring it down the stairs in one arm, Uki in the other, hanging limp and self-consciously attractive. Moe thinks we are moving again, and goes wild. The jacket is made into a nest in the seat of the conversation-piece chair in the kitchen, Uki is shown his toilet. Idella says, "Now we'll see how good our man is." I sleep long and hard and Idella brings coffee this morning groggily. She has had hardly a wink of sleep. Uki had yowled and scratched so at *her* door, that she gave up and opened it. He spent the night in the middle of her narrow bed, thumping down every now and then when the mice *did* come into the kitchen. He caught nothing at all, and now will not speak to me after my cruelty.

. . . Oh, about the television, it was the first I had seen. I wouldn't have a set in the house for love or money. My eyes ached for an hour afterward. The Milton Berle[1] program, too, and it seemed like high school theatricals.

Haven't heard from Julia again, but a note from Norman Berg said he expected to be driving Julie to Vermont the first week in June and would try to stop over-night. Sha'n't get in touch with Julia until I know about the Bergs, as I don't want them over-lapping. Am not keen about having Julia just now, but having invited her, will let her come when she wants to.

My love,

1. MKR is referring to the *Milton Berle Hour*, one of the earliest comedic shows on television.

. . . .

(TLS, 7 pp.)

Van Hornesville, New York
June 4, 1949

Dear Norton:

. . . I 'phoned Julia this morning, and she is coming early this next week for a long week-end. I hadn't wanted to call her until the Bergs were out of the way. She is taking Hildy[1] with the nurse to Far Hills on Monday, to be parked for the summer. Julia said she was walking with a cane, as she lifted the hefty Hildy and sprained her back. She is most anxious to come. It will be wonderful to have her. I shall be slapped down again, of course, but at the moment I am so blithe about my work that nothing can interrupt or disturb me for long. I am even blissful to have Idella here, and work happily at the desk in the dining-room, and don't even hear her when she moves around.

It is all my relationship with you is worth, to prove you wrong, but for many reasons, I am delighted to report that I had a wonderful letter yesterday from Sigrid Undset, and all is well about her letters to me. As well as writing her my plans for the disposition of her letters I had said that I had read some of them to friends who would appreciate their quality. . . .

I understood that a woman, a writer, who had won the Nobel prize for literature, would know that any letter she ever wrote was literature, too, and so would have a value. Her never speaking, in this last letter, of this, shows, I think, how much we are *en rapport*, Sigrid and I.

. . . In this morning's N.Y. Herald Tribune, it would seem that my strange interviewer and pseudo-friend, Whittaker Chambers, is committing suicide. A psychiatrist in the employ of Alger Hiss' defense, evidently a Hiss friend, from the newspaper report, is taking notes on Chambers, as you will have read. Whittaker Chambers is certainly a mystic, a most serious person, but it may well be that he had gone so far into the esoteric realm that he is not responsible. I predict that if Hiss is absolved, Chambers will kill himself. Such a grubby little man, all their raking up of his living with a girl when he was seventeen, is absurd. . . .[2]

My love,

1. Hildreth Bigham, Julia Scribner Bigham's child.
2. Alger Hiss, a former state department official, was accused by Whittaker Chambers, a magazine editor and confessed member of the Communist Party, of helping him deliver confidential documents to the Russians. MKR is reflecting here upon the first trial of Hiss, which ended with no decision in July 1949. Hiss was retried and found guilty in January 1950. The trials created public controversy, in part because it was suggested that the FBI tampered with evidence that led to Hiss's conviction.

. . . .

(TLS, 2 pp.)

Van Hornesville, New York
June 3, 1949

Dear Norton:

Norman and Julie[1] arrived at 4 yesterday afternoon and left at 8:30 this morning. They were crazy about the place. . . . Julie is very much of a person. Great charm and poise. I like her immensely. . . .

My love,

1. Norman and Julie Berg.

. . . .

(TL, 4 pp.)

Van Hornesville, New York
July 1, 1949

Dear Norton:

It was such fun, your being here, and the New York trip, everything.

. . . Julia and I went down to the Young's last night after dinner, and Louise was all upset, swearing that I had said Julia wasn't arriving until yesterday.

. . . Julia thought the Audubon was lovely, the frame, too, and is sure Buzzie[1] will like it. She said the apartment is not completely furnished for him, as the family took out most of the stuff, and Buzz and fiancé gloat over every household gift.

She really wants to be my literary executor, said that anything technical that might arise could be referred to some expert at Scribner's. So I shall write Phil May to make it definite, and shall either screw up my courage later to tell Cliff Lyons I am not naming him, or just let him cuss me out when I am not on earth to hear it.

. . . You are such a sweet darling, and I think we both feel better about everything from your having made the visit here. However queer I may be, however difficult, just always remember that I do love you. . . .

1. Buzz, a nickname for Charles Scribner Jr.

. . . .

(TLS, 3 pp.)

Van Hornesville, New York
July 5, 1949

Dear Norton:

The Fredericks have mowed the meadows across the road, and the field does look so attractive. Good walking now, too, no thistles.

I picked my currants yesterday and made jelly, and the new edition of Fanny Farmer all but ruined the jelly, and me. I should have followed my own memory. . . .

Gertrude is doing a fine job of cleaning up, but she is having such a good time at it that she takes forever, and it is going to cost me as much as to have Idella do everything. . . . The strange disharmony between me and all things mechanical has already blown a kitchen fuse and wrecked the automatic coffee maker. . . .

On my way home Sunday afternoon, all the traffic was stepping along, and I found myself doing 70. Also found the State Police at my side, motioning me to the side of the road. The patrolman driver came over and I said, "I was going too fast, wasn't I?" Icily, "Yes, Ma'am. Florida, eh? Where are you staying right now?" "My—my summer home is the other side of Van Hornesville." "Registration card and driver's license, please." I hauled them out, and the policeman said, "Why, you're the writer, aren't you? We check your place in the winter. Say, the Sergeant would give anything to meet you. Can I bring him over and introduce him?" Me, gulping, "I'd be delighted." So the Sergeant comes with out-stretched hand and the boys are to stop by to be shown through the inside of the house. This pleased Mr. Young no end, and when that night we had illegal fireworks and an illegal bonfire at the Case's 4th of July picnic on their cabined hill, Mr. Young said we didn't have to worry, if the police showed up he'd just turn them over to me. I assured him that I figured I had used up my luck, and from now on, it was every man for himself, and I'd be the first to run. . . .

Much love,

. . . .

(TLS, 2 pp.)

Van Hornesville, New York
July 11, 1949

Dear Norton:

Had a sheet of Cross Creek stationery in the typewriter to write Talmadge DuPree, ending my association with him, but decided to wait a bit and study the figures further. Wish you were here to go over them with me. Instead of the check I have been expecting from him, I have a bill for $1201.60. Of course, he sent me checks for the Creek fruit, about $1,000 or a bit more, but since most of my fruit went to market after the California freeze, my lack of more than a $100 profit, say, seems unreasonable. No, it is $100 or so deficit, isn't it.

Talmadge sent me itemized accounts of the Creek grove expenses—in Chet's handwriting, I noticed—but there were no itemized i.e., really detailed bills for the Big Hammock expenses. And Big Hammock is supposed to be my money-maker. Talmadge also wrote, "I surely would appreciate a check at your earliest convenience as payroll money is now getting scarce down here." I just don't like it, but don't want to make a fool of myself.

I could always sell my fruit on the trees for a much better figure than I have been getting, but that leaves me without anyone to do the cultivating, spraying and fertilizing, if I break with Talmadge. The grove has been slipping behind in the years that I have abandoned it, old trees should have been replaced with young ones, pruning has not been properly done, although I have paid Talmadge well for presumably doing it, yet I can't let it go without such attention as he does give it. I am most disturbed. Hugh Williams and Doug Whidden are out of the question, both thoroughly crooked.

The letter from Pearl Primus[1] from the heart of the Belgian Congo was most moving. Will save it for you.

Much love,

1. Pearl Primus, Trinidad-born American dancer, choreographer, and anthropologist, who helped establish the importance of African dance in American culture.

. . . .

(TL, 4 pp.)

Van Hornesville, New York
Evening July 12 [1949]

Dear Norton:

. . . Still don't know how to write Talmadge.

Had a note from young Charlie Scribner's bride-to-be, thanking me for "the very large old print." I should have sent the ash-trays—.

In settling the estate of Julia's grandmother, they found it was her habit to keep what Julia called a sizeable bank balance, in fact had $90,000 in the bank, "in case of emergencies. . . ."

Much love,

(TLS, 6 pp.)

Van Hornesville, New York
July 14, 1949
Evening

Dear Norton:

... The Langston Moffetts, with two sons, were due to arrive at Louise's today, to stay probably over the weekend. Rather odd people, don't you think, for Louise to invite? ... I am to take the 4 Moffets out to dinner tomorrow night.... I'll take the Moffetts to the Sportsman's Tavern.

My love,

. . . .

(TLS, 6 pp.)

Van Hornesville, New York
July 18, 1949

Dear Norton:

... Am working hard, but in such anguish. I have set myself an almost impossible task, I fear, for my own man is supposed to be almost inarticulate, and I am doing it through his *thoughts*, with the danger of having an equally inarticulate mess on my hands—. God, Max could have told me right now—into my third chapter, whether I am making sense or not. Do not write me soothingly—.

My love,

. . . .

(TLS, 3 pp.)

[Van Hornesville, N.Y.]
July 20, 1949

Dear Norton:

... Late yesterday afternoon I cleared out my desk and dashed off answers to a dozen or more duty-letters and throwing away stuff I decided did not have to be answered, including a formal slip from WHO'S WHO asking if the address marked were still correct for me. Lewis Gannett's[1] column on the amusing bits in the British WHO'S WHO remarked that while they the British weren't so hoity-toity, the American publishers throw you out of the volume if you don't answer their communications. So in a moment I shall go through the vast pile of rubbish, as yet unburned, to retrieve the item and answer it. I am striving for a greater purity and humility, but getting myself thrown out of WHO'S WHO would seem to be leaning over backward.

The horrible realization came to me that I have been through a siege of the swelled-head. Arthur tried to indicate it to me, yet it is the sort of thing one has to see for oneself. And I loathe it so in other people—. It is a sort of germ that pounces when you aren't looking.

... Worked so hard yesterday, decided not to force it, so picked and arranged flowers, and finished reading a choice book Julia sent me, "Diary of a Country Priest...."[2]

My love,

1. Lewis Gannett, columnist for the *New York Herald Tribune*.
2. Georges Bernanos (1888–1948), *The Diary of a Country Priest* (New York: Macmillan, 1937).

. . . .

(TLS, 3 pp.)

[Van Hornesville, N.Y.]

July 27, 1949

Dear Honey:

... And did I write you about giving a lift to a young man on the road—guess not—for I hoped nothing would come of it—and he was working on a farm near-by, but wanted to be a writer, and had a book finished. He said, "If I could get up my nerve, I'd take it to Mrs. Baskin. She lives up on Mt. Tom, wrote 'The Yearling.'" I thought, this is once where I get out of it. He said, "They tell me she's very pleasant." Of course, that melted my hard heart, and I said I was Mrs. Baskin, and it ended with my telling him to bring his g-d- manuscript. Which he did, and left it with me for a week.

I was amazed, the fellow could really write....

... The question of integrity is fascinating. (This, because I just had a letter from Phil May saying that he would send a rough draft of my will this week.) I think I wrote you that I had further proof of Cliff Lyons' lack of it when I stopped with them on the way up, anent Bert Cooper.

And I have the creeps about Edie's being left alone with my files, and the deposit slips etc. in the desk—. Julia would never look at a thing, you would not, Norman Berg would not—not that there is anything that anyone couldn't see without my objection—but I'll guarantee that Edie couldn't resist peeping into things.

Norman has offered to look at my work, saying that he really is a good critic, and of course he is, but—it seems to me I wrote you this earlier—he could not but ask where I'm going, and so on, and I have to battle this thing out in my own way. You are a good critic, too, but you would be too generous. I need Max, and I don't have him, and that's that.

I think that the brash Gene has a genuine writing talent, and it is too bad that he is evidently a homosexual. Though of course other homosexuals, such as Gide, Proust, Oscar Wilde, have done fine work....[1]

My love,

1. Gene Baro. André Gide, French writer and editor; Marcel Proust, French novelist; and Oscar Wilde, Irish poet, dramatist, and novelist.

(TLS, 2 pp.)

Van Hornesville, New York
July 28, 1949

Dear Norton:

. . . A letter from Julia today, with her usual laments which are so amusing. Charlie Jr's[1] wedding did not bother her (she was a bridesmaid) as some of the ushers were old friends and admirers of hers, and she said the other bridesmaids were so homely that for once Vera felt Julia did her credit, and she didn't give her the customary hell.

. . . We picked the gooseberries yesterday, and when I found that both ends of each berry had to be clipped with scissors, I gave Gertrude sugar and the berries and had her take them home to put up on shares. The huge wild blackberries are ripening, and if it hadn't stormed, I was going to begin picking them this evening, to make jelly, which I love. I have enough raspberry jam for other people.

. . . The work goes better, but strange people are appearing and taking over. I shall certainly have to rewrite most of the first part later, but that won't matter.

1. Charles Scribner Jr., aka Charles Scribner IV.

. . . .

(TL, 3 pp.)

Van Hornesville, New York
Aug. 1, 1949

Dear Norton:

The check books came just now, and a good letter from you, and one from Idella. She says she is ready to come any time, just to let her know and send her enough more money (she had $13 left from the trip down) and that she won't get lonesome, or if she does, she won't let me see it. She said she has lots to tell me some day. I suppose life with Bernard is almost unbearable. Which won't help when her Cooperstown friends have left in the fall—. I think it is her Reddick family that is the real pull. . . .

We may find that she just announces to Bernard that I have been taken suddenly and desperately ill, and clear out the next day—. If about that time of the month he asks solicitously after my health, you'd better shake your head mournfully and say you're terribly worried. It does make me uncomfortable to have her so deceitful, or sly, with him, for of course I wonder when it will happen again to me.

As a matter of fact, I probably *would* become ill, from malnutrition, if she didn't come, for I cannot bring myself to cook for myself alone. I forced myself to broil a small steak Saturday night, just nibbled at it, and will ask Gertrude to make a steak pie for me today, and perhaps I can get some down. Have found the window-bench by the cherry table in the kitchen by far the coziest place to eat. . . .

(TLS, 5 pp.)

[Van Hornesville, N.Y.]

Aug. 2, 1949

Dear Norton:

I was so charmed with the dishonest idea of Idella's telling Bernard I was ill, that I suggested it to her myself. At least, I have written her that if it would help her make an easy get-away, I could wire her two or three days before the agreed date, that I was in trouble and needed her. I said that would be true, I was always in trouble without her, especially now that I'm actually at work.

. . . I had noticed that "The Wizard of Oz"[1] movie was playing in Ft. Plain, so went back last night for the 7 o'clock show. An old movie, I gathered, but how I enjoyed it. Bert Lahr as the Cowardly Lion was delicious. Imagine you saw it years ago.

. . . And we both know that to keep from going quite mad, I'll be at the Creek to get on with the book. Am only averaging about a page a day at present, but the time will come when I'll average two or three pages. I hope to have the first draft completed by late next spring, so that perhaps when I return here I can stop in New York and let Charlie Scribner and Wallace Myer[2] read it, and then do the re-writing next summer.

Poor Norman Berg. I had sense enough not to send you the depressed letter I wrote recently, but did mail a similar one to Norman. I had just come out of an extremely bad time, but thought it was apparent I had come out of it. My momentary despair about my work registered too well, and he wired me, "I love and need you very much. Don't ever leave me." You should have heard the ice in the voice of the Western Union man who read me the message! I wrote Norman thanking him, and saying that while I had always been certain of his affectionate friendship, I couldn't see at first how he possibly *needed* me, but that I realized that as with Max Perkins, it was a matter of vital importance to him that I, and two or three other writers and friends in whose literary integrity he believes, should continue to write, and honestly. I started to say to him, but didn't, that I also thought that since he had abandoned his own attempt at creative work, he was living vicariously in the work of a few of us.

And of course Norman doesn't know, as you do, that no matter how far I go into the abyss, I always claw my way out again. . . .

Did the first long job of work in several days. In one of his occasional bitter poems, Robert Frost asks: ("A Question")[3]

> If all the soul-and-body scars
> Were not too much to pay for birth."

Question indeed. Sometimes yes, sometimes no.

My love,

1. *The Wizard of Oz* (1939), starring Judy Garland and Ray Bolger.
2. Wallace Meyer, an editor at Scribners.
3. MKR first met Frost when he came to the University of Florida, but it was during the Van Hornesville days that they became close friends.

. . . .

(TLS, 8 pp.)

Van Hornesville, New York

Aug. 9, 1949

Noon

Dear Norton:

. . . In late afternoon, I realized it would be my first birthday quite alone, that I could remember, so phoned Mr. Young asking if he and his would come up for drinks. He said No, Louise hadn't gotten in from the Garden Club, but for me to come down there, and I accepted with thanks. Everyone had arrived, and Louise simply insisted that I stay for dinner. She meant it, and I was delighted. So at dinner, I told them it was my birthday. Louise immediately turned it into a party, in spite of the main dish of plain stew, changed dessert to ice cream, she and Clare[1] disappeared, it proved later for Clare to slip across to the store to buy the only cake they had, on which Louise dashed some frosting and four lighted candles. Louise produced a large bottle of Mary Chess toilet water that I love so, the kind you gave me, and Mr. Young brought up from his cellar cache a bottle of 20-year. . . . So I had a fine time after all.

. . . Phil May finally sent me an outline of my will. He said when he got to the matter of the literary executor, he couldn't find out the legal status or what are the functions, etc., but is getting information while I make my corrections. Meantime, he has me leaving all my papers and material outright to Julia, which is not the way it works, I know. Such stuff is not *given* to a literary executor, it is still part of an estate. Mr. Young verified this. Phil said we must arrange the joint ownership of the cottage and contents as soon as I return to Florida, but he has taken care of it in the interim by a paragraph to the effect that if this has not been arranged at the time of my death, cottage and contents are yours outright, aside from other provisions. The only thing would be that either of us would have to pay (unjustly) inheritance tax. Unless we make the arrangement first. He also said, as before, that a notation should be made on the Castle Warden mortgage, indicating how much represents our two different holdings. I imagine you could take care of that without me.

. . . An almost unintelligible letter from Martha at the Creek, asking, "Miss Baskin what Must I Do with the Butter it is here and get old Every Day I told some Peter (people?) a Bout it But I in sold But 4 Pound yet the stocks is Getting a lond Find Miss Baskin sissie is in trobel a Bout that Boy ar her he has Give her trobel this is all I an find and will to"

If you or Idella can't get to the Creek—maybe she can go this week-end—better write Martha to give away or use the old butter, and reduce the price on the fresh, to get rid of it, unless you now have room in the deep-freezer for it. . . .

Also, Adrina[2] is Getting a Find But the Doctor in turn her a lose yet.

. . . Arthur sent me a pair of salt and pepper shakers from Alaska, made of carved walrus ivory. I suppose it is a birthday present, but the rascal has not written me in months.

My love,

Damn this tiny paper—I seem to be out of the larger. (over)

My dear kind Norton, what I want to avoid is having you suffer with me. You don't *enjoy* suffering, the way eccentrics, such as Norman and I do!

1. Clare Brown, wife of Stanley Brown, who was Louise Young's son by her first marriage.
2. Adrenna Mickens.

. . . .

(TLS, 2 pp.)

Van Hornesville, New York
[14 August 1949]

Dear Norton:

. . . Just heard the ghastly news about Margaret Mitchell.[1] Am ill—poor little thing. It doesn't seem possible she can come through it—. Have sat in the car thinking the radio would have further news, but nothing more.

1. Margaret Mitchell was struck by a car in Atlanta and died on 16 August 1949.

. . . .

(TLS, 2 pp.)

[Van Hornesville, N.Y.]
August 15, 1949

Dear Norton:

. . . I spent today working on a gloomy verse—.

The morning news on Margaret Mitchell seemed to hold great hope, and I wired John Marsh, as I could not bring myself to do, before. . . .

August 16

Spent the morning re-writing the gloomy verse. . . .

[I] feel, as Browning, "All's well with the world."[1] And then I begin to disintegrate, either from taking drinks too early, or from frustration over the writing. My inability to write for several days came from the shock of finding myself once again off-key. I see now that all I have to do is tear up two pages, and start over.

Gertrude has a radio, and she tells me that Margaret had a relapse last night, but is "holding her own." Did you see the two unspeakable newspaper photographs in the N.Y. Tribune, one of darling Peggy sprawled on the pavement, the other of the moron who had hit her, hands on his hips, a smirking grin on his face? The pair of pictures seemed to me a total indictment of the human race. The first picture, of the catastrophe, printed by such a conservative paper as the Tribune, shows the *pleasure* human beings take in seeing injury to others, which accounts for War. And the picture of the idiot driver sums up all human stupidity. I am sure that he was, and always will be, delighted to be able to say, "*I* am the guy who hit Margaret Mitchell."

I have always considered myself on the side of the angels, and if I manage to avoid suicide, it will be because I cannot bear to depress others, but my secret feeling is that we are past saving. . . .

Now this time, you see, I am letting you suffer with me—.

1. Robert Browning (1812–1889), *Pippa Passes* (1841): "God's in his Heaven—/ All's right with the world."

. . . .

(TNS, 1 p.)

Van Hornesville, New York

Aug. 16, 1949

. . . Am beginning to get a depressed feeling about Peggy Mitchell. It might so much better have been me, since I still cannot decide whether "all the soul and body scars are worth the price of birth."

. . . .

(TLS, 1 p.)

Van Hornesville, [N.Y.]

Aug. 19, 1949

Norton my dear:

I have written you two depressed letters since Margaret's death, torn them up, and I assure you, you haven't missed anything.

This is only a note to say that I am on my feet again, and am working hard, and, I believe, well. The pattern begins to take shape.

Idella is a black angel. The last two days I have done my writing in bed, and it has gone so much better, no thought of a drink, and I do believe, as I have said to you before, that my back has something to do with it, as when I sit on a straight chair—necessary at the type-writer—an hour or so turns me into a mass of screaming nerves.

. . . She told me that Ruby[1] said to her, "Now don't you go back up North. You stay here, Norton needs you. . . ."

My love,

1. Ruby Dillard, a maid at Crescent Beach.

(TLS, 6 pp.)

Van Hornesville, New York

Aug. 20, 1949

Dear Norton:

... Dale Willis,[1] whose last letter said that he was roaming around looking for a job, has another baby. He was such a little man when I knew him in Carolina, at the age of twelve, and I wonder whether I could have put him on his feet if I had taken him home with me, as he wanted. If he had been younger, I should have certainly done it, but as with Edith's[2] Peggy, it seemed too late to do a good job. If we ever turn Cross Creek into an orphanage, we must catch them young.

A brief note from Norman Berg says that he went back from Florida to attend Margaret's funeral, but that he is returning to Florida and will see you.

... Idella has given me a most gloomy picture of conditions at the cottage. ...

I realize that the cottage silver is not adequate for the numbers of people who descend on you, but Idella reports that my set of choice dessert silver is being ruined, the delicate fork-tines bent from having them used to cut ham or what-not. She left this dessert service separately wrapped in cloth, so please tuck it away, and when you have a number of guests, just supplement with Dolphin silver. I don't mean to be selfish, but the dessert silver that I bought in Natchez is really irreplaceable. The set we brought here is 1801, but the set at the cottage is 1796.

My love,

1. Dale Willis, the orphan boy from North Carolina whom MKR immortalized in "A Mother in Mannville," *Saturday Evening Post* 209 (12 December 1936): 7, 33.
2. Edith Pope.

. . . .

(TLS, 3 pp.)

[Van Hornesville, New York]

[22 August 1949]

Norton, my poor dear fellow:

... Your life doesn't sound to me worth living. And I do not see why you let people impose on you so.

... I asked Idella if Bernard was saving anything, and she said I knew as much about it as she did, but she doubted if he saved a nickel. He tells her, and her family, that unfortunately he can't save, because of taking care of his little children. Yet Idella knows that all he gives the mother (judge's ruling) is $6 a week for the three kids, which as she says would hardly keep them properly in milk. And she found by accident that he told his mother that he couldn't save, because he gives his money to Idella! When she is there, he gives her $5 a week, out of which she pays for his own laundry and for their breakfasts and food together, entertainment etc.[1]

I should certainly have stopped you about the deep freeze for the Creek if I had known. As you say, it's too late now. You make me feel so horribly guilty about my inadequacies as a wife. Don't tell me that's what you're up to!!! No, you're just too ridiculously generous. . . .

. . . Gene also phoned from Vermont yesterday, and he and Stadler arrive day after tomorrow, the 24th. I shall make myself go on with Chapter V before they come.[2] I had been suffering over the idea of giving them my own bedroom, but I was so out-done by their dawdling along, and by seeing the trouble you get into by being over-hospitable, that I told Idella they would definitely have to sleep on the perfectly comfortable living-room couches, ordered for just such semi-welcome guests. After all, they can't be much more than half my age, and in their Bohemian ramblings must have slept on much worse beds.

A follow-up letter from Phil May about my will says that there is considerable doubt whether the Florida Endowment Corporation, my residuary legatee (doesn't that sound impressive) can act as executor in Wisconsin (where I have about $20,000 in stocks and bonds) and in New York, where I have this place, (of doubtful value to anyone but me) and so Phil suggests that I make you co-executor, as you could function anywhere. . . .

I thought, too, that Margaret's death would keep me from writing, but I so exhausted my anguish, ending with the day I *felt* her going, and the next day, when I *knew* from the paper that she was gone—I may have said this before—that I was left feeling even more vitally about life, not that I like it more, but that I felt an added sense of hurry in saying what I want to say.

1. Bernard Young worked for NSB at Marineland but was finally fired for his errant ways (Parker, *Perfect Maid*, 101–2).
2. Gene Baro and Albert Stadler. MKR began this letter on a sheet of paper number "44 V," which would have been page 44, chapter 5 of the manuscript of *The Sojourner*.

. . . .

(TLS, 2 pp.)

Van H[ornesville, N.Y.].
Aug. 23, 1949

Dear Norton:

I received recently two copies of the U.S. Army sponsored Japanese editions of "The Yearling" (that is, published by a Tokyo house[1] but O.K.ed by the Army, and arranged for by them) and this edition is in two volumes. My name is still misspelled—. And today I have my first Japanese fan-letter on "The Yearling." From a high school girl, in very good if quaint English. "I hope you won't be angry with me when you come to know I am your truthful friend."

. . . Julia writes that she longs to come in the autumn, if I'm sure it wouldn't interrupt me, and I can fore-see such a fine arrangement, whereby she would come by train ahead of you, (she didn't mention Tom's coming, praise be, although I invited him most cordially and definitely) and then she would drive me back to New York to meet you, and you and I would see the shows we wanted, and perhaps let Carl Van Vechten[2] have his mixed black and white party for us, and then you'd drive back here in the fine weather for as long as you could stay and you would go on to Fla. THEN, Idella would help me close the house for the winter, and we'd, Idella and I, come on South with dog, cat and jams and jellies. We must keep our fun separate from our animals.

I shall probably never again stop off with the Lyons.'

. . . I am still stuck at the beginning of Chapter V, when I wrote you yesterday. This whole week may be lost, as I have to go to some town to lay in supplies for the gourmand-gourmets Baroff and Stadler, due here tomorrow.

Thank you for everything, your mental gifts, your gift of yourself, above all, the gift of your understanding. I'll hope to make it up to you some-day.

My love,

1. *Iyaringu* (Tokyo: Hibiyashuppan, 1949). *The Yearling* was and still is especially popular in Japan (see Tarr, *Descriptive Bibliography*, 252–55).
2. Carl Van Vechten, American critic, editor, and novelist.

. . . .

(TLS, 4 pp.)

Van Hornesville, New York
Aug. 28, 1949

Dear Norton:

. . . As I wrote you, I couldn't decide whether Gene Baroff was a homosexual or not, and I came on the facts in such an odd way. I did find that he and Stadler had been friends since they were boys. I did my stunt of reading their palms, all non-sense, of course, but suddenly I *knew*. They are practically an old married couple. Strangely, the big coarse Gene is the female element, and trim little Stad is the aggressive male. Stad proves to be much more of a person than Gene. But they both have extremely fine minds, and we had good solid talk on the one hand, and roars of laughter on the other.

. . . I had a note from Norman from St. Petersburg, as gloomy as the one I had written him. He said that he found himself most disturbed after attending Margaret Mitchell's funeral.

You know, I have the most uncanny feeling that I was quite wrong about what would happen to John Marsh, and that he may prove to be another Edith Willkie.[1] Since he was able to attend the funeral and to appear in court to testify about Margaret's killer—both of which would have been beyond the crushed, numb John I pictured—it may well be that he will come to life again as Edith did after Wendell's death (and promptly, too!) and go running around with a supercharged ego, after having been submerged so long in or by a much stronger personality. . . .

All my love and thanks,

1. Edith Willkie, wife of Wendell Willkie, who died on 8 October 1944.

. . . .

(TLS, 2 pp.)

Van Hornesville, New York
Sept. 2, 1949

Dear Norton:

. . . The Popes seem more and more depressing, don't they? I just haven't been able to write Edie since I've been here. Verle and Mildred Pepper[1] should have mated young. Norman seems to have come off a bit better than usual. . . .

From the cool, somewhat harsh North, the South seems at this distance so chaotic. At the moment, I long to stay here straight through the winter. Yet I do have sense enough to know that since Idella could not possibly be here and that I should be marooned for several days at a time, perhaps without lights and water, that I could easily be in definite danger, with an eerie wind howling over the physical discomfort and the loneliness, of "ending it all," especially at a despairing moment on the book.

Helen Crosby writes me that Chet reports that great damage was done at the Creek, many trees down, and at least 30% of my crop destroyed.

Phil May writes me that the U. of Florida Endowment Corp. could not act as executor of my will, so you will have to take on that job. . . .

The entire Young family is coming here this Sunday night for buffet supper, about 27 in all.

After that, no more company of any sort.

. . . And a letter today from Cliff Lyons, so stuffy, so pedantic. It is terrible to have one's beloved friends fade away into the limbo—.

Much love,

1. Verle and Edith Pope; Mildred Pepper, wife of Congressman Claude D. Pepper of Florida; Norman Berg.

. . . .

(TL, 2 pp.)

Van Hornesville, New York
Sept. 5, 1949

. . . Virginia[1] is here, and is working on a companion piece to her water-color of the house.

. . . We had our usual buffet menu, ending with ice cream and mangoes. Gertrude helped Idella, and very nicely. It was an unusually successful and *happy* party. Faith[2] was charming.

. . . Mr. Young sat in the rust brocade chair, with your pipe tray handy, a very great patriarch indeed, and beamed and beamed. I am sure that such gatherings seem to him the most tangible success of his life

One of Esther Young's[3] sons had brought along a sheaf of her poems, six sonnets, one each for Charlie, herself, and the three sons and the daughter, called "Family Portrait." Esther had showed them to me a few days before, and if I am not too prejudiced, they are as fine personal poetry as I have ever read. Esther is so shy about her work that she reads rapidly and badly, and she refused outright to read them, so Davie brought them for me to read aloud. Everyone was in tears, and Charlie, who had seen the other poems, but not the one about himself, had to leave the room. The Judge had me read two of them over again, then he took over and read two more himself, stood up, a bit wobbly, and embraced both Esther and me. I shall ask Esther to let me have copies. The Judge quoted T. S. Eliot, I brought out the "Collected Poems" and we pounced on our favorite lines, and he is sending me the "Quartets."[4]

. . . There are already signs of autumn, a maple here, a dogwood there, shows signs of color, and the mornings and evenings are deliciously crisp.

1. Virginia Powis Brown Greene.
2. Faith Young, wife of Philip Young, son of Owen D. Young.
3. Esther Christensen Young, second wife of Charles Young.
4. T. S. Eliot (1888–1965), *Four Quartets* (New York: Harcourt Brace, 1943), a cycle of poems involving religious and philosophical meditations.

. . . .

(TLS, 3 pp.)

[Van Hornesville, N.Y.]

Sept. 6, 1949

Dear Norton:

. . . Shortly after, I ate supper, and was surprised by a phone call from the Cases, saying the family was waiting for me, for the reading of the annual family magazine, "The Dumpling," in which Dick used my "Lament of a Siamese Cat."[1] I had no idea I was expected. . . .

Here I am free again to work on the book, and all I want to do is verse. I have done two more, and am itching with another.

My love,

1. "Lament of a Siamese Cat," *Dumpling Magazine* 11 (4 September 1949): 8.

(TLS, 2 pp.)

Van Hornesville, New York

Sept. 7, 1949

Dear Norton:

An enchanting letter, as always, from James Cabell, thanking me for the MONITOR interview and for Miss Twitter's, approving both, and saying that Miss Twitter[1] did depict me "with a larger veracity."

. . . I got back to the book again.

. . . My dear, the Maine woods are out of the question for our next house, as Chuck Rawlings is living there—. Incidentally, in the Sunday Tribune magazine section, the gentleman had a short story about a deer eating a tender and much needed crop—.

My love,

1. MKR on occasion used the non de plume Lollypop Twitter.

. . . .

(TLS, I p.)

Van Hornesville, New York

Sept. 9, 1949

Dear Norton:

. . . It was 43 this morning. Went on to the movie, Paulette Goddard in "Bride of Vengeance,"[1] and some bobby-soxers and I took turns hooting. Have never seen anything so ghastly. . . .

Much love,

1. *Bride of Vengeance* (1949), starring Paulette Goddard. The film was a flop, and Paramount used the occasion to cancel her contract.

. . . .

(TLS, 2 pp.)

Van Hornesville, New York

Sept. 12, 1949

Dear Norton:

I am evidently never to be free of Dora Rolley. It was such a gorgeous morning that I was up betimes, started Idella on preparing crab-apples for making jelly, and was out in the garden in a house-coat and slippers, soaked to the knees from the dew, cutting flowers, when a car passed, backed up, and the usual Helen Hokinson type of woman[1] got out and minced over to me, and I hope to God she gets pneumonia. She asked, "Could you tell me how far it is to Miss Rolley's place?" I said I was sorry, I didn't know of anyone by that name. "Oh dear, I was looking for Miss Rolley, the one that wrote 'The Yearling,' and I have a great fan of hers with me, and of course I'm a fan, too, and this place looked so nice, I just didn't know whether it was the one or not."

I, colder than ever, "I am Mrs. Baskin. My name was once Mrs. Rawlings."

"Oh, dear. I'd hoped to find Miss Rolley's places. Rawlings? Could *you* (doubt and insult) *possibly* be the lady who wrote 'The Yearling'?"

I, trapped, "Yes."

"Oh, how wonderful. My friend has read all your books, and I haven't read them, but I've seen *all* your movies, and I just adored the last one, 'The Silver Lining.'"[2]

I, "I thought it was a lovely movie, too."

I said to Idella my books must be lousier than I ever dreamed of, to appeal to those bitches. It discouraged me so that I went for the bottle and didn't work....

All my love,

1. Helen Hokinson, a well-known cartoonist for the *New Yorker*, was known for her sly and scathing drawings of frivolous women.
2. *Look for the Silver Lining* (1949), starring June Haver and Ray Bolger. The film was actually about the Broadway career of Marilyn Miller.

. . . .

(TLS, 4 pp.)

Van Hornesville, New York
Sept. 15, 1949

Dear Honey:

You don't mind, do you, if I laugh merrily over your anguish? You must have meant that "remorse" is in *inverse* ratio to one's sins, for surely no one that I know has less to be remorseful about. Your besetting sin is too great and casual a generosity.

No, I have given up on turning you into Rodin's "The Thinker."[1] I am taking all that out on the principal character in my book. You are *Norton*, and we all love you for what you are, a sensitive (if too sensitive, perhaps, for my inquisitive raucousness) beautiful soul. Probably no one would be more upset than I if you turned into a chronic chest-beater.

... You have every reason to feel coldly about my book, but you cannot separate me between woman and writer, and that is just our mutual tough luck.

Anyway, all my love,

1. *The Thinker*, a sculpture by Auguste Rodin.

(TLS, 3 pp.)

Van Hornesville, New York
Sept. 17, 1949

Dear Honey:

. . . I have kept forgetting to answer your kind question about my hair. It is certainly not an Ingrid Bergman[1] bob, but everyone approves of it. It is at least not messy.

. . . A letter from Julia this morning, saying that she and Tom were taking a vacation next week, driving here and there, so I 'phoned her, asking them to spend some time with me. Praise God, they will not, but Julia wants to come alone some time in October, which will be wonderful. So it may still work out for me to meet you in New York, Julia driving my car one way, and you, the other. I still want you to have a spree with me here during the best of the autumn weather, but not to punish yourself by driving south with me and the animals.

All my love,

. . . Mean to order Ham Basso's book, "The Greenroom,"[2] which is getting superb reviews. It looks as though he might have a success and I notice it is NOT a Scribner book. He probably felt they didn't advertise him properly before.

. . . Got off-key on the book again, and am stuck, but shall go on tomorrow. Feel like Channel swimmer—.

All my love,

1. Ingrid Bergman, Swedish actor.
2. Hamilton Basso (1904–1964), *The Greenroom* (New York: Doubleday, 1949).

. . . .

(TLS, 3 pp.)

Van Hornesville, New York
Sept. 23, 1949

Dear Norton:

We have an awfully sick Uki, and I'm fighting hard for his life. The 19th day of his pneumonia, and this morning between 2 and 5, I thought he was going. . . . Moe got jealous of Uki's getting so much attention in the middle of the night, so while I was shut up in the bathroom, had a nice pile waiting for me to clean up when I came out. Anyway, hope last night was Uki's "crisis."

. . . A letter from Arthur, I do love him so, and miss him, and he is about the most *impossible* human being I have ever known. He is *considering* marrying— but *not* the Seattle Miriam. I begged him not to marry anyone at this stage of his work.

He will have to spend the winter in Seattle again, overhauling his brand-new Diesel engine. Says he is all right financially, but didn't get much new film this summer, due to extremely bad weather. He bought a little place at Juneau, but was able to rent it for the winter when he found he would have to be away.

My love,

(TLS, 2 pp.)

Van Hornesville, New York
Sept. 24, 1949

Dear Honey:

. . . I know what you mean when you say that you envy me my work as my raison d'etre, and it is both astute of you, and sad, that you put it that way. I am never done with being faintly puzzled about anyone who does not have a type of work that he or she feels deeply obliged to do, for better or for worse. And I, in turn, also faintly envy any such, for he or she is spared unspeakable torments. Yet I cannot, for myself, imagine living without the torment of writing.

As for you—you are a border-line case, like Julia. You are both completely understanding from the critical angle, yet do not have an out-and-out means of artistic personal expression. Perhaps it is worse to live in such a half-world. I don't know what to call my world, for all its single intent. I have thought of myself as a schizophrenic, but it is more as though I had been put through the atom-smasher.

The "hurdle" on the book, of course, was not as terrific as I thought at the moment. I knocked down at least the top bar. But while the book will have to be totally re-written, I feel that I am baying on the trail. (As the New Yorker says, "Stop those metaphors!")

I never heard such nonsense as your saying that "God knows" you share my financial returns. Is this a part of your gentle hypocrisy, to force me to remind you that while I paid $4500 or $5500, I don't remember, for the cottage, you have spent, by now, nearly $20,000 on turning it into a mansion? And that you have made me the most enormous gifts? And I do almost nothing for you?

Let us be as honest with each other as possible. . . .

My love,

. . . .

(TLS, 1 p.)

[Van Hornesville, N.Y.]
Tuesday A.M.
[4 October 1949]

Dear Norton:

. . . Uki is improving rapidly, and it seems like a miracle. Even his breathing is better. He must be a tough little rascal, after all. I had said, "Good-bye, Uki," several times. My hands are scarred from the battle of the pills and bowels (he had to have enemas the last three days). He thinks Idella is his only friend and that I am a bitch of the first water, little wotting [knowing] how I have fought for his life. . . .

Love,

(TLS, I p.)

Van Hornesville, New York
Wednesday
[5 October 1949]

Dear Honey:

. . . God, I am really working up a breeze on the book. My goal is 100 pages (35,000 words) or almost a third of the book, before Julia comes next week. Have just finished page 88, and think I'll make it. You will be coming so soon after her, that I'll be ready to enjoy any and every thing when you arrive, if I have done my self-appointed stint.

Louise has barked off to N.Y., leaving Mr. Young alone. I had drinks with him last night, and he is coming up for supper here tonight. He has the most magnificent ideas about China, about the coal and steel strikes—. He should be in on the high-policy aspects of the State Dept.

. . . Idella, bless her heart, rejoices with me over the progress on my work.

My love,

. . . .

(TLS, 2 pp.)

[Van Hornesville, N.Y.]
Oct. 7, 1949

Dear Honey:

I can see my goal in sight, 100 pages before Julia arrives next Thursday. . . . Now how I shall feel about the time I leave here will depend altogether on the weather, since I'll have enough work done to feel warranted in not doing any more until I am settled at the Creek. I was saying to Idella this morning, that once we have a killing frost, and my darling garden is done for, I'll probably be ready to high-tail it South. (I wrote a poem called "Mignonette" about a quite different sort of woman than I am, beginning, "She was trapped by the garden.") . . .

. . . The day before, afternoon, I got restless, and took Idella to Cooperstown to the movies, which proved an utter antique, "SHE,"[1] with Helen Gahagan and Randolph Scott, both young and beautiful. . . .

Mr. Young failed me for dinner last night, had his secretary phone that he couldn't come, and I was so disappointed. . . . The evening before, we had the most wonderful talk, he has the solutions for our relationship with Communist China, and for the steel and coal strikes, and on a drunken impulse I sat down and wrote Henry Luce,[2] suggesting that under the guise of offering Mr. Young his 75th birthday congratulations on Oct. 27, if he sent a top-notch interviewer, he might find himself with a great and timely story. Actually, I suppose, Mr. Young's ideas should go to the top-level of the State Dept. rather than to the casual public. They are the last thing one would expect from a capitalist-industrialist. . . .

1. *She* (1935).
2. Henry Luce, publisher, then editor of *Time*.

(TLS, 2 p.)

Hawthorn, Florida

Dec. 1, 1949

Dear Honey:

Martha was so relieved to see me drive in as she was all set for hog-killing yesterday, when the moon was right, meaning the meat will not "swink." The hogs were much better than I expected, 4 hams, 3 shoulders and 4 bacon sides weighing in at 147 lbs. at the curing plant in Gainesville.

Am just back from Hawthorn, where Mr. Gay[1] put the sausage meat through his electric grinder, saving Martha at least a full day of difficult hand-grinding. Idella was the Lady of the Manor yesterday during the hog-killing, holding aloof from the butchering hoi-polloi—and will be the first to dive into the finished product.

Chet's crew is picking tangerines and some oranges. I lost 20 good, large trees in the storm, which at last will give me a sizeable capital loss on income tax.

. . . A letter from Arthur, and at the moment he is hell-bent on marrying the new woman. He says he "wants some happiness, no matter what the price, in those years remaining to me and fifteen alone have been most inadequate. The woman I'm considering has enough fine attributes and few enough faults so that I feel I'm not to be able in the future to do better." Says he's not in love with her but very fond of her. Says "Her worst fault is her poverty." By which I wonder if he means she has a large and impoverished family he would have to help! Did you ever hear of a drearier prospect for a marriage? He will get fed up with her in no time, and have to split his property in half once again.

I shall say nothing further, however, to him. But he can just sweat this one out alone.

. . . March[2] paid off a good chunk on the truck. Martha announced with that manner that brooks no denying that March wished to see me. Thought it was about finances, but he was simply so proud that he had set out a row of lettuce — . . .

Much love,

1. Mr. Gay, grocer in Hawthorne.
2. March Mickens.

. . . .

(TL, 2 pp.)

Hawthorn, Florida

Dec. 2 1949

I was just finishing my supper of sandwiches and milk last night at 6:45, Idella had called "good-night" from the kitchen to go to Reddick, when Gene and Stad drove in. Poor Idella was exhausted from the day's cooking and freezing. . . .

Idella decided to go to the cottage for the week-end, so am sending my letters by her, as they might not reach you Sat. now. Am having her take pork goodies to Aunt Ida, but you'll have to come here for yours. My liver pate tastes very good, and the boys ate almost a small jar on crackers before their supper.

. . . .

(TLS, 2 pp.)

> Hawthorn, Florida
> Monday
> [5 December 1949]

Dear Honey:

So glad you can come Saturday. The boys are fun, but are rather strenuous intellectually without some help. Think I have impressed it on them that they'll have to let me know when they are coming for dinner. Of course, Idella is so rotten spoiled, and I should never get upset when *she* is upset when we have unexpected company.

. . . Have done the most terrific amount of duty-correspondence over the week-end, and will get back to the damn book tomorrow.

. . . Chet took Moe hunting yesterday afternoon and said Moe was perfect. Retrieved, did everything right.

. . . Mail has come, and am appalled. Thought I was caught up but another great pile of stupid letters to be answered.

. . . .

(TLS, 2 pp.)

> [Cross Creek, Fla.]
> Wednesday
> [7 December 1949]

Dear Honey:

. . . Stad bought one of his paintings to show me, "County Jail," really terrific. He charges only $150 dollars for a portrait or any painting (he is definitely a genius) so I told him to do a symbolistic portrait of me, not factual, God forbid, and he will make sketches to submit, and will read everything I've written (he only read two of my books) and will try to put down my complicated and unfortunate nature in paint. One thing only I asked of him, that he put somewhere in the painting a terrific blue-green color that occurs and reoccurs in my nightmares.

. . . I am sorry to have to report that I have been drinking again. I have re-read my manuscript once again, and while I am certain I shall have a good book in the end, I am crushed by its inadequacy, to say what I want to say, in fluent prose.

. . . I should have done better to have stayed at Van H. to finish the ghastly book. . . .

> My love,

(TLS, 4 pp.)

Hawthorn, Florida

Monday

[12 December 1949]

Dearest Norton:

It is too bad that you had to grab your (rum) balls and run—.

. . . As I told you, I have to go to Phil May next Saturday afternoon, to finish up my will. I plan to come to the cottage very early Sat. A.M., and if you could possibly go with me to the May's new home in the afternoon, it would be fine. Phil and Lillian are so touchy about your never visiting them. You could rave with Lillian over the house while Phil and I worked—it won't take very long, as the last draft he sent me is about right—we could have one drink—or two—and then you *always* have to get back to Marineland for Sat. night. Anyway, don't worry if you can't, or are unwilling to go.

. . . I went to Dr. Hook yesterday for one of his superb deep massages, a solid hour. . . . I took Martha along in search of an eye specialist. . . . He . . . said what the country doctor had told her, said it was definitely glaucoma. . . .

Wish I could say the same for Leonard's little girl. I went to Dr. Strange's[1] hospital Monday afternoon, and Leonard and Margaret and Jean[2] were all there, Margaret worn to the bone, Leonard in tears. St. Vincent's had confirmed the leukemia, and sent the child back where her family could be with her all the time. The great horror of it is her suffering. Aside from an almost constant fever of 105, she has begun to swell, and since the bone-marrow is affected, she is in utter agony. One of Leonard's hunting friends had also had a specialist, formerly from Chicago, now retired near Tampa, come up.

Relatives of other patients in the hospital had heard that little Grace had said she wanted Santa to bring her a red wagon, and a man was assembling it when I was there. The child scarcely knew what it was when they put it on the bed, she was so delirious and in such pain. She has to have a blood transfusion almost every day, to keep her alive, and Leonard said he had almost given out of donors. They have used so much of his blood, which types with hers, that they won't let him give any more for some time. I thought I had better 'phone the laboratory at the Ocala hospital before I trekked in, as the very nice and capable nurse said I would need a new check on my blood, to establish the RH factor. I have my blood type written on my car insurance card, but had never had the RH factor checked. Was glad I 'phoned first, as aside from the RH, my type wouldn't do for the child at all.

I went again yesterday afternoon, taking Margaret at her request. Leonard had told me that when he was here (the week I was ill at the cottage) Martha gave him 50¢ "to get something for the sick chile." He was touched, as he is by everyone's kindness. Grace was having a blood transfusion when we got there. . . .

Leonard knows there is no cure, no hope, but I was appalled yesterday when Margaret showed me a lovely little dress she had bought for Grace. She said, "It's a little too big, but I'll take the hem up, and she'll grow into it."

When the child has probably only a few more days to live—. . . .

Much love,

1. Dr. J. L. Strange of McIntosh.
2. Leonard, Margaret, Jean, and Grace Fiddia.

. . . .

(TLS, 3 pp.)

Hawthorn, Florida
Dec. 31, 1949

Dearest Norton:

. . . I have been working like mad on correspondence, in order to get back to the book Monday morning. At about the 20th letter yesterday—I think it was one to a Greyhound Bus Driver who wanted help in marketing the novel based on his life—I began nipping, and at about the 30th letter was suddenly overcome with remorse about Aunt Maggie Turner, Fred Tompkins' sister, who has been patiently waiting for some three or four years for me to say the word for her to visit me, with her notes on Fred's life, so that I may write it up as a "testimonial. . . ."

I thought I was *days* ahead of Idella on her time off, but according to her lights, I am scarcely even. The time she was sick did not count, and I agree with that. But she took the day after Christmas as her right, and the more than half-day Tuesday, and so on, and she said, "You 'keep talking' about 'the use of the car,'" and it seems that the "use of the car" means nothing to her, only the absolutely technical and rigid servant's afternoon-and-evening and Sundays "off." I think that fixing Sunday morning breakfast and making the beds is against the code. We almost had a quarrel yesterday, but in spite of my having nipped heavily, I had sense enough to say that it was wonderful that we could always talk things over. I really wanted to fire her then and there.

Of course, the "use of the car" is a great guarantee of her staying with me, and probably she is too well aware of that.

At the moment, I feel that I could do without her altogether. I have always done my best work when I was not being "taken care of." I thrive on adversity.

. . . Well, I have done my griping, shall finish all the dreadful duty-letters today and tomorrow, and get to the book the next day, come hell or high water.

. . . My anxiety and my guilt about you really are holding me up on my writing. Please tell me that you get along without me.

My love,

1950

1950 was a year of closure and renewal. In March, MKR announced that she would leave the bulk of her papers to the University of Florida. Perhaps more important, she was asked to write a review of the just-published Perkins letters, *Editor to Author*, which resulted in her tribute to Perkins, "Portrait of a Magnificent Editor as Seen in His Letters," which appeared in *Publishers Weekly* on 1 April. She was also responsible for introducing a publisher friend, Margaret Freeman, to James Branch Cabell; and the two were married in April. Buddy Bass stayed with her, which rekindled her maternal instincts. MKR seemed to be revitalized in spite of the fact that her good friend and neighbor Tom Glisson accidentally drank poison and died a "horrible death." As she was about to depart for Van Hornesville, there came another shock: Idella Parker left her without warning. MKR was never able to deal with the loss of her "Perfect Maid," this time gone forever. Van Hornesville brought some comfort, however. She was visited by Robert Frost and was a special guest when Colgate University gave him an honorary degree. As always, the Youngs brought solace. In late September, MKR completed the first draft of *The Sojourner*. And when she returned to Cross Creek for the holidays, another major event presented itself: Irita Van Doren wrote to ask if MKR would consider writing a biography of Ellen Glasgow.

. . . .

(TLS, 1 p.)

Hawthorn, Florida
Jan. 1, 1950

Dear Honey:

A happy New Year to you. I woke up at what I thought would be about midnight, to think about you, and by Heaven, it was 6:30, and day a-breakin,' and Martha coming in with orange juice.

And a happy New Year to me, too—after getting off prodigious numbers of duty-letters this past week, did 38 today! Am really exhausted, but unless a suspicious pile on the N.E. corner of the big porch table is from bus drivers and school children, I am *through*.

Was reading last evening when Chet Crosby appeared with 5 doves and a quail.

It was embarrassingly plain that it was his only way of giving me a present, and my Christmas to him and his family was no more than a decent thank-you for all the kindness he does me, so although I felt it was taking meat from his children's mouths (he said 6 birds wouldn't make "a mess") I raved with genuine enthusiasm. . . .

Much love,

. . . .

(TLS, 3 pp.)

[Cross Creek, Fla.]
Monday morning
[30 January 1950]

Dear Norton, alias Honey:

. . . Jack "got shot." Martha's favorite grandson, Adrenna's son. "Jack wasn't doin' a thing, another boy wanted to shoot another boy, and Jack tried to stop him and caught the bullet." Dr. Strange could not be roused, "Pinky" drove Jack to the Ocala hospital. It has cost $45 already and March is to move Jack today to Dr. Strange's hospital. With people getting blown up and shot up all around me, I am lying low.

I asked Martha for a scrambled egg this morning and thought I described quite well the appearance of an English muffin. She had never noticed Idella toasting one for me, and I explained that it was to be cut across just like an orange, buttered on the inside only, and the two halves browned under the broiler. After some time, she showed up with one of those un-baked rolls, cut across just like an orange, true, a dot of butter in the center, and not browned at all, merely an unhappy dried mass of raw dough. I sent her back to hunt for the English muffins, which I had seen last night in the middle front of the ice-box when I put away the meats. She was gone so long that I ate my egg. Uki was starved and I had to divide even that with him after he mopped up his own. She reported she could not find anything resembling English muffins. I wondered if she sensed that I was about to ask her to prepare other meals than breakfast, and thought she'd nip that in the bud right now. The early morning, and I do mean early, was chilly, and after orange juice I lit the heater. As time went on and I just couldn't get warm, I found that after her last appearance she had left the bathroom door wide open. I still don't want to bother with 'Liza Mae.[1]

Decided to eat on the road, nothing was open, and I turned in to the Glenn Bass' café[2] and found it in full swing, clean and welcoming. Had very good fried chicken, French fries, beets and marvelous hushpuppies. They didn't want me to pay but of course I insisted, Buddy Bass, the youngest or middle, I'm not sure, anyway, the smart and likable one, sat down with me for chit-chat and was induced to have a bite with me. I don't remember whether it was his idea or mine, but we were agreed that we would be miserable without each other's company.

He was ready to go right then, but Elma said she did need time to get his clothes together. He is coming on the school bus this after noon and if all goes well will spend the week. I woke up this morning thinking, "What is it nice that is happening?" and remembered it was Buddy. I hope he doesn't get homesick and also that we haven't hurt the other boys' feelings. Elma said, "I'm warning you, he'll drive you crazy," I said I thought not, it wouldn't matter in any case, this was a love affair. She said, "I can see that." He's in the fourth grade and will go back and forth to school. If he can buy his lunch at the school, I'll give him money for it rather than put it up. I think what finished me was his saying gravely over his drum-stick, "It must be very hard work to write a book."

My love,

1. Eliza Mae Thompson Bickers.
2. Run by Elma Marie Bass, wife of Erwin Glen Bass, at Lochloosa.

. . . .

(TLS, 2 pp.)

Hawthorn, Florida
Monday evening
[30 January 1950]

Dear Honey:

. . . Went to G. to stock up on food suitable for a small boy, the school bus came and went, and no Buddy Bass. Guess his mother was too afraid he'd be a nuisance, I am so disappointed. Don't know whether to go after him or not.

Gave Martha all the cash I had to bail Jack out of the Ocala hospital. The bullet entered the inside of his lower arm and was taken out on the outside upper arm, having shattered the arm-bone. He has accident insurance, and the boy who wanted to shoot another boy is in jail. Martha has pitched in nobly since she got back, is cooking us collard greens and corn-bread. The threat of Eliza Mae was all that was needed to send her into action. . . .

Love,

. . . .

(TLS, 2 pp.)

[Cross Creek, Fla.]
Jan. 31, 1950

Dear Honey:

I drove to Lochloosa last night after supper and brought Buddy back with me. His mother had been so afraid I wasn't serious about his visit. He knew I was, and had been in tears. With his pitiful little paper bag of clothing, new tooth-brush and comb his mother had slipped out to buy, he marched in the house, remarked, "You have a beautiful home," and with the air of the Duke of Windsor surrounded by luggage, said, "If you'll show me to my room, I'll put my things away." He trotted around the back bed-room, commented, "A fire laid. If I get cold in the morning I'll light it. And this is my private bathroom."

We sat down in the living-room for a formal visit. He sat very straight on the davenport. Apropos of nothing, he said, "I never use bad words. If I hear bad words, I just walk away. And I simply love to go to Sunday school." This filled me with horror. I should not have been nearly so shocked if he had pulled out a pocket-knife and ripped open the davenport, should, in fact, have preferred it. It is too soon to know whether I have taken a little viper to my bosom. I don't know whether it would be more depressing to find him a genuine little Lord Fauntleroy[1] (most ungrammatical and with not enough clothing) or a young Bert Cooper, who has discovered that so-called "goodness" brings nice results. I must not judge one of his age by one appalling statement. He may have wished only to reassure me that he would not be an undesirable guest.

He asked me to begin reading "The Yearling" aloud. Whether or no[t] this was cunning flattery, he listened with complete attention. I had not quite finished the first chapter when he said, "Thank you very much, it's a lovely story, but I'm suddenly sleepy." I escorted him to his suite, he drew his own bath, asked how far away I would be, and if Moe couldn't sleep with him. I had expected this, said of course, if Moe would stay, and brought Moe's blanket to put beside his bed. He said, "Don't you think it would be much better if we put his blanket on top of the bed? I can take better care of him." I agreed, and to my surprise, Moe was perfectly contented all night. When I called Buddy this morning, he said he had gotten cold in the night, but Moe helped him keep warm, and he showed me the top sheet split from end to end, and I am sure that Moe ended up in between the sheets with him.

Martha fixed his breakfast, he ate heartily, said he had some trouble getting to sleep, as he wondered if we'd be robbed or murdered, but once asleep, had had no more worries. We had stopped to see the school bus driver, and he came to say good-bye before going to the road to wait for the bus. He waved from the door and said, "Well, happy day." I said "The same to you," and he said, "You'd better have a happy day, because it'll be all over when I get back." I said politely, Not at all, I looked forward to his return, and he said, "I know you do."

I suddenly remembered that school-children usually had home-work. He has not forgotten, but had not brought his books, and since he has three Exams tomorrow, I have to go over questions with him tonight in language, arithmetic and spelling. He has reached long division, and I warned him I would probably be unable to cope. He said cheerfully that he expected to fail in arithmetic anyway. I told him you would be able to help him if you come while he is here.

We go to Ocala late this afternoon to have Moe's stitches taken out and Buddy asked if he might bring a friend from the Creek. I want to get him some pajamas and a warmer sweater, and will treat the friend according to how ragged he seems. Buddy's things are whole and clean, but inadequate.

Martha is much taken with him, is very cheerful and willing, much amused by the sheet business. She said, "That pair must of really tangled."

I think I can start up on the book this morning, enough at least to snap out of my inertia.

My love,

1. Francis E. Burnett (1849–1924), *Little Lord Fauntleroy* (New York: Scribners, 1886).

. . . .

(TLS, 2 pp.)

Hawthorn, Florida
Feb. 4, 1950

Dearest Norton:

. . . One trouble with a little boy around, he doesn't stay that way. He accumulates not only dirt, but other little boys. When I came out to the porch this morning, here were three of them. They look like the "little people" that call on Cookie and walk in on Dagwood's bath.[1] I rather foolishly let Buddy bang on my typewriter yesterday, and he was so fascinated that he was up before the sun—even before Martha—and turned on a porch light and pecked away until breakfast.

. . . Buddy put on another song and dance to stay. At the Sunday school he claimed so to love, they do nothing but read a Bible story, hardly worth while, he insisted. But I am taking him home today. Have had enough for a while.

Don't know what to say about coming over before the 17th. The turn the book has taken is a complete mess. I am most discouraged. I know what is to happen in twenty years, in the narrative, but seem to have nothing to say in the meantime, yet the intermediate years should help develop the theme. Damn, I just can't *write*. Somebody else must have written "The Yearling." Or it happened in my sleep. 'Twa'n't Elmer, 'twould o' woke me.[2]

I think I even read 'A Long Day's Dying"[3] at the cottage, have decided I never brought it here. Seem to remember reading it in the yellow chair in the studio. Have begun the Ronald Firbank's.[4] A bit too precieux for me so far.

If you see your way clear to come here before the 17th, it would be nice to have you alone, sans Gainesville boys or Lochloosa and Cross Creek boys, though of course we would be stuck with the Member of the Wedding.[5]

Much love, darling.

1. Characters in the comic strip *Blondie*.
2. Elmer Fudd, a *Looney Tunes* cartoon character.
3. Frederick Buechner (1926–), *A Long Day's Dying* (New York: Knopf, 1950).
4. Ronald Firbank (1886–1926), *Five Novels* (Norfolk, Conn.: New Directions, 1949).
5. Carson McCullers (1917–1967), *The Member of the Wedding* (Boston: Houghton Mifflin, 1946).

(TLS, 2 pp.)

Hawthorn, Florida
Feb. 12, 1950

Dearest Norton:

And a happy Lincoln's birthday to you! You see, I swing like a pendulum, and yesterday I longed for you no end. I finished a bit more than my day's stint (of writing), had lunch, was restless, and on an impulse drove to Salt Springs to see if I could get crabs, taking both Moe and Uki! I bought four dozen crabs, cooked them in Martha's wash-pot, and was suddenly stricken with nostalgia for our old days. Idella helped me clean them, without picking out the meat, and I said, "Oh dear, I wish Mr. Baskin would come this evening." I didn't have my supper until 7:30, hoping you would appear. . . .

My love,

. . . .

(TLS, 3 pp.)

Cross Creek, [Fla.]
Tuesday afternoon
[21 February 1950]

Dearest Norton:

The idea of rushing to the Creek for peace and quiet is absurd. Found a note in my mail from a Mrs. Bowen, asking for $5 to buy food. Had a bite of lunch, made up a box of groceries of what I had on hand, and Martha and I drove across the Creek to see what was what. They live in a hut near the old Balknight place. Mr. Bowen did some carpentry work for me some years ago, and when I found him, a perfectly worthless drunk, loafing and actually cheating, we had the most terrific row, and he "quit" in hauteur. Martha of course knew all about every-thing, and that he had a stroke three weeks ago. With the idea of getting County help for the family, I asked Martha on the way over how long he had lived here-abouts, and hadn't he worked for me before you and I were married. She said, "No'm, it was after, he done made the chicken-pen Mr. Baskin got shut up in."

To make a long story as short as possible, they were really "on starvation." They have one adult son who ran away with a married woman, from whom they have not heard in some time and have no idea where he is, and who left behind with them three little boys, two of them in school. I left the box of food and $5 and went on to Gainesville to see what I could do. Found the County Welfare Board and such a nice woman in charge and told her the story, and she will send a worker out to investigate, and will do everything possible for the children at least, and meantime, I certainly can't let the family go hungry. . . .

. . . Found here four copies of the French edition of "South Moon Under" en-titled "Le Whisky du Clair de Lune."[1] French for boot-legging, I assume.

A statement from Scribner's, on royalties, will receive about $2,000. in June.

Did think I got royalties in Feb. No '49 income tax statement. Think I had better wire. Such lovely people, and not at all business-like. You remember, one year they wrote me that they found they owed me $1,000.—I should never have known.

Sam Sweet,[2] Estelle's husband, was waiting to see me. The [In MKR's hand: "<Jesus Christ> A queer whirring sound of a spring going hay-wire——my typewriter is broken!!!"]

Feb. 22 Morning

Knowing everything would be closed today, a holiday, I was floored yesterday when my typewriter broke down. I dashed in to Island Grove and 'phoned Baroff and asked them[3] to come out and eat shrimp and take my Portable back to Gainesville for repairs. This was 5:30 P.M., too late to go to town myself. They came, and Gene, bless his heart, brought his own Portable and insisted on leaving it for me until mine is fixed.

And confusion worse confounded,[4] something is wrong with the plumbing, toilet only half flushes, electric pump running day and night, Idella has to keep priming the hand pump to have any water at all. Will send her to Island Grove to mail this. . . .

Oh, about Sam Sweet. The cold ruined the strawberry crop where he was working, and he is coming here to get the moss and mistletoe out of the pecan trees, which they are killing. . . .

Thanks for everything, and all my love.

1. *Le Whiskey du Clair de Lune* (Paris: Michel, 1950).
2. Sam Sweet was married to Estelle Mickens, Martha's oldest daughter.
3. Gene Baro and Albert Stadler.
4. MKR is quoting John Milton (1608–1674), *Paradise Lost* (1667): "With ruin upon ruin, rout on rout, / Confusion worse confounded" (2: 995–96).

. . . .

(TLS, 2 pp.)

Cross Creek, [Fla.]
Sunday night, and I do mean
night
[26 February 1950]

Norton dear:

. . . Martha claims that no car never comes to the gate, she doesn't catch it—. Four cars came to the gate. No Martha, and people came into the yard, gathered oranges and tangerines. She appeared for the last one, with her psychic sense for a tip. A doctor from Arizona and his wife wanted to take pictures. I was working in bed, but Martha came to ask permission for them. I said, God, yes. They were all over the place for two solid hours. They gave Martha a dollar. We agreed it wasn't enough—.

. . . Wish you could have made the trip with me. How I love that scrub country.

(TL, 1 p.)

Hawthorn, Florida
Feb. 27, 1950

Dear Baskin:

In our ill-assorted, but, I hope, in the long run, happy marriage you have been doing two things that irritated me above all else. One has been your rage whenever I asked you simply "When?" You cannot endure being pinned down to dates, and I respect this. I cannot respect, I go utterly insane, when it happens, your writing me on my own private stationery. To receive a letter from "Mrs. Norton Baskin, Crescent Beach, St. Augustine, Florida," accents too ominously my schizophrenia. . . .

Worked hard all morning, and am headed for Gainesville to get a surveyor to run the fence line where the Hamon's[1] fire burned the fence between us. Had a conference with Mrs. Hamon yesterday, about putting up a new fence, but there'll be no peace until Old Will and Martha are satisfied that the Hamon's aren't stealing a strip of my land, and of course, they may be doing so.

1. Hoyt Haymans owned Cow Hammock, which was south of MKR's property.

. . . .

(TLS, 1 p.)

[Cross Creek, Fla.]
Tuesday noon
[28 February 1950]

Darling Norton:

Have passed a critical moment in the book. Have also realized that I just must not be in such a frenzy to finish the first draft by the end of April, must work more quietly, with no sense of haste. Most of the bad writing has been done in hurry. After all, I can go to Van Hornesville in early May, finish up, and re-write at leisure. I am too conscious of "Time's winged chariots ever drawing near." (Quotation not quite accurate.)[1]

I am also appalled at my ill-advised choice of words in writing you yesterday. When I spoke of our "ill-assorted" marriage I had in mind your sociability and my increasing lack of it, yet God knows how I may have wounded you. I am at once callous and sensitive, as no one knows better than you. You must always forgive me.

Robert Frost is to be in Gainesville March 3 to 6. . . . You would be utterly enchanted by him, to listen to his charming wisdom. . . .

My love, in spite of all my nastiness!

1. MKR is quoting from Andrew Marvell (1621–1978), "To His Coy Mistress" (1681): "Time's winged chariot hurrying near" (line 22).

(TLS, 1 p.)

Hawthorn, Florida
March 1, 1950

Norton dear:

God is good. A letter from my ex-brother-in-law, Wray Rawlings, and he and his wife cannot come to Florida this spring. It seems he was involved with the grounding of the battle-ship "The Missouri" off Newport News, to the extent that he was one of the marine engineers working on the odd submarine electrical "lanes" for the "Missouri," so now he is stuck, he reports, with working out the problems for at least another eleven months. . . .[1]

No word from the Young's and Cases. If it were not that Robert Frost so hates our dear Owen D. Young, we could have all of them at the Creek together. . . .[2]

My love,

1. The battleship *Missouri* was aground off Norfolk, Virginia, for sixteen days in January 1950.
2. MKR is revealing an enmity not generally known. While at St. Lawrence University, Owen D. Young dated Elinor White, who at the time was also dating Robert Frost, whom she later married. This no doubt was the cause of Frost's jealousy. See letter of 14 June 1950.

. . . .

(Postcard)

[Cross Creek, Fla.]
Wednesday 5:30 P.M.
[1 March 1950]

. . . Robertson's[1] on the phone from Mr. Gay's store. They are hogging Robert Frost and will not bring him to the Creek at all. Since I do want so much to see him, I accepted their invitation for supper at their house Sat. 6:15 P.M. You are invited too. There will be 25 "Honor students" there, so depressing, don't imagine it tempts you. Yet perhaps, as Frost's talk is worth any punishment.

Much love,

1. Charles A. Robertson and Alleyne Robertson; the former was chair of the English Department at the University of Florida.

. . . .

(TLS, 3 pp.)

Hawthorn, Florida
March 14, 1950

Dearest Norton:

The portrait[1] is really fascinating. When Stad set it up on an easel for inspection, my first reaction was to burst into raucous laughter. Stad beat his fist on his forehead, said "Oh God" and staggered away. My second reaction was to find it rather frightening. Then Stad set it in its frame and put it over the living-room mantel and the three of us sat without a word for half an hour, studying it. Suddenly, I saw with what art Stad had indeed portrayed a schizophrenic soul. What had seemed a meaningless distortion resolved itself into *two* faces, two aspects of the one soul. The left side, Stad said later, when he saw that I began to understand the painting, is an "inner mask" that he called "the dreamer." The eye is closed and the effect is soft, even tender, and mysterious. The open eye on the other side, at a higher level, is objective, penetrating, quite cold. The mouth and chin are accurate and bind the whole together. I found this encouraging, as it seems to preclude actual insanity! The composition itself, in line and substance, is striking.

Idella had an almost instant perception of the painting, liked it at once. Martha seemed rather floored and would only say, "That's her chin, all right. That's her."

Perhaps I shouldn't' have described it before you see it.

. . . If you find that you can "live" with the portrait, over the fire-place in the studio is certainly the place for it. . . .

Much love,

1. Albert Stadler's surreal portrait of MKR.

. . . .

(TLS, 1 p.)

Hawthorn, Florida
March 14, 1950

Dear Norton:

I asked Martha this morning to tell me exactly how she felt about Stad's portrait of me. I pretended to be making notes about something else, and as she spoke, I wrote down *exactly* what she said. This is it, and it seems to me rather fabulous.

"Ain't got my mind composed, but it means a whole lot to me. The way it's looking direct, just like you fixing to pray. Wish he could of had your hands in it. Your hands has meaning."

"Just to stand up and look at it, makes you think way back, way back."

"He couldn't of done a better thing."

"It brings a half-sorrow to me."

. . . I made these precise notes because Stad wanted to know her true re-action, and he wants especially to have yours. He said that with this painting, he thinks he has begin to reach his individual style in which he will work from now on.

(TLS, 3 pp.)

Hawthorn, Florida
March 22, 1950

Dear Honey:

... I was disturbed to find no work being done on the fence, and that Sam[1] had told Mrs. Hayman that I didn't tell him to work on it with her, and he had to have orders from me, whereupon she drove off in a huff. (I'm sure I told you that she planned to work with him in place of hiring another man.) I said to Martha that I was sure I had told her, at least, to tell Sam the fencing was yesterday's project. She said I had, then blurted out, "Mrs. Baskin, Sam ain't goin' back in them woods to work with a white woman."

With a sense of horror, I understood at once. And Mrs. Hayman should have understood, for she is the sort who would join the hue and cry in a lynching—. Makes you feel a bit ill, doesn't it?

Gene arrived early, as he found a friend to drive him out. I was on the porch entertaining two of the little Cross Creek boys who call on me too regularly. The older one said he had just been giving information to a woman tourist who had stopped and asked questions about me, and he had told her that I was about to write a book about the cattle country. I said, No, I was not, and the boy said, "Buddy Bass told us you were going down to the cattle country to write a book about it, and you were going to take him with you." !!!!! Perhaps Buddy's trouble is that he, too, wants to be the member of the wedding, but I must say, he carries it pretty far.

... Gene brought some of his poetry, as I had asked, and I was really astonished by its quality. Most of it is difficult reading, it is like Stad's portrait, one has to study and re-study, to get it, and very few readers or viewers give themselves that far to an art that is obscure, but on the second or third reading of Gene's stuff, I found in most cases a crystal clear theme, and really, genuine poetry. The boy is probably right in cutting loose from his teaching in order to write, but there is still so much of the element of chance in getting anywhere in writing, that I am rather sorry to see him cut his moorings.

... Gene also told me a great deal about his adolescent years with Stad, and it is a strange story.

John Marsh sent me a photograph of Peggy[2] and me, said he didn't know when or where it was taken, but thought I should have it. . . . He speaks of "My Peggy," and I cannot help wondering whether you husbands of writers don't derive a greater satisfaction from the *idea* of us, than from our troublesome reality. As I indicated about Stad's portrait—. Of course, Margaret Mitchell was a better wife than I could ever be. But she and John began earlier in life than you and I.

My love,

1. Sam Sweet.
2. Margaret Mitchell.

(TLS, 2 pp.)

Cross Creek, [Fla.]
April 3, 1950

Dear Honey:

Martha and Moe and I are just back from Gainesville. . . . Martha shopped for a dress for Adrenna's Betty Jean. Betty Jean, at the age of six, is now singing over the St. Petersburg radio.

. . . Idella and I ran into one of our misunderstandings Saturday night. I had not eaten a square meal since the Thursday luncheon in Gainesville, and Saturday afternoon . . . I foolishly tried to catch up on my banal correspondence, to be ready for work this morning, and "nipped" as I corresponded. When Idella announced dinner, I was suddenly through and excused myself to go to bed. Sometime or other I had brought the keys of my car into my bedroom, with the purpose, which I only remembered much later, of having Idella drop my stamped letters into the slot at the Island Grove post-office, for it was understood that she was to go home to Reddick that night after dinner, Martha to fix Sunday morning breakfast.

I went sound asleep, and it seems the girls sang with Martha and Idella etc. then went to bed. The next thing I knew I was awakened out of a deep sleep by a flashlight in the room. It was of course Idella asking me about the car keys. I was on my feet in an instant, in a savage rage, demanding how she dared wake me up with a flash in my face, and I almost threw the keys at her, crying, "Go, go, go!"

She was deeply offended, and was on hand the next morning to fix breakfast in deep indigo. Then she sat at the kitchen table ostentatiously reading the Bible. I asked her forgiveness. She retired to her quarters. Chet Crosby stopped by to give me fish—he and the man with him had caught 50 in a few hours—and to humble myself properly, I cleaned the fish, cutting myself of course, laid a big tray with best linen and silver, fried fish, (parsley), covered bowl of grits, fresh-baked rolls, jelly, broccoli, ice water, salad (I peeled the tomato) pie, and a small bouquet. I struggled over to Idella's rooms with it, only to have Martha call from a window that Idella had taken the 1 o'clock bus!

By the time Idella was brought back by her sister yesterday morning I had figured out that quite aside from being tight, I had some reason for having been angry, for I had reverted to the days, or nights, of long ago when there actually was some dangers here for me alone, with rough characters at large, and I unpopular because of "Cracker Chidlings"—when Fred Tompkins offered to sleep on the place with his gun handy.[1] I had not been *frightened* by being wakened with a flash in my eyes, but I was certainly *startled*. . . .

Much love,

1. "Cracker Chidlings," *Scribner's Magazine* 89 (February 1931): 127–34. MKR's first story offended some locals, who thought she was being critical of Cracker life. Even the *Ocala Evening Star* entered in to the fray. MKR responded in a letter to the *Star* on 2 February 1931, saying that she had no such intention and was in fact portraying the inherent qualities of character of the Crackers.

(TLS, 2 pp.)

Hawthorn, Florida
April 11, 1950

Dear Honey:

. . . Idella was the height of cheer, chatted amiably all the way over. I said she might as well go to Reddick early last evening, as all I wanted was fresh green beans for supper, and she said she would really love to leave as soon as possible after lunch, to go to Silver Springs for some sort of colored school-children's celebration for Mrs. Bethune.[1] Did you know Silver Springs has set aside a colored beach and recreation area? Probably down the Run. I was only too pleased to cooperate—. Nothing was said about Bernard,[2] and I'll let things rock along. From her attitude, I feel most hopeful.

The Rumer Godden[3] book is indeed beautiful. Wouldn't we love going to such a place in India!

It seems Idella is to give her annual "program" at her Reddick church this Sunday, so think it will be smart under the circumstances to stay here over the weekend, so she can have the car. If you can come over, I'll bake a cake! Much love, and thanks for a lovely Easter.

Idella spoke to Mrs. Bethune, who always remembers her. Mrs. B. asked her what she was doing, and Idella said, "You know—I'm companion to Marjorie Kinnan Rawlings."

I was a bit taken aback. When I want to make Idella feel good, or in impressing any of her friends, I refer to her as my housekeeper. On checking the facts, I could hardly deny "companion" as an accurate description of her job. Yet it was a severe test of my liberation from race prejudice!

It seems that Mrs. Bethune cried out, "Wonderful, wonderful! She's a wonderful woman. I only wish she had come today, too."

1. Mary McLeod Bethune, noted black educator.
2. Bernard Young.
3. Rumer Godden (1907–1998), *A Breath of Air* (London: Joseph, 1950).

. . . .

(TLS, 3 pp.)

Hawthorn, Florida
April 12, 1950

Dear Honey:

. . . Another thing has come up which makes it definite that I will not come to the cottage this week-end. I had asked Leonard to see me before I go north, to check over the many jobs he will do this summer, especially the new back porches and repairing the shattered cattle-gap. A note from Margaret asked if I would be here this Sunday, for Leonard to talk with me. I have answered that I will be, and asked the whole family to have noon dinner with me. I told Idella this would not hold her up, as with Martha's help, I could easily bake the fresh pork ham from the last pig, bake sweet potatoes, and have ice cream for dessert. It would certainly not bore you to come over Saturday, would it, spend the night, and stay, or not, for the Fiddias, though the chances are that they will not all come.

. . . Aside from having eaten a few things I shouldn't have, I became so distressed yesterday when I wasn't able to pick up work on my book. I go crazy when I work too long at a time, and I go crazy when I interrupt myself and lose my train of thought. I go crazy, period—. I did think I was ready to continue where I left off. Yet I realize that I have not exactly decided where I am headed on the next two chapters. I'll have to make the decision before I go on. Also, I have misplaced my notes for the book, and suddenly find I need them badly. . . .

Much love,

. . . .

(TLS, 1 p.)

Cross Creek, [Fla.]
Monday morning
[17 April 1950]

Dear Honey:

I got into an interesting light book after you left, so that the evening wasn't as lonely as I feared. It was the Daphne du Maurier book, "The Parasites,"[1] and I don't think the reviewers did it justice. Extremely good reading, in any case. I'll bring it when I come.

I should have looked more closely at "Slick But Not Streamlined."[2] It was Julia who sent it to me. It is odd as can be, and most of it utterly delightful. Will bring that, too. I want to take the Maria Edgworth[3] to Van Hornesville. It's the sort of book that belongs there, and it will assure you of having something meaty to read when you're there.

Last night I walked down to the Glisson's, and found Mrs. G. being most brave. All the kin-folks had gone. . . .[4]

Much love and thanks,

1. Daphne du Maurier (1907–1989), *The Parasites* (London: Gollancz, 1949).
2. John Betjeman (1906–1984), *Slick But Not Streamlined* (New York: Doubleday, 1947).
3. Maria Edgeworth (1767–1849), Irish novelist.
4. Tom Glisson had died after accidentally drinking poison from an unmarked jug. After his death, MKR invited his son, J.T., to spend the night with her. They reminisced through the night, with MKR saying at one point about Tom, "He was one hell of a man" (Glisson, *The Creek*, 254).

(TLS, 3 pp.)

[Cross Creek, Fla.]
Monday 2 P.M.
[24? April 1950]

Dear Honey:

... Moe almost went crazy as we got near Island Grove, and I caught him here just as he was slipping away over the cattle-gap to look for his girl friend, so I shall just have Chet put him with the other dog in the roomy place he has, and send Moe's rations along with him. Better that, than having him keep on the highway, with all the traffic.

... Martha asked, of course, "Where is Idella?" I said, "Didn't she come here Saturday or yesterday to pick up clothes?" No, she had not been here. I said she had joined Bernard in N.Y.C. Martha said that the last time Idella's sister and brother-in-law were here, (a week ago last Friday) that she had seen them putting a lot of stuff in the car—. So she had made her plans that long ago. Martha knows where Idella's key is, to her rooms, and I shall go over and see if she left her uniforms behind. If she did, it is proof positive that she is not going to Van Hornesville. On the other hand, if they are not there, it would not necessarily mean that she plans to go to Van H., but could only have prepared herself if she takes a domestic job with Bernard.

Now I don't want to be too hasty, but I really feel that I have had enough. I was SO concerned over darling Idella's transportation Saturday, begged her to use my car and bring it back Sunday and I'd drive her to the train for N.Y. I said, "But it will be so late when you reach Reddick, after changing from the St. A. bus at Gainesville, and how will you get to Cross Creek to get your clothes there?" She said that Thelma and her husband would drive her to the Creek to get her things—.

Well—. I stopped right here and went over into Idella's quarters. Every stitch of her clothes, all her personal belongings, are gone. Every one of her uniforms is still hanging in the cupboard—. Eight in all, from her oldest worn ones that I ordered last summer, up to her two fancy and expensive white ones, one poplin, one a $16. nylon.

Now just how much of a sap am I called on to be? Can you think of any possible explanation for this? I'll wait to act until I hear from you, in case you CAN think of anything that makes sense. It does not hold water that she planned to write me to bring or send the uniforms, for she knew that there was a strong possibility that I'd be leaving for Van H. the end of this week or the first of the next, and there just wouldn't be that much time for correspondence about the uniforms.

My idea—and I felt sure I was right even before I found the uniforms left behind—is to write her to the address she gave me—if it is accurate—and if not, I can get a letter to her through her mother or one of her Cooperstown friends who will know where she actually is—saying quite simply that I have taken all I can of her double-crossing and dishonesty, and that she can never return to me under any circumstances.

If she was expecting to be met at Ft. Plain at her convenience later in the summer, to have a gay few months (if so, perhaps she expected to have some of her folks come to the Creek to get and mail her uniforms) I prefer not to give her that pleasure, for I will be much better off by setting on some white woman up there who will do what is necessary all the summer through, until I have completely finished my book. I can adapt myself to almost anything except uncertainty.

Now I am assuredly not trying to put on you any onus of agreeing with me that I would be a complete ass not to be done with her at once, or of urging me to wait for her, which might make even worse confusion this winter. I ask only, can you think of any reasonable explanation for her having left her uniforms behind, and lied to me about picking up her clothes at the Creek? Just yes or no, and then I'll decide. I almost think that whatever alibi you could think of, I shall have to be through with her anyway. For the uniforms here DO MEAN that she will not be at Van. H. SOON. . . .[1]

Much love,

1. Idella did in fact leave MKR to join her husband, Bernard, in New York, although the details of the departure differ in Idella's account. Idella says that MKR and NSB "took me to the bus station in St. Augustine. . . . As the bus pulled out, she [MKR] waved and smiled, and that's the last time I ever saw Marjorie Rawlings" (Parker, *Perfect Maid*, 113). As the following letters indicate, MKR tried to persuade Idella to change her mind. Idella wrote saying that she "would no longer be working" for MKR. "It was hard for me to write that letter after so many years together. Hard for me, and hard for her. But it had to be done" (114).

. . . .

(TLS, 2 pp.)

The Creek
[Cross Creek, Fla.]
May 1, 1950

Dear Honey:

I am writing you on the stationery I have just used for a letter to Idella—.

I asked her mother for Idella's addresses, saying that I had promised to let her know when I left for Van Hornesville. Mrs. Thompson[1] produced it, from a letter she had received from Idella, and it is the Brooklyn address of Bernard's brother. I realized that since Idella is double-crossing Bernard just as hard and fast as in my case, she could not have a letter from me arrive for Bernard's scrutiny or challenge. SO, I have written Idella only a chatty letter, telling her when we are leaving, stopping in Alabama, reaching Van Hornesville probably Saturday May 13. . . . I am mailing the letter from Ocala tomorrow on plain paper with no name or return address, so that even if Bernard intercepts and reads it, it is inno-

571

cent on the surface, yet she will be able to read between the lines. I did not dare say anything more, because of the Brooklyn address....

Love,

1. Ethel Riley Thompson, Idella's mother.

. . . .

(TLS, I p.)

Van Hornesville, New York

May 26, 1950

Dear Honey:

Finished my stint on the O. Henry stories[1] and mailed it off today and promptly got lonesome....

Much love,

1. MKR was a reader for the O. Henry Memorial Prize competition for the best short story of the year.

. . . .

(TLS, 2 pp.)

[Van Hornesville, N.Y.]

Van H. May 30, 1950

Dear Honey:

... I have finished "Debby"[1] and Margaret Kennedy's "The Feast,"[2] the latter simply delicious. I'll send them on.

... Don't forget to look at my Will. I see no alternative but being through with Idella for good. If it didn't matter to her to abandon me at this point in my work, I could never depend on her to see me through my life—.

The most *exasperating* letter from Arthur. He spoke of having "stuck his neck out," of knowing that he might always be counted on to do "the questionable thing," that he had been through "a terrific battle" but it hadn't hurt his health, as he weighs 195, and when he had more time, he'd write me all the details! I could kill him. Obviously a woman-mess, for he said of his boat only that he finally had all the "bugs" out of his Diesel engine, and was about to take out the only party he has lined up so far.

Much love,

1. Helen Fern Daringer (1892–1986), *Debby of the Green Gate* (New York: Harcourt, 1950).
2. Margaret Kennedy (1896–1967), *The Feast* (London: Cassell, 1950).

(TLS, 3 pp.)

Van Hornesville, New York
June 2, 1950

Dear Honey:

. . . "Stage Fright"[1] was in Ft. Plain last night, and I drove down for the 7 o'clock show and enjoyed it. Had not eaten first, so went over to the Colonial Hotel afterward, where we ate that noon, and had a straight Bourbon, delicious beef-stew, Polish bread and butter, all for 90¢.

. . . . I haven't checked, of Iturbi,[2] the most ghastly slop already written for me, "Adds Sight to Sound," writes Marjorie Kinnan Rawlings about José Iturbi, "my" statement ending, "I wish I could write color as Iturbi plays it!"

Also enclosed, two "testimonials"—this is a revolting advertising scheme for pushing certain RCA records—one allegedly by John Marquand[3] calling Marian Anderson[4] "A Ruby Swathed in Velvet," one even more allegedly by Hemingway, titled "Whispering Volcano," about Horowitz,[5] "There must be *two* Horowitzes. One man cannot possibly play as whisperingly and as softly as the fall of a petal—and yet be able to summon the tension of Mt. Vesuvius in action—. They say Liszt[6] played like Horowitz. I wouldn't know who is the greater. I only know that Horowitz is great."

Is that Hemingway's style or isn't it?

These horrible people are paying $150 just for signing 60 words. Would Hemingway permit a public prostitution of his famous style for 150 bucks? These commercial devils may have counted on the inherent laziness of writers, such a temptation, 60 little harmless words already written out for you, just sign, probably nobody will notice—.

By God, I noticed, and was so upset, and put in a call for Carl Brandt, to find the name of the actual, not the titular, head, of J. Walter Thompson, so that I might speak my mind to him about this obscenity. Futile in any case, of course, futile, but it does seem to me that high-tension American advertising is doing almost more damage to us in the eyes of the world than anything else, is harming us, too, "selling" material standards—.

1. *Stage Fright* (1950), starring Jane Wyman and Marlene Dietrich.
2. José Iturbi, concert pianist.
3. John P. Marquand, American author.
4. Marian Anderson, American opera singer.
5. Vladimir Horowitz, Russian-American pianist.
6. Franz Liszt, Hungarian composer and pianist.

(TLS, 3 pp.)

Dear Norton:

It is amusing that I "decided" to be done with Idella, since she is done with me.

One of her Cooperstown friends, Hattie, who works for Senator Stokes,[1] 'phoned me last night to say that if I didn't have anyone to help me, she, Hattie, had a fine colored woman in Albany lined up for me, a good cook and house-keeper, drives a car, and would go to Florida with me. I asked Hattie if she had heard from Idella, and whether Idella had asked her to find some one for me. Hattie said yes, she had had a letter from Idella, asking her to find someone nice "To take care of me."

It is clear that Idella and Bernard have found their joint job as a high priced couple—which won't work out for too long a time, for several reasons. However, lining up a woman who would go to Florida with me was certainly serving notice that Idella thinks she is sitting pretty, and is through. I wonder how much brag-ging about their jobs with us she and Bernard did, to get what they wanted.

. . . A typically cute letter from Charlie Scribner, taken home and finished with a drunken pencil. Ernest's book[2] is now in final revised galleys, and Charlie said it is a fine job. He had had "another tragic letter" from Marcia,[3] and he wrote wist-fully, "I went all the way to Lake Como to impregnate her with at least a book but she kept a delicate veil between us."

Love,

1. Walter W. Stokes of Cooperstown, a state senator for New York.
2. Ernest Hemingway, *Across the River and into the Trees* (New York: Scribners, 1950).
3. Marcia Davenport.

. . . .

(ALS, 3 pp.)

Dear Honey:

. . . All about me, all about me—. I must be unendurably self-centered—. I hate being that way, but something has happened to me, I am not so brave any more after fighting hard for so many years, I must be taken care of, or down a whole bottle of Phenobarbitol—.

Monday morning I go to Colgate University, only because my adored Robert Frost is accepting another honorary degree there, and he will probably return here with me Monday afternoon and spend the night, and I shall take him to Albany Tuesday to his train back to the "Homer Noble" Farm in Vermont. He is evidently enchanted by the name of the original owner of his place, so I think I shall continue to call mine "The Root Place."

(TLS, 5 pp.)

Van Hornesville, [N.Y.]

June 14, 1950

Dear Norton:

Robert Frost has come and gone, and as always, provided such rich nourishment that I shall feel fed for a long time. I love him with the same tearing tenderness I feel for Owen D. Young, my heart turned over when I saw him on the "honorary" platform at Colgate, with his mortar-board altogether too askew on his noble head, and while it is impossible to decide which is the greater, as a *man*, Robert has this edge on Mr. Young when it comes to conversation, No, monologues!, where they are both so superb: Owen D. *gives* to his immediate audience with a definite consciousness that he is giving; Robert is a great flowing fountain, and if he ever becomes aware that all sorts of people are lapping there, is probably more grateful than proud. He has been terribly wounded by people, surely most of all by his own children, especially his daughter Leslie, who announced to him firmly after his wife's death that she wouldn't have him living with her— my God, *I* should consider it a privilege to take care of him in his old age. So I couldn't help wondering, with all he gives to others, through his poetry, his personality and his wisdom in talk, whether it is possible that we others have anything to give him in return, and I believe that we do. He kissed me and touched my hand, with tears in his eyes, when I left him at the Albany railroad station.

In a way, I regretted that Owen D. was not "in residence," to have gotten the two together for a terrific battle of minds, yet I could not have endured to have either hurt the other, which might have happened.

Mrs. Theodore Morrison[1] wrote me for Robert that he would reach Utica at 11:08 last Sunday night, and would come on from Colgate Monday to stay with me. She said that in the Vermont mountains she didn't know whether it would be daylight-saving or standard time, and that sent me to the R.R. time-table, where I could find no such train. I 'phoned the Everett Case's, and Everett said, "That train hasn't run for two years," so they sent a car to meet him at Albany.

The commencement exercises at Colgate were most stirring, the graduating class of more than three hundred mostly veterans, *old men* in contrast to the boys with whom I went to college, who did fight the first World War. Another honorary degree besides that to Robert Frost was to Phillip Jessup,[2] a grand person. I sat next to his wife, a lovely woman, and she will stop by the cottage this winter.

After Robert Frost had been "presented" for his honorary degree by the head of the English Dept., Everett began his secondary eulogy before the hood was looped over Robert, and after Everett's first words, I saw that Frost was saying something, and that Everett was really rocked back on his feet. Afterward, I asked what Frost had said, and Everett had begun his actual bestowing of the degree by quoting from one of Frost's great poems beginning, (I quote from memory) "Some say the world will end in fire, Some say in ice,"[3] whereupon Robert said to

Everett, "Which side are you on?" Everett said he had never been so thrown off his stride, having memorized his "tribute."

After the big show, we all went to the Student Union for lunch. Josephine[4] said to me and Dick Young, "You won't be at the head table. Just sit down anywhere." Everett said, "Why isn't Marjorie at the head table?" and Josephine said, "Because there isn't enough room." As the luncheon ended, all the recipients of honorary degrees were called on to speak, a dirty trick, I must say, and Robert Frost was the last, to provide the climax, as Everett said. So Everett announced, "We have saved the best for the last, and Robert Frost is here only because of a writer whom we all admire, who is a friend of Colgate, Marjorie Kinnan Rawlings."

I was appalled, as Frost would have come for his degree in any case, and when I understood that Everett was just dragging me in for a bit of undeserved glory, to make up for my being placed "below the salt"!!

... I asked if anyone knew where Ripton, Vt., was, as it occurred to me that if I could make the round trip in a day, it would be better for Robert Frost to drive him to his door, rather than have him changing trains or trying to take another mythological one. . . .

... I said some little harmless thing about Cliff Lyons to Frost, and evidently he has felt the same disappointment that I have, for later he spoke of some college's looking for a vital teacher, "The sort of person," he said, "we once thought Clifford would be.")[5]

So Robert came here with me, and I asked the Jim Case's[6] to join us for drinks and dinner, as it seemed presumptuous not to offer him somebody besides just me (and they had great mutual friends in the Hervey Allen's)[7] and it worked out nicely. I had planned a turkey dinner, and "Edith" had her daughter in to help, and serve, and all went well in country style. Jim Case was less pedantic, more of a nice human being, than I've ever seen him, and they stayed until about 10:30, and Robert so enjoyed Heering's Danish cherry brandy, which was new to him, that I couldn't get him up to bed, and he talked until after midnight. His witticisms, his casual words of wisdom, come so thick and fast that no one can remember them afterward. I recall only a few.

I felt like a dog, but I did ask him to add a little something to my copy of the limited edition of his complete poems, and he wrote in several of his poems, with a comment for me.

He loved my place here, and we walked up the road to Mt. Tom, and he told me of the rare flowers I might expect to find in the woods there.

He fell in love with the portrait of Maria Bogardus Schuyler,[8] and asked me if I would consider giving it to him. I all but swooned. I gathered myself together and said that I should gladly give it to him if he wanted it more than I did. (He had asked about it and I had told him the story.) I asked him what the portrait meant to him, and he said that he just liked the woman's looks, that the portrait seemed to him definitely of the period of Gainsborough and Reynolds,[9] and what did the portrait mean to me—. I said that having felt insecure all my life, it seemed to give me a feeling of having roots, and that I just liked her, too, and because she looks so sad, I worry about her. He said that was all nonsense, but he wouldn't take her away from me.

He was most interested in seeing Owen D. Young's house, the "home farm," Josephine's house, the school and village. No one was at the home farm, and I told him of Owen D.'s telling of standing as a boy on that snow-bound hill-top, cut off from the world, and of how his whole life, more than that of anyone I had ever known, derived from and was still tied to, his boyhood. Robert was really touched.

He told me more of the trouble of old, and he is only indirectly bitter at Owen D. Another man is the real culprit. He doesn't want me to talk about it to Owen D. He wants me to get him one piece of information but NOT from Mr. Young, so do not mention any of this.[10]

June 15

I went to Cooperstown last night to the early movie and ran into a double feature and had to wait very late to see the one I had gone for, my favorite, Gene Kelly, in "Black Hand."[11] Most exciting, but did I have nightmares!

. . . Haven't got back to work since Mr. Frost was here, read over the last chapter and it seemed such inferior stuff, I was disheartened again. . . .

Much love,

1. Kathleen Morrison, Frost's secretary, and wife of the poet Theodore Morrison.
2. Philip Caryl Jessup, an authority on international law.
3. Robert Frost, "Fire and Ice."
4. Josephine Young Case.
5. Frost had met Clifford Lyons when the latter was chair of English at the University of Florida.
6. James H. Case Jr., president of Washington and Jefferson College and then of Bard College, younger brother of Everett Case.
7. Hervey Allen, the writer who had died in 1949.
8. Maria Bogardus Schuyler, a distant ancestor of MKR (*Selected Letters,* 304–5).
9. Thomas Gainsborough and Joshua Reynolds, eighteenth-century British artists especially known for their portraits.
10. Owen D. Young admired Elinor White while both were at St. Lawrence University, which apparently caused Frost to become jealous. In the end, Elinor rejected Owen Young and became Mrs. Robert Frost. In 1935, Frost did not appear at St. Lawrence to receive an honorary degree, but that was because Elinor was ill.
11. *Black Hand* (1950), starring Gene Kelly and J. Carrol Naish.

(TLS, 3 pp.)

Van Hornesville, New York
June 20, 1950

Dear Norton:

Your sympathy for "poor Idella" is most touching, and as far as I am concerned you know what you can do with it and where you can put it.

I understand her left-over slave-psychology too, but I had hoped that in nearly twelve years of treating her like a white woman, of talking with her about the reasons for race prejudice—on both sides!—she might have brought herself to tell me something *approximating* the truth, in leaving me this last time.

Yet there is something else. Idella is more thoroughly selfish and self-centered than you and I ever dreamed of being, and that's saying something. I realize that our life together, hers and mine, has always operated more for her convenience than for mine. It has been a rare occasion when she sacrificed a Fête or a meeting at Reddick, etc., to stand by me, while on the other hand, as you know, I have changed all sorts of plans to make things comfortable for her. On this last departure, she was balancing values for herself, taking the main chance, is undoubtedly making a large salary for the moment, and was just short-sighted enough not to realize that she would have come out better in the long run by sticking with me.

... I have gotten deep into the work, and nothing else matters.

John Marsh sent me a copy of the Georgia Historical Society magazine, a Margaret Mitchell memorial issue, and I have never seen anything in such ghastly bad taste. Incredible.

Love,

. . . .

(TLS, I p.)

Van Hornesville, New York
June 21, 1950

Dear Norton:

It may have reached the St. Augustine papers by now, but I just had a note from James Cabell, signed by him and by Margaret, saying:

"We are hoping it may interest you, if but as particeps criminis, to know that after being, as the newspaper put it, wed twice, upon 15 June and 17 June, our married life continues as yet to be not unhappy."

... I really feel good about it, and think they will both be very happy. If they can keep Ballard[1] out of the marital bed——.

Love,

1. Ballard Cabell, the retarded son of James Branch Cabell by his first wife, Priscilla.

(TLS, I p.)

Van Hornesville, New York
June 22, 1950

Dear Honey:

I'm in a better mood than when I wrote you last, and will use my remaining hour or so this afternoon mostly to answer things in your letter of today. . . .

. . . With their dinner being paid for, it wouldn't kill Aunt Ida to shell out a quarter of her own on a blistering day. I'm afraid she will become more and more difficult. She is certainly looking a gift horse in the mouth when she's so ugly to Miss Grace. Can you think of any separate things I could do for Bugbee to compensate? Of course, with HER big mouth and lack of tact, she'd only throw it in Aunt Ida's face and start trouble all over again—. Guess I'd better send Aunt Ida $5 as a distinct "taxi fund," and let *her* pay the driver—with a nickel tip—with her grand flourish—.

. . . Had to write Carl Brandt about some business, thanked him for not bothering me about the book, said I expected to have it entirely done by the end of November, and while it was not suitable for serialization, would let him see a copy then. So he writes back promptly asking if he can't come in late August to read what I've done!!! Damn, if I'm not going to let any of the good Scribner people, or Norman Berg, see it before re-writing, I can't fool with Carl and his commercial ideas.

Am working terribly hard and making adequate progress.

Much love,

. . . .

(TLS, 2 pp.)

Van Hornesville, [N.Y.]
[28 June 1950]

Dear Norton:

. . . I have just finished the most enchanting book, "The Tiger in the House," by Carl Van Vechten.[1] It was first published more than thirty years ago, and I had an order with Scribners Rare Book Dept. to watch for a copy. I saw a note in the N.Y. Times that it had just been re-issued so I wrote for it at once. How "Cousin Carl" can live without a cat, after writing so definitively about them, I do not understand.

. . . I think I wrote you that Robert Frost wanted me to visit him in August, and I said I'd love to, then it was all spoiled by a letter from Theodore Morrison, the poet-husband of the woman[2] who has been all-in-all to Robert since his wife's death, saying that Robert said I was coming, and would I give one of the "evening talks," for $200, at the Bread Loaf Writers' conference at that time. I had to write back that this frightened me off completely. The book is going to be so much longer than I expected. Later, I shall take both axe and scalpel to it—.

The impoverished Gene Baroff 'phoned me yesterday from New York, and must have talked five dollars' worth, which he can't afford. He is doing short stories and poems and hasn't gotten into his projected novel or play. I'm afraid that the year he has allowed himself for writing, under pressure, won't work out. He is too sociable, besides, yet he is so young, and seems able to write at night even after a party.

I think I shall ask her [Edith, the maid] to do as she did when Robert Frost and the Jim Case's were here for dinner, come in the afternoon of Friday instead of morning, straighten up, and cook dinner. . . .

I am working steadily, but without joy.

Love,

1. Carl Van Vechten (1880–1964), *The Tiger in the House* (New York: Knopf, 1920).
2. Kathleen Morrison.

. . . .

(TLS, 1 p.)

Van Hornesville, New York

June 30, 1950

Dear Honey:

As I told you over the 'phone, I dreaded the visit from Gene and Stad, mostly because of Edith's hours, which left me stuck with dinners. But the brave little old lady, in such a panic over Robert Frost's visit, when she had to have her daughter in to help, seems calmer, especially since I told her it was just two boys coming who wouldn't be "company. . . ." It may or may not be, a mistake to have let them come at this time. The Young household is so chaotic that I have had no solace (about my work) and almost no conversation with Owen D., and aside from Robert Frost, I haven't really talked with anyone but Edith and Moe and Uki. I find myself using the sign language—. But usually, I find Gene stimulating. . . .

Much love,

. . . .

(TLS, 3 pp.)

Van Hornesville, N.Y.

July 13, 1950

Dearest Norton:

Sunday morning . . . I went to the fields to pick wild strawberries. They were there by the millions, but rain was threatening, and I was a few days late, as they had just passed their prime. I picked until noon, then went down to the Fredericks' tenant farmer, who has all those puny children, and asked for volunteers to pick more berries for me, saying I would pay well. The family was eating its Sunday dinner out-doors, and all they had was bread and a coarse potato salad.

The oldest child, a red-headed boy about eight or nine, the healthiest-looking, I suppose because he has had more years of the school lunches, spoke up and said he'd take over.

Three hours later, he appeared, with three younger ones, and with a prodigious amount of strawberries. I had not hulled my own basket, waiting for them, and think they would have so few that I'd do the whole job at once. My red-head looked at my gatherings and said, "That's pretty good for a lady your age." And so it was—. My back was all but broken. I paid off in relation to how much each kid had picked, then served ice-cream and cookies. I left them alone with the tin of cookies and had to be urged to take more along with them. The red-head will help me later on with wild raspberries and blackberries. Blast these heart-breaking little boys—.

Picked my currants yesterday. Gooseberries are ready.

Have not yet gotten back to the book. Read over the last chapter I had written before Gene and Stad descended on me, and it was so bad that I was utterly discouraged.

A letter from Julia, and she is in trouble, too.

Esther Young and I got together on the subject of our beloved Negroes' walking out on us, for her Raymond, who had been with her 18 years, had left her as Idella left me, tolled away by his wife to the same sort of high-price couple-job. I spoke of the necessity of your firing Bernard,[1] of his having stolen liquor from the bar and filling the bottles with water, and Esther exclaimed, "That accounts for it!" She said that when they were at your place in the Spring, the Martini served her tasted like dish-water, and she ordered something else, which proved equally weak as to alcoholic content. So evidently Bernard was still up to his thieving and watering tricks at that time, even after your all-but impasse with the liquor inspector. It would seem that Bernard would have been frightened away by all the commotion that ensued. It occurs to me, although I think we are all convinced that Bernard was the culprit, that since Bernard SHOULD have been scared off, someone else may have been doing the thieving and the substituting. . . .

Am living in a consistent hell.

1. Bernard Young.

. . . .

(TLS, 2 pp.)

Van Hornesville, N.Y.

July 15, 1950

Dear Norton:

Edith Hulburt announced yesterday that she can't stay with me longer than the end of this month. . . . I have been so numb since Idella left that it doesn't really matter. . . .

. . . Julia 'phoned me yesterday afternoon and begged me to come to New

Marlboro for the week-end. Her domestic problems have straightened out (the new nurse and the cook had been fighting) and the relatives wished off on her by her mother and aunt aren't coming for another two weeks. Since she won't be able to come here for some time, and if I don't get adequate help would rather she did not come, and she really wants me and says she'd adore to have Moe and Uki, I have decided to drive over. It appears about a 3 hour drive, and it is gorgeous cool weather. Julia had extra tickets for the Berkshire Music Festival tonight and tomorrow afternoon, and in my depressed state of mind, think it will be smart to go.

The Gilkyson's seem to be only about 30 miles from New Marlboro, and I may possibly 'phone them and spend Monday with them if they want me.

I have kept forgetting to pass on an incident that is both terribly funny and tragic. Actually, Gene and Stad and I agreed that we had been in on the very beginning of a serious neurosis. The first morning they were here we drove to Bridgewater for a turkey I had ordered. The smallest boy, five, I think, greeted Moe cordially, but Moe was all absorbed with the Walsh's dog. The little boy was sitting down, held out his hand to Moe and called him by name. As Moe dashed past him, Moe h'isted and let him have it right on his little bare legs. The child sat perfectly stunned for several minutes, disappeared in the house, and then there came the sound of the most awful sobbing. There was no acceptable explanation, and he would accept no comfort. He wasn't angry, merely heart-broken, utterly *crushed*. No telling how much damage will be done him! I said that all his life he would be subconsciously haunted by the thought, "I'm the kind of person that dogs pee on." Gene said no, it was a matter of betrayal, that he had offered Moe the right hand of fellowship—and look what he got for his trouble! . . .

Much love, and wish you were going with me.

. . . .

(TLS, 2 pp.)

Van Hornesville, N.Y.
Tuesday-July 18, 1950

Dear Norton:

. . . I am evidently getting queerer and queerer, for I did not really enjoy my visits to Julia and the Gilkysons. I am uncomfortable with Tom Bigham. The Gilkyson's were more than cordial, but I felt I shouldn't have stopped off with them. And I have never come so close to starving to death, in both households.

. . . Most of the music Saturday night and Sunday afternoon at the Berkshire Festival was marvelous. It fed my soul.

The Gilkyson's were going to the music Sunday afternoon and we arranged to meet there. I could only introduce Tom as "Father" Bigham, the title he uses. He is so High Church, and Julia has fallen in line with it, that he says a standing grace, and then he and Julia cross Hell out of themselves.

Went Monday, yesterday, morning, to the Gilkyson's. For lunch we had canned soup and thin sandwiches made of delicatessen ham. They took me for drinks in the afternoon to Efraim Zimbalist, son of the Violinist Zimbalist and Alma Gluck, and half-brother to Marcia Davenport.[1] For dinner we had small portions of rice and tiny piece each of liver. Bernice said, "Won't you have something else?" and I said some bread might be nice, and I filled up on that.

I insisted on leaving this morning before breakfast. Stopped at ten o'clock on the road and really ate.

. . . Shall get back to work tomorrow.

Love,

1. Efrem Zimbalist, Russian-American violinist and composer. Alma Gluck [Reba Fiersohn], Rumanian-American opera singer and mother of MKR's novelist friend Marcia Davenport.

. . . .

(TLS, 2 pp.)

Van Hornesville, New York
July 19, 1950

Dear Honey:

. . . You remember that Dr. Damon told me that only about one out of five women who were sent to him for a hysterectomy actually needed it. And even he was mistaken in thinking I had a cyst on one ovary, which turned out to be just scar tissue at the sigmoid from attacks and one or more abscesses. It is a hellish operation at best. . . .

Much love,

. . . .

(TLS, 2 pp.)

Van Hornesville, N.Y.
July 22, 1950

Dear Norton:

Yes, I decided some time ago—I wrote you about it but tore up the letter—that Bernard and Idella had their plot cooking *before* you fired him. She may have even been the one to put him up to getting himself fired, to make her subsequent actions seem more plausible. I can't tell just when she made up her mind to slip out, but almost think it may have been when Bernard did such a poor job of blowing himself up. I think he worked her sympathy then for all it was worth. I think he had decided that she was not going to spend the summer here with me if he had to kill her to stop her. And if he convinced her that he would really save his money with her, toward a home etc., the high New York wages would be irresistible bait. As I look back on it, in the light of her having already packed every stitch she owned, she was altogether too glib and blithe toward the end about staying with me to the end, and going to Van Hornesville.

Such an enthusiastic note from Julia about my visit, it made me feel better about it, and evidently my boredom—except for the music—went unnoticed. Did I write you that I have never seen a stronger personality in a child than 3-year Hildy? Actually alarming. Her automatic answer to "Do you want, or want to do, so-and-so?" is a quick firm "No." Then half the time she turns around and accepts or does it without a word. She is gay and friendly when she accepts you, but seems to have no need or desire for demonstrative affection. Julia says when they come home she runs down the hall to meet them—and stops short a foot away. Will not stand for being kissed. Yet she is not a brat at all. Very likeable.

... Glad you're getting some company you enjoy. But as Julia wrote, "There is nothing nicer than *invited* guests."

Much love,

. . . .

(TLS, 4 pp.)

Van H[ornesville, N.Y.].
July 24, 1950

Dear Honey:

... Please send me "The Horse's Mouth"[1] when you are through with it. Will eventually send you Gerald Johnson's "Incredible Tale" and "Comes the Comrade,"[2] both loaned out now to Mr. Young. Called on the Young's last night, and for the first time he talked about doing his memoirs. I mentioned Lincoln Steffens' Autobiography[3] and "The Education of Henry Adams"[4] and remarked (with Charlie Young present) that nobody gave a damn where he, Mr. Young, had gone to school, who his teachers were, or how many children he had. Mr. Young said that his memoirs (and I do think he plans to do them) would have to begin with the little isolated boy standing on the snowy hill at the "Home Farm." I said, brashly, that I had never known a man whose whole life so derived from his frustrated boyhood, as his. He said, "Quite so, and the story has to be of a road taken out, and of coming back in again on the same road."

... Read over my whole manuscript so far, about 102,000 words, and feel more hopeful. The thread seems to be coming fairly clear and the style for the most part isn't as sickening as I remembered. Seem to see a glimpse of daylight at the end of the longest darkest tunnel I've ever crawled through on my belly.

Hit so many spots that offended me, and found the answer was usually quite simply, "Take it out!" More a matter of deletion than re-writing.

Much love,

1. Joyce Cary (1888–1957), *The Horse's Mouth* (London: Joseph, 1944).
2. Gerald Johnson (1880–1980), *Incredible Tale* (New York: Harper, 1950); Alexandra Orme, *Comes the Comrade* (New York: Marrow, 1950).
3. Lincoln Steffens (1866–1936), *Autobiography* (New York: Harcourt, Brace, 1931).
4. Henry Adams (1838–1913), *The Education of Henry Adams* (Boston: Houghton Mifflin, 1918).

(TLS, 2 pp.)

Van Hornesville, New York

July 31, 1950

Dear Honey:

Everything I write seems to be about *me*, and I wonder if I am a complete ego-maniac, if that is the word. But I know you want news of me, as I do of you. Seems to me 'tain't egoistic, just plain friendly!

... Having no idea how long Pearl Primus will stay with me, and being such a sissy about a bit of cooking, I 'phoned the Sportsman's Tavern and the Mahaqua Farms, to ask if an artist guest of mine, black as the ace of spades, would be acceptable for dinner. Both proprietors said, of course, we should be welcome.

Much love, darling,

. . . .

(TLS 3 pp.)

Van Hornesville, New York

Aug. 2, 1950

Dear Honey:

... Am sending you "Comes the Comrade." Mr. Young was not interested, said he's heard all he wanted to about the Russians. Yet the book seems valuable to me for its revelation of the common Russian character, along with the *variances* in that character. It seems to give a clue as to the sort of propaganda we could use on them. In talking about his memoirs, Mr. Young said he had learned the secret of contentment, and I said, "Is it possible you can be at peace at this moment?" and he said, Yes. I could only echo Norman Berg for once and say, "You shouldn't be. No man is done with his job until he's put away in the ground."

He lifted his eyebrows and banged his pipe and dropped hot coals on Louise's rug, and I felt very fresh and impudent.

Had a post-card from Marjorie Stoneman Douglas[1] from Bennington, Vt., not too far away, giving her address there, which I took as a hint to invite her here. Much as I love her, I just can't do it. Pearl Primus is another matter. I feel about any book she may write as I do about Mr. Young's, that it would be worth while to drop my own work if I could be of help.

My dear, I am clinging to a precipice with bleeding fingers. If I can work just a little harder, I'll have the first draft of the book done in another month or six weeks, then, as I have written you, the re-writing isn't going to be as painful as I thought—or so it seems now. But I have so little reserve strength, entirely a mental and emotional thing, I know, for I am strong as a horse. I am just plain ashamed of myself.

Much love,

1. Marjory Stoneman Douglas (1890–1998), Florida novelist, newspaper writer, and environmentalist, in particular, a defender of the Everglades.

(TLS, 8 pp.)

Van Hornesville, New York

Sunday August 6 [1950]

Dear Norton:

. . . Got into the oddest trouble while Pearl Primus was here. Wonder if it is a subconscious protest against any company and interruption. She was the easiest guest imaginable, and I enjoyed her. I had four bad nose-bleeds in two days, never had such a thing in my life before. . . .

Had planned to drive Pearl to Albany for the 4:30 train yesterday afternoon, and while she wanted to stay through today to take care of me, I knew she had commitments, so Johnny Redjives took her to Albany in my car. . . .

. . . What is on my mind—. I had a letter day before yesterday from Arthur's third wife. Yes.

The letter, on Arthur's stationery, written on his well-known typewriter, began "Dear Mrs. Baskin." I thought "What the hell" and turned quickly to the signature, which was "Grace Kinnan." What the hell even more!

They were married in a Methodist Church in Seattle on *March 25*. She went with him on the boat to Alaska in April. She has been married before and has a 7-year son. Don't know whether the boy is with them or not. She was a social worker. She and Arthur are expecting an offspring in January—.

. . . Of course, what hurts me terribly is that when Arthur and I have been so close, he'd wait all this time and then let his pregnant bride give me the information. She made excuses for him, and I do understand his reluctance, but I think he's a cowardly bastard just the same. He also had not written the Arizona aunties,[1] who expect him to visit them a long time this winter, as they consider him, as per Mrs. Grace, "such a lonely man." She seems to have a nice sense of irony. She enclosed a picture that a friend took in front of the marriage altar, and she is trim and attractive, looks about 35. Is certainly intelligent.

Am also trying desperately to recall what I have written Arthur these past months, as I could tell that she had read my letters to him. Have written him often, knowing that he was in some sort of trouble, and have always written him *most* freely.

Have just written her, very pleasantly, saying that I am sure she is right for him, and that as to his being right for her, I hope that his great lovability will compensate for the Kinnan neuroticism. Also felt obliged to say that Art need not expect news of me through exclusive correspondence with her, that if I don't have a letter from him at reasonable intervals, he won't hear from me.

. . . Hope you aren't sending anything for my birthday, as from now on I'd like to forget it. Louise asked the date and I said it was past. Aunt Ida sent an ash-tray and a set of nice table-mats. . . .

Had wondered about Mrs. Johnny and the black guest, and asked her if she had any race prejudice, any feeling against Negroes, and she said simply, "Why no, I'd be ashamed to." She is quite a person. She was a WAC and served 18 months in France and Germany, working mostly with codes. . . .

Pearl Primus brought me gifts from Africa, an antique knife the Congo male dancers wear as ornaments, and a pair of book-ends from Nigeria, elephants carved out of ebony, with little ivory tusks and inlaid ivory toe-nails. Her problems that she wanted to discuss are too involved to write about, but it's mostly a matter of Pearl Buck's[2] trying to take her over in every way, harmful to her career.

Louise invited me to show her the weaving-hall etc. and bring her to the house. . . . Leonabel Jacobs[3] the portrait painter was there, and tried her best to get Pearl to stand up in the living room and "perform." Pearl said she could not, without the drums. Leonabel said, "But I could beat on the sofa for you." !!!

The first morning, Pearl got into her tights and did her necessary exercises. She talked me into putting on a play-suit and doing the easier ones with her, showing me especially exercises for reducing stomach and hips. Thought surely she would kill me, but I wasn't the least bit sore afterward. Then she tried to teach me one of the African dances of welcome. I could remotely manage the steps for the feet, I could approximate the gestures of the hands, but when it came to co-ordinating the two, I was sunk. I wound up my old-music box, afraid she would be bored, but she was enchanted. When one piece began a mazurka, I think, she said, "Why, I can do an African dance to that," and she did the most charming thing I've ever seen.

Her tales of her African experiences are fabulous. If she can avoid self-conscious over-writing, she should have a superb book. As I may have told you, her hope was to trace the cultural roots of the American Negro. She found a great deal of really beautiful "superstition," if you want to call it that. For instance, some of the African tribes believe that there is a vast Divine out in space, and a touch of that Divine in each individual. A man or a woman would go out alone into the Bush to meditate, reaching out to the big Divine, and if contact was made, the little Divine inside would come out and sit on the left shoulder, like a bird or butterfly.

In some tribes, the women have dances against war. In most, there are dances against evil.

Pearl is now training her own company for her Broadway performance, and at the Young's (I must say, she held them spell-bound) she spoke of one of the mating, or engagement dances she learned. She said that in the so-called "savage" Bush, boys and girls, men and women, do not dance together in couples, this being considered immodest. So in this dance, two boys or two girls simulate the engaged couple. She said that in adapting the dance, while she disliked being unfaithful to the original, she was obliged to use a boy and a girl together for an American performance. Leonabel said, "I don't see why." I wonder if the hard-boiled Leonabel knows the facts of life, for as Pearl said to me later, such a "true" performance would give the effect of homosexuality, to our "advanced" civilization.

It would take pages more to pass on all the fascinating things she told me. Well, I am happy in writing to you, propped up comfortably in bed, so I'll tell you more stories, for I know you love to have stories told you.

Pearl was born in Trinidad, and her mother tried to teach her an ancient Trinidad dance, not being a dancer herself. Pearl would go so far from the bare description and her mother would say, "Your hands are not right," or, "The foot movement was to the left, not the right," and so on. So Pearl came to one tribe, and she said they were the ugliest people she had seen, the women emaciated, with hard faces, and when they finally agreed to dance for her, they did stupid simple things with an obvious European influence, except that in one dance she recognized two or three movements of the Trinidad dance her mother had tried to teach her. So she said (everything had to go through interpreters, she speaks French as fluently as English, and French is used by many Africans, so her "boy" would speak French, then, if he did not know the dialect of a particular tribe, someone else would translate, and sometimes communication went through four interpreters) "Not far from my village (the real Bush people knew nothing of America or nations, it was all a matter of one's "village") there is a dance. I shall dance it for you." So she did the Trinidad dance, and there was such a silence that she was terrified, thinking she had violated some tabu. Then the villagers shouted, lifted her on their shoulders and carried her a couple of miles. So it came out that the Trinidad dance had originated there, and they had recognized it, and after the excitement died down, they showed her the spots where her dance was not correct, and taught her the rest of the dance, for Pearl's mother had only remembered it up to the point where the priest started the procession and the villagers rushed out of their huts to follow, and there was much more to be danced.

(While I think of it, don't mention the Pearl Buck business.) Will explain later.

Let's see. Pearl Primus was invited to become a wife of the Emir of something, in northern Nigeria, and refused with some regret. She visited his harem, and said the women and their way of life was simply beautiful. Each one has her own house and attendants, the walls are decorated with coral and ivory carvings, the costumes rich and gorgeous, the couches covered with magnificent hand-woven fabric, an exquisite perfume always in the nuptial room, just in case, and when the Emir does come, the favored one's attendants play very soft stringed music outside the door.

The wives have fits if the Emir doesn't take a new one at least once a year, for it is a sign of his wealth, and so, their own prestige.

There is an enormous difference in culture and looks among the different tribes and sections. In contrast to the art made of love-making in that place, in the cruder tribes the man just strides into the hut and it's a matter of "Ready or not, here I come," pounce. Think there's probably as much variance in these United States!

Fried caterpillars are a great delicacy in some places. Turn out quite crispy. Pearl ate anything they served her and often had to fight hard not to woops [*sic*]. Everything is so heavy with fiery hot pepper that you can't tell whether you're eating fish or potatoes. Usually a mercy, she said. Wonderful fruits, which the natives don't eat. Huge mangoes, six for a penny.

She said if my view here from the front of the house had palm trees and little mushroom-shaped thatch huts, it would look exactly like much of Africa.

She thought it was dreadful that I didn't have adequate help all the time, and is going to try to find the right person for me. . . .

Much love,

1. Grace Kinnan and Wilmer Kinnan.
2. Pearl S. Buck (1892–1973), American novelist.
3. Leonebel Jacobs, a portrait painter and close friend of Louise Young. She painted several portraits of Owen D. Young, whom she found an elusive subject.

. . . .

(TLS, I p.)

[Van Hornesville, N.Y.]
Aug. 8, 1950

Dear Honey:

. . . A birthday letter from Arthur, never mentioning his marriage, so evidently he didn't even know that his pregnant bride had written me.

Am feeling wonderfully well, but naturally upset about other things.

Will get back to the book tomorrow, come hell or high water. . . .

Much love, and hope to have the first draft done in another month or so, and that you can come then for a visit. . . .

All love and all thanks,

. . . .

(TLS, I p.)

[Van Hornesville, N.Y.]
Aug. 9, 1950

Dear Honey:

By the grace of God, I got back to work today, took a hurdle on a change in the book, and did the stint of 1,000 words.

I can keep going as long as I can write—. . . .

Many thanks and all love,

(TLS, 2 pp.)

Van H[ornesville, N.Y.]

Aug. 14, 1950

Dear Norton:

... I remembered how touched I was by the most gracious remark I have ever heard, which I know I must have told you at the time. Phil May and Mattie Broome and Jack and I were prowling in the woods of Gadseen Co. with their cousin Fant, when we came on a bush of Silver Bells. Cousin Fant broke a spray and gave to me. I said, "But won't it die?" and he said, "Yes Ma'am, but it'll die in yo' hand."

... Thought I was writing hot stuff on the book, and had to tear up *pages*. Still think another month will finish the first draft. Then we'll see whether to order a double bottle of Phenobaritol. As a matter of fact, think I can face life better if the book is NOT any good, for it isn't "fitten," I'll be mad as hell and want to fight, while if it should prove remotely acceptable, I'd feel committed to write another, and by God, I can't take it!

Much love,

....

(TLS, 2 pp.)

[Van Hornesville, N.Y.]

[August 1950?]

[Missing first page]

... You hurt my feelings yesterday afternoon when I 'phoned you in my cups, you were so cold, would think you would have recognized the compliment I paid you in wanting to hear your voice when in trouble. Had worked so hard on the book that morning, was relieved that the hospital check-up showed that I was well, but still no explanation for the nose-bleeds, and I go back next week for further tests. ...

Can't seem to find a doctor who will forbid drinking and smoking. ...

And you, poor dear, you are so troubled yourself, and can't help me—.

... You so offended me in my trouble yesterday that I swore I should not write you for weeks and weeks, but I can't get away from it, I need you, and if I am too much for you, you'll have to be the first to say so.

....

(TLS, 3 pp.)

Van H[ornesville, N.Y.].

Monday morning

[21 August 1950]

Dear Norton:

Twelve hundred miles seems to me just about the right distance for quarreling—.

... Three weeks more will see the end of my first draft, and it could even be two weeks, as I usually get "hot" toward the end and work day and night—. ... I still cannot decide whether the Scribner folks should see the material before I re-write, or not. So much of it will be an entirely different book after the editing and re-writing, and only Max could have actually helped me at the un-revised stage. On the other hand, I recall the fiasco of the second movie story[1] I wrote, where, if I had let Carl Brandt and the M.G.M. people see the first draft, I would have been spared so much, the thing not being acceptable for an accidental reason. In this case, if the book simply is no good, even potentially, it would be better to know it now. Yet again I kid myself, thinking that it will be good after re-writing and tightening etc.

In any case, it will certainly be wise to take a week off in between, if for nothing more than to gain perspective, and if they are still working on your road, you won't be having any business, and it would be grand if you could come up to play around, either here or in New York, if I decide to let Scribner's see my shame. If the neurotic horse, or should I call her "mare," becomes adjusted to me, we might even ask Julia and Tom for a couple of days while you're here. I can't bear not to have them come.

... A letter from Martha, which I quote as received:

Dear Mrs. Baskin

How are you to day Fine I hope as this leaves me not Feling so well I have Ben goning to the Dorctor ever sence you left Dora got Kill by lighting on 14th of aug. when you come home I think I will go of For a little While hope to see you soon with much love

From Martha

I do think I had better write Martha just to dry up Chrissie, and "go of For a little While." I suspect Martha of deliberately not letting Chrissie get bred, and the poor cow has been milked way too long for her own good, more than two years. I sha'n't be much at the Creek this winter anyway. Think I might as well offer it to the Gilkyson's again. ...

Much love,

1. *A Bad Name Dog*, written in 1948, was not produced.

. . . .

(TLS, 7 pp.)

Van H[ornesville, N.Y.].
Aug, 23, 1950

Dear Norton:

... Charlie Scribner sent me an advance copy of Ernest Hemingway's book,[1] and I have had to set it aside after reading three chapters. It makes my stuff seem worse than ever. Charlie is inclined to think that I'd better do my re-writing before they see my material.

Believe it or not, I took another tumble down my stairs yesterday. This time, forward instead of backward. Was cold sober, going down for cigarettes. . . . About the third step from the bottom, and that bad ankle of mine gave way, and down I went. No damage at all, except for the usual strained ligaments, was already stiff in the shoulders, so went to the nice little chiropractor in Cooperstown, and he fixed me up.

. . . I finished reading Ernest's book, couldn't resist it, and it is the same moving sort of thing as "Farewell to Arms."[2] But Norton, what that bearded genius has done to Martha Gellhorn! "All the characters in this book are fictitious"—. Shit-fire, honey. He has torn Martha limb from limb. The way he has done it indicates to me that he still hasn't got her out of his system, but I think he has made a mistake in teaching his wives to shoot, for Martha would be justified in drawing a bead on the beard, and accurately.

He has also ripped into the High Brass, and by name. Charlie wrote me that Hemingway was having trouble in going on with what he considers his major book, worrying about the responses of the critics to "Across the River and into the Trees." I am writing Charlie that Ernest should have nothing to fear from the critics, only a serious danger from various Generals and from Martha.

My own work goes up and down, one day decent, the next day utterly obscene—.

I wrote Charlie that the whole value of my book depends on whether my man came to life, and he wrote back, "Your man will come to life if you sleep with him long enough, of course, figuratively speaking."

I am trying to work into my book a statement by one of my characters that is actually my own, and if I can manage it artistically, it will be this:

"I cannot accept the idea of immortality. Living one life has almost killed me."

Do you have the Aubrey Menen book (Prevalence of Witches) "The Backward Bride"?[3] Will send it if not. Be sure and answer. Will keep the new Hemingway for you to read here. Please send me "The Horse's Mouth." Charlie Scribner and Norman Berg send me books, besides a new batch Gene Baroff bought for me (I must send him some more money) but I do well if a book lasts me one late afternoon and evening, and I am about out.

Now this really matters, and I hate to bother you. I need badly and *right away*, two or three books I bought several years ago in connection with my manuscript. One, Lecomte de Nouey's "Of Human Destiny,"[4] . . . [a]nd Sir James Jean's "Our (or "The") Changing Universe,"[5] and a book by a scientist named Eddington.[6] So sorry, I can't remember where these are, but presumably in the living room. Would be ready to use the Encyclopedia you gave me when I re-write, but decided I can just as well do my checking of facts and make the corrections when I work on the proofs this winter at the cottage—provided the book is fit to print.

I think my bifocals caused both spills. I have never become adjusted to them. Distance is grand, but close reading is blurred and maddening. Since the last fall, have gone up and down stairs, and onto the stone steps from the wood-shed, without glasses.

I couldn't possibly let Norman see my book right now, He is only (or mostly) interested in *ideas*, and if those please him, according to his own standards I am afraid he is not too good a judge of the literary quality. And if my book isn't remotely of literary quality, it hasn't been worth writing. Ideas only can't carry it.

Also, so much of the book is execrably written, that I'd be too ashamed for anyone at Scribner's to read it now. Was relieved that Charlie said to wait for re-writing.

Now, *Arthur*, you did not say a word about coming up when the first draft is done. . . . New York City is out for me until I go to Charlie in November with my manuscript and my tail between my legs. I need and want you. . . .

All my love,

1. *Across the River and into the Trees* (New York: Scribners, 1950).
2. *A Farewell to Arms* (New York: Scribners, 1929).
3. Aubrey Menen, *The Prevalence of Witches* (New York: Scribners, 1949); *The Backward Bridge* (New York: Scribners, 1950).
4. Lecomte du Nouy (1883–1947), *Human Destiny* (New York: Longmans, Green, 1947).
5. Not located.
6. No doubt Arthur S. Eddington, who authored a number of scientific studies.

. . . .

(TLS, 5 pp.)

Van Hornesville, [N.Y.]

Aug. 30, 1950

Dear Norton:

I have just finished a long and I pray, wise letter to Arthur, which I wanted to do the first thing while I was fresh. I was simply crushed by a short letter from him in the afternoon mail yesterday.

He had not left it up to Grace to inform me of the marriage, but had *no intention* of telling me or the aunts for some time—for the reason that *two days* after what he calls "this very hasty marriage" he decided that he didn't know, and still doesn't know, whether he can "cut it or not"—!!! He said he felt he wanted to wait until he had the answer before telling any of us. He said, "Grace's announcement to you was in no manner altruistic, but steeped with understandable hurt and *vengeance*." (Under-scoring mine.) If ever there was a lack of malice or vengeance, it was in that poor woman's intelligent letter, so full of love for Art and the desire to help him. I could not remotely criticize Art, for I am on such thin ice, and am hoping that my approval of the girl will help him to accept her. But I tried to indicate that she had only done the *honorable* thing in informing me, a little hurt perhaps, but vengeful never.

. . . You know, I begin to feel as poised as Plato, compared with Art. In some obscure way, he is partially demented. I am so frightened for him, and so helpless. After the two wrong wives, then ditching the Seattle "Miriam"[1] he told us about, who seemed so nice, getting involved with a brand-new Canadian woman (in her letter Grace had told me that part of Art's complication with this one, was that as she was a Canadian citizen, he was *sponsoring* her in Alaska) how in hell could he have made "a very hasty marriage"!!! He had the odd trait as a tiny boy of being utterly blind to consequences when he wanted something at the moment. For instance, Mother or Father would explain patiently why he would regret it if he spent the money given him for the circus the next day (and they were very stern with us about the use of money, and didn't have much to give us) on an ice cream soda binge or a fragile toy, that day. He would apparently listen, then say, "But I want it." He has evidently never gotten over the characteristic. Not too bad about a little boy's circus, but another matter when it comes to a grown man's wives—and *their* babies.

I feel that I am betraying him in talking so about him, even to you, but I am sick at heart, and while you can't help me any more than I can help him in this trouble, it is a great comfort to me to be able to unburden myself to you. As a matter of fact, you did help me, and I followed your suggestion about the line to take in writing him. It would be fatal to express to him my true feelings, which I had been tempted to do, for my *objective* sympathy is entirely with this Grace. My blood and bones, of course, cry out with distress for Art, wrong and half-crazy as he may be. And with all the punishment I've given you, I think I told you once before that you and Art are the only people who really exist for me. . . .

Much love, my darling—

1. Miriam was a prostitute in MKR's "Miriam's Houses," *New Yorker* 21 (24 November 1945): 29–31.

. . . .

(TLS, 2 pp.)

Van H[ornesville, N.Y.].
Sept. 2, 1950
5:30 P.M.

Dear Honey:

. . . I told Dick Young that I had nothing for "The Dumpling" this time, . . . as my year's work was an incomplete manuscript. . . .

Then I remembered out of no-where a first line of an ancient poem, so I wrote a set of verses to go with the flowers in the muddy shoes. The verses seemed rather amusing, and I 'phoned Dick, and he came up this noon, and was amused too, and is using them in "The Dumpling." I enclose a copy.[1]

I used both alliteration and puns, but thinking of the younger Young's, changed certain words, also punning, not to be embarrassing. You will recognize these. "Bwitch" instead of bitch, and Dick said we could answer, if questioned, that it was a misprint for "witch." "Hoarish" is "whorish. . . ."

Much love,

1. "Dubious Praise in Dubious Battle; or, 'Who Said That—and Why?'" *Dumpling Magazine* 11, no. 8 (1 September 1950): 7.

. . . .

(TLS, 3 pp.)

Van H[ornesville, N.Y.].

Sept. 8, 1950

Dear Honey:

I sent a telegram yesterday to Bernard and Idella Young at his brother's Brooklyn address, telling them to notify you immediately where they had left the key to their former quarters at Crescent Beach. About ten days ago I decided to be just mean enough but not too mean about the coat and hat Idella had left here, so wrote her a note to that address saying that she knew how I hated to wrap packages, but perhaps one of her Cooperstown friends could come and get the things and mail them to her. It's a very nice coat, I've worn it twice, but I have heard nothing, so wondered if Bernard had intercepted my note on the theory that *any* contact between us was undesirable! So I sent the wire in his name, too.

. . . Well, I had a very long letter from Arthur, telling the whole story at last. He is either crazy as a bed-bug, a liar, or the unluckiest man going. He drew up a full indictment against the woman, which seems pretty much an indictment against him, for if it's all true, he was a prime ass not to have found out or noticed some of it beforehand. Aside from charges of selfishness, a vile and violent temper when upset, lack of cooperation, a certain mental and physical shiftlessness, etc. etc. etc. his main gripe is her previous sexual experience, most of which he *did* know about. She had had two previous husbands, and he said she gave plausible reasons for divorcing them, and for "a few affairs," then it turns out there'd been more than she had mentioned. He said she shows no outward signs of her immoral nature, shows no coarseness, only he spelled it "courseness," and knowledge of her promiscuity is just too much for him, only he spelled it "permiscuity." His spelling irked me as much as his absurd attitude. This is the same trick he tried on the second wife Winifred, having known all about her two affairs before he married her, then deciding he didn't approve.

I am afraid he is six feet four of adolescence, no Galahad he, but hell bent on having, I presume, a passionate virgin. Says this girl trapped him when he was badly burned by the Canadian woman, "urged" sex on him before saying that she loved him, and conceived against his wishes and knowledge. He's an awfully big boy now to be trapped and urged.

Don't know whether it would give him any perspective if I kid him by drawing a picture of what he should do about his fourth wife. She should have been raised in a Catholic orphanage so that she will be frugal and appreciate everything he does for her. She should have her virginity officially tested and attested to, not by one doctor, for then later Art might suspect she had been intimate with the doctor, who was protecting her, but by the whole College of Physicians and Surgeons. Then when he instructs her in the delights of love, he must explain to her that he is the only man in the world who has such a gadget. About the time she begins to enjoy it, she should refuse firmly to allow him to ever touch him again, and then he will be able to respect her. (He just can't *respect* Grace.) And about that time he'll be ready for another Winifred or Grace—.

It is very funny, if it weren't so tragic, and I should be whipped for betraying him to you, but I know you won't let it go any farther.

... The end of the book is coming fast, and I'm getting more and more frightened.

Much love,

. . . .

(TLS, 2 pp.)

Van H[ornesville, N.Y.].
Sept. 19, 1950

Dear Norton:

Began my last chapter this morning.

Along with the poor present quality of the manuscript, which I can improve if I don't literally get caught dead with it, I am fighting my anguish about Arthur. Cannot put it in writing, but Aunt Wilmer came up with a possibility that makes my hair stand on end. Didn't mention it to you, but the new wife had two other men on the string along with Art, a Jewish doctor with whom she admitted intimacy, and a "mariner" with whom she denied it. This was part of what came out two days after the marriage—. If Wilmer is right in her suppositional question, Arthur is not crazy, but has been "had" in a big way—. Then again, yesterday, another letter from this "Grace," who has returned to her parents near Spokane with her boy, which sounds completely plausible and everything kind and considerate of Art—.

Wilmer is pretty cute. In my first letter to her, after she had analyzed Art's not writing any of us because he found himself in a mess, but before he had written her that the bride was pregnant, and the child presumably due in January, I ended up, "God, Wilmer–." So Wilmer write back, "Now Marjorie, just 'God, Wilmer' won't do. It takes stronger language than that."

Now this week will see the end of my first draft. I won't need time in between. I don't want to go to New York....

Love,

(TLS, 3 pp.)

Van H[ornesville, N.Y.].

Sept. 20, 1950

Dear Honey:

The beginning of my last chapter, which I reported so proudly, had to be torn up today. I began again, and it is more nearly right. I had not ripped the other out of my blood and guts. If this book is any good at all, you will see why I have had so to punish both you and me in the writing of it.

. . . Worked hard again this morning, and will work through Sunday, and the first draft will be finished then, perhaps even before. . . .

Much love,

. . . .

(TLS, 3 pp.)

[Van Hornesville, N.Y.]

Oct. 16, 1950

Dear Honey:

A wonderful Owen D. Young evening yesterday. . . .

I imagine that almost everything said was not to be passed on, as Mr. Young was giving Everett[1] a superb briefing, and telling him the two or three people to go through, to have his ideas reach Marshall[2] and Truman,[3] by-passing Acheson.[4] I am sure it is still confidential, but Everett has been asked to head the committee to draw up the Japanese peace treaty. Mr. Young said, "Good grief, I hope you refuse." No, he had accepted, and when he explained why, Mr. Young agreed. Mr. Young discussed the Far East on that high level that only he seems to reach. "Face and food," he said, are the two vital factors in the Orient. He had an idea so good that I'm afraid nothing will come of it—. *Don't breathe a word*, but part of it is to induce Truman to ask Gen MacArthur[5] and Nehru[6] to get together to draw up a plan for the Far East. Who would ever have thought of that combination? Much of it was over my head. But how fascinating to sit and see history possibly influenced, from the Root house dining-room.

After supper, I couldn't budge Mr. Young from the dining-room. He and Everett talked until nearly eleven, and I was one with Louise in being a dumb clod on the side-lines. . . .

Much love,

1. Everett Case.
2. George C. Marshall, then secretary of defense, known especially for the European Recovery Program (the Marshall Plan) devised in 1947.
3. Harry S. Truman, thirty-third president of the United States.
4. Dean Acheson, then secretary of state.
5. General Douglas MacArthur, then commander of the United Nations troops in Korea, whom Truman removed from command in 1951 for his public statements urging stronger military action against Communist China.
6. Jawaharlal Nehru, Hindu political leader, prime minister of India.

(TL, I p.)

[Van Hornesville, N.Y.]

Oct. 19 [1950]

. . . Find myself in pure Hell on the re-writing—. You see, I just read you the few chapters that did not offend me too much. The rest is ghastly. I can manage actual editing, deleting the most revolting phrases and paragraphs, but am absolutely stymied on several major issues, especially at the very end. I am so many months behind, if I only had three months more for re-writing, but the weather here is bound to close in on me.

The book is not *fluid* enough. I make too many awkward jumps in time. At one point, Ase's children are no more than adolescent, then in the next chapter they are middle-aged and he is old, and it won't do. And so much of the thing is dull and plodding, and now I must add even more stupid chapters, just to cover the time element—.

Carl Brandt has annoyed me no end. I had written him some time ago that I could not let anyone see my first draft, but now he writes that he is so thrilled that I have done that, and when I am ready to let him see it, he will set everything else aside, to read and consult—.

. . . Have ordered the new Joyce Cary book,[1] have received the Lockridge book, "Cats and People," a complete disappointment.[2]

1. Joyce Cary (1888–1957), *A Fearful Joy* (London: Joseph, 1949).
2. Frances Lockridge (1901–?) and Richard Lockridge (1898–1982), *Cats and People* (Philadelphia: Lippincott, 1950).

. . . .

(TLS, I p.)

[Van Hornesville, N.Y.]

Oct. 25, 1950

Dear Honey:

Had just a note from Arthur, from Edwall, Wash., where he is staying for 3 or 4 weeks with his wife and her parents, planning to head then for Phoenix. Probably because of the biology which you said had trapped him, he was actually fatuous about the woman, and inclined to turn on *me*. . . .

He said Wilmer was "convinced" the child was not his. I thought she gave no such impression, but was only showing him how to protect himself against the possibility. I felt that I must wash my hands of the whole matter, in the face of his new, or present, attitude. I do not see how I can even answer him, especially to that address. But what a fool not to wait, not to give her a chance to put one over in his absence, if she has made a dupe of him.

Much love,

(TLS, 1 p.)

[Van Hornesville, N.Y.]

Sat. Oct. 28, 1950

Dear Honey:

I'm so sorry I'd had too much to drink when you called yesterday. I had really been behaving well until then. I got so tense and restless, the leg hurt but I stayed downstairs out of boredom, and to be near the dictionary, and had the bottle too handy. The silver lining was the first good sleep this week, and this morning the leg feels very much better and I am no longer worried about it.

I had thought previously about our anniversary—I do know the date—but had lost track of time. . . .

Much love,

. . . .

(TLS, 1 p.)

[Van Hornesville, N.Y.]

Oct. 30, 1950

Dear Honey:

Am totally out of Van H. stationery.

Think I called the turn on Arthur's "biology," as today I have a brief note from him saying that he is back in Seattle. And, "my marital status is bad, very bad, but too soon *into a late development* (italics mine) to report definitely on it."

Of course, I pounce on every excuse for not getting my own job done, (writers both love and loathe their work) and I have indeed been upset by this and that, yet I do want to report that I am so close to the end of my re-writing that I may be able to finish by the end of November, as I planned. . . .

So, Cheerio.

I must admit that it has been Hell, trying to work.

. . . .

(TLS, 2 pp.)

Van H[ornesville, N.Y.].

Nov. 1, 1950

Dear Honey:

. . . Thought I had no jitters from the wreck, but yesterday a car darted out from a side road and Stad just missed it, and I had a minor convulsion. . . . Will be damned glad to have you do the driving to Florida.

Have almost decided not to try to get my manuscript exactly as I want it (or as well as I can do it) but to begin copying it right now. I have so many questions in my mind about it that it may be better to let Scribner's see the moderately revised draft, then plan to do more re-writing later. If not too serious, this could even be done in the proofs. . . .

Much love, and do write as often as you can.

(TLS, 5 pp.)

Van H[ornesville, N.Y.].
Nov. 3, [1950] I guess

Dear Honey:

... I realized that the last 20 pages are so far off, that I have to begin again entirely at this point, p. 392, I wasted two days trying mere editing. Actually, I feel better about it. My dis-satisfaction with the last two chapters was so great that it was slowing me up on emending the rest. If I can make it come right, I'll have more courage to begin the copying. I feel more and more that it would be smart to do the copying at the cottage—if I can be totally without interruption, and you can find a maid. . . .

Realized how dreadfully I exaggerated in describing my alarm while riding with Stad. It was not nearly a close call with the other car, and what I had was certainly not a minor convulsion—only what Martha calls "the all-overs." You and I both can't resist dramatizing an episode—

So amusing that March has never made a payment to you. I suppose the common marital financial mistrust among Negroes of that sort makes him feel very clever that he is waiting to put the money only in my hands. Am glad Martha is really getting away. I wrote that I'd make it all right with Old Will if he would "stand guard." Hoped the challenge would keep him on the place as much as the pay.

I wrote Leonard, and he wrote that it had been all but impossible to get to the Creek to do the repairs, as the road from Eureka to the Ocala highway has been torn up for re-paving all summer, and he broke a spring etc. when he tried to get over it, so he has been working in Ocala, which he reaches by way of the new Salt Springs road. . . . Am glad Pearl Glisson has been nice to Martha, after J.T.'s ugliness to old Will. Shall write her.

I think that Gene Baroff was perfectly serious, after asking me what I paid Gracie for her few hours of harum-scarum help, when he said he'd like the job! Said he was a far better cook, could do his own work downstairs while I stayed upstairs, and he needed the money! From an odd remark he made to Stad, as though I were not in the room, I'm afraid he is a congenital homo, and it seemed never to occur to him how Van Hornesville would feel about a male cook, housekeeper and companion! He and Stad pay only $38 a month for their apartment, with heat and hot water, but his Government pension of $80 something a month can't go very far in N.Y.C., especially with his extravagant tastes. He was so innocent in his offer that I couldn't give him the true objection, and only said that Gracie would tide me over until I went to Florida. He said that he would like to do book reviews to make some money, and I have written Irita Van Doren[1] asking her to give him a trial, telling her of his accepted writings etc. as I do think he would do a good job for her. . . .

Now see, I could have worked on my manuscript while I was chatting with you. But I preferred to write you. The personal and affectionate angle of a writer's life is always in conflict with his work.

So again I say, if you can protect me from people, and can acquire adequate help, I'd like to come soon to the cottage. Your Ego is as strong as mine—sometimes I think more so—and aside from the classic example of Edward's renunciation of a throne for the woman he loved, there is the example of Boissevain, who dropped everything to help Edna St. Vincent Millay[2] in her career. Part of what has depressed me is that you have made not too many concessions to my various needs (until very lately) which has made me feel that you did not consider my work important enough for you to adapt yourself to me. With my own doubts about my writing, this has been an extra hazard. You have a great critical faculty anent literature, and if my stuff didn't seem worth while to you, so that you would not join me at the Creek, etc., I did feel sunk.

When you said when you were here, and I read you the least shameful of my book chapters, "But Marjorie, this is a *big* book," I was tempted to snap at you, "What the hell did you think I've been sweating about all these years, another scenario for Lassie?" I tried to give you a hint in a letter some weeks ago when I wrote you that if I could remotely finish the book to my satisfaction, you would see why I had been obliged to punish both you and me in the doing of it.

I have examined my egoism in relation to you, decided a while ago that I must subject mine to your happiness, since you are such a lovely person. So, I can only say, that you must subject your egoism to mine if you think it is worth-while.

I do feel that we have a, what shall I say—*gracious* love between us.

1. Irita Van Doren, book review editor of the *New York Herald-Tribune.*
2. Edna St. Vincent Millay (1892–1950), American poet. Eugen Boissevain was her husband.

. . . .

(TLS, 3 pp.)

[Van Hornesville, N.Y.]
Sunday noon
[5 November 1950]

Know you will be furious to see that I tore off the beginning of a letter I wrote you last Friday night. I tried to apologize for the previous letter, then I thought, "Other neurotics get drunk and abuse their loved ones, why can't I?" I did come apart at the seams toward the end of the week, delayed shock from the crash, Arthur's mess, dread of having to leave here before re-writing is done, excess drinking result rather than cause of general confusion and uncertainty. You are just supposed to put up with it all—.

I wonder so about Edna Millay. Why was she all alone with no help at all, only a caretaker who found her some eight hours later? Boissevain was very wealthy— unless his abandoning his own business to nurture her, had impoverished him.

I know that Millay had become a hard drinker. Some years ago, an interviewer called on her and Boissevain in a N.Y. hotel, and she poked her head from around the bathroom in their suite, waved a bare arm, and said, "You know, gin never lets you down."

. . . The hills are stark and bare, the bones of the earth protrude, telling a skeletal truth, the wind whistles through my doors and windows, and God, how I love it. I am perpetually torn between courage and cowardice. I am afraid all of the time—of what, I do not know—and when I am most frightened, suddenly I exult in the danger.

Yesterday I did begin the new two last chapters, trying to get a greater simplicity and what I can only call a greater *purity*.

I *must* stay here to finish, if it is possible.

. . . Am so disgusted with myself to have gone a bit to pieces. There is certainly no rush on finishing my book as far as Scribner's is concerned, it is only that I am getting to the limit of my own energy, and cannot quit until I have done at least a fair job on the re-writing. And since the accident, two weeks ago this Sunday, I have done only about two days of real work. Would give anything if I could stay here to finish, but realize it will probably be impossible.

. . .[T]his noon I really began hitting the bottle, but think that you will agree that even so, this letter is most coherent, in contrast to the maudlin thing I sent you yesterday, after drinking only half as much. . . .

My love,

. . . .

(TLS, 3 pp.)

[Van Hornesville, N.Y.]
Wed. Nov 8 [1950]

Dear Honey:

. . . My re-writing simply crawls. . . .

Well, I'll see if I can sweat out a few paragraphs.

Much love,

. . . .

(TLS, 2 pp.)

[Van Hornesville, N.Y.]
Monday early afternoon
[13 November 1950]

Dear Honey:

Your letter in my heavy mail today. . . . Please don't ever hold up what seems to you a "trivial" letter. I always need to be pulled back to earth from the half-mad world in which I live too much of the time. And I enjoy and want every scrap of news about you.

A letter from Arthur in answer to mine—. Actually, no answer. He asked me to write him so that he could read part or all of my letter to Grace, who is with him in Seattle—. Which tells part of the story—. I shall do so, and I swear, shall never again mention to him in any way his "problems. . . ."

Much love,

. . . .

(TLS, 6 pp.)

Van H[ornesville, N.Y.].
Wednesday 6:15 P.M.
[22 November 1950]

Dear Honey:

Twenty pages copied so far today, and I shall have a bite of supper and do another five or ten, afterward.

Friday noon
[24 November 1950]

I waited for the Ed Murrow[1] broadcast Wed. night and was so tired I went right to bed—. Leaving Wednesday, my Gracie said, "I suppose you want me to come tomorrow?" and I was staggered, wondering if in my absorption in my work and the consequent vagueness I had fired her, of if she had quit, as I was sure "tomorrow" wasn't going to be Sunday or even Saturday, when on occasion she joins her husband. I said, "What is tomorrow?" and she said "Thanksgiving," and I said of course not to bother to come. None of these holidays have much meaning any more, and I decided to forget all about it. I was amazed to find my heart leap[2] with delight when Mrs. Three Feathers[3] 'phoned, asking me to join them for Thanksgiving dinner. I accepted almost too avidly. . . . A couple of hours after that surprisingly welcome invitation, Josephine Case called me, asking me to join them at the Hamilton, and I refused with no regrets at all, much as I love the Case family. . . .

Three Feathers' dinner was superb, and I ate like a horse, and I had copied ten pages of my manuscript in the morning, and expected to get back to work again after the 2 P.M. dinner, but found I was expected to stay longer. . . . Three Feathers said, "Such an honor, you come to us," and I hope I made them understand my gratitude, for it was more like the Thanksgivings of my childhood than anything for many years.

. . . The last two nights there has been a phenomenon. Restless, I have aroused in the late night, and seen a milky whiteness, the whole atmosphere nacreous, no snow falling, no sleet, no rain. Only this great suspended whiteness—. And in the morning, the bare trees have been covered with what the local denizens call "Frost." It is in depth a quarter of an inch or more, it is not ice, it is not snow, it is evidently a condensation overnight, and the result is that the trees, the bushes, the shrubs, the grass, are outlined in a silver filagree. It is as though there were winter leaves and blossoms of this crystal.

Saturday morning

... My copying has slowed down. I have begun running into places that are so bad, and when I have to stop and figure out a new angle or re-write *again*, it sometimes takes hours out of the working day. . . . I should be insane to make a break and try to start all over again at the cottage, with new help etc. My ultimate peace of mind would make it worth your while for me to see this through, here. What I should do is to take my three copies to New York—or perhaps send them express a day or so ahead of me—and wait in N.Y.C. while Charlie Scribner and Jack Wheelock and Wallace Meyer each reads a copy, so that I can talk the book over with them on the spot. Then I'd just leave the first carbon behind with Carl Brandt, to keep my promise to him, for he won't be ale to sell it serially.

Julia has begged me to stay with her. . . .

Bernice Gilkyson has had a wonderful thing happen, I forgot what the award was, but she has tied with Robert Frost for first prize in some important poetry contest. I am so thrilled for her. . . .

I *must* write Edie.

About Arthur, I did write casually as per request to the poor devil, and he wrote by return mail, thanking me, but meantime his Grace had cleared out of Seattle where she had been with him, raising a whirlwind in the going. At the moment, her temper-tantrums seem to bother him more than her immoral nature. He said she showed them before they were married, and at the time he thought they were cute. He will not leave before Christmas, so perhaps the paternity of the child will be evident by then. He says he is sure it is his own, but even if not, he can't walk out on the situation. . . .

Well, must try to knock off some more pages—.

Much love

1. Edward R. Murrow, broadcaster for CBS radio.
2. MKR is alluding to William Wordsworth (1770–1850), "My Heart Leaps Up" (1807).
3. Ruth Redjives.

1951 was a year of revision. In February, Norman Berg read the manuscript of *The Sojourner* and sent MKR extensive criticisms. She took them in the spirit they were given, but always with the knowledge that he could not replace Maxwell Perkins. She continued to revise at Cross Creek, on occasion distracted by the plight of her seemingly always destitute brother, Arthur, who continued to write to MKR about his unhappiness with his third wife and new baby. In April, she went to New York to meet with Charles Scribner and John Hall Wheelock about her manuscript. The verdict was simple: it needed extensive revision. Julia Scribner was there to soften the blow. In May, MKR went to Van Hornesville. NSB continued to worry about her excessive drinking, which had become a serious issue between them. Although she tried repeatedly to get it under control, it was a problem she could not overcome. Revision of *The Sojourner* continued, and in October, NSB came to visit. By December, she was back at Cross Creek trying to finish the "bloody book," which led her to opine that NSB was again "abandoned" as she worked.

. . . .

(ALS, 9 pp.)

Harkness Pavilion
[New York, N.Y.]
Saturday afternoon
[21 April 1951]

Dear Norton:—

I no sooner got on the train than I wondered why on earth I hadn't *begged* [underlined twice] you to come up with me. Yet as things are working out, it wouldn't have been much of a joint spree, as Dana thinks it will probably take me through Wednesday for all the tests. . . .

Dana was so apologetic—for being busy—for not having it register on him in Florida when I mentioned my eyes then (he had totally forgotten it, and telling me to use lots of Vitamin A)—and for not having a De Luxe room for me in the part of the Harkness where you and I have hitherto previously luxuriated. I am in a new wing of Harkness, only open for the last couple of weeks. . . .

As a matter of fact, the room is so desirable and comfortable, even with a view of the river, that I told him later to leave me here. It would be absurd to go into one of those high-priced rooms when I don't need any coddling. Also, they need those other rooms for people who are having operations or babies or who are seriously ill.

. . . I located Julia at Far Hills. She is coming back to town Tuesday morning and we'll get together some time. Charlie was out, and I asked her to tell him that I'd call the Scribner office later and would drop in for a talk with him and the boys.

. . . Pearl Primus is on a dance trip, will return Monday—! I do want to see her. If she had been in town, I might have gone out tonight, but as it is, I shall be very happy at the Harkness Hotel. . . .

Much love to all,

. . . .

(TLS, 3 pp.)

[Van Hornesville, N.Y.]
June 4 [1951]

Dear Norton:

. . . About your tomato plants. I think they should have the irregular fronds or branches trimmed off, making one tall stalk. And staked. Yes, tomatoes ripen when picked green, but they are so much better when ripened on the vine, and obviously, you are having too much foliage. Honey, you don't like rutabagas. . . .

. . . .

(TLS, 4 pp.)

Van Hornesville, [N.Y.]
June 11 [1951]

Dear Norton:

I enclose my last letter from Arthur, which has so outraged me that I am still trembling. Return it, please, after you have read it and have given me your general feeling and opinion.

I scarcely know where to begin.

The wife Grace, however much of a bitch and hysterical as she is, certainly has not had a fair deal from Arthur. Do you remember—of course you do—my sending for you from Ocala, before we were even intimate, to tell you of Arthur's turning on his second wife, Winifred? Having known her first as the mistress of one of his closest friends, recognizing her as an intelligent, attractive *chippie*, he marries her, THEN he turns on her, and cannot accept her past. It is part of the way Arthur has always been, wanting something for the moment, then turning against it the moment he has it. How I have survived his blind adoration of me, I do not know.

I can understand this new wife's resentment of Arthur, even the "tantrums," since he did indeed "reject" her, as he "rejected" Winifred. And if I tell him of himself, he is likely to turn on me, or at least to feel that his last fortress has fallen—. If he were only a friend, and not my brother—I should wash my hands of all of him, including his son.

What made me furious in his letter was his selfish and casual remark, "So, I'm planning to be ready to whisk Jeff away, from here or wherever we may be, *get him placed, possibly with you*," (Italics mine) etc, etc. At this point the odd and bitter matter involves not only Arthur and the admittedly affectionate mother, Grace, but your life and mine. To say nothing of the unfortunate baby.

. . . I'll just have to skip any of our own difficulties *without* a child in the household—the strange tension that has *always* existed between us—and so on. I know that you feel that a child would be a stabilizing influence on me, and perhaps it would. Yet you have made possible our going on with the marriage by giving me a long enough rope and enough freedom not to make me feel trapped at the cottage, where the type of life and the physical setting are alien to the very roots of my nature.

If I were pinned down by a child—and as I told you, I shouldn't drag one around like the dog and cat—I don't know whether I could stand the added frustration. ESPECIALLY, and this is where you must think deeply, if Jeff is a temporary, come-and-go proposition.

Arthur seems to me to be considering only his own desires. His idea is evidently to *park* the baby with the most suitable and complaisant party available, us or the aunts, fight it out with the woman, then perhaps when Jeff is old enough to be with him, to "whisk" him back again. If we allow Arthur to follow out this project, the involvements, emotional, legal and financial, would be unspeakable.

My first thought is that I should write Arthur, under no circumstances to "whisk Jeff away." That is kidnapping, and the woman would have every right to raise hell—and Arthur would have to foot the bill. Or we would—.

Don't you agree on this?

Second, my own instinct is to shoot the works. To inform Arthur that we will take Jeff only if he is to be ours permanently. At the moment, I suppose neither Arthur or Grace would consider that.

If we take that baby on the basis of "tiding Arthur over," we couldn't help becoming so attached to him that it would be utter cruelty to take him away from us later. And if we went on for some years, on a vague basis, the mother would have to have the child for certain periods, Arthur might want to do the same, and every damn one of us would end up crazy.

It would perhaps also be extremely cruel to Arthur, even unfair, to demand the child outright or not at all. He has a right to his own son if he wants him. But if he only wants to park him for a few years, providing again the mother would give him up, I say, better to board him near Arthur in some kindly, reliable family, than tear *our* emotions to pieces.

And there is this to think of on the other hand, knowing Arthur's nature. Absence might make him lose his devotion if not his interest, as it did with his girls. He had periods of coolness toward the poor little creatures, then sudden spurts of longing for them and suffering over them, then he'd decide they were just like their mother and entirely undesirable as daughters. If and when he leaves this Grace, he'll go on the hunt for another woman, this time no doubt, for a suitable mother for Jeff. And I wouldn't trust him to pick a foster mother for a rabbit.

If he reached the point where he was perfectly willing to give up Jeff to us completely, well and good, but the uncertainty meantime would make life a definite hell instead of a vague purgatory.

Now let me know how far you go along with me on these angles. I shall not write Arthur until I hear from you.

The few pages I did on my book were forced and valueless. The characters are utterly dead to me. An irresistible idea for a short story came to me (not the monkey one) and I have nearly finished it. I know it can't be any good for the simple reason that I've had *fun* writing it. It's straight narrative and slightly humorous.

I'm tired of beating my brains out. I know I must return to it, but I shall try to be more relaxed when I go at the manuscript again. My nervous tension has affected my eyes. . . .

Love,

. . . .

(TLS, I p.)

[Van Hornesville, N.Y.]
June <16> 15 [1951]

Dear Norton:

. . . I hope you understand that my last letter was not an ugly outburst, only an attempt to get straight some of the facts. I'd give anything if you had the sort of analytical nature that dotes on talking things out. But if you were that way, you wouldn't be Norton, and it is Norton whom I do indeed love, unsatisfactory as our relationship may be. The question I pose to myself is, "Do you want life without Norton?" and the answer is "No."

Love,

(TLS, I p.)

[Van Hornesville, N.Y.]

June 19, 1951

Dear Norton:

If I live long enough, I may learn to give the reins of my subconscious when I am lost, and trust Old Faithful to get me home. All this time, nearly a month now, that I've been trying to force the first of my re-writing, I've been on the wrong road all together, and by *balking*, my subconscious has been trying to tell me so.

I suddenly understood that the second chapter, which I have been trying to *patch*, has always been, in its very concept, nothing short of *fatal* to the whole book. And I know *why*, and now I know exactly the approach I must make. I am not out of the woods on it, as there is still the trifling matter of entirely fresh rewriting, but there is no question but what I'm on the right road at last.

I feel so homeward bound that it has been no problem for two days to drop the drinking completely. It won't last, of course, but I may be good for several weeks.

Max would have seen what I had done, almost at once. It is *obvious* now, that while there is *some* excuse for the writer's lack of perspective, I see none for objective editors.

If you didn't happen to notice it, go back to your Saturday Review of two weeks ago, the one with the picture of Irwin Shaw,[1] I think, on the cover, and read Struthers Burt's story about Max.[2] I went to the Perkins' Letters[3] to check on Burt's statement that Max gave him no editorial comment ever, and found, what had meant little before, several letters from Max to James Jones.[4] These are at the end of the book. You'd be interested in reading them now.

Love,

1. Irwin Shaw (1913–1984), American dramatist and novelist.
2. Maxwell Struthers Burt.
3. *Editor to Author: The Letters of Maxwell E. Perkins*, ed. John Hall Wheelock (New York: Scribners, 1950).
4. James Jones (1921–1977), American novelist. When he died in 1947, Perkins had at his bedside the manuscript of Jones's *From Here to Eternity*.

. . . .

(TLS, 3 pp.)

Van H[ornesville, N.Y.].

June 20, 1951

Dearest Norton:

. . . I followed your advice, even stole two or three of your phrases, and insisted that Arthur not "whisk Jeff away" at any time or under any circumstances. I spoke of the first hysteria he has built up to, which I said was painfully familiar to me, as an affliction of my own and of Wilmer, and in her life, of Aunt Madeline, and tried to analyze it. The focal point you gave me was his necessity to come to a definite decision of some or any sort, and stick to it. I said that it must be his own, but my personal hope was that he might decide to make the very best of things, to be kind and pleasant when he'd rather kill, until Jeff was of school age, at six, or perhaps even at four. Then, if the situation was impossible, to arrange for a dignified divorce, with full custody if he could get it, or he might then want you and me to take Jeff over.

. . . If in writing Arthur yourself, you had in mind telling him he was interfering with my work and causing me utter emotional agony, please don't. It would only mean that he'd keep everything from me, and the next thing we knew, he might do something completely rash without saying a word, when he could have stopped in time if he felt free to spill everything to me. I did say to him myself, after finishing my analysis of the tension that builds up in us, that while we usually only harmed ourselves, often we harmed others even more so, and "In your present indecision about Grace, in your torment of attraction and revulsion, you are doing great damage to yourself, to Grace, to Jeff, to me, and to an extent, I imagine, to the aunts."

It doesn't hurt us neurotics to be reminded that our tail- spins don't take place in a self-centered vacuum! (Vacuum has no center, does it? But you know what I mean.)

Anyway, I did my best.

. . . As if you meant to tell him that you don't think it would be good for *me* to take on Jeff, temporarily or permanently, absolutely not! I said nothing to him of the heart-break it would mean to take the child for a little while or on an uncertain basis, as I did to you. If he will hang on for three or four years, the whole thing may work out for him, or if not, and he would give us Jeff for our own thing, that would be worth-while, and since it would be a *stable* thing, I could make an adjustment that would not wreck me or my damned writing. It would be uncertainty that would be ruinous.

I wrote Arthur calmly, but toward the end, I suppose I was keyed up without knowing it, and thought I would die without a drink. Dora and I argued it hot and heavy, and I decided to flip a figurative coin for it. I said, "All right, go and weigh yourself, and if you've lost two pounds these last three days of virtue, No drink. If you haven't lost, you may have one."

I had lost *three* pounds, and Dora slunk away muttering. . . .

Much love and many thanks,

(TLS, 5 pp.)

[Van Hornesville, N.Y.]
Monday morning
[25 June 1951]

Dear Norton:

... I wondered myself about ordering the McCullers, but since we have her three novels already, the omnibus volume didn't seem worth-while for a few short stories, most of which I imagined we've read. I have a new order in at Scribner's and will send on things like "Man and Boy" and "The Watch."[1] I got so desperate for reading matter that I asked Jo if I might borrow from Mr. Young's books. I was after some of the classics I never read, but couldn't locate the sort of thing I wanted. I found a couple of Galsworthy's I'd never read and was delighted with them.

Bernice[2] sent me her book of poems, publication July 16. I have noted a dozen or so that I want to speak of particularly when I write her to thank her, both for the book and the dedication to me. These seem to me true poetry. Gene Baroff 'phoned me yesterday, and among the assignments for reviewing that Irita Van Doren had given him, was Bernice's volume. He said he tried to beg off, but she was insistent that he do it. He said it isn't his kind of verse at all, but he thought he had been able to say some good things. Bernice will be upset whatever he says, to have her space in such an important paper as the Tribune given to one she considers so young and brash. I must let her know that I had nothing to do with it.

... So after thinking it over for several days, I have written Arthur a note, saying that in an *emergency*, we would take Jeff at any time, and for any length of time. I repeated that he must not do anything precipitous or anything that would put him in the wrong. And said we were behind him. (I don't feel that he deserves one scrap of sympathy or one scrap of help, and I don't believe in this blind family "standing-by," it only makes the weak weaker. I believe in fighting one's own battles. Paying for one's own mistakes. When things go unavoidably wrong, then help should be given at any cost to oneself. But all of this is his own fool fault, when God knows he is old enough to have known better. He won't live too long, he will burn himself out, and I am more concerned about the little boy than I care to admit. The "Kinnan" means nothing to me, I'd feel the same about any nice boy baby that I happened to know about, and that seemed to be in for a needlessly rugged time.)

If it was a girl, he could drown her, for all of me—. . . .

Love,

1. Morris Wright, *Man and Boy* (New York: Knopf, 1951); James Agee (1909–1955), *The Morning Watch* (Boston: Houghton Mifflin, 1951). Carson McCullers, *Ballad of the Sad Café: The Novels and Stories* (Boston: Houghton Mifflin, 1951).
2. Bernice Gilkyson [Kenyon], *Night Sky and Other Poems* (New York: Scribners, 1951).

(TLS, 4 pp.)

[Van Hornesville, N.Y.]

Friday June 29 [1951]

Dear Norton:

... Gene's career is moving fast. He has sold two stories and several poems, has commissions from Harper's Bazaar and Mademoiselle for articles, and Knopf signed a contract for a novel which he outlined to them, with a $1,000 advance. He said he had hoped to be with Scribner's when the time came, but they made no overtures, and Knopf made all of them.

... I have muffed it with Arthur, just sort of the serious damage I was afraid of. He had just returned from an expedition and answered me at once, three large sheets typed single-space, all re-hashing his grievances against Grace. My urging of calming himself in order to come to some decision did not register at all. It will probably be impossible for him as long as he is so torn about the woman herself. ...

He was angry with me in the cold, hoity-toity way he can act—he pulled it on Dessie and me in Alaska when he announced that we were not treating his wife with proper consideration and respect! (Totally untrue.) He says that I have "only a glimpse of the overall picture. So don't judge too harshly, too conclusively." And "I assure you I won't do anything outlandish and detrimental to Jeff, and will not involve you or any of my family except to ask you to continue to believe in my integrity, honesty and conscience which have, despite my failures, been pretty steady." And "Now just forget my problem—I'll not bother you again until I have it licked." He says that "Never, ever, even once, have I considered turning over Jeff to you or anyone else. Being unable to cope with Grace's tyranny, being completely unnerved and at a loss myself I felt and have always felt during those sieges that I must escape, just escape, and then I'd be able to regroup my forces and face the situation. I could only think of placing Jeff in safe hands while I made my stand."

... And oh yes, he took the occasion to point out my shortcomings as a wife to you. You are my husband, and you need my companionship. I should not be apart from you.

I just wanted to get all this off my chest. I have been through *my* emotional crisis about him and about the child, and am free at last. I shall not write him again any way but casually. ...

Love,

(TLS, 6 pp.)

[Van Hornesville, N.Y.]

July 6 [1951]

Dear Norton:

... Do you have the Whitney book "Lone and Level Sands," "Man and Boy" and "The Season of the Stranger?"[1] If not, I'm through with them, and will send them on. "Man and Boy" is delicious.

I also have Carlo Levi's "The Watch,"[2] but you can read it here some time, as I consider it worth keeping in my permanent library....

Saturday

[7 July 1951]

I read the Mary Garden[3]—what a mess, but how I envy her self-confidence. I read the Crichton,[4] which should have been terribly funny, but I couldn't be amused to save me. I felt too conscious all the time of the author saying, "Isn't this cute?"

I look forward to the A. E. Coppard....[5]

Love,

I had a letter from Katie Mickens, March's wife, asking me "Mrs. Baskin, will you sell me your Rest room out door. Martha say she don't use it and mine is gone to the bad."

She means the old outhouse! I suppose they really were the original Rest rooms! ...

Love,

1. Cornelius Vanderbilt Whitney (1898–1974), *Lone and Level Sands* (New York: Farrar, Straus, and Young, 1951); Stephen D. Becker (1927–), *The Season and the Stranger* (New York: Harper, 1951).
2. Carlo Levi (1902–1975), *The Watch* (New York: Farrar, Straus, and Young, 1951).
3. Mary Garden (1874–1967) and Louis Biancolli (1927–), *Mary Garden's Story* (New York: Simon and Schuster, 1951).
4. Kyle Crichton (1896–1960), *The Marx Brothers* (New York: Crown, 1951).
5. A. E. Coppard (1878–1957), *Collected Tales* (New York: Knopf, 1951).

. . . .

(TLS, 3 pp.)

[Van Hornesville, N.Y.]

July 13 [1951]

Dear Norton:

... Arthur wrote me in answer to my note saying we were behind him and would take Jeff for any necessary period. He was all buoyed up by this and had kind words for me, the son of a bitch.

... A cute letter from James Cabell. He and Margaret are having fun writing stanzas every day or so for a long poem "The Ways of Women." He says, "Her tendency toward the obscene, I regret to say, prevents the result's being sent through the mails, but I am trusting that, with Norton's leave, you may blush over it some day. . . .

I made an even dozen half-pint jars of wild strawberry jam, and have begun on currants and raspberries, with wild raspberries just about ready. I grew enough cherries for a little cherry tart (sounds like the beginning of a child's rhyme!) and the damn birds got every one ahead of me. I have to pick the currants before they are quite ripe, as they are stripping the bushes. . . .

Love,

. . . .

(TLS, ALS, 3 pp.)

[Van Hornesville, N.Y.]

July 18 [1951]

Dear Norton:

. . . I am having no trouble about the liquor. I had drinks on the 4th with the Case's, then went back on the wagon the next day without difficulty. I fix my frugal supper about 5, sometimes as early as 4. No comment, please. Louise was telling me yesterday how different I looked, and as I prayed that she'd keep her mouth shut, she said, "Now you *must* stay on your diet and you *must* not drink," and I wanted to scream and tear my hair—and hers.

I'll send on the books. Please send me anything you have. Just hope we don't duplicate. Am sending Mailer's "Barbary Shore". . . .[1]

Love,

1. Norman Mailer (1923–), *Barbary Shore* (New York: Rinehart, 1951).

. . . .

(TLS, 2 pp.)

[Van Hornesville, N.Y.]

July 25, 1951

Dear Norton:

. . . I feel that I never want another maid who is around all the time, especially in such a small place as this. I love my free afternoons and evenings, getting my own light supper in a clean kitchen, and settling down with a book without being conscious of a possibly lonesome creature off in the back. And now that I feel so wonderfully well, in every way, there is no anxiety that I might need waiting on at night. . . .

Love,

(TLS, 4 pp.)

[Van Hornesville, N.Y.]
July 30, 1951

Dear Norton:

Thanks for the Michener.[1]

. . . I don't know why I'm so cross, but I could bite nails. It isn't the work. What I am doing at this stage is not re-writing or editing or changing, but brand-new writing, which makes hard, slow going, but since I feel sure I am on the beam, I am reasonably satisfied that way. It may be the nagging physical effect of the terribly slow but sure reducing. Now I don't expect justice in life, but when I follow scientific rules I do expect results. As a matter of fact, what irks me is that the reducing is *not* sure. . . .

The diet costs me a pretty penny on my meat bills, as Gertrude is crazy about meat, and eats pound for pound with me. I have to have the steak and chops to get the low calorie proteins. But God knows I make it up on the liquor bill.

No, I don't mind not using salt at all. I don't use it on anything.

How can Edie be so bitchy? And what on earth does she have against Gene? I know he's young and brash, but he does have a whale of a good mind and he can *write*.

. . . I'm so sorry I said I'd take Idella back. To give *that* bitch the satisfaction of thinking I can't get along without her! . . . Perhaps since spring Idella has found a good-paying job that she does like. . . .

Love,

1. James A. Michener (1907–1997), *Return to Paradise* (New York: Random House, 1951).

. . . .

(TLS, 2 pp.)

[Van Hornesville, N.Y.]
August 1, 1951

Dear Norton:

. . . I'll enclose the letter I received yesterday from Idella, but please return it to me when you have read it, as I want to answer very carefully. It seems awfully mealy-mouthed and hypocritical to me, when she knows that I must have "forgiven" her to have told Hattie[1] I'd take her back. As to her "really getting it" unless I was in "the right mood," I have never bawled her out in my life.

Evidently she was unable, for lack of capital or engagements, to take up the catering when she finished her course, and has gone back to the same people she had been working for. . . . It was the job Hattie said she didn't like because of the big very late dinners every night, the generally hard work, and the isolation and not too much time off.

I would assume, wouldn't you, that her tone, and her writing at all, mean that she is working up to being invited to return? I do not think for a minute that she wants to spend her life with me. I am sure she sees the chance of a trip back to Florida, and possibly, as I have said before, eventually trying to stick me for money to go her own way again. There will of course be other men, with the familiar complications. I could never feel the same toward her again, and without my complete approval and affection, our relations might not be at all pleasant.

...I want to be at the Creek a great deal this winter, and the willing Adrenna would make me perfectly comfortable....

Love,

1. Hattie, a maid and Idella's friend from Cooperstown.

. . . .

(TLS, 2 pp.)

Van Hornesville, [N.Y.]
Aug. 6, 1951

Dear Norton:

A batch of checks for deposit. The large one, nearly $2,000, from Brandt and Brandt, is amazingly for French royalties on "The Yearling." It is in the third edition, and while I can't figure the number of copies sold, the gross royalties in francs are 868,885.00, so that in France, just think, I might well soon be a millionaire! I notice that the value of a franc is $.002845!!!

I have recently received copies of the French "Cross Creek," called "Le Pays Enchanté,"[1] and I find I can follow the translation easily. Unfortunately, it seems to me extremely literal and pedestrian, and even in my waning French, I could have done better here and there. The translator also took extreme liberties, omitting now and then, and changing the sense occasionally. I suppose some allowance has to be made for different national attitudes, but for instance, where I have Martha saying, "I was a fast breeder. I got sympathy for a woman is a fast breeder," the French is "I was a good breeder. I like (or admire) a woman who is a good breeder"!!!!

Virginia evidently won out with Mr. Young, as she returns to her job on Wednesday. She and Mr. Young came to me for dinner last night, and the poor things said it was the best dinner they'd had in weeks. It was simple, too, standing rib roast (very good and tender), baked potatoes, creamed new corn, hot rolls, jelly, spring onions, radishes, celery, ice cream and mangoes. (I had only roast beef and radishes and celery and mangoes!)....

Thank you for the two books. I am enjoying the Bagnold.[2] I am sending you Irwin Shaw's "The Troubled Air."[3] I am puzzled by what I remember of the reviews on it. I don't see it as very left-wing and radical at all. It seems to me only that he hates the type of fascism we are getting here just a fraction more than he hates the present Russian form of Communism, but he certainly has no use for the latter.

...I am anxious to have your reaction to Idella's letter. I feel quite cool to the idea of having her back....

Love,

1. *Le pays enchanté*, trans. Jeanine Parot (Paris: Michel, 1951).
2. Enid Bagnold (1889–1981), *The Loved and Envied* (New York: Doubleday, 1951).
3. Irwin Shaw (1913–1984), *The Troubled Air* (New York: Random House, 1951).

. . . .

(TLS, 3 pp.)

Van Hornesville, [N.Y.]

Aug. 9, 1951

Dear Norton:

I am so glad the folks are reaching the cottage at last. Hope you can make them finish up the jams and jellies, as I have quite a new crop. And don't forget there are more canned mangoes in the filing cabinet room. There should still be some quail in the deep freeze, and they might tempt your mother.

I was sure the Young's would not think of my birthday. . . . I must admit it was a very pleasant surprise when Gertrude greeted me with "Happy birthday. . . ."

My place at the table was heaped with gifts, as the Young family always does it, and it makes for great fun. One box the size and weight of candy was labeled "For a good girl," and it was a package of my damned prunes. The Case's are at Martha's Vineyard, but they had left a gift of an hour-glass egg-timer, with the note "Two minutes and forty seconds, you perfectionist." Think I'll have to wire them "I get two minutes and thirty-nine seconds. Can timer be exchanged for a more accurate one?" There was a huge wrought-iron "B," with the note "She knows A from B," and it was part of a set of initials Louise had used at her business entrance, I think in the Philippines. There was an old horse-shoe to put over the hop-house door. There was a 2-inch carved wood black cat with arched back, and spitting, and it looks cute facing one of the porcelain Siamese, as though it had encountered a stalking monster. Rather detracts from the artistic effect of the porcelain—. Louise, of all people, had written a birthday poem to me.

Aug. 10

Glad to have your letter yesterday. Guess you are right about Idella. I'll write her. However, if she can't or won't or just doesn't come when Gertrude leaves, I sha'n't fool with her. Once I finish this damn book, I'll be independent as a hog on ice.

. . . I had to laugh at your saying I was such a hard person for whom to buy a present. Just for fun, I wrote out a list of things and types of things I'd *enjoy* being given, and there were 23 different items. . . .

. . . A frantic air mail note from Aunt Ida that she had forgotten my birthday, but would get off a card. . . .

That Cecil—. And that Bob—.[1] How can they fritter away their lives so? Bob talked of the mural for the DuPonts two years ago when we talked on the 'phone—.

And that Dessie! I did think she wouldn't bother with more marrying unless it was extremely worth while. An orange grove is small potatoes for her.

. . . Am stuck on the book again, couldn't work yesterday or today. Feel at this point there's no use in forcing stuff that would have to be done over *again*. Have to get it right now as I go along.

Love to all,

1. Cecil Clarke and Bob Camp.

. . . .

(TLS, 3 pp.)

[Van Hornesville, N.Y.]
Aug. 15 [1951]

Dear Norton:

It's too bad we both bought "Lucy Carmichael,"[1] it's as close to nothing I've read in a long time. I didn't know you had bought the Bagnold and the Iron Mistress[2] just for me, so I'll send them on. Think I said that I have "White Man Returns" by Agnes Keith,[3] and "The Cruel Sea."[4] I'll send them unless your next letter tells me you have them. I now have a nice reading reserve of a lot of Stendhal[5] which I ordered, but I want to keep that here.

I wrote to Idella and said there was no point in beating around the bush, that if she wanted to come back, I'd be glad to have her—if she would come here in mid-September. Said my need of her would not be so great after this fall. Said I would have to know soon, in order to make other arrangements if she isn't coming then. I'll give her two weeks, then if I don't hear, or she is evasive, I'll arrange for someone. . . .

. . . Oh, this wicked, slow reducing. A week of Louise's scientific diet took off only a pound and a half. . . . And my big blackberries are ripening, and I want a blackberry pudding.

. . . Finished an important section of new writing, and now am afraid it isn't right, either. It leaves a bad taste in my mouth. . . .

Much love to all,

1. Margaret Kennedy (1896–1967), *Lucy Carmichael* (New York: Rinehart, 1951).
2. Paul I. Wellman (1898–1966), *The Iron Mistress* (New York: Doubleday, 1951).
3. Agnes N. Keith, *White Man Returns* (Boston: Little, Brown, 1951).
4. Nicholas Monsarrat (1910–1979), *Cruel Sea* (New York: Knopf, 1951).
5. Stendhal [Marie Henri Beyle] (1783–1842), French novelist and critic.

(TLS, 4 pp.)

[Van Hornesville, N.Y.]
Aug. 20, 1951

Dear Norton:

You paint a pathetic picture of your family. Odd, isn't it, the tension they all live under, for all the simplicity of their lives. With their finances so much better, a nice home of their own at last, you'd think they could relax a bit. . . . I know you enjoyed having them at the cottage, and were probably relieved, too, to return to the quiet of peace and the papers.

. . . I never thought the day would come when I'd pray that Idella did *not* return, but that's about what has happened. I may be mistaken, but I think I have found the answer to the sweet, capable, lifelong-loyal help that I once thought I had in Idella. Her name is Katherine Mulligan. . . .

Much love,

. . . .

(TLS, 2 pp.)

[Van Hornesville, N.Y.]
Aug. 23, 1951

Dear Norton:

I have written Idella and will mail it before getting my incoming mail, so that if there should be an answer from her today, the matter will have already been settled. I left the way open for winter contact, although I really don't think I want her then, even if I don't take Katherine south. I was actually joyous yesterday when there was still no word from her.

. . . The not-drinking has certainly been all to the good in every way but one— I just can't get sleepy. . . .

Love,

. . . .

(TLS, 1 p.)

[Van Hornesville, N.Y.]
Aug. 24, 1951

Dear Norton:

Your box was in the mail yesterday. I couldn't believe my eyes when I opened it. "Nicer slips and nighties than I would buy" were the second item on my secret list! These are simply lovely and I am so pleased with them—and with you. I had looked at a somewhat similar nightgown in the spring, wanted it, but wouldn't pay the price. I love that fine plaiting. I love fancy slips. It is a great satisfaction to be fluffy-ruffly underneath. Many, many thanks.

. . . There was still no letter from Idella, and I am glad I didn't wait for her. I had written her in the first place that all she need do was give me a simple Yes or

No, but that seems quite beyond her. It convinces me that she was set for free transportation to Florida later, and was probably willing to be with me for the winter in order to see her family again. She gets very homesick for them. And I do think she meant to hit me for money, using some wild story, in order to take up her catering. She plots quite far ahead.

Love, and thank you, thank you.

. . . .

(TLS, 2 pp.)

[Van Hornesville, N.Y.]
Aug. 24, 1951

Dear Norton:

. . . Well, I had a letter from Idella in the mail yesterday. She spoke of the "joy" of having my letter, which is nonsense, as I had taken two-thirds of it to give her hell. In offering her the job back and telling her I could only pay her $30, I said I knew it wasn't as high as the N.Y. and Long Island pay, but I was sure there were compensations in not having the long bad hours and in having some time off and more general freedom. Now I know she is with the same family as when Cooperstown Hattie talked to me, and Hattie said the big late dinners and the isolation irked Idella no end. So, Idella paints such a picture of her life there as to make me think she is practically the daughter of the family instead of the cook. . . . At the end of the letter, in the same lofty Queen of May manner, she says rather casually that about coming here, she must honestly say No. However, happy and ideal and well-paid as she is, she has no intention of living in the north. "I do like it in Florida in spite of the salaries, so that's where I soon shall be."

I wouldn't take a thousand dollars, literally, for having gotten in *my* rejection first. And I'll have to be more desperate than I can possibly imagine, to take her on this winter or any other time. . . .

Charlie Scribner is about over his shingles. He says Julia's baby will probably come this week, lightening his mind and body. She does get enormous. He said she is well. I'll 'phone her today or tomorrow.

Love,

. . . .

(TLS, 3 pp.)

[Van Hornesville, N.Y.]
Aug. 31 [1951]

Dear Norton:

. . . I had a wire from Tom Bigham, and Julia's baby was born at Harkness Wednesday afternoon and she and child are well. Another girl, damn it. Mary Kirkpatrick.

This is the big week-end for the Young doings. Everyone is here. Tomorrow afternoon there is a dedication party at Mr. Young's new office, and from there we go to Faith and Philip for dinner and band dance. Sunday afternoon, the Family Show at Charlie and Esther Young's, and from there everyone comes to me for buffet supper. . . .

I called Katherine Mulligan again to ask her to begin on Monday Sept. 10. . . . Katherine more than agreeable, and this time I tried to analyze her voice. It is extremely high, every phrase ending on an up-note like a question, and it gives the impression of oncoming *hysteria*, as though an Irish Ophelia were just about to go off the deep end. . . .

Much love,

. . . .

(TLS, 4 pp.)

[Van Hornesville, N.Y.]
Sept. 8, 1951

Dear Norton:

. . . Heavens, Verle and Edith[1] are trying friends.

. . . I am fatuous to expect to finish the book at all soon.

. . . The office-warming [for Owen Young] was a moving ceremony. Dick made a good speech, with poise and humor, and then Mr. Young spoke. He said that on that very spot he had made his first speech, in the little schoolhouse, at the age of seven, and this was likely to be his last public speech. He was so noble and beautiful and I wept copiously. All the work-men were there, and a few of the other villagers.

My party went off splendidly, I am sure, as far as the guests were concerned, but it was a fatality for me. I couldn't get anyone to help me. . . . At 4 o'clock, having had nothing but fruit and black coffee for breakfast, I still had the flowers to cut and arrange, lettuce to pick and wash, the table to set, Martinis to mix, dishes and silver and glasses to set out, myself to bathe and dress, and a token appearance at the Family Show to be made. I reached for the Old Forrester as automatically as a rabbit breeds—. I didn't eat supper, either—and it was ready without flurry on the dot of 7—and I was sober enough to make Sanka separately for Mrs. Powis when I made coffee for the others, after supper. I thought no one noticed, (!!!!) but the next day Louise said with arched eyebrows, "Are you on the wagon again?" I was so furious with myself, and depressed, that I drank again on Monday, then stopped it short with no difficulty. . . .

I talked to Julia on the 'phone at the hospital and she and Mary Kirkpatrick are doing well. She has to go home day before yesterday.

I didn't expect to like "The Catcher in the Rye,"[2] because of the tone of even the favorable reviews, but it was a lovely sensitive job. "The Autumn Garden"[3] left me perfectly cold. It seemed an aimless hodge-podge.

. . . I probably shouldn't have told you about my fall from grace, but wanted to get it off my chest. I understand it is to be expected to slip once or twice while taking the cure.

Much love,

1. Verle and Edith Pope.
2. J. D. Salinger (1919–), *The Catcher in the Rye* (Boston: Little, Brown, 1951).
3. Lillian Hellman (1906–1984), *The Autumn Garden* (Boston: Little, Brown, 1951).

. . . .

(TLS, 3 pp.)

[Van Hornesville, N.Y.]
Sept. 11, 1951

Dear Norton:

You might be amused by a first day's report on Katherine. The voice is not going to be troublesome. . . . Katherine is lonely, *hungry* and perpetually anxious. I am sure she is the soap opera audience incarnate. It isn't a hunger for man-love, just a lostness and longing for kindness and something to which she can attach herself without getting nothing but abuse for her pains. . . .

Much love,

The work is going well at present.

. . . .

(TLS, 3 pp.)

[Van Hornesville, N.Y.]
Sept. 13, 1951

Dear Norton:

. . . I have never seen such a worker as Katherine. I can't stop her. . . .

I enclose a letter from Henry Heyl. It is one of the most tragic things I have ever known. And his courage—. I have taken his address and shall write him, and I know you will want to, too, hard as it is. He would enjoy being told any amusing incidents, in other words, a normal, friendly letter. I shall try to write him every now and then as long as he lives.[1]

Much love,

1. Heyl developed a tumor and was left a paraplegic.

. . . .

(TLS, 3 pp.)

[Van Hornesville, N.Y.]
Sept. 20, 1951

Dear Norton:

. . . My work has gone very slowly this week, mostly because I have had to have Katherine a great deal on my mind and have had to give her quite a bit of help because of her burned hand. . . .

My dinner for the Young's . . . went off very nicely indeed. The helper that Katherine arranged for was a wonder. How I'd love to have *her*, but she has a husband and a 4-year-old-girl. I got the turkey stuffed and ready, odds and ends prepared, and went at my flowers, which I had cut and put in water the evening before. . . .

. . . Well, you are a sweet darling, and bitch that I am, I do appreciate it. . . .

Much love,

. . . .

(TLS, 4 pp.)

[Van Hornesville, N.Y.]

Monday

[24 September 1951]

Dear Norton:

Katherine's burn is nearly healed so that she can do more, and she seems to love trotting up and down stairs. She is quite maternal, which would be fine if she had a good mother's firmness, but she can never make up her mind about anything, and has to present all sides of the simplest question for my decision. Even when I've made it, she thinks up some other angle. . . .

Anyway, she could not be sweeter.

. . . Well, I guess I'll ask Katherine about Florida. I could not find anyone cleaner or nicer, and she has been such a dear the two days I've been laid up that I can feel myself becoming attached to her, and once I like 'em, I can put up with their oddities. And it would be a sort of insurance against Idella! Of course, the idea might frighten Katherine to death. . . .

Love,

. . . .

(TLS, 3 pp.)

[Van Hornesville, N.Y.]

Friday noon

[28 September 1951]

Dear Norton:

Got back to work yesterday in good fashion. And again this morning. Such a relief.

Was dreadfully upset yesterday by a note from Arthur, almost physically ill. He said that when he got back from a hunting expedition, he found Grace had double-crossed him. "She took legal steps, has me completely tied up, even cash in bank. Jeff too. She did this to her first husband. My chances now of getting Jeff are virtually nil. In this frontier country the man is almost never given custody."

Very little more, didn't say exactly what she'd done.

I wired him not to give up the fight for a moment, that he could certainly prove everything and win, and did he need ready cash. Felt much better when answering wire from him came over the 'phone first thing this morning, "Have recovered composure, cash and sense of humor. Situation black but not hopeless. Need nothing from you but what your wire already gave, confidence."

He did say in his note that he should have followed his long inclination to "take Jeff and start elsewhere afresh with him." I wrote him that he was still much better off to have stayed in the legal right, and that the very snideness of Grace's action now was in his favor. I can't help being glad the issue has come to a head. He would have gone completely batty if he'd gone on with the woman. But he *must not* lose that boy.

. . . It was necessary to speak to Katherine about Florida after all. . . . For sweetness, willingness, workingness, even the very servant-ness, I couldn't do better, and in time I may be able to make an efficient cook and housekeeper of her, which she certainly is not now.

Oh, yes, she seemed to like the idea of Florida, and will talk it over with her family this week-end. They'll probably object, but we'll see. I told her that I needed someone permanent, to go back and forth with me. If her family keeps her from going, I'll engage her for next summer, and will *not* try to get Idella for winter. I'll have Adrenna at the Creek, and in my good health will be all right at the cottage with just the cleaning woman. Expect Adrenna would go back and forth, as a matter of fact, I will *not* let Idella use me. . . .

Much love, and wish you were coming next week.

. . . .

(TLS, 5 pp.)

[Van Hornesville, N.Y.]
Oct. 4, 1951

Dear Norton:

My Katherine—. I don't know. She makes me so nervous I could yell, but I haven't given up hope. . . .

A letter from Arthur. Grace is suing not for divorce but for separate maintenance, $150 a month, the Juneau house, and custody of Jeff. He indicates that he was partly to blame this time. I should guess that when he went off on that last fatal trip, he left her with sneers or what-not, and she pounced. He says he is trying for a reconciliation, until he can get himself in a more favorable position. Says if he can get the case moved to Seattle he stands a much better of chance of getting Jeff. The Judge for the Juneau court, who is the sole authority, has a famous blind-spot in the matter of custody. Always gives it to the mother no matter what she is. Of course, if Arthur does manage this, it would be pretty much of a double-cross in itself. And again, he may not really be through with the woman yet, within himself. I feel utterly ill about it, but refused to get stirred up about it. Art said that if he lost, we'd just have to consider it as an unavoidable car accident in which Jeff was a victim. Says he will settle if he has to for reasonable visiting privileges. Says he doesn't mean to sound defeatist, as he intends to fight tooth and nail to the end. But if he should settle for visits, the same thing will happen with the oldest daughter Marjorie Lou whom he was equally in love with, the mother will turn the child completely against him and after years of suffering he'll gradually just give it up. Jeff sounds too good to let this happen. And to be brought up by such a woman. You may yet see me getting into the act. . . .

Much love,

. . . .

(TLS, 3 pp.)

Van H[ornesville, N.Y.].
Oct. 11, 1951

Dear Norton:

. . . I think I know what Martha was so mysterious about. All of six weeks ago Hugh Williams wrote me asking to rent or buy my land adjoining the Valencia grove across the road from the house, for winter pasture for his increasing herd of beef cattle. Said I could keep Chrissie with them, and made a great to-do over Chrissie's present visit with his cattle to be bred to his wonderful registered Hereford bull. I didn't know what the devil to tell him. Anyone else would be welcome, but he is such a bastard and has never kept up with his rent on my 16 acres back of him, and I'm sure for one year's rent he'd consider the stud fee on his bull sufficient. I am also not keen about a flock of cows next to the grove, as they always break down fences, though he said he would keep fences in repair as part of rent. Again, the less business I have with him, the better. But I didn't want to make him sore, either. And I just never answered him. Knowing his cheek, I'll bet that he went ahead and moved his herd, and Martha is waiting with joy for me to come out shooting. She wants to give the news of my arrival so that she can enjoy the fireworks. Which I have no intention of providing.

I could wring her neck about Chrissie anyway. She swore she could get Chrissie to Mr. Williams' bull or vice versa the next morning after I left the Creek. I didn't write her until August, I think, and I answered her about Chrissie. She didn't answer for a couple of weeks, and then reported proudly "Mr. Crosby take Chrissie to Mr. Williams bull this morning." That means that Chrissie will come fresh next May or early June, after I've put in a winter buying milk and cream and butter. The whole summer to go, then, with Chrissie giving gallons of milk and pounds and pounds of butter doing me no good.

Bill Franzen writes that he'll have the place painted by the end of November. Said he could finance his payroll for a while, but would I advance half his price earlier and pay him the rest when he has finished. Suppose that is fair enough. However, I'll have to ask you to go to the Creek at least once to check on his progress. He said he would begin work the first of the week.

... Finished a brand-new chapter and thought I could get it nearly to the last chapters with editing only, when I hit a place again that calls for two new interpolated chapters because of too much lapse in time. God knows when I'll finish the thing.

I have practically decided to run down to New York for a few days at the end of the coming week or the first of the next one. I want Charlie and Jack Wheelock to see what I've done. If they approve so far, it will encourage me. If not, I'll know that I'm stuck for the winter. I'll buy a few clothes. Don't want to wait until it is too cold. Julia has to go to Nantucket the end of the month and I do want to see her, too. ...

Arthur has a sort of truce and temporary reconciliation with Grace, but she is balking on going to Seattle. She may well smell a mouse. I do think Arthur, too, still hopes that the psychiatry may straighten her out so that he can live with her. He obviously enjoys her bed no end.

Love,

. . . .

(TLS, 2 pp.)

[Van Hornesville, N.Y.]
Nov. 8, 1951

Dear Norton:

... I have been reading over my manuscript and am ready to go on working again. Haven't quite made the diet and the wagon yet but am inching up. ...

Much love, and thank you for everything.

. . . .

(TLS, 2 pp.)

[Van Hornesville, N.Y.]
Nov. 10, 1951

Dear Norton:

Just think, this old, old man is my young brother—.

Destroy his letter after you've read it.

I shall ask him, if he *can* get away without Grace, if he'd like to come to Florida. He could even go to the Creek ahead of me. God knows I couldn't cope with *her*.

... I had dinner at the Young's last night. I am greatly concerned about him. Either something is on his mind, or he thinks he has heard the beating of dark wings.

Louise had a superb dinner, to my surprise. A rich oyster stew, fricasseed chicken with gravy, home-made rolls, mashed potatoes au gratin, whole artichokes, ice cream. ...

I have worked to a new point where I have to do some new writing, so will knock off for the week-end and go at it Monday....

Love,

. . . .

(TLS, 3 pp.)

[Van Hornesville, N.Y.]

Nov. 13 [1951]

Dear Norton:

... Had a little visit with Mr. Young in his office. He swears there is nothing on his mind. Said this summer just wore him out....

C. has just come in with the accumulated mail. *Two* boxes from Tiffany's, which frightened me to death. I must admit I'd rather be in on your love affair with Tiffany's, rather than Lewis and Conger, but for your sake, I trust you will get over this mad infatuation. It would be much less expensive to be in love with Rita Hayworth. I'm sure Mr. Harris saw that you were about to bid on the Tiffany diamond.

Well, you did what I knew you would, send me a watch so much nicer than I need. (It is odd, the old one is rusted past much help, the jeweler said.) This one is wonderfully handsome, Norton. It will be stunning with my ring, which wasn't right with the cheap silver metal. I remember seeing a Tiffany Sunday ad, and admiring this style, especially the bracelet. Also remember dismissing it from my mind! And I thank you more than I can say, and this will be my present for Christmas and for my next birthday. And the adorable heavy silver spoons, gold-lined—they will be the next anniversary present. I have grieved over the disappearance of Mother's light-weight set—they were undoubtedly thrown out with the garbage once upon a time—and I do need them, for "company," including you, but again, they are much choicer than necessary. But greatly appreciated, and though I scold you for the watch, I just can't for the salt spoons. ...

Again, thank you, my sweet dear, with much love,

. . . .

(TLS, 3 pp.)

[Van Hornesville, N.Y.]

Monday

[19 November 1951]

Dear Norton:

...You don't know how I dread making the always fatal break, it usually means a month's halt in the work, besides being stuck with inadequate help when I get there. But I am getting Florida-minded in spite of myself, and the nightmare on the ice yesterday morning didn't help any. ...

Much love,

(TLS, 2 pp.)

[Van Hornesville, N.Y.]

Nov. 27 [1951]

Dear Norton:

Got my chore [for Voice of America] done, and Mr. Young's Irene came up and copied it for me, with carbons. It's most inadequate, but the best I could do. Now I'm sweating for fear the man will 'phone and say it's not useable. Incidentally, it's very spooky when he calls, he just says in a deep tone, "This is the Voice of America." Much more impressive than the A & P....

Much love,

. . . .

(TLS, 2 pp.)

[Van Hornesville, N.Y.]

Nov. 30, 1951

Dear Norton:

. . . Well, the Voice of America is coming here today, on the 2:28 at Ft. Plain. After he read the script he 'phoned and said it was "magnificent," "beautiful"— —BUT. Said it was too short, too objective, that I had been too modest in avoiding talk of myself and my work. What I finally realized, after all the soft soap, was that the script simply wouldn't do at all. . . . I do dread the whole business, with Monday still to be gotten through with. I did quite a bit of this kind of thing during the war, and it upset Max Perkins dreadfully. He said writers just shouldn't try to do those political propaganda things, that whatever we have to say, we should say in our books. But this seemed something I couldn't refuse, and didn't really want to, if I can get the script right....

Much love,

. . . .

(TLS, 3 pp.)

[Van Hornesville, N.Y.]

Dec. 1, 1951

Dear Norton:

The Voice of America wore an elegant, conservative gray suit. His light top-coat looked somehow seedy, as though he had only been able to afford one expensive item of dress, and the suit, to be seen from behind his desk, was more important. He had the manner of a banker or an industrialist. He was kindly, beautifully spoken, as poised as his employer Mr. Acheson,[1] and I recognized him as stricken. He was perhaps sixty-three or four.

The new script I had written was nearly right. The Voice had made some notes and I brought out the introduction to the school edition of "The Yearling," and a certain passage from "Cross Creek" and these were exactly what he had in mind.

It took us only an hour to put the combination through the mix-master, and then I took him upstairs to my typewriter and left him alone and he made three copies. I think he was genuinely pleased with the result. He said, "Now *this* comes from the author of 'The Yearling.' The other did not."

Much love,

1. Dean Acheson, then secretary of state.

. . . .

(TLS, 2 pp.)

[Van Hornesville, N.Y.]
Dec. 4, 1951

Dear Norton:

. . . Am sending Stark Young's book[1] of memoirs that Scribners sent me. It is about as damn *Southern* as you can get and annoyed me no end. If your mother feels up to reading, it might be up her alley.

The book in page proofs that I am sending, too, is a hair raiser. It reminds me of "The Lottery."[2] You will like it, as I did.

I found I had read the Steinbeck "Sea of Cortez,"[3] and I sent it to Henry Heyl.

. . .

Much love, and thank you for calling.

1. Stark Young (1881–1963), *The Pavilion* (New York: Scribners, 1951).
2. "The Lottery," a story by Shirley Jackson (1919–1965).
3. John Steinbeck (1902–1968), *Sea of Cortez* (New York: Viking, 1951).

. . . .

(TLS, 3 pp.)

[Van Hornesville, N.Y.]
Dec. 6, 1951

Dear Norton:

Katherine finally drove me to it. Violence. Her motives are the kindest in the world, but I am exhausted from never getting my way. I ask for one or two pieces of Canadian bacon and she brings four, saying, "I thought you might eat it." Yesterday, I said I'd have a piece of Arnold dry toast, and she said, "I already have a muffin fixed." After lunch, I planned to stay in bed to catch up on correspondence, and I got those two blasted boxes of Fanny Farmer and lit into them again. She was taking the car to be with her mother the rest of the day and evening and she came up for final questions. I told her to take the Fanny Farmer boxes home with her.

"Oh no, Mrs. Baskin, you'll want some again."

"That's just it. Take them."

"Oh no, Mrs. Baskin, I'll just put them in the cupboard and then you can have it when you want it. I won't take them home."

"Then hide them some place and use them yourself."

"Oh no, Mrs. Baskin, I'll just leave them here. You might want some more to-day. Good-bye now."

Off she goes down the stairs, and in pure joy, not at all in rage, I rise from the bed, pick up the two boxes and hurl them to the foot of the stairs. She picked up the butter creams and chocolate almonds from three rooms.

I said, "If I ever see them again, the next time I'll throw them right at your head."

...I did write to Idella. Told her to let me know within a couple of weeks, as I'd probably get cold feet and holler to go to Fla. shortly before Christmas.

Finished "Requiem for a Nun"[1] last night. Magnificent, but I thought Faulkner went rather maudlin at the end.

Much love,

1. William Faulkner (1897–1962), *Requiem for a Nun* (New York: Random House, 1951).

. . . .

(TLS, 1 p.)

Van H[ornesville, N.Y.].
Dec. 8, 1951

Dear Norton:

The 20th is definite then, and I'll have the car packed and everything ready to clear out the morning of the 21st. . . . . .

Well, I am on the wagon at last. It would have been much easier to wrestle a grizzly bear. . . .

Katherine came into her own in planning the house-closing. She is an expert on it. It will be grand just to walk out. It is definite that she is to be with me next summer.

Love,

1952

1952 was a year of end and beginning. February was a particularly cruel month. Charles Scribner III died suddenly on 11 February, just as MKR was polishing the final draft of *The Sojourner*. The shock was great, as she had lost a good friend and editorial connection to Maxwell Perkins. In mid-February, she suffered a coronary spasm at Cross Creek, was taken to Flagler Hospital in St. Augustine, and was released after three weeks with the warning that she must change her living habits. She convalesced at Crescent Beach, to be closer to NSB, and by mid-April completed *The Sojourner*. The bankrupt life of her brother, Arthur, continued to distress her, however. In early May, NSB took her to Van Hornesville, where she edited proof. In June, her beloved Aunt Ida died. In July, the hapless Arthur came to stay at Crescent Beach with NSB, and in September he came to Van Hornesville to confront his destitution with MKR. In early October, MKR and NSB left for England and from there to Ireland. Upon return, she stopped at Richmond to make living arrangements for her research on the biography of Ellen Glasgow. Christmas at Cross Creek seemed happier this year, no doubt accentuated when MKR received advance copies of *The Sojourner*.

. . . .

(TLS, 2 pp.)

[Cross Creek, Fla.]
Thursday morning
[3 January 1952]

Dear Honey:

Your wire came in the mail just now, and it did make me feel much better about what had already been done. "I proposes and Martha disposes." When I said on arrival yesterday that we'd give Idella the rest of the week to appear, and then decide, Martha said firmly and reprovingly, "Adrenna come here for the 'spress purpose of he'ping you and keeping me company. She told the Williams[1] right off that when you come back, she was working for *you*." That ended it, and it was no longer a question of either Idella's or my making up our minds. So I said, all right, we'd forget all about Idella, Adrenna was to give the Williams her notice at once, but could finish out the week for them, while Martha took over.

All is rosy, and Martha is working like a thirty-year-old. When I got up and said she could do my bedroom, she said, "Yessum, but I has to go to the house first for a little dip of snuff."

Have been very lucky on the help. Leonard had been here and fixed the lights, and came again just now to put new cords on the porch shades and to make them work. The woodman has brought vast piles of good wood, it seems enough for two years, $39, and Martha got her mysterious word to March to be on the job today. He is setting out the plants in well-manured ground. He worked in the manure several months ago.

Your tea olives here are in full bloom, so fragrant.

Two car loads of "fans" caught me almost on arrival. One pair was from Ky., and the man is the one who took my hush-puppy recipe and commercialized it in package form! He didn't even have a bag for me. Said when he read the recipe in my Cookery, he realized at once it could be marketed!

Stopped by Guthrie's[2] to order a turkey, and March picked it up this morning—21 lbs. Can't possibly get it in my roaster.

Shall we plan on your coming over week-end after this?

Much love,

1. Hugh and Flora Williams.
2. James Guthrie's property was on CR 346, between CR 325 and the River Styx (Stephens, 54).

. . . .

(TLS, 2 pp.)

[Cross Creek, Fla.]

Monday

[7 January 1952]

Dear Honey:

. . . Poor Adrenna looks pretty shabby. She is happy, and doing her best, which included, as I found this morning, carefully pulling out the cord from the bottom of the electric blanket. I awoke in the night simply frozen, and could not understand it, as the light glowed.

. . . Saturday evening Bernie Bass and his father came by. They had taken Glenn to Dr. Strange's hospital, where he was not expected to live the night. I went over, and while he has not died yet, it won't be too long. He was skin and bones, looking a corpse already. Dr. Strange told me the sclerosis had reached the nerves of the lungs. They were giving him oxygen.

Gene did not appear to eat, and except for lunch yesterday, have been alone with a 21 lb. Turkey. Am getting enough for once.

. . . I spent the morning in bed, as I finally got the room warm (it was bitter cold) reading my manuscript. It is more badly *written* than I remembered. It will take another day to do the slow reading.

... A tragic letter from Arthur.

Much love, and I'll look forward to your coming Saturday.

... And do bring me another $100 in fives and tens. I don't know where the money goes, but of course, I don't care as long as it holds out.

. . . .

(TLS, 1 p. + written note, 1 p.)

[Cross Creek, Fla.]

Jan. 16 [1952]

Dear Norton:

Just a note to say that all goes well. I got into the work yesterday.

... Adrenna finally got Buddy in, and I am keeping him in the house until he gets over his bouts of panic. I found Moe shagged him when out of doors.

Love,

Wed. Evening

... The Dreiser "American Tragedy" movie,[1] I forget the movie name, is in Gainesville, and I am going in now to catch the first show. Will mail this from there. Did a modest amount or work this morning.

1. *A Place in the Sun* (1951), starring Montgomery Clift, Elizabeth Taylor, and Shelley Winters, based on the novel *An American Tragedy* by Theodore Dreiser (1871–1945).

. . . .

(TLS, 1 p.)

[Cross Creek, Fla.]

Friday noon

[18 January 1952]

Dear Norton:

... I have just finished a brand-new chapter that helps the book (I think!) more than almost any of the other new writing. I am all set to go on to one more new intermediate chapter following on the heels of this one, and I see it quite clearly. Then I go into some simple revision and editing, and after that the home stretch—the last three or four chapters that are so vital, and since the old ones were so bad, I shall not even read them over. I may even destroy them first, so that they will never be found among my "effects"!

... I have had nightmares, one about Aunt Ida, and it seems so callous of me not to be near her, to say nothing of the much more important matter of failing you in every respect, but I can't help it, Norton, I can't help it. I see my way out of the dark forest, and I shall literally die if I turn aside from the path.

... Now about Mr. Young and Mr. Watson,[1] and the possibility that they might want to come by the Creek. That would be the one exception I would like to make to interruption on a week-day. But as a matter of fact, I can take almost anything in the afternoon or evening. I think I told you of meeting Mr. Watson at Rollins College, and of our *entente cordiale*, and of my saying to him, "I wish there were more business men like you in the world," and of his answering, "I wish there were more writers like you in the world." Of course, he may not remember me at all.

Love,

1. Thomas J. Watson, president of International Business Machines.

. . . .

(TLS, I p.)

Cross Creek, [Fla.]

Hawthorn, Florida

Jan. 21, 1952

Dear Norton:

... My work continues to go well, but I'm damned if I can see how and why, as Adrenna is driving me absolutely insane.

I know that on the whole I've had more of life than I deserve, but on the other hand, I don't feel that I deserve the punishment of Adrenna at this time.

. . . .

(TLS, I p.)

Hawthorn, Florida

Jan. 22 [1952]

Dear Norton:

... I am so deep in my work that any loneliness is momentary, and can be assuaged by almost anything to read. (I'm sure you will not mind my substituting Proust for you.) I may not even come for the Sadler Wells ballet—. And I am praying that Mr. Young does not take me up on my invitation to bring Mr. Watson by for a drink or a meal—. I am just that absorbed—. . . .

Love,

. . . .

(TLS, 3 pp.)

[Cross Creek, Fla.]

Jan. 23, 1952

Dear Norton:

I don't know whether or not I mailed you an uglier than usual of my ugly letters. I was prevented from writing the President very firmly only by being totally unable to finish the letter. I asked Martha to pray for me, and I did "real good" Sunday, just had two small drinks in the evening. Monday and yesterday were beyond the pale, and I asked Martha if she quit praying after Sunday, and she said she had. I told her to get back on the job. Having driven to Gainesville in the afternoon yesterday and mailed half a dozen letters, Heaven knows to whom or about what, I turned spiritual and noble, had supper with Martha and Adrenna in the kitchen, read the Bible aloud, and Martha prayed. Have the feeling the Lord didn't pay his usual attention to her, as instead of referring to me as "this woman" or "this sinner," she felt obliged to call me "Mrs. Baskin" in addressing Him on my behalf, and that probably doesn't "set good" in higher circles.

Actually, I am not as repentant as I should be, for if I get this job done, I don't care what it takes, and I should sacrifice you, me, anybody and anything to that end, and I *am* forging ahead, and that is all I give a damn about. I am in the ghastly state of tension when I finish the morning's work, and getting pie-eyed at least knocks me off early to sleep. Then of course I wake up fresh as a daisy, with no proper punishment at all, ready to go at it again. I am going so fast that at the moment I almost think I can meet Charlie's subtle deadline of April first, finishing the writing by the end of February, and leaving me March for the copying, with or without help. And when I wake up about 4 A.M. with the usual heebie-jeebies, I think about the last few chapters, and sometimes turn on the lights to make notes....

Oh, Christ God, Adrenna—.

. . . .

(TLS, 2 pp.)

[Cross Creek, Fla.]
Jan. 24, 1952

Dear Norton:

... Have done a good morning's work of revision, having finished re-writing until I get near the end.

... And I MUST NOT let Adrenna bother me so. I am such a carping fool. But her coffee and her wood are her only two satisfactory bits of help. I simply cannot stop her from dashing in to report on the people she has driven away. I understand her pride in her accomplishment and all that, and try to respect it. And her total inability to cook the simplest things—and my having to outline every step in detail—after which it doesn't come out right, in such odd ways. And her early morning gloomy reports—. "O-o-o-oh, I jes' couldn't sleep, I dreamed bad, and I set up in a chair rest of the night."

... March Mickens came with his figures, a credit of $220 on the truck, but he needed $80 in cash. He said that in 20 days he hoped he could pay you back what he borrowed. Only hope last night's cold didn't mess him up again on his truck crops.

Martha had a guilty conscience and brought me $2.80 to pay for her chicken feed, which, along with her hog feed, had been charged to me all summer and fall.

Love,

Editor's note: Written on the back of the envelope: "Adrenna *almost* [underlined three times] got the idea this noon about the creamed chipped beef, and it was not *too* [underlined three times] unbearably pasty, and she *did* [underlined twice] serve it on a separate *flat plate* [underlined twice], *not* a bowl, as requested, and the large serving spoon asked for turned out to be a pie knife.

How stupid of me to *mind* [underlined four times].

. . . .

(TLS, I p.)

> [Cross Creek, Fla.]
> Monday morning
> [28 January 1952]

Dear Norton:

I am desperately out of books. Yesterday I hunted out old Harper's and Gourmet's for articles I had not read. At night I went through my book case and found nothing appealing—I am not much of a re-reader—but decided on W. H. Hudson's "Afoot in England,"[1] and enjoyed it more than when I read it years ago.

Yesterday I was sitting on the porch and a woman came to the door from a car full and said, "Is the place open?" The doors were all wide and I stared. She stammered and said, "I understand Mrs. Rawlings' place is open to the public." I couldn't decide whether I felt like a caretaker or a ghost. And in spite of Martha's insistence that she don't let nobody in the house, I'll just bet she's been giving guided tours.

. . . I stayed sober yesterday, and for reward feel like the dickens this morning, with a touch of diverticulitis I expect I have been working with too much intensity.

> Love,

1. W. H. Hudson (1841–1922), *Afoot in England* (London: Hutchinson, 1909).

. . . .

(TLS, 3 pp.)

> [Cross Creek, Fla.]
> Jan. 29, 1952

Dear Norton:

I was depressed at not hearing from you Saturday or yesterday. . . . I had decided that my letter must have been even worse than I remembered it.

But my dear patient friend, you'd be amazed at the letters I DON'T mail!

I am so sorry to find that I stopped you from coming last Sunday. I had the idea from a faintly snappish letter of yours that it was too much of a sacrifice to be away on Sunday. . . .

The envelope you forwarded from Carl Van Vechten was an issue of the Yale Library Gazette, the long first essay by cousin Carl about his Memoir, for it was also for me an *aide memoire*, and I wrote him pages and pages of my own reminiscences of some of the woman writers and magazines he had mentioned, The DIAL, for one, where the DIAL's acceptance of a poem of mine, and my withdrawal of it, turned me from potential poet to novelist.

So this morning I put the whole business in the fire.

. . . Another letter from Arthur—. Confusion worse confounded, and I see clearly where he fails, and I see to a certain extent where I fail, and I feel more strongly than ever that our father should have been castrated, and our mother spayed.

. . . .

(TLS, 2 pp.)

> Cross Creek, [Fla.]
> Hawthorn, Florida
> Jan. 30, 1952

Dear Norton:

. . . Heavens, it was cold last night. Don't think my electric blanket is working right. Believe one reason my nerves are so frazzled is that Moe wakes me up so many times in the night to re-cover him. *Six* times last night. Think I shall try him on his blanket on the davenport in the living room.

Arthur's story is too long to write. Will wait until you come over.

Adrenna said this morning, "You know, I b'lieve I jus got to wipe off your mantel." It has been dusty ever since she began here. And yesterday I had only toast and coffee, and the tray was loaded with silver, including a big serving spoon, knife, fork, two teaspoons. She said, "I know I got too much on the tray, but some day you going to need it and I wants to keep in practice."

Then patooey with the stuff into the fireplace—.

The work goes steadily but I have slowed down. And I'm turning out a lot of tripe that will have to be re-written once again. . . .

> Love,

. . . .

(TLS, 1 p.)

> [Cross Creek, Fla.]
> Jan. 31 [1952]

Dear Norton:

. . . A wire from Wray Rawlings, forwarded via Hawthorn, you might know, says that Jim,[1] perhaps mercifully, had died that morning. Am sure I told you of his ghastly operation.

> Love,

Editor's note: Written on the back of the envelope: "At least twice every morning Adrenna pokes her head in the door, to say, 'I'm going to run to the house.'" Just now, 2 P.M., I was splashing in my bath, and she opens the door to say, "I'm going to run to the house." Started to repeat my answer, but can't do it here.

1. Wray Rawlings and James Rawlings, brothers of Charles Rawlings, MKR's first husband.

. . . .

(TLS, 1 p.)

[Cross Creek, Fla.]
Monday afternoon
[4 February 1952]

Dear Norton:

. . . Adrenna said she was so lonesome for me Saturday night she almost cried. I told her she could certainly go with me next time.

Martha reports that Mrs. Glenn Bass was here Sat. night and will come again this Wed. or Saturday. I do think she should repay that loan. The fact that she appeared would indicate good intentions at least. Of course if she brings her Buddy with her, I'll probably get cold feet.

. . . Read "The Ape in Our House"[1] in bed last night. Fascinating but somehow creepy. Do you want it back, or shall I send it to Henry Heyl?

Dwye Evans[2] wants to include "The Yearling," cut by a third, and with the dialect simplified, in their "Windmill" series for schools. Wrote him O.K. but asked to see the cuts. Carl Brandt told me years ago I'd be surprised how the royalties from all those foreign things add up over the years, and I'm glad to have a new source, as it should be steady, though small. The Brandt income for '51 was something over three thousand as against Scribner's something over one thousand.

The "awful" Aunt Mabel[3] was on her way to Arizona to stay until into April. Poor Wilmer and Marjorie and Grace. They don't like her, either.

Thank you for a restful week-end, and love,

1. Cathy Hayes, *The Ape in Our House* (New York: Harper, 1951).
2. Dwye Evans, editor. The abridged edition was published by William Heinemann in 1953 (Tarr, *Descriptive Bibliography*, 81).
3. Mabel Traphagen.

. . . .

(TLS, 2 pp.)

[Cross Creek, Fla.]
Feb. 12, 1952

Dear Norton:

. . . Yesterday's work was most encouraging. Can't seem to get going this morning. (Later, did a fair stint.)

I am fascinated by our discovery of the difference in our approach to life. When you said, "But you can't *plan* a life," I thought I had never heard such heresy, for I do not know what one would do with a life except *to* plan it. You remember Mr. Young's saying, "The goal may change, but there must always be a goal." Things happen that you can't control, you have to change your plans at times, but I'd just give up altogether if I lost the incentive to try to keep the upper hand. As far as I'm concerned, it's a battle, with only an occasional truce in which to catch breath. How I must wear you out—.

Love,

Mail did come, and in it telegrams from Julia and from Whitney Darrow that Charlie Scribner had died suddenly. Then just now Mrs. Williams brought your message, and I understood that wires had come to you, too. It is unspeakable. To lose Max and Charlie together in so few years. I don't see how I can bear it. I did so want to justify myself to both of them, but never mind that, it is a dreadful loss, once again. Charlie was so sweet, so sensitive, proving a fine editor in his own right—.

. . . And to think, that I was afraid it might be Aunt Ida who would die at a bad moment—! For me—! Am I a completely self-centered egoist? Pray God, not.

. . . .

(TLS, 2 pp.)

Cross Creek, [Fla.]
Hawthorne, Florida
Wed. afternoon
[3 February 1952]

Dear Norton:

. . . And in the mail today, so shocking, was what must have been one of Charlie's last letters. Dictated at the office Feb. 8, but he had evidently taken it to Far Hills with him (from where it was mailed) and had done his usual delightful scribbling all around it in pencil.

He was so pleased that the end of my book was in sight, said he and Vera were leaving in a couple of weeks for London, and he'd be back in N.Y. just about the time my manuscript would come in, and he was sure it would be good, that there hadn't been too much wrong with it in the first place. And he had too much to do and was so tired, and he looked forward to Charlie Jr.'s return from his Navy stint, as he was a tower of strength. Etc.

And a letter from Arthur, and he did lose the waterfront place, and he has finally accepted advice from a good lawyer, who convinced him he must above all not grab Jeff and run away.

And he is divorcing Grace "soon" (if he only doesn't get cold feet again, or let her pull another fast one first!) and the lawyer thinks that by giving her a bit better settlement than a court might allow, he may get other concessions, such as having Jeff for the six summer months, with the hope that sooner or later Grace will be only too glad to let him have him all the time. He seemed reconciled to accepting what he called "Just a piece of mis-judgment and bad luck," says he feels relieved for the first time, and can go on with his life and work. . . .

Love, Marjorie ('scouse me, pen and pencil in front room)

. . . .

(TLS, 2 pp.)

Van Hornesville, N.Y.
June 4, 1952

Dear Norton:

Have written two long letters, trying to suggest ways out of our apparent impasse (cannot admit for a moment that there is no solution) but tore them up.

Have never had so long a period of depression.

. . . Scribner's wants proofs done by June 19. Don't think I can possibly make it.

. . . Dana had sent the prescription for Dexedrine. Said it was likely to make one very jittery, "more so than usual!" he said, and/or to cause insomnia. I didn't dare try it, as I have never been so jittery in my life, anyway, and having to take a pill every night. Really thought I would blow up, literally. Simply could not stand it so Saturday began drinking again, and after knocking myself out last night, feel relaxed this morning for the first time. Will go back on the wagon again today.

. . . Well, if I can hold out these two more weeks, maybe life will seem remotely worth living again.

Odd, I used to enjoy working on proofs. . . .

. . . .

(TLS, 1 p.)

Van Hornesville, N.Y.
Saturday late morning
[7–14? June 1952]

Dear Norton:

Have just finished as much editing as I would ever be able to do, on exactly the first half of my proofs. So I can see that I can make Scribner's June 19 deadline all right, and probably so much to the good, as the longer I work with this, the more nervous I get.

I *cannot* put up with Katherine much longer. . . .

. . . .

(TLS, 2 pp.)

[Van Hornesville, N.Y.]
Saturday A.M.
[21 June 1952]

Dear Norton:

. . . Saw a small notice of my book in the Tribune, and it couldn't have sound *duller*!

(ALS 11 pp.)

Van H[ornesville, N.Y.].

July 3, 1952

Dear Norton:—

    ... Gertrude said the aunties had 'phoned from Phoenix, early last week and would 'phone again. Wilmer called me yesterday. They had had a letter from Arthur which supplemented his 'phone call to me. They were in a state of complete hysteria. (Letters from Wilmer and Marjorie were waiting here for me, and they evidently got upset when they had no answer.) They were certain that Arthur was about to be the first Kinnan ever to go to jail (they have no idea how close *I* [underlined three times] have come) and Wilmer said tearfully, "Peaches, we couldn't raise the bail amongst us all, for such a crime as kidnapping."

    Well, while their letters had suggested that Arthur and Jeff *really* [underlined three times] hide out somewhere (he had written them that his wife had reached Seattle and was hunting for him) Wilmer on the 'phone demanded that I leave *at* [underlined twice] *once* [underlined three times] for Seattle (we all have the name and address of his friend there) and sit down and say to Arthur that I refused to move until he returned Jeff to the mother, and then fought legally and properly for custody of the boy.

    Wilmer said they would help pay my expenses. I asked if she had talked with a good lawyer, and she said no, but with "a smart man who knew a lot"!!!

    I said I felt I had meddled once too often in Arthur's affairs anyway, and I had no intention of tearing off to Seattle without expert legal advice. . . .

Love,

. . . .

(ALS, 2 pp.)

[Atlanta, Ga.]

[8 July 1952]

3 P.M.

Dear Honey:—

    The train is as bad as we thought. So jerky and swaying, it is all I can do to read. Stops at every milk station.

    ... Did finish the Maritta Wolff[1] and will mail it first chance I get.

    ... Wish you were coming along. And don't despair of me, or us.

Much love,

1. Maritta Wolff, *Back of Town* (New York: Random House, 1952).

(TLS, 2 pp.)

Van Hornesville, N.Y.

July 9, 1952

Norton, my dear:

I suppose no one but you could understand the terrific relief that has swept over me. Arthur's troubles have disturbed me more than I would admit even to myself. I feel that with you he has come into harbor, and that with you giving the major help, between us we can save him.

As I said on the 'phone, it will be the greatest kindness of your life to keep him with you at the beach for a while, and to try to restore his sense of proportion.

I can see so many possibilities working out pleasantly. You and Arthur and Jeff might drive up here in your car in the fall—leave Arthur and Jeff here with Moe and Uki, to return to Cross Creek in my car when they are ready—you and I to go on in your car, perhaps to catch a boat in New York for foreign parts unknown—etc. etc.

. . . I am so happy.

I called the aunties at once forgetting how early it was in Arizona, and Wilmer literally wept for joy. She said, "*DO* you realize how wonderful Norton is?"

I know nothing about MGM option, though someone else spoke of seeing notice. I had wired Carl Brandt not to try for movie sale, and would write him, and did not. I felt it would cheapen peoples' advance conception of the book if a movie sale was announced.

. . . The Young picnic was very small, 17 instead of the usual 30-odd, no fireworks, but all very pleasant. . . .

My one regret in the splendid turn of circumstances is that Arthur arrived when you had your family there. But you always take such things in your stride.

Hang on to him and to Adrenna.

I got off 2/3 of the page proofs today, and after the last small batch still due, will be free as the wind, and open to any and all suggestions.

Much love,

. . . .

(TLS, 2 pp.)

Van Hornesville, N.Y.

8 o'clock

Monday morning

[14 July 1952]

Dearest Norton:

This is total nightmare. Yesterday and last night I thought I could not go through with it. To recall that I thought that when I was really done with my book, I should have peace!

However, if Arthur will do as I ask, and give me a little time, perhaps as long as a month, I shall be all right and can take over from you.

Before he arrived in Florida, I had asked Julia and Tom to come for a few days, and she accepted with real delight. . . .

I want the Gilkysons for a week-end.

I want to go to Vermont to spend a couple of days with Robert Frost.

For the first time, I need people, that is, a very few certain people. In between, I also need some quiet and rest.

As I see it now, the thing to do is to have Arthur and Jeff come here *by train* as soon as I am in shape. I should be on the wagon by then, which will certainly be necessary for coping with such a situation.

. . . It seems to me best for him to be at the Creek this winter. If he can bring himself to a final break with Grace, he would put in his three months of residence and get a counter-divorce. If she got a divorce meantime, he would have to do something about fighting for custody of Jeff, but we'll cross that bridge when we come to it.

I am so angry at him that it took all my strength to write him as restrained a letter as I have just done—. If you insist that he is not actually demented, he has certainly lost all touch with reality. For practical purposes, this amounts to much the same thing!

Anyway, he cannot and must not wander about like an Ishmael. I kept myself from remarking acidly to him that Mother is not in Madison—. I have wondered if that is what he is hunting so futilely—the Puritan Mother who impressed it on him that a "nice" woman is not "passionate."

I am sure you have reminded him, if anything at all can penetrate the miasma in which he moves, that starting a new business or taking a job *anywhere* is impossible while Jeff is still so untrained and so dependent on him.

. . . Arthur's persistent and apparently *in*sistent stupidity in muffing his life puts me in a rage. I must not think about it.

It is of course a hideous imposition on you, but as you realize, you are helping me as much or more than Arthur, by giving me a chance to get myself together. The middle of August, roughly, should see me entirely ready, able and willing to have them come here. Then I'll be ready to escape with you as early in September as you wish. . . .

Much love,

. . . .

(TLS, 4 pp.)

Van Hornesville, N.Y.
July 21, 1952

Dear Norton:

Your saga about Arthur and Jeff and you is one of the funniest things I have ever read. . . . Of course, it isn't really amusing at all. Arthur is an addled ass, and I do not see how I *could* love the child.

Tell Arthur that if tantrums are hereditary, Jeff gets it straight from him. Art was famous for them his first few years of life. He would kick and scream to be carried downstairs, Mother would simply *drag* him down the stairs, and he would turn right around and scramble *up* again, and kick and scream to be carried down—.

It all seems too dreadful. I don't think there *is* any helping Arthur. How could a man let a woman so terrorize him that he would throw over a successful work that he had spent five years perfecting, and the life he always wanted to live?

. . . I have a new kettle of raspberries and sugar soaking, (having just come from Jordanville) for more syrup. Wild raspberries are ripe and ready, and Gertrude and I shall set out in jeans the first clear day. I bought my own jeans for wild strawberry picking, and while I could get them on, I could not possibly bend nor stoop in them, but they will serve for high-picking. Gooseberries are ready, and my first green beans and peas. Wish you were here! It is a time of plenty. . . .

Much love,

. . . .

(ALS, 4 pp.)

[Van Hornesville, N.Y.]
Late Wed. afternoon
[23 July 1952]

Dear Norton—

. . . I am *certain* [underlined twice] at the moment of only one thing, and that is, that you and I must let nothing short of family illness or death interfere with our fall trip, preferably abroad.

Aside from that, I must decide what I can and should do for Arthur and the boy. I am disgusted with Arthur, but no one understands better than you that some family troubles *have* [underlined twice] to be faced, and helped.

Ideas—

. . . What about Arthur's leaving Jeff here with me while he goes West to settle things?

What about my going West with the two of them, to lend moral support?

What about Jeff's staying with me, and then when you come up, you and I take him West?

My health is perfectly good, nerves rapidly improving. Unfortunately, I began having an occasional cigarette with Lois,[1] and ended with from 1 to 2 packs a day. It is certainly all or nothing with me, and I *must* [underlined three times] quit again!

It is hard for me to be objective about Arthur, for while I see him and his self-induced situation clearly and extremely coldly, I do love him, and you just don't let your brother down unless you're harder-boiled than I can manage to be.

It is hard for you to be objective about it, too, for you have fallen for the child, for one thing, and are considering only my welfare, for another.

Try to reverse the picture in your mind. If you were in my shoes, what would you consider your duty? Don't pass this off lightly—think it out from that angle.

God, what a *mess* [underlined three times] it all is. Probably my punishment for letting myself get so selfish. . . .

Much love,

1. Lois Hardy.

. . . .

(TLS, 1 p.)

[Van Hornesville, N.Y.]

July 26, 1952

Dear Norton:—

I am suddenly most anxious to have Arthur and Jeff here—couldn't stand it if they don't come.

Meantime, will you go through the files and get together all of Arthur's letters to me, dated since his marriage in March 1950. You can send the packet by him—or perhaps better make a parcel and mail it. He might take the notion to destroy them, and if admissible evidence, they should be of value in his court fight.

Am so glad Phil[1] has taken over.

Much love,

1. Philip May.

. . . .

(ALS, 6 pp.)

[Van Hornesville, N.Y.]

Wednesday 3:20 P.M.

[30 July 1952]

Dear Norton:—

I had a call for Arthur in Baltimore all day Sunday. . . .

I suppose he is capable of having headed straight for Seattle instead—.

He could hardly be more difficult to help—.

It was partly probably being upset about Arthur at the same time, but Julia's and Tom's three days tired me very much. . . .

I couldn't take them out to dinner, as I wanted to do especially Sunday night, as Tom had forgotten to bring any sort of jacket, and said he couldn't go in a public place. But he is very sweet indeed, and seeing Julia was a joy as always.

. . . I do think it is inconsiderate of Art not to have gotten word to me by now.
. . . How are you progressing about the administration of Aunt Ida's estate?[1]

. . . Arthur just 'phoned from Grand Central Station—They will be in at 9:29 P.M. tonight.

He sounded so understandably weary!! Anyway, it is lovely and cool here—had to turn up the furnace last night and this morning!!

Much love, and I'll 'phone you Sunday morning.

1. Aunt Ida Tarrant, actually Charles Rawlings's aunt, but MKR's friend for thirty-five years, had died in June.

(ALS, 3 pp.)

July 31, 1952—Thursday
Van H[ornesville, N.Y.].

Dear Norton:—

I have never seen anything so pitiful as that great hulking stricken ruined man, looking twenty years more than his age, nursing so tenderly the beautiful child. Arthur's love for, and obsession with, the boy, is actually terrifying. . . .

Jeff is not the problem. The problem is Arthur.

At breakfast, Gertrude and I had prepared a Pablum cereal, with strained banana and cream and sugar, and Jeff began eating, when Arthur announced that Jeff would not eat it. Jeff dropped his spoon and reached toward the plate of cookies, doughnuts and blueberry muffins I had for Arthur, who said he himself had almost nothing but coffee for breakfast. I also had wild strawberry jam to tempt Arthur. Jeff reached (over) toward the plate of sweet things, and I broke off a bit of a plain molasses cookie to give him. Arthur took it away and said it had probably had too much shortening in it, which was bad for babies.

So what happens?

Arthur ends by feeding Jeff a whole blueberry muffin, with lots of butter and wild strawberry jam—

Jeff points to Art's coffee cup (cream and sugar in it) and Arthur in his first show of firmness, says sternly, "NO, NO, no coffee"—and thereupon dips the tip of the spoon in it several times and gives it to Jeff—

Jeff has had no tantrums, but begins to fuss and whimper if remotely thwarted. At one point Art said, "He's a *huge* [underlined four times] success, and it's all my doing, all mine."

Gertrude is wonderful + tried to go outdoors with Jeff to give Art some time with me, whereupon Art goes out and brings Jeff in.

. . . It is all totally mad.

The child is indeed adorable. Instead of stopping cigarettes and liquor, I have just bought a fresh carton and a fresh bottle—

It will not floor me at all, but I stand aghast.

Much love,

. . . .

(AL, TLS, 14 pp.)

[Van Hornesville, N.Y.]
Sunday Afternoon
[10 August 1952]

Dear Norton:—

. . . Robert Frost was upset that I did not spend another day, for he had just begun one of his long and wonderful monologue spells. But I told him Henry Heyl's story and he felt better about my leaving. The Heyls also begged me to stay longer, but you and I are both one-day visitors, I think, and while I loved my visits, I was ready to be on my way.

As I told you, Mrs. Morrison said frankly that she didn't think Robert would want me to stay with them, and I only hope she isn't jealous of his affection for me, for which I am so grateful. Talk about your dominating women, she is a dilly. Yet she is doing a noble job in looking after him and protecting him from onerous details (and people.) There is something oddly treacherous about her—she told me all about his difficult moods, etc., etc., all meant to show, I assume, how magnificently she and she only can handle them. God, the viciousness of the human ego—In the long run, it probably does more damage than wars.

She took me up to Robert's separate cabin for us to talk, after I arrived in mid-afternoon, left us "to have a good private talk," then came by on horseback in half an hour to say that it was five o'clock, which seemed needless, as she had set his alarm clock for five-*thirty*, the time we were to break it up, as guests were coming for drinks at six.

We had an amazing dinner, *fried* steaks (they have a country cook) that Robert had bought especially on my account, which she stressed, quoting the price, and which were tough as tripe; (over) mashed potatoes, peas, store ice-cream, and that was literally all.

At the last moment I had put the page-proofs of my book in my birthday suitcase, and when Robert asked me infinite questions about the book, I said I'd read a couple of chapters aloud if he'd like me to! So I did, and the next morning he said I should either have read most of the book, or nothing at all, as he had stayed awake, "wondering what you're up to and where you're coming out."

(And by the way, Buzz Scribner took Julia a semi-bound copy of cut page-proofs, and has promised to send me several such early things, for you, Robert Frost, Mr. Young, Dr. Atchley and Henry Heyl. I am telling each of you that you are getting the first copy!!)

Friday A.M. Robert was to come down to Mrs. Morrison's[1] place at 9 o'clock to see me off. He did not come, and she went up to him and was away a long time. He was in a switchet, doing a chore he had said the night before he *could* [underlined four times] *not* [underlined three times] do.

That depressing, liquid-eyed minor poet Joseph Auslander, a poor poet in two ways, had the gall to ask me to be his emissary to Frost, (over) to ask "if he could find it in his heart to write a few words of welcome" for a volume Joe is making up for his infant son.

I should have refused of course, should have told Auslander to write Frost himself. (Am sure I wrote you that the Auslanders are in one of the teacher's houses, Louise's bright idea. They have no car, are marooned with the 3 mos. baby and Collins' Grocery Store, and Louise had ignored them until the wife had a nervous collapse and seems now to have taken over.) (I am not drunk, but am trying to write on my lap, and the paper is about an inch deep in its box.)

So when Robert finished his *charming* [underlined twice] note for the Aus-lander baby, it was nearly 11 A.M., and *then* [underlined three times] he began talking to me, and read his latest long poem, which raises the hair on your head.

And was I torn—I must write Robert what I did not have the wits to say, that I expect him to be on earth longer than Henry Heyl, and that while I had nothing to give him, Robert, (over) I did think I might cheer Henry a bit.

And so it proved.

The whole drive was beautiful, going and coming, although some of the mountain roads terrified me.

The pain in Henry's lower back is a bit better, but he has developed involun-tary spasms in his legs, so that he sits in his wheelchair and his whole body seems to go into convulsions. He says the spasms are "a bit painful." Their farm set-up is beautiful and Kit is *superb* [underlined four times].

Henry is putting up a magnificent fight. I told him that Robert Frost and I had discussed our spells of depression and that I had said to Robert that what kept me going was the feeling that one was obligated to fight in one's small way on the side of the creative, not the destructive, forces, and Robert said, "I've never quite committed suicide. I figure as long as you can *make* [underlined three times] something, if it's only a basket, the whole business is worth while." (I forgot to say that Henry had told me that his first problem had been to decide whether his family would be better with, or without him. His next problem still is, to engage himself in a creative work.) Oh yes, I told Henry of what Frost and I had said, and Henry said, "Count me in on that club."

To revert to the spasms, he is waiting to see if therapy will help them. The al-ternative is, as he put it, to have the nerves and muscles "butchered." In that case, his leg would be totally immobilized, and he [MKR was interrupted and contin-ued later in typescript].

Monday A.M.

(Virginia Brown and her guest came to call and stayed a long time for drinks. After I had cooked and eaten my dinner, I was tired and just read.)
continued:

would never be able again to use crutches. As a matter of fact, he can't use them now, for when the spasms hit, they throw him off balance and he falls.

When their good nurse comes back from vacation, they want to take a 3 or 4 day trip, and if the downstairs bathroom door is as wide as 26½ inches, to ac-commodate his wheelchair, I really think they may come here. They seemed re-ally pleased to be asked. Henry of course is afraid of being a nuisance and a bur-den, but I said that he certainly wouldn't be any burden to me, and that Kit took it all in stride. He is not in the least morbid about the whole business, has ac-cepted it in a completely mature way. He is more of a man, existing only from the waist up, than Arthur's whole six feet four.

I expect Arthur to phone any day, reproaching me for not writing or calling. But I don't see how I can write, for I have nothing to offer but hell, and ass-child that he is, it still isn't fair to kick him when he's down—and suddenly basking in what he considers proper appreciation—.

When I do get in touch with him, I shall have to be explicit as to what I meant when I quoted you that we would stand behind him morally and financially. Actually, what we meant was that we wouldn't see him go hungry, but I can't deflate his precious ego by saying that! What I told him for myself, was that money was of no use except to make a bit more comfortable the difficult business of living; that I wouldn't enjoy my profits from my new book if he was in trouble; and that he must promise me not to take some undesirable step just for the lack of a few thousand. I certainly never meant that we would finance him in whatever venture he decided on, and I hope he hasn't told his "important" Syracuse friends that he has the unlimited backing of a fabulously wealthy sister and brother in law.

What I had in mind was that he must not sell his boat and equipment for less than their value, to get ready money. I shall let the subject rock along without saying anything, if possible, for he is apt to throw the scheme over, just as he did the Alaska lumbering one.

About my bonds. I am reasonably sure I have 10 or so thousand in the kind that you buy at a rate of $17.50 and that return $25 on maturity, which I thought was in ten years, not twelve. If so, maturity is probably 1953.

I shall deposit Aunt Ida's $1566.90 into my account, although I do not consider it "Automatically" mine, for she intended it to be used to pay for her final illness and funeral expenses. Of course, when you figure that I spent a *minimum* of $500 a year on her for at least the last ten years, it seems fair enough to use this, at a moment when I am short.

Since the money you have loaned me (aside from paying my share of income taxes) has gone into my A.T. & T. investment, I wish to and can, pay you back the $3,000, is it? with the Castle Warden money. Was it $2,000 you deposited for me earlier, and then $1,000 lately? I didn't think I had accumulated $3,000 in my Special Account. I enclose a signed check, leaving the amount blank, for you to fill in, when you check on the amount again.

Also, I see no earthly reason why I should not take an advance from Scribner now, of $5 or 10 thousand. That would not interfere with the 80% that must come in, in one year, to make me eligible for pro-rating the book income over 3 years.

I was prepared to sign whatever British contract was offered me, feeling guilty at taking money from poor England anyway, but to my amazement the contract is so much more generous than Scribner's that I shall have to tell the latter what other people are doing! After 15,000 copies, I get 17½%, with apologies that 20% is no longer possible! Also, for book clubs, outside use of all sorts, I am to get

75%, with Heinemann's taking only 25%, as against Scribner's splitting such things 50-50.

I don't see why Willard fools with the two Ocala men who signed Aunt Ida's will, when Mr. Nutter has the original, and as named executor, can testify to her signature.

No, Charlie Riley was white, and is dead. Lulu is very much alive, and always sent Aunt Ida a Christmas card with a note on it, and Aunt Ida did have her address, and wrote her once a year.

I assume that Gene has gone to England. I kidded him when he wrote that he was sailing on the Queen Elizabeth, and at the same time said he might try for a Fulbright, as he needed some financial security, I said that even if he went steerage, which I doubted he meant to do, he could save enough by going on a freighter instead of the Queen to live in England for two or three months. He phoned me from New York, said that freighter rates have gone up since they became chic, and that he had passage on the new boat Flandre for $70 less than a freighter. When the Flandre was delayed, I don't know whether he waited for her or not, but probably so, as I have heard nothing since. He said things were too hectic to get time to see you.

Well, guess I have about covered the waterfront for now. Better wait to send the crib until you see whether Art stays in Syracuse or flits on.

I had hoped to dodge birthday fuss, but this morning Gertrude brought me a really handsome copper etched tray that she made for me at the Home Bureau. I was so touched. Was ready to be sore if you gave me anything, after the suitcase, but am of course thrilled to have the tree peony coming. What color is it, and where will be a good place to plant it?

Much love,

[Postscript handwritten] Am also a bit uncertain about exact amount in joint account of Aunt Ida's. Please check and fill in, and deposit to my regular account. (over) [underlined four times] Realize I don't know how to make out check, for depositing Aunt Ida's money to my regular checking account.

1. Kathleen Morrison, Frost's secretary, friend, and, finally, lover.

. . . .

(ALS-TLS, 13 pp.)

[Van Hornesville, N.Y.]
Aug. 18, 1952

Dear Honey:—

My goodness, I'm lonesome! It looks and feels like fall—imagine. Am just back from taking my good colored boy home, and came by way of Jordanville to pick up the very last box of raspberries of the season. The goldenrod is out, and the wild white asters, and some of the small shrubs are already turning color. It is

62° at 6 P.M., gray and windy, and while I love it, I did get a sad feeling. Had to turn on the furnace.

I finished and mailed my chore for the Guild Magazine. Have not heard from Irita Van Doren as to whether she still wants me in her fall authors' number, since my book isn't to be published until later, but will go ahead and write (over) the piece anyway, to be done with it. That clears up everything except some correspondence.

Will you 'phone the Grafstrom number on St. George St. and ask for Katrina? If they are still there, I think I could send her my accumulated mail with just *notes* as to how to answer (she did that kind of stuff for me 2 or 3 times, you know) along with *signed* paper, and envelopes and if she will do it, I'd get the whole thing off my hands that way.

Of course, I'm wondering what will pop up next to interfere with all that freedom I was going to have!

Sgt. Cunningham's daughter gave a birthday dinner for him Saturday night, at Sherry's restaurant in Cooperstown. Capt. Gay, head of the troopers at Sidney, was there, lots of people (18 in all) I didn't know, and Senator Stokes and his mealy-mouthed Hannah Lee. She sat next to me and spoiled everything (She sent you her best.) I think the Senator hates every inch of her guts.

"The Sarge" asked three of us to his house afterward. There was a sound of commotion in the Trooper's part, and the Sarge and a couple of young troopers kept going in and out (over) and it seemed they were jam-packed with prisoners of all varieties, and evidently at least one case was serious. I said to the man guest when he and his wife and I were left alone for a few minutes, "It's sort of creepy. The place is crawling with prisoners."

He said, "The place is crawling with State Troopers, too."

I had had the Auslanders alone for lunch last week, and Saturday noon I had them again with Josephine and Everett. Did I tell you the Heyls gave me a 3-lb. Chunk of frozen fresh Nova Scotia salmon? It was partly unfrozen when I reached home from Vermont, so I steamed it at once in a court bouillon, the first I ever made, using a full quart of white wine along with the herbs, onions, etc. etc. You can save the bouillon and use it again, but I knew I wouldn't be having any more fresh salmon, so I experimented. I strained the liquid through a fine sieve, added lemon juice and gelatin, boned the salmon and put it in the big iron fish-shaped casserole the Cases gave me, to make an aspic or galantine or what-not.

With home-made mayonnaise, it was really grand. I thought (over) of saving it until you come, but it was taking up too much room in my deep-freeze, and it really was not a dish for the northern autumn. But I shall do the same thing in Florida with a large bass or something of the sort, red snapper, maybe.

Mrs. Rankin is hounding me to keep my promise to go to Rochester and spend a day and night. I don't want to go at all, but she is past 80, and I suppose I'd feel guilty if she dropped dead and I hadn't gone. Maybe I'll do it next week.

Now, Mr. Baskin, I shall be ready ANY TIME to do whatever you want to do!

Jo and Everett say that early Sept' is a bit too soon to go abroad. They said, "Let the tourists come home first."

They urge the idea of Greece, after England and Ireland, as the climate stays lovely in Greece later they say, and they are mad about it. But I *don't* [underlined three times] want to *tour* [underlined three times], and I think if we do go just to England and Ireland, we would enjoy taking our time.

Julia is working up a list of places in Ireland for us. (over)

Of course a lot depends on how long you can be away. We'd better begin planning. I don't know what to do about Moe and Uki. It would seem foolish for me to return clear to Cross Creek to park them with Adrenna, and then go back to N.Y.C. to take a boat.

Gertrude can stay with me until almost the end of September. I'd sort of like to have you come here as soon as you can after Labor Day and spend some time here first.

I could board Uki very nicely at Gertrude's house if we do go abroad, and then return here to pick up the car, the raspberry syrup and wild strawberry jam, and the animals. Young Gertrude is crazy about cats. They (the Sandvolds) live on enough of a side road so that Uki wouldn't be in much danger from traffic.

Moe is a more difficult problem. I don't think I could bear it to leave the old fellow shut up at a Vet's. I could board him at Gertrude's, too, if Halvor would take him to work on the truck with him, but the cars go like mad through Van Hornesville, and I know that Moe would come trekking up to the Root house all the time, looking for me.

Well, think about all the angles and let me know.

I still don't know what to say to Arthur about "standing back of him financially." His second letter from Syracuse said that probably this is not the right territory after all for starting the gun business, which he said he would explain to me soon. I think I might well wait, as I said before, to see which way he jumps.

On the other hand, I feel that perhaps I should clarify our attitude about financial backing, to avoid his suddenly wiring for some thousands, which I should feel obliged to refuse under his chaotic circumstances, and in which case he might feel, and say, that I, or we, had reneged on a promise and had failed him. I think I wrote you that in his first letter from (over) Syracuse, he said he would only let me turn in my mortgage amount from the sale of his boat, to the new venture, "with proper security" for me. "Proper security," my eye—There is no such thing as far as the poor devil is concerned.

[MKR continues on p. 13 in typescript] Have kept forgetting to tell you that the M.G.M. option on my book was all Louella Parsons' own wild idea.

It was 48 this morning! But bright and sunny and beautiful. Johnny President came to work again, and the garden should look fairly well when you come.

Just 'phoned Irita Van Doren, and goody, goody, I don't have to do the article.

She is using only authors who are being published this fall. My January date would be almost three months out of line.

Told her I had decided to try the Ellen Glasgow biography. She said she had seen Ellen's sister, and Anne Virginia Bennett, Ellen's long-time companion, and they were both pleased at the idea of my doing it, and said they hoped I would. So, I'll plan to go to Richmond in the fall after we get through whatever tripping we decide to do. Interviews of that sort should be done in leisurely fashion. There will also be considerable research, I should imagine, and it might be best to take a little apartment for a month. Well, we'll see.

Had something else to tell you, but can't remember.

Much love, and hurry along now.

Editor's note: Written at the top of page 1: "Check is for Judge—Southern Book Parade."

. . . .

(TLS, 4 pp.)

Van H[ornesville].
Aug. 26, 1952

Dear Norton:

I returned at 12:30 noon yesterday from Syracuse and Rochester, feeling as though I had been around the world. Moe and Uki thought so, too. I had dreaded both visits but am glad I went.

Arthur was out when I reached his boarding house in Syracuse early Friday afternoon. I sat waiting for him in utter despair. The house, the neighborhood, were of a shabby middle-class dinginess that I had never really known before. The landlord slept (not at the moment!) in an unmade bed in the living-room, behind a square piano. There were magazine cover pictures of Judy Garland and kittens on the walls, sagging overstuffed furniture, an oilcloth cover visible on the dining room table across the bare hall. The landlord came in and visited with me, and he had been obliged to put Arthur and Jeff out the day before! All quite amicably, and he had found another place for them, and moved them in his car. He had given Arthur kitchen privileges, and he summed up by saying, "Nice as the man is, and the boy, too, I couldn't stand the organized confusion."

I had arranged to have a room there for the night, when I had 'phoned Art, and when I took my things up, it seemed to me, coming from my luxury, that I was Ase Linden, going into Benjamin's slum room to find the lost brother. The room was actually not that bad. It was clean, but the ragged shades, the one glaring electric bulb, with a cord leading to a so-called bedlight that fell off when you pulled the light chain, shocked me. Oh, how spoiled you and I have become! I thought I simply could not spend the night there. I also realized that I could not possibly enjoy a decent hotel, with Art in some other shabby room.

It occurred to me that when it is impossible to live graciously, clean, bare cabins like Snow Slater's and Leonard's are infinitely more attractive and livable than such places, with their poor attempt at pretentiousness, for the overstuffed furniture is not cheap as to cost.

Arthur came, and we went to a cheap restaurant and talked all afternoon over coffee. My heavy burden lifted, and I felt so much better about him. He had gotten himself together, saw daylight ahead on showing his pictures this winter, and his gun proposition, which he would work up gradually, sounds entirely solid. It would not require any large original capital investment. He had his sense of humor back, and more of a sense of proportion about everything. He had taken my harsh letter very well, and said that what the rest of us did not realize was that he himself saw the danger in the way he was handling Jeff. He planned to see one more lawyer, a very close friend, in Wyoming, and if he too agreed with all the others, he, Arthur, would accept it and go on to fight the court battle, but with little hope. He said that losing Jeff would be a practically unbearable misfortune.

He asked me to give him my explicit opinion, and I could not do it. I said that objectively I could only agree with the lawyers, that I could see no way for him to do anything at all in a business way, or to make a home for Jeff, until the domestic mess is straightened out. I also said that I could not be objective, that I felt so close to him that I understood his love for Jeff and his suffering in the matter, and that possibly anything in the world was better than having to give him up.

He said that he thought Grace and her lawyer were bluffing in many ways, including the threat against the boat, and that Phil was unduly alarmed. (This has proved to be so, with a letter waiting for me from Kenneth Cole saying that no action is pending that would jeopardize my interests.) If any action is taken, Arthur has only to produce his records of my loans to him over the years (he says he has all his books and records in perfect order) to show that the mortgage is a legitimate one, and not, as Grace is claiming, an attempt to evade his creditors.

Arthur said, "I'm afraid Phil is rather impulsive."

I said, "Isn't that the pot calling the kettle black?" and he laughed with me and agreed. Of course, Phil is!

We drove out then to see Jeff, and he has improved a great deal. We took a long drive with him, for Arthur to do some business, and while Art was away from the car for at least twenty minutes, Jeff made absolutely no fuss of any sort. And that night, when we went to their boarding house after our dinner, Jeff came to where I was sitting and put his arms around me and kissed me.

I had written Art that he was likely to make Jeff not only totally unadapted to normal living, but even a homosexual. He had cut Jeff's hair, and he was all tough boy, and Art grinned and said, "Well, had we better begin calling him 'Homo'?"

In the new place, the woman, who has taken many of the Welfare children and made a study of children, was taking care of Jeff.

Arthur and I both felt so much better about everything. One reason he hadn't wanted to go to Seattle was that he has enough money for about six weeks of that sort of living, to send for his pictures and work on them and the sound effects etc., ready to make at least a living with them, and if he goes to Seattle, it will absorb most of that money. I told him that was exactly where I came in, that what I had meant originally was that he must not sell his stuff at a sacrifice or do something unsuitable, for lack of just those few hundreds, and he saw it, and agreed to call on me that way.

I thought we said good-bye that night, but when I came down with my bags at 7:30 the next morning, he was waiting, having taken a bus clear across the city, to drive me out of Syracuse until I hit my road.

I was too tired yesterday to call him, but 'phoned this morning, and he has his ticket and reservations to leave for the west tonight. He goes by way of Wyoming, then to Idaho to see another man about the gun business, then to Seattle. I should feel wonderfully, except that he said he was a little confused again—. He needs, as I do, a real rest with absolutely no responsibilities.

I reached Rochester in the late morning Saturday. Again, I thought I should die if I couldn't get right out. I considered faking illness, or making a call to Gertrude that would puzzle her no end, but from which I could report that I had to get back at once, but knew it would do no good, that Araminta would give me no peace until I had "visited" her. It was a combination of claustrophobia and my horror of all suburbs. The houses so close together you could spit from your living room into the neighbor's, the sense of masses of people all doing the same things at the same time, people on a treadmill, "Point of No Return." Now these houses are "nice" houses, they sell for $13,800, and the small rooms gave me the creeps. The dining room 9x11, living room 9x14. And dark, dark, dark. They are so close together, and Rochester goes in for heavy vegetation, and much as I love *trees,* I don't want them smothering me. I always hated the place, and as I looked at the house next to Araminta's where I had lived in hell, I thought with immense satisfaction that I had certainly escaped from one of my life's major and most repulsive traps.

Wednesday morning

Now you have just called, and I am so glad. We'll just have to take a chance on the trip's proving no help to my depression. We could always come home! But we do have a good time seeing scenery together, and I think a completely carefree period may be what the doctor ordered. Getting the animals comfortably parked is my main problem.

Before I forget it, if Mr. Nutter will 'phone Agnes McDonough, or MacDonough, I don't know the spelling, on S.E. Sixth St. in Louisville, next door to where Aunt Ida and Uncle Joe used to live, she would know where to reach Lulu. Or the Catholic church in that section of Louisville could give him Agnes' exact name and address etc. if my spelling is too far off. But her name is pronounced that way.

To get back to my Rochester visit, Araminta and Marguerite were darling, and the next door neighbor told me it would probably put ten years on Araminta's life to have had me, as she had fretted so because I had not come. But as I told you just now, she is no more "satisfied" than Aunt Ida was, and I felt frantic when she said, "now the next time you come—."

I felt the other thing I should do was to see Jim Rawlings' widow, and was THAT a strange experience! We drove down early Sunday afternoon and at first I thought Olive was perfectly adorable. I still don't know what's the matter with her, but she gave me the jitters. She told of Jim's illness and death and every single morbid detail, with a sort of *relish*, and everything she told showed how noble and loving and perfect *she* had been. She had the oddest sort of complacency. The older girl, nine, Marcia, is the spitting image of Mother Rawlings, but ugly as a mud fence, where Mother Rawlings, except for those evil black eyes, was a rather handsome woman. It seems she is a "problem," which became understandable in the light of two things: the six-year-old, Marjorie Kinnan (Godamnit) looks like Jim and is quite pretty and is the whole show, the most terrible exhibitionist and as mealy-mouthed as her mother; and with the two little girls playing in the next room and hearing, I know, every word that was said. Olive said that Marcia was exactly like Mother Rawlings, and with Chuck's meanness, too, and that she and Marcia were at cross purposes all the time. (Driving away I said to Araminta and Marguerite, "The horror of Mother Rawlings' being on earth again!") Actually, the poor little brat doesn't have a chance, period. Wray Rawlings and his wife evidently saw the situation, and planned to take Marcia with them, to keep, after Jim's funeral, but the child refused to go at the last minute. A pity.

Marjorie Kinnan was all over me, asked if she might kiss me, snuggled beside me, announced that I was her great-aunt and that she was named for me, and said, "You didn't send me anything for my birthday." As you know, I have never done anything for my namesake, and I am sure that Olive had made a crack to the effect that Aunt Marjorie could have least have sent MK something for her birthday—. The whole set-up gave me the same sense of gold-digging that I get from Arthur's daughters. Marguerite, who is nobody's fool, said, "Marjorie, you've done your duty to Jim, and you'll be awfully smart if you drop the whole thing right now."

Jim evidently left Olive comfortably off, as she plans to stay in the large and expensive house. Its seems that Chuck ignored Wray's letters and wires during Jim's ghastly illness, never wrote him (even I wrote the poor devil twice), never came, although Wray, with a regular job, stayed with Jim almost night and day for six weeks. Then Chuck appeared for the funeral. Clive said that when they all came back to the house after the services, Chuck asked her what she was going to do, and she said, "Why, carry on," and he said, "I didn't think you had brains enough." Jolly warm comfort at such a time, eh?

I was happy to make my getaway early Monday morning, and the drive back was beautiful. As I said, I was tempted to call Geneva and swing by to spend a few hours with the Pooles, but thought you might enjoy taking that drive with me later. However, since you can't get away until October first, and we'll want to be heading out, I may see if they'd like me alone for a day. I get so damned restless and want to hit the road. Will probably ask the Gilkysons here for a couple of days, too, without waiting for you. And Julia has begged and begged that we both come to New Marlboro, and I may go there alone, for a day or two at the most. Or Julia might like to come here alone. She too has had company all summer.

Winifred Spofford is having a luncheon and bridge at Louise's inn today and I said I'd go. The place is about halfway open, and there have been four guests staying there.

The Literary Guild floored me by sending an 8-page questionnaire to be filled out, for publicity uses, beginning with age, height, weight, date of first published stuff, and ending with "What do you consider the major world problem today? The major domestic problem? How would you solve them?" !!!!!!!!!!!

Am hoping that Buzz Scribner will soon have several rough copies of my book for me, and will send the first off to you. (Along with the first to Henry Heyl, Dana Atchley and Mr. Young! Don't give me away.)

Just received copies of "The Yearling" in Burmese. Am sure Burmese is similar enough to Urdu so that you can read it fluently.

Much love,

. . . .

(TLS, 1 p.)

Van Hornesville, N. Y.
Aug. 28, 1952

Dear Norton:

Just a note to say that Gertrude is going to room-and-board Moe and Uki while we are away, and anticipates no trouble at all. While I was in Florida Moe got so lonesome that she took him home with her part of the time, and he stayed around her, perfectly contented. And Uki will have the use of their bathroom. Now I begin to feel real enthusiasm for our trip.

Also, Jean Hardy and the charming young Princeton professor are being married in Louisville Oct. 25. I am lending them the house here for their very brief honeymoon. In accepting, Heath wrote me that because of their short time, they had expected to stay at some Pennsylvania inn, and that he would be happy to escape "the hot and cold running bellhops."

I shall have ready-to-thaw-and-serve entrees in the deep freeze, and Gertrude will come every afternoon from 3:30 to 5 to clean up.

Had my usual loathsome time at the ladies' party yesterday, but Virginia, who is running the Inn, really put on a delicious luncheon, chicken curry à la Louise. The place is going to be most attractive.

None of the younger Youngs but Phillip and Faith will be here over Labor Day, so I am not having my buffet this year, thank God.

Much love,

(TLS, 6 pp.)

[Van Hornesville, N.Y.]
Saturday
[30 August 1952]

Dear Norton:

... A package will shortly reach you in your name, from Scribner's. This is the first unrevised Mss. of my book. I don't want it to go to the Florida library until well after publication, so please just park it as is, in the filing room.

... Mr. Tiffany wrote that under the circumstances, full credit would be allowed me on my wrist watch. I did write them that with the last failure, I could never enjoy the watch again, and that the tough clasp on the bracelet had driven me crazy, having to be opened with a nail file, after broken finger nails.

Yesterday the credit slip came in (amazingly, made out to *MRS*. Baskin) and I all but fainted. Who do you think you are, a millionaire? How appalling to have bought anything so expensive! I absolutely forbid a Christmas present this year.

... Shall we allow a day in New York for shopping when we reach there from here? My idea is to leave the car in N.Y.C.[1]

The House of Scribner is making me a present of the last remaining set of the Virginia edition of Ellen Glasgow, 12 volumes, in levant, retailing for $300. I know the richest people!

Monday Sept. 1

... I must write James and Margaret Cabell, and ask Margaret to find me a place in Richmond. I should prefer to have the animals with me. I could even have Adrenna come to me for the month or two of my research. . . .[2]

Everyone says by no means take an American ship. Louise says the Dutch ships have always been her preference, and everyone seems to think the Maasdam a fine idea. Most of the "family" thinks the tourist class on that is preferable, because of the saving and because the whole ship is almost entirely tourist. I myself am not keen about being shut up with only 39 people (think of the 39 people we dislike the most, and suppose they were all there) on a penthouse deck! The one and only thing that would make me vote for first class on the Maasdam would be, I suppose, private bathrooms. I know that [in] tourist there are community showers only. Mr. Young thought this important, but nobody else did. . . .

I'd just as soon leave it up to you as to what class we take on the Maasdam. I really think tourist is perfectly safe. And if we find we aren't keen about it, we can probably switch to first for the passage back—or take some other boat back.

If we spend a night at a hotel in N.Y., let's try the Chatham. It may be just what we've been looking for. Louise likes it. I remember it from getting drunk at their terrace, Chatham Walk, with Max Perkins and Tom Wolfe, and it is an old sort of Victorian smallish place, in a convenient location, a few blocks from Scribner's. . . .

Love,

1. MKR and NSB were about to embark on a trip to England and Ireland.

2. MKR is referring to her research for her biography of Ellen Glasgow.

. . . .

(TLS, 2 pp.)

Van Hornesville, N.Y.

Sept. 16, 1952

Dear honey:

Will just have to tell you about the Cabell rumpus when I see you. It would take pages. And I find I have more than 100 letters to be answered. . . .

Have written Art asking how much he will need to tide him over. Told him it will be best to limit his debt entirely to me, even if I had to borrow from you. I enclose his last letter, which you can file. I really boil when I think of paying for getting him out of his third mess! It will cost him plenty if he hires a high-powered lawyer. . . .[1]

Much love,

1. Arthur Kinnan had gone bankrupt for the third time.

. . . .

(TLS, I p.)

Van Hornesville, N.Y.

Sept. 22, 1952

Dear Norton:

. . . Also letter from James Cabell clearing up fascinating impasse over Ellen Glasgow's biography. (Will tell you the story when I see you.)

. . . Will be at Hotel Chatham, Vanderbilt Ave. and 48th St., unless you hear otherwise.

. . . Had to pay Talmadge DuPree full $1556, have sent Arthur checks aggregating $1,000, so please check my St. A. account. I plan to take $1500 in travelers' checks. . . .

Love,

. . . .

(TLS, I p.)

Van Hornesville, N.Y.

Sept. 24, 1952

Dear Honey:

. . . Johnny Redjives will drive me to N.Y. in his car as I messed mine up yesterday. Irene[1] phoned in early afternoon that she had some stuff ready for me, and I lit out way too fast and skidded around the curve between me and Redjives, lost control of the car (undoubtedly jerked it too sharply from side to side in trying to straighten out) went through Redjives barbed wire fence and over stone wall, and took down a telephone pole, snapped right in half. Car motor all right but left fender and headlight well smashed. . . .

Neither Moe nor I hurt at all. I have one bruise on shoulder and bridge of nose is a bit sore, otherwise OK, but so provoked with myself. Told the telephone repair man to have someone come today so I can pay for the pole before I leave. Shall not bother with red tape of insurance co. but just pay for everything myself.

If I could lose as much as you do, I'd do the two-day prunes once a month! But 2 lbs. is about all I can get off and it isn't worth it. I have gained a lot again.

Don't want to look fancy in poor England, so may knock around in old fur jacket and then get new one on return, or early 1953 when I feel rich again. . . .

Much love,

1. Owen D. Young's secretary, whom MKR used on occasion.

1953

1953 began in triumph and ended in tragedy. *The Sojourner* was officially published on 5 January and was picked up by the Literary Guild. MKR was relieved, even though it received mixed reviews. She went on the lecture circuit in late January and February. In May, NSB drove her to Richmond, where she rented a house and began to interview the intimates of Ellen Glasgow, which resulted in a large file of notes. During her stay, MKR was treated as a celebrity. In April, she returned to Florida, and in April-May her five-part autobiographical account appeared in the *Los Angeles Times*. At the end of May, NSB drove her to Van Hornesville, where she began to sort though her research on Glasgow. NSB came in September to take her to Richmond for final interviews. In November, she and NSB planned a return trip to Ireland, where she hoped to begin writing on the Glasgow biography. Fate intervened. While playing bridge with the Owen D. Youngs at Crescent Beach, MKR suddenly fell ill and was taken to Flagler Hospital, where she died on 14 December as the result of a ruptured aneurysm in the brain. She was buried at Antioch Cemetery, near Island Grove, not far from her beloved Cross Creek.

. . . .

(TLS, 2 pp.)

> 5 Paxton Road
> Richmond, Va.
> Feb. 5, 1953

Norton dear:

 . . . I realized I was only three blocks from Anne Virginia's[1] apartment, so I walked there, and she saw me, much to Margaret's[2] amazement when she 'phoned me last night, as Anne V. has been refusing to see anyone. Anne V. simply has not gotten over Ellen's long illness and death,[3] and she naturally finds her life a void. Mr. Glasgow[4] had written Josephine Clarke,[5] who has 'phoned Anne V. to say how pleased Mr. Glasgow had been with me. But I am in terror—Anne Virginia has gotten qualms about telling me *anything personal*. If she decides that it is her duty not to speak freely of Ellen, I am sunk on some of the most important details. It will not be a matter of winning her confidence, for I have that, but of what she considers an ethical decision. I did say that I felt if Ellen and I had been able to be together, that Ellen would have spoken freely to me.

... Bert Cooper dropped in about five o'clock. His new position with the State department sounds splendid, and is not going to work as great a hardship on Connie as we had feared. He goes to Washington for two months of training, is to spend two months probably in Paris, then back to Washington for two years, where he will settle the family. He then goes on more or less permanent assignment somewhere abroad taking the family. He says the salary is extremely good, future prospects excellent, the job permanent if he wants it, and it may well be just the proper life and work for him. He is extremely gray, but his little mustache is still red. He looks most distinguished and manages an air of prosperity and good tailoring. I was glad to see him. He is coming for dinner this evening, and leaves for Charlottesville Saturday morning. He wants me to see three people in Charlottesville who knew Ellen well and have letters from her. He has also traced some Glasgow material for me in the Un. Of Va. Library. He would have been invaluable help to me on technical detail.

James[6] is much better. The doctor said the strong sleeping pills he had been giving him often gave some people nightmares and made them most jittery, and he stopped them. James was up half a day yesterday. . . .

Much love,

1. Anne Virginia Bennett, Ellen Glasgow's secretary and companion.
2. Margaret Cabell, second wife of James Branch Cabell, who was helping MKR make contacts with those closest to Ellen Glasgow, in order to enhance MKR's projected biography.
3. Ellen Glasgow, died on 21 November 1945.
4. Arthur Glasgow, Ellen Glasgow's brother.
5. Josephine Clark, Ellen Glasgow's niece.
6. James Branch Cabell.

. . . .

(TLS, 3 pp.)

5 Paxton Road

Richmond, Va.

Feb. 9, 1953

Dear Norton:

... Friday afternoon he [Bert Cooper] took me to the U. of Richmond library, where the librarian had lined up some splendid material. I shall have to find a typist to copy much of it. Bert would have saved me infinite technical trouble. However, he insisted that for a book of my sort, I do not need a definitive bibliography. He said that to list just the sources I use myself, is sufficient. A true bibliography he said would be short book length itself. . . .

Margaret and I have just made a nice arrangement, if James continues to improve. . . .

... What is troubling Anne Virginia at this point (and she told me not to breathe a word to anyone—I suppose because she doesn't want the press to come to see her) is that she has just had to have put to sleep the dog Bonnie that was her and Ellen's last dog. It was Anne V., you know, who was really crazy about dogs, and took care of them. She seems needlessly morbid about it. She wrote me a note, saying "It is over. I don't want anyone ever to mention it to me." I had written her asking her to spend a week here when it happened, as being possibly a little easier to be away for a while. She wrote that she could not come now, but would rest in bed at her own apartment, and would let me know when she could talk with me. She suggested that meantime I talk with Carrie Duke.[1] Margaret said that Anne V. spent two years in a sanatorium and that her friends think she is ready for another trip. God forbid.

Saturday Margaret and I and a cute little old lady Mrs. Dashiell, now living in the Episcopal old ladies' home, who used to work with Ellen on the SPCA,[2] had lunch at Miss Roberta Welford's.[3] It was a charming interlude that might have occurred seventy-five years ago. I asked Mrs. Dashiell if she minded my smoking, and she said not at all, that for herself, she took it out in liquor. Then Miss Welford didn't even serve sherry! When I go to see Miss D. I shall certainly take her a quart of Bourbon. She must be past ninety. She was at Ellen's party for Gertrude Stein[4] when the strange woman crashed the gate, was at Ellen's side when the impasse occurred. James said she would be accurate about it; the woman, hatted, in a street dress, when the *invited* women were in evening dress, came up to Ellen and said, "I've had a lovely time at your party." Ellen said, "I'm glad you enjoyed it, as long as you came." The woman turned away without another word. James said he had asked Ellen about the famous incident and she laughed and said, "Oh, I behaved like a lady." Carl Van Vechten[5] and others had told me that Ellen said to the woman, "I don't believe I know you. I think you had better go." James trusts the Dashiell version.

Miss Welford told us a delightful story. Miss Mary Lee, General Lee's last daughter, as an old lady moved in with the Stuarts.[6] They left her sitting by the fire one Sunday morning, in a study whose walls were covered with at least five hundred "tributes" to various members of the Stuart family, including testimonials with crossed Confederate flags etc. The Stuarts returned from church to find that Miss Mary Lee had had a whale of a fine time. She was sitting happily with folded hands, having taken down every last "tribute" and burned them in the fire. Said Miss Welford, "No one ever said a word to her. Miss Lee was royalty."

I suppose I am not yet adjusted, for I am quite lonely and not at all happy. I have written to Col. Anderson, Dr. Freeman,[7] etc. and should have answers soon. Saturday night (I had let Mary off after breakfast, as she had not had her Wednesday) I called a cab and went to the Ballet, Frederic Franklin, Danilova,[8] etc., expecting a treat. It was most inferior ballet. Joan Bennett and Zachary Scott are here in "Bell, Book and Candle"[9] and Audrey Hepburn comes next week in "Gigi"[10] and I shall try to go to both, asking Margaret for matinee of the latter.

...I am dreadfully shocked at the appointment of Clare Boothe Luce[11] to the ambassadorship at Rome. Not only highly unsuitable, in a non-feminist country, but so obviously a paying of a political debt.

...I'll wait until afternoon to send this, as the afternoon paper will probably have an interview and picture. When the Times-Dispatch photographer got me in profile and aimed his brutal flash, I knew what would happen—....

Much love,

1. Carrie Duke, Ellen Glasgow's lifelong friend.
2. Glasgow was devoted to the SPCA (Society for the Prevention of Cruelty to Animals) and directed the income from her trust fund be given to the Richmond branch in memory of her dog Jeremy, given to her by Henry Anderson.
3. Roberta Wellford, close friend of both Glasgow and Carrie Duke.
4. Gertrude Stein, American expatriate, who in Paris became famous as a patron of the arts, and her companion, Alice B. Toklas, visited Glasgow in February 1935. Glasgow was not impressed and wrote in her Journal that Stein was a "wise overgrown child, as obvious as an infant" (Goodman, 210). During the dinner at Glasgow's home, a young woman, obviously uninvited, came forward and asked Glasgow to sign a book.
5. Carl Van Vechten, critic and novelist, arranged the dinner.
6. The descendants of J.E.B. Stuart, the Confederate general.
7. Henry Anderson, a suitor of Ellen Glasgow. Douglas Southall Freeman (1886–1953), who was the editor of the Richmond News Leader and the biographer of Robert E. Lee.
8. Frederic Franklin, British-born ballet master; Alexandra Danilova, Russian-American ballerina.
9. Bell, Book, and Candle (1950), a comedic play written by John Van Druten (1901–1957).
10. Gigi (1951), a play written by Raymond Rouleau.
11. Clare Boothe Luce (1903–1987), playwright, member of Congress, and ambassador to Italy.

. . . .

(TLS, I p.)

5 Paxton Road
[Richmond, Va.]
Feb. 10, 1953

Dear Norton:

Carrie Duke is coming to lunch alone today, and since I must learn those down-town streets, I shall try to drive in for her myself. She says that Anne Virginia will probably go to the hospital for a couple of weeks, to have electric shock treatments that brought her out of her last nervous-breakdown. Carrie thinks that she will set her up again and that I will be able to talk with her.

I did go alone last night to "Bell, Book and Candle," and Pyewacket is incredible. He *answered* Joan Bennett *on cue*, he growled on cue, and at one point where she has him help to put the spell on the man, he opens his mouth *wide* and *hisses*. The rest of the time he is impassive as a porcelain cat, with only the Siamese flickering of the end of the tail now and then to assure you that he is really alive.

Joan Bennett looked very handsome, but the lines in her throat are deep and old, and her complexion is very bad. I was second row center, to be close to Pyewacket.

I went shopping down-town yesterday. . . . Buying card index etc. at Miller and Rhodes, and the clerk was not understanding what I wanted, I said something about filing research notes, and she said, "Why, you must be Mrs. Rawlings, doing the Glasgow book." Buying at the counter, the third book I was offered was "The Sojourner"[1] and I said I had a copy, as I had written it. The heads of the department were called and I was most welcome. . . .

I forgot to tell you about Bert Cooper and Cliff Lyons. Bert said that he had never been as hurt in his life [as] by Cliff, who simply turned into a stone wall and a stranger when Bert went to him for moral solace in his unhappiness at Chapel Hill. Bert said, "I was humbled and broken, and I had no one to turn to but Cliff, and I got less than nothing." I was tempted to tell him what Cliff had said to me, with a trace of guilty conscience, I think, "I was new myself and had my own way to make, and I couldn't carry anyone else along with me." It explains Cliff's "climbing" but I said nothing, as I was afraid it would depress Bert even more, as showing that Cliff considered him an undesirable burden. I said that I had seen Cliff's pomposity overtaking him, and that I myself was through with him, while hating to lose Gladys, and Bert said, "Marge, I love you. . . ."

Much love,

1. *The Sojourner* (New York: Scribners, 1953).

. . . .

(TLS 4 pp.)

5 Paxton Road
Richmond, Va.
Feb. 12, 1953

Dear Norton:

. . . A box of books came Special Delivery from Scribner's, and I was horrified to find they were all "The Sojourner". . . .

. . . My luncheon here and long afternoon's talk with Carrie Duke were most successful. She knows a lot, told a lot, and I think the rest will come out gradually, under the influence of good food and drink. She is really as cute as a bug's ear. Said early that she was 71, then when dates began to come out, said with no embarrassment that she was 77. She dresses snappily in mostly inherited expensive clothes, and I swear she looks younger than I. She is great fun and I see how she made a perfect foil and friend for Ellen. Says that Ellen and Henry Anderson were definitely engaged when he went abroad and fell into the clutches of Queen Marie;[1] did not write Ellen all during that time, which brought Ellen great suffering. She also knows about the first man, Ellen's greatest love, was plainly staggered when I mentioned him, said, "it was an infatuation, only an infatuation." She tried to shunt me off by speaking of a secondary and Platonic romance, and

I said, "No, Pe[a]rce Bailey wasn't the name." Carrie sat like a little ramrod, staring at me, then snapped, "His name was Mulhern. Irish. Terribly virile. Not good enough for Ellen."[2]

There was the usual tone of adoration and reverence, and then in answer to a question of mine about something innocuous, out came a hard answer from another copperhead—. And "the sweet Virginia flower" is the microphylla rose, pale yellow, almost cream, very fragrant.

There have been moments when I have decided that I don't want to do this biography at all. It can only be brutal in many of its aspects. Yet the body of Ellen Glasgow's work is still unavoidably important, so I suppose I shall try to see it through. . . .

Anyway, love,

Feb. 13 [1953]

A note from Col. Anderson, in answer to one of mine, said that he would like me for luncheon this week if and when his butler recovered from the flu, otherwise he would 'phone and ask to come here for tea the end of this week. I wired him please to come for luncheon here this Saturday or Sunday, as my inherited maid did much better on an actual meal than at tea, having used tea-bags instead of properly steeped tea when I had a guest (a woman who brought me her splendid thesis and map on the Virginia background of Ellen Glasgow's novels.) Col. Anderson just 'phoned me, asking me to come to him tomorrow for luncheon, as his doctor does not want him to go out. The Colonel said, "I have a touch of the flu, and there's no telling what will happen." I hope this means that he WANTS TO TALK!

I have just sent Arthur Glasgow yesterday's News-Leader story and picture of me (story dull, picture not too bad). . . .

1. Henry Anderson, Glasgow's suitor, met Queen Marie of Rumania, the daughter of Queen Victoria of Britain, in September 1917. Richmond gossip assumed that they had become lovers, and Glasgow was devastated.
2. Glasgow's biographer Susan Goodman does not mention Mulhern, nor does Glasgow in her autobiography, *The Woman Within* (1954). Pearce Bailey might be the mysterious lover from Glasgow's youth, the one she called Gerald B.

. . . .

[TLS, 2 pp.)

5 Paxton Road
[Richmond, Va.]
Feb. 16, 1953

Dear Norton:

. . . Well, Col. Anderson won't talk. I got blunt and he got blunt. I had tried to lead him on—fatuous fancy—by wondering why Ellen never married. He said she gave everything to her work. He had spoken of her stern principles and a certain Presbyterian viewpoint, and I said that perhaps her restraint had kept her from marrying. He said, "She was very much in love with a man in New York in her early days." I said I knew all about that, but had no intention of using it in my book. He said, "Dr. Bailey was very much in love with her and wanted to marry her," and I said, "Yes, Dr. Pe[a]rce Bailey. She wasn't interested in him." He glared at me. I said, "One story is that you and Ellen were engaged when you went abroad." He said, "I have no intention of talking about anything like that. I learned at my mother's knee never to talk about a woman." I said, "I thought a man learned that at his father's knee." He snapped, "My father was very busy."

Norton, I had to change the subject very quickly. He began to have trouble breathing and turned purple. He tapped his chest and muttered something about the constriction that hit him. I had visions of his dropping dead from a heart attack, which would have been hard for me to explain! I got him soothed, we are to talk further, he will come here when he feels better, and the subject is to be Ellen's book "One Man in His Time,"[1] on which he worked with her.

He did give himself away about Ellen in some respects, but I believe, in view of things Irita[2] knows from the memoirs, that he told me an out and out lie. I shall write him a letter giving my reasons for asking him to consider giving me a plain simple statement about their relationship. I shall also say that if he does not admit the validity of my reasons, I promise never to mention the subject to him again.

After lunch, when I was asking him to describe Ellen's appearance in her early days, he said he had a photograph of her that had never been used, that he considered the best and most typical. He suggested that we go upstairs to his library. I used the stairs while he went up in a one-man lift. His bedroom door was open, and the oil painting over the mantel was of a young girl, probably of his mother, done later from a photograph. It was definitely neither Ellen nor Queen Marie. But over the mantel in his library, where we finished our visit, was a large oil painting—of himself—in middle age, rather heavy and hard-looking—and on either side of it, with a pair of candlesticks that could be lighted in honor of him or of her, were two huge signed photographs of Marie. So that is the truth of *that* legend. If anyone in Richmond asks me questions, I shall be all ignorance. Everyone is dying of curiosity.

He brought the photograph of Ellen from his bedroom, and it is most lovely. He said I might borrow it for the book. He had another picture of her on his desk.

If I could get him mad enough, he'd talk, if only to refute me, but I am certain it would also kill him. He has my dander up, and I'd even enjoy being told a provable lie. However, I feel that he will be adamant.

Margaret Cabell calls me two and three times a day. I don't know whether she thinks I am lonesome, or just wants to talk because she is so confined, with

James' illness. Her hysteria is really overpowering when it goes on long enough. She has always been more or less that way, but it seems worse now. She had two women in to meet me yesterday afternoon, and one of them, a good friend of Ellen, had some perfectly charming anecdotes. We are to meet again, and I think she will have a great deal of the lively sort of *harmless* personal stuff that gives a certain sparkle to a biography.

Bert Cooper found about twenty marvelous letters from Ellen Glasgow, to Mary Johnston[3] etc., in the U. of Va. library, and sat right down and made typed copies and sent them to me.

Only Anne Virginia and the Colonel are holding me up.

Much love,

1. Ellen Glasgow, *One Man in His Time* (Garden City, N.Y.: Doubleday, Page, 1922), one of a series of novels intended to depict the political history of Virginia from 1850.
2. Irita Van Doren, one of Glasgow's closest friends, advised Glasgow on her literary career.
3. Mary Johnson, American novelist.

. . . .

(TLS, 3 pp.)

> 5 Paxton Road
> [Richmond, Va.]
> Feb. 19, 1953

Norton poor dear:

I think that having Nike[1] here will encourage me to do really concentrated work, so that I can have everything ready, noted and annotated and filed away. I hate the idea of packing up, going away and coming back again. However, I would never be so physically comfortable here again and I must make hay while the sun shines. I must take a real rest when I have this material safely in shape. The trip abroad[2] had just begun to get me on my feet, and I really wasn't quite ready to tackle anything like this. Having James not well enough for me to work hard with him, having the Colonel and Anne Virginia getting the vapors on me, have all been depressing, too. However, two people whom I was warned I should have to handle with kid gloves called up and volunteered everything. One woman did a thesis on the definite backgrounds of all of Ellen's books, that she had not let anyone use, and she brought this to me on loan and I am to copy as much as I want. That will be Nike's first job. Mrs. Wilkins also gave me a copy of the map she had made of the locales, most valuable. An old lady in Charlottesville, sister of Mary Johnston the novelist, whom Bert was afraid would be difficult, called me and is having Ellen's letters to her sister photostatted for me. The articles in the two Richmond papers did a great deal of good.

Imagine, Theodore Pratt came through on a deed of terrific human kindness. He sent me a copy of a letter he wrote the Saturday Review, raising pure hell about Bromfield's review,[3] or what he called "alleged" review. He made exactly the points I was concerned about. His letter was a dilly.

A rented typewriter and table are to be delivered today. I shall give Nike the front bedroom and have her move to another if I have a real guest, and shall put her typewriter in the other unused front room so that I won't hear it so plainly, and where she can keep the paper mess out of sight. James laughed at my description of her vague, ghostly quality, so that you wouldn't feel surprised if she passed dimly through a door without opening it. Margaret was concerned that I might have to drag her everywhere with me, and I assured her that she doesn't have to go anywhere with me at all, and for any one vital person lunching alone here, she needn't appear. I shall explain the situation to her at once and I know she will understand. . . .

Carrie Duke is having a cocktail party for me on Monday, and didn't invite Margaret, who knew all about it. I said I was sure Carrie was just having a few people who might have some Glasgow material and Margaret says No, that it's something of a brawl, with even the Pres. of the Writers' Club, whom Margaret has been keeping off my neck.

. . . Give my love to Moe and Adrenna, and lots to you.

1. Nike Grafstrom, MKR's typist.
2. In the fall of 1952, after MKR had submitted final proof of *The Sojourner*, she and NSB embarked for England and Ireland. Upon arrival back in New York, she went immediately to Richmond, the period represented by these letters.
3. In his review of *The Sojourner* in the *Saturday Review* 36 (3 January 1953): 9–10, Louis Bromfield wrote that it was a "good book," a "solid book," but lacked "excitement and fire" (10). Theodore Pratt (1901–1969), the novelist who once bragged that he had written twenty-two books about Florida.

. . . .

(TLS, 3 pp.)

5 Paxton Road
[Richmond, Va.]
Monday Morning
[23 February 1953]

Dear Norton:

. . . I have time for just a note, as Col. Anderson comes to luncheon today, when the fatal question will or will not be answered. . . .

Carrie Duke is having a cocktail party for me this afternoon.

I have lost my sense of despair, with Grafstron working steadily and quietly eight hours a day. She is, and will continue to be, exactly the sort of help that I need. She would like to stay no longer than three weeks, and it begins to seem that we can cover the ground in that time. I will still have the personal talks to finish, including the ones at Charlottesville and Lexington. The material continues to pour in.

I spent an hour and a half alone with Douglas Freeman[1] Saturday afternoon. He went at once into the most vicious diatribe against Col. Anderson and poor

Anne Virginia. He spoke as if he knew everything in the Memoirs, and I was never so grateful that I had not read them, for he was simply trying to pump me. He is utterly despicable. He has nothing of value for me, and I must keep out of his clutches.

. . . Margaret Cabell had us both for supper last night. James was in bed, but I talked with him. . . .

Love,

Feb. 24, 1953

Failure.

Results probably more interesting than success.

. . . The Colonel said he had gotten out of bed to come. "I couldn't sleep last night. I got to worrying about things." He had brought copies of his speeches, letters, relating to his political theories which Ellen used in "The Builders."[2] The talk was entirely of this. We had had drinks in the living room, but had demitasse in the study, and went over the papers. I knew he would leave at 3. At a quarter of, he said he would have to be going, as he was very tired. I kept my side of the bargain and didn't say a mumblin' word.

At ten of three, he began that alarming breathing again, his chin sank on his chest, and each obviously painful breath ended in something like a groan.

He said, "About that question you asked me. I said I'd rather see you, than write about it. I can't possibly answer you. It would violate the ethical principles of a lifetime."

I said, "You are not willing to make a direct statement as to whether or not you were ever engaged?"

H.A.: "If I told you that, I'd have to tell you why it was broken off."
!!!!!!!!!!!!!

He realized he had trapped himself and said hastily, "If there ever was—" and just dropped it there.

He was as miserable as an old gentleman could possibly be. I felt like Lady Macbeth. Who would have thought the old man had so much blood in him?

He said something feebly and unhappily about another of his speeches I had asked for, as though he was sure I was through with him now. I assured him that I wanted it very much, that its date was important, as a probable influence on Ellen for "The Builders," that when I had correlated the speeches with the book, I should like to talk with him further, and he brightened as if reprieved, and I wanted to pat his clean sparse white hair with the sun shining through it.

He stayed until 3:15, and something led to his offering with absolute delight to have his partner's wife alone for luncheon with him and me. Everyone has spoken of Ellen's famous formal dinners, but no one remembers how the table was set, what foods and wines were served. It seems that Mrs. Randolph Williams[3] has a microscopic memory, and he said she would be able to tell even what flowers Ellen had on the table for any specific occasion. He left, a much happier old man, and with, I think, a certain grateful affection for me.

Imagine our mutual astonishment when we met again at Carrie Duke's cocktail party! I had not mentioned the party, and he had said he was going to bed, (which it seems he did, in between) and although I was the guest of honor, I doubt if he knew that beforehand, or that I would be there. Neither of us referred to our joint ordeal—. He took a seat beside me and said that he had found the missing speech, and William would deliver it today. Carrie Duke sat on his other side and he said, "I've had an awful day. An awful day."

I am sure that he was referring to the state of his health, or *thought* he was, but I wanted to say, "I've had an awful day, too, pal. I know what you mean."

He left the party without quite finishing one old-fashioned.

The party was charming. Carrie's lived-in antique shop was bright with open fires and flowers and red damask and Carrie in red and sequins and fabulous special Virginia twisted cheese straws and paper-thin cookies from an old recipe. Martha Byrd Porter[4] took me and brought me home, and I am going to them alone for drinks this afternoon. They live in a large old house near here, you remember. He is the doctor who knows of Ellen's morbid animal activities, and who said, "She had an unhealthy personality." The rest of that story will come out today, I am sure. I shall get the other side from Mrs. Parker Dashiell, whom I shall have here for lunch alone soon. She is the one living in the Episcopal home, who didn't get her toddy at Miss Roberta Wellford's. Miss Roberta was at the party of course, said she wanted to talk with me alone, wanted me to come to her for luncheon again, but she is coming here Thursday.

. . . I am exhausted today, and shall do nothing more but read Harry Anderson's speeches.

Love,

1. Douglas Southall Freeman (1886–1953), most famous for his biography *R. E. Lee* (1934), for which he was awarded the Pulitzer Prize.
2. Ellen Glasgow, *The Builders* (Garden City, N.Y.: Doubleday, Page, 1919).
3. Maude Williams.
4. Martha Byrd Porter, Virginia writer.

. . . .

(TLS, 2 pp.)

5 Paxton Road
Richmond 26, Va.
Feb. 28, 1953

Dear Norton:

I have time for just a note before dressing to go to lunch to Col. Anderson today to meet Mrs. Williams.

Don't know when I have had as much fun as when Miss Roberta Wellford was here for luncheon Thursday. She reminds me a little of "votre petite tante," dresses well, weighs 73 pounds and put down a meal like a trencherman. Apropos of something or other, said, "My chest is flat but discreet." She had delightful stories about Ellen and some good material and we are to get together again soon. I told her that Col. Anderson was having me for luncheon today, and why, and she said "That's splendid. Maude talks freely and most indiscreetly. I do hope she invites you for lunch *alone*."

Carrie Duke 'phoned last night, and Rebe Tutwiler[1] wants the two of us to come to Lexington soon for a week-end. In a way I should prefer to go alone, but for the first time this may well be better, as Carrie was even a closer friend of Rebe than of Ellen in childhood and girlhood, and they should, with proper leads, get into reminiscing. I said that the week-end after this would be fine for me. . . .

Irita Van Doren sounds ready to come for a week-end any time, but it will be best to wait until Nike leaves, I think. Also, I'm not ready to give a party. It would be more suitable shortly before I leave.

Love,

1. Rebe Tutwiler, Glasgow's sister.

. . . .

(TLS, 2 pp.)

5 Paxton Road
Richmond, Va.
Mar. 3, 1953

Dear Norton:

. . . Last Saturday's luncheon meeting with Maude Williams at Col. Anderson's brought out an interesting supposition. The old gentleman had gotten out of bed against his doctor's orders and was having sharp pains in his right lung area where he had the operations. He sat with us perhaps twenty minutes after lunch then went to bed, telling us to stay and talk as long as we wished. He said to Mrs. Williams, "I want to give Mrs. Rawlings any help I can, but I told her that when it came to talking about my personal relations with Ellen, 'I just ain't going to do it.' I learned at my mother's knee 'Never talk about a woman.'"

I said, "And wasn't I very nice about it?" and he said, "You were indeed. You said you appreciated my position and would never mention the subject again, and you haven't said another word."

THEN, as he left for upstairs, he said to Mrs. Williams, "Now you tell Mrs. Rawlings everything you know about Ellen, only she mustn't print it."

I am going on the assumption that since he knows he was to blame for their marriage's not going through, he could not talk about it himself, *but has no objections to its being told by someone else.*

He had scarcely had time to get up the stairs when "Maude" stage-whispered,

"My dear, Ellen was simply WILD about Henry Anderson. Do you suppose anybody can hear us?"

I said I was sure that Archer, the butler, could, and that it was best to talk some time when we were alone somewhere else. It didn't seem cricket to me to let her gossip under the man's own roof. In about fifteen minutes Archer came down to say that the Colonel was comfortably in bed, and if we wanted to ask him any questions, we could come up to him!!! I said that we must be leaving.

"Maude" came here avidly in more ways than one, to luncheon yesterday—. She is a large, jolly, rather gross woman who spilled Mexican pumpkin seeds, served with my Martinis, down her ample bosom from pudgy, well-diamonded hands. She wears extremely handsome large hats from Mme. Germaine. I don't know whether she comes from aristocratic or mixed stock, but her type of coarseness rather seems that of one whose position is so secure that she doesn't have to trouble to be delicate about anything, pumpkin seeds or people.

It was she who brought Ellen and Henry Anderson together. She says they were definitely engaged, that his romance with Queen Marie threw the monkey wrench in the works, that he hurt Ellen dreadfully, that while he was once as much in love with Ellen as so cold-blooded a man could be, she doesn't really know whether Ellen's hurt and pride broke the engagement, or whether by that time he was not only dubious about taking on an ill, deaf wife but dubious about marriage altogether. After the post-war and post-Marie breach was healed, they were platonic friends, and he went to Ellen every Sunday evening for supper until the very end. Did I write you that Douglas Freeman said he would never forget the sight of Henry Anderson standing in the doorway at the services for Ellen in her house. "The ladies" who were running the services and funeral had not invited him. "He stood there tall and proud, half defiant and half crushed."

There WAS a portrait of Queen Marie! "Maude" doesn't remember in which room he kept it. It was done by de Laszlo (sp.?).[1] Not long ago Il[l]eana[2] was in Richmond and spent some time with the Colonel, and he gave her the portrait of her mother, as she had none, and he felt that none of his nieces or nephews would appreciate it as would Il[l]eana. "Maude" is not certain, but thinks the dates are wrong for Henry to have been Il[l]eana's father.

"In any case, my dear, Henry was always too cautious to have fathered *anyone*."

Miss Roberta Wellford, who knew "Maude" was coming, warned me that while Maude would tell all she knew, I myself must be most discreet and not add a single bit to Maude's repertoire, and I was caution itself. I go to Miss Roberta's for luncheon again this Saturday to meet a Mrs. Scrivenor, who knew Ellen well. This afternoon I go to see Mrs. Dashiell, who does not feel well enough to come here. All she will have for me is Ellen's side of the S.P.C.A. story, which will make a nice contrast with Dr. Porter's side. Miss Roberta sent me a box of choice candy after she was here for luncheon, the cute thing.

Carrie Duke 'phoned again to say that this week-end isn't possible for Rebe Tutwiler to have us at Brushwood, but that we will probably go the following week-end.

Anne Virginia is getting the electric shock treatments four times a week. She gets a lift and feels better afterward, then lapses into moroseness. I am terribly concerned, for she is the one person who can sift fact from fiction for me. Carrie Duke keeps telling me just to wait, but I do feel the impulse to write Anne V. now and then, in a general and cheery way, perhaps telling her some of the things that others have told me. I don't know her psychology well enough to know whether this would help or harm the situation. What do you think?

Dr. Porter[3] just 'phoned to say that Dr. Alexander Brown, who was Ellen's personal doctor, will be glad to talk with me as often as I wish. Everything goes well except poor Anne Virginia.

My love,

Editor's note: The following poem by MKR about one of her cats is inserted on a separate sheet:

A DEFENSIVE DITTY FOR A DEFENSELESS DITTY

I have a cat whose name is Ditty,
Admittedly uncouth, un-pretty.
I'VE been called names, so I have pity.
And ah, we both detest a city.

We have so many things in common.
We share indifference to Mammon.
We play at Scat, but not backgammon.
We both adore a nice fresh salmon.

We watch the birds. (Our reasons vary.)
We're alternately sad and merry.
O'er mild and gin we love to tarry.
We will not fetch nor will we carry.

We recognize our serendipity.
We think each other wise and witty.
What's in a name when one's a kitty?
HE calls ME "Meow." THAT's worse than "Ditty"!

1. Philip Alexius de Laszlo, the Budapest-born British portrait painter. The portrait of Queen Marie was done in 1924.
2. Rumor about Richmond at the time, which had a deep impact on Ellen Glasgow, had it that Illeana was the illicit daughter of Queen Marie and Henry Anderson.
3. William Porter, M.D.

(ALS, 4 pp.)

5 Paxton Road
Richmond Va.,
Mar. 7, 1953

Dear Norton:

Ditty is now a man. The adit's adit. He was the most astonished cat in the world. He dove under the bed immediately afterward to think it over. Chi-Chi rolled luxuriously a bit, had a terrific wash, and went sound asleep.

. . . The time of the birthing, if Ditty was as good as he now thinks he was, will take me to Van Hornesville later than usual, which I am sure suits you.

The pictures came from Carl Van Vechten[1] and they are interesting, I think, quite different from the professional ones.

Carrie Duke thinks the prospects are good for my seeing Anne Virginia. If I can only have a few days with her, I can be through by March 27. In that case, it would be best for you to come as far ahead of them as possible, for me to have a party for you, and for us to see Ellen's house and poor Walter McCormack's[2] dominant tomb-stone.

I forgot to tell you that last Sunday I took her [Nike] to Williamsburg and we had a grand time. The Inn is superb. We had a marvelous dinner and champagne cocktails, the only drink available. Expensive, but worth it. We went through only one house, the George Wythe house (he had been tutor to Thomas Jefferson) and Margaret Cabell said afterward that we had lit on the *one* [underlined three times] authentic house, furnishings and all. And lo and behold, in the dining-room was a pine hunt board *exactly* [underlined three times] like the one Margaret got me for Van Hornesville, but only half the width. I told her that I felt I had a treasure, and she said, "Yes, it's a very good piece."

At noon today I go to Miss Roberta's for luncheon. Carrie Duke comes here for dinner tonight. If it is pleasant tomorrow, I shall take Nike to Monticello, which I have never seen, either. We will take a picnic lunch to save an extra 20 miles going in and out of Charlottesville to eat. It will be a 160 mile round trip at best.

Nike types steadily six days a week, sometimes 9 or 10 hours a day. We did catch Harrison and Palmer in "The Four Poster"[3] at the neighborhood movie. Don't miss it if you haven't seen it.

. . . I drove in yesterday afternoon to talk with a dear old gentleman who had been one of Ellen's doctors, fought traffic, and had to park four long blocks from his house.

Colonel Anderson and I are now as one. His last note was delightful.

James is a trifle better. Margaret is really wonderful.

Much love,

1. Carl Van Vechten (1880–1964), American writer, was a distant cousin of MKR and friend of Glasgow's.

2. George Walter McCormack, once married to Glasgow's sister, Cary, committed suicide. Cary had a monument erected in his memory, which to some became an object to ridicule.

3. *The Four Poster* (1952), starring Rex Harrison and Lilli Palmer.

. . . .

(TLS, I p.)

> 5 Paxton Road
> [Richmond, Va.]
> Monday
> [March 9, 1953]

Dear Norton:

. . . Not much material from Mrs. Scrivenor at Miss Roberta's, but she gave me more facets, unwittingly, of "the Richmond picture. . . ."

Very gay dinner here with Carrie Duke. I have fallen in love with her, as well as with Miss Roberta. Nike said afterward that she couldn't believe that Carrie and I weren't life-long friends. She reported that Carrie told her she was "just crazy" about me, said, "Isn't she *sweet!*" !!!!! Carrie called last night to say that I can see Anne V. in the hospital this afternoon. I had told her to ask about it and to say that I wanted to make only a short social call and not to talk about anything serious.

. . . It is a disappointment to me that the work here is not relaxed and leisurely as I had expected. It is a terrific strain. I try to plan my dates for every other day, as I give out in between . . . puzzles.

> Love,

. . . .

(TLS, I p.)

> 5 Paxton Road
> Richmond, Va.
> March 10, 1953

Dear Norton:

. . . I spent an hour with Anne Virginia at the hospital yesterday afternoon. I tried to leave twice and she wouldn't let me. She seemed in quite good condition to me, was not in bed, and is anxious to return to her apartment. She asked how long I would be here, and said that she would hope to see me soon. If I can have several days with her, with her mind clear, I shall not have to return. Grafstrom is doing a superb job of correlating material, and the rest of her week here we shall spend together at the libraries. Then when she leaves, I shall concentrate on people again.

. . . Col. Anderson 'phoned to ask to come out at 4 this afternoon. He is going over my notes that connect his speeches and letters with Ellen's book "The Builders." I had planned to spend the afternoon at the U. of Richmond library with Nike, but must study up on my notes, in order to ask the Colonel intelligent questions, so shall just drive her out to the library after lunch, get her started and leave her. She now knows as well as I what I want and need.

No one could have done a better job for me than she has. I feel most fortunate. We have vast, well-coordinated files that will make it easy for me to do my writing whenever I feel ready. She got on my nerves just once, Sunday afternoon, and I simply left her in the study with the open fire and came to bed with a book.

Poor Jack Wheelock was so anxious to help me, so sure that taking 80% of "The Sojourner" in one year would do it, and I believe it was a ghastly mistake. The three year pro-rating will not be sufficient compensation, as it only adds to an already fairly high income in the last three years. And when you realize that the book represents ten years' work, and that each book I finish brings me closer to the grave, it seems grossly unfair that a *capital* return is charged as *income*. The flow of successful writing is as uncertain as the flow of Texas oil wells. . . .

Love,

. . . .

(TLS, 1 p.)

5 Paxton Road
[Richmond, Va.]
March 11, 1953

Dear Norton:

I am so glad that you can come for me, and do come as far ahead of the 27th as possible, so that we can go to Glasgow House and to pay our respects to poor Walter MacCormack, and to have Carrie Duke and Miss Roberta Wellford here *separately*. We could have one for lunch and the other for dinner, the same day, if necessary.

I just talked to Miss Roberta on the 'phone, to ask her to the party, and told her that after reading about her in my letters, my husband had asked if she was available for adoption. She said, "I should adore to be adopted. You can take me right back with you. And I am most anxious to meet a man with that much imagination."

Try and keep folks away from the party! The Virginius Dabneys[1] and the Douglas Freemans have to call me back, but everyone else has accepted, including Col. Anderson.

Irita[2] would have preferred to come week-end after this, but was most sporting about it. It seems that Rebe Tutwiler just has to have some painting finished before Carrie and I can come. So we go to her March 21–22, which gives me very little time with her, as it is a half-day's drive each way.

. . . Had a pleasant hour here with Col. Anderson yesterday, the first time he'd been out of bed in ten days. I think for two cents he would have kissed me when he left—probably out of gratitude that I didn't torment him about Ellen.

Love,

1. Virginius Dabney, a historian.
2. Irita Van Doren.

677

(TLS, 5 pp.)

5 Paxton Road
[Richmond, Va.]
March 17, 1953

Dear Norton:

I am in the midst of copying fourteen letters from Ellen Glasgow to Anne Virginia, that the latter had saved after all. Ellen's handwriting is difficult to decipher, just short of Walter Gilkyson's, and it is proving a full-day job. I have just had an early lunch on the tray in bed, and shall try to bring you up to date before going back to these letters. I scarcely know where to begin. Since this is Virginia, I suppose from the social angle—

My Friday afternoon cocktail party for Irita Van Doren seemed to be a success. Everyone invited came but the Virginius Dabneys, who were involved elsewhere. There were eighteen.

(I stopped here and went back to the letters, which I have just finished. It took me six *solid* hours. I am exhausted, but will try to go on, as I must use tomorrow for seeing people, including returning the original letters to Anne Virginia. I am too tired to consider dressing and going to her today.)

. . . Col. Anderson monopolized Irita, and even Douglas Freeman let him get away with it.

On Saturday, Irita and I lunched at Carrie Duke's, and there was no other guest except, of all people, Anne Virginia, who had left the hospital the day before. Irita did a superb job in taking such people aside individually to say what a superb job she felt I was doing and would do, hoping that it would help to loosen them up for me.

Saturday afternoon Margaret Cabell had her cocktail party, and James was dressed and on hand, then once again when he could get Irita away from Col. Anderson, he took her into his room for a private talk.

Sunday afternoon Irita and I spent an hour alone with Henry Anderson, and he showed us his Balkan decorations, mostly from Marie, I gather. Then he showed us a Roumanian silver case like a large powder compact, which, opened, revealed a beautiful colored miniature of the Queen. She had had it made for him. He remarked, "She was very nice to me," which is perhaps the under-statement of the season.

She and I went on from there to the Douglas Freeman's tea. Others left, and there were six of us for what Mrs. Freeman had said would be "a simple supper." This was an elaborate dinner, with a special old wine, and champagne with dessert. I had planned to drive Irita to the train at 10:30 P.M., but it was raining and she knew I was about done for, and refused to let me do it, but called a taxi instead. I was infinitely grateful.

I should have given a great deal to stay in bed all Monday, but I had an engagement to go with Carrie Duke at 11 A.M. to see if a sofa a dying antique dealer told me over the 'phone had belonged to Ellen Glasgow, was authentic. The woman had first called it a chaise longue, and I thought it might be wonderful to have for my bedroom at Van Hornesville. Also, Mrs. Hull[1] was supposed to have a vast amount of clippings about Ellen, which she said she would be glad to give me outright. It proved a water-haul. The sofa was an Empire sofa, hard as a rock and narrow, and Carrie said that while it had indeed been Ellen's, she had not used it in any of her important rooms, but had relegated it to the back hall. It was in very bad condition and Mrs. Hull wanted $200 for it. The clippings which she pressed on me were an assortment of material, including letters, from Mrs. Hull's dead husband's family, and of no interest to anyone, not even, I should think, to Mrs. Hull. I shall return them.

I reached home about twelve-thirty, to find a message that Anne Virginia wanted me to call her. I did, and she asked me to come to her apartment to look over material. I spent from 2:30 to 6 with her. Her mind is as clear as mine (what am I saying!), anyway, she is in very good condition. (There is evidence that her mind, or memory, *does* lapse, however.) She had some interesting things to tell me, and will have more, as we manage just to visit. On certain subjects she simply closed up as tight as a clam, and I think she will *never* discuss them. About Henry Anderson, she would happily talk until the Last Judgment, and on that occasion I expect to find her fighting her way to the Seat to get in her licks about him before he shows up. In her hate and contempt for him, her resentment of the way he made Ellen suffer (while insisting that Ellen really never cared deeply for him at all) she let drop some extremely fascinating things. She did not mind my making notes, as she talked of the dogs and such matters, and I managed to slip in the H.A. notes quietly.

She read aloud the fourteen letters she had saved, from Ellen to her, finally agreed with me that there was no reason why I might not make copies, as I had remarked that they were no more personal than the many ones Arthur Glasgow had turned over to me—and then put them back in the leather box Ellen had always used for keeping her own immediate letters—and firmly closed the lid—. (While reading aloud, she stopped once to say, "Oh dear, Ellen didn't know I would ever be reading these to anyone.") How I squirmed—. Several letters were marvelous, including one which described her tea with the widow of Joseph Conrad,[2] whom she had known and visited, and the Thomas Hardys,[3] (not too long before his death). I had to press my point, and I gathered my courage and, taking it for granted that I might have copies of the letters, asked whether she preferred to have my secretary do it, or to have me send in a good typist who has been recommended to me. It ended with her handing me the letters—. I decided that I did not dare take the time to send them to Nike, as Anne V. might change her mind and call to ask to have them back, and that is why I spent the day doing the copying myself.

Oh yes, the instance of Anne V's lapse of memory. At Carrie Duke's luncheon,

Anne V. answered my question about the gifts Henry Anderson had made to Ellen. She said then that while he had never given her a ring, he had given her infinite amounts of other jewelry, pins, bracelets, etc., sapphire and diamond, topaz and diamond, onyx and diamond, and that SHE HAD THEM. She said *then*, that, her hospital and doctors' bills having recently been so heavy, she was tempted just to sell them all. I said that I should like very much to buy some piece, if she did. SO, at her apartment yesterday, after she had showed me many things, and I was about to leave (she kept saying, "Don't go") I said, "I'd love to see the jewelry that Henry Anderson gave to Ellen." "Oh," said Anne Virginia, "I don't have it. Rebe Tutwiler took it, She wasn't going to give it back to Henry Anderson, and she didn't want it herself, and she sent it all off to Baltimore and sold it." !!!!!!!

Anne Virginia and I are *en rapport*—up to the point where she will *not* talk about some matters. She will come here as soon as she feels well enough, and I think she would be glad to have me come every day, to her. But I have other irons in the fire—.

Once again, there is so much to tell that I don't know where to begin—.

For a start—I telephoned Irita the day before she was to arrive, that I thought I was ready to read Ellen's Memoirs. I felt I had gone as far as I could at the moment in getting Ellen's *very few* close friends to talk. Irita got the autobiography[4] out of the Harcourt, Brace vaults and brought it with her. I have not yet finished the reading, but went far enough while Irita was here to talk over many things with her, while she in turn was reading all my vast notes and all the Glasgow copied letters that Nike had done. NOW, NOBODY knows that I have read this, or that I have it. I am still protected from the people who themselves know little about Ellen but pretend to know all, while trying like mad to pump *me*. Even James and Margaret don't know. Perhaps especially James and Margaret—. (Last night, when Margaret 'phoned me, as I told you she does regularly, once or twice a day, she asked me so many questions, including some that James wanted asked, about everything that Irita and I had done and talked about, that I made a note to find the proper simile or metaphor—it would be something like Uki's holding down a live chipmunk with one paw while he ate out its insides, or something like Margaret's pinning me, perhaps a soft-shell crab, to the plate, while she used her fork to get out every last scrap of flesh. Dear Heaven, the Richmond story! I wrote Carl Van Vechten a rough report on my progress, and he answered, "You will have material enough for another book, NOT about Ellen Glasgow.")

Well, I had told Irita that instead of finding this research easy and relaxing and leisurely, I was in a state of constant tension, and somehow distressed all the time. On the two nights she was here, we visited back and forth between our rooms, each with something to read to or check with the other, and Saturday night I went to her with a few sentences from Ellen's Memoirs, which said that she, Ellen, was writing frankly, else the autobiography would have no value. I asked Irita if perhaps that did not clear the way for me to do a biography with equal frankness and fullness. The next late morning, after I had driven to the blessed Broad St. Station to get the Sunday N.Y. papers, and Irita and I were reading them, she said suddenly, "Marjorie, perhaps I know why you are so tense about all this. I think it may be because you are having such a mental conflict about probing these people for material. If so, Ellen's own statement should relieve you completely. Since she herself has written so freely, you need have no qualms."

She was right, and a great load was lifted from my shoulders, for I have felt myself a hypocrite and sneak. I have always been able to draw people out—someone here, at some party, said to me, "You make anybody want to talk to you."

A great blow—. Anne V. will not talk of some things, as I have reported. I shall have a chance to tell Carrie Duke what Irita said, so that I think Carrie will talk more freely on our trip to Lexington this week-end—but Miss Roberta Wellford who knows more than anyone of some important matters about Ellen Glasgow, was to leave this morning, as she called me yesterday to say, for perhaps two weeks. She knows more, would tell more, once she knows how much I know, than anyone. She has already verified some.

I am in torment, not knowing whether it will be necessary for me to return here after April 8th. There are people I must see in Charlottesville, Va., who will have Ellen Glasgow letters for me.

I MUST talk with Miss Roberta again.

And James Cabell—. I thought I was being kind in not pressing him to talk, as he has been so ill and miserable, but I began to sense that he and Margaret were offended by my talking with everyone else and not with him. Irita verified this. I had a fortunate chance to see James alone Sunday morning, when I took him magazines and papers on my way back from the Broad St, Station, and Margaret had taken Ballard to church. I think that Margaret had not passed on to him my message as to why I had not bothered him—. Anyway, I go to them tomorrow for dinner, for James to begin talking with me. And it seems that he himself has already written of his connections, literary, personal and social, with Ellen Glasgow, and it is quite possible that he wants to keep all this material for whatever book he may be working on.[5]

I 'phoned Nike Grafstrom last night, to report that her missing cigarette lighter had been found, and in telling her of my hectic week-end, she said that the tension of my work and interviews had begun to make her tense, too. . . .

Love,

Perhaps you do it anyway, but it might be a good idea for you to keep my letters to you from Richmond, as I often write you details that I don't have in my notes.

If you *could* come early enough next week, would you like to go with me on my necessary trip to Charlottesville? As I think I told you, I can't combine seeing three vital people there with my trip this week-end to Rebe Glasgow Tutwiler, as

Carrie Duke is going with me in my car, and she cannot leave until 10 A.M. this Saturday and must be back Sunday night. I dare not go to Charlottesville this week beforehand, as Anne V. is available, and I am seeing her again this afternoon. . . .

1. Mrs. Hull, not identified.
2. Joseph Conrad, the novelist, whom Glasgow found to be a "brilliant talker" when she visited him in the summer of 1914 (Glasgow, 201).
3. Thomas Hardy, the British novelist and poet, whom Glasgow visited in the summer of 1914 and again in 1927. She found him "still gentle, considerate, with a poetic fire" (Glasgow, 199).
4. *The Woman Within.*
5. Cabell later did publish his memories, *As I Remember It* (New York: McBride, 1955).

. . . .

(TLS, 3 pp.)

Van H[ornesville, N.Y.].

June 13, 1953

Dear Norton:

Peggy[1] came up last night for a good long visit, and let loose on Louise with both barrels. She told half a dozen instances of Louise's smallness. . . .

Mr. Young had called Peggy to ask her to come and fix him a bite of lunch, as Louise had disappeared, and asked her if she would mind straightening their bedroom, with clean linen. The bed had evidently not been changed since their arrival, and the bathroom towels were equally dirty and shocking. The next time she saw her, Louise said, "Seems to me you're awfully extravagant with linen."

Then it was agreed that Peggy was to go to the Youngs at 9:30 yesterday morning, to pack Mr. Young's bag to drive to Boston with Dick for the big Harvard doings. She found Dick white as a sheet, but he only said that he was disturbed because his father was so upset. Louise had arisen at 6 A.M., made a pot of coffee and that was all, and had taken off for the Inn, she said in a note. The men said it was too late to trouble about breakfast. Peggy began hunting for the things for Mr. Young's bag, and there was not a whole or clean or decent night-shirt anywhere. Peggy picked the best one and sewed on buttons. She found the cuff lining of his good blue suit loose and hanging out, and sewed that hastily. Mr. Young asked her if she would mind seeing that he came home to some clean shirts and underwear. She said she had never seen him in such a state, that he was actually trembling.

He will be 79 in October. To think that that great man cannot be comfortable in his old age—. . . .

Much love,

1. Margaret Carey Eagan.

(TLS, 4 pp.)

[Van Hornesville, N.Y.]

June 22, 1953

Dear Norton:

... I really think we had better fly to Phoenix in November.

Wilmer[1] plans to fly back, only 13 hours without changing 'planes. She says TWA has a grand safety record. She does not think it advisable to try to come here. She has at least four more weeks in the hospital.

My visit to her was just what she needed. She is really doing remarkably well, after such a serious operation. ...

You can send any books you won't want to keep, to her. Don't send the Rumer Godden, as I am sending that, also "The Echoing Grove."[2]

... Wilmer told me reluctantly that Barbara, his [Arthur's] younger daughter, ran away with a married man, leaving behind a child four years old and a six-months baby. To my amazement, Wilmer turned away and burst into racking sobs! She said, "Nothing like this has ever happened in our family before."

Of Mabel,[3] the Christian-hearted son of a bitch, she said, "Mabel spends all her time going around looking for sin." I said, "It's right easy to find. What does she do when she finds it?" "She preaches to them, and it makes them so mad they go out and sin a lot harder."

Much love,

1. Wilmer Kinnan, MKR's aunt.
2. Rosamond Lehmann (1901–1990), *The Echoing Grove* (New York: Harcourt, Brace, 1953).
3. Mabel Traphagen, MKR's aunt.

. . . .

(TLS, 1 p.)

Van H[ornesville, N.Y.].

June 23 [1953]

Dear Norton:

I had a letter from Gene Baro saying that he had Martin Dibner's new book[1] to be reviewed for the Herald Tribune, and he was both impressed and disappointed.

I had a charming letter from Doris Nash Wortman, who does the Kingsley Acrostics now, in answer to mine about her use of "The Sojourner". ...

Much love,

1. Martin Dibner, *The Deep Six* (Garden City, N.Y.: Doubleday, 1953).

(TLS, 3 pp.)

Van H[ornesville, N.Y.].

July 7, 1953

Dear Norton:

. . . I should be so happy about paying income tax etc., if I could say where my hard-earned money would go. Not for atom bombs, for an incredibly stupid set of men in power, but for helping all over the world. We have a "surplus" of wheat and of corn, while other nations are starving.

I may end up as a revolutionary (not a Communist, as they are more reactionary, more feudal, than our capitalists) but as—I don't know what. I am annoyed with people and with life. My life.

. . . .

(TLS, 2 pp.)

Van H[ornesville, N.Y.].

July 8, 1953

Afternoon

Dear Norton:

. . . Out of my terrible and constant depression, it came to me that part of it was the hideous correspondence, on which I am always behind. . . .

I enclose more checks for deposit, and two contracts for filing.

. . . I keep forgetting to answer your question. Yes, I attended the Young family picnic on the 4th of July. . . . I got sleepy and had to leave before the bonfire.

The reason why Miss Roberta[1] couldn't come was that she thought our time would not fit. I have written her that it will, if she wants it to. . . .

. . . Let me have news of Edie. You know, I decided that we should not be offended ever by her lady-authorship, as, by God, she is truly a lady author, if there ever was one.

Love,

1. Roberta Wellford.

. . . .

(TLS, 3 pp.)

Van H[ornesville, N.Y.].

July 9, 1953

Dear Norton:

I am simply enraged by Gene's letting you do so much for him and his satellite,[1] while they sat around and did not even move dirty glasses to the kitchen.

I was not already infuriated with him—and have carefully *not* written him to that effect—since he had mentioned that the grass at the Creek was deep in sandspurs, which annoyed him no end, as March had not been there to cut the grass since his wreck. Gene said he supposed he himself could cut the grass, but it just didn't appeal to him. Again, there sit two healthy males on their hunkers, and with a new and simple power mower in the barn, won't stir themselves to use it.

The whole business has helped me to decide what I want to do this winter. I want to be at the Creek. I have just written Gene that I must have it back then.

Ireland in the dead of winter would be silly. If I *should* be ready to start on the Glasgow thing, I should also have to have American libraries at hand, even if it meant trips to N.Y.C.

... And I want to get the Creek house in shape again.

... I may be too optimistic, but I seem to feel day light coming!

Love,

1. Albert Stadler.

. . . .

(TLS, 2 pp.)

Van H[ornesville, N.Y.].

July 20, 1953

Dear Norton:

... I do not know what it wrong with me, but I have not been able to settle to work any sort, short stories or the studying of the Glasgow material. I don't seem to give a damn about anything. My garden and the kittens are my sole pleasures. . . .

Love,

. . . .

(TLS, I p.)

Van Hornesville, N.Y.

July 27, 1953

Dear Norton:

Buzz Scribner[1] sent me a fat box of new Scribner books, including the Scribner Treasury and the new Alan Paton,[2] which you will have had through the B. of M. club. He also sent the new Audry Menen.[3] It is short (and delicious) and I'll keep it for you to read here. It is non-fiction, and marvelous irony.

Arthur does intend to hide out forever, if possible. He writes that a year ago his lawyer in Seattle—wonder which one!—told him that the longer he kept the boy, the better would be his chances of not having him taken away, if the woman catches him. . . .

Love,

1. Charles Scribner Jr.
2. Alan Paton (1903–1988), *Too Late The Phalarope* (New York: Scribners, 1953).
3. Audrey Menen, *The Ramayana* (New York: Scribners 1954).

(TLS, 2 pp.)

Van H[ornesville, N.Y.].

July 29, 1953

Dear Norton:

. . . I have made syrup so far from 50 qts. of raspberries, and there will be at least two more pickings, one today. I want to make some more of the raspberry shrub, which I forgot to have you taste. I have the brandy and rum ready for it. It has the same amazingly fresh flavor of the syrup, but with the alcoholic fillup. . . .

Love,

. . . .

(TLS, 2 pp.)

[Van Hornesville, N.Y.]

July 31, 1953

Dear Norton:

I was glad to hear from you at all, as I always get a thrill when I see your envelopes, but I must agree with you that you offered very little comfort. I thought you rather hit below the belt in throwing my own words back at me, and in making the crack that in my "mood" I wouldn't even believe you when you say you wish you could help me. It would have been much less depressing if you had said you wished you could help, and left off the stinging tail. But I know I have worn your patience to the bone. Also, you must be extremely tired and tense, yourself, from the long heat and no relief from your job.

This horrible thing that gets me in its grips is of course a form of mental illness. No one knows a thing about it who isn't subject to it, and such another person could scarcely help, except that everybody could cry together. I have just finished the Sherwood Anderson letters,[1] and he went through the same thing. A great part of it is the writer-not-at-work.

I can put my finger on several matters that I know are causing me distress, but if they were all cured, there would still be no guarantee that I would be all right. . . .

Yesterday morning I threw away Phil and Lillian's[2] letters about the Blender and the cook-book, wondering why I had ever kept them. It was, of course, to send to you. I am sure they thought I would do so, as they were especially pleased that you sent a recipe book to go with the Blender. They are delighted with both.

. . . I do hope that you can get some relief and not only catch up on your bookwork, but get away for a few days for a real rest. Your nerves are less on the surface than mine, but they eat into you just the same. If only you did not so go into your shell about me—.

Love,

1. Sherwood Anderson (1876–1941), *Letters* (Boston: Little Brown, 1953).
2. Philip and Lillian May. MKR had sent them, through NSB, a Waring blender as a gift.

(TLS, 2 pp.)

Van H[ornesville, N.Y.].

Aug. 4, 1953

Dear Norton:

I enclose an encouraging letter from Arthur and Wilmer's letter to him! She gets really hysterical, and will never learn that she can't run other people's lives. I think Arthur has totally twisted Phil May's advice. "There are none so blind as those who will not see." But he does have a point, and if he can make money at real estate, it suits me fine, as I should not be keen about financing his law suit....

Much love,

. . . .

(ALS, 4 pp.)

[Ritz-Carlton Hotel]
Boston
Aug. 6, 1953

Dear Norton:

She [Wilmer Kinnan] enjoyed your "Edwin Booth"[1] very much....

Love,

1. Eleanor Ruggles (1916–), *Prince of Players: Edwin Booth* (New York: Norton, 1953).

. . . .

(TLS, 1 p.)

Van Hornesville, N.Y.

Aug. 22, 1953

Dear Honey:

Carrie[1] leaves Wednesday morning. I am driving her to Albany to take an 8:05 A.M. 'plane to Washington, D.C....

Much love,

1. Carrie Duke, who came to give MKR more material for her biography of Ellen Glasgow.

. . . .

(TLS, 4 pp.)

Van H[ornesville, N.Y.].

Aug. 27, 1953

Dear Norton:

I enjoyed Carrie very much.... [S]he is really a dear, and the best company.

Carrie and I had drinks at the Youngs, and Saturday she and I and Louise and Virginia[1] had luncheon and bridge at the Inn.

... Later, Carrie said, puzzled, "You know, Mrs. Young doesn't seem like the wife of Owen D. Young. She seems like a peasant woman."

... Carrie had very little material to give me. She repeated her few tales of Ellen and that was about all, with one important exception. Grafstrom, I found, in reading over my notes and material before Carrie arrived, had failed to copy many of my hand-scrawled notes from Richmond, among them the names and facts about "the" man in Ellen's life. I had to pretend that I had this written down somewhere but just couldn't remember, for Carrie to come across. She was ready to cooperate, but is just a bit too scatter-brained to have much to offer. Anne Virginia is my next vital source, and since she and Carrie are so close, Carrie's delight in her visit here will help me that way. I don't mean to sound horrid about Carrie, for I came truly to love her.

... Oh, yes, a story that Bee McNeil told me, which you may of heard:

"Clare Luce was in audience with the Pope,[2] and the audience went on and on. Finally one of the nervous guards heard the Pope say, "But Mrs. Luce, I AM a Catholic."

Love, and please answer my questions,

1. Louise Young's daughter, Virginia Brown Green.
2. Pius XII.

. . . .

(TLS, 4 pp.)

Van Hornesville, N.Y.

Sept. 4, 1953

Dear Norton:

... Scribner's sent me some figures, and my income from them will be almost exactly $40,000, so there will be only the extras of a small grove profit, Brandt and Brandt etc., which should be absorbed by pro-rating the Sojourner royalties over the past 3 years. . . .

Much love,

. . . .

(ALS, 6 pp.)

Van H[ornesville, N.Y.].

Sept. 9, 1953

Dear Norton:

... I won two prizes at the Young's Family show. . . . One entry was 3 stages of the "The Sojourner" (I had almost sent most of the stuff to the U. of Fla. Library)—my original notes; a carbon of the carpeted manuscript; and a copy of the printed book.

Love, and write or phone me.

(TLS, (3 pp.)

The Jefferson [Hotel]
Richmond, Virginia
Oct. 20, 1953

Dear Norton:

. . . I had the depressed feeling that things here were going too slowly, then I realized that it is only Tuesday, and I have seen the Cabells, who are coming here for dinner tonight; had a good visit yesterday afternoon with Anne Virginia, who will probably come here for luncheon and the afternoon tomorrow; talked with Roberta Wellford on the 'phone, who said she would call me for a date after I get myself together. Have been to Carrie's twice. Anne Virginia and Roberta are now my last hopes, and I can't hurry them.

. . . James Cabell is very much better.

This is rather a second-class hotel, although considered the best and most fashionable here. Even Arthur Glasgow stays here often. . . .

Anne Virginia is also in splendid health, and was most cordial. Time will tell—. If I can get what I want, I'd like very much to get out in two weeks. . . .

Much Love,

. . . .

(TLS, 4 pp.)

The Jefferson [Hotel]
Richmond, Virginia
Oct. 21, 1953

Dear Norton:-

. . . James and Margaret had dinner in the rooms with me last night. Anne Virginia had luncheon with me here this noon. (She talked freely, and I am most hopeful for future talks.) Roberta Wellford comes here for dinner tonight. (Yesterday she sent me some choice cocktail tid-bits and a box of choice local candy.) Tomorrow night I go to Carrie's for dinner, and Friday night she comes here for dinner.

I am gradually getting some *select* [underlined twice] *dirt* [underlined three times], and also some sweet and charming stories. Everybody either hates or mistrusts everybody else, except Carrie, who loves the world.

Also called this afternoon on Mrs. Dashiell in the old folk's home, the one who gave me her delightful water-colors of Richmond. It was she who told me the *nice* [underlined twice] stories.

Margaret and I ordered our main dish, and then she said, after James had mentioned things that appealed to him, "James will have chicken a la King." I said, "My God, let the man order for himself," and she snapped back, "You aren't the one who has to get up in the night when he's made himself sick" ——!

... I have just an hour before Roberta arrives, and must try to remember and write down everything Anne Virginia said.

Love,

. . . .

(TLS, 2 pp.)

The Jefferson [Hotel]
Richmond, Virginia
Oct. 23, 1953

Dear Norton:-

Oct. 24, afternoon

Am seeing everyone *except* [underlined three times] Anne Virginia and Roberta Wellford ——. I don't need much more from them, but that little is vital. Roberta will probably take a trip after this coming week. However, she will probably come here for supper tomorrow, Sunday, night.

... Maude Williams sends her best to you—said she found you so attractive, "one of those things," She is cute & wicked.

Love,

. . . .

(TLS, 3 pp.)

The Jefferson [Hotel]
Richmond, Virginia
Sat. 11:30 A.M.
[Late October? 1953]

Dear Norton:

I planned to call you this morning, but one of the most interesting people I have yet met 'phoned, and living next door, came right over, and has just left. She is Francis Williams, a writer, and a cousin of Ellen Glasgow. I can't imagine how I had missed her. She gave me much valuable material mostly from the literary angle.

I leave after an early lunch to drive to Norfolk to have cocktails (and I hope they ask me to dinner!) with a couple who knew Ellen very well, and are supposed to be brilliant. The man I think had been one of Ellen's lawyers. Tomorrow morning I go for all of the mid-day, to spend with Josephine Clarke, Ellen's niece to whom she left some choice things, and the only close member of the family I have not met. I had hoped Anne Virginia would go with me, but it made her sick after our last long session, and she doesn't feel up to it. I am spending the night at what I find is a dreary hotel, the Monticello, but just to sleep, it won't matter. Josephine lives 25 miles from Norfolk at Virginia Beach.

Found this Miss Williams has a small hotel and tea room at Va. Beach (closed for the season) and she was taking the bus as far as Williamsburg, which I have to go through, so she is driving with me that far, which will be a great help on the roads. We leave at 1:30.

Anne Virginia has lost every trace of reserve, has given me more most valuable letters, and has told me *more* than I need to know. She told me of one incident that is so shocking—and you know I am almost shock-proof—that I simply don't know what to do about it. Ellen was innocent, but her reaction throws a strange light on her character—I can't go into it by mail. If I use the incident in the biography—and how can I not?—it will create a scandal to rock all Virginia, and will make my book too lurid for my own taste.

I shall have to talk it over privately with Irita Van Doren, in person.

. . . James[1] and I had a wonderful visit. He is absolutely sweet in his own home. He loaned me two more fine Glasgow letters.

. . . Was very tired last night, but Carrie came over for dinner with me, and then I saw her home and turned out the lights for her. . . .

Love to all [underlined twice],

1. James Branch Cabell.

. . . .

(TLS, 2 pp.)

> The Jefferson [Hotel]
> Richmond, Virginia
> Nov. 4, 1953

Dear Norton:

. . . After lunch, Carrie Duke and I went calling in my car, the visits including the old lady who did the water-colors, so brave but pitiful in the old people's home, and Mrs. Douglas Freeman, who is brave, too, but not at all pitiful. I was so tired that I did not see how I could get to the Cabells last night, where I was due at 7 for dinner. Oh yes, before I picked up Carrie, I walked to Ellen's home, and entering un-noticed, sat on the back steps of the old gallery over-looking the garden which was once so beautiful. There were no ghosts there, and even the garden is so changed that I felt nothing. Then I walked on to a dear old second-hand book-shop. I merely asked whether the old proprietor could find me a copy of the Ellen Glasgow poems,[1] but he said, "Oh yes, Mrs. Rawlings, I saw your ad in the Sunday paper. You should have come to me first. If the book is obtainable, I can get it for you for less than the ad cost you. I only charge $5 for it." He is now probably my best bet.

. . . Anyway, I took a cab to and from the Cabells. I had a perfectly delightful time with James. He was never more adorable. He looks very well, and said that he yearned to drive to Ophelia with us, but knew it would be too much for him. (Don't think I reported on what he said one day when I had been there to lunch. I said I must go, and he looked at the clock, and said, "I didn't realize you had been here so long. It's two hours. Really, you wear very well."!!!) Margaret said that if I didn't mind driving a bit out of the way, we would pick up oysters near Ophelia, and I would stay for supper of her superb oyster stew, thick with cream, lightly spiced, and laced with sherry. (When we get back to Richmond.)

4 P.M.

Anne V. has just left. Unless she could visit me for a couple of weeks—and I did invite her to Florida, but I know she will not come—I feel that I have gotten as much personal material as will ever be possible. She began *repeating* her anecdotes, as Roberta Wellford did on Monday.

It is a pity not to have gotten more from these few still-living friends and relatives, but I imagine that when I go over my card file, I will find that I have a great deal. . . .

Love,

1. Ellen Glasgow, *The Freeman and Other Poems* (New York: Doubleday, Page, 1902).

. . . .

This is the last known letter from Marjorie to Norton. She returned to Florida just after this letter was written and died suddenly on 14 December 1953, at the age of fifty-seven. In the years following, Norton—always her courtier—became her quiet champion. He died peacefully on 15 August 1997, at the age of ninety-five.

Bibliography

Acton, Patricia N. *Invasion of Privacy: The "Cross Creek" Trial of Marjorie Kinnan Rawlings.* Gainesville: University Presses of Florida, 1988.

Baker, Carlos. *Ernest Hemingway: A Life Story.* New York: Scribners, 1969.

Case, Josephine Y., and Everett N. Case. *Owen D. Young and American Enterprise.* Boston: David R. Godine, 1982.

Glisson, J. T. *The Creek.* Gainesville: University Press of Florida, 1993.

Glasgow, Ellen. *The Woman Within: An Autobiography*, edited by Pamela R. Matthews. Charlottesville: University Press of Virginia, 1994.

Goodman, Susan. *Ellen Glasgow: A Biography.* Baltimore: Johns Hopkins Press, 1998.

Hemingway, Ernest, and Maxwell E. Perkins. *The Only Thing That Counts: The Ernest Hemingway/Maxwell Perkins Correspondence 1925–1947*, edited by Matthew J. Bruccoli. New York: Scribners, 1996.

Hurston, Zora Neale. *Zora Neale Hurston: A Life in Letters*, edited by Carla Kaplan. New York: Anchor Books, 2002.

Kinser, Brent. "'the least touch of butter': Marge and Emily on Manners." *Journal of Florida Literature* 10 (2001): 1–9.

Parker, Idella. *Idella: Marjorie Rawlings' "Perfect Maid."* Gainesville: University Press of Florida, 1992.

———. *Idella Parker: From Reddick to Cross Creek.* Gainesville: University Press of Florida, 1999.

Rawlings, Marjorie Kinnan. Autobiographical Sketches. *Los Angeles Times*, 26 April 1953; 3 May 1953; 17 May 1953; 24 May 1953.

———. *Blood of My Blood*, edited by Anne Blythe Meriwether. Gainesville: University Press of Florida, 2002.

———. *Cross Creek.* New York: Scribners, 1942.

———. *Max and Marjorie: The Correspondence between Maxwell E. Perkins and Marjorie Kinnan Rawlings*, edited by Rodger L. Tarr. Gainesville: University Press of Florida, 1999.

———. *Poems. Songs of a Housewife*, edited by Rodger L. Tarr. Gainesville: University Press of Florida, 1997.

———. "Portrait of a Magnificent Editor as Seen in His Letters." *Publishers Weekly* 157 (April 1950): 1573–74.

———. *Selected Letters*, edited by Gordon E. Bigelow and Laura V. Monti. Gainesville: University Presses of Florida, 1983.

———. *Short Stories,* edited by Rodger L. Tarr. Gainesville: University Press of Florida, 1994.

Scribner, Charles, Jr. *In the Company of Writers: A Life in Publishing.* New York: Scribners Sons, 1990.

Silverthorne, Elizabeth. *Marjorie Kinnan Rawlings: Sojourner at Cross Creek.* Woodstock, N.Y.: Overlook Press, 1988.

Stephens, James M. *"Cross Creek" Reader's Guide.* Privately printed, 2003.

Tarr, Carol A., and Rodger L. Tarr. Introduction to *Cross Creek,* by Marjorie Kinnan Rawlings. Jacksonville, Fla.: South Moon Books, 1992.

Tarr, Rodger L. *Marjorie Kinnan Rawlings: A Descriptive Bibliography.* Pittsburgh: University of Pittsburgh Press, 1996.

———. "Marjorie Kinnan Rawlings and the Rochester (N.Y.) Magazine *Five O'Clock.*" *American Periodicals* 1, no. 1 (Fall 1991): 83–85.

———. Marjorie Kinnan Rawlings and the *Washington Post."* *Analytical and Enumerative Bibliography,* n.s., 4, no. 4 (1990): 163–68.

———. "MKR and the FBI." *Rawlings Newsletter* 11 (June 1998): 2–5.

Index

Hemingway, Martha E. *See* Gellhorn, Martha E.

Hemingway, Patrick, 505, 505n

Hemingway, Pauline Pfeiffer, 505, 505n

Hendricks, Joe, 471, 471n

Henry V (Shakespeare), 482

Hepburn, Audrey, 663

Hepburn, Katharine, 435n

Herrick, Mrs., 58

Hersey, John, 280, 280n

Hers to Hold (film), 16, 133, 134n

Heyl, Henry, 110, 111n, 134–35, 146, 152, 287, 290, 329, 360, 374, 392, 426, 512, 622, 622n, 629, 638, 646–48, 651, 657

Heyl, Kit, 646, 648, 651

Hiss, Alger, 531–32, 532n

History of Nora Beckham, The (Pennell), 523, 524n

Hitler, Adolf, 61, 128, 128n, 161, 165, 314, 366

Hobe Sound, 94

Hodgins, Eric, 496, 496n

Hoffman, Malvina, 45, 45n

Hokinson, Helen, 547, 547n

Holden, William, 337n

Hollywood, 16, 256, 519

Holmes, Justine, 403

Homer Noble Farm, 574

Hook, Dr., 448, 472, 554

Hoover, J. Edgar, 10, 144, 154

Hope, Bob, 444n

Horne, Callie, 106

Horne, Ray, 269

Horowitz, Vladimir, 573, 573n

Horse's Mouth, The (Cary), 584, 584n, 592

Horton, Edward E., 350

Hour with the Masters (radio), 287

House of Commons, 208n

Houston, Alfred, 175, 176n, 304, 345–46

Houston, Ruth, 304, 346

Howatt, Frank, 189, 189n, 346n, 430

Howatt, Virginia, 430

Howatt, Willard, 115, 189n, 345–46, 346n, 347, 398, 470, 470n, 650

Huckleberry Finn (Twain), 1

Hudson River, 61

Hudson, W. H., 636, 636n

Hughes, Langston, 165, 166n

Hulburt, Edith, 576, 579–81

Hull, Cordell, 150, 150n, 168

Hull, Mrs., 679, 682n

Human Comedy, The (Saroyan), 76, 76n

Human Destiny (du Nouy), 522, 522n

Hunta Hunta Hara, 131, 132n, 271–73

Hunter's Horn, The (Arrow), 528, 528n

Hurston, Zora Neale, 4, 6, 114, 115n, 208–11, 217, 217n, 482, 485, 523, 524n

Huston, Audrey B., 79, 79n, 166, 237, 254, 273, 280, 394–95, 399–400, 465, 465n

Huston, Clarence M., 79, 79n, 103–104, 117, 117n, 166, 198, 236–37, 254, 273, 287, 323, 342, 344–46, 377, 394–95, 400, 465, 465n, 490

Huston, Robert, 79n, 198, 342, 344, 377

Huston, Walter, 435n

"Hyacinth Drift" (MKR), 6

I Dream of the Day (Milne; intro. by MKR), 17, 114, 115n, 131–32

Iberia (Debussy), 178

IBM, 634n

Idella: Marjorie Rawlings' "Perfect Maid" (Parker) 69n, 543n, 571n

Idella Parker: From Reddick to Cross Creek (Parker), 179n, 223n

Idiot, The (Dostoyevsky), 202

"If You Want to Be a Writer" (MKR), 488, 489n

"I heard a Fly buzz" (Dickinson), 170n

Ileana, Princess, 673, 674n

Incredible Tale (Johnson), 584, 584n

Indigo (Weston), 144–45, 145n, 182, 261, 262n, 286

Information Please (radio), 119n, 444

Institute of American Genealogy, 217

International Business Machines. *See* IBM

"In the Heart" (MKR), 38n

Invasion Diary (Tregaskis), 251n

Invasion of Privacy: The Cross Creek Trial of Marjorie Kinnan Rawlings (Acton), 254n, 467n

Irene (secretary), 628, 659, 660n

Iron Mistress, The (Wellman), 618, 618n

Isaacs, Emmy, 344, 346n

Isaiah, 209

Ishmael (character), 643

Iturbi, José, 573, 573n

Iyaringu (*The Yearling*), 544, 545n

Jackson, Charles, 305, 305n

Jackson, Clint, 347, 348n

Jackson, George, 347, 348n

Jackson, Shirley, 629, 629n

Jacksonville Gun Club, 186

Jacksonville Naval Air Station, 134

Jacksonville Times-Union, 315, 347–48

Missouri (battleship), 564, 564n
Mitchell, Margaret, 1–2, 10, 16, 58, 59n, 124, 240, 245, 262, 448, 530, 540, 540n, 541–44, 566, 578
Mixon, Samuel, 446, 446n
Modern Library (publisher), 127, 149
Moe (dog), 75, 77, 83, 86, 91, 93, 96–97, 102–4, 106, 111–13, 118–20, 128, 140, 145, 150, 152, 159, 162, 168, 176–77, 187–89, 192–94, 196, 198, 202–3, 213, 215, 219, 221, 224, 232, 238, 246–48, 252, 260–61, 263, 266–67, 271, 284, 287–89, 290, 294, 298, 300, 303–5, 308, 312, 325, 327, 332, 336, 340–41, 356, 358, 361–62, 364–67, 372–73, 376, 382, 386, 388–90, 394–95, 400–402, 405, 414, 417, 421, 424–26, 432, 434, 437, 442, 446, 452, 473, 476, 491, 493, 501, 504, 511, 520, 530, 549, 553, 559, 561, 567, 570, 580, 582, 633, 637, 642, 652–53, 655, 657, 660
Moffett, Claudia, 458, 458n, 535
Moffett, Langston, 10, 321, 347–49, 458, 458n, 535
Mohawk Valley, 490
Monitor (magazine), 547
Monsarrat, Nicholas, 618, 618n
Monticello Hotel, 690
Moody, Minnie Hite, 294, 295n
Moon Is Down, The (Steinbeck), 205, 206n
Moore, Noel, 473, 474n
Morgan, Helen, 213, 213n
Morning Watch, The (Agee), 611, 611n
Morris, Marguerite, 655–56
Morrison, Kathleen J., 575, 577n, 578, 578n, 647, 650n
Morrison, Theodore, 577, 578n
Morrison, Tom, 422, 423n, 451, 452n
Moscow Conference, 168, 168n, 176
Mother Hubbard (character), 453
"Mother in Mannville, A" (MKR), 4, 465, 542n
Mountain Prelude (MKR), 465n, 476, 476n, 479–83, 485, 489
Mt. Tom, 519, 521, 536, 576
Mt. Vesuvius, 573
Mountbatten, Louis Francis, Lord, 116, 117n, 132, 141, 330, 337
Mountbatten, Philip, 509, 509n
Mozart, Wolfgang Amadeus, 516
Mr. Blandings Builds His Dream House (Hodgins), 496, 496n
Mrs. Knightley (character), 156
Mrs. Nickleby (character), 446, 446n

Mrs. Three Feathers. *See* Redjives, Ruth
"Muggs and Skeeter" (Bishop), 188n
Mulhern, Mr., 666, 666n
Mulligan, Katherine, 619, 621–24, 627, 629–30, 640
Munro, H. H. [Saki], 105, 105n
Murphree, John, 120, 121n, 122, 253, 254n
Murrow, Edward R., 603, 604n
"My Bonnie Lies over the Ocean" (song), 150
Myers, L. H., 510, 510n
"My Heart Leaps Up" (Wordsworth), 603, 604n
Myrdal, Gunnar, 297, 298n, 332–33, 354

Naish, J. Carrol, 577n
National Broadcasting Corp. (NBC), 402
National Cemetery (St. Augustine), 116, 119–20
National Council of the Teachers of English, 36, 46, 46n
National Geographic, 283
National Institute of Arts and Letters, 36
National Lampoon (magazine), 9
Nazis, Nazism, 154, 269, 304, 314, 315n
NBC. *See* National Broadcasting Corp.
NEA (syndicate), 403–4
Neagle, Anna, 67, 67n
Negro Problem and Modern American Democracy (Myrdal), 297, 298n
Nehru, Jawaharlal, 597, 597n
Neil, Mr., 463, 464n
New Deal, 127, 154
New Testament, 161
New World A-Coming: Inside Black America (Ottley), 164, 166n, 246
New Yorker, The, 43, 43n, 119, 123, 125, 196n, 232, 240, 302, 354, 384n, 433, 433n, 454, 526, 548n, 550, 594
New York Herald-Tribune, 117, 117n, 132, 291, 305, 311, 403, 423, 431, 531, 535, 536n, 541, 547, 601n, 611, 640, 683n
New York Post, 36
New York Times, 289, 294, 305, 311, 416, 579
New York Yankees, 146
Nicholas Nickleby (Dickens), 277, 277n
Nichols, H. C., 194–95, 195n, 196
Night Sky and Other Poems (Kenyon), 611, 611n
Nimitz, Chester W., 280, 280n
Nine Lives with Grandfather (Longstreet), 334, 335n

Randolph Field, 312

Rankin, Araminta, 442, 442n, 444–45, 651, 655–56

Rankin, Charles M., 42, 42n

Ration Board: Gainesville, 83, 103, 229, 234; St. Augustine, 115, 254, 304n

Rationing, 95, 127, 137, 147, 150, 152, 154, 180, 191, 194, 206, 218, 233–35, 238, 241, 275, 283, 450

Rawlings, Charles, Jr. (MKR's first husband), 2, 14, 59n, 257–58, 299, 324, 325n, 339, 355, 423n, 482, 483n, 547, 638n, 645n, 656

Rawlings, James, 58, 59n, 122, 355, 637, 638n, 656

Rawlings, Marcia, 656

Rawlings, Marjorie K. (MKR's niece), 656

Rawlings, Marjorie Kinnan: *accidents*, 215, 219, 299; *airplane spotting*, 104, 111, 128, 131, 134, 140, 256; *alcohol*, 2, 4, 9, 12, 14, 17, 39, 41, 42, 44–46, 48–49, 53, 58, 74–75, 95, 102–4, 111–12, 131, 139, 141–42, 153, 159–69, 189, 182–83, 185, 189, 201, 216–17, 224, 228, 231–32, 245–48, 255, 268–69, 303–7, 318, 320, 355, 359, 364, 369, 370n, 374–75, 384, 386, 389, 402, 411, 421, 425, 441, 452–53, 453n, 470, 478, 488–89, 491, 496, 502, 522, 529, 541, 548, 551, 553–55, 567, 593, 599, 600–602, 605, 609, 614–15, 619, 621–22, 626, 630, 634, 636, 640, 646; *anti-Semitism*, 10, 48, 76, 132, 144, 154, 161, 259, 284, 287, 319, 360; *boys*, 4, 56, 236–37, 297, 337–38, 542, 542n, 556–60, 581–82, 607, 610; *bravery* (war), 96; *censorship* (war), 125–26, 136–37, 161, 203, 106–7, 282–83, 320, 358, 376; *charity*, 12; *chronology of life and works*, 19–23; *cigarette smoking*, 4, 17, 74, 113, 139, 142, 212, 228, 306, 308, 359, 419, 459, 522, 590, 644, 646; *citrus grove*, 77, 83–87, 190, 203–4, 206, 245, 247, 250, 257, 261, 265–66, 275, 277, 279, 308, 330, 334, 337–38, 355, 371–72, 389, 420, 444, 446, 456–57, 469, 487, 533–34, 552, 625, 659; *Crackers*, 2, 6–8; *critic*, 15–16; *death*, 3, 661; *diverticulosis*, 6, 35–36, 42, 64, 69, 71, 81, 91–92, 139, 221, 374, 405, 424, 495, 507–9, 511, 514, 518, 521–27, 636; *faith*, 243, 268, 434, 635; *finances (royalties, taxes)*, 2, 109, 188, 218, 310, 325n, 327–40, 374, 412, 457, 459–60, 476, 550, 561–62, 569, 616, 638, 649–50, 677, 684, 688; *fishing*, 6, 59–60, 85, 91, 197, 265, 275, 277, 288–89, 294–

95, 299, 300, 310, 365; *food*, 4, 41–42, 64, 75, 80, 85, 230, 242, 245–48, 252, 255–56, 259, 273–74, 306, 369, 371, 383–84, 389–90, 400, 415–16, 452, 462, 465, 488–89, 491, 495–96, 498, 502, 522, 527, 552, 557, 567, 569, 582–83, 610, 614–16, 618, 626, 629–30, 644, 651, 660, 686; *gifts*, 103, 182, 195, 214, 227, 249–50, 309, 327, 627, 658; *girls*, 106, 611, 620; *health*, 35n, 36, 61–63, 71–73, 73n, 74–82, 90, 98, 156–57, 206, 440, 509–10, 520, 583, 631; *homosexuality*, 12, 102, 536, 543–44, 588, 600, 654; *honesty*, 4, 169, 181, 224, 234; *honorary degree*, 46; *hunting*, 6, 134, 184, 187, 193–94, 197, 224, 260–61, 263, 265, 271, 310; *jealousy*, 9, 12, 15, 88, 117, 196, 367; *language*, 3–4, 6, 12, 16; *lawsuits*, 5–6, 17, 35n, 69, 71, 75, 75n, 80, 89, 92, 106, 108, 137, 157, 184, 189–90, 209–10, 214, 216–18, 221, 223, 226–27, 227n, 228–29, 232, 234–35, 237–38, 253, 254n, 256, 257, 325, 327, 332, 351, 362, 364, 385, 400–401, 403, 430, 454, 459–61, 464, 466–67, 471, 476–77, 479, 484–86; *lectures*, 36–37, 42, 45, 47, 441–42, 506; *loneliness*, 2, 13, 38–39, 41, 49–50, 58, 62, 70, 76–79, 92, 95–96, 104, 115, 118, 120, 131, 162, 174, 202, 207–8, 232, 234, 238, 240, 255, 272, 279, 303, 312, 326, 337, 360, 370–71, 468, 500, 572, 634; *love*, 197–98; *love (NSB)*, 4, 17, 36, 39, 49–50, 57, 92–93, 157, 167, 170, 202, 207, 233, 372–73, 608; *mail* (war), 120, 129–30, 141n, 144, 188–89, 228, 237, 242, 365, 377, 387–88, 418, 553; *marriage*, 3, 12–13, 38–40, 47, 49–50, 57, 60–61, 63, 65–66, 76, 198, 372–73, 449–50, 563, 566, 590, 601, 608, 612, 633–34, 636, 638–41, 686; *mental state*, 3–4, 14, 17, 41, 49–51, 61–65, 73, 112–13, 130, 171, 206, 208, 214, 220–21, 228, 233, 291, 307–8, 357–59, 379–80, 385, 401, 450, 456, 458, 522, 527, 538, 540–41, 543, 550, 563, 565, 569, 574, 577, 582, 586, 601–2, 607–10, 614–15, 623, 635–36, 639–40, 653, 655, 669, 680–81, 684–85; *poetry*, 44, 503, 514, 519, 528, 540, 637; *politics*, 9–10, 127, 208, 407–8, 431, 523–24, 527; *pregnancy*, 4, 319; *racial issues, racism*, 2, 4–6, 12–14, 48, 100–101, 114–17, 119, 146, 155, 162, 164–65, 171, 175–76, 185, 194, 198–99, 200, 204, 208–11, 213, 224, 241, 244, 246, 256, 264, 266–70, 274, 279, 282, 284, 299, 317–19, 328–29, 331–335, 354, 360–61, 366, 369, 371–72, 381, 400, 403–5, 407, 413, 427, 430,

517, 533, 537, 540, 545–46, 615, 617, 641,
   646, 650, 652, 655, 657
Sandvold, Halvor, 503, 504n, 516n, 652
Santa Claus, 184, 213, 554
Saroyan, William, 76, 76n, 336
Saturday Evening Post, 38, 38n, 43, 43n, 258,
   398, 465n, 482–83, 485, 489, 511, 516, 519,
   526n, 542n
Saturday Review of Literature, 609, 668,
   669n
Schuyler, Maria Bogardus, 576–77, 577n
Sciuscià. See *Shoe Shine*
Scott, Martha, 337n
Scott, Peter, 359, 359n
Scott, Randolph, 551
Scott, Zachary, 471n, 663
Screwtape Letters, The (C. Lewis), 248–49,
   249n
Scribner, Charles, I, 172, 173n
Scribner, Charles, II, 263
Scribner, Charles, III, 9, 11, 15, 47, 47n, 72,
   74n, 78, 127, 175, 297, 323–24, 325n, 360,
   360n, 361, 367, 387, 456, 478, 479n, 480,
   483, 490–91, 509, 517, 523, 532, 538, 574,
   591–93, 604–6, 620, 626, 631, 635, 639
Scribner, Charles, IV, ("Buzz," aka Jr.),
   532–33, 533n, 534, 537, 537n, 639, 647, 657,
   685, 685n
Scribner, Charles, Jr. *See* Scribner, Charles,
   IV ("Buzz")
Scribner, Julia, 8–9, 11–12, 42, 47, 53, 53n, 62–
   64, 70, 70n, 72–77, 79, 95, 98, 104, 107, 110,
   126–27, 134–35, 152–54, 168, 172–74, 197,
   203, 205, 220–21, 227, 237, 253, 257–78,
   280–99, 300–301, 306–7, 309–10, 317–19,
   324, 326, 329, 350, 352, 359–61, 374, 393n,
   397, 410, 416, 426, 432, 439, 443, 478, 497–
   99, 500–501, 503–4, 508–9, 512, 524, 527,
   529–32, 532n, 536–37, 539, 543–44, 549–51,
   569, 581–84, 591, 604–6, 620–21, 626, 639,
   643, 645, 647, 652, 657
Scribner, Vera, 9, 47, 47n, 74, 74n, 78, 104,
   174, 483, 498, 509, 537, 639
Scribners (publisher), 1, 9, 11, 15, 35, 37, 42,
   44, 47, 100n, 103, 173, 186, 190–91, 257,
   323–24, 328, 338–39, 352, 356–68, 387, 412,
   426, 471, 485, 487, 499, 500n, 528–29, 532,
   539n, 549, 561, 591, 593, 599, 602, 606, 611–
   12, 629, 638, 640, 649–50, 658, 665, 688;
   Rare Book Dept., 579
Scribner's Magazine, 328n, 567n
Scribner Treasury, 685
Scrivenor, Mrs., 673, 676

Scruggs, Sigsbee Lee, 71, 451, 466, 467n,
   468–69, 472, 479, 480n
Seaboard Railroad, 44, 355
Seals and Pennington (accounting firm),
   109
Sea of Cortez (Steinbeck), 629, 629n
Season and the Stranger, The (Becker), 613,
   613n
Secret River, The (MKR), 9, 485–87, 487n,
   490, 490n
See Here, Private Hargrove (Hargrove), 173,
   173n
Selected Letters (Rawlings), 73n, 78n, 393n,
   449n, 513n, 577n
Sender, Ramón José, 294, 295n, 361, 361n,
   363
Seraph on the Suwanee (Hurston), 114, 115n,
   523, 524n
Seton, Anya, 409, 410n
Settle, Glenn T., 417
Shakespeare, William, 201, 357, 482, 621, 670.
   See also individual plays
Shands (farm), 220, 355
Shaw, George Bernard, 333, 334n
Shaw, Irwin, 609, 609n, 616, 617n
Shaw and Keeter, 194
She (film), 551, 551n
"She Dwelt Among the Untrodden Ways"
   (Wordsworth), 278, 279n
"Shell, The" (MKR), 123, 123n, 196n, 433n
Shenton, Edward, 35
Sherry-Netherlands Hotel, 45
Sherry's (restaurant), 651
Shoe Shine (film), 508, 508n
Shortridge, R. J., 143, 147, 150, 194, 195n, 199,
   274, 285, 318, 445, 445n
Shortridge, Thelma Tompkins, 76, 76n, 77,
   84, 143, 146, 146n, 147, 150, 154, 180, 194,
   199, 224, 238–39, 244, 318–19, 355, 445,
   445n, 451–52, 471–74, 474n
Short Stories of Saki [Munro], 105, 105n
Sickler, Mary, 514–15, 517
Silver Glen Springs, 289–90, 360, 427
Silver Springs, 484, 568
Silverthorne, Elizabeth, 1
Simpson, Wallis Warfield. *See* Windsor,
   duchess of
Sinatra, Frank, 150, 176
Sisk, Robert, 482–83, 483n, 517, 517n
Sitwell, Osbert, 420, 420n
Skinner, Cornelia Otis, 37, 38n
Slater, Annie ("Widow Slater"), 49n, 442,
   443n, 473

Traphagen, Ethel, 100, 102n
Traphagen, Fanny Osmun, 101, 102n, 128, 129n
Traphagen, Ida May (mother). *See* Kinnan, Ida May Traphagen
Traphagen, Mabel, 218–19, 220, 638, 638n, 683, 683n
Traphagen, William, 101, 102n
Traphagen family, 71, 100, 101, 160
Travels Through North and South Carolina (Bartram), 438, 438n, 529, 529n
Tree Grows in Brooklyn, A (B. Smith), 341, 342n, 370
"Trees for Tomorrow" (MKR), 70, 70n, 112, 112n, 524, 525n
Tregaskis, Richard, 250–51, 251n
Troubled Air, The (I. Shaw), 616, 617n
Truman, Harry, 9, 278n, 279n, 425, 443, 514n, 597, 597n, 634
Turnbuck (character), 10
Turner, Maggie Tompkins, 75, 75n, 143, 146, 146n, 150, 239
Turnipseed, 319
Tuskegee Institute, 115n
Tutwiler, Rube, 672, 672n, 674, 677, 680–81
Twain, Mark, 1
Tweeny (character), 140n
Twink Weatherby (character), 449
"Tyger" (Blake), 293, 293n

Uki (cat), 516, 519–20, 520n, 530–31, 549–50, 557, 571, 580, 582, 642, 652–53, 655, 657, 680
Ulysses (Joyce), 15, 149, 149n, 150, 158
Uncle Sam, 242
Under Cover (Carlson), 154, 154n
Undset, Sigrid, 10, 98–99, 99n, 177, 178n, 283, 371, 457
United Electrical Securities, 495n
United Nations Atomic Energy Commission, 525n
United Service Organizations (USO), 333
United States Army, 252, 334, 364, 430, 433, 514, 543; Fifth, 130, 206; Medical Corps, 111n; Seventh, 187
United States Coast Guard, 188–89, 254
United States Congress, 112, 168, 176, 278, 278n, 331, 332n, 334
United States Department of the Interior, 56
United States Forest Service, 70n
United States Marine Corps, 257, 264, 310, 396, 453
United States Military Academy, 175

United States Navy, 366, 391, 393, 410, 427, 434, 639; Pacific Fleet, 280n
United States Post Office, 370, 471
United States State Department, 252, 551, 662
United States Supreme Court, 331, 489
United States Treasury, 195, 459
United States War Department, 119
University of California, 146
University of Chicago, 146
University of Florida, 3, 5, 7, 11–12, 38n, 47n, 96–97, 459, 464, 467, 481, 539n, 556, 564n, 577n, 688
University of Florida Endowment Corp., 543
University of Louisville, 42n
University of North Carolina, 478
University of Richmond, 662, 676
University of Virginia, 662
University of Wisconsin, 1, 47, 59n, 102n, 140n, 204n, 426
Upchurch, Frank D., 10, 331, 332n
"Use of Sitz-Bath, The" (MKR), 490, 490n
USO. *See* United Service Organizations

Van Doren, Irita, 556, 600, 601n, 611, 651–53, 667, 668n, 672, 677–78, 680–81, 691
Van Druten, John, 664n
Van Loon, Hendrik, 325, 326n
Van Vechten, Carl, 544, 544n, 579, 579n, 636–37, 663, 664n, 675, 680
Venus, 400
Venus de Milo, 400, 401n
Vichy government, 187n
Victoria (queen of England), 666n
Victoria Grandolet (Bellamann), 250, 251n
Vidor, King, 315, 315n
Vinson [later Prescott], Dessie Smith, 6, 58, 81, 106, 109, 126, 138, 147, 180, 209, 262, 289, 312, 351, 459, 471, 473, 484, 612, 618
Vinson, J. C., 126, 126n, 473
V-mail, 104, 153, 248, 259, 252, 257, 387, 428
Vogt, William, 523, 525n
Voice of America, 628

WACS. *See* Women's Army Corps
Wagner, Richard, 247, 248n
Walden (Thoreau), 380, 380n, 384–85, 390
Waldorf-Astoria Hotel, 170, 222, 426
Walker, Danton, 54, 54n
Wallace, Henry A., 425, 425n, 514, 514n
Walter Reed Army Hospital, 287